DATE DUE

NY 19 '04			
JE 9 '04			

DEMCO 38-296

The New Christian Right

Political and Social Issues

K

The New Christian Right
Political and Social Issues

Edited with introductions by

Melvin I. Urofsky
Virginia Commonwealth University

Martha May
Western Connecticut State University

GARLAND PUBLISHING, INC.
New York & London
1996

Library of Congress Cataloging-in-Publication Data

The New Christian right : political and social issues / edited with
    introductions by Melvin I. Urofsky, Martha May.
        p.   cm.
    ISBN 0-8153-2581-9 (alk. paper)
    1. Christianity and politics—History—20th century.
    2. Christians—United States—Political activity.
    3. Fundamentalism—History—20th century. 4. Conservatism—
United States—History—20th century. 5. United States—Politics
and government—1993– 6. United States—Social policy—1993–
I. Urofsky, Melvin I.   II. May, Martha.
BR115.P7N37   1996
320.5'5'0973—dc20   96-24441
                                                   CIP

Printed on acid-free, 250-year-life paper
Manufactured in the United States of America

Contents

Social Issues

Introduction

To Europeans the United States is a most difficult country to understand, because it often appears as a bundle of unresolved contradictions. They recognize it as a democratic society, yet one whose government can often appear paralyzed, stopped dead in its track by determined minorities. Used to parliamentary systems where the executive and the legislature are always controlled by the same party, they wonder how the American people can so frequently elect a Congress dominated by one party and then choose a president from the other. But nothing confuses them as much as the role of religion in American society.

The First Amendment proclaims that there shall be no establishment of religion, nor any interference by the government in an individual's free exercise of his or her faith. Yet religion is a pervasive influence in the United States, and almost every issue can pick up religious connotations. For a society in which there is no established church, and where no single faith commands more than a fraction of the population, the voices of religious advocates often appear to dominate public discourse. Never has this been truer than with the rise of the New Christian Right in the last decade.

Religious fundamentalism, however, is not a uniquely American phenomenon. While the media may emphasize those associated with the Christian Coalition, the Satmar Hasidim and the Gush Emunim of Israel are every bit as dedicated to their particularized views of religion and the world. Sunni Muslims in Egypt and the Sudan, Shi'ite Muslims in Iran and Iraq, the Jamaat-i-Islami and the Tablighi Jamaat in South Asia, Sikhs and Theravada Buddhists in India, the Soka Gakkai in Japan, and the Catholic Society of Saint Pius X are but the best known of modern fundamentalisms.

Using those two words together, "modern" and "fundamentalism," may strike some as an oxymoron, but fundamentalism today, while certainly connected to the past, also has an eye on the present and to the future. For many fundamentalists—be they Christian, Jewish, or Muslim—the "end of days" is rapidly approaching. Fundamentalists worldwide seek to reshape political life through devout adherence to the laws of a God, whether that deity is understood as Allah, Jehovah, or as Jesus Christ.

Modern religious fundamentalism is not an easy term to define, however, and there is substantial disagreement about both definition and terminology among people who study the matter. Some scholars insist on a careful delineation of the differences between the Moral Majority's fundamentalist Jerry Falwell and the pentecostalist vision of Pat Robertson, for example. While such distinctions color discussions among conservatives, they obscure the more basic similarities within modern fundamentalism. Perhaps most important, variations in religious belief have not diminished the fervor or significance of fundamentalist efforts. For outside observers, Justice Potter Stewart's conclusion about pornography may hold equally true of religious fundamentalism: if it is hard to define, most people still "know it when we see it."

First of all, these movements—even while opposed to many of the forces that they denounce as modern—have established a symbiotic relationship with the modern, using its technology and mass media to further their own ends. The Christian Coalition may advocate restrictions on the internet, for example, but the organization offers political commentary, speeches, and daily updates over the World Wide Web. The political power of America's Christian Right since 1985 stems in good part from a vigorous use of computer and satellite technologies to deepen grass-roots support and mobilize its constituency.

Second, they are overtly and defiantly religious, in that they believe that some sort of divine world plan directs human activity, and that in order for men and women to lead a moral life they must adhere to the teachings and obligations of that plan. Religious practice takes on a distinctly public character, and personal identity for fundamentalists is continually shaped by the profession of faith.

Martin Marty and Scott Appleby have characterized fundamentalists in terms of "*fighting.*" First, they are "*fighting back*" in that they see themselves as victimized by secular society and deprived of their rights and status. Not all revert to bullets, such as the Islamic Jehad or the murderers of abortion providers, but they are not offended by the term "militant."

They are also "*fighting for*" their particular worldview. While this view varies from group to group, it includes very specific ideas on the proper roles of family, gender roles, and the education of children, among other things.

Next, they are "*fighting with*" certain resources, which are in a way weapons. These groups are called fundamentalists because they have reached back into their real or presumed pasts, to real or imagined conditions, and have chosen what they consider basic—that is, fundamental.

Fourth, these groups "*fight against*" others, the others being any and all who either attack their basic tenets or who refuse to join with them. They have no middle ground, no neutrality—one is either with them or against them. God, they believe, does not like fence-sitters.

Finally, fundamentalists "*fight under*" God, in the case of theistic religions such as Islam, Christianity, and Judaism, or under some transcendent referent in the case of militant Buddhism or Confucianism. They see themselves as the soldiers of God, and because they battle for the divine cause they are invincible and can do no evil.

*   *   *   *   *

The tale of religion in America and how different sects were treated by the majority is a long and often convoluted story, and at times a not very pleasant one. The current conflicts between the religious right and the liberal tradition grow out of that historical soil. Contrary to popular wisdom, today's fundamentalists are not an entirely new phenomenon on the American religious, social, or political scenes.

Members of the religious right see the ills of society—crime, drugs, homelessness, a decline in international prestige, and especially the disintegration of the American family—as all due to the abandonment of God and religious values. Pat Robertson of the Christian Coalition, Jerry Falwell of the Moral Majority, James Dobson of Focus on the Family, and others all preach that what is wrong with American society today is that it has lost God. To them a people who do not rely on divine guidance is a nation that is not only morally bereft but politically adrift as well. Some leaders of the Christian Right even point to an exact day on which America began straying from God's path—June 25, 1962—the day the Supreme Court banned mandatory prayer in public schools.

Pat Robertson typifies this sentiment when he charges that "the Supreme Court of the supposedly Christian United States guaranteed the moral collapse of this nation when it forbade children in the public schools to pray to the God of Jacob, to learn of His moral law or even to view in their classrooms the heart of the law, the Ten Commandments."

Without belaboring the point, it seems clear to most analysts that problems such as crime, illegal drugs, and homelessness have roots far deeper than the absence of morning prayers in the nation's classrooms. Yet the Christian Right continues to cite religious commitment as the solution for America's troubles. From godly devotion, fundamentalists declare, the country will regain its lost habits of hard work and personal responsibility. This regeneration will restore an orderly and prosperous United States idealized from the past. If others seem unwilling to share in the religious agenda, Christian conservatives remain eager to politicize their dogma into policy and legislation, whether the subject be prayer in the schools, the rejection of evolution, restrictions on gays and lesbians, or penalties against unmarried mothers.

The fundamentalist right objects to the whole development of contemporary society away from what it perceives as "traditional" values and social forms: a nuclear family centered around the "natural" dominance of the husband and a community in which authority can appear simultaneously democratic and hierarchical. Issues of gender and sexuality, from women's leadership roles to open homosexuality, raise particularly anxious responses from the right. To them abortion is murder, a woman's place is in the home, and single parent households are morally inferior to nuclear families headed by a father. Some Christian Right activists also imply that there are too many Americans who are not native-born, white, Protestant and middle class.

From a historian's point of view, this is not an unfamiliar pattern. We can see the growth of right-wing fundamentalism in this country every time there has been a major social upheaval. The Ku Klux Klan in the 1920s, the John Birchers and their allies in the 1950s, and the Moral Majority in the 1980s all share common characteristics both in terms of their membership as well as their complaints. They object to the social changes, often triggered by war, that threaten their traditional values and status in society. Religion, of course, is one of those basic values.

What is different today is that other voices have entered the debate in concert with the Christian Right, voices that were absent in the 1920s and 1950s. Among these voices are conservative intellectuals both within and outside the academy who, while not echoing all of the claims of the fundamentalists, nonetheless agree with them on many issues. No respectable university professors endorsed the Ku Klux Klan program in the 1920s or the charges of the John Birch Society in the 1950s; in the 1980s and 1990s, however, highly respectable academic and lay writers have argued the wrongness of the Supreme Court's decisions, and have joined in the charge that at least part of the current social unrest is due to the expulsion of religion from public discourse. If such intellectuals reject the specific religious tenets of fundamentalism, they share a similar moral language, and make common cause in renouncing the decline of "family values."

Politicians, too, have given greater legitimacy to the Christian Right. Mainstream conservative politics in the past avoided close association with "fringe" groups, such as the Klan, the fascist organizations of the 1930s, or the Birchers of the fifties. Political hopefuls in earlier decades drew carefully and selectively from the rhetoric of the far right. Today's Christian conservatives enjoy a more eager reception. In 1995, Republican presidential candidates actively sought audiences at the Christian Coalition's annual convention. Former Senate Majority Leader Robert Dole conspicuously appealed to Christian fundamentalists by rejecting contributions from the gay Republicans of the Log Cabin Coalition, and denounced sexually explicit films to bolster his "family values" image. Some political pundits wondered openly if a Republican could win the presidential nomination without such performances. The one Republican rebel from the ideal of a "Christian nation," Pennsylvania Senator Arlen Specter, withdrew from the race when he was unable to generate moderate support.

From the 1980 election of Ronald Reagan, the Right, as "New Right" or "Religious Right," has played an influential role in national politics. Reagan actively courted the religious right, and when he largely ignored their social agenda, the president earned their cautious criticism. George Bush opened his bid for re-election in January 1992 with an appearance at a convention of the National Religious Broadcasters, a group representing Christian television and radio stations. The president declared: "I want to thank you for helping America, as Christ ordained, to be a light upon the world. . . . One cannot be America's president without a belief in God, without a belief in prayer." Bush then went on to cite the teachings of Jesus Christ as the moral justification for the previous year's war against Iraq. In fact, in June 1991, immediately after the hostilities had ended, the Episcopalian Bush flew to Atlanta for the annual meeting of the nation's largest Protestant group, the Southern Baptist Convention, where with tears in his eyes he told how hard he had prayed at Camp David before ordering the attack.

At the 1992 Republican convention, Bush wrapped himself not only in the American flag, but also in the embrace of Jerry Falwell, Pat Robertson and other evangelicals. Bush's references to God were not unusual; every president from George Washington to Bill Clinton has sought divine guidance. Jimmy Carter openly acknowledged his own evangelical beliefs. What is unusual is the growing enthusiasm of Republican politicians for the religious right, and their willingness to shape programs in accordance with fundamentalist views on school prayer, abortion, and "family values." Other modern presidents not only showed a sensitivity to religious pluralism, but glorified it as one of the basic values that a democratic society holds dear.

Observers outside of the Republican party (and some inside of it), both Christian and non-Christian, have voiced concern over this particular kind of connection between church and state. Barry W. Lynn, executive director of Americans United for the Separation of Church and State, has argued that the Christian Coalition "won't rest until they usher in an officially Christian America." Coalition director Ralph Reed has countered such claims by reassuring audiences that the Christian Right wants to be "a voice in the conversation that we call democracy." Yet Reed has also declared that "by the year 2000, when you wake up and look back at this decade, the movement that will have etched the contours of politics ... will be these people."

Finally the Christian Right's persistent emphasis on gender and sexuality makes it distinctive in twentieth century conservative politics. The insistence on morality parallels reform movements of the nineteenth century far more than it echoes the dominant notes of conservatism in this century. Citing the need for a "pro-family agenda, the Christian Right returns repeatedly to domestic causations, tenaciously defining issues as wide ranging as crime, taxes, health care and international policy within the context of "family values." The Christian Coalition's Ralph Reed connected the nation's health care crisis to "marital discord, sexual promiscuity" and the need for a "loving home," for example. Even more typical is the connection drawn by Christian conservatives between crime and family structure: without a two parent family, they maintain, violent crime will rise. Dire warnings are frequently accompanied by graphic examples.

The Christian Right has also become a forceful opponent of recently expanded acceptance for gays and lesbians. Attempts to deny homosexuals equal access to jobs, housing, and health care have been couched in biblical condemnations. The most vociferous response to sexuality, however, has been provoked by the arts, including film and television. The national campaigns of Donald Wildmon's American Family Association have been especially visible as the organization works to expose the "excessive, gratuitous sex, [and] violence. . . . " As political analyst James Davison Hunter notes, however, the battles over obscenity and art remain symptoms of a larger debate over "art as a symbol of conscience" and "art as a symbol of immorality." The Christian Right's insistence that any expression of sexuality beyond marital relations is immoral means that the boundaries of acceptability remain narrow and the possibility of dissension wide.

Admonitions about violence and complaints over liberal sexuality from the Christian Right betray a curious contradiction, however. Even as Christian conservatives condemn crime and immorality, they utilize vivid examples of rape, infidelity, and murder to make their case. It is as if the act of condemnation provides a legitimate cover for titillation, exploration of what they believe should otherwise be forbidden. The result is exhortation which both provokes and represses, a mixed message of excitement and restraint.

The construction of gender by the Christian Right poses a similar contradiction. Insistence on monogamy, the privileges of husbands, and the "natural" maternal desires of women would seem to be, at least to some observers, a "pro-family agenda" far more attractive to men than to women in the 1990s. Yet many female Christian activists accept these limitations and find opportunities within them. As Kathleen Blee notes in her study of Klan women, that organization opened doors for women beyond the home even as the Klan celebrated women's domestic roles. The same kind of duality exists for women of the Right who advocate women's subordination to husbands but who maintain a very public and independent profile. Beverly LaHaye of Concerned Women of America, Phyllis Schlafly of the Eagle Forum, and others speak enthusiastically of women's destiny as wives and mothers centered in the home, even as they pursue lives as speakers, reformers, and politicians. Perhaps ironically, women remain the "typical" members of the Christian Coalition.

* * * * *

Until recently, fundamentalists, perhaps more than any other group, advocated strict separation of church and state, and eschewed politics. They based this policy on the belief that the world was sinful and not a worthy place for holy people to expend their energies. Rather, they tried to lead morally upright lives and prayed for the early arrival of Jesus' Kingdom, which would end the corrupt and evil secular society. The Rev. Billy Graham was the first evangelical to bring religious fundamentalism into contact with political realities, and until the 1980s many on the religious right condemned Graham for betraying the true faith.

As conditions in the United States and elsewhere seemed to worsen, evangelical leaders began to speak out more forcefully about what they saw as the lack of a religious dimension in modern life, and their followers responded avidly. The cynic and the realist might denounce such sermons as simple-minded and simplistic; crime and other problems plagued the United States even in the supposedly golden era when it was a "God-fearing country." Yet the Christian Right persists in romanticizing this American past drawn from the 1950s, when, they suggest, families were comfortable and pious, crime a problem of the inner city and the nation strong internationally.

In elevating the fifties to the status of a "golden age," religious leaders of the Right, and conservative politicians such as House Speaker Newt Gingrich, reveal a certain bias. The historical record of the 1950s includes widespread racial discrimination, high levels of poverty, and a claustrophobic domesticity. In applauding the fifties, the Christian Right focuses on an exclusive America, the "American dream" of a white middle class. This world of a devout Ozzie and Harriet hides racial divisions, inequalities of opportunity, and the widening gulf between classes that shape our most recent social problems.

Differing views on the fifties reflect the substantial gulf between religious conservatives and more secular Americans. The two groups, the true believers and the secularists, have never been able to communicate because they speak different languages. To the former, all problems have a religious component and can be resolved only through divine dispensation; to the latter, prayer is a private matter, and neither an appropriate nor an efficacious way to deal with contemporary social difficulties. The differences extend into beliefs about work, child rearing, and even the environment. Where Christian Right activists see the hand of God and the sin of man, liberals have cited the more complex human constructions. As a result, the religious right has declared war not only on liberal groups, such as the American Civil Liberties Union, the American Jewish Congress, People for the American Way, the National Organization for Women, and the Federal Council of Churches, but on the liberal tradition as well.

The extent of fundamentalist involvement in politics could not be missed in the 1994 mid-term elections. In Virginia, Oliver North's campaign for the Senate was termed a crusade by his religious backers. The religious right captured the Republican Party machinery not only in Virginia, but in Texas, Minnesota, Oregon, Iowa, Washington, and South Carolina as well. Moreover, in countless towns and cities, the Christian Coalition and its allies have orchestrated sophisticated and for the most part little publicized campaigns to win control of local school boards. In Florida, after gaining a majority on one district board, the fundamentalists voted to implement a curriculum that declared American culture to be superior to that of any other country's.

In Minnesota, the evangelicals turned against Republican governor Arne Carlson because he favored abortion and gay rights, and denied him renomination. Instead the party named Allen Quist, a corn and soybean farmer who embraced the fundamentalist platform—he opposed abortion and gay rights, denounced evolution, and claimed that there is a "genetic predisposition" for men to be heads of households.

In Texas, Dolly Madison McKenna, a Houston business executive and the moderates' candidate for chairperson of the state Republican Party, told the convention that "There are those people in this audience who want the Republican Party to be a church." Amid catcalls and boos, she continued "You are very welcome in the Republican Party. But the Republican Party is not a church." The delegates defeated her and elected instead Tom Pauken, whose backers held placards that read "A Vote for Pauken is a Vote for God." As for moderate Republicans who favored such things as abortion rights, one delegate put it quite simply: "They should leave."

*   *   *   *   *

The very extremism of the fundamentalist right has led some people to downplay its significance. "America is diverse and is growing more so," goes one line of thought, "and the religious right has about as much chance to reverse that trend as King Canute did to hold back the waves." In fact, after the scandals involving Jim and Tammy Bakker and Jimmy Swaggart a few years ago, some commentators rushed to write obituaries for the religious right. The highly respected historian Naomi Cohen noted in 1993 that "by the end of the 1980s it seemed as if the political force of the New Christian Right was spent." But while so-called "televangelism" has played an important role in the rise of the religious right, it is not the same thing. Many of the leaders of the Christian Right, such as Falwell and Robertson, began their careers as television preachers, and then have used that base to expand into other activities. Both men, as well as Oral Roberts, founded universities where students could receive appropriate Christian education and be free from the temptations of modern society. They also used their television base, and the money it brought in, to branch into politics. There is a big difference, however, between a Jimmy Swaggert and a Jerry Falwell, and to lump all of the Christian televangelists into one category is to make a serious mistake.

If we were to look at any one of the fundamentalist groups in detail, that would have to be Pat Robertson's Christian Coalition, founded in 1989 after Robertson's failed bid to capture the Republican nomination for the presidency. Since he burst on the religious scene in the 1970s, Robertson, the son of a former U.S. Senator from Virginia, has created a multimillion dollar conglomerate, for there is no other word for it. An early televangelist, Robertson's "700 Club" became the basis for his Christian Broadcasting Network (CBN), which airs programming for both domestic and international markets twenty-four hours a day. CBN has more than 1500 radio stations and nearly 350 television outlets. In addition, Robertson launched the Family Channel, which broadcasts reruns of popular television shows such as "I Love Lucy" and "Gilligan's Island." Recently Robertson paid $68.5 million for TVS Entertainment; TVS owns MTM Productions, which created "Lou Grant," "Hill Street Blues," and the "Mary Tyler Moore Show." Robertson uses these shows to attract viewers, who he hopes will then stay tuned for his evangelical message.

Critical to the Christian Coalition's plans is Regent University in Virginia Beach, which trains graduate students in education, religion, and communications to build theological and political alliances. At the heart of Regent University is its law school and the American Center for Law and Justice. There students are trained not only in the "Christian basis" of law, but also how to use the law for particular social ends. The Center, which is modeled on the work of the American Civil Liberties Union, litigates cases involving parental rights, sex education curricula, school prayers, and abortions. According to its chief counsel, Jay Sekulow, the Center seeks to protect the "rights of Christians" in America.

In order to circumvent the Supreme Court ruling banning mandatory school prayers, the Center, along with the Christian Coalition since 1991, has organized "See You at the Pole" rallies, where high school students gather at the flagpole in front of their schools for voluntary prayer. According to Sekulow, "We are on the offensive. We will no longer stand for Christians being victims." In August 1993 the Center moved into a new building called the Strategic Command Center, a name chosen to symbolize the battle that Robertson claims he is waging for the soul of America. Regional offices have been opened in Georgia, Arizona, Alabama, Kentucky, and Washington, D.C.

In terms of theology, the Christian Coalition has a very particular agenda, and a particular view of what it means to be Christian. It wants to reorder the nation's political structure under the authority of a "Christian" government. The leaders subscribe to a philosophy called "Christian Reconstruction" or "Dominion Theology," which was originally articulated in 1973 by Rousas John Rushdoony. Most of the leaders of the major right-wing religious groups subscribe to this theology, and also belong to a secretive clique known as the Coalition on Revival, which is headed by Jay Grimstead.

It is impossible to summarize Christian Reconstruction in only a few sentences, but in essence its adherents believe pluralism of any sort is wrong, be it racial, ethnic, or religious. People who espouse religious arguments different from them are not only wrong but have no claim to religious freedom. Toleration merely means exposure to theological error. As Rushdooney put it, "In the name of toleration, the believer is asked to associate on a common level of total acceptance with the atheist, the pervert, the criminal, and adherents of other religions as though no differences existed." Byron Snapp put it even more harshly: "The Christian must realize that pluralism is a myth. God and His law must rule all nations. . . . At no point in Scripture do we read that God teaches, supports or condones pluralism. . . . Clearly our founding fathers had no intention of supporting pluralism for they saw that the Bible tolerates no such view." And, of course, there is the famous comment by Bailey Smith to the Southern Baptist Convention in 1980, "God Almighty does not hear the prayer of a Jew."

From this rejection of any form of diversity, the Reconstructionists propose a new society that would eliminate most forms of government and leave citizens accountable to church authorities for their moral behavior. Taxes would be replaced with mandatory tithing, and what few social services would exist would be provided by church agencies. Security and police would be provided by local militia. Crime would be severely punished, and the death penalty would be administered for a variety of felonies, including adultery, "unchastity," and sacrificing to "false gods."

Rushdoony has written: "To the humanistic mind these penalties seem severe and unnecessary. In actuality, the penalties, together with the Biblical faith which motivated them, worked to reduce crime. Thus, when New England passed laws requiring the death penalty for incorrigible delinquents and for children who struck their parents, no executions were necessary; the law kept the children in line."

While not all conservatives subscribe to all of the tenets of Reconstructionism, one can see the appeal it has to those who want harsh penalties imposed upon criminals, who believe the government ought to be shrunk to little more than police and army forces, who want to do away with the entire public social service system (including public education), and who want the government out of the private sector completely. Whether or not captains of industry, who are often rampant individualists, would be happy living in a theocracy is another question.

How Robertson views the United States can be seen in his 1991 book, *The New World Order*, in which he presents a rather distorted view of American history to prove that the country is a Christian nation that must be governed in a Christian manner. His model is colonial Massachusetts, in which the clergy controlled society and government. Robertson's efforts to gain control of the Republican Party, primarily through control of local organizations, is designed to provide him with a vehicle by which this Christian view of American can be imposed upon the nation.

Young dedicated members of the Christian Coalition are gaining control of local Republican organizations and forcing moderates out of the party councils. Moreover, Robertson is not all that secretive about his plans. Politicians "who believe in Judeo-Christian values are better qualified to govern Americans than Hindus and Moslems," he declares. But the Pennsylvania Action Plan includes the following advice for organizers: "If someone asks you what group you represent say 'A local group of concerned citizens' . . . never mention the name Christian Coalition." Ralph Reed, the executive director of the Coalition, gained instant notoriety when he spoke about "stealth candidates." Reed remains one of the most skilled political organizers in America today and has been credited with the growing influence of the Christian Coalition nationally. When the Coalition announced its "Contract with the American Family," Reed stood with House Speaker Newt Gingrich in the Capitol, a reflection of his expanded political authority.

*   *   *   *   *

Although most of the political agitation has been by Protestant Christian activists, Roman Catholicism, Judaism, and Islam all have their fundamentalist wings as well. While less visible and therefore less well-known than their Protestant counterparts, at least in the United States, these groups play an important role in contemporary political-religious affairs.

Islam is the fastest growing religion in the United States today, and all of its local leaders are trained in foreign seminaries where fundamentalist Muslim doctrine is preached. The Catholic Church has seen a resurgence of strong conservatism, in some areas bordering on schism, as traditionalists fight liberal proposals.

A little over a year ago the Supreme Court handed down a decision involving an ultra-orthodox Jewish sect, the Satmar Hasidism, which had successfully lobbied the New York state legislature to create a special school district that would be comprised entirely of Satmar.

While Protestants comprise the bulk of the visible religious right, they are not alone, and their basic rejection of the liberal tradition is shared by fundamentalists of other faiths as well. In addition to social change and upheaval, there is one more consideration to take into account in looking at the sudden rise to political power of the fundamentalists, and that is a sense that the end of days is approaching. The magically numbered year 2000 will soon be upon us, and even among non-Christian fundamentalists—indeed among secularists—one can find eschatological notions.

Among Jews, for example, the Lubovicher Hasidim declared that the messiah, if not already here in the person of the Reb, would certainly be here when Reb was resurrected after his death, and devout followers remain on vigil next to his grave in Jerusalem. The Gush Emunim believe that the prophecies of redemption are nigh, and will be fulfilled as soon as they settle the biblical boundaries of ancient Israel.

Many Christian fundamentalists believe that the prophesied "end of days" is upon us. In his various mailings inviting people to join his groups, Pat Robertson says, "We have been chosen since the foundation of the earth for this day and this time. To help usher in the Second Coming of our Lord Jesus Christ." To Robertson and others, events such as the Israeli recapture of Jerusalem in the Six-Day War and the Gulf War against Iraq in 1991 are lead-ins to the Second Coming.

(In fact, in 1990, John Walvoord published *Armegeddon, Oil and the Middle East Crisis*, in which he declared that the Biblical prophecies foretold of an imminent war, in which "great armies from the north, south, and east will have reached the Middle East. . . Jerusalem will be under attack . . . and the entire world will then be stopped in awe.")

On a more extreme level, the Branch Davidians in Waco, the Covenant, Sword and Arm of the Lord, and other groups retreat into closed communities to await the millennium. These communities, unlike earlier particularists like the Shakers, are willing to confront the authority of the state with armed resistance and to die fighting for their beliefs.

The notion of an end of days is not new. Karl Barth wrote over sixty years ago that "Christianity that is not entirely and altogether eschatology has entirely and altogether nothing to do with Christ." Even before that Albert Schweitzer had proclaimed that Jesus came to proclaim the end of this world and the beginning of the kingdom of God.

But just as for centuries Jews saw redemption as something mythic, in the far future of God's time, so Christians also viewed the end of time in mythic terms. But following World War II, and the Cold War threat of nuclear annihilation, eschatological sentiment increased dramatically, and found a ready home among a group already predisposed to literal belief, Christian fundamentalists.

*   *   *   *   *

There is no question but that the New Christian Right will be a significant force in American society and politics for a number of years. Although some commentators believe that the very narrow focus of their concerns will prevent groups like the Christian Coalition from ever becoming a majority party, they have already demonstrated that they can gain power at the local and state level, and can influence the Republican Party on the national level.

But the attraction of the Christian Right is that its leaders focus on a few push-button issues through the invocation of "family values." Even if they secured constitutional amendments putting mandatory prayer back in schools or prohibiting abortion, the general social problems that upset them would not disappear. Prayer in the school will not solve the problems of drugs, poverty, and crime. Limiting aid to unmarried mothers will have nothing to do with putting out brush-fire wars in Africa or resolving the trade deficit with Japan. Telling women that their husbands should control decisions in the home will not assure family harmony.

In times of social upheaval and turmoil, people do not want to hear how difficult and complex problems are; they do not want to look beyond the surface symptoms to find the root causes of social unrest. In a media age of advertisers exhorting Americans to instant pleasures, citizens have become reluctant to accept complicated explanations. They want to hear that the old-fashioned virtues are good, and that the problems of the country all stem from the abandonment of those precepts, chief of which is adherence to fixed religious beliefs. In that mindset is the strength of the New Christian Right, as well as its weakness.

Political Issues

Although the First Amendment separates church and state, religion and politics have been intertwined in this nation's history from its founding in the early seventeenth century. The settlers who came to Massachusetts wanted to establish a godly kingdom, a "city upon a hill," where the political realm would be ruled by the righteous followers of God's law. Although the Englishmen who settled in Virginia differed on theological matters from their Puritan cousins to the north, they accepted as a basic social premise that there should be an established church, and the Church of England enjoyed that status until the Revolution.

Throughout American history, religion has played a significant role in politics. In the nineteenth century, presidential candidates went out of their way to placate particular religious groups and to show that they were more God-fearing than their opponents. In this century anti-Catholicism played an important part in the presidential campaigns of 1928 and 1960.

But these were general manifestations for the most part, and Christians, who make up well over 95 percent of the population, did not expect more from political candidates other than that they believe in some religion and at least pay lip service to divine authority. The more pious the religious sect, the less contact its adherents had or wanted to have with the nitty-gritty of political life. For them only God's kingdom mattered, and they took literally the biblical injunction to render unto Caesar; they would leave politics to the less faithful, while they awaited God's final judgment.

This began to change in the late 1960s. Billy Graham was the first major fundamentalist to try to establish contact with the broader secular society, and this effort, successful as it proved to be, initially brought down on him contumely from fellow evangelicals. But the seeming deterioration of American prestige resulting from Vietnam, the turmoil caused by the various rights movements, and the dramatic increase in crime and social polarization led a number of conservative Christians—conservative both in secular and religious beliefs—to call for what they considered a reestablishment of religious values into secular life. Only by reversing what they saw as the anti-religious nature of American society could the America they loved be saved. And the only way to achieve that was through political action.

Jimmy Carter was the first presidential candidate to openly court the religious right, and in 1980 both he and Ronald Reagan actively went after the religious vote. By the following year Terry Eastland could write in a major journal that religion belonged in American life and discourse, and Paul Weyrich could look forward confidently to a new and stronger conservative movement challenging the then-dominant liberal-moderate coalition.

During the following decade many people failed to distinguish between the political activities of the Christian right and the prosletyzing efforts of televangelists; in some instances this is not surprising, since men like Jerry Falwell and Pat Robertson mixed politics and piety together. Then came the scandals, and as Sean Wilentz points out, this created a crisis for all the television preachers. For Falwell it eventually meant the abandonment of the Moral Majority and a return to his pulpit; it did not mean the end of his political involvement.

The focus for Christian Right political action became Pat Robertson and the empire he built based upon the 700 Club. This empire, as John Taylor points out, gave Robertson the dollars and the communication links to reach millions of people with his message. He also founded the Christian Coalition, which by 1993 was looking to become a mainstream political force. Ralph Reed, Jr., the young bright executive director of the Coalition talked about casting a "wider net," but as the articles by Chip Berlet, Rob Boston, Joseph Conn, and others show, the older strategy of winning school district by school district, precinct by precinct, had not been abandoned.

But the influence of the New Christian Right grew enormously in the early nineties, and several of the articles, such as those by Sara Diamond, Matthew Moen, John Persinos, and Erin Saberi, analyze its impact and strength on the national stage.

One reason the New Christian Right has gained such influence, according to some analysts, is that the old conservatism had played out and proven unable to conquer the liberal-moderate coalition that has governed the nation since the 1930s. Michael Lind talks about the death of the old conservatism, while William Kristol directs his remarks to what he sees as the conservatism of the future. While these articles are not focused directly on the religious right, they limn out the general political and intellectual context in which the Christian Coalition and its allies have flourished.

Social Issues

When asked, Americans are quick to define family values. Most see them as ideals of nurture and support among family members, financial comfort and security, and a good future for their children. Yet another kind of "family values" has emerged as the convenient shorthand in the 1990s for a political agenda of the Christian Right and its conservative allies. This set of "family values" includes selective state intervention in private life, policies that emphasize "responsibility" rather than assistance, and a renewed celebration of feminine domesticity and nurture. The increasing success of conservative politicians who invoke the symbolic terms of "family values" represents a critical shift in American domestic politics.

The rhetoric of "family values" appeared from a loose coalition of conservative Republicans and Christians in the late 1970s; by 1992 it had grown powerful enough to shape the controversial pronouncements of the Republican National Convention. Marilyn Quayle, wife of then Vice President Dan Quayle, offered her listeners a critique of women who rejected a "natural" role as wife and mother. Pat Buchanan, former speechwriter to President Richard Nixon, cited protection of family and faith as the rationale for a "holy war" on liberals and Democrats. The public rejected this vitriolic assault on working mothers and others who were not "born again," but while conservatives embracing "family values" may have lost that skirmish, the larger battle over family and policy continued.

The 1994 elections crystallized the growing power of a new alliance between Christian political activists and Republican politicians who seek to reduce the size of the federal government and promote business development. Conservative intellectuals such as Charles Murray, George Gilder, Adam Bellow, William Kristol, and William Bennett, along with columnists including George Will and radio personality Rush Limbaugh, provide analysis and philosophical fire for this diverse conservative constituency. Leaders of the Christian Right, from Pat Robertson and Ralph Reed of the Christian Coalition to Donald Wildmon's American Family Association, insist on a religious mission. Others, such as Gary Bauer and the Family Research Council and the Heritage Foundation, make common cause in the defense of "morality." If elements of this conservative force sometimes express discomfort with the views of others within the "big tent," it remains a fluid affiliation of individuals and organizations sharing similar goals and shaping a new political ideology and restoring "family values."

The readings in this section illustrate the fluidity of this conservative coalition. Although Charles Murray, for example, is not a religious leader of the Christian

Right, his writings remain widely cited by Christian conservatives. Similarly, Barbara Dafoe Whitehead's article in *The Atlantic Monthly* in 1993, "Dan Quayle Was Right," has been repeatedly mentioned by Christian Right activists in their criticism of single mothers.

The roots of today's Right stretch through many facets of American history and culture. As Mathew Moen notes, elements of conservative religious tenets date back to American Puritanism, but more recent events such as *Roe v. Wade* (1973) and the development of a gay rights movement also influence this political movement. By concentrating on gender and sexuality, the Christian Right has tapped into profound anxieties within American culture.

William Rusher, former publisher of National Review, included among "pro-family issues" opposition to abortion, pornography, and gay rights; concern over busing, drug use, and crime; advocacy of gun rights and capital punishment; and "general support for the institution of marriage." James Q. Wilson offered a similar definition in 1993, declaring

> To many conservatives, family values is the mainline of resistance against homosexual marriages, bureaucratized childcare, and compulsory sex education in the schools. For some conservatives, the family means a defense against the very idea of a planned society.

James Dobson of Focus on the Family more recently defined the concerns of the Christian Right as "the killing of babies, the spreading of homosexual propaganda to our children, the distribution of condoms and immoral advice to our teenagers, and the undermining of marriage as an institution." The Christian Coalition's "Contract With the American Family" ranges from prayer in public places to asserting the legal rights of biological parents over those of children.

The "family values" rhetoric of the Right centers on a devout, male-headed family. Michael Lienesch provides an important analysis of how the Christian Right has defined an ideal manhood and a proper femininity. Elizabeth Kadetsky's interviews with women who identify themselves as members of the Christian Right find that these roles offer benefits and significant sacrifices. Both Judith Stacey and Katha Pollitt level angry criticisms at conservatives who would extend a restrictive ideal of womanhood throughout society.

It is the very articulation of gender politics within "family values," the ways in which the Right energizes a social agenda centered around gender, that makes this conservative movement unique. Certainly many New Right activists share the ideal of "traditional" domesticity that was popular throughout American society during the 1950s; some, such as House Speaker Newt Gingrich, still praise a sentimentalized and suburban fifties family. Yet reverence for Ozzie and Harriet in the 1990s cannot be the same as conformity to middle-class family prescriptions during the 1950s. Feminist and gay politics in the 1960s and the 1970s reshaped the ways in which Americans perceive and practice their intimate lives, and the politics surrounding gender and sexuality are vastly different now from what they were in that earlier time. Women may have entered the labor force without fanfare in the 1950s and 1960s, and without directly rejecting domestic ideals. In the 1990s women understand the economic importance of their waged work and how gender shapes it, from issues of sexual discrimination and harassment to the need for quality day-care. Feminism in the 1960s transformed expectations about work and relationships as it changed the political landscape. To discuss family ideals in the 1950s or to name "family values" in the 1990s is to evoke different symbols and social relationships.

The emergence of a movement for gay and lesbian rights also changed the context of "family values." The sexual politics of gay rights has made its deepest impact on culture, from "queer theory" sessions at the Modern Language Association convention to popular plays such as "Angels in America." Part of the agenda of the Right includes efforts to restrict the acknowledgment of gays and lesbians and to limit their unique legal rights, an unforeseeable scenario in the closeted fifties. Although a few openly gay writers within the Right criticize the apparent tolerance among conservatives generally toward anti-gay rhetoric, the ability of the Christian Right to define this discussion of sexuality persists. The moralism at the center of "family values" remains a struggle over the meanings of gender and the legitimate forms of sexuality: about claims to equality within the family, about recognition of specific family forms, and ultimately about the power and privilege of women and men, the terms of femininity and masculinity. If the New Right pronouncements about family ideals sound like a celebration of "Father Knows Best," they nonetheless occur in a world with much more resemblance to "Rosanne" or "Grace Under Fire."

The social debate between the Christian Right and its critics also serves to address broader issues of citizen and state, and to defend a particular organization of capitalist economy. Thus "family values" encompasses more than home and hearth, and who bakes cookies; it raises questions about how the state mediates among classes and how resources are appropriated by gender and, indirectly, by race. The "family values" debate allows the Right to employ gender to achieve a variety of political goals, in other words, including some that would at first glance seem only vaguely connected to family life. As a result, the ongoing battle over "family values" reveals a deepening disagreement over the nature of the modern American state. As sociologist James Davison Hunter has noted, the "culture wars" over media and art

> reveals a conflict over world views—over what standards our communities and our nation will live by; over what we consider to be 'of enduring value' in our communities; over what we consider fair representation of our times. . . . But even more, these battles again lay bare the tensions between two fundamentally different conceptions of the sacred.

To legitimate their efforts, Christian Right activists and conservatives have declared that a "crisis" exists in American family life that threatens national stability. James C. Dobson, president of Focus on the Family, defines it as "a great Civil War of Values"; William Bennett, co-director of Empower America, states simply that "a lot has gone wrong in America." Bennett lists increases in crime, abortion, suicide, child abuse, and the rise of illegitimacy, along with a troublesome welfare dependency as symptoms of a deeper illness. "The answer to much of what ails us," he says, "is spiritual and moral regeneration" to be achieved through family life. Other conservative commentators have cited acceptance of homosexuality and legal obstacles to school prayer as symptoms of national decline. Such descriptions of faltering "family values" depict a grim urban society gripped by crime and secular cynicism, while the solutions offered by the Right center on a revival of spiritual order and Christian ethics, pursued vigorously through legislation and propaganda.

Two persistent themes accompany the discussion of "family values" among Christian activists and their associates: the need to reduce or redirect the influence of the federal government, and a call for individual "responsibility." Conservatives denounce the inefficiency of federal agencies and argue that bureaucracies inherently corrupt or limit individual freedoms. William Kristol, the influential advisor to former Vice President Dan Quayle, contends, for example,

> that citizens should take care of their own lives and not be intimidated by the so-called 'experts'—the government bureaucrats, social welfare providers, therapists, and their friends in the media, who are trying to radically limit the ability of families and individuals to control their own destiny.

Illinois Representative Henry Hyde, a longtime member of Congress, says that government erodes family authority and personal responsibility, "as if the two are perched on opposite ends of a seesaw," while Nevada Republican John Ensign names a "system of Government programs that have helped create a moral decline in this country." Former Republican presidential candidate Phil Gramm offered students at Virginia's Liberty University a similar argument, proclaiming that "government programs established to help our people have changed the way we behave, corrupted our values, and diminished our virtue."

The support of capitalists for this agenda became clear through the 1990s. Some corporate leaders such as Joseph A. Coors provided seed money for conservative foundations in the 1970s, and through the Reagan years many industrialists learned that there would be great rewards in sustaining the conservative agenda. By 1995, corporate lobbyists discovered themselves drafting legislation and sitting at congressional tables during regulatory hearings. Such eager laissez-faire politics reverses the "corporate liberalism" that has been dominant for much of this century. But if it is not surprising that capitalists should recognize an advantage and pursue it, it is remarkable that the potential protections of corporate liberalism, such as social stability, are now dismissed as excessive regulation and dangerous federal control.

The link drawn by the Right between federal authority and family leads with an apparent inevitability to discussions of welfare and dependency, which have become the symbols of federal intrusion and misdirection. As William Kristol describes it, "conservatives want to liberate civil society from the therapeutic welfare state." Although criticism of state assistance has persisted to some degree throughout the century, in the 1970s and early 1980s conservative dissent gathered force. Conservative writers such as George Gilder and Charles Murray popularized attacks against federal aid to the poor, arguing that relief itself generated poverty by encouraging immoral or inappropriate behaviors. The Reagan administration sought to limit federal aid while President Reagan openly condemned "welfare queens" who took advantage of American taxpayers. Despite this rhetoric, and despite federal initiatives to reduce welfare programs, Americans in the early 1980s continued to support assistance to the elderly and the poor. If such negative proposals seemed outrageous to many Americans in the 1980s, by 1994 they had become part of the legislative package promoted by Christian conservatives and pursued by congressional Republicans as their "Contract With America."

As the debate over public assistance unfolded in the 104th Congress, advocates of "welfare reform" spoke of "tough love," hard work, and industry. They implicated the "welfare state" in the decline of morality and proclaimed that assistance as we have known it has ended; in Gingrich's words, there would be no government "escalator" of support for the poor. The rhetoric of "family values" persistently informed these pronouncements, even as it implied a more substantial question about the relations embodied in state assistance and the construction of community obligation.

The welfare debate that has unfolded concerns far more than policies for public assistance, however. Advocates of dramatic cuts in aid speak of laziness and a lack of initiative among the poor while suggesting the pain of the middle class. Opponents of reductions use Save the Children scarves and ties to confront the debate, and talk of innocence and community. Each side of this issue invokes different meanings from what had been once shared symbols. For the Right, children no longer serve as a metaphor for the future, but become rather a measure of past failures and moral flaws. As James Davison Hunter noted in 1990, within the debates between liberals and the Right "the main actors are talking past one another. . . . They are not talking on the same plane of moral and political discourse." Yet political scientist Mathew Moen perceptively points to the Christian Coalition's eager use of the language of liberalism even as they seek to unravel liberal policies. The "Contract with the American Family" reverberates with the language of "rights," even as the Coalition eagerly seeks to limit the rights of women and children on behalf of "family values."

If, as some historians suggest, the "welfare state" represents the more humane face of capitalism, a necessary promise that industrial conditions would not relegate the mass of American workers to extreme privation, the erosion of these guarantees suggests a transformation in political economy in its broadest sense. What has transpired that would allow Americans to accept the prospect of an estimated one million children living in desperate poverty without public aid? One part of the very complicated answer to that question lies in the success of a conservative coalition eager to challenge previous cultural assumptions about poverty and dependency on behalf of "family values." These debates over public assistance, family life, and culture reflect larger ideological battles over gender, authority, and social structure.

The New Christian Right

Political and Social Issues

THROUGH A GLASS DARKLY

Is the Christian Right Overconfident It Knows God's Will?

THOMAS C. ATWOOD

The Evangelical Protestant Right is reawakening. Conservative charismatics, Fundamentalists, and other born-again and Evangelical Christians were briefly confused and demoralized by the demise of Jerry Falwell's Moral Majority, the failure of Pat Robertson's presidential campaign even in the South, the Jim Bakker and Jimmy Swaggart scandals, and the slow start last year by pro-life forces in most parts of the country after the Supreme Court's *Webster* decision partially returned abortion decisions to state legislatures. But now the Evangelical Right is back, better organized for state and local politics and less dependent on highly visible national leaders, and more effective because it works through broader-based organizations not explicitly identified with Evangelicalism.

A panoply of activist organizations has emerged, ranging from local, single-issue, "kitchen-table" operations to national organizations with grass-roots networks throughout the states. Some of the highly visible organizations with strong Evangelical Right support, such as Focus on the Family, Concerned Women for America, and Eagle Forum, downplay their religious identification, choosing instead the more inclusive strategy of emphasizing issues and values. Focus on the Family has two million members, has formed pro-family coalitions in 18 states through its Family Research Council, and syndicates James Dobson's highly popular radio show to 1,400 stations. Concerned Women for America has 700,000 members and a sophisticated national network of phone trees, prayer chapters, and trained lobbyists. The membership of Phyllis Schlafly's Eagle Forum is smaller (80,000) but remarkably efficient in mobilizing through phone trees, newsletters, and lobbyists.

Grass-Roots Revival

Earlier this year, these and other pro-family groups, such as Mississippi minister Don Wildmon's American Family Association, joined with more explicitly evangelical organizations such as the National Association of Evangelicals, the Christian Life Commission of the Southern Baptist Convention, and Pat Robertson's Christian Broadcasting Network in arranging a blitz of phone calls that convinced Congress to remove biases against

religious and informal child-care from federal day-care legislation. More recently, these groups have been at the forefront of the massive public protests against federal funding of obscene and blasphemous art.

Evangelical and other pro-life forces have meanwhile gathered momentum around the states; leaders expect to introduce major pro-life legislation in all but a few state legislatures in 1991. Where comprehensive bans with few or only life-of-the-mother exceptions are judged not to be achievable, most pro-lifers plan to put forth passable legislation that targets the pro-choice "hard cases"—banning gender-selection abortions, postviability abortions, and taxpayer funding of abortions, and requiring parental consent, informed consent, spousal notification, viability testing, and professional standards of hygiene for abortion facilities. They expect to be able to make examples of state legislators who vote against such popular restrictions by "hanging a few scalps on the wall," as Paul Weyrich is fond of saying. This has already happened in Illinois where post-*Webster* pro-life legislation was bottled up in committee by one vote, and a pro-life primary candidate unseated the Republican leader of the House, a 20-year veteran who had voted against the measure.

Other priorities for the Evangelical Right over the next year or two include abstinence-based curricula in sex education classes, vouchers for private school and home-school students, and enforcement of the laws protecting voluntary prayer groups at public schools, while opposing gay rights and contraceptive counseling at school-based clinics. Family tax issues are also on the agenda—restoring the allowance per dependent to 1940s levels (adjusted for inflation) and making adoption-related expenses tax-deductible. And crisis pregnancy counseling centers will continue to be a priority; the Christian Action Council already has 400 centers in the United States and Canada and plans many more.

Beyond these specific goals, the central challenge for

THOMAS C. ATWOOD *is managing editor of* Policy Review. *Formerly controller of Pat Robertson's presidential-campaign exploratory committee, he is now a district chairman in the Fairfax County, Virginia, Republican Party.*

the Evangelical Right is to move from cultural isolation to cultural leadership. Most of the movement's victories so far have been defensive—protecting the tax-exempt status of Christian schools when the Internal Revenue Service threatened to take it away, protecting the religious liberty of students who wanted to form voluntary after-hours prayer groups at public schools, pressuring Presidents Reagan and Bush to name Supreme Court justices who would overturn *Roe* v. *Wade*, stopping public funding of abortion and abortion counseling, stopping convenience stores from openly displaying pornography, stopping state and local "gay rights" legislation in many jurisdictions. But conservative Evangelicals have been less successful in persuading the public of their most important civic values—the affirmative obligation of the state to protect human life, the right of parents to make the most important decisions about educating their children, the right of communities to establish wholesome environments by restricting certain kinds of non-political expression, and the state's obligation to reinforce the institution of the traditional family.

The isolation of the Evangelical Right has also kept it from positions of leadership in government and mainstream politics. The problem is especially severe in the Republican Party, where angry factionalism divides GOP regulars from the Religious Right in many locales, and Evangelicals have failed to win either influence or offices commensurate with the number of enthusiastic activists they have brought into the party.

This isolation is explained partly by widespread bigotry against conservative Evangelicals. Anti-Fundamentalism is probably expressed more commonly and more openly today than either anti-Catholicism or anti-Semitism. But the isolation is also of the Evangelical Right's own making. Conservative Evangelicals have made a number of major political errors that have hampered their effectiveness. And underlying these political errors—paradoxically for a movement that takes religion so seriously—has been a set of theological positions dissonant with Evangelical Christianity.

Overestimation of Strength

A major strategic error of the Evangelical Right has been the overestimation of its own strength. Thinking they had "enough votes to run the country," as one conservative Evangelical leader put it a decade ago, all too many Evangelical Right activists and leaders have spoken in unrealistic terms about what the movement would accomplish. This overconfidence discouraged conservative Evangelicals from following basic rules of politics, such as respect for opposing views, an emphasis on coalition-building and compromise, and careful rhetoric. Thus they often came across as authoritarian, intolerant, and boastful, even to natural constituents. And high expectations made the Evangelical Right look worse for its failure to live up to them. Fear-mongering by groups such as People for the American Way and the American Civil Liberties Union and media exaggerations of Evangelical Right strength also contributed to the general impression that America might be taken over by "moral majoritarians."

A common fallacy during the 1980s was to cite Gallup

St. Jerome seeking guidance as he translates the Bible. Even with the tools God has given us to help discern His will, believers are required to be reverent and cautious about speaking for the Lord.

polls indicating that between 50 million and 80 million Americans call themselves "born-again Christians," as if this self-description somehow equated to acceptance of the Evangelical Right's political agenda. But Evangelicals are hardly monolithic in their political beliefs or voting and party identification. As political scientist Stuart Rothenberg has written, "Politically, Evangelicals cut across the spectrum. While more conservative than the population in general, their ranks also include many liberals. A 1984 survey by the Free Congress Foundation...found that they oppose government funding of abortions overwhelmingly, but they also back the Equal Rights Amendment and support the availability of birth-control information in the public schools. And Evangelicals are split on issues such as defense spending and the morality of abortion." George Gallup Jr. and Jim Castelli confirm this political diversity within Evangelicalism in their 1989 book, *The People's Religion.* For example, many Baptists strongly oppose prayer in public schools, and some of the most prominent evangelical preachers, such as Billy Graham, have kept their distance from the Evangelical Right. And significantly, more Evangelicals voted for George Bush than for Pat Robertson in the early 1988 Republican primaries.

The Evangelical Right probably numbers in the millions rather than the tens of millions. While this still constitutes a powerful political base, especially because so many conservative Evangelicals are willing to become political activists, it also means that the Evangelical Right cannot achieve much political influence without forming coalitions.

New Ecumenism

One of the major organizational achievements of the Evangelical Right has been its coalition-building with conservatives of other faiths. Shared defensive interests have bound conservative Evangelicals together in common cause with theologically and politically conservative Roman Catholics and Jews. As George Weigel of the Ethics and Public Policy Center has said, "The 'new ecumenism'...is the result of a shared perception that the systematic effort to strip American public policy discourse of any relationship to the religiously based values of the American people portends disaster for the American experiment." Conservative Evangelicals and Catholics have cooperated rather harmoniously in the pro-life movement. Through its strong support for Israel

The Evangelical Right never built a strong relationship with the evangelical establishment as represented by Billy Graham, *Christianity Today*, and the National Association of Evangelicals.

on biblical grounds, the Evangelical Right has also developed good ties with a number of Jewish organizations. These coalitions are quite remarkable considering historic Protestant animosities toward Jews and "papist" Roman Catholics.

The Evangelical Right is also itself a coalition across evangelical theological streams that have often been antagonistic toward one another. All Evangelicals share the belief that one must personally accept Jesus Christ as Savior to enjoy eternal life, and almost all maintain the infallibility of Scripture. Many, although not all, identify their conversion with a specific born-again experience. In the past, though, heated divisions among Evangelicals have arisen over Fundamentalism (the belief in a literal interpretation of the Bible); eschatology (whether Christ will come before or after His Kingdom is established); and the Pentecostal or charismatic belief in spiritual gifts, including glossolalia (speaking in tongues), prophecy, and healing. Nevertheless, during the past dozen years, political conservatives from these various evangelical streams, along with conservatives

from mainline Protestant denominations, have generally been able to put aside their theological disputes in making common political cause.

Missed Opportunities

This model of coalition-building has not been replicated elsewhere within Evangelicism, however. The Evangelical Right never built strong relationships with the mainstream evangelical establishment as represented by Billy Graham, *Christianity Today* magazine, and the National Association of Evangelicals. Another missed opportunity has been the failure of white conservative Evangelicals to build effective political relationships with black Evangelicals.

On moral and social issues white Evangelicals are closer to black Evangelicals than they are to white non-Evangelical Protestants. Moreover, a number of items on the agenda of the Evangelical Right could be highly appealing to blacks if framed correctly—particularly parental choice in education and abstinence-based sex education in public schools. An alliance between white and black Evangelicals would also probably be the single most effective way of dispelling derogatory stereotypes of the Evangelical Right.

Leaders of the Evangelical Right have made some efforts to build bridges to blacks. Jerry Falwell has often preached in Watts and other black neighborhoods. Pat Robertson opened his presidential campaign in the predominantly black neighborhood of Bedford-Stuyvesant, site of his first ministry, and chose a black man, Ben Kinchlow, as his co-host on the *700 Club*. Those blacks who have joined the Evangelical Right have been welcomed with open arms.

For the most part, though, black Evangelicals have kept their distance. One reason may be that black churches are often deeply involved with the politics of the Democratic Party and are generally supportive of government welfare programs. Black Evangelical preachers may therefore not want to antagonize their political allies on economic and social-welfare issues by allying with conservatives on moral and family issues.

Another explanation is that the Evangelical Right hasn't given much thought to practical solutions to the problems of special concern to blacks—poverty, unemployment, discrimination, educational inequality, drug addiction, and the deterioration of the black family. Black Evangelicals could tell what conservative white Evangelicals were *against* with respect to "black" issues—redistribution of wealth, allowing capable people to be dependent on welfare, racial quotas, busing, softness on crime, and government-created economic incentives for the dissolution of the family—but they couldn't really tell what white Evangelicals were *for*.

Cognitive (Im)modesty

Coalition difficulties have also lessened the effectiveness of conservative Evangelicals in the party of Lincoln, which has become a "tent divided" in many jurisdictions. Antagonism in the GOP between Republican Party regulars and the Evangelical Right, particularly at the state and local levels, is hurting both parts of this still uneasy coalition. State and local GOP leaderships have in many cases been too resistant to the armies of hard-working activists that the Evangelical Right can offer and the party desperately needs. In some cases, Republican leaders have resorted to dirty tricks, lockouts, and even physical violence and threats to keep these newcomers out. But many conservative Evangelicals have also been unwilling to engage in the compromises and give-and-take so crucial for effective coalition-building. Although some of these mistakes can be traced to inexperience, others stem from misapplications or misinterpretations of evangelical theology in the political context.

Conservative Evangelical activists are now notorious for displaying an overconfidence in their ability to discern the Divine Will at any time, in any situation. Certainly, most people can and should respect Evangelicals' conviction that believers can discern God's will through prayer, Bible study, wise counsel, and the gentle promptings of the in-dwelling Holy Spirit. But some Evangelical activists, at both ends of the political spectrum, have been too quick to put words into the mouth of the Almighty in the political context. Evangelical theologian Carl F. H. Henry said it well when he criticized the Evangelical Right for "its confusion of the inerrancy of Scripture with the inerrancy of its own interpretation and application of Scripture."

In recent years some well-meaning Evangelical Right organizations have applied biblical "scores" to candidates' positions on such issues as the INF Treaty, South Africa sanctions, tax reform, and Contra aid. And politically liberal evangelical leaders use the same Bible to argue for the opposite positions, or even more radical positions such as liberation theology. Well-intentioned though they are, one has to question whether some of these uses of Scripture aren't violations of the command-ment against taking the name of the Lord in vain. From a strategic view, such arguments can be counterproduc-tive, because so many hearers are offended by the presumption of speaking for God.

This overconfidence was especially noticeable among charismatics, who became prominent in the Evangelical Right in the mid- to late 1980s. Charismatics, or Pentecostals, hold that believers are able to discern God's will and word through prophetic gifts, without reference to the authority of Scripture (as long as the "word from

To become cultural leaders, conservative Evangelicals must minister healing, compassion, and justice to the culture, not simply condemn its fallen nature.

noncharismatics.

Similarly, a misinterpretation of the Evangelical belief that God answers prayer led some to a simplistic notion that the truly faithful would achieve their specific, desired political result through public prayer and con-fession, "speaking the word of faith." This has led at times to claims of God-ordained electoral victory, only to be followed by defeat.

Another effect of spiritual overconfidence among Evangelical Right activists has been a tendency not to engage forthrightly the ideas of non-Evangelicals or liberals or even other Evangelicals or conservative Republicans with different views, but rather to dismiss them as ungodly and unworthy of response or discussion. The attitude would tend to be, "Why bother to pay attention to anyone else's ideas if we've already heard from God?" Or as the bumper sticker reads, "God said it, I believe it, that settles it." But the American people expect to hear policy issues openly and publicly debated; indeed they need those kinds of debates in order to make well-considered decisions.

A more biblical (and ultimately more effective) at-

Spiritual warfare is conducted primarily through prayer, evangelism, and ministry, not politics.

the Lord" does not contradict Scripture). But one can believe in prophetic gifts and still acknowledge that they are too subjective for use as an authoritative reference in political argument—and impractical strategically be-cause of the perplexed reactions they generate among

5

titude to replace this spiritual overconfidence would be one of "cognitive modesty—an awareness of the limitations of our knowing," in the words of Richard John Neuhaus in *The Naked Public Square*. An underpreached verse in Scripture is appropriate here: "For now we see through a glass, darkly; but then face to face; now I know in part; but then shall I know even as also I am known" (I Corinthians 13:12). This is not to say that we know no truth, simply that our knowledge is only partial until "the perfect is come" (verse 10), until the Kingdom of God is come. "In this light, modesty and provisionalism are not the result of weak-kneed accommodationism but are required by fidelity to claims of the gospel" (Neuhaus again). Even with the generous tools God has given to help us know Him and discern His will, believers are required to be reverent and cautious about speaking for the Lord, especially in the volatile, darkly glassed world of politics.

Faithful Compromise

A second misapplication of evangelical theology by conservative Evangelicals has been a tendency "to apply to politics the same absolutism and purity they appropriately apply to their religious doctrine," as Brian O'Connell of the National Association of Evangelicals puts it. Evangelical Right activists have sometimes excluded potential coalition partners because they do not share their conservative theism. And, making the opposite error, all too many conservative Evangelical activists have judged a person's sincerity and orthodoxy of faith by his politics. I observed this at the 1990 Fairfax County, Virginia, Republican Convention where one delegate was told that he was "not a Christian" because he was supporting the "wrong" candidate for county chairman. In all fairness, most Evangelical leaders and activists frown on such pronouncements. But even their occasional occurrence perpetuates party factionalism and the negative stereotype of Evangelicals.

A common fallacy was to equate the numbers of born-again Christians—50 million to 80 million—with the political strength of the Evangelical Right.

This political orthodoxy has led to taking a hard line on virtually every issue, and an unwillingness to compromise on tactics. Rather than define and pursue a realistic, achievable agenda of incremental progress, conservative Evangelicals have expected too much too fast, sometimes displaying an almost martyr-like relish for taking extreme positions without concern for results.

Such efforts have generally gone down in flames.

Many conservative Evangelicals have learned from these experiences: the perfect should not be the enemy of the good. It is not necessarily unprincipled to take incremental steps toward a desired policy goal. Nor is it unprincipled to base political decisions, in part, upon the perceived potential consequences of those decisions. Relentless insistence on the once and for all achievement of the "perfect" policy—and on working only with candidates and coalition partners committed to that standard—can leave the Evangelical Right without achieving even a "better" policy. It can also leave them without political allies.

Controversial political issues usually take years, often decades, before they are ultimately settled. For a political movement to be successful, it must have some advocates who articulate the long-term goal (like the abolitionists), despite the controversy such advocacy stirs up; but, as Lincoln was well aware, a politician will not survive if he gets too far ahead of public opinion. A politician can only hope to achieve what is politically achievable in his time, and trust the ultimate resolution to Whom Neuhaus calls the "Arbiter Absolute." In this light, settling temporarily for less than the ideal but moving incrementally toward it can represent both moral progress and an act of faith in God.

Servant-Leadership

A third theological error has been the idea that the people of God—and specifically Evangelical Christians—should *rule*. Two passages from Scripture often used to justify this "dominion mandate" are Genesis 1:26-28, calling on man to rule the earth, and Deuteronomy 28:13, "And the Lord shall make you the head, and not the tail; and you only shall be above, and you shall not be underneath." The triumphalist idea of Evangelical Christian rule, of "putting the righteous in authority" as an end in itself, has been widespread.

But this triumphalism is in conflict with Christ's own definition of leadership: "Whoever would be great among you must be your servant, and whoever would be first among you must be slave of all" (Mark 10:43-44; also Matthew 20:26-27). Christians are not called to rule or "lord over" the people, but to *serve* the people. Leadership is to be earned and maintained through service, not domination. This is not to say that conservative Evangelicals should become servile to the Republican establishment or other prospective coalition partners. True service, like love, requires toughness sometimes. But the truth *can* be spoken in love. One *can* play political hardball with a heart of love and service toward God, neighbor, and even toward political adversaries.

Conservative Evangelical activists who have been most successful at getting and staying ahead in the Republican Party have done so by quietly and diligently earning the trust and respect of both conservatives and moderates. This has been happening with greater frequency as the Evangelical Right's experience grows. But those Evangelical Right activists who have won GOP leadership positions simply because their faction controlled a majority have lost influence when their newcomer fellow activists failed to sustain their political involvement (like

6

the seeds planted on shallow ground that shoot up quickly, but then wither in the heat of the sun).

Most conservative Evangelicals know and believe in this principle of "servant-leadership." For example, Pat Robertson wrote an entire chapter on it in his popular 1982 book, *The Secret Kingdom*. Yet conservative Evangelicals' devotion to this principle has not always been evident. Too often, the implicit rallying cry of the Evangelical Right has been "Christians, take over," instead of "Christians, serve." Too often the rhetoric has seemed to express anger and condemnation. To become cultural leaders, though, conservative Evangelicals must minister healing, compassion, and justice to the culture, not simply condemn its fallen nature.

In practical terms, too, one wonders if the Evangelical Right would be more effective today had its message been more widely understood as "We're here to serve; what can we do to help our party's candidates get elected, or what can we do to help solve the problems of the black community?", instead of "We're the Christians and we're here to take over; are you with us or against us?"

The Law Written on Our Hearts

A fourth theological error that has hindered the effectiveness of the Evangelical Right in coalition politics has been a failure to distinguish between the means of special grace and common grace, and between the authorities of special revelation and general revelation.

An alliance between white and black Evangelicals would probably be the single most effective way of dispelling derogatory stereotypes of the Evangelical Right.

Special grace is that grace available through God's *redemptive* order, that grace available to believers through faith in Christ. Its blessings are salvation, deliverance from sin, a personal relationship with God through prayer, and eternal life in the Kingdom of God. The church's primary charge is to witness to this grace. Special revelation is that revelation which explains the redemptive plan of God—historically considered to be found only in Scripture, but some today might also include the uniquely personal revelation available through prayer, and charismatics would include revelation from true prophecy.

Common grace is that grace available within God's *created* order; it is afforded to all people regardless of religious belief. This created order includes not only physical nature but also aspects of metaphysical nature, including the created moral order. The law of gravity

Despite symbolic overtures such as Pat Robertson's opening of his 1988 presidential campaign in a black Brooklyn neighborhood, the Evangelical Right has not done enough to build bridges with black Evangelicals.

and the "falling of the rain on the just and the unjust" are examples of common grace. Another example, according to Christian (and Jewish) teaching, is that all people are created in the image of God, and are therefore capable of giving and receiving love and of acting unselfishly. The blessings of common grace are the provision, tranquility, and satisfaction that can come from living in harmony with God's created order.

General revelation is universally knowable wisdom that points to God as Creator and to the order of His creation. God's "eternal power and deity [can be] clearly perceived in the things that have been made" (Romans 1:20). His created moral order is knowable by examining "the law written on our hearts" (Romans 2:15). This is the law by which all candid people know that murder is wrong, for example. It is the law by which our consciences, if they are not too cauterized and traumatized by sin, judge us. Kenneth Myers, author of a forthcoming book discussing the importance of common grace to the formulation of a Christian public philosophy, summarizes the distinction between the two types of revelation as follows: "General revelation has to do principally with creation, and special revelation deals uniquely with redemption, although it obviously deals with creation as well." To this summary Myers has added the following important point, "Scripture itself implies that there is no reason to suppose that truth is exhausted in Scripture. That is, if God speaks in creation as well as in His redemptive work and words, then we ought to listen to Him everywhere....[T]here is a biblical mandate for *not* attempting to solve all cultural and social problems with deductions from Scripture."

Many Evangelical Right activists have not recognized the authority of general revelation, and instead have liberally referred to special revelation in their political arguments. Quoting chapter and verse, they would attempt to deduce their policy goals from biblical principles, "government by the Book," as one Freedom Council publication is titled. Their communications would also often use redemptive rhetoric to rally the

7

troops, exhorting them to band together to "take America for Christ" or "restore America to righteousness." This language has been understandably alarming to people of other faiths, even to many Christians, who feared the Evangelical Right would impose its beliefs on everyone else. Such rhetoric also limited the potentially broad appeal of the Evangelical Right's arguments, which could easily have been phrased in general revelation terms, but were instead tuned out by Americans irritated by "Christianese."

"Christian America"

Even many Evangelicals have been disturbed by the Evangelical Right's overuse of redemptive vocabulary and concepts in public policy arguments, which imply, contrary to Christian teaching, that the state has a redemptive capability. The government described in

---

"There is a biblical mandate for *not* attempting to solve all cultural and social problems with deductions from Scripture."

Romans 13 is clearly an institution of common, not special, grace. Its role is the mitigation of evil in a fallen world, not the redemption of man's sinful nature. Politics can help by providing public forums for discussions of morality, and good law does influence public moral behavior, but the primary means of restoring righteousness will always be spiritual and moral revival in the hearts of people, which is a task for God Himself and for a Holy Spirit-led Church.

Many Christians have also been disturbed that the overuse of special revelation in policy debate politicizes the Gospel, thereby competing with the Gospel's redemptive purpose, distracting and confusing disciples and potential converts alike with cacophonous voices, and diluting its power to save. As Michael Cromartie, co-editor of *Piety and Politics: Evangelicals and Fundamentalists Confront the World*, says, "Many people are looking for the bread of life and instead some Christian leaders only give them a 'political stone.'...But our very best political efforts will not reconcile us to the Father."

Many conservative Evangelicals have referred to America's Christian heritage in justifying their reliance on scriptural arguments as well as their calls to restore America to her Christian roots. However, despite the Founding Fathers' biblical ethos and worldview, their finest piece of political advocacy, the *Federalist Papers*, contains scant reference to God and Providence, let alone biblical chapter and verse. As Regent University (formerly CBN University) associate professor Gary Amos points out in his book, *Defending the Declaration*,

when the Founders did appeal to God or Providence, as in the Declaration of Independence, it was to God as Creator, the Endower of unalienable rights, not as Redeemer. Moreover, during conservative Protestantism's heyday in the mid-19th century, when the calls for a "Christian America" had widespread support, the goal was generally a Christian "people," "society," or "civilization." There was no establishment of any religion even at the state level after 1833. Most 19th-century Americans viewed a Christian "state" as an indirect result of a Christian people or nation, not the other way around, as it might seem with some Evangelical Right activists' heavy emphasis on politics.

Reformed Rhetoric

One of the virtues of the Evangelical Right has been its sincere effort to learn from its mistakes. The theological and political lessons mentioned in this article are frequently discussed within the movement. The biblical philosophy of political involvement these lessons suggest would consist of five principles, all now recognized in much of the literature of the Evangelical Right: cognitive modesty, or sensitivity to the limitations of human knowing; faithful, principled compromise and political realism; servant-leadership; consensus-building by appeal primarily to general revelation; and recognition of the limited spiritual authority and capability of government. More specific recommendations arising from these principles include:

• Use scriptural references more judiciously and stop using messianic rhetoric to describe and motivate the movement. Appeal instead primarily to general revelation; the term "commonsense public values" would be a good one to add to "traditional" and "Judeo-Christian" values. Effective commonsense arguments can be made for every Evangelical Right agenda item. Sparing use of Scripture can be effective in illustrating a point, but let God's Word speak for itself. Don't preach it or use it argumentatively; the hearers are not likely to change their opinions of the authority of Scripture based on its use in a political statement.

• Keep discussion of "spiritual warfare" to a minimum in political communications. After all, spiritual warfare is conducted primarily through prayer, evangelism, and ministry, not politics. And calling opponents ungodly usually backfires. So does referring to "secular humanism" as an established religion, an argument that falls on deaf ears outside the Religious Right. Don't exaggerate anti-Christian bias; given the freedom of religion, the proliferation of religious broadcasters, and the rapid growth of evangelical churches in America, indiscriminate charges of persecution against Christians can jeopardize credibility.

• Calm down fund-raising communications, which are too often inflammatory and apocalyptic, thus setting the wrong rhetorical tone for grass-roots activists, who often repeat in public what they read in these letters, to their causes' detriment. (According to some letters, western civilization should have ended several times by now.) Many managers of direct mail fund-raising still speak of the need to appeal to the emotions of anger, fear, and guilt in order to generate response. But the most effective Evangelical Right nonprofits in the long run will be those that operate on the assumption that their activists are spiritually mature, and can be motivated by the obligations of responsible citizenship, compassion and love for one's neighbor, and stewardship of traditional American values.

As Charles Colson puts it in a recent article, "Don't Swing That Bible," in Focus on the Family's *Citizen*: "A broken world will see either our faces twisted in hate and anger or the face of Christ, listening, serving, speaking the truth in love." In that same issue readers are advised to avoid "Christianese," such as, "The Lord told me to attend this protest and call lawmakers to repentance and righteousness"; to avoid inflammatory and derogatory language, such as describing homosexuals as "perverts"; and to "display love for your neighbor, the media, and the opposition through kind gestures."

Pilgrims' Progress

• Make tactical compromises in order to achieve longer-term objectives. For example, pro-lifers' plans to target maximum achievable pro-life legislation, state by state, will save some lives right away; they will also turn the legislative and public relations momentum in the movement's favor and perhaps eventually lead the public to support a comprehensive ban. A pro-life candidate who wants both to be elected and to be faithful to his or her principles may find it useful to refer to the final will of the people as the sovereign in making major policy decisions. When, in advocating an intermediate position on abortion, the candidate is asked the inevitable question, whether there should be a ban, he or she might respond, "Yes, I believe there should be a ban, and as state legislator I hope to lead the people to that same conclusion. Ultimately, though, the people will decide this question, not me. Right now the people of our state are undecided about the most fundamental question, whether to ban, but they are decidedly pro-life on these intermediate positions I am proposing. During this term these are the measures I will be advocating." This approach allows the honesty and straightforwardness the

Conservative Evangelicals should appeal primarily to general, not special, revelation in political arguments.

tive Evangelicals have confidence in their ideas, they should not fear testing them in frank, but respectful, public exchanges. The public requires this kind of debate in order to make good decisions.

• Reach out to the large number of Americans who morally oppose abortion but presently believe that it should remain partly or mostly legal. Certainly, there are no possibilities for cooperation with the radical leadership of pro-abortion organizations, but joint efforts to discourage abortions and provide alternatives to them may be possible with this "middle" group. For example, many Americans not yet willing to embrace the ultimate pro-life goal of a comprehensive ban on abortion may be prepared to join pro-lifers in working the pro-adoption principle into pregnancy counseling, sponsoring support services for unwed mothers who place their babies for adoption, discouraging abortion in sex education, or promoting pre- and post-natal health services for low-income mothers. Many would also support limited rollback measures, such as banning gender-selection and post-viability abortions, banning taxpayer funding, and requiring professional standards of medical hygiene at abortion facilities. Perhaps most important, pro-lifers and this middle group could voice common opposition to abortion, thus strengthening cultural sanctions against the practice, regardless of its legal status.

• Work overtime building the ranks of conservatives in local and state parties. The frontlines for most Evangelical Right issues are in campaigns for state legislator.

The central challenge for the Evangelical Right is to move from cultural isolation to cultural leadership.

---

electorate expects, while placing the accountability for the decision where it belongs in a representative democracy, with the people.

• Seek courteous exchanges of ideas with potential allies and even opponents on key issues. These exchanges could take place both in private, or in public, say, in conferences, seminars, or debates, or in guest appearances on evangelical TV and radio talk shows. If conserva-

For success in these campaigns, it is just as important that conservative Evangelicals serve the public on local tax, law enforcement, infrastructure, and environmental issues as on the moral and pro-family issues. It is also important to play hardball—targeting liberal incumbents in state legislatures much as the National Conservative Political Action Committee did so successfully with Congress in the late 1970s and early 1980s.

• Whether Democrats or Republicans, conservative Evangelical activists should support their party's nominees whenever possible, but *always* get something in exchange. Even when the nominee is a moderate, a decent-sized conservative constituency still has the opportunity to negotiate commitments from him or her

---

Temporarily settling for less than the ideal policy, but moving incrementally toward the ultimate goal, can represent moral progress and an act of faith in God.

---

that, if implemented, would incrementally move certain key policies in the right direction. If local conservative Evangelical leaders go to the candidate shortly after the nomination and offer their support in exchange for certain realistic, politically viable, minimum positions on their three or four top priority issues, they may still be able to make progress toward their goals.

• When organizing in political parties, Evangelical Right activists should not overemphasize their faith. Setting up as the "Christian bloc" essentially requires all other party activists to make a choice for or against the bloc. The "Christian" label discourages potential non-Evangelical coalition partners from joining and offends other Christians who resent the commandeering of the term. It also promotes rigid factions. This segregation could lead to conservative Evangelicals' being relegated to the status of a special interest group, rather than having their people and ideas ultimately accepted and assimilated into party leadership and direction. The most relevant concerns in developing political relationships are potential coalition partners' reliability and views on

issues, not their faith. This doesn't mean Evangelical activists should hide their faith or abandon their personal evangelistic responsibility. Nor is there any reason they should refrain from using whatever lists or networks are available for recruiting volunteers and delegates, including church lists.

• Look for opportunities to build coalitions with black Evangelicals. Useful issues include privatizing public housing, abstinence-based sex education and opposition to school-based clinics (most of which are going into poor, minority neighborhoods, often against parents' wishes), and educational choice for inner-city kids, so they can get a decent education and work their way out of the ghetto, or better yet, help revive it. This latter issue appears to blend black and white Evangelicals' interests particularly well, especially given the courageous leadership of black state legislator Polly Williams, who is bringing education vouchers to Milwaukee. Williams would make an excellent guest on evangelical TV and radio talk shows.

• Continue the trend toward decentralized leadership. A movement whose fate is closely tied to the fate of one or two individuals is vulnerable; one person is easier for adversaries to pick off than an entire movement. Moreover, the highest priority issues for the Evangelical Right are state and local issues; the kind of social and moral change conservative Evangelicals are looking for is only going to happen from the ground up, not the top down.

Onward Christian Citizens

When Jerry Falwell shut down Moral Majority he was criticized for saying its work was done; obviously the policymaking work of the Evangelical Right is incomplete. He was right, though, in saying, "We have raised up a generation of fighters and leaders and activists." The organization had outlived its usefulness; the political baggage it carried made it an easy target for opponents to use to perpetuate a negative stereotype of Evangelicals. Moral Majority—and Pat Robertson's presidential campaign—can be likened to the grains of wheat that had to fall to the ground and die, in order to bring forth new life. Both were flawed, but in the end both served the vital purposes of reviving the spirit of citizenship in a disaffected people and training their followers in the school of hard political knocks. Conservative Evangelicals can yet be the cultural leaders, the salt, light, and fruitful grain, they are called to be, but only by persistently applying the lessons of the '80s. "Servant-leadership" may not have the dramatic ring that a "moral crusade" for political power does, but it is the true call of Christian citizenship.   ☎

10

The Right Rides High

BY CHIP BERLET

As the United States slides toward the Twenty-first Century, the major movements offering a critique of the bipartisan status quo are to be found not on the left of the political spectrum but on the right. The resurgent Right is made up of several different strands, but together, ultraconservative organizations and dogmatic religious and political movements pose a grave threat to democracy in America.

The Religious Right has come to dominate the Republican Party in at least ten of the fifty states. As part of its aggressive grass-roots campaign, the Religious Right is targeting electoral races from school boards to state legislatures, as well as campaigns for the U.S. Senate and House of Representatives. It is a social movement that uses a pious and traditionalist constituency as its mass base to pursue the political goal of imposing a narrow theological agenda on secular society.

Along with the Religious Right, two other significant right-wing political movements threaten democracy: Regressive Populism, typified by diverse groups ranging from members of the John Birch Society to followers of Ross Perot, and Racial Nationalism, promoted by Pat Buchanan and his shadow, David Duke of Louisiana, and increasingly influential in conservative political circles closer to the mainstream.

Finally, there is the militant, overtly racist Far Right that includes the White Supremacists, Ku Klux Klan, skinheads, neo-Nazis, and armed right-wing revolutionaries. Although numerically smaller, the Far Right is a serious political factor in

some rural areas, and its propaganda promoting violence reaches into major metropolitan centers where it encourages alienated young people to commit hate crimes against people of color, Jews, and gays and lesbians, among other targets. The electoral efforts of Buchanan and Duke serve as a bridge between mainstream conservatives and these Far Right movements.

All four of the right-wing movements are antidemocratic in nature, promoting in various combinations and to varying degrees authoritarianism, xenophobia, conspiracy theories, nativism, racism, sexism, homophobia, demagoguery, and scapegoating. There are constant differences and debates within the Right, as well as considerable overlap along the edges. The relationships are complex: The Birchers feud with Perot on trade issues, even though their other basic themes are similar, and the Religious Right has much in common with Regressive Populism, though the demographics of their respective voting blocs appear to be remarkably distinct.

Despite the differences, however, one

goal has united the various sectors of the antidemocratic Right in a series of amorphous coalitions since the 1960s: to roll back the limited gains achieved in the United States by the civil-rights, antiwar, feminist, environmental, and gay-rights movements.

Each wing of the Right has a slightly different vision of the ideal nation:

¶ The Religious Right's ideal is a theocracy in which Christian men interpret God's will as law in a hierarchy where women are helpmates, children are property of their parents, and the Earth must submit to the dominion of those to whom God has granted power. People are basically sinful, and must be restrained by harsh punitive laws. Social problems are caused by Satanic conspiracies aided and abetted by liberals, homosexuals, feminists, and secular humanists. These forces must be exposed and neutralized.

Newspaper columnist Cal Thomas, a longstanding activist in the Religious Right, recently suggested that churches and synagogues take over the welfare system "because these institutions would also deal with the hearts and souls of men and women." The churches "could reach root causes of poverty"—a lack of personal responsibility, Thomas wrote. "If government is always there to bail out people who have children out of wedlock, if there is no disincentive for doing for one's self, then large numbers of people will feel no need to get themselves together and behave responsibly."

¶ For Regressive Populism, the ideal is economic Darwinism, with no regulations restraining entrepreneurial capitalism. The benevolent despot rules by organically expressing the will of the people. Social problems are caused by corrupt and lazy government officials who are bleeding the common people dry in a conspiracy fostered by secret elites, which must be exposed and neutralized.

Linda Thompson, a latter-day Joan of Arc for the New Patriot movement, represents the most militant wing of Regressive

Chip Berlet is an analyst at Political Research Associates in Cambridge, Massachusetts. He wishes to acknowledge the input of researchers and activists who met last year at the Blue Mountain Conference Center in upstate New York (including Suzanne Pharr, Loretta Ross, Russ Bellant, Skipp Porteous, Fred Clarkson, Robert Bray, Tarso Ramos, Scot Nakagawa, Marghe Covino, and others); Lumiere Productions (with Frances Fitzgerald, Leo Ribuffo, John C. Green, and George Marsden), and Political Research Associates (with Jean Hardisty and the late Margaret Quigley), as well as private conversations with Sara Diamond, Holly Sklar, and Matthew N. Lyons. For a Defend Democracy & Pluralism kit, including an extensive bibliography and resource guide, a list of groups fighting the Right, and a copy of the Blue Mountain statement, send $5.00 to Political Research Associates, 678 Massachusetts Avenue, Suite 702, Cambridge, MA 02139.

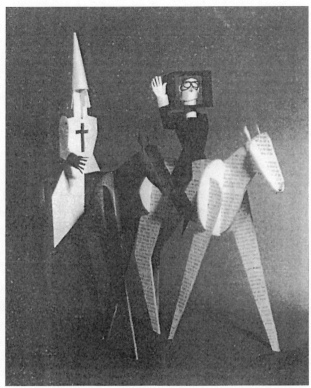

Populism. She has appointed herself "Acting Adjutant General" of the united militias that have formed armed cells across the United States. Operating out of the American Justice Federation of Indianapolis, Thompson's group warns of secret plots by "corrupt leaders" involving "Concentration Camps, Implantable Bio Chips, Mind Control, Laser Weapons," and "neuro-linguistic programming" on behalf of bankers who "control the economy" and created the illegal income tax.

¶ The Racial Nationalists' ideal oscillates between brutish authoritarianism and vulgar fascism in service of white male supremacy. Unilateral militarism abroad and repression at home are utilized to force compliance. Social problems are caused by uncivilized people of color, lower-class foreigners, and dual-loyalist Jews, who must all be exposed and neutralized.

Samuel Francis, the prototypical Racial Nationalist, writes columns warning against attempts to "wipe out traditional white, American, Christian, and Western

Culture," which he blames on multiculturalism. Francis's solution: "Americans who want to conserve their civilization need to get rid of elites who want to wreck it, but they also need to kick out the vagrant savages who have wandered across the border, now claim our country as their own, and impose their cultures upon us. If there are any Americans left in San Jose, they might start taking back their country by taking back their own city. . . . You don't find statues to Quetzalcoatl in Vermont."

¶ For the Far Right, the ideal is white revolution to overthrow the corrupt regime and restore an idealized natural biological order. Social problems are caused by crafty Jews manipulating inferior people of color. They must be exposed and neutralized.

The Truth at Last is a racist Far Right tabloid that features such headlines as JEWS DEMAND BLACK LEADERS OSTRACIZE FARRAKHAN, CLINTON CONTINUES MASSIVE APPOINTMENTS OF MINORITIES, and ADOPTING BLACKS INTO WHITE FAMILIES DOES NOT RAISE THEIR IQ, which

concluded that "only the preservation of the white race can save civilization. . . . Racial intermarriage produces a breed of lower-IQ mongrel people."

Ll of these antidemocratic tendencies are trying to build grass-roots mass movements to support their agendas. Across the Right one hears calls for a new populist revolt. Many people presume that all populist movements are naturally progressive and want to move society to the left, but history teaches us otherwise. Populism can move to the left or right. It can be tolerant or intolerant. In her book, *Populism*, Margaret Canovan defined two main branches of Populism: agrarian and political.

Agrarian populism worldwide has three categories: movements of commodity farmers, movements of subsistence peasants, and movements of intellectuals who wistfully romanticize the hard-working farmers and peasants. Political populism includes not only populist democracy, championed by progressives from the LaFollettes of Wisconsin to Jesse Jackson, but also politicians' populism, reactionary populism, and populist dictatorship. The latter three antidemocratic forms of populism characterize the movements of Ross Perot, Pat Robertson, and Pat Buchanan, three straight White Christian men trying to ride the same horse.

Of the hundreds of Religious Right groups, the most influential is the Christian Coalition led by televangelist and corporate mogul Pat Robertson. Because of Robertson's smooth style and easy access to power, most mainstream journalists routinely ignore his authoritarianism, bigotry, and paranoid dabbling in conspiracy theories. Robertson's gallery of conspirators parallels the roster of the John Birch Society, including the Freemasons, the Bavarian Illuminati, the Council on Foreign Relations, and the Trilateral Commission.

In Robertson's book *The New World Order*, he trumps the Birchers (their founder called Dwight Eisenhower a communist agent) by alluding to an anti-Christian conspiracy that supposedly began in ancient Babylon—a theory that evokes historic anti-Jewish bigotry and resembles the notions of the fascist demagogue Lyndon LaRouche, who is routinely dismissed by the corporate media as a crackpot. Robertson's homophobia is profound. He is also a religious bigot who has repeatedly said that Hindus and Muslims are not morally qualified to hold government posts. "If anybody understood what Hindus really believe," says Robertson, "there would be no doubt that they have no business administering government policies in a country that favors freedom and equality."

Robertson's embrace of authoritarian theocracy is equally robust: "There will never be world peace until God's house and God's people are given their rightful place of leadership at the top of the world. How can there be peace when drunkards, drug dealers, communists, atheists, New Age worshipers of Satan, secular humanists, oppressive dictators, greedy money changers, revolutionary assassins, adulterers, and homosexuals are on top?"

Mainstream pundits are uncertain about the magnitude of the threat posed by the Religious Right. Sidney Blumenthal warned recently in *The New Yorker* that "Republican politics nationally, and particularly in Virginia, have advanced so swiftly toward the Right in the past two years that [Oliver] North's nomination [for the U.S. Senate] was almost inevitable." But just a few years ago, after George Bush was elected President, Blumenthal dismissed the idea that the Religious Right was a continuing factor in national politics.

"Journalists like Blumenthal are centrists who believe that America always fixes itself by returning to the center. They have the hardest time appreciating the danger the Right represents because they see it as just another swing of the political pendulum," says Jean Hardisty, a political scientist who has monitored the Right for more than twenty years. "As the McCarthy period showed, however, if you let a right-wing movement go long enough without serious challenge, it can become a real threat and cause real damage. Centrists missed the significance of the right-wing drive of the past fourteen years as it headed for success."

The Right has now managed to shift the spectrum of political debate, making conservative politics look mainstream when compared with overt bigotry, and numbing the public to the racism and injustice in mainstream politics.

When, for example, Vice President Dan Quayle was asked by ABC what he thought of David Duke, Quayle sanitized Duke's thorough racism and said: "The message of David Duke is . . . anti-big-government, get out of my pocketbook, cut taxes, put welfare people back to work. That's a very popular message. The problem is the messenger. David Duke, neo-Nazi, ex-Klansman, basically a bad person."

The pull of the antidemocratic Right and its reliance on scapegoating, especially of people of color, is a major factor in the increased support among centrist politicians for draconian crime bills, restrictive immigration laws, and punitive welfare regulations. The Republican Party's use of the race card, from Richard Nixon's Southern Strategy to the Willie Horton ads of George Bush's 1988 campaign, is made more acceptable by the overt racism of the Far Right. Racist stereotypes are used opportunistically to reach an angry white constituency of middle- and working-class people who have legitimate grievances caused by the failure of the bi-partisan status quo to resolve issues of economic and social justice.

Scapegoating evokes a misdirected response to genuine unresolved grievances. The Right has mobilized a mass base by focusing the legitimate anger of parents over inadequate resources for the public schools on the scapegoat of gay and lesbian curriculum, sex education, and AIDS-awareness programs; by focusing confusion over changing sex roles and the unfinished equalization of power between men and women on the scapegoat of the feminist movement and abortion rights; by focusing the desperation of unemployment and underemployment on the scapegoat of affirmative-action programs and other attempts to rectify racial injustice; by focusing resentment about taxes and the economy on the scapegoat of dark-skinned immigrants; by focusing anger over thoughtless and intrusive government policies on environmental activists, and by focusing anxiety about a failing criminal-justice system on the scapegoat of early-release, probation, and parole programs for prisoners who are disproportionately people of color.

Such scapegoating has been applied intensively in rural areas, and there are signs of an emerging social movement of "new patriots" who are grafting together the conspiracy theories of the John Birch Society with the ardor and armor of the para-military Right.

These Far Right forces are beginning to influence state and local politics in the Pacific Northwest and Rocky Mountain states through amorphous sovereignty campaigns, county autonomy and "posse" movements, and some portions of the anti-environmentalist "wise use" effort. The same regions have seen contests within the Republican Party on the state level between mainstream Republicans and the Religious Right. The political spectrum in some states now ranges from repressive

corporate liberalism on the "left" through authoritarian theocracy to nascent fascism.

Spanning the breadth of the anti-democratic Right is the banner of the Culture War. According to current conspiratorial myth, liberal treachery in service of godless secular humanism has been "dumbing down" schoolchildren with the help of the National Education Association to prepare the country for totalitarian rule under a "One World Government" and "New World Order."

The idea of the Culture War was promoted by strategist Paul Weyrich of the Free Congress Foundation. In 1987, Weyrich commissioned a study, *Cultural Conservatism: Toward a New National Agenda*, which argued that cultural issues provided antiliberalism with a more unifying concept than economic conservatism. *Cultural Conservatism: Theory and Practice* followed in 1991.

Earlier, Weyrich had sponsored the 1982 book *The Homosexual Agenda* and the 1987 *Gays, AIDS, and You*, which helped spawn successive and successful waves of homophobia. The Free Congress Foundation, founded and funded with money from the Coors Beer family fortune, is the key strategic think tank backing Robertson's Christian Coalition, which is building a grass-roots movement to wage the Culture War.

For Robertson, the Culture War opposes sinister forces wittingly or unwittingly doing the bidding of Satan. This struggle for the soul of America takes on metaphysical dimensions combining historic elements of the Crusades and the Inquisition. The Christian Coalition could conceivably evolve into a more mainstream conservative political movement, or—especially if the economy deteriorates—it could build a mass base for fascism similar to the clerical fascist movements of mid-century Europe.

John C. Green is a political scientist and director of the Ray C. Bliss Institute at the University of Akron in Ohio. With a small group of colleagues, Green has studied the influence of Christian evangelicals on recent elections, and has found that contrary to popular opinion, the nasty and divisive rhetoric of Pat Buchanan, Pat Robertson, and Marilyn Quayle at the 1992 Republican Convention was not as significant a factor in the defeat of Bush as were unemployment and the general state of the economy. On balance, he believes, the Republicans gained more votes than they lost in 1992 by embracing the Religious Right. "Christian evangelicals played a significant role in mobilizing voters and casting votes for the Bush-Quayle ticket," says Green.

Green and his colleagues, James L. Guth and Kevin Hill, wrote a study entitled *Faith and Election: The Christian Right in Congressional Campaigns 1978-1988*. They found that the Religious Right

was most active—and apparently successful—when three factors converged: (1) the demand for Christian Right activism by discontented constituencies; (2) religious organizations who supplied resources for such activism, and (3) appropriate choices in the deployment of such resources by movement leaders. The authors see the Christian Right's recent emphasis on grass-roots organizing as a strategic choice, and conclude that "the conjunction of motivations, resources, and opportunities reveals the political character of the Christian Right: much of its activity was a calculated response to real grievances by increasingly self-conscious and empowered traditionalists."

How did we get here? The current right-wing avalanche began when a group of conservative strategists decided to brush off the flakes who had burdened the unsuccessful 1964 Goldwater Presidential campaign. Such activists as Phyllis Schlafly and John Stormer had helped engineer Barry Goldwater's nomination at the Republican convention. Schlafly was a convention delegate in 1964, and went on to found the Eagle Forum, which fought the Equal Rights Amendment. Stormer wrote a book called *None Dare Call It Treason*. Their aggressive anticommunist militarism worried many conventional voters, and their conspiracy theories of secret collusion between corporate Republican leaders and the communists—Schlafly called them the "secret kingmakers" in her pro-Goldwater book, *A Choice Not an Echo*—brought the Far Right out of the woodwork as Goldwater supporters, which also cost votes.

Most influential Goldwater supporters were not marginal Far Right activists, as many liberal academics postulated at the time, but had been Republican Party regulars for years, representing a vocal reactionary wing far to the right of many persons who usually voted Republican. This reactionary wing had an image problem, which was amply demonstrated by the devastating defeat of Goldwater in the general election.

If reactionaries wanted to dominate the Republican Party, they had to face their image problem. This meant creating a "New Right" that distanced itself (at least publicly) from several problematic sectors of the Old Right. Overt white supremacists and segregationists had to go, as did obvious anti-Jewish bigots. The wild-eyed conspiratorial rhetoric of the John Birch Society was unacceptable, even to William F. Buckley Jr., whose *National Review* was the authoritative journal of the Right. While the Old Right's image was being modernized, emerging technologies and techniques using computers, direct mail, and television were brought into play to build the New Right. Richard Viguerie built the first right-wing direct-

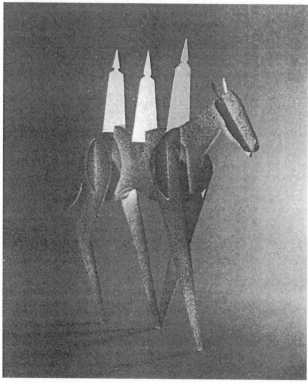

MICHAEL DUFFY

tion and enforcing policies that take rights away from individuals perceived as sinful. Matters of money are interpreted to persuade the sinking middle class to cheer when the rich get richer and the poor get poorer. Toward these ends, questionable statistics, pseudoscientific studies, and biased reports flood the national debate through the sluice gates of the right-wing think tanks.

Thus, the Right has persuaded many voters that condoms don't work but trickle-down theories do. The success of the Right in capturing the national debate over such issues as taxes, Government spending, abortion, sexuality, child-rearing, welfare, immigration, and crime is due, in part, to its national infrastructure, which refines and tests its rhetoric by conducting marketing studies, including those based on financial response to direct-mail letters and televangelist pitches.

But corporate millionaires and zealous right-wing activists can't deliver votes without a grass-roots constituency that responds to the rhetoric. Conveniently, the New Right's need for foot-soldiers arrived just as one branch of Christianity, Protestant evangelicalism, marched onward toward a renewed interest in the political process. Earlier in the century, Protestant evangelicals fought the teaching of evolution and launched a temperance campaign that led to Prohibition. But in the decades preceding the 1950s, most Protestant evangelicals avoided the secular arena. Their return was facilitated by the Reverend Billy Graham, perhaps the best known proponent of the idea that all Protestants should participate in the secular sphere to fight the influence of Godless communism at home and abroad, and others ranging from the international Moral Re-Armament movement to local pastors who helped craft theological arguments urging all Christians to become active in politics in the 1950s and 1960s.

mail empire by computerizing the list of Goldwater contributors. And to reach the grass-roots activists and voters, right-wing strategists openly adopted the successful organizing, research, and training methods that had been pioneered by the labor and civil-rights movements.

When Richard Nixon was elected President in 1968, his campaign payoff to the emerging New Right included appointing such right-wing activists as Howard Phillips to Government posts. Phillips was sent to the Office of Economic Opportunity with a mandate to dismantle social programs allegedly dominated by liberals and radicals. Conservatives and reactionaries joined in a "Defund the Left" campaign. As conservatives in Congress sought to gut social-welfare programs, corporate funders were urged to switch their charitable donations to build a network of conservative think tanks and other institutions to challenge what was seen as the intellectual dominance of Congress and society held by such liberal think tanks as the Brookings Institution.

Since the 1960s, the secular, corporate, and religious branches of the Right have spent hundreds of millions of dollars to build a solid national right-wing infrastructure that provides training, conducts research, publishes studies, produces educational resources, engages in networking and coalition building, promotes a sense of solidarity and possible victory, shapes issues, provides legal advice, suggests tactics, and tests and defines specific rhetoric and slogans. Today, the vast majority of "experts" featured on television and radio talk shows, and many syndicated print columnists, have been groomed by the right-wing infrastructure, and some of these figures were first recruited and trained while they were still in college.

Refining rhetoric is key for the Right because many of its ideas are based on narrow and nasty Biblical interpretations or are of benefit to only the wealthiest sector of society. The Religious Right seeks to breach the wall of separation between Church and State by constructing persuasive secular arguments for enacting legisla-

A more aggressive form of evangelicalism emerged in the 1970s, when such right-wing activists as Francis A. Schaeffer, founder of the L'Abri Fellowship in Switzerland and author of *How Should We Then Live?*, challenged Christians to take control of a sinful secular society. Schaeffer (and his son Franky) influenced many of today's Religious Right activists, including Jerry Falwell, Tim LaHaye, and John W. Whitehead, who have gone off in several theological and political directions, but all adhere to the notion that the Scriptures have given dominion over the Earth to Christians, who thus owe it to God to seize the reins of secular society.

The most extreme interpretation of this "dominionism" is a movement called Reconstructionism, led by right-wing Presbyterians who argue that secular law is always secondary to Biblical law. While the

Reconstructionists represent only a small minority within Protestant theological circles, they have had tremendous influence on the Religious Right (a situation not unlike the influence of Students for a Democratic Society or the Black Panthers on the New Left in the 1960s). Reconstructionism is a factor behind the increased violence in the anti-abortion movement, the nastiest of attacks on gays and lesbians, and the new wave of battles over alleged secular humanist influence in the public schools. Some militant Reconstructionists even support the death penalty for adulterers, homosexuals, and recalcitrant children.

The Coalition on Revival has helped bring dominionism into the Religious Right political movement. Militant anti-abortion activist Randall Terry writes for their magazine, *Crosswinds*, and has signed their Manifesto for the Christian Church, which proclaims that America should "function as a Christian nation" and that the "world will not know how to live or which direction to go without the Church's Biblical influence on its theories, laws, actions, and institutions," including opposition to such "social moral evils" as "abortion on demand, fornication, homosexuality, sexual entertainment, state usurpation of parental rights and God-given liberties, statist-collectivist theft from citizens through devaluation of their money and redistribution of their wealth, and evolutionism taught as a monopoly viewpoint in the public schools." Taken as a whole, the manifesto is a call for clerical fascism in defense of wealth and patriarchy.

While dominionism spread, the numbers of persons identifying themselves as born-again Christians was growing, and by the mid-1970s, rightists were making a concerted effort to link Christian evangelicals to conservative ideology. Sara Diamond, author of *Spiritual Warfare*, assigns a seminal role to Bill Bright of the Campus Crusade for Christ, but traces the paternity of the New Right to 1979, when Robert Billings of the National Christian Action Council invited rising televangelist Jerry Falwell to a meeting with right-wing strategists Paul Weyrich, Howard Phillips, Richard Viguerie, and Ed McAteer. According to Diamond, "Weyrich proposed that if the Republican Party could be persuaded to take a firm stance against abortion, that would split the strong Catholic voting bloc within the Democratic Party." Weyrich suggested building an organization with a name involving the idea of a "moral majority."

While Falwell's Moral Majority began hammering on the issue of abortion, the core founding partners of the New Right were joined in a broad coalition by the growing neoconservative movement of former liberals concerned over what they perceived as a growing communist threat

and shrinking moral leadership. Reluctantly, the remnants of the Old Right hitched a ride on the only electoral wagon moving to the Right. The New Right coalition was built around shared support for anticommunist militarism, moral orthodoxy, and economic conservatism, the themes adopted by 1980 Presidential candidate Ronald Reagan.

The first attempt to build a broad Religious Right movement failed in part because Jerry Falwell's Moral Majority, with its Baptist roots and pragmatic fundamentalist Protestant aura, had only a limited constituency; it failed to mobilize either the more ethereal charismatic and Pentecostal wings of Christianity or the more moderate branches of denominational Protestantism. Apart from the abortion issue, its appeal to conservative Catholics was microscopic.

But as early as 1981 Falwell, Weyrich and Robertson were working together to build a broader and more durable alliance of the Religious Right through such vehicles as the annual Family Forum national conferences, where members of the Reagan Administration could rub shoulders with leaders of dozens of Christian Right groups and share ideas with rank-and-file activists. This coalition-building continued through the Reagan years.

When the scandals of Jimmy Swaggart and Jim Bakker rocked televangelism and Pat Robertson failed in his 1988 Presidential bid, some predicted the demise of the Religious Right. But they overlooked the huge grass-roots constituency that remained connected through a Christian Right infrastructure of conferences, publications, radio and television programs, and audiotapes. Robertson lost no time in taking the key contacts from his 1988 Presidential campaign and training them as the core of the Christian Coalition, now the most influential grass-roots movement controlled by the Religious Right.

The genius of the long-term strategy implemented by Weyrich and Robertson was their method of expanding the base. First, they created a broader Protestant Christian Right that cut across all evangelical and fundamentalist boundaries and issued a challenge to more moderate Protestants. Second, they created a true Christian Right by reaching out to conservative and reactionary Catholics. Third, they created a Religious Right by recruiting and promoting their few reactionary allies in the Jewish and Muslim communities.

This base-broadening effort continues, with Ralph Reed of the Christian Coalition writing in the Heritage Foundation's *Policy Review* about the need for the Right to move from such controversial topics as abortion and homosexuality toward bread-and-butter issues—a tactical move that does not reflect any change in the basic belief structure. Sex education, abortion, objections to lesbian and gay

rights, resistance to pluralism and diversity, demonization of feminism and working mothers—these will continue to be core values of the coalition being built by the Religious Right.

Most Christian voters who had previously voted Democratic did not switch to Reagan in 1980. But by 1984, the New Right had persuaded many traditionally Democratic but socially conservative Christians that support for prayer in the schools and opposition to abortion, sex education, and pornography could be delivered by the Republicans through the smiling visage of the Great Communicator. Reagan did try to push these issues in Congress, but many mainstream Republicans refused to go along.

During Reagan's second term, some key New Right leaders, including Viguerie and Phillips, began denouncing Reagan as a traitor, especially over his negotiations with the Soviet Union. The New Right saw Bush as an Eastern elite intellectual, and even his selection of Dan Quayle as his running mate to pacify the Republican Right was not enough to offset what they perceived as Bush's betrayal over social issues.

Still, the Religious Right kept its ties to the Bush White House through chief of staff John H. Sununu, who worked closely with the Free Congress Foundation and even sent a letter on White House stationery in July 1989 thanking Weyrich for his help and adding, "If you have any observations regarding the priorities and initiatives of the first six months or for the Fall, I would like to hear them." The Bush White House also staffed an outreach office to maintain liaison with evangelicals.

The strongest glue that bound together the New Right pro-Reagan coalition was anticommunist militarism. Jewish neoconservatives were even willing to overlook the longstanding tolerance of racist and anti-Jewish sentiments among some in the Old Right who dubbed themselves paleoconservatives. This led to some strange silences, such as the failure to protest the well-documented presence of a network of emigre reactionaries and anti-Jewish bigots in the 1988 Bush campaign. The neocons could not be budged to action even when investigative writer Russ Bellant revealed that one aging Republican organizer proudly displayed photos of himself in his original Waffen SS uniform, and that Laszlo Pasztor, who had built the Republican emigre network, was a convicted Nazi collaborator who had belonged to the Hungarian Arrow Cross, which aided in the liquidation of Hungary's Jews. (Pasztor is still a key adviser to Paul Weyrich.)

However, the New Right alliance eventually collapsed. That became clear during the Gulf War, when Buchanan's bigotry was suddenly discovered by his former al-

MICHAEL DUFFY

lies in the neoconservative movement. Now, neoconservatives who championed the anti-Sandinista Nicaraguan contras are offered posts in the Clinton Administration. And Barry Goldwater, toast of the reactionaries in 1964, has lambasted the narrow-minded bigotry of the Religious Right, which owes its birth to his failed Presidential bid.

If the left of the current political spectrum is liberal corporatism and the right is neofascism, then the center is likely to be conservative authoritarianism. The value of the Culture War as the new principle of unity on the Right is that, like anticommunism, it actively involves a grass-roots constituency that perceives itself as fighting to defend home and family against a sinister threatening force.

Most Democratic Party strategists misunderstand the political power of the various antidemocratic right-wing social movements, and some go so far as to cheer the Religious Right's disruptive assault on the Republican Party. Democrats and their liberal allies rely on short-sighted campaign rhetoric that promotes a centrist analysis demonizing the "Radical Right" as "extremists" without addressing the legitimate anger, fear, and alienation of people who have been mobilized by the Right because they see no other options for change.

That there is no organized Left to offer an alternative vision to regimented soulless liberal corporatism is one of the tragic ironies of our time. The largest social movements with at least some core allegiance to a progressive agenda remain the environmental and feminist movements, with other pockets of resistance among persons uniting to fight racism, homophobia, and other social ills. Organized labor, once the mass base for many progressive movements, continues to dwindle in significance as a national force. It was unable to block the North American Free Trade Agreement, and it has been unwilling to muster a respectable campaign to support nationalized health care. None of these progressive forces, even when combined, amount to a fraction of the size of the forces being mobilized on the Right.

"It's a struggle between virtual democracy and virulent demagoguery," says author Holly Sklar, whose books on Trilateralism document the triumphant elitist corporate ideology implemented in the United States, Europe, and Japan. Trilateralist belt-tightening policies have caused material hardships and created angry backlash constituencies. The Right has directed these constituencies at convenient scapegoats rather than fostering a progressive systemic or economic analysis. Ironically, among the right-wing scapegoats is a conspiratorial caricature of the Trilateralists as a secret elite rather than the dominant wing of corporate capitalism that currently occupies the center and defends the status quo.

Suzanne Pharr, an organizer from Arkansas who moved to Oregon to help fight the homophobic initiative Measure Nine, is especially concerned that even in states where the Religious Right has lost battles over school curricula or homophobic initiatives, it leaves behind durable right-wing coalitions poised to launch another round of attacks. Pharr says, "Progressives need to develop long-term strategies that move beyond short-term electoral victories. We have to develop an analysis that builds bridges to diverse communities and unites us all when the antidemocratic Right attacks one of us."

Obviously, individuals involved with the antidemocratic Right have absolute constitutional rights to seek redress of their grievances through the political process and to speak their minds without Government interference. At the same time, progressives must oppose attempts by any group to pass laws that take rights away from individuals on the basis of prejudice, myth, irrational belief, inaccurate information, and outright falsehood.

Unless progressives unite to fight the rightward drift, we will be stuck with a choice between the nonparticipatory system crafted by the corporate elites who dominate the Republican and Democratic parties and the stampeding social movements of the Right, motivated by cynical leaders willing to blame the real problems in our society on such scapegoats as welfare mothers, immigrants, gays and lesbians, and people of color.

The only way to stop the antidemocratic Right is to contest every inch of terrain. Politics is not a pendulum that automatically swings back and forth, left and right. The "center" is determined by various vectors of forces in an endless multidimensional tug of war involving ropes leading out in many directions. Whether or not our country moves toward democracy, equality, social justice, and freedom depends on how many hands grab those ropes and pull together.■

P<u>OPERATION</u> RECINCT✝

Watching a tidal wave of Religious Right activists carry controversial Iran-contra figure Oliver North to a Senate nomination during last month's GOP convention in Virginia, Greg Eanes could not hide his disgust.

"The Republican Party has buried itself today," Eanes, a party official in rural, south central Virginia's Nottoway County told *The Washington Times*. "They buried the Constitution when they nominated Oliver North." Eanes said he was so upset he planned to resign his party office and later told *USA Today*, "We're going to bolt. I'd rather see a Democrat in Congress than a traitor."

Eanes was not alone. While thousands of North delegates packed the Richmond Coliseum to assure the former Marine lieutenant colonel's victory, many disgruntled Virginia Republican moderates seemed on the verge of mutiny. There was open talk of supporting the upstart candidacy of J. Marshall Coleman, a former Republican attorney general who is running an independent campaign.

To followers of the Religious Right, many of whom are affiliated with TV preacher Pat Robertson's Christian Coalition, such talk bordered on blasphemy. They were for North 100 percent and would brook no criticism of their hero. "Ollie is being set up by the media and Beltway insiders," Elaine Beachy, a Prince William County resident and North delegate, told *The Washington Post*. "They don't want to have him in the Senate, and they're using any means possible to keep him out. They're afraid of his tough stand for smaller government, keeping people honest, holding their feet to the fire." Beachy and her husband, David,

After Years Of Grassroots Organizing In The GOP, Religious Right Forces Are Playing A Major Role In The Republican Party

by Rob Boston

told the newspaper they got involved in GOP politics after attending a Christian Coalition meeting in 1991.

What happened in Virginia the weekend of June 4 is the most high profile example of the Religious Right flexing its political muscle during this election season. The pattern is being replayed in many states, and the conflict has become the focal point of a heated national debate on the role of religion in political life.

Here's why. From Minnesota and Iowa to Oregon and Texas, the Religious Right is on the march. Its goal is nothing less than a complete takeover of the GOP from the ground up. Step one began a few years ago when ultra-conservative, mostly fundamentalist-oriented forces began seizing control of GOP county units. Seizing control of the party at the state level is step two.

The 1994 mid-term elections look to be the Religious Right's first real test of its newfound power, and movement leaders are pulling out all the stops to ensure victory and bring about a closer relationship between church and state. In a recent fund-raising letter, Robertson promised to

distribute 40,000,000 voter guides and congressional scorecards "to ensure an informed Christian vote, so that Christians aren't fooled into voting for candidates who say one thing to get Christian votes, and then work in Washington to undermine the moral values you and I share."

Robertson also pledged to hold 100 "Citizen Action Training Schools" across the country to train people in intra-party politics and "mobilize the Christian vote" as well as launch a television advertising campaign to double the Christian Coalition's membership from one to two million.

Estimates vary, but most observers agree the Religious Right already has control of the Republican Party in seven states. *The New York Times* recently listed Virginia, Minnesota, Texas, Oregon, Iowa, South Carolina and Washington. Religious Right forces are said to be on the verge of consolidating GOP takeovers in Florida, New York, California and Louisiana. They are active in numerous other states as well, notably Pennsylvania, North Carolina, Alaska, Hawaii, Kansas, Wisconsin, Georgia, Oregon, Kentucky, Oklahoma, Colorado and New Mexico. Fledgling movements even exist in states not previously known for Religious Right activity, such as New Jersey, New York and Massachusetts.

Such frenetic activity has put the Religious Right—and by extension, the movement's top leader, Robertson—in an excellent position to dictate who the GOP nominates for president in 1996. Numerous Republican hopefuls, among them Kansas Sen. Robert Dole, Jack Kemp, William Bennett, Dan Quayle and Dick Cheney, are acutely aware of this and are already actively courting the Religious

---

20

Right vote. Cheney and Bennett kept high profiles during the Virginia convention. Bennett gave a banquet speech attacking "the liberals," and Cheney sang the praises of home schooling activist and unsuccessful lieutenant governor candidate Michael Farris, a Religious Right point man in Virginia GOP politics. Remarked Cheney, "I know there's great things in Mike's future." After North's victory, Kemp called and offered to do anything he could to help him win.

Democrats watching the developments appeared gleeful in the media, relishing the prospect of a Republican Party civil war and asserting that North is unelectable. In private, however, they admit to being concerned about North's phenomenal ability to raise money. North brought in $6 million during the primary alone—much of it from out of state. He is expected to continue accumulating cash during the summer and fall, right up until election day; he may ultimately spend an additional $12 million or more.

The Democrats are also troubled by the heavy political baggage incumbent Sen. Charles Robb carries. Dogged by allegations of marital infidelity and other misconduct, Robb is considered so vulnerable that an "independent" Democrat, former Gov. Doug Wilder, has entered the race.

Political analysts in Virginia say the prospect of a four-man race throws the election wide open. "Neither party is responding to the voters of Virginia," Mark Rozell, a professor of political science at Mary Washington College in Fredericksburg, told USA Today. "In a four-way race, I could imagine a scenario in which any candidate could win."

No matter what the eventual outcome, Republican politics in Virginia will never be the same. Religious Right activists who now control the party are already plotting their next move: They hope to oust Sen. John Warner, a Republican who has been harshly critical of North. Warner backed North opponent James C. Miller before the convention and has now thrown his support to Coleman. (The Religious Right

Reed and Robertson: Aboard Ollie's trolley

hopes to punish the three-term senator by nominating Farris in his place in 1996.)

North's controversial past may trouble Warner, but, ironically, it has failed to bother most moralists on the Religious Right. In the wake of Iran-contra, North was convicted of two counts of lying to Congress and one count of accepting an illegal gratuity. (The convictions were later overturned on a technicality.) North, then a government employee, was given a $16,000 security fence by retired Gen. Richard Secord. When the scandal broke, North back-dated two documents to make it appear that he had paid for the fence. The Reader's Digest and other publications have also charged that North has lied about or exaggerated other activities.

Some Religious Right activists have bent over backwards to excuse North's behavior. Last March David M. Hummel, a Republican Party official in Virginia Beach, told The Paper, a publication of the Regent University journalism school, that it was okay for North to violate the laws of the U.S. government because he was serving "God's higher law." According to Hummel, who serves as Second District GOP Chairman, North should be forgiven for committing the offenses since at the time he was allegedly battling Communism in Latin America. Communism, Hummel explained, denies the existence of God and the deity of Christ and kills those who do believe.

Religious Right leader Farris took a similar approach, telling The Paper repentance is the key issue. "If we have an unrepentant person," he said, "that is not good." Farris said he believes North has

repented of his past deceptions.

Some Religious Right activists, however, were less sure. Farris told World magazine that 100 delegates came up to him on the day of the vote and said they were having trouble making a decision in the race between North and Miller.

According to World, Farris ventured that at least North's lies were told with the best interests of the country in mind. "I don't want to be too glib about sin," he said. "But motives count too." Farris added that some delegates felt "what Ollie North did was basically the moral equivalent of what the spies and Rahab did in Jericho. Rahab lied to protect lives." (Farris was referring to an Old Testament story in which Rahab, a Canaanite woman, lies to the king of Jericho to protect two spies sent into Canaan by Joshua.)

Ralph Reed, executive director of the Christian Coalition, came up with a less theologically oriented excuse for North. Citing Democratic opponent Robb's ethical lapses, he asserted, "The character issues cancel each other out."

Warner is not the only Republican displeased with North's ascendancy. Others have offered at best lukewarm endorsements of the controversial nominee. Appearing on CBS News' "Face the Nation" the day after the convention, Minority Leader Dole said, "it's going to take a while" before he decided whether or not to support North. "There may be another candidate in the race," Dole said. "A Republican may enter the race as an independent....So we're not certain what's going to happen....It makes it very difficult for some in the Republican Party."

Washington Post columnist Mary McGrory reported that Warner and former Nevada Sen. Paul Laxalt, a North critic who now lives in Virginia, had allegedly convinced Dole to endorse Coleman. But the plan collapsed when three of the GOP's most conservative Senate members—Jesse Helms, Phil Gramm and Trent Lott—warned Dole he had better

21

climb aboard the North bandwagon or risk alienating the Religious Right.

Dole, who is already planning a 1996 presidential run, did a quick about-face. Within a week of the broadcast the Senate minority leader had not only endorsed North but had contributed $5,000 to his campaign.

Perhaps the most curious response came from Republican Sen. Charles Grassley of Iowa. Urging Republicans to respect each state's nomination process, he remarked, "The bottom line is there have been a lot of nuts elected to the United States Senate, and they've come out of this system. Ollie North might be a nut, but I don't know."

The hedging around North underscores the Republicans' dilemma: How to keep the Religious Right's votes, and their diehard political activism, without alienating moderates and economic conservatives. State by state the same drama is being played out as Christian Coalition members and their allies wrestle with GOP moderates for control of the party. The outcome could have grave implications for this November's elections and the presidential race in 1996.

Moderate Republicans are clearly concerned. In the wake of the 1992 presidential election, a group of GOP moderates pulled together to form the Republican Majority Coalition (RMC), a nationwide organization designed to fend off the Religious Right. RMC members insist that Republicans win when they stress what the group calls the "traditional Republican issues"—lowering taxes, reforming welfare, reducing federal spending and adopting a "tough on crime" stance.

"That's what's going to get them elected," Bob Meyerson, executive director of the RMC, told *Church & State*. "Concentrating on the issues that divide the electorate won't get them elected." Meyerson points to the 1993 gubernatorial victory of Christine Whitman in New Jersey and GOP wins in mayoral races in Los Angeles and New York City as proof. In all three races, the candidates emphasized crime and tax issues while adopting moderate positions on abortion and gay rights.

"Extremism on either side is a bad thing," Meyerson said. "The American people have spoken on these issues. They are fiscally conservative and socially moderate, period. If we continue to tap into that, we'll do well....We see that abortion and gay rights and creationism are not where the American people are now. The American people want a sound economy and safe streets. Until these issues are resolved, everything else will take a back seat."

But the Religious Right sharply disagrees and insists that most Americans favor their brand of "traditional family values." While the movement's leaders are paying more attention to issues such as taxes and crime, activists in the trenches continue working in state GOP units to make abortion, homosexuality, school prayer and other social concerns litmus tests for potential officeholders.

A round-up of Religious Right activity in key states follows:

Minnesota: Minnesota is an example of the kind of state where the GOP is vulnerable to a Religious Right campaign. Long a Democratic bastion, its Republican Party is weak—and thus easy to manipulate. Earlier this year ultra-conservative sectarian activists consolidated control of the GOP apparatus and immediately pounced on incumbent Gov. Arne Carlson. Carlson, a moderate Republican, is pro-choice on abortion and favors civil rights protections for homosexuals—two issues that are anathema to fundamentalists and their allies. At the GOP state convention June 17, Religious Right forces voted by a wide margin to endorse Allen Quist, a soybean farmer and former state legislator who hawks the Religious Right's line on social issues.

"This is a complete religious takeover," Carlson told *The New York Times*. "Quist sees himself as the Messiah—that he'll decide right and wrong. And these are people that are very fervent in their support of a pro-life position. So now the issue is, really, 'Are you one of us?'"

Carlson gave up hope of winning an endorsement from Minnesota's Republican Party before its convention met but still believes he can win the Republican primary against Quist in September. Republican Party moderates in Minnesota are infuriated.

Quist's views echo many of the Religious Right's pet causes. A former professor at Bethany Lutheran College in Mankato, Quist supports parochial school vouchers, opposes abortion, wants "creation science" taught in public schools and has drawn fire for a remark he made to the *Twin Cities Reader* that men have a "genetic predisposition" to be the heads of households. He is the father of 10 children.

Iowa: Four-term Republican Congressman Fred Grandy challenged three-term incumbent Gov. Terry Branstad, in part because of his concerns that the Iowa GOP had become dominated by the Religious Right. Earlier this year, Christian Coalition operatives took control of the Iowa GOP central committee.

Coalition members favored Branstad, a convert to Roman Catholicism who has pushed through tax breaks for private religious education and made common cause with anti-abortion groups and other "pro-family" organizations. Although Grandy was careful to avoid criticizing fundamentalists too pointedly during the race, he told *The Washington Post*, "If that is now the Republican Party in Iowa, you have to ask yourself if it's worth the struggle. A lot of this campaign is to recapture the heart and soul of this party." Grandy is considered a leading GOP moderate in the House.

Grandy narrowly lost the race to Branstad, 52 percent to 48 percent. The day after the election, Grandy's wife bitterly lashed out at the Religious Right, telling the *Des Moines Register*, "The fact is, the Republican Party is controlled by the Christian Coalition. Terry Branstad played Pied Piper to them....[Branstad] turned Fred into the devil. He had them pass out leaflets in church. He had priests writing letters saying there would be no private schools if Fred was elected. He basically led a campaign of lies, fronted by the Christian Coalition...."

Moderate Republicans are worried that Grandy backers will stay away from the polls in November or vote for Democrat Bonnie Campbell. As a concession, some Iowa GOP leaders have suggested toning down the party's militant platform, which takes a hard line on abortion and homosexuality and calls for teaching creationism in public schools.

Kentucky: Religious Right activists are on the verge of completely taking over the state Republican Party. At the state GOP convention last June, delegates affiliated with the movement pushed through a number of resolutions on social issues. One called for a school prayer amendment to the Constitution, while another opposed abortion and asserted that "life begins at conception." A third endorsed tuition tax credits for private schools.

The Religious Right movement in the Bluegrass State was given a boost last May when Ron Lewis, a fundamentalist Christian preacher, defeated Democrat Joe Prather in a race to fill the congressional seat of the recently deceased William H. Natcher in western Kentucky. In a low turnout race, Lewis defeated Prather 55 percent to 45 percent, thanks in part due to mobilization by the Christian Coalition. The seat had been held by Democrats for 129 years.

Texas: Christian Coalition activists and their allies have been flooding the Republican Party for months in response to an appeal from Pat Robertson. Earlier this year, state party chairman Fred Meyer resigned under pressure from fundamentalists who complained that he was too moderate. At June's state GOP convention, the Religious Right consolidated its control and elected one of its own as state GOP chairman.

In a three-way race, Dallas lawyer Tom Pauken, who had the endorsement of Christian Coalition leader Dick Weinhold, easily defeated two other candidates to become chairman. Pauken, a Roman Catholic long active in right-wing politics, faced challenges from Joe Barton, a former House member who is also conservative, and Dolly Madison McKenna, a pro-choice Republican who ran as a protest candidate.

Addressing the delegates before the vote, McKenna warned of the dangers of mixing religion and politics. "There are those people in this audience that want the Republican Party to be a church," she declared to rising boos and catcalls. "You are very welcome in the Republican Party, but the Republican Party is not a church."

Hurtt: California kingmaker

Despite McKenna's passion, she was never considered a serious contender for party chair. The race all long was between Barton and Pauken. (McKenna received only 11 percent of the vote in a caucus session.) Both men were deemed acceptable by the Texas Christian Coalition, leading group director Reed to gloat to *The Washington Post,* "We've already won before the first ballot is cast. It's a win-win situation."

The state Republican Party platform now tilts sharply to the right. It opposes all abortions, except when the mother's life is in danger, endorses vouchers, tuition tax credits and home schooling, opposes "secular humanism" and calls for corporal punishment, prayer and "creation science" in public schools.

Hard-right delegates rejected an effort to give a mere nod to inclusiveness in the preamble to the party rules. Delegate John Mouldin introduced language urging Republicans to "agree to disagree" on some issues and asserting that the GOP "is not a church" or a "social club."

Observed the Mouldin motion, "It is inappropriate to require a certain type of religious expression for leaders, candidates, delegates. Many people who hold identical positions and values will have different religious expressions....A Republican should never be put in the position of having to defend or explain his faith in order to participate in the party process." Mouldin withdrew the motion

after it was shouted down on a preliminary voice vote.

The Religious Right takeover of the Texas GOP was carefully organized. According to *The Dallas Morning News,* Texas Christian Coalition members received a mailing from Robertson last November imploring them to join "Operation Precinct." The first step was to attend one of eight local politics workshops offered around the state. The response was overwhelming. An estimated 70 percent of the 6,000 convention attendees were affiliated with the Religious Right.

Coalition activists had already taken power in many GOP districts in Texas. Some districts passed resolutions asserting that abortion is "the shedding of innocent blood which will surely bring God's judgment upon our nation." Another resolution called for quarantining AIDS patients.

Many worried Republican moderates in Texas have rallied around a newly formed group called Take It Back. "As the official position of the party becomes more strident, and more exclusive, and more castigating of people who don't agree with their particular religious beliefs, it portends more and more Republicans losing elections at all levels," said George Dutton, chairman of Take It Back.

Christian Coalition supporters shrug off that type of criticism. Weinhold, chairman of the Texas branch of the Christian Coalition and one of four national directors of the group, told the *Morning News* Coalition supporters are not fanatics, but rather "just average Texas citizens concerned about what is happening in the state and nation."

Moderates are also worried that Religious Right forces will eventually turn on GOP Sen. Kay Bailey Hutchinson. At the state convention, the platform committee voted 29-2 against a pro-forma resolution honoring Hutchinson and Sen. Phil Gramm. Some Religious Right delegates refused to endorse Hutchinson because she is not 100 percent anti-abortion. (Earlier this year Hutchinson angered the Religious Right by voting in favor of a bill that makes blocking access to abortion clinics a federal crime.)

Even the conservative Gramm felt the

23

Religious Right's wrath. Branded a Washington insider, he was embarrassed by a poor showing in a straw poll delegates held to determine a favorite for the 1996 presidential race. The top vote getter was former education secretary William Bennett with 25 percent. Gramm came down near the bottom of the list with 9 percent.

Democrats, meanwhile, hope to use the resurgence of the Religious Right against the Republicans. In a fiery speech before the state Democratic convention last June, Gov. Ann Richards charged that the "radical Religious Right" had taken over the GOP and launched a "witch hunt."

Remarked Richards, "They have invited a Trojan horse into their midst. They have created a tremendous danger, both to them and for all of us. They have turned the party of Lincoln into the party of Operation Rescue.

"This is not about faith," Richards continued. "My faith and my church, they are as important to me as they are to you. But my faith and your faith do not call on us to make enemies of our fellow citizens and victories at any means necessary. This nation was founded on free speech and the freedom to live our lives in whatever fashion we choose."

Richards faces George W. Bush, son of the former president, in the November election. The younger Bush is desperately trying to keep both moderates and Religious Right activists happy, but appears to know which way the winds are blowing in Texas' GOP. According to the *Post*, Bush has already invited the Christian Coalition's Weinhold to join him in the owner's box at the Texas Rangers' new stadium in Arlington.

California: Religious Right activists, led by state Sen. Rob Hurtt Jr., continue to make heavy inroads in the California Republican Party. Six social-issue conservatives seeking Assembly seats easily won GOP primaries. Among them was Steve Baldwin, the architect of much of the Religious Right's crusade in San Diego County. (Baldwin ran for the same 77th Assembly District seat in 1992 but was defeated by Democrat Thomas Connolly in a close contest.)

Moderate Republicans failed to express great interest in the Assembly races.

A Republican Party official in Virginia Beach said it was okay for Ollie North to violate the laws of the U.S. government because he was serving 'God's higher law.'

Joe Justin, an advisor to victorious Religious Right candidate Howard Kaloogian in District 74, said that factor was significant. "The right wing of the Republican Party came out in large droves," Justin told *The San Diego Union-Tribune*. "Moderates just couldn't compete. Combine that with low turnout, and it's a dead ringer for victory."

Hurtt, a multi-millionaire who represents District 34, is expected to pour hundreds of thousands of dollars into the races. His goal is to pack the state legislature with like-minded allies and eventually be elected Senate minority leader—or even majority leader if enough seats change hands. Hurtt tried to win the post last year but settled for finance committee chair instead. (Hurtt faced only token opposition in the June GOP primary, trouncing opponent Frank L. Adomitis, 78 percent to 22 percent.)

Observers of the Religious Right in California say Hurtt is one of the movement's leading figures. He and three other wealthy businessmen have bankrolled the fundamentalist resurgence in the state through political action committees and direct donations. He helped found the Capitol Resource Institute, the state political arm of radio counselor James Dobson of Focus on the Family. Hurtt was also a major financier of Proposition 174, a pro-voucher initiative rejected by the voters in 1992.

But not all Religious Right-backed candidates for state Assembly won. In Riverside County's District 66, Bruce Thompson defeated Trudy Thomas after a mean-spirited campaign that included ugly religious slurs. Galen Walker, a Riverside anti-abortion leader, sent a letter on Thomas' behalf blasting Thompson for being a Mormon. The letter sought the "active support of every Bible believing pro-life/pro-family Christian" and called Thompson "a member of a leading anti-Christ cult." Thompson won the four-person race with 36 percent of the vote, while Thomas came in third with 23 percent.

Three Hurtt allies won GOP primaries in Senate races. They are Maurice Johansson and Joe Ghougassian, both of whom ran unopposed in the 4th and 40th districts respectively, and Ray Haynes, who in the 36th district defeated Cois Byrd 57 percent to 43 percent.

While several congressional incumbents who had been endorsed by the Religious Right in Southern California won easily, other ultra-conservatives did not fare as well. Incumbent Gov. Pete Wilson, whom the Religious Right perceives as too moderate, easily defeated wealthy businessman Ron Unz, who held the endorsement of the *Southern California Christian Times*.

In the GOP Senate primary, the Religious Right was unable to muster much enthusiasm for former congressman William Dannemeyer, who faced first-term congressman and multi-millionaire Michael Huffington. Dannemeyer, who during his years in the House was known best for gay bashing, pushing school prayer amendments and raging against abortion, lost to Huffington, a moderate, by a nearly 2-1 margin.

Religious Right groups were also interested in the race for state superintendent of schools. They backed Wilbert Smith, a conservative who had endorsed vouchers during the vote on Proposition 174. Smith came in third in a crowded field of 12 candidates. The two top vote getters, Delaine Eastin and Maureen G. DiMarco, will face each other in a runoff this November. Both are Democrats.

The recent round of GOP conventions and primaries should erase any doubts about the Religious Right's ability to influence the Republican Party and in some cases determine the nominee of the GOP in statewide races. But the larger question

24

of whether the Religious Right can transform those victories into wins during the general election will remain unanswered until November.

Democrats at the national level hope to turn the Religious Right's gains against the GOP. In late June, Rep. Vic Fazio, a California Democrat, attacked the "subterranean tactics" and "stealth campaigns" of the Religious Right during a Washington speech. The "radical right" he asserted, wants to "forget there's a separation between church and state." '

"The Republicans accept the Religious Right and their tactics at their own peril, for these activists are demanding their rightful seat at the table, and that is what the American people fear most," said Fazio, who serves as chairman of the Democratic Congressional Campaign Committee.

GOP leaders quickly fired back. In a letter to President Clinton, Sen. Dole and all 43 fellow Senate Republicans called on Clinton to repudiate the Democratic attacks on the Religious Right.

Clinton, however, was far from intimidated. In a radio interview the next day, he lambasted Jerry Falwell and other far right broadcasters for spreading "scurrilous and false charges" against him. While he reiterated his support for evangelical Christian participation in the political process, he criticized those who "put on the mantle of religion and then justify anything they say or do." (See "President Clinton Hits Religious Right Tactics," People & Events, page 15.)

The Religious Right, not surprisingly, is confident its candidates can win. Leaders of the movement insist they represent mainstream American political thought. Robertson, Reed and other movement leaders also insist that the Republican Party cannot win elections without courting the votes of religious conservatives. Moderate Republicans remain skeptical of the claim.

"They told me that; they told me they delivered the vote in '92," says Meyerson of the moderate Republican Majority Coalition. "Well, they certainly did, but there was one small problem: Bush lost. I don't know if that [the claim Republicans can't win without the Religious Right] holds true."

Although Meyerson and other moderates speak optimistically of reaching accommodation with the Religious Right, that sentiment usually does not cut both ways. Religious Right leaders want no compromise and often speak of shutting down the GOP's "big tent" philosophy on issues such as abortion.

The challenge the Republicans face is best summed up in the words of David Schnittger, a fundamentalist pastor and North supporter in Virginia. Schnittger told *The Washington Post* he was energized by the Farris campaign and insists the GOP will win only by becoming even more conservative.

"Bush lost in '92 because he sought to be too bipartisan," asserted Schnittger. "I think the Republican Party needs to be more forthright in a pro-life position. It needs to get rid of this idea that we need to be broad and inclusive." □

25

The Election is About Who We Are

TAKING BACK OUR COUNTRY

By PAT BUCHANAN, *Presidential Candidate and Columnist*

Delivered at the Republican National Convention, Houston, Texas, August 17, 1992

WHAT a terrific crowd this is. What a terrific crowd. This may even be larger than the crowd I had in Eligay, Georgia. Don't laugh. We carried Eligay.

Listen my friends, we may have taken the long way home, but we finally got here.

The first thing I want to do is to congratulate President Bush, and remove any doubt about where we stand: The primaries are over, the heart is strong again, and the Buchanan brigades are enlisted — all the way to a great comeback victory in November.

My friends, like many of you last month, I watched that giant masquerade ball up at Madison Square Garden — where 20,000 radicals and liberals came dressed up as moderates and centrists — in the greatest single exhibition of cross-dressing in American political history.

One by one, the prophets of doom appeared at the podium. The Reagan decade, they moaned, was a terrible time in America; and they said the only way to prevent even worse times is to entrust our nation's fate and future to the party that gave us McGovern, Mondale, Carter and Michael Dukakis.

Where do they find these leaders? No way, my friends. The American people are not going to go back to the discredited liberalism of the 1960s and the failed liberalism of the 1970s — no matter how slick the package in 1992.

No, the malcontents of Madison Square Garden notwithstanding, the 1980s were not terrible years in America. They were great years. You know it. And I know it. And everyone knows it except for the carping critics who sat on the sidelines of history, jeering at one of the great statesmen of modern time, Ronald Reagan.

Remember the time of Jimmy Carter's days of malaise? Ronald Reagan crafted the greatest peacetime recovery in U.S. history — 3 million new businesses created, and 20 million new jobs.

Under the Reagan Doctrine, one by one, it was the communist dominos that began to fall. First, Grenada was liberated by U.S. airborne troops and the U.S. Marine Corps.

Then, the mighty Red Army was driven out of Afghanistan with American weapons. In Nicaragua, that squalid Marxist regime was forced to hold free elections — by Ronald Reagan's contra army — and the communists were thrown out of power.

Fellow Americans, we ought to remember, it was under our party that the Berlin Wall came down, and Europe was reunited. It was under our party that the Soviet Empire collapsed, and the captive nations broke free.

You know, it is said that every president will be remembered in history with but a single sentence. George Washington was the father of our country. Abraham Lincoln preserved the Union. And Ronald Reagan won the Cold War. And it is just about time that my old colleagues, the columnists and commentators, looking down on us tonight from their sky boxes and anchor booths and sky boxes, gave Ronald Reagan the full credit he deserves — for leading America to victory in the Cold War.

Most of all, my friends, Ronald Reagan made us proud to be Americans again. We never felt better about our country; and we never stood taller in the eyes of the world than when the Gipper was at the helm.

But we are here tonight, my friends, not only to celebrate, but to nominate. And an American president has many, many roles.

He is our first diplomat, the architect of American foreign policy. And which of these two men is more qualified for that role? George Bush has been U.N. ambassador, director of the CIA, envoy to China. As vice president, George Bush co-authored and co-signed the policies that won the Cold War. As president, George Bush presided over the liberation of Eastern Europe and the termination of the Warsaw Pact.

And what about Mr. Clinton? Well, Bill Clinton couldn't find 150 words to discuss foreign policy in an acceptance speech that lasted almost an hour. You know, as was said of another Democratic candidate, Bill Clinton's foreign policy experience is pretty much confined to having had breakfast once at the International House of Pancakes.

You know, let's recall what happened. Let us look at the record and recall what happened. Under President George Bush, more human beings escaped from the prison house of tyranny to freedom than in any other four-year period in history.

And for any man, let me tell you for any man to call this the record of failure is the cheap political rhetoric of politicians who only know how to build themselves up by tearing America down, and we don't want that kind of leadership in the United States.

The presidency, my friends, the presidency is also an office that Theodore Roosevelt called America's bully pulpit. Harry Truman said it was preeminently a place of moral leadership. George Bush is a defender of right-to-life, and a champion of the Judeo-Christian values and beliefs upon which this America was founded.

Mr. Clinton, however, has a different agenda.

At its top is unrestricted, unrestricted abortion on demand. When the Irish-Catholic governor of Pennsylvania, Robert Casey, asked to say a few words on behalf of the 25 million unborn children destroyed since Roe v. Wade, Bob Casey was told there was no room for him at the podium at Bill Clinton's convention and no room at the inn.

Yet a militant leader of the homosexual rights movement could rise at that convention and say:

"Bill Clinton and Al Gore represent the most pro-lesbian and pro-gay ticket in history."

And so they do.

Bill Clinton says he supports school choice — but only for state-run schools. Parents who send their children to Christian schools, or private schools or Jewish schools or Catholic schools need not apply.

Elect me, and you get two for the price of one, Mr. Clinton says of his lawyer-spouse.

And what does Hillary believe? Well, Hillary believes that 12-year-olds should have the right to sue their parents.

And Hillary has compared marriage and the family as institutions to slavery and life on an Indian reservation.

Well, speak for yourself, Hillary.

Friends, my friends, this is radical feminism. The agenda that Clinton and Clinton would impose on America — abortion on demand, a litmus test for the Supreme Court, homosexual rights, discrimination against religious schools, women in combat units — that's change, all right. That's not the kind of change America needs. It's not the kind of change America wants. And it is not the kind of change we can abide in a nation that we still call God's country.

A president of the United States is also America's commander-in-chief. He's the man we authorize to send fathers and sons and brothers and friends into battle.

George Bush was 17 years old when they bombed Pearl Harbor. He left his high school graduation, he walked down to the recruiting office, and signed up to become the youngest fighter pilot in the Pacific war.

And Mr. Clinton? And Bill Clinton?

I'll tell you where he was. I'll tell you where he was.

I'll tell you where he was. When Bill Clinton's time came in Vietnam, he sat up in a dormitory in Oxford, England, and figured out how to dodge the draft.

Let me ask the question of this convention. Which of these two men has won the moral authority to send young Americans into battle? I suggest, respectfully, it is the American patriot and war hero, Navy Lieutenant J. G. George Herbert Walker Bush.

My fellow Americans, my fellow Americans, this campaign is about philosophy, and it is about character; and George Bush wins on both counts.

And it is time all of us came home and stood beside him.

As his running mate, Mr. Clinton chose Albert Gore. But just how moderate is Prince Albert? Well, according to the Taxpayers Union, Al Gore beat out Teddy Kennedy, two straight years, for the title of biggest spender in the U.S. Senate, and Teddy Kennedy isn't moderate about anything.

I'm not kidding. I'm not kidding about Teddy. How many other 60-year-olds do you know who still go to Florida for spring break?

You know, at that great big costume party they held up in New York, Mr. Gore made a startling declaration. Henceforth, Albert Gore said, the central organizing principle of governments everywhere must be the environment.

Wrong, Albert!

The central organizing principle of this republic is freedom.

And from the ancient forests of Oregon and Washington, to the Inland Empire of California, America's great middle class has got to start standing up to these environmental extremists who put birds and rats and insects ahead of families, workers and jobs.

One year ago, my friends, I could not have dreamt that I would be here tonight. I was just one of many panelists on what President Bush calls

"those crazy Sunday talk shows."

But I disagreed with the president; and so we challenged the president in the Republican primaries and we fought as best we could. From February to June, President Bush won 33 primaries. I can't recall exactly how many we won.

I'll get you the figure tomorrow.

But tonight I want to speak from the heart, to the 3 million Americans who voted for Pat Buchanan for president. I will never forget you, nor the great honor you have done me. But I do believe, I do believe deep in my heart, that the right place for us to be now — in this presidential campaign — is right beside George Bush.

This party is my home. This party is our home, and we've got to come home to it. And don't let anyone tell you any different.

Yes, we disagreed with President Bush, but we stand with him for the freedom of choice religious schools. And we stand with him against the amoral idea that gay and lesbian couples should have the same standing in law as married men and women.

We stand with President Bush for right-to-life, and for voluntary prayer in the public schools.

And we stand against putting our wives and daughters and sisters into combat units of the United States Army. And we stand, my friends, we also stand with President Bush in favor of the right of small towns and communities to control the raw sewage of pornography that so terribly pollutes our popular culture.

We stand with President Bush in favor of federal judges who interpret the law as written, and against would-be Supreme Court justices like Mario Cuomo who think they have a mandate to re-write the Constitution.

My friends, this election is about more than who gets what. It is about who we are. It is about what we believe and what we stand for as Americans. There is a religious war going on in this country for the soul of America. It is a cultural war as critical to the kind of nation we shall be as the Cold War itself, for this war is for the soul of America.

And in that struggle for the soul of America, Clinton and Clinton are on the other side, and George Bush is on our side.

And so, to the Buchanan brigades out there, we have to come home, and stand beside George Bush.

In those six months campaigning from Concord, New Hampshire to California, I came to know our country better than I had known it ever before in my life, and I gathered up memories that are going to be with me the rest of my days.

There was that day-long ride through the great state of Georgia in a bus Vice President Bush himself had used in 1988 called Asphalt One. The ride ended in a 9:00 p.m. speech in a tiny town in southern Georgia called Fitzgerald.

There were those workers at the James River Paper Mill, in northern New Hampshire in a town called Groveton — tough, hardy men. None of them would say a word to me as I came down the line, shaking their hands one by one. They were under threat of losing their jobs at Christmas. As I moved down the line, one tough fellow about my age just looked up and said to me,

"Save our jobs."

Then there was the legal secretary that I met at the Manchester airport Christmas Day who came running up to me and said,

"Mr. Buchanan, I'm going to vote for you."

And then she broke down weeping and she said,

"I've lost my job, I don't have any money, and they're going to take away my little girl. What am I going to do?"

My friends, these people are our people. They don't read Adam Smith or Edmund Burke, but they came from the same schoolyards and the same playgrounds and town as we came from. They share our beliefs and convictions, our hopes and our dreams. These are the conservatives of the heart. They are our people. And we need to reconnect with them. We need to let them know we know how bad they're hurting. They don't expect miracles of us, but they need to know we care.

There were the people, of Hayfork, a tiny town up in California's Trinity Alps, a town that is now under a sentence of death because a federal judge has set aside 9 million acres for the habitat of the spotted owl — forgetting about the habitat of the men and women who live and work in Hayfork.

And there were the brave people of Koreatown who took the worst of those L.A. riots, but still live the family values we treasure, and who still believe deeply in the American dream.

Friends, in those wonderful 25 weeks of our campaign, the saddest days were the days of that riot in L.A., the worst riot in American history. But out of that awful tragedy can come a message of hope.

Hours after that awful tragedy can come a message of hope.

Hours after that riot ended I went down to the Army compound in south Los Angeles where I met the troopers of the 18th Cavalry who had come to save the city of Los Angeles. An officer of the 18th Cav said,

"Mr. Buchanan, I want you to talk to a couple of our troopers."

And I went over and I met these young fellas. They couldn't

have been 20 years old, and they recounted their story.

They had come into Los Angeles late in the evening of the second day, when the rioting was still going on, and two of them walked up a dark street, where the mob had burned and looted every building on the block but one, a convalescent home for the aged. And the mob was headed in to ransack and loot the apartments of the terrified old men and women inside. The troopers came up the street, M-16s at the ready, and the mob threatened and cursed, but the mob retreated because it had met the one thing that could stop it: force, rooted in justice, and backed by moral courage.

Greater love than this hath no man than that he lay down his life for his friend. Here were 19-year-old boys ready to lay down their lives to stop a mob from molesting old people they did not even know. And as those boys took back the streets of Los Angeles, block by block, my friends, we must take back our cities, and take back our culture, and take back our country.

God bless you, and God bless America.

PLAYING BROADWAY

With A Little Help From New York's Cardinal John O'Connor, Pat Robertson Has Taken A Bite Of The Big Apple

by Joseph L. Conn

A s the New York City school board elections approached last May, Ralph Reed had a song in his heart. Swiping a few lyrics from the familiar tune "New York, New York," the Christian Coalition leader warbled to reporters, "If you can make it here, you can make it anywhere."

Reed was feeling buoyant because he and the Christian Coalition seemed to be making it in America's largest city. In an unprecedented and remarkably successful foray into New York City politics, Pat Robertson's religio-political machine had hit the big time.

Usually thought of as a fundamentalist Protestant movement with little appeal in urban areas, the Christian Coalition had formed a tactical alliance with Cardinal John J. O'Connor and the Roman Catholic Archdiocese of New York, which had promised to distribute thousands of the Coalition's voters' guides in all 213 of its parishes. The Coalition also won support from a handful of other unusual allies, including a smattering of African-American and Orthodox Jewish leaders.

Reed was triumphant. Calling this ecumenical partnership of the right "the most significant amount of cooperation we've ever had," he said New York "has become a laboratory for this experiment and a very successful one."

What brought about this unusual coalition? The alliance had its origins in an ongoing battle in New York City over how the public schools should deal with such touchy topics as AIDS, sex education and homosexuality.

School Chancellor Joseph A. Fernandez, while praised by many for his education reform skills, had alienated Cardinal O'Connor and other conservative religious leaders by advocating the distribu-

tion of condoms as part of a high school AIDS prevention program. He added fuel to the fire by promoting "Children of the Rainbow," a multicultural curriculum that celebrated not only racial and ethnic diversity, but also encouraged tolerance of homosexuals.

Fighting for these programs, Fernandez ran headfirst into adamant opposition from some of the city's 32 local school boards, the nine-member community-based panels that oversee elementary and junior high education in New York. The fracas centered on District 24, a middle-income and working-class section of Queens where the school board has long been dominated by members with close ties to the Roman Catholic hierarchy.

As far back as 1970, the majority of school board members had been elected on a slate chosen more for its loyalty to the Catholic Church and Catholic parochial schools than for its support for public education. (See "Captive Schools," September 1986 *Church & State*).

Although District 24 is nearly three-fourths black, Hispanic and Asian, many of them immigrants, critics noted that the school board is all white, native born and

Roman Catholic. One member, the Rev. John J. Garkowski, is a Roman Catholic priest (although Vatican rules supposedly prohibit priests from holding public office). The board majority reportedly maintained its control by distributing slate cards at friendly neighborhood churches. With voter turnout very low—rarely more than 7 percent of eligible voters—a well-organized slate had little problem holding power.

Board 24 President Mary Cummins became something of a media celebrity by defying Fernandez on the Rainbow curriculum. Working with a well known lawyer provided by the cardinal, Cummins and her associates stymied the chancellor's attempts to implement his policies.

While the local board's stance was sparked by ties to the cardinal, sentiment against Fernandez and his curriculum was also felt by many parents in District 24 who thought elementary school children were too young to learn about controversial topics like homosexuality. Parental concern was heightened by inflammatory videos produced by Concerned Parents for Educational Accountability, a local Religious Right outfit that charged the curriculum was a vehicle to recruit children into the homosexual lifestyle.

The controversy over the Rainbow curriculum as well as other factors soured relations between Fernandez and the New York City School Board, the citywide governing body. With O'Connor and company urging them on, board members voted 4-3 last February not to renew the chancellor's contract. (During a hearing on Fernandez, Katherine Hickey, the cardinal's parochial school chief, urged the board to "purge ideologies of hedonism and secularism from the school system.")

According to the *Daily News*,

30

O'Connor's leading role in the ouster triggered debate about the church's excessive influence over the public school system. *New York Times* columnist Anna Quindlen, herself a Catholic, blasted "church officials who clearly overstep the bounds between moral guidance and politicking, acting more like lobbyists than spiritual leaders." Some observers speculated that O'Connor was trying to return to the days when the cardinal's residence in New York was known as "The Powerhouse," the most influential political precinct in the city.

But the New York prelate was undeterred by the criticism, and instead quickly moved to solidify his political advances. In February, O'Connor announced plans to target the upcoming school board elections around the city. Arranging a voter registration drive and encouraging parishioners to sign up as candidates, O'Connor told his flock that voting in school board races may be "more important than voting for president of the United States."

Into this burgeoning fray stepped Pat Robertson's Christian Coalition. With a rudimentary organization already in place in New York, Robertson and company saw the school controversy as a perfect opportunity for Christian Coalition organizing.

Robertson's forces have always done best in low-turnout races where few citizens vote and ever fewer take the time to figure out who the candidates are. Emotional and polarizing issues such as abortion and homosexuality also help rally the faithful. In other words, the New York City school contests were ideal.

The school board election system seems designed to turn away voters. Held separately from other major elections, citizens are required to rank candidates for the unpaid posts in order of voter preference. This proportional system is supposed to guarantee a better mix of board members, but in fact, it makes the process hard to understand. Fewer than 10 percent

Robertson and O'Connor: We are one

of New Yorkers cast ballots in most recent school board elections compared to 75 percent in New Orleans and 68 percent in Miami.

"The whole system is so byzantine," said Barbara Handman of People for the American Way's New York office. "They could not have made it more difficult for people to vote."

In mid-April, however, voter interest was piqued by the dramatic religio-political entente. A spokesman for Cardinal O'Connor told *The New York Times* that the archdiocese would distribute Christian Coalition voters' guides in all the Catholic parishes in Manhattan, the Bronx and Staten Island. As tax-exempt entities, churches are not allowed to endorse candidates, but the IRS has not forbidden congregations to distribute voters' guides that list candidates' stands of a broad range of issues. This loophole left just enough leeway for the cardinal and the television preacher to slip through.

The alliance between Robertson and O'Connor came as surprise to some New York media, but it shouldn't have. The two religious leaders have long harbored a hostility for church-state separation, as well as an admiration for each other. Shortly after his 1988 presidential cam-

paign collapsed in May of 1988, Robertson traveled to New York and met with O'Connor. After a closed-door half-hour meeting, the pair emerged as friends. Touting the same stances on social and moral issues, Robertson told the press, "We are one."

On a more practical level, Monsignor John G. Woolsey of the archdiocesan Family Life/ Respect Life Office told reporters that he has worked with the New York affiliate of the Christian Coalition for the past three years on issues such as abortion.

The political machinations of O'Connor and Robertson dramatically raised the level of concern among church-state separationists, mainstream clergy and others who thought the public school system ought not be dominated by any particular religious denomination or combinations thereof.

In an unprecedented move, Mayor David Dinkins spent $635,000 in city funds to send election notices to New York voters. "I am tremendously concerned with the suggestion that Pat Robertson has injected himself into this campaign," Dinkins said in a radio broadcast. Condemning Robertson's shrill political rhetoric, the mayor said, "That's instilling fear in folks. It's just plain wrong." The American Civil Liberties Union, Americans United, People for the American Way, teachers' organizations and other groups also criticized the O'Connor-Robertson alliance. Progressive forces formed PACs and conducted information drives to educate the electorate and encourage voting.

Meanwhile, the Clergy Council, a group formed to address the issues in the school board race, held a press conference to challenge sectarian encroachment into the political process. "God should not be taking sides in this election," said Rabbi Balfour Brickner of the Stephen Wise Free Synagogue. Others concurred. Warning of the Religious Right's repressive agenda, the Rev. Finley Shape of Prospect Park United Methodist Church quipped, "When Jesus said, 'Beware of

31

ravenous wolves in sheep's clothing,' he was referring to people like the Rev. Pat Robertson."

Other clergy took a different tack. According to the *Daily News*, the Rev. Timothy Mitchell of the Ebenezer Baptist Church told a meeting of the Baptist Ministers' Conference, a coalition of black churches, that disproportionate Roman Catholic influence over the public schools should be resisted.

Henry Siegman of the American Jewish Congress chided the archdiocese for teaming up with Robertson and "turning every school board election into a holy war." He warned that the Catholic Church appeared to be ignoring the IRS strictures on tax-exempt organizations by endorsing candidates.

O'Connor indignantly spurned the criticism. In a full-page viewpoint column in his archdiocesan newspaper *Catholic New York*, the cardinal denied that he was trying to tell anyone how to vote. "I can't imagine that anyone would listen to me if I did try," he quipped.

O'Connor said he only wanted to "let voters know in an unbiased manner the respective positions of *all* candidates on the issues." The Roman Catholic prelate heatedly denied that he had joined forces with "right-wing-religious extremists," and he never mentioned Robertson or the Christian Coalition by name.

But critics charged that the Christian Coalition voters' guides were anything but unbiased. Candidates were queried on issues such as "voluntary school prayer," condom distribution and teaching about AIDS and homosexuality. No attention was given to classroom overcrowding, ways to improve academic performance and other issues that many New Yorkers consider much more important.

"Their voters' guides are hardly a non-partisan tool," said Skipp Porteous of the Institute for First Amendment Studies. "These are highly biased guides that point out 'pro-family' or extreme conservative candidates as much as possible."

In a particularly audacious move designed to deflect criticism and skirt IRS regulations, the Christian Coalition included a line on its voters' guide that said, "This guide is not intended to influence

"God should not be taking sides in this election."

—Rabbi Balfour Brickner

the outcome of the election." In bold print, the booklet added, "Christian Coalition of New York does not advocate the election or defeat of any candidate, and does not endorse any political party."

Ironically, despite all of the public angst, Robertson's forces found only a fraction of the city's school board candidates willing to respond to the questions in their guide. Only 160 candidates out of 543 were profiled in the eight-page document. Of that number over 100 said they support "voluntary prayer" in schools, while 108 said they opposed the Rainbow curriculum. *The New York Times* estimated that only 90 of the candidates running in 27 of the 32 school districts actually fit the Christian Coalition's desired "pro-family" profile. Nonetheless, some 100,000 copies of the guides were distributed in Catholic parishes, with another 390,000 handed out in Protestant churches and other houses of worship.

To no one's surprise the May 4 elections drew large numbers to the polls—almost double the number of voters that came out four years ago. But the paper ballot counting, which was still going on as *Church & State* went to press three weeks later, showed decidedly mixed results.

According to incomplete returns, District 24 reelected Cummins and other anti-Rainbow candidates. Conservatives also were running well in the Bronx' District 8, Staten Island's District 32 and some other neighborhoods.

But liberal slates also were doing well in several districts, including Brooklyn's District 15. Robertson and O'Connor must have been especially appalled that their polarization of the electorate resulted in a backlash that catapulted two avowed lesbians and a gay man to school board seats, the first open homosexuals to

hold such positions in the city.

The *Times* speculated that the new school boards will "reflect the ideological diversity of their neighborhoods." But regardless of the final tallies, the New York City elections are likely to mark an important watershed in the story of the Christian Right.

For the first time, Robertson, a charismatic Protestant, has won significant support from a major Roman Catholic religious leader. If other bishops follow suit and similar alliances form in other communities, Robertson will have gained an unprecedented amount of political clout through his much-sought ecumenism of the right. The non-sectarian public school system and other cherished American institutions are sure to feel the heat.

Although church-state separation has always been a touchstone of the American way of life, the New York religio-political alliance demonstrates that divisive sectarian forces can still be unleashed in the political system.

Many observers see the New York battle as part of a larger "culture war" over the role of organized religion in public life, especially its relationship to politics. Anti-separationists also see the Catholic-Protestant cooperation in New York as a model for communities across the country. Former U.S. education secretary William Bennett hosted a "town meeting" about the election, which was broadcast nationally on National Empowerment Television, right-wing activist Paul Weyrich's growing communications network.

Ultimately, control of the political process—and of the public schools—may be at stake. Chancellor Fernandez told *The New York Times* the school board battle was precipitated by the same forces that caused his firing. "I think you can't separate what happened to me from their agenda on a national level," he said. "My colleagues all around the country are telling me they are very concerned about this issue."

District 24 School Board President Mary Cummins agrees. "Knocking out the chancellor was just a skirmish," she told *The Times*. "There's a war going on—not in District 24, but all over the country." □

32

TROUBLE IN TEXAS

How The Christian Right Seized Control Of The Houston GOP

by Joseph L. Conn

iberty, says Dr. Steven F. Hotze, is "the freedom to do what is biblically right," not "the freedom to act irresponsibly." And Americans, in his opinion, are missing the mark badly.

"Our transgressions as a people against God's laws are innumerable," he contends, "and are leading us inexorably to moral and economic bankruptcy....If we are to survive as a nation and maintain our liberties, then we must get back to the basics and restore our nation to its Christian heritage."

Hotze's views sound familiar; the stance has been repeated many times in recent years by Pat Robertson, Jerry Falwell and other leaders of the Religious Right. But the 42-year-old Houston physician is more than just another spokesman for the Religious Right, he's the newly elected leader of the Republican Party in Harris County, Texas, a GOP bastion and current home of former President George Bush.

In a political coup last year, Hotze and his fundamentalist precinct allies seized control of the Republican Party from County Chairwoman Betsey Lake. Lake was elected to the party post last spring by voters in the GOP primary, but her "big tent" stance on abortion and her willingness to work with gay Republican groups were anathema to the Religious Right insurgents. In September, Hotze and supporters censured Lake and firmed up plans to strip the elected party official of her power. Then at a GOP conference last December Hotze was chosen as head of a new advisory board that will run the party apparatus.

Lake appeared at the December gathering, but only to announce that she is forming a new "Republican federation" where party mainliners can go to regroup. Her announcement was met with open derision from many of the 400 precinct chairmen present. According to press accounts, Lake left the meeting after being shouted down.

How did the Republican Party organization in Texas' largest city fall into the hands of theocracy-minded political extremists? Local observers say Religious Right activists used the same process they have used elsewhere: quietly organizing conservative churches into a formidable political machine and then ousting mainline GOP activists—secular conservatives and moderates alike—who didn't see the Religious Right juggernaut coming.

Hotze, who also serves on the state GOP executive committee, has played a key role. The Houston native, who converted from his childhood Catholicism to a conservative Presbyterian denomination, is the founder of a local group called Citizens for American Restoration.

In 1985 Hotze helped organize the "Straight Slate," a group of candidates for Houston city government who opposed civil rights for homosexuals. The slate's nominees lost, but Hotze went on to additional work in the anti-abortion movement and other right-wing causes.

Hotze's ties to radical Religious Right groups suggest a far-reaching theocratic agenda. The Houston physician is an activist with the Coalition on Revival (COR), and he serves as Houston coordinator for COR's political unit, the National Coordinating Council, as well. Both organizations are heavily influenced by Christian Reconstructionism, a radical movement that rejects democracy and seeks to impose a harsh version of biblical law, including Old Testament strictures, on all aspects of modern American society. (See "Hard COR," January 1991 *Church & State*.)

Reconstructionist leaders call for the death penalty for adulterers, practicing homosexuals, blasphemers, "incorrigible" children and others who violate their understanding of the Bible. Some even advocate stoning as the biblically preferred means of execution.

Hotze also serves on the board of directors of *Biblical Worldview*, a publication of Christian Reconstructionist Gary DeMar. Hotze's Houston group uses DeMar's "God and Government" study series to train local activists on how to bring civil government into line with the "biblical worldview."

Aware that such close ties to radical

GOP's Hotze: Theocrat?

33

organizations could hurt his party takeover efforts, Hotze is now downplaying his relationship with these groups. He told the *Houston Post* he does not consider himself a Reconstructionist. "I'm a restorationist," he said. "I want to restore America to its Christian heritage."

Hotze's agenda, however, is clearly theocratic. Both church and state, he insists, must conform to "God's Law-Word." "Every civilization has a religious foundation that defines its people's code of conduct," observed Hotze in a *Houston Chronicle* essay. "A nation's laws simply enact that code. Israel was founded upon the Jewish religion, Saudi Arabia on Islam." America, he insisted, was founded on "faith in the God of the Bible and His Son, Jesus Christ" and must return to its religious basis.

Hotze waxes nostalgic about early American settlements such as the Puritan theocracy in Massachusetts where Christianity was imposed by force of law. He excoriates "government schools" and denounces Supreme Court decisions that bar government-sponsored worship there. No abortions should be permitted, he says, for any reason. He wants to eliminate the welfare system, the Internal Revenue Service and the Federal Reserve.

Despite the movement's professed Christian character, many of Hotze's allies have a mean streak. Attendees at Christian Right gatherings and GOP party functions have distributed fliers that said "no queers or baby killing femi-nazis."

The radical character of the Houston movement has not prevented its standard bearers from winning some public support. John Devine, a "Christian" write-in candidate for a local judgeship, collected 39,183 votes in the November elections. It wasn't enough to win the post for Devine, who was endorsed by Hotze and company, but the Religious Right write-ins proved to be the margin of victory for four other judgeship candidates and a legislative nominee. According to the *Chronicle*, Hotze claims a mailing list of about 35,000 voters.

Many Houston citizens are alarmed. "To try to Christianize America by means of the political process—to use the state to propagate a particular kind of Christianity—is a frontal attack on religious liberty which threatens us all," observed the Rev. William L. Turner, pastor of the South Main Baptist Church, in a *Chronicle* response.

Jo Martin, a Houston activist, agrees. "As far as I'm concerned," she said, "Dr. Hotze's a Reconstructionist. Don't let him fool you; I don't think he has any respect for democracy." Martin and her husband David formed a watchdog group, Pro-SOCS (the last four letters stand for separation of church and state), to work with other concerned citizens in Houston and alert the general public about the Christian Right onslaught.

Meanwhile, Republican mainliners are working hard to regain control of the GOP. "I am mad," said Lake, "and I want my party back."

Observers agree that the outcome of the Houston battle could be a bellwether for the role of the Religious Right in the Republican Party across the country.   □

WATCH ON THE RIGHT

How "Radical" Is the Christian Right?

Going on two years since Patrick Buchanan delivered his infamous "cultural warfare" speech at the 1992 GOP convention, I am still invariably asked on radio talk shows: hasn't the Christian right's "extremism" become a liability for "mainstream" Republicans? My answer, also invariably, is both "yes" and "no."

The Christian right's flamboyant convention antics scared a lot of television viewers but, at the same time, signified the movement's arrival as the Republicans' biggest and most reliable constituency. As the Christian right continues to march steadily, though less noisily, toward assuming political power, movement leaders are now debating their future—as unyielding moral crusaders, as rank-and-file Republicans, or as some combination of both.

While the Christian right stands to mature in the process of charting its own course, critics of the movement seem to be wearing blinders; they continue to depict politically active evangelicals as "extremists" somehow outside or not belonging to "mainstream" culture, let alone everyday party politics. But opponents of the Christian right stand to lose if they do not recognize that, while the movement indeed has some wild policy goals, the agenda is supported by millions of people as common as the neighbors next door.

Take last fall's elections in the state of Virginia. The Democrats tried to turn the election into a referendum against Christian-right-backed candidates, and that strategy failed. First-time candidate Michael Farris, a home-schooling activist and former attorney for Concerned Women of America, was pilloried as a raving "extremist"; he lost the race for lieutenant governor but still managed to raise $1 million and win 46 percent of the vote. On the other hand, Governor George F. Allen and Attorney General James S. Gilmore III, both moderate Republicans, won largely because of support from right-wing evangelicals. (After the election, Allen appointed prominent anti-abortion activists to his transition team and sought to nominate Family Research Council Vice-President Kay Cole James as Virginia's secretary of health.) In fact, Democratic gubernatorial candidate Mary Sue Terry saw her poll ratings plummet following negative TV ads and speeches portraying Allen as a darling of the Christian-right "extremists." In a state where a third of the voters identify themselves as evangelical Christians, the Democrats' name-calling smacked of religious bigotry. Post-election commentators drew the lesson that, for mainstream Republicans, Christian-right backing helps more than it hurts.

That's because negative campaigning has limited appeal and because—like it or not—the Christian right genuinely represents a solid minority of Americans. In some parts of the country, that minority is a majority. Last summer, six Oregon counties passed preemptive measures banning civil-rights protections for gay citizens. The measures were sponsored by the activist Oregon Citizens' Alliance, but they won because thousands of voters share the Christian right's homophobia. To call them all "extremists" will not change the vote tallies.

Why, then, do liberal critics of the Christian right persistently resort to broad-brush slogans like *extremism* and a related epithet, the *radical right?* I can offer a few reasons. These terms were first popularized during the 1950s and 1960s when prominent political scientists, in dutiful service to the liberal wing of the Cold War establishment, labeled Senator Joseph McCarthy and his admirers as paranoid "radicals," alien to the American body politic. In reality, McCarthy drew his support from the same Republican faithfuls who had elected President Eisenhower. Popular right-wing groups like the John Birch Society emerged only in the late 1950s, well after political elites had turned the pursuit of "communist subversion" into a national religion. By then, polite society was keen to depict wild-eyed Birchers as "extremists," even as they played by democratic rules and helped win the Republican nomination for Barry Goldwater.

Academia's warnings about "radical right extremism" held influence when the massive Christian right mobilized in the late 1970s. Throughout the 1980s and continuing now, liberal outfits like People for the American Way have promoted a view of dangerous "radical right" Christians as something separate from the U.S. political and economic system itself. But there is nothing particularly "radical" about most politically active evangelical Christians. To be "radical" means to seize the roots of social problems, to advocate and work for profound change. The Christian right, on the contrary, supports existing conditions that effectively maintain inequality between rich and poor, white and black, men and women. More directly, the Christian right of the 1980s enlisted in a full gamut of U.S. military operations abroad and now in the 1990s is working to forestall gay civil rights and provisions for accessible abortion within the Clinton health-care plan.

Still, liberals organized against the Christian right can make hay by exploiting the "radical right" paradigm. While performing the valuable service of monitoring electoral races, People for the American Way, for example, needs to ensure its own financial resources and prominence in the media limelight. It can do so most efficiently by projecting its spokespeople as legitimate democratic players battling Christian "extremists" and by sticking to simplistic formulas that avoid controversy. Were liberal critics to analyze the Christian right as a natural ally of corporate Republicanism, they might find themselves labeled as "radicals." The *New York Times* and CNN would stop calling, and the foundation dollars would dry up.

Then again, the Christian right's own avowed strategy—until recently—has played right into the hands of liberals looking to find "extremists." The idea of secretly running Christian-right-backed candidate slates to take over city councils and school boards was hatched by "dominion theologists" with grandiose plans about implementing biblical law in every sphere of secular society. I first heard about the "county-by-county" stealth takeover plan at the 1986 convention of the Coalition on Revival. COR leaders, among others, were then laying the groundwork for Pat Robertson's 1988 presidential bid. During that effort and the simultaneous TV preacher scandals, the press made laughing-stocks of politically active evangelicals. That reinforced the Christian right's collective martyr complex and also the wisdom of the stealth strategy.

By 1990, Robertson's Christian Coalition was boasting of its steadily increasing membership rolls while, at the same time, encouraging its local campaign functionaries to keep low profiles lest they be blasted by secular humanists. Through stealth campaigns, the Christian right won countless elected offices, but the cloak-and-dagger routine also became a public-relations liability, particularly Christian Coalition director Ralph Reed's way-out threats about "flying below radar" and operating like a guerrilla warrior. At best, stealth campaigns can work only for first-time challengers, and increasingly voters are wary of candidates with little-known public policy positions and affiliations.

In 1992, sneaky and undemocratic stealth tactics became the dominant theme in press coverage of the Christian right. After Clinton's election, the Christian Coalition hired a public-relations firm to help the movement project a more "mainstream" image. Recently, Ralph Reed told *Charisma* magazine that he regrets having fostered the stealth model. More significantly, Reed

published, in the Heritage Foundation's *Policy Review*, a widely discussed article, "Casting a Wider Net," calling for the Christian right to broaden its base by granting bottom-line economic concerns as much priority as the "moral" issues. To attract more diverse constituents, the Christian Coalition has also announced its intentions—thus far unrealized—to recruit heavily from minority churches.

Critics of the Christian right might dismiss Reed's new mainstream soft-sell as the public-relations device it most certainly is. But the mainstream gambit has helped the Christian right solidify alliances with the most dominant faction of the Republican Party. After Clinton's election, pundits predicted that moderate Republicans would ditch "extremists" like Pat Robertson, and a handful of pro-choice moderates joined forces under former Congress member Tom Campbell's Republican Majority Coalition.

Thus far, though, this faction has been unable to wield much influence. Instead, the most successful new Republican Party faction has made clear its

37

intentions to court right-wing evangelicals. In early 1993, Jack Kemp, William J. Bennett, Jeane Kirkpatrick, and former Minnesota Congress member Vin Weber launched Empower America. One of their goals has been to dampen Patrick Buchanan's popularity; in the 1992 Republican primaries, Buchanan won 25 to 30 percent in most states, largely because of Christian right backing. Empower America and Buchanan's own American Cause Foundation are diametrically opposed on issues of free trade and U.S. military intervention abroad. Both factions seek to represent the Christian right on the "family values" front, but Empower America has a far richer corporate donor base than Buchanan's group. Last fall, Empower America joined forces with the Christian Coalition in the failed effort to pass a "school choice" initiative in California.

Over this and other questions involving the proper role of the state, the Christian right is divided between those who want to broaden the movement's agenda and those concerned about the pitfalls of collaboration with "mainstream" Republicans. Following Ralph Reed's *Policy Review* article, the debate went public. In a September 1993 *Washington Post* column, Christian Action Network President Martin Mawyer chastised Reed for casting too wide a net and, essentially, for selling out "pro-family" concerns (school prayer, opposition to gay rights and abortion) to what he called "unrelated" issues like the North American Free Trade Agreement and health-care reform. In sync with his allies over at Empower America, Reed had endorsed NAFTA, although, as Mawyer reports, the audience applauded when Patrick Buchanan denounced NAFTA at a Christian Coalition conference. Mawyer concluded that broadening the coalition's legislative agenda will not translate into victories on salient "moral" issues.

For its part, CAN has focused on single-issue campaigns. CAN was front and center in last year's lobbying to maintain the bans on gay military personnel and on federal funding for poor women's abortions. CAN also took credit for persuading Congress to cut the budget of the National Endowment for the Arts by $8.6 million.

Though CAN opposes subordinating Christian right activism to the interests of the Republican Party per se, there is nothing particularly "extreme" about its tactics. CAN uses direct mailing lists to mobilize phone calls and letters to Congress members. That CAN pursues a narrow-issue focus and the Christian Coalition hopes to make itself indispensable to the Republican Party is, if anything, a sign of the Christian right's maturity. Social movements are successful to the extent that activists and leaders with divergent strategies can each find a niche. The public debate between Ralph Reed and Martin Mawyer was inconsequential for a movement that now effectively accommodates both single-issue and party-oriented organizations. Both types of groups are successful because they exploit elements of routine electoral politics: Congress members' response to constituent lobbying and persistent low voter turnout, both of which are advantageous to the highly mobilized evangelical minority.

It does no good, then, to see the Christian right through the blinders of a "radical/extremist" paradigm. It is outrageous that the right wants to padlock gays in the closet, deprive women of reproductive freedoms, enforce antiquated and monolithic school curricula —the litany is well known. But in the coming season of local and statewide elections, the Christian right will hold the high ground as well-organized, well-heeled, and genuinely discontented opponents of the Clinton era status quo. To crudely blast politically active evangelicals as "extremists" will only increase their claimed underdog status. The only way for opponents to beat back otherwise inevitable Christian right gains will be to disavow name-calling and instead—with cool heads—conduct grass-roots voter education on the true policy aims of the Republican/ Christian right alliance.   ⬛

Sara Diamond, Ph.D., is the author of Spiritual Warfare: The Politics of the Christian Right *and a columnist for* Z Magazine. *She recently received her doctorate in sociology from the University of California at Berkeley.*

In Defense of Religious America

Terry Eastland

"RELIGION in American life, Mr. Cadwell. We need it." That is the concluding line of a radio commercial which for some, perhaps providential, reason I have had occasion to hear several dozen times over the past year. It is not an advertisement for any particular religion, just religion itself, which presumably could be Christian or Jewish or Muslim or Hindu or—though I think the commercial's sponsors did not quite have this in mind—the Reverend Sun Myung Moon's. It is an innocuous ad, so ecumenical as to be able to effect no conversion to anything. But concerned as it is with religion in American life, the message serves beautifully as a kind of theme song for our times. It implicitly raises the question brought up by the activities of so many others in the past year, from Jerry Falwell to the American Civil Liberties Union: what should be the place of religion in American life? What, that is, should be the place of religion, not so much in the life of any one individual American as in American civil society?

Discussion of this question has not been especially enlightening. It has centered almost exclusively on the First Amendment, and the reflections on the First Amendment have themselves been unhelpful. Columnists and politicians have been content to repeat the mythology most famously (though not originally) articulated by Chief Justice Earl Warren when he said that the First Amendment "underwrote the admonition of Thomas Jefferson that there should be a wall of separation between church and state." The Chief Justice had a way with history, but for the sake of accuracy—and much else besides—it should be noted that Jefferson said what he said in 1802, when he was President, in a letter to the Danbury Baptists. However interesting Jefferson's thoughts may be, and however much we may wish today to regard his views as authoritative on church-state matters, this letter is simply not relevant to a consideration of the framing of the First Amendment and its original intention—unless of course Jefferson had been sitting in Congress in the summer of 1789 (in fact he was in Europe as Secretary of

State and would not return until the autumn).

The invocation of Jefferson obscures history by implying that the Founding Fathers were hostile to religion, since in today's usage the idea of a wall connotes antagonism and suspicion between the two sides thus separated. As a matter of historical fact, the Founding Fathers believed that the public interest was served by the promotion of religion. The Northwest Ordinance of 1787, which set aside federal property in the territory for schools and which was passed again by Congress in 1789, is instructive. "Religion, morality, and knowledge being necessary to good government and the happiness of mankind," read the act, "schools and the means of learning shall forever be encouraged."

It is only from history, not from clichés about history, that we can understand what we once were as a nation in regard to religion, and what we have since become. Let me therefore start with these propositions: that there was a principal religion in American life from 1620 until roughly 1920; that this religion was Protestant Christianity; and that Protestant Christianity has been our established religion in almost every sense of that phrase.

The one sense in which Protestant Christianity was *not* established, of course, was as our national religion. There never has been a Church of the United States, complete with a bishop and supported by tax revenues, as in England. Nor can there be one: the First Amendment to the Constitution did make sure of that. But nothing *more* than that.

The intention of the framers of the First Amendment was not to effect an absolute neutrality on the part of government toward religion on the one hand and irreligion on the other. The neutrality the framers sought was rather among the sects, the various denominations. Accordingly, as Michael J. Malbin has shown, although there could be no national establishment of a sect, there could be state aid to religious groups so long as the assistance furthered a public purpose and so long as it did not discriminate in favor of some or against others; all sects, in other words, would have to be benefited.*

TERRY EASTLAND, co-author (with William J. Bennett) of *Counting by Race: Equality from the Founding Fathers to Bakke and Weber*, has recently been named editor of the *Virginian Pilot* (Norfolk).

* *Religion and Politics: The Intentions of the Authors of the First Amendment* (American Enterprise Institute, 1978).

The perspective of colonial history in the period dating from the Great Awakening makes it all the more clear that the First Amendment could not have been meant to enforce neutrality by government as between religion and irreligion. The Society for the Propagation of the Gospel, a sort of missionary arm of the Church of England, had been in business in America since 1701. For three-quarters of the 18th century, and especially in the years just prior to the Revolution, a widespread religious attitude in America was fear—fear that the Crown would establish the Anglican religion. The principle of non-establishment of a particular denomination was a product of this historical period, and the First Amendment applied this principle at the national level. Throughout the late 18th and early 19th centuries the principle was similarly applied at the colonial and, later, the state levels. As at the national level, so at the state level: no one denomination was to be given state support; there had to be neutrality among sects.

Thus, if Anglicanism could not reign in a given colony or state, neither could Congregationalism. The Anglican establishments in Maryland, South Carolina, North Carolina, and Georgia were wiped out before 1776, and Virginia's died finally in 1802. Congregationalism held on long past 1791 in Massachusetts, Connecticut, and New Hampshire, but by 1833 had lost its privileged status in all of these states.

It should be noted that although these establishments were of different sects, they belonged to the same religious family tree—that of Protestant Christianity. This is hardly surprising. The original colonies were English, and their English settlers were primarily Protestant. The non-English minorities—the Scots, the Scotch-Irish, the French, the Dutch, the Swedes, the Germans—were also mostly Protestant. There were only a few Catholics, mostly in Maryland, and even fewer Jews. This relative mix would endure until well past the middle of the 19th century.

The heavily Protestant orientation of the churchgoers of early America should not obscure the fact that many if not a majority of Americans were unchurched in the 18th century. But with a very few exceptions these unchurched were not freethinking atheists or agnostics. Hence, while the principle of non-establishment could be extended to prohibit the establishment of one particular religion (and not just the sects within a religion), few people were sufficiently bothered, as a practical or theoretical matter, to make this extension. The prominent exception was Madison, who believed that Christianity should not be favored over any other religion. Yet even Madison agreed on the general proposition that so far as the public interest was concerned, religion itself was better than irreligion.

THE particular sects, then, had been disestablished at the state level by 1833. But Christianity had not been, and would not be, until much later. In the early part of the 19th century, states set up both by constitution and statute provisions declaring it the duty of all men "to worship the Supreme Being." States also regulated membership in Christian denominations, imposed fines for failure to fix the worship hour on Sundays, and even mandated that elected officials believe in "the Christian religion."•

State courts did their part to support the Protestant faith. In 1811 the New York state court upheld an indictment for blasphemous utterances against Christ, and in its ruling, given by Chief Justice Kent, the court said, "We are Christian people, and the morality of the country is deeply engrafted upon Christianity." Fifty years later this same court said that "Christianity may be conceded to be the established religion."

The Pennsylvania state court also affirmed the conviction of a man on charges of blasphemy, here against the Holy Scriptures. The Court said: "Christianity, general Christianity is, and always has been, a part of the common law of Pennsylvania . . . not Christianity founded on any particular religious tenets; nor Christianity with an established church and tithes and spiritual courts; but Christianity with liberty of conscience to all men."

States also required the teaching of the Christian religion in state colleges and universities, and in prisons, reformatories, asylums, orphanages, and homes for soldiers. Furthermore, public aid was given to church-run hospitals and orphanages. Last, but certainly not least, many states required Bible reading and prayers in the elementary and secondary public schools.

Religion was far more integrated into the actual curriculum than these religious exercises might suggest. Textbooks referred to God without embarrassment, and schoolteachers considered one of their major tasks the development of character—an aim quite consistent, as we shall see, with America's brand of Protestant Christianity. The influence of William Holmes McGuffey (1800-1873), a Presbyterian educator and philosopher, was remarkable. His *Eclectic Readers* were published in 1836, and from that year until 1920—two years after Mississippi became the last state to institute a public-school system—his books sold more than 120 million copies, a total that put them in a class with only the Bible and Webster's Dictionary. McGuffey's *Readers* stressed, as the Northwest Ordinance did, "religion, morality, and knowledge," in that order.

As with the public schools, so with almost every area of American life. The establishment of Protestant Christianity was one not only of law but also, and far more importantly, of culture. Protestant Christianity supplied

---

•For this and following references, see Harold Berman, "The Interaction of Law and Religion," *Humanities in Society*, Spring 1979.

the nation with its "system of values"—to use the modern phrase—and would do so until the 1920's when the cake of Protestant custom seemed most noticeably to begin crumbling. But before coming to that moment we should reflect on the content of the particular religion that held sway in American life for the better part of 300 years, and remark more precisely on the significance of its "cultural" establishment.

As a general metaphysic, Protestant Christianity was understood in ways Catholics and Jews and deists could accept. Not only Protestant Christians but most people agreed that our law was rooted, as John Adams had said, in a common moral and religious tradition, one that stretched back to the time Moses went up on Mount Sinai. Similarly, almost everyone agreed that our liberties were God-given and should be exercised responsibly. There was a distinction between liberty and license.

Beyond this it is possible to be much more specific. Protestant Christianity was Reformed in theology, Puritan in outlook, experiential in faith. It was also evangelical in its orientation toward the world. These propositions held true of not only the denominations of Puritan origin (such as the Congregational, Presbyterian, and Baptist churches) but also those with more highly qualified views on the issue of predestination (such as the Methodist church) and those we might today consider "High Church" (such as the Episcopal church). Almost everyone drank from the same Reformation well, which happened to be the Westminster Confession of 1643. Reformation theology placed emphasis on the sovereignty of God and the depravity of man. It was a religion of the book—the Bible—that demanded the individual conversion of man and, in consequence, the living of a changed life.

This point had enormous social and political consequences. It is unlikely that a predominantly Catholic or Jewish America would have given birth to the type of society that eventually evolved by the late 18th century. The reason is that neither would have emphasized to the degree the American Puritans did the importance of personal development in the moral (and for them spiritual) sense of character formation. The Westminster Confession describes the preaching of the word as "an effectual means of driving them [sinners] out of themselves" and "of strengthening them against temptation and corruption, and of building them up in grace."

That is doctrine that will shape a man, and the shaping, molding emphasis of the American Puritans, the character-building emphasis, can even today be seen—literally seen—in needlework shops where samplers bearing the old, straightforwardly didactic Protestant American messages can be found. Often such messages take the form of unedited Bible verses (from the King James version). Scripture was not incidental to the Puritan American. It was to be considered, meditated upon, learned by heart. "As a man thinketh in his heart," says the Bible, "so is he." The Puritans did not think only with their heads.

The American Protestant characteristically was driven out of himself, not only into Christ but also into the world. Hence the description—"this-worldly ascetic"—so often applied to individuals in Reformed communities. The change in the history of Christianity that this phrase suggests is seismic. After Luther it was no longer necessary to withdraw from the world (and into a monastery) to serve God. A man could serve God in the secular world. ("What is the chief and highest end of man?" asks the first question of the Larger Catechism of the Westminster Confession. "Man's chief and highest end is to glorify God and fully to enjoy Him forever.") Every job had a purpose, every man a calling, a vocation, no matter how lowly or how exalted. Working in *this* world, furthermore, men could transform the society about them, as the New England Puritans tried to do in their Bible Commonwealths. Though these societies failed according to their own ideals, the impulse to change society remained and would manifest itself in numerous ways, including the voluntarism of the 19th century, which became such a mainstay of American life.

AMERICAN Protestantism not only taught spiritual virtues but also the less heroic ones of sobriety, honesty, prudence, temperance, and diligence. In the context of these virtues, as Irving Kristol has often pointed out, capitalism made ethical sense. Protestantism was understood to tame and direct a man's interests, including his economic ones, toward worthy ends. Man was understood to be a steward upon earth, and he was to use his liberty and his talents responsibly (and diligently; there was to be no idleness, no sloth). There may be no more interesting text on this than Question 141 of the Larger Catechism of the Westminster Confession, which even as late as 1844 was described by Philip Schaff, a German writing on America's religious life, as "the reigning theology of the country." The question refers to the Eighth Commandment ("Thou shalt not steal") and asks what duties it requires:

The duties required . . . are: truth, faithfulness, and justice in contracts and commerce between man and man; rendering to everyone his due; restitution of goods unlawfully detained from the right owners thereof, giving and lending freely, according to our abilities, and the necessities of others; moderation of our judgments, wills, and affections, concerning worldly goods; a provident care and study to get, keep, use, and dispose of those things which are necessary and convenient for the sustentation of our nature, and suitable to our condition; a lawful calling, and diligence in it; frugality; avoiding unnecessary lawsuits, and suretyship, or other like arrangements; and an endeavor by all just and lawful means to procure, preserve, and further the wealth and outward estate of others, as well as our own.

This answer offers much to reflect on; there is, for instance, the implicit approval of both commerce and the creation of wealth, even of one's own wealth. But the principal concern is man's duty, which is to have moderating effects upon his commercial activities. Tocqueville observed that the law allowed the American people to do everything, but that there are things which their religion prevented them from imagining and forbade them to dare. Religion—the Protestant religion here described—was thus a major source of the virtues a nation conceived in liberty always would need. It shaped the society and the individuals within it. Protestant Christianity helped answer the oldest of political questions: what kind of people, having what kind of character, does a society produce?

Tocqueville therefore was right to say that religion was America's "foremost political institution." It was the branch of government that the Constitution, based on self-interest and envisioning a commercial Republic, obviously could not create. Yet it was the branch essential to the maintenance of the Republic. It provided a check on the liberty guaranteed by our conventional political institutions. It was responsible for the character of the people. And as this "informal" branch of government, as our "foremost political institution," Protestant Christianity enjoyed its most significant form of "establishment."

I N THE past sixty years, we have witnessed the disestablishment of this religion. One could argue that it was bound to happen. Good American theory—as given by Madison —holds that the more factions the better for the Republic's chances of survival. This theory applies not only to economic interests but also to religious ones. Despite the fact that the nation had been settled by Protestants, other religious peoples could settle here, too, and eventually they did. The great immigrations from Southern and Eastern Europe after the Civil War brought millions of Catholics to the United States, and by the end of the 19th century a sizable number of Jewish and Eastern Orthodox communities were also flourishing.

Meanwhile, something was happening to the old Protestantism itself. Evangelical Protestant Christianity (revitalized by the Second Awakening in the early years of the Republic) had held on strongly throughout the first half of the 19th century, but after the Civil War the tendencies toward Arminianism—i.e., the belief in divine sovereignty *and* human freedom—that had been present even in the 18th century became far more pronounced.

On the one hand, a liberal variety of Protestantism developed. Liberal theology had little interest in Original Sin; indeed sin to it was nothing more than mere error. Liberal Protestantism emphasized instead man's freedom and his natural goodness. Dogma and the sacraments were slighted, and there was immense optimism about the human race. Influenced by Kant, liberal Protestants reduced Christianity to morality; they had no prophetic voice, to speak of (or with). Liberal Protestantism was an accommodation to culture. H. Richard Niebuhr perhaps best described its God as One "without wrath" Who "brought men without sin into a kingdom without judgment through the ministrations of a Christ without a cross."

Liberal Protestantism was not the only accommodation to culture. More conservative Protestants—the keepers of the old religious flame— proved to be poor stewards of it. The old Protestantism descended into revivalistic orgies, as brought to us most sensationally by Billy Sunday. Christianity was presented as something dulcet and sentimental, and as often as not it was allied to the pursuit of profit. Frequently the old Protestantism was served up as a civil religion—a heresy, as Jonathan Edwards, but not Billy Sunday, would have recognized. Here too, and not surprisingly, dogma was neglected. A remark by Dwight Moody's perhaps best captures this. "My theology!" he exclaimed, when asked about it. "I didn't know I had any."

In the 1920's H.L. Mencken would acidly but correctly assert that "Protestantism is down with a wasting disease." One of the deepest reasons for its condition was that the Enlightenment had finally made its way to America. By the end of the 19th century the higher biblical criticism had disturbed the Protestant theologians' confidence in their ultimate authority, the Bible. So had the modern sciences, not only the physical sciences (especially biology in the form of Darwinism) but also the newer, social sciences. Truth no longer seemed absolute but relative to time and place, and the insights into personality and society provided by psychology and sociology seemed at least as plausible as those found in the Bible.

The half-decade following the Civil War had been the great age of urbanization. The rise of the city had also seen for the first time in American history the development of an intellectual class, and it was not kind to the old Protestant faith. By the 20's it had become intellectual fashion not to believe in God and, if one were a writer, to attack "Puritanism."

W ITH the great immigrations, the decline of the old Protestant religion, and the rise of an intellectual class not merely indifferent but hostile to religion, the stage had been set by the 1920's for the cultural disestablishment of the old faith. Indeed, it had begun earlier. The end of World War I in 1918 had inaugurated a period of laxity in morals and manners. This is typically what happens after wars, but the decade of the 20's eventually would prove to be a dramatic break from the past. For it was not followed by a recovery of the old morals and manners, as also typically happens after social upheavals; the Victorian era stayed firmly in the past. Church attendance declined throughout the 20's. People lost their fear of Hell and had less interest in Heaven. They made more demands for material fulfillment.

Such demands, of course, are as American as the Declaration of Independence, which after all sanctified the idea of the pursuit of happiness. That idea owed more to the Enlightenment than to the Bible; certainly it did not sail to America aboard the Mayflower Since the Declaration of Independence America had held its commitments to liberty and to virtue in tension. By the 20's it was clear the tension had begun to resolve itself in favor of liberty. Americans now insisted, as William Leuchtenburg has noted, not only on the right to pursue happiness but also on the right to possess it. The 20's saw the beginnings of the installment-buying plan; it is impossible to imagine such a purchasing scheme in the American culture of 200 or even 100 years earlier.

Since the 20's the disestablishment of the old Protestant religion has taken place most obviously in the intellectual, governing, bureaucratic, and cultural classes, and to a lesser but no less real and increasing degree in the rest of society. Today the disestablishment is perhaps most easily detected on the college campus. Logical positivism may have long ago fallen out of favor among philosophers, but as a cultural attitude among intellectuals and academics it is still going strong. Godtalk (the literal meaning of theology) is not fashionable, not even, it sometimes seems, in a college chapel.

The campuses of the old Protestant culture emphasized the importance of the Christian faith. Now their chapels still stand, but university policies have changed. There is probably no more striking instance of this than at Princeton University, over which both Jonathan Edwards and John Witherspoon once presided. Last year Princeton went looking for a new Dean of the Chapel. A Presbyterian of deep commitment and faith had retired, and his retirement provided the occasion for a reevaluation of the Dean's function. A trustee report came forth with a new job description: henceforth the Dean should be a person of "deep religious faith" but "above all, he or she must be personally gracious and open, and his or her own religious commitment must include sensitivity to the vulnerability of human finitude and the particularity and relativity of the views he or she espouses." The clauses following "above all" say everything that needs to be said about the distance Princeton has traveled.

Other evidences of disestablishment abound. Today the old idea that law has its roots in the Judeo-Christian ethic, as was believed at the Founding and throughout most of American history, is no longer much discussed, let alone believed in by many American legal philosophers and judges. The public philosophy of America, as Harold Berman has pointed out, has in the past two generations "shifted radically." Law is in theory no longer religious but secular; no longer moral but political and instrumental; no longer communitarian but individualistic. (People increasingly engage in "unnecessary lawsuits.") It is no wonder that Aleksandr Solzhenitsyn, at Harvard for the commencement address three years ago, left his audience stunned when he spoke of law in a religious context.

MEANWHILE, liberty, like law, has been severed from its religious basis. What Jefferson once called the "firm conviction" in the minds of Americans that their liberties derive from God is hardly so firm anymore, certainly not among political scientists, columnists, television personalities, and others who influence public opinion. Having been given its own existence, ontologically speaking, liberty fairly runs riot now. The distinction between liberty and license transmitted to us by the old Protestant culture has faded almost completely among the educated classes. Consider again the college campus, where the old doctrine of in loco parentis is out of fashion. Administrators now run their campuses as if there is no God, since virtually everything is permitted. Probably the most libertine societies in America today exist on those very campuses that were originally the creations of the old Protestant culture.

To be sure, many other parts of America are closing fast on the campuses. It is the style nowadays not only among the college-educated but also among many blue-collar workers who are economically conservative but socially and morally liberal. This, translated, means balance the budget but decriminalize marijuana and cocaine and let us have abortion on demand. If the liberalism of the 60's has a definite legacy, it is found in the far more liberalized and hedonistic lives many Americans, including many older Americans, and indeed many political conservatives, now lead.

The "Me-Decade" has been well chronicled. Perhaps less obvious, but no less significant, is the change in ethical *thinking* that has occurred throughout society. A book could be written on what has happened to the idea of character. People in authority—teachers, parents, and even ministers—resist the fact that they are in authority. They will not "impose" their values; the idea is to let the young "clarify" *their* "values" (now considered as relative as any matter of taste). Moral education is no longer rooted in the virtues of courage, temperance, prudence, and the like. It is full of form but empty of content. What matters is that you feel sure the "option" you have chosen for yourself is the right one for you. I have seen a course in "values clarification" offered to adults in a Presbyterian Sunday School curriculum—and as an "option," no less!

Perhaps because the old imperative of "America the Beautiful"—"confirm thy soul in self-control" —has become too hard to follow, ethical teaching, while studiously neutral about personal life, is assiduously assertive in social matters. Where once the major emphasis was on tidying up the individual soul, on making it conform to reality, now the focus has shifted to the external world, to tidying up the laws that regulate the public lives of man and man (or woman). Where people, whether of secular or religious disposition, seem to feel most comfortable, and certainly most confident, is in talking about "social injustice" or "racism" or "poverty" or "exploitation." Recently I joined a panel at a major university on the subject of religion and virtue. A participant who was a professor of theology centered most of his remarks on "corporate sin." I don't recall his once mentioning the idea of virtue, let alone any particular virtue. Sometimes it is hard to find a difference between what ministers and theologians say and what many secular intellectuals say.

THIS, then, is the picture so far of an America that has experienced the cultural disestablishment of its old religion, the dissolution of its once "foremost" political institution. Consideration of a few trends within the Supreme Court will help complete the picture.

In 1947 the Supreme Court, in *Everson* v. *Board of Education of Ewing Township*, said the First Amendment "requires the state to be neutral in its relations with groups of religious believers and non-believers." This new doctrine of neutrality not only would seem tó forbid the establishment of a religion—as Madison would have had it—but also the establishment of religion in general over non-religion and thus irreligion.

With its doctrine of neutrality, the Court has denied substantial public aid to elementary and secondary church-related schools. And by striking down prayers and Bible readings and now, this past fall, even the posting of the Ten Commandments in the public schools, it has acted according to an implicit doctrine that the public schools should be secular—and "value-free."

In 1961, in *Torcaso* v. *Watkins*, the Court so enlarged the definition of religion that an observer might say irreligion had now become a religion. The Court decreed that neither a state nor the federal government can "constitutionally pass laws nor impose requirements which aid all religions based on a belief in the existence of God as against those founded on *different beliefs*" (emphasis added). A footnote listed "Ethical Culture" and "Secular Humanism" among other examples of "religions" founded on "different beliefs."

In other contexts the Court has said that virtually anything may qualify as a "religion," so long as the "religious person" believes in whatever he believes in with, as Justice Black put it, "the strength of traditional religious conviction." This definition of religion celebrates individual conscience. It is hardly surprising that in cases involving "privacy" the Court has reduced public restrictions on private choice (as with its abortion decision in 1973). The legal trend here, like the cultural trend, has been toward a pronounced individualism in matters of religion and morals.

These trends of the Court round out the portrait. We are all "pluralists" now. And it should be stipulated that this is not altogether a bad thing. I doubt that any serious religious believer would wish a return to the days of intolerance that were an admitted ill of the old Protestant culture. But people who take religion seriously—and I mean here religion that has social and historical dimension, not merely something you might believe with "the strength of traditional religious conviction" in the midst of a Saturday night drunk—will find much in this picture that is disturbing. For the disestablishment of the old Protestantism has meant defeats not only for Protestants but for Catholics and Jews as well.

By contradicting the historical meaning of the establishment clause of the First Amendment, the Court has said, in effect, that promotion of religion is not in the public interest. Daniel P. Moynihan has correctly written that the recent decisions based on the establishment clause are "an intellectual scandal," and it is perhaps not too much to hope that the Court will one day reverse itself on this matter. Meanwhile, however, the severing of both law and liberty from their historic rooting in religion has serious and more immediate implications. Instrumentalists may argue that obedience to law can be brought about solely through the threat of coercive sanctions, but, as Berman has written, what is far more important is "the tradition of being law-abiding, which in turn depends upon a deeply or passionately held conviction that law is not only an instrument of secular policy but also part of the ultimate purpose and meaning of life."

As for the loss of the religiously-grounded distinction between liberty and license, we have all witnessed the proliferation of rights with no concomitant responsibilities that has been the result. With traditional religion now pushed to the margin of our public life, not only thanks to the Court's doctrines of neutrality and secularism but also, and more importantly, thanks to the pedagogy of school and college teachers alike, religion is less able to exercise its historic role as a political counterweight, as the voice of constraint and responsibility.

The shift in ethical thinking away from character formation toward personality adjustment and values clarification on the one hand, and social problems on the other, is perhaps the most disturbing change of all. The emphasis on virtues that the old Protestant culture provided was precisely what the Founding Fathers acknowledged their new Constitution could not provide. And yet the Founders also knew that just these virtues were what the best thinkers in antiquity had thought necessary to the maintenance of a republican order. If the old evangelical Protestantism had a special fire in it that burned the ancient virtues into the souls of men, the virtues themselves were not special to that faith. For these were virtues agreeable to Catholic and rabbinical tradition, to the Deists of the Founding period, to the Greeks and Romans. The old Protestant religion understood, as ancient philosophy did, that politics is ultimately about the cultivation of character. It is unclear today that our modern culture even understands this point, let alone wants to deal with it.*

Even so, it is answered, by default if not by design. Protestant Christianity is no longer America's "foremost political institution," but this fact does not obviate the need for a system of values in which Americans can move and live and have their commercial (and now leisure) being. If our morality is not engrafted upon Protestant Christianity, it will be engrafted on something else—God only knows what. The brilliance of the Founding Fathers did not anticipate this situation, but surely they did not believe that any institution could ever be "value-free." We are all the time engrafting our way of life upon *some* set of values.

I F WE ARE today a secular society, we are still also a liberal society. And in the current groping toward what inevitably will be our public philosophy, the religious person is entitled, if not to prevail, at least to be heard. The religious person can expect to be allowed a voice in matters of public policy. He can expect that his religion will not disqualify him from speaking on political matters, and that if he offers a religious or ethical justification for his position on a public issue, it will not *ipso facto* be considered out of the bounds of public discourse. The question here is ultimately one of where you get your basic beliefs. If, as Michael Novak has written, we should be willing to let people get their politics as much from the Bible as from Gloria Steinem, then biblical or religious values should be permissible in public debate. Unless the free exercise of religion, vouchsafed in the First Amendment, is to mean only trivial whispers, something practiced in the closet, then it must mean a voice equal to that of anyone who is not religious.

The trends go against even this minimal kind of free exercise of religion. It has been argued by serious public philosophers that only a rational, utilitarian morality should ever be enforced by law, and that this morality by definition would exclude any influenced by or grounded in religious considerations. Today this argument, spoken by non-philosophers, is used against the Moral Majority and their kind. You cannot legislate morality, it is said, meaning you cannot legislate a particular kind of morality—the kind having to do with religion as traditionally conceived.

History is not irreversible, but the trends for the past hundred years suggest that traditional religion will have an increasingly marginal influence on our public life. America is still one of the most religious countries in the world, and yet church affiliation (40 percent of Americans profess one) continues to decline, as Seymour Martin Lipset and Earl Raab noted recently in these pages ("The Election &. the Evangelicals," March). These are just the circumstances to expect in a country to which the Enlightenment came late. The much-touted religious renaissance of recent years does not promise to change this state of affairs, at least not soon. Lacking is what has been lacking in much of American religious life for the past hundred years—solid theological content—and on this score the seminaries that have brought us the "death of God," "liberation theology," and other similar inspirations cannot inspire hope. As for the turning of a few scientists toward God, this is hardly a full-blown theological revolution. To postulate, as Sir John Eccles has done, that the brain is the product of evolution but that only God could have created the mind may prove an invaluable service to religion. But we are still a long way from any *Summa*, and a longer way from a great cultural movement.

One need not hold a brief for Jerry Falwell, nor for his cousin evangelists who appear on the television screen in the shank of the evening, to acknowledge what they have done, which at the least has been to flush the anti-religious bias out into .the open. The early reaction to Falwell was dominated by comments from civil libertarians who implied, ironically enough, that Falwell had no right to speak out on public issues. Such was not the reaction when the Reverend Martin Luther King wrote his letter from a Birmingham jail, but the hypocrisy is less interesting, I think, than the secular bias that produced it.

If, someday, people with traditional religious views should be effectively banned from public debate, not only will the free exercise of religion have been denied but a new religion will have been culturally established as our "foremost political institution." It would no doubt look very much like what the Supreme Court alluded to in its *Torcaso* ruling—the religion of "secular humanism." God save us from that.

---

* Can a government, asks Francis Canavan, "committed to absolute neutrality among 'religions' . . . be capable of educating anyone? . . . The right questions were raised, but not answered, by Justice Jackson in his dissenting opinion in *Everson* where he said: 'Our public school . . . is organized on the premise that secular education can be isolated from all religious teaching so that the school can inculcate all needed temporal knowledge and also maintain a strict and lofty neutrality as to religion. The assumption is that after the individual has been instructed in worldly wisdom he will be better fitted to choose his religion. Whether such a disjunction is possible, and if possible whether it is wise, are questions I need not try to answer' " ("The Impact of Recent Supreme Court Decisions on Religion in the United States," *Journal of Church and State*, Vol. 16, No. 2, 1974).

CATHOLICS & THE 'RELIGIOUS RIGHT'

GEORGE W. GERNER

WE ARE BEING WOOED

Last September, weeks before the 1994 congressional elections, Christian Coalition President Pat Robertson addressed 3,000 cheering followers in Washington, D.C.: "We're seeing the Christian Coalition rise to where God intends it to be in this nation as one of the most powerful political forces....in the history of America." The coalition, Robertson asserted, reflects the moral values of "a mighty army" not only of 40 or 50 million evangelical Protestants, but of "30 to 40 million profamily Roman Catholics" as well.

This claim of moral alliance with what approximates the nation's total adult Roman Catholic population will strike many Catholics as inflated and highly improbable. After all, doesn't the "religious right" consist primarily of Protestant evangelicals, most of them Southern and rural, with a long history of virulent anti-Catholicism? Though Robertson's numbers are almost certainly inflated, a convergence of social interests across denominational lines is not as unlikely, on some issues, as theological differences might suggest.

Christian conservatism is an amalgam of the diverse. In a July 1994 *New York Times*/CBS national poll of 1,339 adults, 9 percent of the respondents identified themselves as members of the "religious right." Their profile contrasts sharply with the stereotype captured in the *Washington Post*'s 1993 characterization of politically conservative Christians as "poor, uneducated, and easy to command." The *Times*/CBS poll shows educational levels approximating the national average. Respondents were as likely to consider themselves Democrats as Republicans. Their positions on trip-wire issues, such as homosexuality and a school prayer amendment, were more conservative than those of the general population by about 20 percent. Although these 9 percent were overwhelmingly Protestant, only half considered themselves to be "evangelical, fundamentalist, or charismatic Christians," labels which many find pejorative. Many Catholics who share the "religious right's" political or moral convictions are likely to reject that label because of the stereotypes to which it is attached.

A 1994 Akron University Bliss Institute for Applied Politics survey found that 27 percent of the U.S. electorate sees itself "close" or "very close" to the religious right on particular issues. "Morally conservative" evangelicals, mainline Protestants, and Catholics account for half of the U.S. population. Whatever distinctions might be made about who is on the religious right, the survey data suggest that the reality of religious conservatism is larger and more varied than the label.

A 1994 *Newsweek* poll found that "the fraying of America's social fabric—once considered the crotchety preoccupation of the cultural right—has become a national (even a liberal) obsession" (*Newsweek*, June 13, 1994). Three of every four adults surveyed believe that the nation is in a moral and spiritual decline. Crime and drug abuse are of far greater concern to Americans than employment or health care. *Newsweek* proclaims a "craving for virtue" that transcends denominational lines. The religious right has provided one of the more coherent responses to this craving, especially among the 64 percent of American voters who say that religious values are "very important" in their lives (Gallup, 1992).

Catholics are among those to whom that message can and does appeal. On specific issues, such as education (tuition vouchers, sex education, condom distribution, school prayer), homosexuality, euthanasia, and abortion, the shared values of Catholics and politically conservative Christians seem clear. Professor William Dinges of The Catholic University of America, who has studied conservative Catholics, sees abortion as "the catalyst which has galvanized the trans-denominational right." The institutional right, in turn, sees the Catholic

GEORGE W. GERNER *is a retired intelligence officer and a free-lance writer residing near Washington, D.C.*

47

vote as a natural, if unfamiliar, potential ally, a massive prize worthy of its wooing.

No other organization on the religious right approaches the Christian Coalition in membership, media capability, political professionalism—or desire to reach the Catholic voter. Pat Robertson established the Christian Broadcasting Network (CBN) thirty-four years ago. It was the first TV network to devote more than half of its broadcast schedule to religious programming. The Family Channel, a 1972 CBN spinoff, is now the nation's tenth largest cable network and reaches 58 million American homes. Robertson's tabloid newspaper, *Christian American*, has a circulation of 270,000. By 1993, CBN annual revenues totaled $140 million, over half of which came from average daily contributions of $240,000. Robertson's International Family Entertainment holding company (in which he owns shares worth $50 million) earned 1993 revenues of $208 million and paid him a salary of $435,000.

Robertson founded the Christian Coalition in 1989, shortly after his costly ($22 million) but unsuccessful bid to win the 1988 Republican presidential nomination. He defeated George Bush in the Iowa caucus but placed a poor fourth on Super Tuesday. To himself and to others, however, he had clearly demonstrated the potency of the religious right and of his personal power over it. Coalition membership grew rapidly— 57,000 in 1991 became 250,000 the following year, and 450,000 by 1993. Membership increased rapidly following Bill Clinton's election, and, by September 1994's Washington "Road to Victory" conference, Robertson claimed nearly 1.5 million contributing coalition members in some 900 chapters throughout the fifty states.

The Christian Coalition has become the dominant influence in more than a dozen state GOP organizations, largely in the South and the Midwest. Realizing that most national elections can be decided by 15 percent of potential voters who actually register for a given election (only 6 to 7 percent in local and state elections), the coalition has worked effectively to see that those who show up at the polls include a plurality of conservatives. Simply put, they are getting out the vote—selectively.

According to Akron University's Bliss Institute, an unprecedented 33 percent of voters in the November 1994 elections were white evangelical Christians, up from 18 percent two years earlier. More than two-thirds of these voted Republican. That increase was due in no small part to efforts by the Christian Coalition to register their constituency and get them out to vote. Among the results: twenty-five House races that would otherwise have seated Democrats were won by Republicans.

In the process of its steady advance, the coalition has put out the welcome mat to Catholics, and the threshold is being crossed. A Catholic approaching the Christian Coalition very quickly discovers that other Catholics have preceded him. A call to its Washington office is answered by secretary Connie Cavanaugh, cheerily efficient and Catholic. Referred to the officer in charge of Catholic Outreach, one is greeted by the unmistakably Boston accents

of Gerry Giblin, Irish Catholic and 1955 graduate of Holy Cross College. Giblin, who retired from IBM after "thirty-plus" years and regularly attends a local Tridentine Mass, encountered the Christian Coalition two years ago at its national convention. Having concluded that "these people share my concerns," Giblin is now a four-day-per-week unpaid volunteer. His Washington predecessor, Marlene Elwell, also an active Catholic, is now the Coalition's executive director in Michigan.

Giblin speaks with satisfaction of "the success we had in the November 1994 elections." The Republican winners included at least forty-four anti-abortion congressional candidates in an election where only 18 percent of the voters said that they voted prolife. As for Catholic participation in the coalition, Giblin notes that 120 Catholic conferees attended Mass at the September "road to victory" conference, points to the active participation of the Legionaries of Christ, a religious order, and remarks that a Catholic priest offered the invocation at the conference's banquet. Major conference speakers included Michael Novak, the Reverend Richard Neuhaus, then-Pennsylvania Governor Robert Casey, and Paul Weyrich (who invented the term "Moral Majority," and designed for the Reverend Jerry Falwell the organization which bore that name). Panel participants included the Reverend Michael Scanlon, president of the Franciscan University of Steubenville, Ohio. Enthusiastic applause greeted coalition executive director Ralph Reed's statement, "I am proud to call myself an ally of Pope John Paul." Reed is a former political organizer for Jesse Helms.

The most detailed and theologically sophisticated statement of a Catholic-Evangelical alliance is "Evangelicals and Catholics Together—The Christian Mission in the Third Millennium." Signed on March 29, 1994, the declaration was the product of eighteen months' consultation between Catholics and evangelical Protestants initiated by the Reverend Richard Neuhaus (a recent convert to the Catholic church who edits *First Things* and heads the Institute on Religion and Public Life) and former White House aide Charles Colson (Prison Fellowship).

Neuhaus says that Vatican officials concurred in the project. Among Catholic formulators and endorsers are Cardinal John O'Connor (New York), Bishop Francis George (Yakima), Monsignor William Murphy (chancellor, Boston), Archbishop Francis Stafford (Denver), Bishop Carlos Sevilla (San Francisco), and Avery Dulles, S.J. Also endorsing the declarations were senior faculty members of The Catholic University of America, Boston College, Fordham, Notre Dame, and Saint Louis Universities, plus well-known neoconservatives George Weigel (Ethics and Public Policy Center) and Michael Novak (American Enterprise Institute). Giblin refers to the declaration as a "document of understanding" between Pat Robertson and Cardinal John O'Connor.

Among other issues, the declaration resolves "to enact the most protective laws and public policies that are politically possible…to reduce dramatically the incidence of abortion"; to oppose euthanasia; to seek transmission in public education of "our cultural heritage, which is inseparable from the influence of religion"; to work for "parental choice" in publicly-supported education; and to oppose pornography. The declaration calls for "renewed appreciation of Western culture," noting that "commonly, today, multiculturalism means all cultures but our own."

The declaration shows the convergence of Catholics and Evangelicals on certain moral and social issues. But, according to Michael Russell at the Christian Coalition's Virginia Beach headquarters, the major vehicle for joint action with Roman Catholics at the institutional level has been the Coalition's voter guides. The coalition spent $2 million distributing 33 million such guides via 60,000 churches of many denominations around the country for the November 1994 elections. As "educational" guides, this $2 million expenditure did not require reporting to the Federal Elections Commission.

The voter guides present single-phrase statements of complex problems with one-word ("supports/opposes") comparisons of candidate positions on issues of concern to the Coalition. Although explicitly denying endorsement of any candidate, the guides make choices simple and obvious. The liberal People for the American Way sees them as devastatingly effective: 60 percent of all candidates strongly supported by the religious right in November 1994 won their races. (Not all candidates endorsed by the Christian Coalition sought its endorsement.)

aced by what they see as compelling moral issues in political campaigns, some Catholic bishops or their chancery staffs have found the Christian Coalition's ready-made guides an efficient distribution system for marshaling the Catholic vote.

The New York City School Board elections of May 4, 1993, was such an occasion. At stake were 288 unpaid community school board seats. Key issues in the election included school-based condom distribution without parental consent and, in the primary schools, the Rainbow Curriculum's sympathetic treatment of homosexuals. In what the *New York Times* labeled "a tactical alliance" between the Christian Coalition and the Archdiocese of New York, the Family Life Office of the archdiocese announced in April that it would allow distribution of 100,000 Christian Coalition-prepared voter guides through its 213 parishes in Manhattan, Staten Island, and the Bronx. (Across the East River, the Brooklyn diocese refused a similar arrangement.) More than half a million voter guides were distributed to over 2,000 New York City churches and synagogues. Fifty-one percent of the coalition-backed candidates were elected.

Even among those Catholics who would not question the appropriateness of diocesan guidance on election issues, there is concern about the ethical character of such actions. Perhaps the most dramatic example of the emerging alliance occurred across the Potomac from the Christian Coalition's Capitol Hill office. The Diocese of Arlington, Virginia, is among the nation's most conservative. As the November 1994 elections approached, the diocese's 270,000 Catholics (13 percent of the population) became a potentially significant factor in one of the most highly contested and nationally significant senatorial races: Republican Oliver North against incumbent Democrat Senator Charles Robb. North, a charismatic Episcopalian, made his religious beliefs a central feature of his campaign.

Having supplied North with indispensable help in winning the GOP nomination, the Christian Coalition actively backed him in his $16.8 million campaign, the second most heavily funded in the nation.

Enter Gerry Giblin's Christian Coalition "Catholic Outreach." In June, four months before the elections, Giblin held a luncheon at which some eight Arlington diocese priests, including the diocese's former vicar general, Monsignor Richard Burke, met with Ralph Reed. Shortly before, Catholic layman Frank Nassetta (a quietly effective federal retiree and father of an Arlington priest) had joined the Christian Coalition. When Nassetta sought diocesan approval for parish distribution of the Coalition's voter guide, Chancellor Robert Rippy anticipated resistance if the guides were presented solely as a Pat Robertson product. Within weeks and with the "blessing of the diocese" was born the League of Catholic Voters, which met for the first time in August 1994—just two months before the elections.

With the prospect of a jointly sponsored voter guide, Nassetta says, the Arlington chancery concurred in its distribution, subject to approval by parish pastors. On November 3, the 47,000-circulation diocesan newspaper, the *Arlington Catholic Herald*, published a full-page "voter guide" attributed jointly to the "League of Catholic Voters and the Christian Coalition." Although the fine print says that the guide's publication was "paid for and authorized by the Christian Coalition," the coalition's Washington office says and the *Herald*'s editor confirms that no payment was made.

The *Herald*'s publication of the voter guide "opened doors," according to Nassetta. Pastors who had previously refused distribution of the guides now agreed. On Sunday, November 6, 30,000 voter guides were distributed at some twenty of sixty Arlington parishes, mostly in the Northern Virginia metropolitan area where support for North was weakest. Lacking pastors' permission elsewhere, Christian Coalition volunteers distributed the guide anyway outside Masses on Sunday.

Several ethical questions arise from these actions:

● Although their stated purpose is "educational," the voter guide's selection of issues and the minimal descriptions of the candidates' positions are skillfully designed to lead to a specific partisan choice. Does this constitute "education" or endorsement? If the latter, it could threaten diocesan and parish tax-exempt status. According to Deacon Chris Baumann of the NCCB, dioceses and parishes engaging in such activity "could be on thin ground."

● Characterizations of Senator Robb's positions were inaccurate and misleading. In response to my query, Ms. Peggy Willhide, Robb's press secretary, documented numerous examples, ranging from misleadingly incomplete to false. (For example, contrary to the guide's claim, Robb favors voluntary school prayer.) Do diocesan officials not have an obligation to ensure the accuracy of factual assertions in the guidelines when published in the diocesan newspaper?

● Distribution of the voter guides only days before the election made any response by misrepresented candidates nearly impossible. Such timing reportedly accords with Christian Coalition guidance. Doesn't this belie the educational, nonpartisan purpose of voter guides?

● Publication of voter guides like those of the Christian Coalition by diocesan newspapers and their distribution through parishes and/or by groups bearing a diocesan "blessing" seem to imply their endorsement by the local church. Does this accord with accepted church practice?

Professor Daniel Cowdin, who teaches social ethics at The Catholic University, says that it does not: "Simplistic caricaturing by the Christian right is fundamentally at odds with the methods of Catholic social teaching. It is disrespectful of the autonomy of its audience. At its best, the Catholic social tradition has been much more sophisticated than that. It preaches issues of doctrine but leaves applications to the practical judgment of the laity—it does not load the dice."

Oliver North narrowly lost to Senator Robb in November (43 percent to 46 percent). However, in spite of one of the largest turnouts in the nation, one-quarter of Virgina voters identified themselves in exit polls as "religiously active, born-again Christians." They voted 57 percent for North and only 37 percent for Robb. As Ralph Reed concluded, "We turned out our vote, and it was overwhelmingly for North." Black voters overwhelmingly favored Robb. Among white voters in an exit poll for news organizations by Mitofsky International the following breakdown was reported:

	Robb	North	Coleman
Protestants	37	49	14
Catholics	42	47	11
Jews	75	21	4

For most of this century, American Catholics have been consistently more politically liberal than Protestants. However, a gradual conservative trend is discernible in the politics of U.S. Catholics. For Professor Dinges of The Catholic University, this is a by-product of Catholic upward mobility. Larger numbers of educated and affluent Catholics have "produced a class transformation that leads inevitably to more of them voting Republican," he argues.

Within the Catholic hierarchy, the trend toward political as well as theological conservatism is even clearer than among the laity. Professor Cowdin observes, "Catholic social thought from World War II through the pontificate of Paul VI was on a trajectory somewhat left of center." This changed with John Paul II, whose encyclical, *Centesimus annus*, served as a rallying point for Catholic conservatives in the same way that John XXIII's *Mater et magistra* did for Catholic liberals thirty years earlier. *Centesimus annus*, in Cowdin's view, "led to an easier merging of Catholic attitudes with those of the religious right."

Constituting nearly one-third of the national electorate, American Catholics were part of the strong swing to the right in the November 1994 congressional elections [*see, Commonweal,* January 13, 1995]. For the first time in recent history, more Catholics voted Republican than Democrat in an off-year election. There are now nearly as many Republican Catholics in the House of Representatives as Democratic Catholics. University of Notre Dame political scientist David Legee sees this as a phenomenon unique to this election and not a permanent change in Catholic voting patterns. Representative Peter T. King, prolife New York Republican, attributed last November's Catholic conservative swing to "the cultural gap between Bill Clinton and the traditional Irish and Italian Catholics."

As dramatic as the national swing to the right was in November 1994, Catholic laity are still not as conservative as other American Christians. Exit polls by Voter News and Surveys show that 55 percent of Catholics voted Republican compared to 66 percent of other American Christians. The Catholic contrast is even greater with the 5 percent of total voters who identified themselves as members of the "religious right,"

90 percent of whom voted Republican in November.

With the exception of the National Conference of Catholic Bishops/US Catholic Conference (NCCB/USCC), no Catholic organization approaches the size, sophistication, or political effectiveness of the Christian Coalition or Dr. James Dobson's Colorado-headquartered Focus on the Family. "The Religious Right," a study published in 1994 by the Anti-Defamation League, listed no Catholic organizations and found "as-yet limited public interaction between Catholic and evangelical organizations and differences in strategy, rhetoric, and impact." USCC's Media Relations officer, Bill Ryan, says that the USCC has "very little" contact with the Christian Coalition.

Although a few conservative Catholic groups have achieved some impact upon specific issues, such as "right to life," most are of nominal consequence in national politics. Professor Cowdin sees that as consistent with Catholic social practice. "The Catholic social encyclical tradition has no constituency. It is not a living tradition in terms of grassroots organizations. Unlike the Christian Coalition, it has not focused on the nuts and bolts of social effectiveness. There's a vacuum there, and that's part of the reason why some Catholics have been flowing into the religious right. The church has not offered them something at a parallel level."

That is what brought Gerry Giblin to the Christian Coalition. "It's a grassroots thing. People like myself and other Catholics, we're disappointed with the bishops. They verbalize, but they don't do much to get the vote out. The K. of C., Knights of Malta, Holy Name Society—they're not doing it either." Giblin seeks new channels to cooperation with conservative Catholics who, like himself, wish to "make a difference."

Clearly, the Christian Coalition is building these channels. Despite important theological and historical differences between Catholics and Evangelicals, the Coalition shares some common ground with the social and moral teachings of the Catholic church. In the current political environment, its efforts to enlist Catholics will probably meet with a degree of success.

Such inroads, however, are likely to be greater in some diocesan chancery offices than among the mass of U.S. Catholics. The laity's persisting liberalism and the widening divergence of their experience from a theologically and politically more conservative hierarchy are certainly among the factors. Any continuing Catholic evolution toward the political right will more likely come "from above" than "from below." It will probably be of limited degree and gradual pace, reflecting the continuing upward mobility of Catholics. As the new conservative ascendancy in Washington moderates its stand on abortion and cuts budgets for a variety of social programs, historical fissures between political conservatism and traditional Catholic liberalism are likely to reemerge. Witness Speaker Newt Gingrich's March 14 removal of an anti-abortion amendment from the budget reduction bill and the severe USCC criticism of the Republican welfare reform plan four days later.

Catholic impact upon the religious right will probably con-

51

tinue to come from active volunteers like Giblin as well as scholars and intellectuals. Catholics tend to be (or at least think they are) more cerebral than Evangelicals in their social theology. Few are likely to confuse Pat Robertson with Karl Rahner. Catholics such as Patrick Buchanan, William Bennett, Richard Neuhaus, Michael Novak, and George Weigel will continue to be ready donors of intellectual substance to the needy religious right. But the religious right's wooing of the Catholic electorate is likely to remain a rather one-sided courtship. □

Transcript of "Life Beyond God" by Leslie Kaufman
New York Times Magazine, October 16, 1994

Life Beyond God:
The Christian right is going secular—
emphasizing taxes and other mainstream issues,
while talking more quietly about abortion.
Can they build a real moral majority?
By Leslie Kaufman*

On a rainy Tuesday night in Big Stone Gap, Va., Mike Farris was running late. By the time he got to the Powell Valley Middle School to kick off a fund-raising dinner for Oliver North, he had already missed "The Star-Spangled Banner," the Pledge of Allegiance and a booming rendition of "Proud to Be an American." The 300 people who packed the cafeteria didn't seem to mind his tardiness: As he dashed up to the dais to introduce North, the Republican candidate for Senate in Virginia, the crowd gave Farris a standing ovation. Tan and handsome in his double-breasted gray suit and blue silk tie, he would blend in far better in the properous eastern suburbs of Arlington or McLean than in this tiny mining town in the far southwest corner of the state. But he is tremendously popular in Big Stone Gap, where he won a substantial majority in his unsuccessful 1993 race for lieutenant governor.

The true hero of Virginia's religious conservatives
is a man who argued that schoolchildren
shouldn't be required to read Anne Frank's diary.

Farris, 43, is a lawyer, an ordained Baptist minister, founder and president of the Home School Legal Defense Association and a likely Republican candidate for senator from Virginia in 1996. He is also the most recent embodiment of what has come to be called the Christian right. After serving as president of the Washington State chapter of Moral Majority, the Jerry Falwell organization, Farris gained national attention during "Scopes II," the 1985 trial of a case brought by Christian fundamentalist parents against the Hawkins County, Tenn., public-school system. (Farris, who had moved to Virginia by this time, argued that requiring children to read parts of "The Diary of Anne Frank" and "The Wizard of Oz," for instance, represented an unconstitutional infringement on their religious beliefs. He won the case, but the verdict was later overturned.) He has labeled American public schooling "A godless monstrosity," and his name appeared as a co-author on a policy paper by a group called Coalition on Revival, which has called for the United States to reclaim itself as a "Christian nation." (Farris says that he only worked on an early draft of the document and that the organization included his name without his permission.)

For all the chatter about the politically reborn Oliver North, Farris is the true hero of Virginia's religious conservatives. His 1993 candidacy brought thousands of Christian supporters into the Republican fold, and many of these men and women, at Farris's urging, have stayed in the party as envelope-lickers, phone-bankers and pamphlet-folders. If North should defeat the Democratic incumbent, Charles Robb, and an independent candidate, Marshall Coleman, on Nov. 8, it will be in large part thanks to their handiwork. Conservative Christians have similarly come to dominate the Republican parties in more than a dozen states, including Florida, Iowa, Minnesota, South Carolina and Texas. Yet, as Farris learned firsthand in his own failed election campaign—when opponents played up the more intemperate aspects of his religious-political history—the imprimatur of the Christian right can scare off the general electorate.

That is why, on this night, the words "God" and "Christian" rarely passed Farris's lips. "When Senator Robb comes across a problem, his solution is always more government," Farris began. He went on to talk about balancing the Federal budget and about his desire to give parents more control over their children's education. There was no mention of abortion (Farris is anti-abortion) or minority rights for homosexuals (he is opposed). The Christian right has learned to concentrate on more secular conservative crowd-pleasers—term limits, tough anti-crime measures and higher tax deductions for families with children.

Offstage, Farris is equally circumspect about his own religious convictions. While quick to acknowledge a personal debt to his Christian faith, he told me, "As a candidate, I can't go to any individual and ask him to vote for me . . . because the Bible says so."

It is certainly the better part of political wisdom for Farris *not* to. In the past, candidates sponsored by the Christian right have routinely been defeated at the polls, often with the not-so-subtle connivance of fellow Republicans. "The fact is, if you step back and ask who has won elections since 1992, it is a bunch of pro-choice Republicans like Christine Todd Whitman in New Jersey—liberal, yuppie modern types," says William Kristol, Dan Qyayle's former chief of staff and chairman of the Project for the Republican Future.

Still, the Christian right has emerged as the single most powerful bloc within the Republican Party. Now, Mike Farris and the movement's other leaders are determined to cash in their grass-roots success for some real power, to convert their devout crusaders into electable politicians. And if that means holding their tongues about abortion and homosexuality—and even God—so be it.

Conservative Christians have come to dominate the Republican parties in more than a dozen states, including Florida, Minnesota and Texas.

The Christian Coalition, founded in 1989 by the televangelist Pat Robertson, is perhaps the best known and most aggressive of the dozens of organizations that make up the Christian right. Ralph Reed, the coalition's executive director, is a baby-faced 33-year-old who hardly looks the part of master political strategist, but he is widely credited with the coalition's stunning growth—it now boasts 1.4 million supporters, a mailing list of 30 million and 1,100 chapters in all 50 states.

Sitting behind an enormous polished desk at the coalition's Chesapeake, Va., office, Reed, who has a Ph.D. in American history from Emory University and 10 years' experience as a Republican operative, explained that modern Christian activism is struggling to enter its third stage. The first, he believes, began in the late 1970's and was leader-centered—he points to Falwell and to Robertson's 1988 Presidential bid. Robertson, Reed says, was prompted by his loss six years ago to reconsider his own prominence and to focus instead on more finite goals. He began the coalition to train Christian conservatives in nuts-and-bolts politicking, and it rapidly became a genuine organizational boon to the Republican Party. "Our folks do the unheralded, uncelebrated, often unrecognized 'three yards and a cloud of dust' grass-roots efforts that flat-out need to be done," Reed said.

Now will come the third stage—or so Reed hopes—during which the election of Christian conservatives is no loner such a rarity. "By the year 2000," he predicted, "when you wake up and look back at this decade, the movement that will have etched the contours of politics . . . will be these people."

Reed, like Farris, realizes that such a goal demands a broad agenda. Conservative Christian voters, as Reed readily concedes, are, like most voters, primarily concerned with crime, taxes and the deficit. Reed claims that exit polls from the 1992 Presidential election show that only 22 percent of voters who identified themselves as "born-again evangelicals" considered abortion a key issue. As Reed admits in his new book, "Politically Incorrect: The Emerging Faith Factor in American Politics," many potentially sympathetic voters simply "tuned out" the "policy-thin and value-laden" rhetoric of the Christian right.

Smaller government and term limits, lower taxes and school choice: Reed is convinced that the coalition's new platform will capture the votes not only of Christian conservatives but of other disaffected groups as well. He recently met with Ross Perot to discuss their respective movements. Reed sees many similarities between the Christian Coalition and United We Stand America, which he calls "an outsider-versus-insider, grass-roots, reform-minded, shake-up-the-establishment movement." And Reed thinks it only natural that, should Perot not run for President in 1996, the 19 percent of the electorate that voted for him in 1992 would find a home with the Christian right. "We are demographically the same kind of voters: middle class with kids and mostly white."

Reed offers this profile of a typical Christian Coalition member, drawn from the organization's own research: a white, Baptist, semi-professional woman, from 30 to 55 years old, with children and some college education. To reach the next, cherished third stage, Reed acknowledged, the Christian right must expand its constituency and retool its image.

The coalition's Road to Victory conference, held last month in Washington, featured such conservative Christian stalwarts as Dan Quayle, Pat Robertson and William Bennett. But Reed also programmed seminars to address the various constituencies to whom the Christian right is trying to extend its reach: "Jews and Christians in Unity," "Catholic-Evangelical Cooperation" and "Building Bridges Into Minority Communities."

In 1988, when the United States Supreme Court refused to hear the "Scopes II" case, Mike Farris issued this proclamation: "It's time for every born-again Christian in America to take their children out of public schools." Because his clients felt that Anne Frank's diary promoted the belief that all paths lead to God and that Dorothy, Toto and company condoned the practice of witchcraft and the occult, Farris had demanded that Hawkins County schools arrange separate reading classes for the children and pay the religious-school tuition for those students who had been suspended for refusing to read certain books.

In his new book, "Where Do I Draw the Line?," Farris describes why he finally began to tone down his rhetoric: "My natural tendencies caused one of my friends who saw me in the midst of a political dispute to say I sometimes react like a 'trained Doberman pinscher.'" After Farris lost his cool on a TV talk show in Seattle, his wife, he wrote, "used an analogy that—afterward—spoke to me: 'Getting your message across is a lot like singing a song. You have to do more than sing the right words. You need a pleasing melody if you want people to listen.'"

Today, Farris carefully avoids framing his arguments in strictly religious terms. In fact, in explaining why he once mounted a campaign against "The Learning Tree," the Gordon Parks book in which a drunken character assails Jesus as a "long-legged white son-of-a-bitch," Farris sounds as if he has appropriated the language of multiculturalism that is anathema to so many conservatives: "Just as I don't think a black kid should be forced to read Mark Twain because of the word 'nigger,' religious Christians shouldn't be forced to read books offensive to them."

Farris no longer invites reporters to his home to meet his wife and nine children (all of whom have been or will be educated at home). He feels such access was abused during his campaign for lieutenant governor. Instead, we met in Washington at Sfuzzi, a sleek Italian restaurant in Union Station. He brought his 16-year-old daughter, Jayme—a National Merit Commended Scholar, he proudly pointed out. Poised and friendly, she sat respectfully through the long interview. Her father was articulate and thoughtful.

Education is still Farris's prime concern; his prescription for public-school reform these days focuses on parent-teacher cooperation. "I want parents, the people who care the most about the education of their children, to be equal partners," he said. If parents object to the curriculum of a sex education course, Farris explained, they should be able to work with teachers to design an alternative.

But what if those same parents don't like the curriculum of a science class, or English, or math? Would the teacher have the right—the responsibility—to develop alternatives for these courses as well?

"I know this works," Farris replied, seeming to find the question impertinent. "I've seen it work, so don't give me a crazy hypothetical."

Unlike some past Christian candidates, Farris is not obsessed with militant feminism or homosexuality. In fact, he thinks that gay teachers are acceptable as long as they don't "promote homosexuality." Farris also believes that the Supreme Court was right to ban official prayer in the public schools—an issue, he said, that is "three parts gimmick to every part of reality. Most evangelicals are far more concerned with the other 5 hours and 59 minutes of the school day than with what happens in the first minute."

Farris's detractors within Virginia's Republican Party—and there are many—doubt the authenticity of his kinder, gentler persona. When Bobbie Kilberg, a veteran of the Reagan and Bush Administrations and Farris's opponent in last year's bid for the Republican nomination for lieutenant governor, rose to address the state convention, she was nearly booed off the podium. Kilberg, who supports the right to abortion (but not at taxpayer expense), was taunted with cries of "Killbaby," and was, she claims, pelted with ice. Witnesses also say one Kilberg loyalist, wearing a "Republicans for Choice" pin, was circled by Farris delegates chanting "baby-killer." Farris denies that any of this took place, but says "it was wrong" if "a few isolated people did those things."

The Christian right, Kilberg claims, is as radical and dangerous as ever. "It is positive to have people of faith—all faiths—participating in the political process and running for office," says Kilberg, who is Jewish. "But I get very nervous when I am told that only Christians, preferably those who are 'born again,' should be elected, that evolution should not be taught in the public schools, and that I am not a Republican if I am pro-choice. I get even more nervous when people tell me that they have been directed by God to support a candidate and that the right to arm yourself with assault weapons is necessary to protect a 'Christian nation' against the heathen onslaught." All of this, Kilberg says, "was said to me on the campaign trail by Farris supporters."

Nowhere has the Christian right's success wrought such discord as within its own party. As Irving Kristol, the godfather of neoconservatism, wrote in The Wall Street Journal, "A struggle for both the soul and body of American conservatism is taking place place before our eyes."

There is scant disagreement among Republicans, Kristol argues, about what is wrong with America—that an ever-expanding welfare state is wasting money and rewarding destructive behavior. The party's fiscal conservatives, though, argue that social disaster is predicated on economics—that women have children out of wedlock because the state rewards them for doing so. Social conservatives, including the leadership of the Christian Coalition, believe that social ruin can be reversed only when the American people undergo a moral and spiritual revival.

Kristol shares some of the fiscal conservatives' concerns about the marriage of politics and religion. But he feels that religious Americans are under siege these days and need a principled defender. What's more, he points out, Republican candidates will have a tough time winning national elections without the support of Christian conservatives. As Ralph Reed often mentions, right-wing evangelicals were the only solid bloc of support for Bush in 1992.

Certain Republican operatives have begun to nurse the relationship between the dueling factions. Differences will endure, argues William Kristol, Irving's son, but "cutting government and expanding the spirit of liberty is consistent with strengthening families." He predicts "a big fight on the abortion plank in 1996," but insists that "it will come within the context of a reasonably united party."

The national Republican Party has evidently decided it must embrace the Christian right, at least with one arm. National Republican Senatorial Committee staffers, some of whom hesitated to work for Oliver North, were told they would be fired if they backed Marshall Coleman, who broke Republican ranks to oppose North as an independent. Freelance consultants were told they'd never work for the national Republicans again if they helped Coleman. Even James A. Baker 3d came to help North raise money, and Bob Dole, the Senate minority leader and quadrennial White House seeker, spent a day campaigning with North after initially refusing, quite noisily, to endorse him. A few days later, several secular conservatives showed up as speakers at the Road to Victory conference—Elizabeth Dole, Phil Gramm and Dick Cheney among them.

Already, the Christian right's efforts to align itself with secular conservatives has paid dividends. Teaming up with the 70,000-member organization U.S. Term Limits, Frank Lucas, a candidate supported by the Christian Coalition, was elected to Congress in Oklahoma last year; Ron Lewis used the same combined sponsorship to win a Congressional seat from Kentucky. Considering the particularly virulent strain of anti-incumbency in the air this year, Democrats are justifiably worried. "The religious right," says Mike Casey, a spokesman for the Democratic Congressional Campaign Committee, "is joining forces with other conservative issue groups to form a single fist with incredible punching power."

North, who may very well win his race, is only the most visible of this year's candidates supported by the Christian right; 10 more Republicans who stand to win Congressional races have been identified by the Democratic National Committee as Christian right candidates.

Given this potential power shift, Mike Farris can afford to drop his newly gentle demeanor for a moment. "If the rest of the Republican Party behaves the way they did in my election, where you get big-name defections every time an evangelical runs, it will be the death of the party," he warned recently. "The patronizing, 'We want your vote, we want your support, but we will not support one of your people,' will not last. It will blow this party apart."

*Leslie Kaufman is an associate editor at Newsweek. Her articles have appeared in The Los Angeles Times Magazine and The Washington Post.

THE FUTURE OF CONSERVATISM

The agenda of American conservatism today can be defined as the construction (or reconstruction) of a politics of liberty and a sociology of virtue. Fifteen years ago, this would not have been the case. At the end of the Carter administration, economics and foreign policy were at the top of conservatism's agenda. But the Cold War is over. And while economic growth remains important today, the case for markets has made so much intellectual and political headway since 1980 that it is hard now to accord economics primacy. Beyond this, most thoughtful observers now agree that noneconomic factors are at least as crucial to our future economic performance as narrowly economic ones. These noneconomic factors involve the politics of liberty and the sociology of virtue.

I am indebted to the sociologist Robert Nisbet for this formulation of the conservative agenda. In a recent essay, Nisbet points out that "a conservative party (or other group) has a double task confronting it. The first is to work tirelessly toward the diminution of the centralized, omnicompetent, and unitary state with its ever-soaring debt and

deficit." The relimiting of government—this is the politics of liberty. "The second and equally important task," Nisbet says,

IN THE U.S.

BY WILLIAM KRISTOL

"is that of protecting, reinforcing, nurturing, where necessary, the varied groups and associations which form the true building blocks of the social order." Strengthening the institutions in civil society that attend to the character of the citizenry—this is the sociology of virtue.

The Politics of Liberty

The phrase "the politics of liberty" suggests that the preservation of liberty is itself a political problem and a political task. Prior to Reagan, the libertarian wing of the conservative movement was primarily concerned with theoretical constructions of the case for liberty. Other conservatives, often bolstered by the findings of social science, sought to demonstrate the failure of particular policies of the welfare state. Both groups gave less

thought to the issue of how to construct institutions and provide incentives for political actors to preserve and strengthen the system of liberty itself.

But in the post-Reagan/Bush era, the politics of liberty has come to the fore. It has done so for the practical reason that conservatives had such limited success in the 1980s in rolling back the huge expansion of government that took place in the 1960s and 1970s. The federal government is as big, as intrusive, and as meddlesome as ever. Many conservatives have therefore become convinced that instead of merely offering critiques of particular policies, they must address the issue of the size and scope of government itself. Conservatives have also learned that it is not enough simply to try to make the case against big government but that we have to think politically and institutionally about how to rally support and create incentives for less intrusive government—for limited government.

There is also a much greater appreciation among conservatives today of the institutional obstacles to cutting government. Electing conservative or Republican presidents has not changed things very much. Nor has the movement of popular opinion toward far greater unhappiness and skepticism about government. This is because sets of relationships and patterns of behavior have been built into the liberal welfare state that are hard to break once they have formed and congealed. George Bernard Shaw said early in this century, "A government that robs Peter to pay Paul can always depend on the support of Paul." And if it doesn't rob Peter too much, and if there are a lot of Peters dispersed throughout the society and only a few Pauls, there will be an endless process of little robberies of Peter to give benefits to Paul. And if the Pauls organize as an interest group, and if they are strong in particular congressional districts, and if limits on governmental action disappear, then the welfare state comes into being and keeps on growing.

Having failed on the whole to curb the growth of the welfare state by fighting it in one policy area after another, conservatives need to think imaginatively about how to challenge it in general. And it may well turn out, paradoxically, to be easier to contain and roll back the welfare state systematically than to fix particular parts of it one by one, as Reagan and Bush tried to do.

After all, polls today show that the American people have a deep distrust of the federal government and its ability to do good. In fact they believe, by substantial margins, that the government is more likely to do more harm than good. We have, therefore, a public opinion that would support a broad attack on government. But we also know that people dislike big government in general more than they dislike its particular policies. Because particular policies have beneficiaries who will fight to keep them, while the opposition to these par-

William Kristol is chairman of the Project for the Republican Future. This is a revised version of his Bradley Lecture, delivered at the American Enterprise Institute on December 13, 1993.

ticular policies is often diffuse, the best strategy for containing or rolling back the liberal welfare state may be to try to cut the Gordian knot, rather than to try to unwind the knot one string at a time. Conservatives are therefore particularly interested in proposals—such as a balanced budget amendment, term limits, various taxing and spending limitations, the devolution and privatization of government functions—that are radical in the sense that they do not seek simply to restore a status quo ante or undo the damage of the Great Society welfare state. They seek to change our political system as a whole to make it more supportive of limited government.

The resurgence of interest in the politics of liberty has also been aided by developments in political science. The Founding Fathers were interested in creating institutional structures, incentives, and relationships that would preserve liberty, and there has recently been a revival of interest in their thinking on those subjects. Public choice economics, with its interest in institutional or constitutional structures that produce outcomes that are favorable to liberty in general as opposed merely to specific policy outcomes, has been influential too.

Consider, for example, the change in the way conservatives tend to discuss federalism. Conservatives no longer have much interest in reviving "New Federalism" efforts. They are interested in *real* federalism, but only if that is understood as part of a general program of relimiting government. They no longer have much faith that state governments are more immune to the entreaties of interest groups than the federal government. They do have a general preference for smaller rather than bigger government, but the fact is that teacher unions in Richmond or Sacramento are virtually as strong as in Washington. Conservatives in 1980 argued for killing the federal Department of Education and returning power to the states and localities; conservatives today continue to favor this, but the key to their agenda goes beyond federalism to

parental choice. The point is not simply to get power back to the state governments, but to get power back to parents. Similarly, whereas once there was a great desire to fight for prayer in the public schools, conservatives today tend to believe that while the public square should be friendlier to religion, the cause of respect for religion will be advanced more substantially by allowing parents greater choice in the kind of schools they can send their children to, including religious schools. Post-Reagan conservatism is thus, in many ways, more radical than pre-Reagan conservatism, because it has learned the lessons of the limitations of his accomplishments.

Similarly, if you look at the conservative agenda today, there is much less talk about restoring the proper interpretation of the Constitution. In 1980 it seemed reasonable to talk about overturning a few years of bad court decisions, but almost 15 years later, those decisions have calcified. There is much greater openness today, therefore, to state initiatives and referendums, constitutional amendments, and other populist remedies to the capture of the federal judiciary by the modern welfare state. Conservatives are far less wary than they once were of these populist remedies, because they seem to be the only feasible ways to address the pathologies of the welfare state. Most striking in this respect is the emergence of term limits as an issue. Term limits were not discussed in the late 1970s by conservatives or by anyone else. The idea, rejected at the Constitutional Convention, had disappeared from our politics for almost two centuries. Today term limits may be the most popular movement in the country. Because no one in Washington likes the idea very much, it still isn't much discussed here. But voters in some 14 states have passed such limits. Seven states and the District of Columbia are petitioning to put term limits on their ballots this November. The remaining states would then have to pass term limits through their state legislatures. This is unlikely to happen, and indeed the courts may strike down state-imposed federal term limits. In either case, the issue would be driven to the national level, in the way that such issues as female suffrage and the 18-year-old vote ascended to the national level when they required a constitutional amendment.

Term limits could thus become a huge issue as early as 1995, an issue on which congressmen, senators, and even presidential candidates could run. And the reason for the interest in term limits is not primarily an abstract belief that Congress will be a better institution if there is more turnover. There is actually more to the case for term limits than this. The Iron Triangle of the welfare state—the politicians, bureaucrats, and interest groups who establish and benefit from its programs—seems at once impervious to change from above, even from a popular president, and impervious to change from below, from public opinion. But term limits threaten the Iron Triangle. The incentives for individual congressmen change once term limits are enacted. The seniority and committee system disintegrates. The balance of power within Congress and between Congress and the other branches of government, and even between Congress and the electorate, changes. That's the argument for term limits. They are ways of getting at the pathologies of interest-group liberalism, and they seem to have more promise than most other ways people have devised to address those pathologies.

Conservatives understand that the politics of liberty has to go beyond a generalized hostility to big government. The conservative task is now to think imaginatively about structural, legislative, and constitutional changes that would restore the principle of limited government and, if at all possible, the practice of limited government. To put it simply: Al Gore and the new Democrats want to reinvent government; conservatives want to relimit it.

For big government is not merely a threat to our economic well-being. It is a threat to a free society because it makes

TODAY'S SOCIOLOGY OF VIRTUE IMPLIES A THINKING THROUGH OF THE WAY IN WHICH SOCIAL INSTITUTIONS CAN BE REINVENTED, RESTRUCTURED, OR REFORMED TO PROMOTE VIRTUE AND FOSTER SOUND CHARACTER.

people less able to govern themselves. Self-government means that communities and citizens and families are able and willing to govern themselves. To enable that to happen, conservatives will have to reassert the wisdom of the old-fashioned idea that there is a private sphere that government shouldn't regulate at all, even for desirable policy ends. The "pursuit of happiness" has to be left primarily to citizens acting freely in civil society; government can secure some of the conditions of such a pursuit, but it cannot make "happiness"—or even "security" in an extended sense—its direct object. The politics of liberty, if pursued, culminates in a case for, and in a commitment to, limited government.

Conservatives do of course favor an energetic government within its proper sphere. But it is precisely as our government has expanded its sphere to encompass all problems that it has become less energetic and less effective where it should be energetic and effective. So the politics of liberty seeks to reconstruct limited and effective government—effective because it is limited.

The Sociology of Virtue

The "politics of liberty" is complemented by the other pillar of today's conservative agenda, the "sociology of virtue." Here too conservatives face a different situation from the one that prevailed before the Reagan/Bush era. The older conservatism was of course also concerned with the issue of the relationship of liberty and virtue. But it tended to speak primarily of preserving our wasting moral capital from the depredations of modern life, of maintaining traditional ideas of law and morality, and of shoring up old institutions that were under modernist assault. The older conservatism was profoundly "conservative," ever defensive, in this respect.

The new conservatism is more concerned with restoring or creating a sociology of virtue than with stemming any further erosion of virtue's moral capital. That erosion has today gone too far for a merely "conservative" approach. Today's sociology of virtue thus implies a thinking through of the way in which social institutions can be reinvented, restructured, or reformed to promote virtue and to foster sound character. Just as important, many Americans have decided they can't wait for political victories to deal with these social problems. They don't in any case have much faith that government can solve our most serious social problems. A successful politics of liberty would make a sociology of virtue much easier—but even a sound political order is not sufficient for a sound society. Such a society would require a resurgence of efforts within the sphere of civil society to grapple directly with social problems, with problems that are ultimately problems of character, problems of virtue.

What is interesting is that such efforts are already happening, and are not waiting for a politics of liberty. There are efforts by inner-city pastors to religitimize and redignify fatherhood, for example, as the beginning of a solution to the terrible condition of our inner cities. There is an authentic religious revival going on in the land, despite the continuous efforts in the public sphere to delegitimize religion and reduce its role. The right-to-life movement is doing a great deal to provide counseling and homes for unwed mothers, trying to convince women not to take advantage of a right they have won due to both the Supreme Court and political action. Citizens are banding together to deal with even so fundamental an area of government responsibility as crime. They no longer think it is their job just to call the police and then get out of the way. We will see more efforts along these lines to solve social problems through civil society, simply leaving government aside, because government is so ineffectual.

These efforts will ultimately have a political effect, of course. Take the area of education. There is a surge in privately funded voucher programs that enable students from poor and lower-income families to go to a school of their parents' choice, with major success stories in Indianapolis and Milwaukee. A new organization in Washington, D.C., recently announced that it already had enough money to send some 50 children to schools of their parents' choice. And once these efforts get off the ground, it should become relatively easy for them to raise money from corporate philanthropists. After all, they are directly benefiting young people who are at risk.

Ultimately, this kind of nonpolitical activity puts political pressure on the public schools to reform. In fact it may well be the most effective way to reform them, given the difficulty of doing so through either legislation or popular initiatives, due to the power mismatch between the well-financed educational status quo and the school-choice proponents.

This new approach might be called the Federal Express Model of Change. Conservatives tried for decades to reform the Post Office, which they decried as an inefficient monopoly dominated by unions. They were right, and nearly everyone agreed the Post Office didn't work well, but it seemed impossible to make a dent in it legislatively. Then, in the early 1970s, Fred Smith started Federal Express. The political fight then became the effort by the Post Office and its allies to strangle Federal Express in its crib. But Federal Express prevailed, since it is politically easier to defend a

THE POLITICS OF LIBERTY AND THE SOCIOLOGY OF VIRTUE ARE TWO TRACKS THAT COULD RUN PARALLEL TO ONE ANOTHER. BUT THEY TEND TO RUN UP AGAINST ONE ANOTHER ON A CORE SET OF ISSUES INVOLVING THE FAMILY.

small business from the government than to break up a huge government monopoly. Now, thanks also to technological developments such as the fax machine, we have a situation where, with no real legal change, the delivery of mail has been transformed. The Post Office is no longer a big obstacle to American competitiveness, and it has in fact probably improved its performance as a result of competition from the private sector.

This sort of approach can be taken in many other areas. Instead of changing government institutions, people will simply go around them. And, if that happens often enough, these institutions will either reform themselves, or they will become relics that don't cause much harm anymore, and will then shrivel up and die. As the Federal Express example suggests, political action *is* necessary to protect these private-sector efforts from government attempts to prevent them from coming into being. This is how the Moral Majority got its start. The federal government was threatening the tax-exempt status of Christian schools, and the Moral Majority was founded as a defensive measure to defend these private-sector institutions against the government. And this experience also shows how defensive efforts on behalf of the private sector, on behalf of civil society, can ultimately become offensive ones that seek to change the political system and the political culture.

So while the sociology of virtue implies pursuing virtue primarily in the private sector through our social institutions, it ultimately has a political agenda and political implications. At the very least, it requires the defense of sound social institutions from attempts by political institutions to suppress or reshape them.

Family Values

The politics of liberty and the sociology of virtue are two tracks that conservatism can and will pursue in the years to come. They are, on the whole, consistent and complementary tracks. Many conservatives favor school choice on grounds of liberty, because they like competition and want to break up government monopolies; others favor school choice because they believe that sound values will be taught in schools that parents have more control over.

Similarly, when conservatives oppose government efforts to regulate day care, and try instead to provide vouchers for parents to use in any private setting they want, we see a politics of liberty seeking to restrict the scope of the federal government and to keep the state out of the private sphere of civil society. But we also see a sociology of virtue in the sense that the quality of day care that families, relatives, and private-sector institutions offer will be friendlier to the values conservatives tend to favor than would be publicly provided day care.

Some hope that these two tracks would simply run parallel to one another, allowing libertarians to fight the federal government and traditionalists to worry about the sociology of virtue. But it turns out that they ultimately intersect, and there is, therefore, some tension between the two. The two tracks can run parallel for quite a while; but they tend to run up against one another on a core set of issues involving the family. Here the politics of liberty runs up against the political impossibility of being neutral about the fundamental arrangements of society; and the sociology of virtue runs up against the limits of what can be done in the civil sphere absent legal or public policy support.

This can be made clear by reflecting on Charles Murray's now-famous October 29, 1993, *Wall Street Journal* article, "The Coming White Underclass." Murray's argument is that we have a terrible problem, one that has moved from black America to become a threat to all America. He argues that the problems of crime, illiteracy, welfare, homelessness, drugs, and poverty all stem from this core problem, which is illegitimacy. Illegitimacy is therefore "the single most important social problem of our time." Doing something about it is not just one more item on the American policy agenda; it should be at the top of the agenda. The broad and deep response Murray's article has received suggests that it struck a chord—and, in fact, it has struck chords in both the politics of liberty and the sociology of virtue.

Murray argues we need a politics of liberty. We don't need more liberal social engineering to solve the problem, we need the state to stop interfering with the natural forces that have kept the overwhelming majority of births within marriage for millennia. While Murray says he is pessimistic about how much government can do (except for getting out of the way), he is optimistic about how little it needs to do. And it mentions making the tax code more friendly to families and to families with children.

So the politics of liberty, presumably supplemented by a private-sector sociology of virtue, would seem to be Murray's recommendation. But near the end of his article he adds the following: "A more abstract but ultimately crucial step is to make marriage once again the sole legal institution through which parental rights and responsibilities are defined and exercised." Indeed, "a marriage certificate should establish that a man and woman have entered into a unique legal relationship. The changes that have blurred the distinctiveness of marriage are subtly but importantly destructive."

But Murray's suggestion that we need to reverse these changes would require

THE POLITICS OF LIBERTY NEEDS TO ACCOMMODATE THE SPECIAL STATUS OF THE FAMILY, AND THE SOCIOLOGY OF VIRTUE NEEDS POLITICAL AND LEGAL SUPPORT FOR THE FAMILY AS AN INSTITUTION.

substantial alterations in federal law and constitutional interpretation, in order once again to discriminate against illegitimacy or against nontraditional family arrangements. Here, in other words, a mere politics of liberty runs up against the political actions needed to combat "the single most important social problem of our time." State welfare policies, for example, cannot today discriminate against illegitimate children. But if it is essential that the law support marriage and the family—if we can't depend simply on civil society in a climate of legal neutrality to produce healthy families and to see to it that children are mostly born into intact families—then we come to the point where the politics of liberty and the sociology of virtue intersect. At this intersection, it would seem that the politics of liberty needs to accommodate the special status of the family, and the sociology of virtue needs political and legal support for the family as an institution. In other words, the political sphere, whose primary goal is liberty, cannot be inattentive to the claims of virtue; and the social sphere, whose focus is virtue, requires some political support. Underlying a commitment to the politics of liberty and the sociology of virtue, in other words, there is a certain view of human nature that cannot but be repressed in law and society.

To support the family, one needs to support the value of the family. To sup-

port the value of the family, one must hold a view of human nature different from the view underlying the sexual revolution, whose effects Murray laments. Murray thinks that public policy should lean against the sexual revolution, perhaps the second most powerful revolution of our time. But implicit in his position and in discussion of the (differing) expectations we need to have for "little boys" and "little girls," is a view, also, that public policy should lean against the most powerful revolution of our time, the feminist revolution. For Murray is willing to acknowledge that the burden of preserving the family inevitably falls primarily on women, and he believes public policy should recognize this fact.

The sexual and feminist revolutions sprang up in civil society, of course. Politicians did not invent them. But the polity helped them along by legitimizing them and delegitimizing those who tried to resist them. Our politics cannot simply be neutral between the sexual revolution and those who would resist it, and between radical feminism and those who would resist it. Our politics should and will be overwhelmingly a politics of liberty; the pursuit of virtue will be primarily a "sociological" matter; but at the intersection of politics and society—at the family—some judgments must be made. These judgments will always be more problematic than the relatively clear and, to conservatives, unproblematic agendas of the politics of liberty and the sociology of virtue; but they cannot be avoided. The politics of liberty and the sociology of virtue can be pursued for quite a way before we reach this point; but at some point neither our politics nor our sociology can ultimately be neutral as to the content of the "laws of Nature and Nature's God." In this sense, a return to "nature" underlies both the politics of liberty and the sociology of virtue.

▲

Michael Lind

WHY INTELLECTUAL CONSERVATISM DIED

The collapse of intellectual conservatism in America has been as complete as it has been swift. Consider a few contrasts. In 1984, the leading conservative spokesman in the media was George Will; by 1994, it was Rush Limbaugh. The basic concerns of intellectual conservatives in the eighties were foreign policy and economics; by the early nineties they had become dirty pictures and deviant sex. In the early 1980s, the *Public Interest* was publishing scholarly analyses of public policy, from a moderate conservative point of view; by the early nineties, it was publishing a potted commentary on the sexual practices of the ancient Greeks and Chinese by a California radio talk show host, Dennis Prager. The *American Spectator*, which in the eighties had striven for respectability by publishing neocon scholars, had by 1994 turned into a semipornographic tabloid of a kind familiar in Britain. Barry Goldwater was a conservative hero in the early eighties; now he is a pariah, considered too far to the left because he supports an end to legal and social discrimination against gay Americans. In the eighties, Peter Berger and Richard John Neuhaus authored a thoughtful monograph on the importance of intermediate institutions; by the nineties, Berger was ranting in *Commentary* about the persecution of smokers, and Neuhaus (a convert to Catholicism) was publishing articles in his magazine, *First Things*, denouncing Darwin and defending the theory that today's animals descend from honeymoon couples aboard Noah's Ark. In the 1980s, conservatives claimed to be defending the color-blind civil rights idealism

of Martin Luther King, Jr.; in 1994, Charles Murray has revived old theories about the innate inferiority of average Latinos and blacks compared to whites in his new book (written with the late Richard Herrnstein), *The Bell Curve*: "Latino and black immigrants are, at least in the short run, putting some downward pressure on the distribution of intelligence. . . . The shifting ethnic makeup by itself would lower the average American IQ by 0.8 per generation."

I was present at the destruction of intellectual conservatism over the past several years, as executive editor of the *National Interest*, published by Irving Kristol, as a research assistant for William F. Buckley, Jr., and as a contributor to such conservative intellectual journals as *Commentary*, the *Public Interest*, and *National Review*. What I observed convinces me that the conventional explanations for the demise of American conservatism as a serious intellectual force are wrong.

It is a mistake, for example, to attribute the death of intellectual conservatism to the end of the cold war. The loss of the Soviet enemy did not cause the right to crack up; on the contrary, the differences among "paleoconservatives," *National Review* conservatives, and neoconservatives have actually diminished in the years since 1989 (as the former center-right has enthusiastically adopted the far right's "culture war"). What is more, it is *only* in foreign policy that there have been any interesting or rigorous debates among conservatives (chiefly in the pages of Owen Harries's *National Interest*). The foreign-policy half of the conservative brain remained alert long after the other hemisphere was clinically dead.

The decline of intellectual conservatism has had less to do with geopolitics than with domestic politics. By far the most important factor has been a process well under way before 1989: the growing power within the Republican party of the Protestant right.

The two main varieties of mainstream conservatism, from the founding of *National Review* in 1955 to the disastrous Houston convention of 1992, were Buckley-type fusionism ("fusing" free-market economics and a sort of high-church traditionalism) and neoconservatism. These corresponded more or less with the Catholic right and the Jewish right. Not all Buckleyites were Catholic (though the non-Catholics tended to convert, like Russell Kirk and Lew Lehrman) and not all neocons were Jewish; even so, the difference between fusionists and neocons was as much ethnocultural as ideological.

For several decades, the chiefly Protestant and heavily southern and western mass constituency of conservatism had, as its spokesmen, Catholic and Jewish intellectuals, most of them Ivy League-educated Northeasterners. This was no accident, as the Marxists say; the success of Buckley and his allies in discrediting the John Birch Society in the early 1960s effectively wiped out the major rival for the leadership of conservative white Protestant Americans. Though the Birchers probably reflected the views of the conservative base more faithfully than people like Buckley or Kristol, the leaders of the Catholic right and the Jewish right became the only *respectable* spokesmen for conservatism.

The disparity in social origins between the conservative base and the conservative elite became even more pronounced in the 1980s, which saw a great influx of Thatcherite British journalists and policy analysts and other foreigners into the upper ranks of American conservatism. One Englishman, Stuart Butler, became the chief social policy thinker of the Heritage Foundation; another, John O'Sulli-

van, became editor of *National Review* (making the United States, to my knowledge, the only democracy in which the editor of the leading conservative journal is not himself a citizen of the country). A Belgian immigrant, Arnaud de Borchgrave, edited the conservative daily, the *Washington Times* (itself controlled by Korean would-be messiah Reverend Sun Myung Moon). Increasingly, conservative leaders like Bill Buckley and Irving Kristol socialized with foreign media tycoons like Rupert Murdoch (Australian) and Conrad Black (Canadian) and Greco-British-American trophy wife Arianna Stassinopolous Huffington, a "Minister of Light" in California cult leader John-Roger's Movement of Spiritual Inner Awareness (MSIA). The complaint of "paleoconservatives" that their movement was being taken over by opportunistic (and in many cases weird) foreigners was not completely without foundation.

Sooner or later, it was inevitable that the conservative masses would find leaders who did not speak with funny upper class or foreign accents. Indeed, this came to pass after 1988, when Pat Robertson succeeded in converting his presidential campaign organization into the Christian Coalition. Here, for the first time since World War II, was the stable infrastructure of a Protestant right with real clout. The institutions and the leaders of the older Catholic and Jewish conservatives suddenly became superfluous. Pat Robertson spoke the language of the conservative masses more authentically than Bill Buckley or Irving Kristol (to say nothing of Her Majesty's loyal subject John O'Sullivan). Who needs the Philadelphia Society when you can have the Christian Coalition? Who needs *Firing Line* when you can watch *The 700 Club* and Rush Limbaugh?

Now that the hitherto silent majority of white evangelical Protestant conservatives has found its own leaders, the Catholic and Jewish (and mainline Protestant and secular) conservatives are at a loss. They have lost an empire, and not yet found a role. Some of them, like R. Emmett Tyrrell, have more or less abandoned serious politics altogether for sensational and lucrative tabloid journalism. A more typical response—exemplified by William Bennett and

William Kristol—has been to seek out a new role for Catholic and Jewish intellectuals as middlemen between the uncouth fire-and-brimstone Protestant evangelicals and the world of serious journalism, policy, and scholarship. The task of the go-between is to formulate a compromise language, a set of ambiguous code words, which can win the fundamentalists over to the GOP without alarming the moderate majority. Thus, "pro-family" as a euphemism for "antigay," and "cultural elite" as a code word for what George Wallace more pungently called "eggheads" and "pointyheads." But this is image-laundering, not thinking. Indeed, the careers of Bennett and the younger Kristol are part of the history, not of American thought, but of American public relations.

The eagerness with which most intellectual conservatives have embraced this degrading new role as image consultants for Protestant fundamentalists took me and many other former conservatives by surprise. A few years ago, I rather naively expected the *National Review* conservatives and the neocons to close ranks, to prevent the takeover of the Republican party by the fundamentalists, whose leaders (not their voters) would be sent packing like the Birchers. Remember, at the beginning of the decade there were signs of a purge of the far right by the center-right. Midge Decter accused Russell Kirk of anti-Semitism, and Bill Buckley more subtly suggested that Patrick Buchanan was guilty of the same offense. The "paleoconservatives" of *Chronicles* broke off and formed their own far-right organization, the John Randolph Society. Neocons railed against the conservatism of "the fever swamps." Only a few years later, however, the fusionists and neocons had themselves adopted "fever swamp" themes, like the so-called "culture war" and the claim that homosexuals are trying to destroy family, religion, and Western civilization. After Bush lost in 1992, the center-right quickly became indistinguishable from the far right.

In hindsight, I failed to realize just how corrupt the conservative leadership had become. I don't mean personally corrupt; as individuals, the conservatives are no better or worse than intellectuals or activists of other political persuasions. (They are, perhaps, more hypocritical, though: the conservative leadership is full of secular Jews recommending Christianity for other people, closeted homosexuals condemning "alternative lifestyles," and divorcees and adulterers praising marriage and family.) The corruption of the conservatives has involved, rather, the sacrifice of intellectual standards.

One reason is nepotism. Anyone spending any time in conservative circles in Washington or New York in the past decade has constantly run across what Charlotte Allen dubbed the "minicons," the children or nieces or nephews of eminent conservatives—little Podhoretzes and Kristols, as well as junior Buckleys and Weyrichs. An intellectual movement that hopes to endure must constantly replenish itself by recruiting the best outside talent and relentlessly purging its ranks of mediocrities. Instead, the leaders of conservatism turned the magazines and institutions of the right, like the Moonie-controlled *Washington Times* and various think tanks, into patronage dumps for their offspring and in-laws. The best jobs tended to go to direct lineal descendants, minicons proper; a second tier of positions was occupied by friends of the minicons (usually, their roommates at Harvard or wherever). The bottom tier tended to be reserved for a mudsill class of wealthy and dense Young Republicans. It is no accident that the most impressive of the younger conservative intellectuals, Dinesh D'Souza, was an outsider, an immigrant from India. Even he owed his rise in part to the fact that he was a friend, at Dartmouth, of Ben Hart, son of long-time *National Review* editor Jeff Hart. Irving Kristol's son William, Dan Quayle's former chief of staff, has been trying to position himself as heir to the leadership of the movement.

Hereditary political aristocracies are not unknown to the left of center—think of the various Kennedys and Galbraiths. The neoconservative intellectual movement might have survived this sacrifice of meritocracy to family values. It could not, however, survive its corruption by excessive partisanship in the service of the Republican party.

The conservatives, one can argue, tried to take over the wrong party after 1955. In many ways, the Democratic party would have made a more natural home for conservatives than the Republicans. This is not as crazy as it sounds. The discrediting and political demise of the southern segregationists in the 1960s left a void on the right wing of the Democratic party that a nonracist conservative movement (anticipating the Democratic Leadership Conference) might have filled. Conservatism would have had to make its peace with the New Deal—but that should not have been all that difficult for a Catholic-influenced American version of European Christian Democracy, with a strong base in the unionized working classes of the Northeast (who tend to be more conservative in morals than the business and professional classes). First-generation conservative thinkers like Russell Kirk, Willmoore Kendall, and James Burnham had little use for laissez-faire capitalism and were comfortable with the idea of a conservative welfare state. Conservatism would have had far more influence as the theory of the dominant wing of the dominant party, and defending congressional prerogatives against presidential Caesarism (a staple of conservative theory in the 1950s) would have been more compatible with conservative constitutionalism than apologizing for the imperial prerogatives of a succession of Republican presidents.

If conservatizing the Democrats was ever an option, it was foreclosed by the "Draft Goldwater" movement, by Nixon's southern strategy, and the defection, one by one, of the Democrats who remained conservative to the GOP. As the conservative movement and the Republican party became identified, conservative doctrine began to be cut and stretched to accommodate the short-term needs of Republican coalition strategy. The debates over first principles that made *National Review*-type conservatism lively in the 1950s and 1960s, and neoconservatism interesting in the 1970s, gave way to united-front solidarity on a growing number of issues important to this or that wing of the Republican party, from tax cuts to the outlawing of abortion.

The point of no return, in my view, came with the adoption of support for supply-side economics as a litmus test for true-blue conservatism. No first-rate economist took the supply-siders seri-

ously—even Milton Friedman scoffed at them. Ominously, for the first time, a theory that most serious intellectuals on the right did not believe became the official doctrine of the conservative movement, because it served the narrow short-term interests of an important Republican constituency, the rich.

Once critical thinking had been abandoned as a threat to the program of massive tax cuts for the super-rich, further sacrifices of rigor and empiricism became easy. By the mid-eighties, conservatives were dismissing very serious objections to the practicability of space-based strategic defenses as "liberal" propaganda (as though there were "liberal" physics and "conservative" physics). As standards of evidence sank, conservative journals opened their pages to previously marginal ideas and thinkers. *National Review* debated the question of whether Shakespeare's plays had been written by the Earl of Oxford. In the once-moderate *Public Interest*, editor Irving Kristol published a rave review of a book by Richard Epstein, a legal theorist who argues that most federal laws against racial discrimination are unconstitutional—a view formerly associated with the John Birch Society rather than the neocons. Another *Public Interest* author argued that the solution to the crime problem is for everyone to own a gun.

Then there is "creation science." The silence of serious conservative intellectuals in the face of fundamentalist campaigns to force public schools to teach the book of Genesis in geology and biology classes has completely discredited the claim of conservatives to be defenders of objectivity and empirical scholarship against politicization. How can intellectual conservatives credibly attack Afrocentrists for distorting history while passing in silence over efforts to teach American children that the dinosaurs lived with Adam and Eve in the Garden of Eden and drowned in Noah's Flood? Even worse, *National Review, Commentary,* and *First Things* have actually run essays attacking evolutionary theory and espousing "guided evolution," "creation science," and similar nonsense. Who would have thought that, at the end of the twentieth century, the remnants of the New York Intellectuals would be refighting

69

the Scopes Trial—from the point of view of William Jennings Bryan?

Kookiness has been joined by complacency. Instead of exploring plausible conservative solutions to genuine problems, the right began to deny that problems existed at all. What pollution problem? What overpopulation problem? What secondhand smoke problem? What falling American wages? What health care crisis? Conservatism—which historically has tended to be pessimistic—in recent years has become strangely Panglossian, adopting, as it were, the motto of *Mad* magazine's Alfred E. Neumann—"What, me worry?"

One aspect of conservative complacency has been a growing toleration of the vicious lunatic fringe. The "no enemies to the right" policy has been symbolized in recent years by annual conservative "summits" in Washington—small, private dinners bringing together people like Bill Buckley, Irving Kristol, Norman Podhoretz, Charles Krauthammer, and the far-right activist Paul Weyrich. At one of these meetings, Weyrich circulated a proposal (which I have held and read) that the federal government secretly lace illegal drugs with substances like rat poison and release them into the black market. Drug addicts would be more easily identified and punished, Weyrich reasoned, if, in public, they went into sudden convulsions. None of the other conservative leaders at the meeting walked out in protest, or insisted that this man be ostracized. On the contrary, at subsequent summits Weyrich has been welcomed by the same conservatives who criticize the NAACP for meeting with Farrakhan.

Such latitudinarianism has become the norm. Bill Buckley recently appeared on television as an ally of Pat Robertson, who in print has accused the Council on Foreign Relations—an organization to which Buckley belongs, and to which he successfully nominated me—of being a secret instrument of Satan's plot to destroy America and condemn most of humanity to eternal damnation. Call me sensitive, but I *resent* that.

By the late 1980s, the conservative movement, drifting into crankiness and complacency under the control of a small number of elderly men,

was in desperate need of a revolutionary renovation from within the ranks, as well as an invigorating transfusion of outside talent. At the very least, there needed to be a searching reconsideration of first principles, a questioning of dogmas like supply-side economics and hypocrisies like the lip service paid to criminalizing abortion.

Such a free and frank debate within conservatism, however, was made impossible by the dependence of the journals of the right on foundation money. One by one, every leading neoconservative publication or think tank over the past decade has come to depend on money from a few foundations—Olin, Smith-Richardson, Bradley, Scaife. Many were started in the first place by seed money from the foundations. Inevitably, this has promoted groupthink. The foundations are the chief reason that *Commentary* sounds more and more like the *New Criterion*, which sounds so much like the new *Public Interest*.

It is not that there is some centralized conspiracy imposing a party line. By and large, the program officers of the foundations, though partisan, sincerely believe in debate among conservatives. They do not deliberately impose an orthodoxy. They do not have to. The editors tend to censor themselves, for fear of appearing "liberal" and losing that critical annual grant. There are a few honorable exceptions—the *National Interest* and the *American Scholar* continue to put the life of thought above the life of the party. For the most part, though, instead of boldly attacking falsehoods wherever they are found, conservative editors tend to print only what they believe will confirm the prejudices of the program officers.

The addiction to foundation dollars has reinforced the disastrous "no enemies to the right" policy. The last thing the foundations want is for one set of grantees to criticize the policy views or intellectual standards of other grantees. The major conservative foundations ended their support of *Chronicles* a few years back when its editors got into a spat with Richard John Neuhaus and the neocons—a lesson that has not been lost on other conservative grantees.

In addition to reinforcing groupthink, the addiction to foundation money has also led to the

70

lowering of intellectual standards. After all, if you, the editor, turn down a piece by a mediocrity or crackpot who is a friend of a program officer, this could have consequences. Once too many Republican hacks start moving into a journal or a think tank, serious thinkers and their audiences go elsewhere. A cycle of decline is set in motion. With foundation money comes the implicit imperative to avoid questioning partisan pieties—but this very avoidance of controversy sends intellectuals away, even as it attracts true believers (the truer they are, the crankier). As third-rate zealots gradually replace first-rate thinkers and intelligent readers, the beleaguered editor places the blame for the decline of his journal's prestige on the "liberals," the "media elite," the "cultural elite"—anyone but himself and his sponsors.

In this way, bit by bit, a number of once-interesting intellectual journals on the right have degenerated into newsletters for Chamber of Commerce Republicans, creationists, and elderly curmudgeons denouncing the music that young people listen to nowadays.

Eventually there may be a revival of serious thought on the political right, but this seems unlikely for at least a generation. For the foreseeable future, American conservatism will be defined by the fundamentalist/tabloid right, with its program of making centrist and liberal Christians, Jews, and secular Americans, working women, nonwhite Americans, gay men and lesbians, and intellectuals scapegoats for the serious problems afflicting American society (problems for which the conservatives I have worked with for a decade have no plausible answers). The new Radical Right of Pat Robertson and Pat Buchanan, which sets the agenda for trimmers like William Bennett and William Kristol, has more in common with the pre-World War II right of Father Coughlin and William Randolph Hearst than with the intellectual conservatism of the decades after the war. The Radical Right has no arguments, only hatreds.

Today, as always, it is possible to be an American intellectual who is politically conservative. But conservatism as an intellectual movement in the United States is dead. □

71

Sociology of Religion 1994, 55:3 345-357

From Revolution to Evolution: The Changing Nature of the Christian Right

Matthew C. Moen

University of Maine

This interpretive essay examines major organizational and tactical changes in the Christian Right, from its origin in the late 1970s to the present. It argues that the Christian Right has passed through several distinctive phases, gradually becoming much more of a traditional political actor following conventional strategies in American politics. This essay also examines popular and scholarly understanding of the movement's rise and evolution, with special attention to paradigms impeding understanding of the Christian Right. It closes with suggestions for further research.

The principal objective of this essay is to explain change in the Christian Right over time; the central argument is that the Christian Right has gradually reconciled and adjusted itself to the secular norms and practices of American politics. Stated alliteratively, the Christian Right has forsaken revolution for evolution, abandoning its quixotic quest to "put God back in government" (Ogintz 1980) for a calculated campaign to infiltrate and influence carefully selected repositories of political power. It has done so on its own rhythm, rather than on the cycle of presidential politics, as one might reasonably surmise from the exhaustive research on the presidential elections of the 1980s and 1992 (Johnson and Tamney 1982; Smidt 1983, 1987; Miller and Wattenberg 1984; Himmelstein and McRae 1984; Brudney and Copeland 1984, 1988; Buell and Sigelman 1985; Sigelman et al. 1987; Wilcox 1987; Jelen 1987; Guth and Green 1991; Kellstedt et al. 1990; Green 1993; Leege 1993; Kellstedt et al. 1993; Johnson et al. 1993).

With a few exceptions (Lienesch 1982; Bruce 1988; Moen 1992), scholars have not really focused on how political activism has shaped the Christian Right, preferring instead to concentrate on how the Christian Right has influenced politics. Neglecting one side of that causal relationship has skewed the literature; scholars know much about the Christian Right's voting behavior, campaigning, and lobbying, but comparatively little about its internal dynamics over time. Yet, it is important to understand the movement's machinations, both for the sake of explanation and prognostication. This essay is a small step in that direction; I deliberately sketch the big picture, providing references along the way to works containing the details.

A subsidiary objective of this essay is to examine popular and scholarly understanding of the Christian Right. This task is approached in a constructive spirit, with the hope of fostering dialogue among scholars; it is not meant to suggest that only my interpretations are correct, nor to replicate solid review essays of the existing literature (Guth et al. 1988; Hertzke 1988a). The time is ripe to assess the state of affairs, in the wake of the Reagan-Bush era and of events that captured the attention of scholars, such as the closure of Moral Majority (Hadden et al. 1987; Hadden and Shupe 1988; Bledsoe 1990) and the candidacy of Pat Robertson (Guth and Green 1991; Langenbach 1988; Green and Guth 1988; Johnson et al. 1989; Green 1993; Hertzke 1993). Many words were penned about the Christian Right during the 1980s and the 1992 elections, making it an opportune time to reflect on some of the things written.

THE RISE OF THE CHRISTIAN RIGHT

The rapid rise of the Christian Right in the late 1970s astonished observers of American politics. Journalists were among the most surprised, writing only two articles during the time the movement was crystallizing (March 1979-February 1980), as measured by the *Reader's Guide to Periodical Literature*. Many politicians were also caught off guard. The "born-again" Baptist president, Jimmy Carter, did not sense the depth of unrest among conservative Christians until it became too late to make amends (Hastey 1981). The whole situation was aptly described years later by Kenneth D. Wald (1987:182): "Of all the shifts and surprises in contemporary political life, perhaps none was so wholly unexpected as the political resurgence of evangelical Protestantism in the 1970s."

The rise of the Christian Right is a familiar story that has been told by historians, sociologists, theologians, and political scientists, among others (Jorstad 1981; Kater 1982; Liebman and Wuthnow 1983; Bromley and Shupe 1984; Bruce 1987; Wald 1987). Common to those discussions is that the Christian Right arose in response to a complex array of liberal and secular trends, ranging from the eradication of religion in the schools, to easy availability of abortion, to tax policies that adversely affected the traditional family.

The rapid rise of the Christian Right spawned a potent and sometimes mean-spirited counterattack from those far removed from the conservative Christian subculture. Liberal activists created groups like People For the American Way as platforms for personal attacks on Christian Right leaders; intellectuals mocked the Christian Right's concerns by penning a "Secular Humanist Declaration"; theologians drew unflattering biblical analogies, with the Rev. William Sloan Coffin suggesting that Christian Right leaders were "jackasses"; government officials reflexively described Moral Majority as a white racist group, and compared Jerry Falwell to the Ayatollah Khomeni, as if one could casually ignore the legal, cultural, and theological schisms separating an American Christian from an Iranian Muslim (Nyhan 1980; Unger 1980; Hyer 1980; Briggs 1981; "Christian Right" 1980). Scholars opposed to the Christian Right also succumbed to the temptation to overstate matters, with one historian comparing the Christian Right of the 1970s to the European Fascism of the 1940s (Linder 1982). The shrill rhetoric and simplistic comparisons shaped the tone of public discourse in the early 1980s, just as opponents hoped. The Christian Right was caricatured as a collection of hillbillies bent on creating a theocracy, and evidence that this view was assimilated by the public could be found in its negative assessment of the Christian Right's leaders, issues, and organizations (Shupe and Stacey 1983; Buell and Sigelman 1985; Wilcox 1987; Sigelman et al. 1987; Guth and Green 1987).

Researchers certainly did not create the negative perceptions that took root; the Christian Right's opponents and even its own leaders accomplished that task, through their miscalculations and mistakes (Moen 1989). Yet, once scholars started explaining the rise of the Christian Right, they contributed to the perception that the movement was suspect. Hadden and Swann (1981) laid the groundwork for many subsequent studies by suggesting that the Christian Right was a technologically driven movement spawned by master manipulators. They identified the modern "televangelist" as the force behind the surge of traditional religiosity. While a plausible explanation, it blinded other observers to the possibility that the Christian Right was more of a grassroots protest than a technological artifact; moreover, such a "top down" explanation implicitly trivialized the concerns of social conservatives, by casting those concerns as the baggage of unsophisticated followers being duped by clever elites.

Journalists subsequently portrayed the "televangelist" label and the "top down" paradigm as gospel, occupying themselves with unmasking the conservative preacher conspiracy afoot. Their work reached its apogee years later, when they blithely associated ministers barely connected to the Christian Right but tainted by scandal, such as Jim Bakker and Oral Roberts, with those responsible for creating the key Christian Right groups (Marz et al. 1987; Ostling 1987). Many journalists never grasped the distinctions among ministries and objectives, equating Jim Bakker's quest to build the ultimate pentecostal amusement park with fundamentalist Jerry Falwell's mission to remake America. (Some still insist on stereotyping conservative Christians, demonstrated by a *Washington Post* article calling evangelicals "uneducated and easy to command"; see Morin 1993). Given this lack of understanding of the conservative Christian community, and the inculcation of the "top down" paradigm, is it any wonder that the "resurgence" of the Christian Right circa 1992 surprised many writers?

Scholars fed the perception that the Christian Right was suspect in another way — by using frameworks that suggested some sort of personal or social strain. For instance, Wald and his colleagues (1989a) borrowed from the psychology literature to examine empirical support for "authority-mindedness" in the Christian Right; other scholars used the status politics and life-style defense paradigms toward a similar end (Crawford 1980; Lorentzen 1980; Lipset 1982; Conover 1983; Harper and Leicht 1984; Wald et al. 1989b). Those paradigms drew criticism for their explanatory power (Simpson 1983; Miller 1985; Moen 1988; Smidt 1988), and also for their presumption of pathological problems among Christian Right supporters (Jelen 1991; Wilcox 1992).

The larger point is that the Christian Right was placed very early into established frameworks that often reflected a liberal understanding of the conservative mindset. The concerns of Christian Right supporters were explained as the by-product of authoritarian personalities or symbolic crusades, rather than taken at face value. One unfortunate result of pigeonholing the Christian Right was that scholars circumscribed their research agendas. They neglected fruitful lines

75

of inquiry, while debating the fine points of value-laden frameworks — the academic equivalent of fiddling while Rome burned. For instance, scholars virtually ignored the Christian Right's infiltration of state Republican party organizations until the Reagan era was over (see Morken 1990; Oldfield 1990, 1992; Hertzke 1993). Those missed opportunities are not easily recompensed because the Christian Right has undergone dramatic changes over time.

PERIODS OF DEVELOPMENT

The Christian Right has passed through two distinctive phases since its rise in the late-1970s, and is in the midst of a third (Moen 1992). This periodization scheme is embellished and refined here to provide a picture of how the Christian Right has evolved. While such a framework is open to criticism, it may serve to synthesize major changes in the Christian Right, including its reorientation to the traditional norms and practices of American politics.

Expansionist Period (1978-1984)

As the label implies, the dominant characteristic of the Christian Right during the expansionist period was steady growth. The National Christian Action Coalition was launched in 1978 and became the first national organization of the Christian Right. It was followed by the Religious Roundtable, Christian Voice, Moral Majority, and Concerned Women for America (1979), the Freedom Council (1981), and the American Coalition for Traditional Values (1983). The proliferation of organizations and their concomitant division of labor signaled steady growth (Hatch 1983).

Reliable membership estimates for each specific organization were difficult to obtain. Christian Right leaders dispensed data, but they had every incentive to exaggerate their constituency's size. Independent assessments varied considerably. With Moral Majority, for instance, scholars suggested membership figures that ranged from 482,000 to 3,000,000; journalists estimated its voter registration campaigns netted 200,000 to 3,000,000 new voters (Liebman 1983; Hadden et al. 1987; Wald 1987; Spring 1984; Harwood 1985). When scholars documented the unpopularity of Moral Majority's issue positions, they implicitly confirmed the lower estimates, although they mostly refrained from such conjecture (Shupe and Stacey 1983; Buell and Sigelman 1985; Wilcox 1987; Sigelman et al. 1987; Guth and Green 1987). Based on Moral Majority alone, though, one can reasonably conclude that the Christian Right consisted of several hundred thousand (if not millions of) citizens. It grew at a remarkable rate early on.

The geometric growth of the Christian Right created a high public profile. Journalists wrote hundreds of stories about its leaders and organizations (Hadden and Shupe 1988), with 75 percent of that coverage coming within three years after an organization was launched (Moen 1992). Since seven of the eleven national organizations composing the Christian Right formed during the expansionist period, the early 1980s were a publicity bonanza.

Owing to rapid growth and high visibility, the Christian Right successfully influenced the political agenda. It helped shift the congressional agenda in fundamental ways, winning votes on constitutional amendments to ban abortion and to permit prayer in schools in the 98th Congress (1983-1984), as well as securing passage of an array of lesser objectives (Hertzke 1988b; Moen 1989). It also altered the public dialogue. The Christian Right placed a cluster of issues involving conventional morality and the traditional family at the political forefront, simultaneously bumping off items that offended, such as the Equal Rights Amendment (Hadden and Shupe 1988; Hofrenning 1989; Dionne 1989; Wald 1992). Some observers missed those indices of influence. Pressman (1984) and D'Antonio (1990), for instance, defined success for the Christian Right in absolute rather than relative terms — it should win elections and final passage of bills, not just alter the terms of debate. Those questionable standards contributed to the erroneous assessment that the Christian Right was spent by the mid-1980s.

Ironically, the Christian Right's agenda-setting success was costly. It convinced many lawmakers that it was time to consider new issues, since key Christian Right objectives were voted upon in the 98th Congress (1983-1984). Concurrently, Christian Right leaders made a host of mistakes while lobbying on Capitol Hill that created a less hospitable environment in the future. Their political amateurishness was yet another defining characteristic of the expansionist period, and it abetted the demise of the early groups.

The expansionist period is also distinguishable by the overt and pervasive religious underpinnings of the Christian Right. It was led by a clique of fundamentalist pastors and laypersons, such as Bob Billings (National Christian Action Coalition), Ed McAteer (Religious Roundtable), Jerry Falwell (Moral Majority), Beverly LaHaye (Concerned Women for America), and Tim LaHaye (American Coalition for Traditional Values). They attracted mostly fundamentalist supporters, who were very conservative and often intolerant of their evangelical and pentecostal brethren (Shupe and Stacey 1983; Wilcox 1986, 1989; Beatty and Walter 1988). The presence of fundamentalists was most evident at the 1980 National Affairs Briefing, where leaders made pronouncements grounded in a literal interpretation of the Bible that jarred many Americans, such as God not hearing the prayers of Jews (Jorstad 1981).

The predominance of fundamentalists during the expansionist period was also evident in the way that leaders handled political issues. They focused on issues with strong moral overtones, such as gay rights, abortion, and pornography; moreover, they declared the correct position on those issues according to Scripture, and attacked alternative views as misguided biblical interpretation or secularism (Heinz 1983). Christian Right leaders also used moralistic language, speaking freely about the need to restore "moral sanity" (Falwell 1980), and defining issues like abortion and pornography in terms of sin. Taking stock of the Christian Right's rhetoric and early activities, Jorstad (1981:8) stated: "The theme brought home in every speech, every sermon, every pamphlet, every request for funds was that of saving Americans by a return to what the leaders called its traditional morality." The early Christian Right was long on morality, but short on skill.

Transition Period (1965-1986)

The critical transition period is often overlooked by scholars intent on explaining the rise of the Christian Right in the early 1980s or assessing its activities in the wake of Moral Majority and Pat Robertson's presidential bid. The distinguishing feature of this period was retrenchment. Table 1 chronicles the fate of the early organizations during this time.

TABLE 1

Retrenchment Among Christian Right Organizations: 1985-1986

Organization	Status	Action by Group Leader
National Christian Action Coalition	dissolved	Bill Billings quits politics
Religious Roundtable	moribund	Ed McAteer runs for Tennessee Senate seat in 1984
Christian Voice	moribund	Robert Grant departs to lead American Freedom Coalition
Moral Majority	dissolved	Jerry Falwell merges group into Liberty Federation
Concerned Women for America	relocated	Beverly LaHaye moves from San Diego to Washington, D.C.
Freedom Council	dissolved	Pat Robertson dissolves group amidst IRS audit
American Coalition for Traditional Values	dissolved	Tim LaHaye dissolves group following allegations of a tie to the Rev. Moon

The breadth of change is striking. Nearly every organization suspended its work, merged with another, or dissolved. (The only new group formed during this time was the Liberty Federation in 1986, which was Jerry Falwell's vehicle for absorbing the Moral Majority and then exiting politics in 1987.) The principal reason for retrenchment was the erosion of a direct-mail base during the mid-1980s (Diamond 1989:59). It was caused by an odd combination of agenda-setting successes that defused the anger of conservative Christians, along with tactical blunders that sapped their confidence in their leaders. Local supporters became weary of constant monetary appeals to fight distant national battles (Moen 1992:27).

Interestingly, this wholesale transformation went virtually unnoticed. The New York Times carried only 16 stories about the Christian Right during the transition period (focused mostly on Pat Robertson's budding presidential candidacy), compared to 132 stories in 1980-1981. The decreased visibility seemed to reflect the institutionalization of the "top down" and symbolic crusade paradigms, which assumed that Christian Right supporters would decrease their activism once they vented their frustrations. The media was so certain that the Christian Right was fading away that it paid scant attention at all, let alone to subtle changes in progress.

As in the expansionist period, one change fostered others. The organizational retrenchment eradicated natural platforms for Christian Right leaders to speak out on issues, and consequently eroded their ability to shape the legislative and public agendas. The retrenchment also destroyed some of the inventiveness that the Christian Right exhibited in its earliest years, when it was on the cutting edge of issues, such as the impact of the tax code on families and the quality of the public schools. Christian Right leaders were relegated to the role of apologists for controversial Reagan-administration positions, including South African sanctions and aid to the Nicaraguan Contras. The movement's agenda withered along with its early organizations, tempting observers to write a political obituary. Yet, Christian Right leaders were using this time of retrenchment to advance a strategic reorientation already in progress. The rapid collapse of organizations and a political agenda simply hastened that process.

Institutionalization Period (1987-present)

The distinguishing feature of the institutionalization period is the existence of several stable and well-positioned organizations. Space constraints preclude a discussion of the role of Christian Right elites in retooling the movement; suffice it to say that during the transition period, they examined their mistakes, assessed the existing political situation, commissioned polls to outline appropriate strategy, and then restructured the movement in major ways (Moen 1992). The present characteristics of the Christian Right contrast sharply with previous periods, and explain why the movement is better-positioned today.

One characteristic is a more predictable financial situation. The early organizations banked on direct-mail for their financial support, an unpredictable wellspring because of the ease with which contributors can turn off the flow (Godwin 1988). It is as easy as tossing out repetitious third-class mail. Cognizant of the difficulty of sustaining stable organizations through direct-mail, Christian Right elites emphasized the utility of genuine membership organizations such as Concerned Women for America and Focus on the Family, replete with established dues, meetings, communications, and benefits. They also quietly accepted money from controversial figures such as the Rev. Sun Myung Moon, who helped launch the American Freedom Coalition (Lawton 1988). The latter tactic is more risky, but it keeps the Christian Right flush.

A second characteristic of the Christian Right is a greater representation of theological orientations. Recall that early on the movement consisted mostly of fundamentalists, whose political conservatism and disdain for evangelicals/charismatics was often intense. Pat Robertson's candidacy attracted evangelicals and charismatics into the movement (Hertzke 1993), thereby increasing diversity. While "religious particularism" is a major obstacle to a unified movement (Jelen 1991), it is not necessarily injurious to achieving common goals, since people can operate within the confines of the theological tradition they find most appealing. Moreover, the sectarian attitudes that have haunted the

Christian Right show some signs of abating. Oldfield (1990) found that political activism had a homogenizing and moderating effect on Christian Right supporters, which portends greater cooperation. Then too, the intensity of the current "culture war" necessitates alliances by those holding "orthodox" views (Hunter 1991), even if they are somewhat uneasy with their coalition partners. This logic follows the Islamic aphorism, "the enemy of my enemy is my friend." Even if sectarianism does not abate, the infusion of evangelicals/charismatics may still prove beneficial because it increases the pool of potential recruits.

A third characteristic is the ability to frame issues to maximize support. During the expansionist period, Christian Right leaders constantly invoked moralistic language, spawning organizations like Moral Majority and Christian Voice, issuing "moral report cards" on elected officials, and peddling issues with a strong moral component, such as abortion, school prayer, gay rights, and pornography. Today the Christian Right employs the more familiar and widely accepted language of liberalism, with its focus on rights, equality, and opportunity. Virtually all of its issues have been recast in that rhetoric. School prayer is framed as a "student's right" to pray or as an issue of equal opportunity (for religious expression in the schools); abortion is a civil rights issue involving opportunity for the fetus or the "rights of the unborn"; gay rights is a case of homosexuals seeking "special rights" as citizens; vocal prayer at graduation ceremonies is a case of "free speech" for those holding religious values; the ability of voluntary student religious groups to meet on school grounds is one of "equal access"; the content of school textbooks involves "parental rights" to instill proper values in their children. Christian Right leaders also use the invective language of liberalism as a political tactic, blaming cultural elites for "bigotry" and "discrimination" against traditional values. The ill-fated campaign of Vice President Dan Quayle to chastise the fictional television character Murphy Brown during the 1992 election was designed to rally religious conservatives with the language they had assimilated. Using the rhetoric that Americans are accustomed to hearing both maximizes the appeal of issue positions and circumvents the problems connected to religious discourse in a pluralistic society.

Pat Robertson's "Christian Coalition" seems to undermine this point, with its overt religious title. Yet, Robertson has been a driving force behind the rhetorical reorientation, often framing issues in liberal language and accusing the media of "bigotry" for its portrayal of religious conservatives. The name "Christian Coalition" is easily explained as Robertson's attempt to rebuild his religious constituency, following a foray into presidential politics that meant distancing himself from the Christian Right and resigning his ministerial affiliation.

It is conceivable that the Christian Coalition signals a new twist to Christian Right activism — groups with religious titles secretly advancing candidates and issues amidst secular trappings. Bruce (1988) has noted the interesting dilemma facing Christian Right leaders, who must simultaneously "play to the faithful" and participate in a secular political arena. One way they can lessen their problem is quietly to organize religious conservatives to achieve secular political objectives — hence the "stealth candidates" of the 1992 election season. (Another way is using liberal language to advance moralistic goals.) Other explanations for the stealth candidates, of course, are the need for a surprise attack by an outnumbered force, or a media that simply "rediscovered" the Christian Right following years of neglect. Religious conservatives appeared on radar because journalists looked again at the screen.

A fourth characteristic is a reorientation to the grassroots. Recall that during the expansionist period, the Christian Right focused on lobbying Congress, and exhibited clout by setting the agenda; during the transition period, it lost much of its power on the Hill. Christian Right leaders knew it was necessary to shift to other venues, spawning groups like the American Freedom Coalition, expressly to organize religious conservatives in the grassroots. The Christian Right soon infiltrated the Republican party in select locales, paving the way for Pat Robertson's strong performance in the caucus states during 1988. By 1992, the party platform reflected the Christian Right's influence, and a variety of local initiatives aimed at instigating and inculcating a sense of activism among religious conservatives were underway, such as the anti-gay-rights referenda in Colorado and Oregon. Those activities grew naturally out of a shift to the grassroots. This local activity is likely to spread and intensify in the future, with issues involving public education topping the agenda (Moen 1993), because of the school's key role in socializing citizens.

In summary, the Christian Right has changed substantially over time. A decade ago, it consisted of direct-mail lobbies, led by prominent fundamentalists, who championed a moralistic agenda on Capitol Hill; it now consists of a variety of well-established membership organizations, whose leaders use mainstream language and organize followers in the grassroots. The strident campaign to "put God back in government" has been replaced by a quiet effort to rally sympathetic citizens and win elections. The Christian Right has adjusted itself to the traditional practices of American politics.

CONCLUSION

Evidence and reason suggest that the Christian Right will march down the same path it has followed since 1987. The forces driving the Christian Right's reorientation in the first place still remain, such as an unfriendly political environment in the nation's capital and a climate of popular opinion that disdains moralism. The Christian Right will continue to offer liberal language and to operate at the grassroots, where its prospects are quite good. It has experienced leaders and ample funds, in part because it draws upon the extensive resources of the Rev. Moon, Pat Robertson, and now James Dobson (Shupe 1990; Fineman 1993); it is engaged in an intense cultural war that motivates followers; it operates outside the realm of a Democratic majority in Washington. Its work would proceed quietly, except for the clamor created by its opponents, who realize that in many ways it is better positioned today than in earlier eras.

At the same time, the Christian Right faces major challenges. It lacks a titular leader who can command immediate attention, like Jerry Falwell could in 1981-1982. It lacks a galvanizing issue comparable to the tax-exempt status of religious schools, the one that ignited fundamentalists in the late 1970s. It still suffers from personal rivalries (Jelen 1991), and now is often blamed for the Republican party's poor performance in 1992 (Leege 1993:23). It faces the same dilemma of virtually all other interest groups: retaining its fervent supporters while trying to broaden its base of support. Striking a balance between purity and pragmatism will remain problematic for a movement containing political and theological cross-currents.

The evolution of the Christian Right and the challenges it faces in its current form provide scholars many opportunities in the years ahead. Guth and his colleagues (1988) call for further research into the mobilization of religious belief, the challenge presented to the state by religion, and the role of religion as a source of social cleavage. More narrowly drawn topics that might be added to their list include the importance of political symbols to sustaining the Christian Right, the success of its grassroots activism, and the effectiveness of its coalition building. Recent studies of the movement's political thought (Lienesch 1993) and the saliency of religion in the political process (Kellstedt and Leege 1993) demonstrate that divergent methodological approaches are beneficial in illuminating different research questions. The task facing scholars, whose research agendas are helping to shape public discussion of religious issues (see Woodward 1993), is to bring those divergent approaches to the still untapped areas of inquiry.

REFERENCES

Beatty, K. M. and B. O. Walter. 1988. "Fundamentalists, evangelicals, and politics." *American Politics Quarterly* 16:43-59.

Bledsoe, W. C. 1990. "Post Moral Majority politics." Paper delivered at the annual meeting of the American Political Science Association, San Francisco.

Briggs, K. 1981. "Evangelical leaders hail election and ask continuation of efforts." *New York Times* (Jan. 28):8.

Bromley, D. G. and A. Shupe (eds.). 1984. *New Christian Politics*. Macon, GA: Mercer University Press.

Bruce, S. 1987. "Status and cultural defense." *Sociological Focus* 20:242-46.

_____. 1988. *The Rise and Fall of the New Christian Right*. New York: Oxford University Press.

Brudney, J. L. and G. W. Copeland. 1984. "Evangelicals as a political force." *Social Science Quarterly* 65:1072-79.

_____. 1988. "Ronald Reagan and the religious vote." Paper delivered at the annual meeting of the American Political Science Association, Washington, DC.

Buell, E. H., Jr. and L. Sigelman. 1985. "An army that meets every Sunday?" *Social Science Quarterly* 66:426-34.

"Christian Right." 1980. "Christian right equated with Iran's mullahs." *Washington Star* (Sept. 24):4.

Conover, P. J. 1983. "The mobilization of the new right." *Western Political Quarterly* 36:632-49.

Crawford, A. 1980. *Thunder on the Right*. New York: Pantheon.

D'Antonio, M. 1990. "Fierce in the '80s, Fallen in the '90s." *Los Angeles Times* (Feb. 4):M3.

Diamond, S. 1989. *Spiritual Warfare*. Boston: South End Press.

Dionne, E. J., Jr. 1989. "Taking measure of the impact that Moral Majority has left on the American landscape." *New York Times* (June 15):B10.

Falwell, J. 1980. *Listen America!* Garden City, NY: Doubleday.

Fineman, H. 1993. "God and the grass roots." *Newsweek* (Nov. 8):44.

Godwin, R. K. 1988. *One Billion Dollars of Influence*. Chatham, NJ: Chatham House.

Green, J. C. 1993. "Pat Robertson and the latest crusade." *Social Science Quarterly* 74:157-68.

_____ and J. L. Guth. 1988. "The Christian right in the Republican party." *Journal of Politics* 50:150-65.

Guth, J. L. 1987. "The moralizing minority." *Social Science Quarterly* 68:598-610.

_____ and J. C. Green (eds.). 1991. *The Bible and the Ballot Box*. Boulder, CO: Westview Press.

Guth, J. L., T. G. Jelen, L. A. Kellstedt, C. E. Smidt, and K. D. Wald. 1988. "The politics of religion in America." *American Politics Quarterly* 41:825-38.

Hadden, J. K. and A. Shupe. 1988. *Televangelism*. New York: Holt.

_____, J. Hawdon, and K. Martin. 1987. "Why Jerry Falwell killed the Moral Majority," pp. 101-15 in M. Fishwick and R. B. Browne (eds.), *The God Pumpers*. Bowling Green, OH: Bowling Green State University Popular Press.

Hadden, J. K. and C. E. Swann. 1981. *Prime Time Preachers*. Reading, MA: Addison-Wesley.

Harper, C. L. and K. Liecht. 1984. "Explaining the new religious right," pp. 101-10 in Bromley and Shupe, *q.v.*

Harwood, J. 1985. "Religious right, GOP sometimes spar." *St. Petersburg Times* (Jan. 28):8.

Hastey, S. 1981. "Carter." *Baptist Press* (May 28):1.

Hatch, O. 1983. "Christian conservatives are a major force on U.S. political scene." *Human Events* (Jul. 9):10-12.

Heinz, D. 1983. "The struggle to define America," pp. 133-48 in Liebman and Wuthnow, *q.v.*

Hertzke, A. D. 1988a. "American religion and politics." *Western Political Quarterly* 41:825-38.

_____. 1988b. *Representing God in Washington*. Knoxville: University of Tennessee Press.

_____. 1993. *Echoes of Discontent*. Washington, DC: CQ Press.

Himmelstein, J. L. and J. A. McRae, Jr. 1984. "Social conservatism, new republicanism, and the 1980 election." *Public Opinion Quarterly* 48:592-605.

Hofrenning, D. 1989. "The agenda setting strategies of religious interest groups." Paper delivered at the annual meeting of the American Political Science Association, Atlanta, GA.

Hunter, J. D. 1991. *Culture Wars*. New York: Basic Books.

Hyer, M. 1980. "Outflanking the right." *Washington Post* (Oct. 21):8.

Jelen, T. G. 1987. "The effects of religious separatism on white Protestants in the 1984 presidential election." *Sociological Analysis* 48:30-45.

_____. 1991. *The Political Mobilization of Religious Belief*. New York: Praeger.

Johnson, S. D. and J. B. Tamney. 1982. "The Christian right and the 1980 presidential election." *Journal for the Scientific Study of Religion* 21:123-31.

_____, and R. Burton. 1993. "Family values versus economy evaluation in the 1992 presidential election." Paper delivered at the annual meeting of the American Political Science Association, Washington, DC.

_____. 1989. "Pat Robertson." *Journal for the Scientific Study of Religion* 28:387-99.

Jorstad, E. 1981. *The Politics of Moralism*. Minneapolis: Augsburg.

Kater, J. L., Jr. 1982. *Christians on the Right*. New York: Seabury Press.

Kellstedt, L. A. and D. C. Leege. 1993. *Rediscovering the Religious Factor in American Politics*. Armonk, NY: Sharpe.

Kellstedt, L. A., P. Kellstedt, and C. Smidt. 1990. "Evangelical and mainline Protestants in the 1988 presidential election." Paper delivered at the annual meeting of the American Political Science Association, San Francisco.

Kellstedt, L. A., J. C. Green, J. L. Guth, and C. Smidt. 1993. "Religious voting blocs in the 1992 election." Paper delivered at the annual meeting of the American Political Science Association, Washington, DC.

Langenbach, L. 1988. "Evangelical elites and political action." Paper delivered at the annual meeting of the American Political Science Association, Washington, DC.

Lawton, K. 1988. "Unification church ties haunt new coalition." *Christianity Today* (Feb. 5):46.

Leege, D. C. 1993. "The decomposition of the religious vote." Paper delivered at the annual meeting of the American Political Science Association, Washington, DC.

Liebman, R. C. 1983. "Mobilizing the Moral Majority," pp. 49-73 in Liebman and Wuthnow, *q.v.*

_____ and R. Wuthnow (eds.). 1983. *The New Christian Right*. New York: Aldine.

Lienesch, M. 1982. "Christian conservatism as a political movement." *Political Science Quarterly* 97:403-25.

_____. 1993. *Redeeming America*. Chapel Hill: University of North Carolina Press.

Linder, R. 1982. "Militarism in Nazi thought and in the American religious right." *Journal of Church and State* 24:263-79.

Lipset, S. M. 1982. "Failures of extremism." *Society* 20 (1):48-58.

Lorentzen, L. 1980. "Evangelical life style concerns expressed in political action." *Sociological Analysis* 41:144-54.

Martz, L., V. E. Smith, D. Pederson, D. Shapiro, M. Miller, and G. Carroll. 1987. "God and money." *Newsweek* (Apr. 6):16-22.

Miller, A. H. and M. P. Wattenberg. 1984. "Politics from the pulpit." *Public Opinion Quarterly* 48:301-17.

Miller, W. E. 1985. "The new Christian right and fundamentalist discontent." *Sociological Focus* 18:325-26.

Moen, M. C. 1988. "Status politics and the political agenda of the Christian right." *Sociological Quarterly* 29:429-37.

_____. 1989. *The Christian Right and Congress*. Tuscaloosa: University of Alabama Press.

_____. 1992. *The Transformation of the Christian Right*. Tuscaloosa: University of Alabama Press.

_____. 1993. "The preacher versus the teacher." *Thought & Action* 9:125-43.

Morin, R. 1993. "Getting a hold on the religious right." *Washington Post Weekly Edition* (Apr. 5-11):37.

Morken, H. 1990. "Religious lobbying at the state level." Paper delivered at the annual meeting of the American Political Science Association, San Francisco.

Nyhan, D. 1980. "Attacks on religious right put its influence in doubt." *Boston Globe* (Oct. 28):1-2.

Oldfield, D. 1990. "The Christian right and state Republican parties." Paper delivered at the annual meeting of the American Political Science Association, San Francisco.

_____. 1992. "The Christian right in the 1992 campaign." Paper delivered at the annual meeting of the Northeastern Political Science Association, Providence, RI.

Ogintz, E. 1980. "Evangelists seek political clout." *Chicago Tribune* (Jan. 13):5.

Ostling, R. N. 1987. "TV's unholy row." *Time* (Apr. 6):60-67.

Pressman, S. 1984. "Religious right." *Congressional Quarterly Weekly Report* 38 (Sept. 12):2315-19.

Shupe, A. 1990. "Sun Myung Moon's American disappointment." *Christian Century* 107:764.

_____ and W. Stacey. 1983. "The Moral Majority constituency," pp. 103-16 in Liebman and Wuthnow, *q.v.*

Sigelman, L., C. Wilcox, and E. H. Buell, Jr. 1987. "An unchanging minority." *Social Science Quarterly* 68:876-84.

Simpson, J. H. 1983. "Moral issues and status politics," pp. 187-205 in Liebman and Wuthnow, *q.v.*

Smidt, C. 1983. "Evangelicals versus fundamentalists." Paper delivered at annual meeting of the Midwest Political Science Association, Chicago.

_____. 1987. "Evangelicals and the 1984 election." *American Politics Quarterly* 15:419-44.

_____. 1988. "The mobilization of evangelical voters in 1980." *Southeastern Political Review* 16:3-33.

Spring. B. 1984. "Some Christian leaders want further political activism." *Christianity Today* (Nov. 9):40-41.

Wald, K. D. 1987. *Religion and Politics in the United States*. New York: St. Martins.
_____. 1992. *Religion and Politics in the United States*, 2nd ed. New York: St. Martins.
_____, D. Owen, and S. Hill. 1989a. "Habits of the mind?," pp. 93-108 in T. G. Jelen (ed.), *Religion and Political Behavior in the United States*. New York: Praeger.
_____. 1989b. "Evangelical politics and status issues." *Journal for the Scientific Study of Religion* 28:1-16.
Wilcox, C. 1986. "Evangelicals and fundamentalists in the new Christian right." *Journal for the Scientific Study of Religion* 25:355-63.
_____. 1987. "Popular support for the Moral Majority in 1980." *Social Science Quarterly* 68:157-66.
_____. 1989. "Evangelicals and the Moral Majority." *Journal for the Social Scientific Study of Religion* 28:400-14.
_____. 1992. *God's Warriors*. Baltimore, MD: Johns Hopkins University Press.
Woodward, K. L. 1993. "The rites of Americans." *Newsweek* (Nov. 29):80-82.
Unger, A. 1980. "TV ads try to offset religious right." *Christian Science Monitor* (Oct. 21):6.

HAS THE CHRISTIAN RIGHT TAKEN OVER THE REPUBLICAN PARTY?

by John F. Persinos

Religion has always infused American politics, from the days when Massachusetts Bay Colony governor John Winthrop proclaimed the virgin continent "a City upon a hill" in 1630, to the 1960s when Protestant, Catholic and Jewish leaders struggled for civil rights, to the growing grassroots power of the religious right today. God's people have never been strangers within the profane environs of Caesar.

Ever since it rose to prominence in the late 1970s, the Christian Right has attracted considerable press interest. Indeed, few political movements have generated so much overwrought commentary. When examined with a coldly non-partisan eye, it turns out that much of the mainstream's reportage on the Christian Right is a hodge-podge of cliches, regurgitated conventional wisdom, and fatuous analysis.

With mid-term elections looming and the Christian Right a bigger factor than ever, now is an opportune time to examine the electoral strength of this widely misunderstood movement.

This "special report" includes results from an exclusive state-by-state survey of the Christian Right's influence within the Republican party; a Republican leader's advice on how the GOP should handle the Christian Right; a Democrat's advice to his party on the same matter; a pollster's demographic overview of it all; and a Case Study of how a Christian Right candidate won the GOP endorsement over a sitting governor.

The Christian Right has re-focused its money and efforts to the grassroots level and de-emphasized national lobbying. So far, one of the consequences of this new strategy is the nomination of philosophically compatible candidates at the state and local levels. But therein lies the rub. The movement these days is garnering greater visibility – a two-edged sword. Moreover, the conservative candidates who emerge from the primaries are often vulnerable in general elections to charges of extremism – usually a death blow if it's made to stick.

87

Who's Got the Power?

Levels of Christian Right Strength in State Republican Party Organizations

State	Minor	Substantial	Dominant		State	Minor	Substantial	Dominant
Alabama			†		Nebraska	†'		
Alaska			†		Nevada	†		
Arizona			†		New Hampshire	†		
Arkansas		†			New Jersey	†		
California			†		New Mexico	†		
Colorado	†				New York	†		
Connecticut	†				North Carolina			†
Delaware		†			North Dakota			
District of Columbia	†				Ohio		†	
Florida			†		Oklahoma			†
Georgia			†		Oregon			†
Hawaii			†		Pennsylvania		†	
Idaho			†		Rhode Island	†		
Illinois	†				South Carolina			†
Indiana		†			South Dakota	†		
Iowa			†		Tennessee	†		
Kansas		†			Texas			†
Kentucky		†			Utah		†*	
Louisiana			†		Vermont	†		
Maine		†			Virginia			†
Maryland		†			Washington			†
Massachusetts		†			West Virginia	†		
Michigan		†			Wisconsin	†		
Minnesota			†		Wyoming	†		
Mississippi		†						
Missouri	†				**TOTAL**	**20**	**13**	**18**
Montana		†						

ABOUT THE SURVEY

Campaign activists, political consultants, news reporters, university professors, and GOP officials from all 50 states were interviewed by the editorial staff of Campaigns & Elections this summer. They were asked to determine the extent to which members of the top Republican party governing bodies in each state (typically the state central committee) consist of people who are directly affiliated with the Christian Right or with organizations commonly associated with religious conservative causes such as pro-life and home-schooling. Responses were confirmed and checked through additional in-depth interviewing to ensure balance, fairness, and accuracy.

Key Codes:

"Minor" = Christian Right strength in GOP state party organization less than 25 percent

"Substantial" = Christian Right strength in GOP state party organization above 25 percent but less than a majority

"Dominant" = Christian Right strength in GOP state party organization constitutes a working majority on major issues

* There is reasonable dispute over whether all of the considerable Mormon influence in the Utah Republican Party organization should be counted as being part of the Christian Right. If it is, then Utah would move to the "dominant" category.

Right Turns

Religious conservatism reached its present course after undergoing three phases. The first, from 1979 to 1984, witnessed the incorporation of activist organizations and an "expansionism" that emphasized legislative lobbying, direct-mail fundraising, and Washington-based issues.

The second phase, 1985 to 1986, was marked by the collapse of the movement's direct mail base. The success of President Reagan's conservative counter-revolution made it harder to get activists to open their checkbooks; it also became difficult to keep voters in the hinterlands agitated enough to give money and time to national causes that seemed remote. Many brand-name groups, such as the Moral Majority, went out of business.

The third phase – grassroots activism within the GOP – started in 1987 with the rise of televangelist Pat Robertson. His 1988 GOP presidential bid attracted hundreds of thousands of small contributors, a base from which he created the Christian Coaltion in 1989. The Coalition is a grassroots organization with over 450,000 members and almost 1,000 chapters located in all 50 states. Led by Ralph Reed, the Coalition organizes local chapters, trains activists and potential candidates, provides voter "information," and supplies resources for mobilizing voters.

The Coalition is credited with spearheading the "capture" of state Republican parties by Christian Right forces and in getting conservative Christians to the polls in support of Republican candidates in many key races, most recently the Virginia state elections and a Republican upset victory in a special Kentucky congressional race.

This still-unfolding "third phase" is alarming many moderate Republicans, notably such veterans as U.S. Sen. John Warner (R-VA), who has openly broken with the Christian Right by refusing to support religious conservative leader Mike Farris for Lt. Governor and Oliver North for the U.S. Senate. Moderates are worried that these Armies of God are poised to conquer the GOP and spark a nasty internecine battle unparalled since the emergence of Barry Goldwater.

Meanwhile, as they face potentially big losses in the November elections, the Democrats predictably cast the movement in stark terms. "Worse than their extremist brand of politics...is the radical right's absolute intolerance of dissenting views and ideas," blasts Democratic Party Chairman David Wilhelm in a memo to party regulars. "Those who disagree with their narrow-minded vision of American society are labeled 'un-Christian' or 'immoral.' We have seen time-and-time again that there is no line that the radical right won't cross in their effort to gain political power."

But the fact is, electoral spoils go to those who organize. U.S. Sen. Nancy Kassebaum (R-KS), noting the growing power of the religious right in her state, perhaps put it best: "Part of the problem is that moderates aren't willing to work in the trenches, while the Christian conservatives have gone door to door and worked hard and won control fair and square. My hat's off to them for that."

Matthew Moen, a political science professor at the University of Maine and a noted scholar on the Christian Right, says the inability of the Christian Right to set the national political agenda in the 1990s does not mean it will be bereft of influence.

"Its political clout simply will be expressed in other ways," Moen says. "The prinicipal way that it will exercise a political impact will be through shaping the Republican party." As Pat Robertson himself has declared: "We want...to see a working majority of the Republican party in the hands of pro-family Christians by 1996."

For candidates everywhere, the stakes of this political Holy War are high indeed. Religious convictions provide voters with a strong source of direction, with clear priorities and policy stances. They are also integrated within a network of churches, television programs, and associations – all of which make these voters readily accessible for political mobilization. Love it or hate it, the Christian Right brings formidable personal and institutional resources to the political arena. Candidates ignore its growing strength at their own peril.

Politicians across America debate whether the Christian Right has, in fact, taken over the leadership structures of the Republican state party apparatus, as some of their adherents claim and some of their rivals charge. In many cases, Christian Right forces have seized majority control of state parties, at least temporarily, and have used their strength to endorse and nominate candidates (the Minnesota case study beginning on page 50 is a prime example), allocate campaign resources, and take controversial policy stands. This fact-of-life cannot be ignored. So why shouldn't it be measured?

The weapon of today's intra-party Republican warfare is *organization*. Forces of the Christian Right are cohesive, mobilized, dedicated, and often well financed. They do what voter groups always do if they're serious about taking power: they *turn out*. It was no idol of the religious right, Woody Allen, who said that 90 percent of success is showing up. That's particularly true in politics. Whether it's a county caucus, a central committee election, a state convention, or low visibility primaries and special elections, Christian Right forces mobilize themselves and are able to exaggerate their popular numbers by skewing turnout.

The ability of "true believers" to get out the vote worries Republican moderates and maddens Democratic antagonists who view this movement as part of a nationwide plot that is fueled by millions of dollars of campaign cash, a stealth network of megalomaniacs, and legions of stoic foot soldiers.

State-by-State Survey

Nevertheless, Ralph Reed, executive director of the Christian Coalition, has no philosophical qualms about his group's widespread efforts.

"All politics is local – that has been the motto of the left; it's now our motto," Reed told *Campaigns & Elections*. "Other movements have gone through phases similar to ours. Civil rights activists and feminists started in the trenches and then obtained mainstream political power. Now it's our turn. If moderates complain, they have to keep in mind that we're the ones licking the envelopes and burning the shoe leather. The only crime that the Christian Right has committed is the crime of democracy."

To measure organized Christian Right influence within state organizations, we interviewed Republican state chairs, party directors, and campaign consultants, as well as a few adversarial Democratic analysts and considerably more objective (though not necessarily more knowledgeable) political reporters and academic researchers. Because definitions and quantitative measurements of this kind are open to endless debate and empirical dispute, it was our mission to rate states within broad groupings that make practical sense. Our task was to ultimately determine whether the influence of the Christian Right within each state party's governing body (usually the elected state central committee) was minor, substantial, or dominant—the politically relevant question.

In this survey, Christian Right strength is classified as "minor" when it is less than 25 percent of the state party's governing body; "substantial" when it exceeds 25 percent but is less than a majority; and "dominant" when it encompasses at least a working majority control on major issues.

Respondents were asked: *What percentage of the governing body of the Republican Party in your state would you estimate is directly affiliated with the Christian Right or with an organization commonly associated with religious conservative causes such as pro-life, home-schooling, and other similar groups?* Responses to that probe constituted estimates of Christian Right influence. Those were separated from Republican party officials who may be generally sympathetic to the Christian Right or with groups commonly associated with religious conservative or with causes but who are not directly affiliated with any of them.

John Green, director of the Bliss Institute for the Study of Applied Politics in Akron, Ohio, has written several empirical articles on the Christian Right and is considered an expert on the subject.

Green acknowledged the difficulties of compiling such surveys, especially when it comes to the Christian Right. "Just keep in mind that certain social issues aren't necessarily synonymous with the Christian Right," he says. "For example, some Catholics are adamantly pro-life but they would take great umbrage to being lumped in with the Christian Right. And of course, the Christian Right is not monolithic. Many evangelicals, for example, can't stand Pat Robertson."

It should be cautioned that this study does not measure rank-and-file religious conservatism in the Republican party or in the electorate as a whole. It was designed only to determine the might of the Christian Right within the statewide Republican party governing organization – which is key not only to this year's elections but also to future party-building efforts, electoral strategies, and control of the 1996 presidential nomination process.

The *Campaigns & Elections* survey found that in 20 states (including the District of Columbia), Christian Right state party leadership strength was considered minor. In 13 states, their influence was measured as substantial. In 18 states, it was rated dominant.

Interestingly, of the 18 "dominant" states, most are spread across the South and West. Christian Right influence in New England and the Northeast is viewed as being the most limited.

If Christian Right organizational influence continues to grow at the rate that it has in recent years, it would be possible that by 1996 many of the states now in the "substantial" category could roll into the "dominant" grouping, thus giving them dominance over a majority, or a near majority, of state party decision structures.

If so, then Pat Robertson will have fulfilled his goal of making so-called family values paramount within the GOP by 1996. However, political "mainstreaming" comes with a price: co-optation. Charles Colson, the Watergate felon who experienced an evangelical conversion, recently summarized this age-old dilemma: "Our well-intentioned attempts to influence government can become so entangled with a particular political agenda that it becomes our focus; our goal becomes maintaining political access. When that happens the gospel is held hostage to a political agenda, and we become part of the very system we were seeking to change."

Determining whether Republican parties have been "taken over" by the Christian Right is a sensitive, politically charged question that digs deep into the various partisan self-interests of political participants of the left and right.

The Christian Right is understandably proud of its influence. They have deeply held principles they want advanced through effective political participation. Loyal Republicans who do not identify with the Christian Right for whatever reason find themselves in a bind on this question: On the one hand, they want the votes of religious conservatives but, on the other hand, they don't want Democrats to have a chance to paint GOP candidates – particularly those who do not hold extreme right views – as part of an out-of-step, fanatical moral minority.

While many Democrats and liberals fear the rising influence of the Christian Right, they're happy about one aspect: it gives them a target. Just as the influence of organized labor within the Democratic Party was an issue Republicans traditionally turned against Democratics, now the left has a "boogey man" to use against the right.

What is the bottom line of the survey? A fair assessment of these findings is that the Christian Right has considerable influence within state Republican Party organizations across the nation. Whether these results prove a party "take over" has been accomplished is highly debatable. Whether a take over is underway, however, is another matter that can be argued both ways. Nevertheless, one thing is clear: the Christian Right, using any yardstick, has leveraged finite voter support into major influence within state GOP party organizations and, consequently, has become a powerful component of the Republican coalition and its tactical support apparatus.

Whether that's a winning or a losing coalition is something only the voters can determine – and they'll be doing that Tuesday, November 8. ☑

State-by-State Survey Verbatims:

"The important thing to remember is that there are factions within factions within factions within the Christian Right."

"The Christian Right is not as big an issue in most states as it may be in, say, Texas."

"I have yet to read a satisfactory definition of 'Christian Right' anywhere."

"Why does the liberal media insist on classifying people in groups?"

"It doesn't take religiosity to care about the decline of values in our nation. Perhaps this is why, despite all the negatives, candidates who wear the religious right label this year are winning."

"Clinton has unified the Christian Right. He's the enemy."

90

CASTING A WIDER NET

Religious Conservatives Move Beyond Abortion and Homosexuality

RALPH REED JR.

During Adlai Stevenson's second losing campaign for the presidency in 1956, Harry Truman met with the embattled candidate to offer him some advice. Mr. Stevenson, then badly trailing Dwight Eisenhower, asked the former president what he was doing wrong. Mr. Truman led him to the window, pointed to a man walking down the street below, and said, "What you've got to do is figure out how to reach that man."

This same dilemma now faces the pro-family movement. Though blessed with talented leadership, strong grassroots support, and enormous financial resources, it has not yet completely connected its agenda with average voters. The pro-family movement still has limited appeal even among the 40 million voters who attend church frequently, identify themselves as evangelicals or orthodox Roman Catholics, and consider themselves traditionalists on cultural issues.

Developing a Broad Agenda

There are many explanations for this political disconnect. One is a basic breakdown in communication. In his incisive critique of the "family values" theme of the 1992 campaign, pollster Richard Wirthlin points out that political communication proceeds on three levels: policy, personal benefit, and values. The pro-family movement's political rhetoric has often been policy-thin and value-laden, leaving many voters tuned out.

Values are important to voters, but values alone are not enough. The successful candidate or movement must promote policies that personally benefit voters—such as tax cuts, education vouchers, higher wages, or retirement benefits. Without specific policies designed to benefit families and children, appeals to family values or America's Judeo-Christian heritage will fall on deaf ears.

A related shortcoming is that pro-family activists have built their movement around personalities rather than policies. Visible religious figures play a vital role in building grassroots membership and generating financial support. But their personal charisma, while an important asset, is no substitute for good policy.

Prominent personalities are always critical in building social movements. Labor unions were dominated in the 1940s and 1960s by controversial figures like John L.

Lewis of the United Mine Workers or Jimmy Hoffa of the Teamsters. Today, however, labor organizers are more likely to be lower-profile political professionals. The same can be said of the civil-rights movement, which no longer has one dominant figure such as Martin Luther King. A similar transition will probably occur in the pro-family movement during the coming decade.

The pro-family movement in recent years has put too much emphasis on political solutions to America's social problems. Political involvement alone will not bring about cultural renewal: it is also important for the faith community to feed the hungry, teach the illiterate, provide loving care for unwed mothers, bring together families, and reawaken the spiritual life of criminals. These require cultural institutions more than election-day mobilization.

The most urgent challenge for pro-family conservatives is to develop a broader issues agenda. The pro-family movement has limited its effectiveness by concentrating disproportionately on issues such as abortion and homosexuality. These are vital moral issues, and must remain an important part of the message. To win at the ballot box and in the court of public opinion, however, the pro-family movement must speak to the concerns of average voters in the areas of taxes, crime, government waste, health care, and financial security.

Attracting a Majority of Voters

The issues of abortion and gay rights have been important in attracting activists and building coalitions. When tactics become ends in themselves, however, social movements falter. Abolitionists spent decades in the early 19th century petitioning Congress in vain for anti-slavery laws before expanding their focus to the free soil movement. Cesar Chavez built the United Farmworkers union in the 1960s with hunger strikes and boycotts. But as he continued the same organizational tactics, membership in his union plummeted, falling to under 20,000 by the time of his death earlier this year.

If the pro-family movement is not to suffer the same

RALPH REED Jr. *is the executive director of the Christian Coalition.*

Cesar Chavez built the United Farmworkers of America with hunger strikes and boycotts, but as he continued these same tactics, membership plummeted.

but about eliminating government waste and abuse.

According to exit polls, 17 percent of self-identified evangelicals in 1992 cast their ballots for Ross Perot, only two percent less than the total electorate. Perot downplayed or avoided stating his support for taxpayer funding of abortion. The centerpiece of his campaign was deficit reduction, an issue that resonates among middle-class families.

Famine in Family Time

Family tax relief is another important issue to churchgoing voters. Members of both political parties are beginning to understand the importance of reducing the tax penalties on savings, capital formation, and jobs creation. The family, too, exemplifies Justice John Marshall's admonition that "the power to tax is the power to destroy."

In 1950 only 2 percent of the income of the average family of four in America went to pay federal income taxes. Today that figure is 24 percent. When state, local, and property taxes are included, the typical family of four spends 37 percent of its income on taxes, more than on food, clothing, housing, and recreation combined.

Higher taxes have torn at the fabric of the American family. In many families, both parents must work just to make ends meet. According to the U.S. Census Bureau, the second income generates an average of only 27 percent of total household income. Because of confiscatory tax rates, therefore, mothers and fathers often work for the sole purpose of paying for taxes, meals, wardrobe expenses, and day care.

Children are the main victims of this financial strain. As employers and the government encroach on the time and attention of parents, children are left to pick up the crumbs from the table. The result is a famine in family time. In 1965 parents spent 30 hours each week in direct, intimate interaction with their children. By 1985 that figure had fallen to only 17 hours per week, and today shows no signs of increasing.

An essential principle that should guide tax policy is that income dedicated to the care and nurturing of children is sacrosanct and should be exempt from taxation. The standard deduction for dependents today is only $2,300. However, if the standard deduction had kept pace with inflation since World War II, its value today would be approximately $8,000. No family of four in America with an income of $32,000 or less would pay federal income tax. One promising step is a bill offered by Representatives Rod Grams and Tim Hutchinson that would provide a $500 tax credit for each child and pay for it with a cap on discretionary domestic spending.

In the late 1970s, the U.S. economy labored under the twin burdens of inflation and sluggish growth. The challenge of fiscal policy at that time was to lower marginal tax rates to generate economic growth and create jobs without inflation. In the 1990s the primary objective of fiscal policy should be to make the tax code more family friendly, allowing parents to keep more income.

Health care is another issue that directly affects the family's pocketbook. It is inextricably linked to the moral health of society. Good health reflects good living; poor health in many cases betrays poor living. Yet this simple

fate, the cluster of pro-family issues must now be expanded to attract a majority of voters. Network exit polls conducted in 1992 are instructive. Only 12 percent of voters indicated that abortion was a key issue in their voting decision. Even more startling, only 22 percent of self-identified, born-again evangelicals—about 24 percent of the total electorate—listed abortion as an important voting issue. And only 16 percent of all voters listed family values as one of the most important issues in their voting behavior.

There is growing evidence that suggests that evangelicals and their Roman Catholic allies are concerned about the same issues as the broader electorate, but with a pro-family twist. Their primary interest is not to legislate against the sins of others, but to protect the health, welfare, and financial security of their own families.

In this sense, the pro-family movement and its natural constituency have passed like two ships in the night. A recent survey by the Marketing Research Institute found that, aside from the economy, the chief concern of voters who attend church four times a month was not abortion, pornography, or prayer in school, but cutting waste in government and reducing the deficit. A poll of GOP voters by Fabrizio, McLaughlin and Associates in January, 1993, also found that the issue that most united evangelicals and fiscal conservatives was the deficit.

The reason is simple. Taxes fall heaviest on middle-class families with children, who must tighten their belts and balance their checkbooks. They wonder why government cannot do the same. The furor over federal funding of the arts in 1990 and 1991 was not about censorship, fact is almost entirely missing from the current policy debate over health care on Capitol Hill.

The United States spends $800 billion a year on health care, roughly 14 percent of its entire gross domestic product. As Dr. Leroy Schwartz of Health Policy International has documented, many of the most expensive items in the health care budget are directly attributable to behavioral problems. Crack babies, with intensive care costs of $63,000 per infant, cost $25 billion. Drug abuse and its associated violence cost the nation additional tens of billions of dollars.

Cancer is the second leading cause of death in the United States. Lung cancer claimed 146,000 lives last year; 90 percent of these victims were cigarette smokers. Recent figures indicate that the direct cost of lung cancer on the economy may be as high as $5 billion, with an additional $10.1 billion of indirect costs such as lost wages. America's 18 million alcoholics suffer from cirrhosis of the liver and a host of other costly ailments.

Hospital emergency rooms overflow with the victims of gang wars, drive-by shootings, and domestic quarrels. Murder, assault, and unintentional injuries run up a bill of $100 billion a year. Sexual promiscuity imposes its own terrible costs, including hepatitis, AIDS, and other sexually transmitted diseases.

Unless these widespread social pathologies are ameliorated, there can be no genuine solution to the health care cost crisis. Poor physiological health is often a reflection of psychological disorders such as stress, loneliness, marital discord, alcoholism, sexual promiscuity, lack of exercise, or poor eating habits. The healthiest environment for persons suffering from these disorders is not a hospital, but a loving home.

Protecting the Children

The key to understanding evangelical and Roman Catholic voters is appreciating their devotion to their children. Voting behavior was once determined by geography or income. Today, the two most predictive demographic characteristics of conservative voting behavior are church attendance and having children present in the home. Survey data reveals that 47 percent of the electorate attends church twice or more a month. Seventy-six percent of churchgoing voters are married, and 66 percent have children.

Crime is a major issue to churchgoing voters because they worry about protecting their children. Parents no longer feel that their children can safely venture more than two blocks from their homes, and no wonder. While U.S. population has increased only 41 percent since 1960, violent crime has increased 560 percent. The number of crimes has increased from 4.7 million in 1965 to 14.8 million in 1990. The U.S. violent crime rate is five times that of Europe, and our incarceration rate is the highest of any major industrialized nation in the world.

The crime problem in America is largely a problem of single men raised in absentee-father households. A child growing up in a home without the father present is three times as likely to abuse alcohol or drugs, twice as likely to drop out of high school, and three times as likely to commit murder or rape. As George Gilder has pointed out in *Men and Marriage*, while single men com-

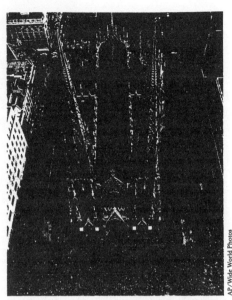

Growing evidence suggests that evangelicals and Roman Catholics are concerned about the same issues as the broader electorate, but with a pro-family twist.

prise only 13 percent of the total population, they account for 40 percent of all criminal offenders and commit 90 percent of all violent crimes.

Many of their victims are children. In Washington state last year, prison officials executed convicted murderer Wesley Alan Dodd as death penalty opponents burned candles at a silent vigil outside the penitentiary. No one bothered to light a candle for the murder victim, four-year-old Lee Iseli. Mr. Dodd was on parole after serving just four months of a 10-year sentence for child molestation when he abducted Lee Iseli from a playground just a few blocks from his home. He took the boy to his apartment, strapped him to a bed, and spent all night repeatedly suffocating him, reviving him, and brutally molesting him. As the sun rose over this horrible scene, Wesley Dodd choked the child to death, hung his body in a closet, and went to work at his job as a shipping clerk.

Such violence will prevail as long as the two-parent family continues its decline as the primary socializing institution in society. As Daniel Patrick Moynihan argued in 1965, "from the Irish slums of the 19th century eastern seaboard to the riot-torn suburbs of Los Angeles, there is one unmistakable lesson in American history: [When] a community that allows a large number of young men to grow up in broken families ... that community asks for and gets chaos." Moynihan added that in such a society, "crime, violence, unrest, unrestrained lashing out at the whole social structure—these are not only to be expected, they are very nearly inevitable."

Today one in five white children is born to an unmarried woman; two out of every three African-American children are born out of wedlock. This social calamity has produced gang violence, juvenile crime, and pathology among our youth that has no parallel in history. Our inner cities have become war zones. An African-American male between the ages of 18 and 35 in the District of Columbia has a greater chance of being killed than an American soldier did in Vietnam.

Liberal solutions to crime, such as rehabilitation and early release programs have failed utterly. Nor are traditional conservative policies—building more prisons, for example—an adequate answer. Since 1975 the United States has quadrupled its rate of incarceration and the prison population has soared from 250,000 to 1.3 million. Yet our streets are less safe and our neighborhoods more terrorized than ever.

The only true solution to crime is to restore the family. Young males raised in homes with male authority will emulate their fathers in marriage and procreation. Through their families, they will have a personal stake in creating a moral climate for their own children. Moreover, the penal system needs reform to allow for redemptive sentencing for non-violent criminals that allows them to work, pay back their victims, and make restitution to society.

Make Schools Safe

Education is another issue that churchgoing voters view primarily through the eyes of their children. Many observers mistakenly believe that the abortion issue gave rise to the Religious Right. In fact, the spark that ignited the modern pro-family movement was the fear of increased government regulation of church schools. When the government begins to threaten their children, evangelicals will pour into the civic arena like a flood, albeit reluctantly. The first goal of education policy should be to make schools safe. Increasing numbers of American children bring weapons to school every day. Stuffed in book bags or hidden in lockers, these weapons are turning schools into combat zones. Violence against teachers is commonplace. In Lorraine, Ohio, a female student attempted to stab her teacher to death after a dare from classmates, who promised her their lunch money if she committed the murder. The knife-wielding student was 15 years old.

In part because of the breakdown in discipline in public schools, churchgoing voters strongly support choice in education. A growing parental rights movement is gaining momentum at the grassroots level. In Chicago a group of parents recently filed suit against the city for failing to provide their children with an adequate education. In Wisconsin earlier this year, Linda Cross, a parent and schoolteacher, narrowly lost her campaign for state superintendent of schools after being outspent 10-to-1 by a union-backed candidate who opposed school choice. Although powerful teachers unions oppose the parental rights movement, citizen groups are pressing for reform. In San Antonio, Texas, the Children's Educational Opportunity Foundation, a nonprofit corporation, provides school vouchers to 934 inner city students for half their tuition. The Golden Rule Insurance Company

began a similar program in 1991 in Indianapolis, Indiana. These citizen efforts will soon test their strength at the ballot box. A choice initiative will be on the ballot in California in November, and both sides have pledged to spend a total of $15 million in the campaign. School choice initiatives will also appear on other state ballots in 1994. As with the tax limitation movement and the success of proposition 13, a victory in California could spawn ballot-measure victories throughout the nation.

Coalition for Common Sense

The parental rights movement found its most dramatic expression recently in New York City. School board elections in New York have historically been sedate affairs. But the 1993 campaign read like a subplot from Tom Wolfe's *Bonfire of the Vanities*, complete with the histrionics, bombast, and larger-than-life politics unique to the Big Apple.

The controversy began with the Rainbow Curriculum, a multicultural curriculum that included instruction about the gay lifestyle to first graders. Mary Cummins, a feisty Irish grandmother and school board member in Queens, successfully resisted the imposition of this curriculum in her community district. She and other Queens school board members were then summarily fired by school Chancellor Joseph Fernandez, who later lost his own job as a result of his role in the growing controversy.

The battle spilled over into the campaign for school board seats in the city's five boroughs and 32 school districts. Parents groups and pro-family organizations distributed 500,000 nonpartisan voter guides informing voters where 540 candidates stood on a broad range of issues, including school choice and more parental involvement in curriculum decisions. The ACLU hysterically called the involvement of people of faith "the greatest civil liberties crisis" in the history of New York City. The Reverend Al Sharpton denounced the parents' efforts as "racist." This campaign of fear and intolerance failed. Over half of the 130 pro-family candidates won, and several school boards in Queens, Brooklyn, and Staten Island are controlled by parental rights advocates.

The New York City experience is important for two reasons. First, to paraphrase Frank Sinatra, if you can make it there, you can make it anywhere. Family-friendly education is as popular in the Big Apple as it is in the Bible belt. Second, it united a multi-racial, multi-ethnic, ecumenical coalition for common sense. Cardinal John O'Connor and the Roman Catholic Archdiocese cooperated with Protestant groups in the distribution of nonpartisan voter guides; civil rights leader Roy Innis joined with white and Hispanic parents in turning out the vote; and Orthodox Rabbi Shea Hecht of the National Committee for the Furtherance of Jewish Education endorsed the campaign of his Christian brethren. The pro-family movement's inroads into the African-American, Hispanic, Catholic, and Jewish communities may be the most significant development since its emergence in the late 1970s.

Reforming welfare to make it more conducive to family formation is an important element in a broad-based pro-family agenda. Just as the tax code penalizes

The key to understanding evangelical and Roman Catholic voters is appreciating their devotion to their children.

marriage and children, so does the welfare system subsidize family breakup. Welfare reform has been put on the back burner by the Clinton Administration, but it is a top priority for many churchgoing voters.

The number of families on welfare has risen from 1.9 million in 1970 to 4.7 million today. Of all the children born in 1980, 22.2 percent of white children and 83 percent of black children will be dependent on welfare before they reach the age of 18. Because women on welfare lose their benefits if they take a job or get married, they face a strong disincentive to work, save, and form a stable marriage. Welfare dependency is stark evidence of the economic inviability of single motherhood. Because children learn what they live, intergenerational poverty is common. This should come as no surprise. The habits that welfare subsidizes and fosters are the same habits that, when inculcated in children, make it difficult to break loose from dependency.

There is a way to break the cycle: subsidize marriage and work while lowering incentives for family breakup. There are many proposals for reform: requiring welfare recipients to find a job within two years; reducing rather than eliminating benefits when a male enters the home; requiring job training or education as a condition of benefits. Probably the best immediate policy goal is to grant waivers and additional funding to states willing to experiment with welfare reform. As with the progressive

reformers of the early 20th-century, pro-family activists should use the states as laboratories, and legislate at the federal level only the reforms that work.

All Things to All People

The pro-family movement will realize many of its objectives if it can begin to speak to the issues that concern the voters. The Bible admonishes to "divide your portion to seven, or even to eight, for you do not know what misfortune may occur on the earth." Diversifying one's investments applies to political capital as well as financial capital. Building a political agenda around a single issue is a risky proposition, because when progress lags on that issue, as it inevitably will, the viability of the entire movement is threatened.

The key to success for the pro-family movement is to discuss a broader issues agenda in the language of the target audience—churchgoers and families with children. In doing so, a social movement until now composed largely of white evangelicals can win natural allies among Catholics and racial minorities. The Apostle Paul said that he had become "all things to all people that I may by all means win some." His methodology made Christianity the dominant faith in the Western world within three centuries. The same technique can make the pro-family movement the most effective grassroots voice in America if properly followed. ☎

From Moral Majority to organized minority: Tactics of the Religious Right

by Erin Saberi

THOSE WHO concluded from the Religious Right's failure to re-elect George Bush that its activist agenda is doomed have overlooked critical new developments within the movement. Many believed that Jerry Falwell's disbanding of the Moral Majority following the televangelist scandals of 1987 and Pat Robertson's failed presidential primary bid in 1988 meant the collapse of the conservative Christian coalition that helped elect Ronald Reagan. In reality, however, the movement has shifted its focus from national politics to local politics. The Religious Right's show of strength at last year's GOP convention was the fruit of a deliberate change in organizing strategy by Robertson and other leaders.

At the forefront of this effort is Robertson's Christian Coalition, which emerged from his unsuccessful presidential bid in 1988. The coalition is estimated to have at least 350,000 members and more than 600 chapters nationwide. According to Ralph Reed, the organization's executive director, the move to the grass roots was a necessary corrective: "We tried to change Washington when we should have been focusing on the states. . . . The real battles of concern to Christians are in the neighborhoods, school boards, city councils and state legislatures" (*New York Times*, October 27, 1992).

During the past three years the conservative evangelical movement successfully waged more than 1,000 electoral battles for local and municipal offices. It then launched an ambitious effort to dominate the national Republican Party by first taking control of local and state party committees. According to Reed, "The future for the pro-family movement lies not in quadrennial millennialistic runs at the White House. It lies in building an infrastructure and a farm team" (National Public Radio, November 6, 1992).

The "farm team" participated in more than 500 local races and referendums across the country in 1992. A few were high-profile congressional races, but most were races for state assembly, city council, zoning commission or school board. The People for the American Way estimates that the Religious Right elected 40 percent of its state and local candidates, and that it constituted George Bush's largest single voting bloc.

IN SPITE of the growth of this network, which spans all 50 states, the movement's "resurrection" at the GOP convention caught both the political and media establishments by surprise. Robertson and his 300 convention delegates seemed to come from out of nowhere, as a bewildered American public watched them flex their political muscle in Houston. How did the media and elected officials overlook this highly developed grass-roots coalition poised to dominate the Republican National Convention?

In their book *Televangelism: Power and Politics on God's Frontier*, Jeffrey K. Hadden and Anson Shupe observe that the mass media often miss significant religious developments such as the New Christian Right because "media personnel generally do not consider religion a significant force in social change, making serious coverage, therefore, unnecessary."

But there is another reason why the news media didn't notice this movement: it intentionally sought to avoid coverage. Having learned that high media visibility often invites public backlash against their agenda, Religious Right leaders adopted a unique strategy of "flying below the radar" of media scrutiny. Reed likens his strategy to guerrilla warfare. He speaks of waging "stealth"

Erin Saberi is a free-lance writer in New Haven, Connecticut.

activity "under the cover of night," where "every moment you disguise your position and your truth from the enemy because the minute you stick your head up, you can be shot."

And although they surfaced in the national spotlight during the Republican convention, they have quickly returned to stealth tactics. Local Christian Coalition activists have declined to be interviewed for news reports. One who did speak to a reporter, Jay Grimstead, director of the National Coordinating Council in California, boasted of winning a majority of seats on the GOP Central Committee in one California county, but declined to say which one: "The county and the liberals and the media won't know it until they take their seats and prove themselves to be what you would call Christian-right people" (*New York Times*, October 27, 1992).

THE HIGH visibility and national focus of the Moral Majority has thus been cast aside in favor of a dual-track approach to political action designed to gain the attention of a select local audience, namely, churchgoers. This strategy comprises an "air war" and a "ground war." Reed's guerrilla tactics, in which the goal is to remain invisible, "to paint [one's] face and travel at night" while mobilizing the grass roots, constitute the ground war. Sophisticated marketing through radio and television ads, videotape distribution, advanced computer systems, phone banks, leaflets and direct mail make up the air war.

Success lies in targeting the media appeals not to the general public but to a select audience that is most likely to be sympathetic and able to be mobilized to vote. Says Reed: "The advantage we enjoy is that liberals and feminists don't generally go to church; they don't gather in one place three days before the election. We can print 25 million voter guides and insert them in the bulletins of 10,000 churches across the country. We can mobilize the people; we can send the message."

The stealth strategy was first successfully implemented in the San Diego County School Board elections of 1990. The approach, now known as the "San Diego Model," enabled conservative Christians to win 60 of 88 specially targeted low-visibility races. These candidates won not because of media attention or appearances at public forums but on the strength of voter registration drives conducted by the Religious Right. According to Steve Baldwin, a principal organizer for the 1990 San Diego slate, "The theory is there are enough Christian voters out there to win most races if they register, vote and vote for who they're supposed to vote for" ("McNeil-Lehrer News Hour," October 29, 1992).

The San Diego organizers collected names from church directories for mailings and telephone banks, conducted voter-registration drives at churches and distributed thousands of flyers in church parking lots on Sundays.

Religious Right leaders are targeting media appeals not to the general public but to a select audience that is most likely to be sympathetic.

The public and local officials had no idea what was happening. According to Carol Albright, who lost her school board seat to stealth candidate Cheryl Jones, "The first time anybody even laid eyes on Cheryl Jones was the day she was sworn in as a board member" (*New York Times*, October 27, 1992).

After taking office, the new officials' conservative agenda became clear. For example, two of the stealth candidates elected to the La Mesa, California, school board opposed a federally funded breakfast program on the grounds that it "violated family values" and was "socialist" (National Public Radio, November 6, 1992).

In 1991 the Christian Coalition used similar tactics to make substantial gains in races for the Virginia state house. The coalition was cited as a key factor in the Republican gain of eight seats in the state. It targeted 12 seats held by Virginia Democrats who did not even know they were targeted until it was too late. "They openly targeted me by using their phone banks starting in July 1991 and getting their voters to the polls, calling them as many as five times," said former State Senator Moody Stallings, Jr. "I would have to say they were a major factor in my defeat" (*Washington Post*, September 10, 1992).

From these early successes Robertson was able to develop the Christian Coalition and raise over $13 million in order to become a major player in the 1992 primary and general elections. Working with other conservative evangelical groups—Phyllis Schlafly's Eagle Forum, Randall Terry's Operation Rescue, the Traditional Values Coalition, the American Families Association and the Christian Voters League—Christian Coalition supporters staffed phone banks, walked precincts and distributed voter guides in campaigns across the country.

STEALTH TACTICS are based on an old political truism: only a small percentage of voters is needed to win any election. The smaller and more local the office, the lower the percentage needed. Christian Coalition National Field Director Guy Rodgers told activists at a January 1992 conference called "Turning Out the Christian Vote in '92" that in most presidential elections about 15 percent of the eligible voters determine the outcome, and in low-turnout elections such as those for school board, city council and county commissions, this number drops to 6 or 7 percent. "We don't have to worry about convincing a majority of Americans to agree with us," said Rodgers. "Most of them are staying home and watching 'Falcon Crest.' They're not involved, they're not voting, so who cares?" (*Nation*, April 27, 1992).

The first step is getting evangelical churchgoers to the polls. According to Rodgers, "We build a conduit into the churches where we can funnel information in and funnel people out" ("McNeil-Lehrer News Hour," October 29, 1992). Videotapes quietly sent to congregations stress that committed Christians can wield power if they register and vote. This message is buttressed by a voter identification process that often involves working with church membership lists. Noted Reed: "You can meet without anyone knowing it, key-punch church lists and match them with voter registration lists. You take the ones that aren't registered and send them voter registration packets."

Sophisticated telephone canvassing techniques are next. In its "pro-family" voter identification efforts during fall 1991, the Christian Coalition distributed telephone canvasser kits and manuals in over 5,000 precincts. In the canvassing procedure, as described by Rodgers, callers ask questions to determine the political biases of the household. If the voter answers that they usually vote Democratic, the call is quickly terminated. According to Reed, "There are no Dukakis Democrats on our lists. We don't want to communicate with them. We don't even want them to know there is an election" (*Nation*, p. 556). If, however, the voter answers that they are inclined to vote Republican, the caller goes on to ask questions about abortion and the voter's "issue burden"—those issues that most concern that particular voter. This information is coded and determines which "personalized" paragraphs will be inserted in direct-mail appeals.

In September 1992, Reed told a *Detroit News* reporter that the Christian Coalition had amassed through phone surveys a computerized file of 1.6 million constituents. These voters were targeted to receive voter information guides and to be urged to vote on election day. In the view of Joe Conason, writing in the *Nation*, these tactics allowed antiabortion candidates in the 1991 Virginia Senate races to "bamboozle an overwhelmingly pro-choice electorate by focusing their direct-mail and phone canvass on such local issues as water shortage, traffic, crime and education."

The candidates also used the tactic of appealing to alternative issues. For example, Christian activist Steve Baldwin downplayed his Religious Right ties in his recent race for the California State Assembly by labeling himself "the pro-business candidate." Before secular audiences, Baldwin campaigned as a tax fighter and did not mention abortion unless asked. According to Darleen Crockett of the Mainstream Voters Project, "They are all tax fighters now. . . . They don't want to talk about . . . this wide agenda, antigay, antiabortion, creationism taught in schools, certain books out of schools, so what they present themselves as is tax fighters" ("McNeil-Lehrer News Hour," October 29, 1992). When

stealth candidates come under the scrutiny of the press and are labeled as being part of the conservative religious coalition, candidates are trained to accuse the news media of exaggerating the influence of Christian activists and of infusing the label "Religious Right" with McCarthyite overtones.

ANOTHER TACTIC used successfully in the 1992 campaign was "in-pew" voter registration. Reed claims to have registered thousands of churchgoers. "Right before or right after the offering is taken we pass voter registration materials right down the pews. Everyone fills them out and when the offering plate goes down the pew, in addition to their contribution to their local church they throw in their voter registration card" (NPR, September 23, 1992).

A better-known tactic is the distribution of voter guides, first used by the Religious Right in the early 1980s. The most comprehensive effort came during the last weekend of the 1992 election when the Religious Right circulated 40 million voter guides to 246,000 churches comparing the three presidential candidates' positions on such issues as abortion, school prayer and homosexual rights. According to Robertson, this effort was unparalleled in the history of the country.

These "ground war" tactics are supported by mass-media communications aimed at a wider Christian audience. For example, last year Robertson conducted a television advertising campaign to "educate pro-family conservatives." Ads were aired on Robertson's family channel and on CNN. Throughout October he emphasized the importance of the Christian vote with rhetoric that invoked images of a holy war. "The 700 Club" conducted telephone polls to gauge voter support of presidential candidates, and Robertson periodically used the results to show "Christian" voting strength for George Bush over Bill Clinton and Ross Perot.

The new tactics employed by the Religious Right represent a significant new stage in use of media. Robertson and the Christian Coalition have moved beyond using television as their principal tool to organizing local communities in ways that bypass mainstream media and thus escape scrutiny. The "700 Club" should be understood less as a mechanism for the conversion of a mass public audience and more as a reinforcement for a growing army of stealth-trained ground troops. Audience size now matters much less than the number of mobilized voters and actual candidates elected.

Patrick Buchanan was not exaggerating when he proclaimed to the Republican National Convention last summer, "There is a religious war going on in this country. It is a cultural war as critical to the kind of nation we shall be as the cold war itself, for this war is for the soul of America."

The Religious Right is neither down nor out. In its transition from Moral Majority to organized minority, the movement has combined the effective use of both mass media and local organization. The surprises and innovations of the 1992 campaigns are only a harbinger of what the Religious Right may bring to the American religious and political scene throughout the 1990s.   ∎

Jesus made him rich. The Christian
Coalition made him powerful. And
now he wants to lay hands on the
next president of the United States.

Pat Robertson's
God, Inc.

By John Taylor

T WAS NOON, which meant it
was time for the daily prayer
meeting at the Christian
Broadcasting Network. These
meetings are held in the CBN
television studio, and except
for the technicians monitoring
the broadcast equipment, all
members of the staff are required to attend. Since Pat Robertson had
just returned from a religious retreat,
there was, on this particular day, a stir of
anticipation in the crowded room.

Robertson, dressed as always in a suit
and tie, but with his cowboy boots providing a subtle rakish statement, stood at
the front of the studio's main set. He is a
tall, powerfully built man, handsome despite his jug ears, short neck, and a certain
Nixonian hunch to his shoulders. While
the things he says may at times seem
harsh, bewildering, even deranged,
Robertson himself has a genial and com-
forting manner. He does not reek of the
trailer park. His background, to the con-

trary, is aristocratic. He speaks in the soft
cadences of the Virginia gentleman.

"Each year, at least for the last
decade, I have said to the Lord, 'What
kind of year is it going to be?' " Robertson, in describing the pattern of his re-
treats, told the assembled employees.
"Each year, the Lord has said to me, 'It's
going to be a good year for the world.' "

But on this last retreat, Robertson
continued, the nature of the message
changed. "I asked the Lord, 'What about
this year?' And I didn't get the same answer. I got a different answer. And he
said, 'It will be a year of sorrow and
bloodshed that will not end soon, for the
world is being torn apart, and my kingdom shall rise from the ruins of it.' "

But Robertson assured his followers
that they had no reason to fear. God had
said he would let them know when the
world would end. Absent any warning,
no event, regardless of how calamitous,
should be deemed apocalyptic. One
morning in the early Seventies, Robert-

101

son went on, he turned his radio on in a Dallas hotel room to learn that President Nixon had scrambled the air defense over Houston as part of a military emergency.

Robertson's first thought was that this was it; the end had finally come. His second thought was, Why didn't I know anything about it?

After all, God had promised due notice. "So I got on my knees, and I said, 'Lord, what is happening?' And I opened my Bible to the Book of Amos, and in the Book of Amos, it said, 'Does the Lord permit anything without revealing it to his servants the prophets?' and I said, 'No, he doesn't.' And he said, 'Did I reveal anything to you?' I said, 'No, you didn't.' He said, 'Did I reveal anything to any of your friends?' I said, 'No.' He said, 'Well, there isn't anything happening.' And, sure enough, nothing happened."

THAT PARTICULAR prayer meeting took place on January 1, 1980. In the intervening years, while expecting the end at any moment, Robertson has run for president, suffered a humiliating defeat that almost bankrupted CBN, built a formidable political organization out of the campaign wreckage, and, on the side, amassed an immense personal fortune. All through that time, he has never renounced either his apocalyptic scenario or his claim to some sort of spiritual priority with God.

With the emergence of Robertson's Christian Coalition as the dominant organizational force in the Republican party, questions about the televangelist's true religious beliefs—questions never fully answered—have assumed renewed political significance. The coalition now controls the Republican party apparatus in at least six states, including Texas and Florida. Although the perception of religious intolerance at the Republicans' 1992 convention is widely believed to have contributed to George Bush's defeat, Christian conservatives will send more delegates to the 1996 convention than they did to the last one.

Some people, including Herbert Titus, whom Robertson fired last year as dean of the law school at CBN's Regent University, believe that Robertson himself is preparing to run for president in 1996. Robertson denies this, and one of his most severe critics concurs. "Pat Robertson is never going to be president, and he knows it," says Barry Lynn, head of Americans United for Separation of Church and State. "But he does believe he can be the kingmaker. Not a Republican around thinks Clinton can be reelected in '96, and Robertson wants to pick the next president."

In an apparent effort to make that ambition more palatable to the rest of the country, Robertson has in the last year moderated his rhetoric—he will now support pro-choice

HIS OWN WIFE once accused him of being a "religious nut" with "schizoid tendencies." Others have called him a prophet, a huckster, a broadcasting genius.

Saving souls in the electronic wilderness, 1966.

ing a "religious nut" with "schizoid tendencies." Others have called him, in turn, a psychotic, a prophet, a cynic, a huckster, an entrepreneur, a broadcasting genius. While he is undoubtedly brilliant at what he does, no one can agree on what that is.

SOMEBODY WITH PROSTATE trouble is being healed by God's power! A bladder infection has been healed by God's power!"

It is the close of another episode of The 700 Club. Pat Robertson sits on one of three sets in the CBN studio, a lavishly appointed, barn-size room. Banks of massed klieg lights crowd the ceiling above the live audience.

On the set with Robertson are his cohosts, Terry Meeuwsen, a former Miss America, and Ben Kinchlow, a middle-aged black man who sculpts his snow-white hair into a modified pompadour. Robertson holds Terry's hand. She holds Kinchlow's hand. All three have their eyes clenched shut. Robertson is praying aloud, and as he prays, messages from God appear unbidden in his mind, and he repeats them aloud. They are messages for people watching on television. They deal with hemorrhoids and varicose veins, gallbladders and psoriasis, neuralgia, chilblains, ague, gout—a veritable Jacobean chronicle of ailments and distemper.

When Robertson has repeated all the messages sent through him, he turns to Kinchlow and says, "Ben, you have something to say."

Republicans—and sought to forge a "pro-family" alliance with non-evangelical blacks, Hispanics, and Catholics. But it's far from certain how genuine Robertson's new, moderate views really are. The "wider net" he and his colleagues now say they want to cast may well be a disingenuous ruse, a variation on the "stealth" tactics they used with much success in the early Nineties.

Robertson himself, of course, cannot be counted on for a candid explanation. On a recent broadcast of his television show, The 700 Club, he discussed the New Testament analogy about the futility of casting pearls before swine: "Jesus said don't put pearls out before people who have no spiritual discernment, because they'll turn around and hurt you. I've seen it done to me time and time again by unbelieving reporters. So I just do not use what is called spiritual idiom when I'm speaking with secular reporters. They just cannot handle [it]."

The most powerful religious leader in the country, Robertson is a man of both extraordinary accomplishments and extraordinary contradictions. He likes to portray himself merely as a pious man in an impious world, a humble minister persecuted by "anti-Christian bigots." But even his own wife once accused him of be-

102

"Someone has a problem on their inner thigh," Kinchlow declares. "God's healing that problem right now in the name of our Lord Jesus."

"Someone else has an esophagus problem," Terry says. "And you have trouble swallowing. The Lord's going to heal that for you."

"Somebody is praying right now for $25,000!" Robertson says. "God is going to supply your need."

As the prayer session draws to a close, Robertson says, "Amen." Then he opens his eyes. "Wherever you are, call in, please." With that, the number to call to contribute to *The 700 Club* appears on the screen.

More than thirty years of such remarkable appeals—"Seeing them, you can be forgiven for thinking Pat's just another religious charlatan," says Skipp Porteous of the Institute for First Amendment Studies in Great Barrington, Massachusetts—have enabled Robertson to build quite an empire. His operations are today housed in a series of neocolonial brick buildings with gabled slate roofs across from a strip mall in the small coastal town of Virginia Beach, Virginia. They consist of the nonprofit CBN (1993 revenues, $140 million); Regent University (endowment, $154 million); International Family Entertainment, the for-profit holding company (1993 revenues, $208 million) that owns, among other things, the Family Channel, Mary Tyler Moore Entertainment, and the Ice Capades; and various other businesses, including the Founders Inn, a smoke-free, alcohol-free hotel and conference center that charges ninety dollars a night.

These operations have made Robertson—who subscribes to what is known as the "prosperity gospel," whereby God showers riches on those he favors—exceedingly wealthy. His annual salary and bonus as head of IFE come to $435,000 (which, as he likes to point out, is low for a broadcast executive). His 3.1 million shares of the company's stock are worth $50 million. He lives on the CBN campus, in a grand brick mansion built with proceeds from his book sales. The Arabian horses he likes to collect graze in an adjoining paddock.

The house is surrounded by a brick wall. Beyond it lies a wooden fence, and beyond that, an electronic fence, which, if breached, summons a guard. An underground tunnel enables Robertson to walk to CBN without going outside. The security may seem somewhat overwrought for a man of faith, but in 1990, he received a letter bomb. And in 1991, a man with a history of psychotic behavior crashed the gates at night and fired shots at a security guard.

O N EACH EPISODE of *The 700 Club*, the 1.5 million viewers are invited to call in and confide their troubles to CBN's "prayer counselors" at no charge. Some of those calling are in moments of crisis, some are in physical pain, some simply need a little reassurance. The prayer counselors, working in gray-carpeted cubicles in a low-ceilinged room on the second floor of the network, offer them "Christian guidance." When I toured the headquarters in August, two of the prayer counselors, most of whom were young women, were singing into a telephone receiver. Others took down prayer messages to be placed in a basket in the CBN chapel, where the staff prays over them. "They're not there to provide real psychological counseling," said the tour guide, Carolyn. "They mostly try to cheer people up or refer them to the Bible."

Although the prayer counselors provide genuine solace, they also represent an effective money machine. A sign attached to the walls of the counselors' cubicles reads, ALWAYS REPEAT AND SPELL BACK ALL NAME AND ADDRESS INFORMATION TO CALLER. The names of the callers go on CBN's legendary mailing list. The callers can then be invited to join the 700 Club (for twenty-five dollars a month), or the 1,000 Club (for eighty-four dollars a month). They are also, from time to time, asked to make contributions to special projects.

Last Easter, for example, Robertson sent out a letter requesting a gift of "a hundred dollars or more over and above your regular giving" to enable CBN to broadcast an hourlong Hanna-Barbera cartoon, *The Easter Story*. "Millions of young people will hear the gospel, and we're believing for tens of thousands of decisions for Christ!" Robertson wrote.

But not all of the money so raised necessarily goes to those special projects. A statement in minute print at the bottom of the letter said, "All funds are used for designated projects and for the worldwide ministry of CBN in accordance with Ezra 7:17–18." That biblical passage reads, "That thou mayest buy speedily with this money bullocks, rams, lambs, with their meal offerings and their drink offerings, and offer them upon the altar of the house of your God, which is in Jerusalem. And whatever shall seem good to thee, and to thy brethren, to do with the rest of the silver and the gold, that do after the will of your God."

The Christian Broadcasting Network reveals very little about its finances. In 1992, it resigned from the Better Business Bureau after failing to meet the bureau's standards for nonprofit organizations, and it has refused to join the Evangelical Council for Financial Accountability, an organization that monitors evangelical ministries for fraud. But CBN's annual report reveals that in 1993, it spent $15 million on overhead and another $15.5 million on fundraising; contributions came to $91 million.

One tenet of the prosperity gospel is that those whom God has blessed with wealth should express their gratitude by contributing generously to Christian charities. So CBN courts large donors. Members of its Christian Financial Planning Department, who are paid by a bonus system, have, according to *The Virginian-Pilot*, raised $1 billion in potential donations by persuading Robertson's followers to make charitable bequests in their wills.

But the unfortunate also need to contribute to Christian charities like CBN, since, by the logic of the prosperity gospel, one way to earn God's favor—and the wealth that

"Somebody is praying for $25,000!": Miracle time at *The 700 Club*.

1-800-759-0700

The Christian Coalition's Ralph Reed once spoke of "stealth" tactics and "guerrilla warfare." Lately, he's been trying to moderate his image.

accompanies it—is through largesse. "If you are in financial trouble, the smartest thing you can do is start giving money away," Robertson has said.

And so money, from the rich and the poor, the troubled and the happy, the thankful and the desperate, flows into the CBN coffers at the rate, roughly, of $240,000 a day, or $10,000 an hour. According to Gerard Straub, a former producer for Robertson who wrote the book *Salvation for Sale*, "We had a small, unmarked, guarded warehouse near our headquarters that received the daily donations that poured into Virginia Beach from all over the world. The volume of mail was so overwhelming that the post office had assigned us our own ZIP code. The bags of money, both cash and checks, were dumped onto a conveyor belt that carried its payload past dozens of people, who opened every letter."

INTERESTINGLY ENOUGH, there is no church on the CBN campus. Although Robertson is a member of the Freemason Street Baptist Church, he has not attended in years. "It is boring. I didn't enjoy going there," he told an interviewer in 1987. "How about that?" But there is no questioning Robertson's religious devotion. He studies the Bible every morning for an hour, prays daily, and regularly converses with God. In his accounts of these conversations, a distinct divine personality emerges. Robertson's God is irascible, sardonic, possessed of a certain wry streak. He is also extremely canny. God, Robertson says in his autobiography, *Shout It from the Housetops*, told him how much to pay for the small defunct television station in Portsmouth, Virginia, with which he began his teleministry: " 'Lord,' I heard myself praying, 'if you want me to take over that station, tell me how much it will cost.' Immediately, a figure came to mind. It was $37,000." In 1969, when Robertson was negotiating the purchase of new television equipment, an RCA executive named Ed Tracy asked him how much he could spend.

"I waited. Then the Lord spoke, 'Don't go over $2.5-million.'

" 'Ed,' I said, 'our top limit is $2.5 million.' "

According to a 1986 Gallup poll, 36 percent of Americans

have such conversations with God on a regular basis. And it seems safe to say they are represented disproportionately on the CBN campus. Employees of CBN and Regent University, who can be heard praying aloud in the small prayer rooms found in many of the buildings, are required to be not just Christians but born-again Christians. And although the Founders Inn is a for-profit operation and therefore, in the view of some, should be prohibited from using discriminatory hiring practices, its job-application form asks candidates to "briefly state your Christian testimony." The testimony should include, according to the form, "(1) My life before receiving Christ. (2) How I became aware of my need for Christ. (3) How I came to Christ. (4) My life since receiving Christ."

Most of those who work on the CBN campus are Pentecostals. They believe in the literal interpretation of the Bible, in miracles, and in speaking in tongues. Robertson has described how, while praying fervently after his son Tim had recovered from a fever, "I became aware my speech was garbled. I was speaking in another language. Something deep within me had been given a voice, and the Holy Spirit had supplied the words. I was aware of the sounds, but they were not of my own creation. It sounded more like some kind of African dialect."

A case can be made that the capacity for this sort of intense religious experience—a conviction, to use William James's phrase, in "the reality of the unseen"—is genetic. Natural selection would favor those born with a gene predisposing them toward religious emotions, since such emotions would make them less likely to despair in the face of adversity or pain. And intense religious conviction is a Robertson family trait.

Robertson was raised in Lexington, a quiet, graceful town in the mountains of Virginia. His father was Senator A. Willis Robertson, who chaired the Senate Banking Committee in the Sixties. Both Pat's grandfathers, however, were ministers, and his mother, Gladys, was so devout that his wife, Dede, initially regarded her as a "religious fanatic."

As a child, Robertson showed no signs of a religious temperament. Going to church was, as he puts it, "primarily social, not spiritual," and he stopped when he left home,

MARTIN SMITH-RODDEN

first to attend a military prep school, then to attend Washington and Lee University, then, in 1951, to serve with the Marines in Korea.

Robertson had his share of fun during those years. Paul Brosman, a marine buddy who later became a professor at Tulane University, has said in a sworn deposition that while in Korea, Robertson "messed around with prostitutes" and at one point "was scared to death he had gonorrhea." Robertson has always denied Brosman's charges, but he has acknowledged that he indulged in "wine, women, and song" before "Jesus Christ came into my life."

When his military tour was over, Robertson enrolled in Yale Law School, but after graduating, he failed the bar exam, and with some friends started a small company that produced electronic components. His mother, a lonely woman who remained in Lexington while her husband was in Washington, wrote Robertson "long, involved, and often preachy letters" about God. "I tossed the letters aside," he confesses.

Eventually, his mother persuaded him to have dinner with Cornelius Vanderbreggen, a wealthy Philadelphia evangelist. During that meal, while Vanderbreggen quizzed him about his faith, Robertson first experienced God as a vivid presence. The next day, he threw away the Modigliani nude that hung in his living room, poured all the whiskey down the drain—Dede, who liked a drink herself, tried unsuccessfully to stop him—and set out to become a minister.

DEDE, A ROMAN CATHOLIC from Ohio, was at first rather dismayed by this turn in her husband's life. "I don't mind you going into the ministry, but all this 'saved' stuff is too much for me," she told him. Particularly disturbing to her was her husband's insistence that if he felt God was telling him to do something, he had no choice but to obey—regardless of how inconvenient or preposterous the command might seem. When the Robertsons had one small child and Dede was seven months pregnant, Pat decided to spend a month on a religious retreat in Canada. His wife begged him not to go. "It's just not normal for a man to walk out on his wife and leave her with a small child when she's expecting a baby any minute—while he goes off into the woods to talk to God," she told him. "God doesn't tell people to do things like that. At least, my God doesn't."

"This is God who's commanding me," Robertson explained. "I have no choice." At the camp, Robertson received a letter from his wife. "Please come back," she wrote. "I need you desperately." Robertson prayed for help, then opened the Bible at random. He interpreted the passage that caught his eye as a sign that he should stay. "I can't leave," he wrote to his wife. "God will take care of you."

A couple of years later, while Dede was visiting her family in Ohio, Robertson, who had just graduated from the seminary, prayed to God for guidance about his future, then opened the Bible. He came across this passage in Luke: "Sell all that ye have and give alms." The next day, without informing, much less consulting, his wife, he sold all their furniture and moved into a parsonage in the Bedford-Stuyvesant slums of Brooklyn. "Oh, Pat, what have you done this time?" Dede sobbed when she found out.

At that point, Dede believed Robertson had become a fanatic. "I recognize schizoid tendencies when I see them, and I think you're sick," she told him. She herself refused to submit to religious discipline. One day, when the Robertsons were still living in the Bed-Stuy parsonage, the "presiding elder" ordered everyone to take a bath. "I have a will of my own," Dede replied. "I'm not one of your slaves."

"Dede's rebellion bothered me," Robertson concedes. But eventually, she expressed a "willingness to submit herself to my spiritual leadership," and he woke one night to find her kneeling at the foot of the bed and chanting incomprehensibly. "It sounded like French—but I knew it was tongues—and I knew she was praising the Lord." His wife had become as much of a "religious nut" as she had previously believed him to be. And her willful disobedience vanished.

FROM THE BEGINNING, Robertson's father had been highly scornful of his son's plans for a television ministry. To his surprise, it became so successful that his son was actually in a position to help him during his 1966 reelection campaign. But Pat, who had been stung by his father's ridicule, did nothing. God, he said, forbade it, because although his father still attended church, Jesus Christ was not for him the all-consuming figure that he should be. "I felt I could have helped my father, but the Lord steadfastly refused to let me." The senator lost the race by slightly more than six hundred votes. "I knew my father's defeat was of the Lord, for his soul was far more important than his seniority in Washington."

In the first edition of his autobiography, which came out in 1972, Robertson wrote that God had told him, "You cannot tie my eternal purposes to the success of any political candidate." But when Robertson reissued the book during his 1988 presidential campaign, the line had been taken out. God had come to favor political involvement. "I have made this decision [to run] in response to the clear and distinct prompting of the Lord's spirit," Robertson said in 1987. "I know this is his will for my life."

Spending $22 million, Robertson beat George Bush in the Iowa caucus but placed fourth on Super Tuesday. His campaign had been dogged by the charge from former congressman Pete McCloskey, a decorated Korean War veteran, that Robertson had used his father's influence to avoid combat. While he attributed his decision to run to God, he explained his withdrawal from the race in more secular terms. "Politics is not fun. CBN is fun," he told one reporter.

Robertson's presidential bid in 1988 was the one disaster in a career otherwise defined by shrewdly successful calculations. It almost destroyed CBN. The number of households watching *The 700 Club*, which Tim Robertson had hosted while his father was away, declined by 56 percent. Contributions fell by $70 million. As a result, CBN had to cut its budget by $34 million and lay off 645 workers. When Robertson returned, the proportion of airtime that *The 700 Club* devoted to raising money increased from 20 percent to 44 percent.

The late Eighties were a confusing period for Robertson as well. To put it simply, events played havoc with his understanding of the global conspiracy. R. J. Rushdoony, a Christian theologian more conservative than Pat Robertson, has written, "The view of history as a conspiracy . . . is a basic aspect of the perspective of orthodox Christianity." Gary North, another conservative Christian minister, explains that "Satan's supernatural conspiracy is *the* conspiracy; all other visible conspiracies are merely outworkings of this supernatural conspiracy."

Robertson has always shared this view of history as satanic conspiracy. For years, he considered Communists the primary satanic forces on the global scene. In 1980, he prophesied a war, possibly nuclear, within a few years between the Soviet Union and the United States in the Middle East. It would, he had foretold, destroy the oil fields and cause worldwide economic collapse. When the Communist regimes in the Soviet Union and Eastern Europe disintegrated in a relatively peaceful manner, he shelved that scenario.

H E NEEDED A NEW ONE, and George Bush's call for a "new world order" in the aftermath of the 1991 Gulf war provided it. The following year, Robertson published his book *The New World Order*, in which he traced the phrase to the eighteenth-century Order of the Illuminati. The secret society of "atheists and satanists" was committed to "the elevation to world leadership of a group of handpicked 'adepts' or 'illumined' ones."

The Illuminati, Robertson explained, went on to penetrate the Masonic order and the Rothschild banking family, provoke the French Revolution, inspire Karl Marx, and arrange the assassination of Abraham Lincoln. Today, Robertson writes, the Illuminati control everything from the Council on Foreign Relations and the Federal Reserve Bank to the new-age movement. "Robertson reminds me of no one so much as Lyndon LaRouche," says Edmund Cohen, author of *The Mind of the Bible Believer.*

Indeed, in perhaps *The New World Order*'s most extraordinary passage, Robertson writes, "It may well be that men of goodwill like Woodrow Wilson, Jimmy Carter, and George Bush, who sincerely want a larger community of nations living at peace in our world, are unwittingly carrying out the mission and mouthing the phrases of a tightly knit cabal whose goal is nothing less than a new order for the human race under the domination of Lucifer and his followers."

In the book, Robertson also forecast economic chaos, a prophecy he repeated that year in his newsletter, "Pat Robertson's Perspective," predicting a "debt implosion" in 1992. The country, he warned, would see "stock values collapse, bonds lose value, weak companies go out of business." Interestingly enough, at the same time he was making these dire predictions, he was planning an initial public offering of the stock of his own company—an offering that would amass him a breathtaking fortune.

Robertson, who is nothing if not innovative, founded

Robertson's Christian soldiers could be Dan Quayle's salvation in '96.

the Family Channel in 1977 as a division of CBN. The first basic-cable television network to be carried by satellite, its primary purpose was to bring Robertson's religious programming to a national market. To fill in the remaining time, it also broadcast old family-oriented movies and television programs like *Father Knows Best* and *The Waltons.* By 1989, the Family Channel had become so profitable that it threatened CBN's tax-exempt status.

So that year, Robertson, his son Tim, and John Malone, the founder of Tele-Communications, Inc., the country's largest cable operator, undertook a classic leveraged buyout of the Family Channel. Malone put up $45 million, Robertson and his son invested a total of $183,000, and their shell corporation issued CBN $250 million in convertible debt. "[Robertson] actually approached us," Malone said in testimony before the Senate Judiciary Committee last year. "[He] said, 'If you'll make an investment in my channel, I'll be able to restructure it, take it out of the church, pay the church for the channel, and retain the format.'"

Just how good a deal this was for the Robertsons can be seen from the fact that in the LBO, they bought 1.5 million shares of a special variety of the company's common stock for 2.2 cents a share. At the subsequent public offering in 1992, the stock was valued at fifteen dollars a share. The very year that Robertson had prophesied upheaval in the stock market, he and his son converted their $183,000 investment into shares of stock worth $90 million.

Robertson vigorously defends the deal. But critics have complained that using charitable contributions made to a tax-exempt organization to create a profit-making enterprise and then selling that enterprise to yourself is, while legal, shamelessly unethical. In introducing a bill last year that would, as he put it, restrict such "self-dealing," California congressman Pete Stark attacked the Robertson LBO, saying, "Assets accumulated by organizations enjoying tax-exempt status are being raided through certain business transactions."

I N THE FALL OF 1990, Ralph Reed, a former political organizer for Jesse Helms, was working as the director of the Christian Coalition. Helms was in the midst of a tight race to retain his Senate seat. Reed had access to tracking polls that shortly before the election showed the senator eight points down. "Pat called me up and said, 'We've got to kick into action,'" Reed later told a reporter.

Within five days, the Christian Coalition had made 30,000 phone calls and distributed some 750,000 voter guides—supposedly nonpartisan pamphlets indicating the candidates' positions on a variety of issues. Many of the pamphlets were placed on the windshields of cars parked in church lots during services. Helms won by a hundred thousand votes. "The press had no idea what we were doing," Jude Haynes, the coalition's southern regional director, said at the time. "But it worked."

Robertson formed the coalition in 1989 from the lists of people who had supported his presidential bid. It set out to ~~ve control of the Republican party "precinct by precinct," as Reed would say. At the same time, having learned from 1988 that many voters recoiled from candidates openly espousing a Christian agenda, coalition members ran for school boards and city councils from New York to California without revealing their true affiliation. "In Republican circles, never mention the name Christian Coalition," declared

106

a handbook put out by the coalition's Pennsylvania chapter.

This Illuminati-like approach to secretly seizing control worked at first. With little public notice, sixty-six religious conservatives won various local offices in San Diego in 1990. "It's like guerrilla warfare," Reed explained to a reporter.

But once in power, the Christian Coalition candidates in San Diego revealed their true agenda—creation science in the classroom, abstinence-based sex education—and as a result the Christian right lost forty-one of forty-two local races two years later. Like the narrowly sectarian message of the Christian Coalition, guerrilla warfare had its limits.

So Robertson abandoned both. At the same time, he launched a campaign to portray all criticism of him as the product of "anti-Christian bigotry." "We are the victims of scorn, slander, and ridicule," he has written. "Soon, I fear, without God's intervention, our protests may seem intolerant. When that happens, and it will, we can expect the same treatment that the Jews experienced in Nazi Germany." In other words, it's the Christians themselves who are threatened by oppression, not those with whom they differ.

"YOU'VE GOT A country filled with drunkenness, fornication, addiction, crime, and violence. What are you going to do with these people, kill them all?"

CBN: The Pentagon in Robertson's war on Satan.

who are living together outside of wedlock, who are engaged in drunkenness, fornication, drug addiction, crime, and violence," he said at that 1980 prayer meeting. "Now, what are we going to do with those people?"

Robertson paused. "Are you going to kill them all?"

He chuckled lightly at this notion, then continued. "Are you going to put them in jail? How are you going to *enforce righteousness* on them?"

As this notion of "enforcing righteousness" suggests, Robertson, for all his talk of Christians and Jesus, seems more drawn to the Old Testament than the New. His God is the wrathful, violent God of the tribes of Israel, one perpetually enraged over the abominable behavior of his disobedient children, one always on the verge of destroying them all.

Robertson himself, steeped in the obscure books of Jeremiah and Ezekiel, hungry for signs and prophetic revelation, has, for all his electronic ministry, many of the characteristics of an Old Testament figure. A judgmental anger—sunstruck and stone-littered in its bleakness—possesses him. He is stirred by the prospect of impending doom. And because he hears the voice of God, all he requires of himself is obedience to that voice. That is why he seems such an unintegrated person, a figure predating Freud, predating even the Enlightenment. For all his prayer and meditation, he never seems to examine his own assumptions, or to try to reconcile his own contradictions.

MEL WHITE takes a somewhat different view. White, the dean of the Metropolitan Community Church in Dallas, ghostwrote Robertson's 1986 campaign book and came to know him fairly well. White is both an evangelical Christian and a homosexual. For years, he fought against his sexual orientation. Finally, he decided to accept it, and last spring published the story of his saga, *Stranger at the Gate.*

In radio interviews during his book tour, the hosts of the shows frequently invited a member of the Christian Coalition to appear to counter White's views. Time and again, when the question of the Christian position on homosexuality was raised, the coalition member conceded holding the belief that homosexual acts did need to be punished with death. This acknowledgment was always made more in sadness than in anger. But the punishment was stipulated in the Bible, in Leviticus 20:13—"If a man also lie with mankind as he lie with a woman, both of them have committed an abomination; they shall surely be put to death"—and since biblical commandments express the will of God, they must be obeyed. Just who was to do the punishing? "That's for the civil authorities," one man told White. "That's why we need to elect more good men of God."

Robertson himself has never actually advocated killing homosexuals. But he has spoken on the subject.

"You've got a country filled with homosexuals, people

While Mel White is alarmed by the political movement Robertson has built, Bill Clinton and his aides hope the televangelist does run for president. When a report by Clinton's pollster, Stanley Greenberg, was leaked to *The New York Times* in August, most of the attention was focused on its recommendation that congressional Democrats could fare better in the midterm elections by distancing themselves from Clinton. But just as interesting was that a greater number of those polled were more worried about the religious right than they were about any putatively "anti-family" legislation the Democrats might push through.

As that suggests, the Christian Coalition may well seize control of the Republican party only to condemn it to the sort of national marginalization the McGovern delegates inflicted on the Democratic party in 1972. The righteousness that makes Robertson so appealing to his narrow if politically significant following is precisely what makes him so distasteful to the larger public. But, in the paradox that defines his political position, to the extent that he dilutes his message to expand his appeal, he risks alienating his core. Like a desert mirage, Robertson and the religious right loom large from a distance but recede as they are approached. Forever threatening but forever peripheral, they may well be, in political terms, condemned to an eternity of Becoming. 🔳

JOHN LOIZIDES

107

Pat Robertson: Apocalyptic Theology and American Foreign Policy

MARK G. TOULOUSE

Marion (Pat) Robertson's 1988 candidacy for United States president raised anew old questions of the separation of church and state. Did Robertson's candidacy threaten that separation? One thing is certain: a clear mixing of religion and politics exists in this individual. But should that concern Americans? After all, Rev. Jesse Jackson also represents a mix of religion and politics, though with different content from both areas. And these two former presidential candidates together simply signify the most obvious of the mixing that goes on between religion and politics in all candidates for public office. Overtly religious presidents are not new; one need only bring to mind names like James Garfield (a preacher), Abraham Lincoln, Woodrow Wilson, and, more recently, Jimmy Carter to recognize that religion and politics have been cohabitants of the White House long before the 1980s.[1]

All Americans should realize that foreign and domestic policies are planned and acted out by people who are, more often than not, religious people. The popular (and misinformed) understanding of the separation of church and state as a demand to keep the influence of religion out of politics misses this point. Obviously, the architects of American institutions were deeply religious people. Pat Robertson and others distort the facts when they claim that the nation's founders were Christian. Americans, however, should not let negative reactions to such fabrications cause them to deny that the architects behind the founding of the nation were religious people who planned for religion to have a continuing impact upon the development of

• MARK G. TOULOUSE (B.A., Howard Payne University; M. Div., Southwestern Baptist Theological Seminary; Ph.D., The University of Chicago) is Assistant Professor of Church History, Texas Christian University. Author of *The Transformation of John Foster Dulles* (Macon: Mercer University Press, 1985). He has also published articles in such journals as *The Disciple, Union Theological Seminary Quarterly Review, Midstream*, and *Journal of Presbyterian History*. He is the author of articles in *Religious Periodicals of the United States* and *Twentieth Century Shapers of American Popular Religion* published by Greenwood Press.
1. See the large bibliography relating to this topic in Albert J. Menendez, editor. *Religion and the U.S. Presidency: A Bibliography* (New York: Garland Publishing Co., 1986).

the nation. Early American leaders like Benjamin Franklin and Thomas Jefferson realized that religion inherently concerned itself with the deepest of human questions. Therefore, Franklin and Jefferson, and others like them, believed that religion had much to offer to policy formulation. These early leaders did not intend for religion to sit on the sidelines in the game of politics; rather, they intended to teach religion how to play the game within certain acceptable and prescribed limits.[2] Three observations might prove helpful in understanding the significance of the Robertson candidacy to the question of the separation of church and state.

First, Americans should not attempt to keep religion out of the public policy arena. It has a right to be there; in fact, it should be there so long as it abides by the same rules of the reasonable public debate that apply to everyone else. In Pat Robertson's case, due largely to his voluminous writings and public remarks concerning the role of religion in politics, his candidacy raised a question concerning whether or not he believes religion to be exempt from the rules of the reasonable public debate. Or, stated another way, in Robertson's view, is the public debate unnecessary because God has already dropped the answers to public policy questions from heaven in some revelatory way, either through scripture or through the last time Robertson personally spoke with God?

Second, Americans should not oppose politicians merely because they also happen to be ministers or religious leaders. In fact, the current Congress boasts of at least three members who are also ordained ministers.[3] These religious leaders possess the same right to run for public office that any other American citizen possesses. In fact, ministers may be more qualified than many others might be to work as public servants.

Robertson's announcement, made during his campaign, that he was resigning his ordination as a Southern Baptist minister was, therefore, not required by the political process itself. Of course, given the public perception of the issue, it was probably a wise political action to take. In order to deflect criticism during the campaign, Robertson and his aides attributed to "reli-

---

2. For a very good description of how religion may work toward the influence of public policy in America without violating the separation of church and state see Franklin I. Gamwell, "Religion and the Public Purpose," *Journal of Religion* 62 (1982):282f.
3. Senator John Danforth of Missouri (Episcopal), Rep. Floyd Flake of New York (African Methodist Episcopal), and Rep. William Gray from Pennsylvania (Baptist).

gious bigotry" any critical questions or comments concerning his religious past.[4] Robertson defined the issue as he resigned his ministry:

The call of God on my life for service has never diminished. It has shifted, however, from service within the church body to service in the nation. As I formally make the transition from service in one to service in the other, I would serve neither well by blurring the distinction that exists between them. . . . I'm running for chief executive officer, not chief pastor.[5]

This announcement resigning ministerial credentials did not seem to attract new supporters, but it did help to stifle media criticism. Robertson's resignation from ministry, shrewd as it may have been, should not cloud the major issue in assessing his fitness for an office like the presidency.

Finally, Americans should recognize that religion has influenced public policy decisions in individual ways. American leaders, just like any other leaders in the world, have world views. Religion happens to play a fairly large part in shaping the world view of individual American leaders. Thus, it is also important to recognize that religion can, and often does, exert a subtle, sometimes not so subtle, influence on public policy in cases where the policymaker entertains a religious view of the world. None of this nation's political leaders are immune to the influence of their personal world views. In fact, if they are healthy individuals, and one can only hope they are, they will make decisions in the context of their own personal world views. The better politicians among them are conscious of their personal religious outlooks and attempt, as Martin E. Marty has expressed it, to "exercise restraint in specific expressions of these, being mindful of how they are regarded and tested in a pluralist society, where not all will share them."[6]

Is Robertson "mindful" of the pluralist society? Does he support traditional understandings of the separation of church and state and is he respectful of the rights of others in the public arena to choose or not choose to relate themselves to religious ideas and their consequences? Jim Castelli has pointed out that Robertson's views of the separation of church and state seem to come in two versions. On the one side, are statements much in

---

4. See "Robertson Downplaying Preacher Past," *Ft. Worth Star-Telegram*, 14 February 1988, Section 1, page 7.
5. *Fort Worth Star-Telegram-P.M.*, 30 September 1987, 6.
6. See Martin E. Marty, "Foreword," in Mark G. Toulouse, *The Transformation of John Foster Dulles: From Prophet of Realism to Priest of Nationalism* (Macon: Mercer University Press, 1985), xiii-xiv.

line with his comment about the dangers of "blurring the distinction" between service to these two spheres. When interviewed by *USA Today*, for example, Robertson noted that "the president . . . is the president of all the people."[7] On the other side, Robertson has often said that the separation of church and state is a Soviet invention popularized in America after 1920 with the help of the American Civil Liberties Union.[8] Robertson told *Conservative Digest* that "people in the educational establishment, and in our judicial establishment, have attempted to impose the Soviet strictures on the United States and have done so very successfully, even though they are not part of our constitution."[9]

This second side to Robertson's expressions regarding church and state are tied to expressions of his "dominion" theology, named after his assertion that God's people are "to take dominion."[10] Over the past several years, in many different contexts, he has stated his understanding that "the righteous" are the most qualified to govern. For example, in soliciting 1986 contributions for his political action committee, the "Committee for Freedom," Robertson expressed his belief that "we all want a time when, as the book of Proverbs puts it, 'the righteous are in authority and the people rejoice.' "[11] On the 1 May 1986 television showing of the 700 Club, Robertson claimed that "God's plan . . . is for his people to take dominion . . . What is dominion? Dominion is lordship. He wants his people to reign and rule with him." This dominion theology is particularly appealing to fundamentalists who have been on the fringes of the polit-

---

7. Quoted in Jim Castelli, "Pat Robertson: Extremist," published by "People for the American Way," p. 8. The article in question appeared in *USA Today*, 1 July 1985.
8. Ibid. This is the topic of discussion on the 700 Club, 30 September 1981. In fact, according to Castelli, "Robertson even commissioned a Gallop Poll" to see how many Americans would identify with the American Constitution the statement "The state shall be separate from the church and church from state," a statement he found in the Soviet Constitution.
9. Ibid., 9.
10. 700 club, 1 May 1986.
11. Pat Robertson in a form letter to potential PAC donors, 8 April 1986, 3. See also, for example, "Pat Robertson Teaches: Three of the Most Important Words Ever Spoken," *Touch Point* (April 1985), 3: "[God] has ordained for those who love Jesus Christ to take over the kingdom. All things are ours." A few months earlier (8 February 1985), Robertson wrote letters soliciting contributions for his Political Action Committee, "Committee for Freedom," saying: "I am persuaded that our Lord has a plan for the next several years which involves lifting His people to a level of responsibility, wisdom, and material prosperity that is unprecedented in history."

ical process for so many years and who have recently mourned America's liberal abortion policies and the passing of prayers and Bible readings from public schools.

Due to the scrutiny associated with a national political campaign, Robertson has occasionally denied, and eventually had to admit, that he has made these kinds of statements. The clearest example stems from the 11 January 1985 remark on CBN's 700 Club. "Individual Christians," he said, "are the only ones really—and Jewish people, those who trust the God of Abraham, Isaac and Jacob—are the only ones that are qualified to have the reign." Ben Kinchlow, his co-host interrupted, "Obviously you're not saying that there are no other people qualified to be in government or whatever if they aren't Christians or Jews." Robertson responded, "Yeah, I'm saying that, I just said it. . . . Yes, I did say that. You can quote me. I believe it."[12]

In September of 1987, Robertson "vehemently denied" having made the remark in an interview with *Time* magazine.[13] According to the *New York Times*, he said "I never said that in my life. . . . I never said only Christians and Jews. I never said that." Later Robertson admitted to the *Times* that he had said it, but said he "made the comment when he was a minister, not in his present capacity as a candidate for President."[14]

The next couple of these kinds of statements to get him in trouble came on the heels of his victory in the Michigan precinct-level delegate elections. After getting the news of his victory, he declared, "The Christians have won! . . . What a breakthrough for the kingdom." Shortly thereafter, he claimed that Christians feel "more strongly" about "patriotism, love of God, love of country, support for the traditional family . . . than others do."[15] Education Secretary William J. Bennett publicly challenged Robertson's comments. After a brief period of denying that he made the statement, Robertson finally tried to place it in a context that would make it less offensive. "I had talked about clear statistical evidence that some Americans do not care about their country as much as believing Christians. . . . We find some appalling things. . . . Our surveys found that those who take drugs, who believe carnal sex is acceptable, and so on, also

---

12. Wayne King, "The Record of Pat Robertson on Religion and Government," *New York Times* (27 December 1987), 1, 30.
13. "His Eyes Have Seen the Glory," *Time* 130 (28 September 1987): 23.
14. King, "The Record of Pat Robertson," 30.
15. Ibid. See also Fred Barnes, *The New Republic* 195 (29 September 1986): 15.

have very little social conscience."[16]

These few examples of Robertson's dominion theology are illustrative of the fact that Robertson is basically an elitist. The gravest implication of his elitism is in the practical threat it poses for the traditional celebration of American religious pluralism. Robertson's elitist reading of the Bible causes him to disdain pluralism and leads him to see it as the major problem with American life today. America has somehow departed from the biblical foundation of its early life and, in his view, pluralism is the result. For example, in 1982, Robertson wrote:

Essentially the country had been founded as a Christian nation, adopting biblical principles and governing itself pretty much under biblical countenance. . . . Today the United States struggles under a social philosophy of pluralism. There is no unified reality. . . . If this continues and the rival factions increase and strengthen, the country will fall quite simply from violation of the law of unity.[17]

The key question raised by Robertson's elitist dominion theology is whether or not as president he could publicly defend the pluralism he has spent a lifetime attacking and still effect his revitalization of biblical moral values in the culture. That seems a tough task even for a miracle worker.

Robertson's elitism, of course, arises out of his particular approach to the Bible. As a fundamentalist, Robertson is a biblical literalist who views the Bible as an answer book. "I frankly believe," claimed Robertson in 1984, "that about 98 percent of all the guidance that you and I need is contained in the Bible."[18] Four years earlier, Robertson described his literal dependence on the Bible with even greater clarity: *"Most Christians deal with absolutes. If God said it, that settled it. We cannot compromise or negotiate away matters of principle. We deal with eternal issues. We hold in our hands the keys to the kingdom of heaven. How can we deal away these things in political bargaining?* [Robertson underlines for emphasis in most of his

---

16. Interview with Patrick B. McGuigan, "The Religious and Political Values of Dr. Pat Robertson," *Conservative Digest* 12 (December 1986): 37.
17. *The Secret Kingdom* (Nashville: Thomas Nelson Publishers, 1982). 177. See also *Touch Point* (May 1987), 3 where Robertson appears to identify American pluralism with the tactics of Satan (a real and powerful being in Robertson's view): "Jesus said a house divided cannot stand. Satan's tactic is to keep Christians divided. He knows that if we are united, we will bind him hand and foot and despoil his house. That's precisely what God intends. He wants Satan to crawl on his belly in the dust of the ground. But God is waiting for His people to come together in unity. So begin right now to pray for unity. Then pray and declare that Satan's power is bound—in your home, your town, your state, your nation, and the world."
18. *Touch Point*, March 1984.

writing; the underlining is maintained as italics in this text and is always Robertson's own emphasis.]"[19]

Since Robertson's commitment to the literal reading of the Bible is combined with his oft-expressed belief that "our form of government came directly from the Bible," he believes that America's problems can only be solved by a return to the Bible.[20] In the spring of 1985, he put it this way:

First of all, it is imperative that Christians, and our entire country return to a faith that is founded in the Bible. We must read the Bible, study the Bible, understand the Bible and live the Bible. . . . Our view of God, of man, of salvation, of redemption, of eternal punishment, of eternal rewards, of holy living, of relationships between the sexes, of the sanctity of life, of concern for the poor, of citizenship and government, of reliance on God, of wealth, of duty, of honor, of man's relationship to the environment, of what is pure and what is impure and of what is sacred and what is secular must all be redefined in light of the clear mandate of the Scriptures.[21]

The bottom line is that the Bible, in the words of Robertson, "is a workable guidebook for politics, government, business, families, and all the affairs of mankind." Recognition of this fact, Robertson says, causes us to "realize that the Bible is not an impractical book of theology, but rather a practical book of life containing a system of thought and conduct that will guarantee success."[22] The significance of these words, published in his book, *The Secret Kingdom*, were made completely clear when, in October of 1985, Robertson told *Newsweek* that his "foreign and domestic policies would be guided by a world view derived from the Bible."

Statements like this one, in combination with his long held

---

19. *Pat Robertson's Perspective* (hereafter *Perspective*), September 1980, 3. One should note here that Robertson's context for this comment is in matters pertaining to what he often calls elsewhere "eternal verities." In the paragraph following this comment, Robertson says, "Since we cannot negotiate away our principles, and are prohibited by Scripture from 'lording' over our brothers, *our unique way of leading is through service. . . . The Christian's chance to lead our nation is not through the levers of political power, but through service to its people and godly example.* As society is changed and people acknowledge the Lordship of Christ, those who are servants will find they are now leading others, who also desire to be servants. There will then be a consensus—neither of coercion or compromise—but, a consensus brought about by the Spirit of God. *Christians should be wary of placing their hopes in non-Christian men and in programs of secular political parties.* (Ibid.)."
20. Quoted in Castelli, "Extremist," 10. The quotation is ultimately from his statements on "Family Forum," 20 August 1984.
21. Pat Robertson, "The American Church at the Crossroads," *Christian Herald* 108 (March 1985): 23.
22. *The Secret Kingdom*, 44.

belief that American government is founded on the Bible, would seem to indicate that Robertson, if elected president, would have utilized the Bible in matters of foreign and domestic policy in much the same way that he utilizes it in matters of religion: as a literal guide.

For five years, between 1977 and 1982, Robertson authored a newsletter, *Pat Robertson's Perspective*, offering contributors to the 700 Club a running commentary on the Bible's relevance to current domestic and foreign policy matters. Proponents for women's rights, education, civil rights, and social programs would, no doubt, be angered by many comments in these forty-one issues. But the point where Robertson's world view and use of the Bible is most disturbing is in the area of apocalyptic theology and its impact upon his understanding of world events.

The word "apocalyptic" describes Robertson's belief that God will bring human history to a close *soon*. In early 1982, Robertson wrote that America needed leadership "at every level, especially in the international realm, as Armageddon looms closer with each passing day."[23] In light of this statement, perhaps the proper name for Robertson's theology might be "armageddon theology." This particular term has been used in the media since the 1985 Christic Institute study of Reagan and armageddon theology.[24] Yet, the term has come to be associated quite clearly with the certainty that Armageddon will be a final nuclear war. There are, in Robertson's writings, traces of this linkage between armageddon and nuclear war, but he hedges just enough on the issue that one cannot claim for sure that Robertson links the two completely. Robertson is not as certain about nuclear war as Jerry Falwell is, and one should be aware of the difference between the two men on this point. Therefore, the term "apocalyptic" avoids the implied connection to nuclear war that has become a part of the popular usage of the word "armageddon."

The best way to arrive at an understanding of Robertson's world view is to explore the way it led him, in the pages of *Pat Robertson's Perspective* between 1977 and 1982, to predict that events leading to the end of the world would more than likely begin in earnest in the fall of 1982. In this newsletter's pages,

---

23. *Secret Kingdom*, 165.
24. Journalist and author Grace Halsell uses the term throughout her book *Prophecy and Politics* (Westport: Lawrence Hill & Company, 1986).

Robertson repeatedly referred to the 1980s as the "decade of destiny."

One should acknowledge, however, that questions can be raised as to whether statements made before 1983 should be given much weight in assessing Robertson's fitness for the presidency. On the one hand, as the Robert Bork hearings demonstrated, the dedication of a lifetime's work to a particular position on the issues should count for something in assessing the appropriateness of a candidate for public office. On the other hand, questions asking about the outdated nature of particular comments ought to be taken seriously. For that reason, one needs to address the question of whether or not Robertson still holds to this world view. The nature of political language does not make this task any easier. Robertson himself put it this way: "Am I more guarded in my statements now? Absolutely ... When [you're] looked at as a potential president and every word is being analyzed ... [you're] conscious of that."[25]

The Decade of Destiny

Though Robertson expressed his belief that "dating events in the future is dangerous," he nevertheless offered his own understanding of why the world seemed so close to Armageddon. Why was Robertson so convinced in the late seventies and early eighties that the 1980s would be a decade of destiny and why was he so intent on believing that 1982 would be a particularly important year in God's timetable?

The answer has to do with his reading of the prophetic materials in Daniel, Ezekiel, and Revelation and believing that current events in the Middle East were fulfilling prophecies made in those biblical books. "The Bible tells us," he wrote in 1977, "that the wise man sees the danger and hides himself and the foolish goes on and is punished. *Christians must stay alert both to the dangers and the opportunities of our age.*" In 1977, Robertson saw dramatic changes coming in the next few years, changes that would "leave us breathless," and therefore, he cautioned, it was "*imperative that we know the voice of God and can recognize what comes from His hand and what does not.*"[26]

This viewpoint caused Robertson to be on the lookout for signs of Christ's coming. As illustrated by his newsletter, he

---

25. Quoted in Michael Kramer, "Are You Running With Me, Jesus? *New York* 19 (18 August 1986): 28.
26. *Perspective*, December 1977, 2.

generally found those signs in world events. The secret to understanding the meaning of world events, Robertson wrote in 1980, is found in Luke 21:24, where *"Jesus Christ gave us the key to modern-day events with these words: 'And Jerusalem will be trampled underfoot by the Gentiles until the times of the Gentiles be fulfilled.'"*[27] Robertson interpreted this verse in a manner consistent with premillennialism as a whole: "Put another way," he wrote, "Jesus was saying that the termination of Gentile spiritual privilege and the power that results from it would take place when the Jews took control of Jerusalem."

In June 1967, "2535 years after Nebuchadnezzar's action" to capture Jerusalem in 568 BCE, the Jewish people took over Jerusalem. June 1967, therefore, for premillennialists like Robertson, *"becomes the prophetic benchmark for the rapid disintegration of Gentile world power."* It was, he says, "as if something turned a corner [in 1967] and the world began to disintegrate."[28] It is interesting to note the way Robertson attempts to verify this loss of Gentile world power: *"Consider,"* he writes, *"these events after 1967*:

a humiliating U.S. loss in Vietnam, the first military loss in our history; virulent worldwide inflation; the fall of the dollar as the great world currency; the worldwide oil crisis; communist advances throughout Africa; upheaval in Iran; panic in world gold markets; lesser-developed countries on the edge of bankruptcy; a Ponzi pyramid in computer-generated Eurocurrencies threatening an international bank collapse; a plague of abortion, homosexuality, occultism, and pornography; widespread family disintegration; genocide in Cambodia; Russian troops and planes in Cuba; the Afghan invasion; impending worldwide depression; potential Middle East war or even World War III.[29]

According to Robertson, the rising power of Russia during the last few decades has hardly been accidental. He pointed to prophecies found in the thirty-eighth and thirty-ninth chapters of Ezekiel that, in his view, clearly indicate that the Soviet Union will attempt to control the Middle East region. According to a Robertson paraphrase of those chapters, "Israel would be living at peace in unwalled villages when *a ruler identified as Gog, the prince of Rosh, Meshech, and Tubal in the Far North (land now occupied by the Soviet Union) would join together with Persia, Ethiopia, Gomer* (Eastern Europe, probably Ger-

---

27. *Perspective*, February-March 1980, 2.
28. Cassette tape, "Pat Robertson Teaches: Biblical Prophecy," side 1B.
29. *Perspective*, ibid. This litany of events, as seen through fundamentalist eyes, has also served as the underlying reason why fundamentalists who used to eschew political and social involvement have now become politically active.

many), and Put (either Somalia or Libya) to seek very important spoil and plunder."[30]

Robertson saw events during these years falling into conformity with this prophecy: *"In 1975,"* he observed, *"Ethiopia fell to communism; in 1979 the Shah of Iran fell and probably before 1980 ends, Iran will be a Soviet puppet; Somalia is a marxist country and Libya tilts to the Soviets; Mideast oil is the key to world domination; the Soviets have moved 200,000 troops into Afghanistan."*[31]

Robertson's analysis of world events like these led him to the certainty that the beginning of the end would come by 1982. In May of that year, he wrote members of the 700 Club the following message:

What's happening is that we are seeing the breakup of world order as we know it. And it cannot continue much longer. This is the zero hour. A great turning point for you. For me. For the entire world. . . . In the fall of 1982, we may well see the entire world engulfed in flames. Purging flames that will consume impurities, and leave only what is precious behind.[32]

One of the more bizarre features of Robertson's apocalypticism is his early eighties description of the role of the feast of Tabernacle in determining the date of the end. The other two Old Testament feasts found New Testament fulfillment: "Jesus was crucified during the Feast of Passover; 120 believers on the day of Pentecost were filled with the Holy Spirit on the Feast of the First Fruits."[33] However, Robertson pointed out in 1980, the Feast of the Tabernacles (Leviticus 23) has not yet been fulfilled.

In seeking the reason why this feast has not yet been fulfilled, Robertson turned to Zechariah, chapter fourteen. There he found that "any who are left of all the nations that went against Jerusalem will go up from year to year to worship the

---

30. Ibid.
31. Ibid., 3; similar lists appear in *Perspective*, March 1979, p. 1; and *Perspective*, June 1979, p. 1.
32. Pat Robertson, "Five Days of Programming You Don't Want to Miss." This brochure was mailed to Robertson's contributors advertising a five-day 700 Club emphasis on the end of the world, to be aired 17-21 May 1982. The programs were entitled "The Worldwide Collapse of Communism!" (Monday); "Surviving the Coming National Depression!" (Tuesday); "Israel: The Key to U.S. Security!" (Wednesday); "Soviet Union: at a Critical Crossroads!" (Thursday); and "The Crashing World Economy and You!" (Friday). During time this author spent at CBN in Virginia Beach during the Summer of 1987, he attempted to view video tapes or hear audio tapes of these programs but was refused access to them.
33. *Perspective*, February-March 1980, 4.

king, the Lord of hosts, and to celebrate the Feast of Tabernacles." This, Robertson asserted, speaks of the millennium.[34] To describe its connection to the apocalypse, Robertson examined how that feast progressed in the Old Testament. First, trumpets were blown on Rosh Hashanna, then a ten-day interval to Yom Kippur. Through sacrifice the people's sins were forgiven and they enjoyed peace with God. After five days of grace to complete the harvest, the feast of tabernacles began. The actual feast symbolized a transition period during which the people lived in transition housing, booths, and tabernacles and made offerings by fire for seven days. On the eighth day, one final sacrifice was made by fire and that sacrifice ushered in the new agricultural season.

Through a description of events related to the June 1967 Israeli invasion of Jerusalem, Robertson put forth a scenario that described the end of the world by 1982:

Suppose that in biblical prophecy and typology one day stands for a year, and *that we can impose an Old Testament model on current events.* Try this one, for instance: *In June 1967 Israel captured East Jerusalem. The Chief Rabbi went to the wailing wall and blew the shofar, the ancient Ram's horn trumpet. Counting ten years from this blowing of trumpets in 1967, we find Egyptian President Sadat journeying to Jerusalem in 1977 and declaring, "we agree to live at peace with you." For the next five years, a time of grace, the Israelis work out and amplify the peace,* and *there is an incredible final spiritual harvest* throughout the Gentile world as millions are added to the kingdom of God. *During the fifth year, in 1982, Russia strikes Israel, is defeated, and for seven years Israel makes symbolic offerings by fire of Russian war materiel.* These seven years are a transition period for Israel and the world. On *the eighth year, there begins a new era*—a new beginning—for Israel and for the world![35]

As time passed and the expected crisis of 1982 failed to materialize, Robertson heard a new message from God. In a letter written to CBN supporters in December 1982, he described why he was discontinuing the *Perspective*:

Last spring the Lord made it clear to me that my job with the *Perspective* was coming to an end. As I waited on Him in prayer a couple of weeks ago, I was praying about the upcoming banking crisis. He clearly spoke, "You take care of My work, and I will take care of the world's crises." His clear direction to me and CBN is to give all of our efforts to our primary mission of bringing the knowledge of the kingdom of God and of His salvation in Christ to entire nations around the world. And as this has happened His anointing upon me to write the *Perspective* has lifted. . . . I have shared with you my concerns that the world's systems are in critical condition and will ultimately fail—to be replaced by God's kingdom.

---

34. *Perspective*, 4.
35. Ibid., 5.

There has been a warning to prepare and a message of hope. . . . Now together we must move forward to claim nations for the glory of the Lord. . . . Perhaps God let me spend five years in intense study of world affairs in order to understand how the principles of God's "Secret Kingdom" can influence the entire world."[36]

Though Robertson stopped predicting direct dates and tried to avoid the apocalyptic topic as he entered politics, there is little doubt he remains committed to this particular biblical vision. In 1984, for example, he wrote, "I firmly expect to be alive when Jesus Christ comes back to earth."[37] In April of 1987, during a visit to Israel, Robertson described Israel as "the place where prophecy has been spoken and fulfilled. Not just for Jesus' time, but for our times as well. God's Word says that Israel and the Middle East will continue to play a vital role in world affairs."[38] Even though his first presidential campaign failed, Robertson's continuing commitment to both apocalypticism and presidential politics raises a very interesting question: What might be expected from a presidential mixture of apocalyptic theology and American foreign policy?

APOCALYPTIC THEOLOGY AND AMERICAN FOREIGN POLICY

Sections two and three of Article II of the Constitution have been interpreted as giving the president of the United States considerable power in the making and conducting of foreign policy in this country. Given this fact, it is a worthwhile exercise to consider how an apocalyptic world view might color the president's look at foreign policy.

Charles Colson, convicted Watergate participant turned born-again conservative evangelical and founder of Prison Fellowship, has written a brief short story exploring the topic from a fictional perspective. Included as a prologue to his latest book, *Kingdoms in Conflict*, the narrative, set in 1998, artfully describes a fundamentalist president's response to a developing crisis in the Middle East as Israeli fanatics, having cut a deal with Israel's leadership, are about to bomb and destroy the Dome of the Rock, one of the holiest Moslem shrines. Unable to shake his understanding that the Bible calls for the rebuilding of the Jewish temple on that spot, the president says, "You can't help but wonder if these could be events we've all waited for." Para-

---

36. Letter addressed to "Dear Partner," and sent to all 700 Club partners.
37. Pat Robertson, *Answers to 200 of Life's Most Probing Questions* (Nashville: Thomas Nelson, 1984), 153.
38. Pat Robertson, "Make No Mistakes Here," *Touch Point*, 2.

lyzed by his apocalyptic theology and its accompanying belief that "this situation is beyond us all," the president could not bring himself to even threaten a move against Israel. After the Dome is destroyed, Colson leaves the president facing Arab and Soviet responses to the incident; the prospect looks like a self-fulfilling prophecy.[39]

Is Colson's scenario out of the question? Perhaps not. Colson claims that his story is based upon "actual public statements" made by premillennial leaders. Robertson's explicit apocalypticism over the years probably provided grist for Colson's fictional mill. His presidential candidacy, even though unsuccessful, raises the possibility that apocalyptic theology is ready to emerge from the obscure corners of American religion to assume a place of prominence in American public life. Robertson has used apocalyptic categories to discuss the Mideast, and the relationships of the United States to Israel, the Soviet Union, the question of peace and nuclear disarmament, and the European Common Market. Examination of Robertson's use of apocalyptic theology in these areas is illustrative of the problems posed by the potential of a premillennialist presidency.

GENERAL CONSIDERATIONS IN THE MIDEAST

In 1977, Robertson wrote that "in truth, from now on world attention will never be diverted too far from what the Prophet Isaiah called 'the navel of the earth [the Middle East]." In 1986, Robertson made the same point, again demonstrating his dependence upon the Bible for his view of the Middle East, when he told Time magazine that the Middle East is "the most volatile area in the whole world, and if you read the Bible, it seems to be considered the center of the Earth."[40] Therefore, for Robertson, the Middle East is a particularly important area for American foreign policy.

Unlike other premillennialists, particularly Falwell, Robertson saw prophetic fulfillment in the Egypt-Israeli talks. In his reading of Ezekiel, the prophet "foretold a period of peace for Israel at the end of time just prior to surprise attack by a vast army led by Soviet Russia."[41] Therefore, the 1980 peace accords

---

39. See Charles Colson, with Ellen Santilli Vaughn, *Kingdoms in Conflict: An Insider's Challenging View of Politics, Power, and the Pulpit* (New York and Grand Rapids: Co-publication of William Morrow/Zondervan Publishing House, 1987), 9-40.
40. *Time*, 16 February 1986. Quoted in Castilli, "Extremist," p. 11.
41. *Perspective*, March 1977, p. 1. According to Robertson, "*Peace in the Middle*

between Israel and Egypt became a sign of the beginning of the end. *"Undoubtedly,"* he wrote, *"Jordan, Syria, Iraq, Lebanon, and the Arab oil states under the pressure of current Soviet aggression will seek peace with Israel soon."*[42] Robertson's apocalyptic theology, therefore, places a high priority in helping to achieve peace between Israel and the Arab nations. As he put it in 1979, *"the United States should use all of its persuasive skills to see to it that peace talks accelerate between Israel and her Arab neighbors."*[43]

About ten years ago, Robertson's understanding of other prophetic texts led him to conclude that Iraq and Syria will ultimately merge to form a new nation, probably to be called Assyria. A passage in Isaiah describes an Israel, "in that day," at peace with both Egypt and Assyria. "If I am reading the Bible correctly, it would seem that the nations of Syria and Iraq are going to forget their quarrels and effectuate a political alliance or merger. Then the new nation, possibly to be called Assyria, will enter into a peace treaty with Israel. . . . *Check on it for yourself in the Bible, Isaiah 19:23-25."*[44]

In other materials providing his teachings on biblical prophecy, he described the probability that Iraq, with Israel as an ally, would move against Syria in war (or *vice versa*). In such a case, he said, Iraq will emerge the victor and Syria will cease to exist as a separate nation. "That's got to happen," Robertson wrote, "It will happen according to the Bible."[45] Such a perspective naturally leads Robertson to a rather favorable view of Iraq's role in the Middle East.[46] For, in his view, "if Iran is successful and Iraq falls, the next target will be Kuwait, Bahrain, Saudi Arabia, the entire Persian Gulf, then Jerusalem. So far the world has assumed Khomeini to be a dottering, old fanatic. It would be a mistake to sell him short."[47]

East must come!" (Perspective, December 1977, 1. See also *Perspective,* March 1978, 2. This contradicts Jim Castelli's comment that Robertson rejects "peace efforts in the Middle East;" see Castelli, "Extremist," p. 15.
42. *Perspective,* February-March 1980, 3; see also *Perspective,* March 1979, 1.
43. *Perspective,* March 1979, 2.
44. *Perspective,* November-December 1978, 3; see also *Perspective,* March 1979, 1. See also *Perspective,* February-March 1980, 4: *"Syria and Iraq must merge into one entity."*
45. Cassette tape, "Pat Robertson Teaches: Biblical Prophecy," side 1B.
46. For Iran, see *Perspective,* September-October 1978, 2; *Perspective,* March 1977, 1-4; *Perspective,* March 1979, 1; and *Perspective,* Fall 1980, 6.
47. *Perspective,* Fall 1982, 3. On 12 July 1985, Robertson told interviewers Cal Thomas and Tom Braden on "Crossfire" that he "knew that Iran would fall into the Soviet Orbit. It said so in the Bible."

Since Robertson's Bible tells him that Ethiopia, Somaliland, and Iran are all to fight with the Soviet Union against Israel, these nations could not expect favorable consideration from a Robertson presidency. This particular apocalyptic vision would no doubt affect the judgment of a premillennialist president even if vital American interests might be served by some future offer of temporary support for these nations.

Further, because of premillennialism's sincere belief that the Soviets will move against the Middle East oil states, a president sharing that view might move to protect the area with, in Robertson's words, *"a massive deployment of men and war material into the region."* Since none of the Arab states in the region are willing to accept major U.S. bases on their territories, Robertson believes that the military build-up of Israel is absolutely essential. He further foresees that *"Haifa will become the ideal port of supply for the United States 6th fleet, and undoubtedly there will be United States air bases in the Negev."*[48] A Robertson presidency would no doubt maintain a sustained and substantial commitment to American military presence in the Middle East.

ISRAEL

Robertson's apocalyptic theology stands behind his firm commitment to support Israeli territorial expansion. An imperialistic Israel is biblically mandated. "From antiquity," he wrote shortly over a decade ago, "Bethlehem, Nazareth, and other West Bank communities have been a part of Israel (or Judah). *There never has been a Palestinian nation as such at any time in history*, and the Jordanian claim to the West Bank Territory was less than 20 years old when it was terminated by the Six-Day War in 1967."[49]

This connection between the Israel of today and the Israel of the Old Testament, combined with Robertson's naive belief that the Arab and Israeli nations will come to peace in spite of themselves, means that he does not much consider the potential for serious conflict that might result from Israeli policies. "Despite Arab-Israeli maneuvers," he wrote shortly over a decade ago, "we are assured that *peace must come to the Middle East.*"[50]

Robertson divides into "two major parts" his discussion of God's plan for the present world. The first is *"the evangeliza-*

---

48. *Perspective*, February 1982, 2.
49. *Perspective*, July 1977, 1.
50. Ibid., 2; see also *Perspective*, September-October 1978, 2.

tion of the world," a long held Christian objective. The second is *"the establishment and development of the nation of Israel."*[51] In other words, the expansion of Israel and its growth as a major power is the secular concomitant to the sacred evangelization of the world, and just as necessary. When Israel invaded Lebanon, Robertson spoke of how the event provided evidence of God's blessing on Israel: "God's blessing on Israel can be seen by the fact that the invasion of Lebanon took place during the Falkland crisis, the Iran-Iraq War, the Versailles Summit, the death of King Khalid of Saudi Arabia, the Polish crisis, and a crisis of leadership in the Soviet Union. A time, in short, when no one was in a position to stop Israel from its mission."[52]

"Only one nation on earth," Robertson proclaimed, "has the spiritual and material capacity and willingness to support both parts of God's program—the United States of America." Nothing *"will be permitted to frustrate God's plan . . . too much of eternal consequence is at stake."* Americans, therefore, must *"redouble our efforts through prayer and hard work* to insure that our nation is both worthy of our high calling and diligent to fulfill it."[53] In other words, in Robertson's view, the general mission of the United States is connected to the protection and development of Israel. The welfare of the United States depends upon its relationship to, and support of, Israel. This attitude is reflected in the title of his 19 May 1982, 700 Club program, "Israel: The Key to U.S. Security." It is also clearly expressed in his many writings over the past decade or so.

For the United States to force territorial concessions on an unwilling Israel at this stage of history would be to invite the wrath of Almighty God to fall on our nation. There is a terrible judgment pronounced in the Bible against the nations that have "divided my land. (Joel 4:2)." *Many Bible scholars feel that the downfall of mighty Britain came about because Britain presumed to "divide His land."*[54]

---

51. *Perspective*, January-February 1978, 2.
52. *Perspective*, Summer 1982, 1.
53. *Perspective*, January-February 1978, 2. In 1979, Candidate John B. Connally's call for the return of half of Jerusalem to the Arabs was enough to provoke Robertson to write: "Since Jerusalem contains the wailing wall, the most sacred spot in Judaism, and since many evangelical Christians regard Jewish control of a united Jerusalem as a major event before the second coming of Christ, ... Connally's statement . . . puts most evangelical leaders firmly in the Reagan camp" (*Perspective*, November 1979, 4). In September of 1980, Robertson said: "The official Israeli annexation of East Jerusalem should trigger an accelerated decline of Gentile world power. In fact, the dispute over Jerusalem may well serve to precipitate the ultimate crisis with Russia in the Middle East" (*Perspective*, September 1980, 1)." He did not elaborate on this statement.
54. *Perspective*, July 1977, 1.

*Our nation is in the balance between God's favor and His judgment.
Nothing in Bible prophecy forces us to believe that the United States must
be drawn into the Antichrist system, or must of necessity taste the plagues
reserved for those who unite against God.* We have the choice of being a
godly nation [aligned with Israel] or of being humiliated and destroyed.[55]

It is clear that, historically at least, Robertson has been more
concerned with the national interests of Israel, and America's
relationship to those interests, than he has been with the national interests of the United States. Israel is the nation to be
glorified in the millennium, not the United States. "The thing
that has been promised for so many years," Robertson told CBN
contributers, is that during the millennium, the nation of Israel
will "govern the world" under the reign of the Messiah.[56] "Apparently," he wrote in 1984, "all governments will be subject to
godly people and, at that time, Israel will be the key nation on
earth."[57]

The implications of such a posture are evident enough. If an
American president gauges American foreign policy based upon
what is best for Israel, legitimate American interests all over the
world would more than likely suffer. All nations operate out of a
concern for self-interest. Since the American nation is not
Christian, regardless of Robertson's views to the contrary,
American self-interest cannot and should not be defined according to the very narrow view represented by Robertson's premillennialist reading of Christianity.

THE SOVIET UNION

Robertson's reading of the Bible enables him to know who is
evil and who is good, largely on the basis of how one is related to
Israel at the end of time.[58] The Bible does not contain a clear

---

55. *Perspective*, May 1981, 3.
56. Cassette tape, "Pat Robertson Teaches: Biblical Prophecy," side 1B.
57. *200 questions*, 160. Robertson's pro-Israel position is currently causing him
some problems, or so he says. Robertson has recently claimed that the "Arabs" are
paying Representative Paul McCloskey's legal bills in the lawsuit brought by Robertson as a result of McCloskey's charge that Robertson's father used his influence
to keep him out of combat in Korea. Why would this be the case, Robertson asks?
"Because I'm so pro-Israel." See *Time*, 28 September 1987, 23.
58. Perhaps Gerard Straub, a former associate of Robertson's for two and one half
years, expressed it best: "Fundamentalists like Pat are engaged in a never-ending
effort to maintain the appearance of goodness and moral purity by denying their
own badness and shortcomings and projecting their 'own' evil onto others. Evil is
seen everywhere but within themselves." See Gerard Straub, *Salvation for Sale:
An Insider's View of Pat Robertson's Ministry* (Buffalo, N.Y.: Prometheus Books,
1986), 294.

enough word on the exact relationship of America to Israel, so he wants to be sure the country is on the right side. This might be one motivation behind his recent quest for the presidency.

Yet, for all other major countries, according to Robertson, the word from the Bible is much clearer. Therefore, American leaders can know whom to trust and help, and whom to fight and oppose. The Soviet Union is, of course, the major foe. "Communism," says Robertson, "is hell on earth."[59] In his 1984 book, *Answers to 200 of Life's Most Probing Questions*, he wrote: "Karl Marx was a satanist priest and . . . his hideous philosophy, which has resulted in the massacre of tens of millions of people, is clearly based on satanism. The persecution of innocent people in the gulags of the Soviet Union and other communist countries are manifestation of supernatural inhumanity. [sic]"[60]

It is obvious in all of Robertson's writings that he views communism as a monolithic entity centered in Moscow. In early 1987, he told a group at a Virginia Beach fund raiser that "it makes no sense to adopt a policy of containment" toward communism; instead, "the only intelligent policy for the United States is the total elimination of communism."[61] During his 1988 campaign, Robertson repeatedly stated his intention to begin "the decolonization of the Soviet empire."[62] "I will," Robertson declares, "initiate specific steps to rock them back on their heels."[63] Robertson makes even Reagan look soft on communism.

In Robertson's view, the Soviet Union has a clear master plan to encircle Europe, take control of Africa, and leave America "alone and helpless."[64] He is convinced that this plan includes an attack upon Israel. Not only does the Bible predict such a move, but one should also be able to see that "Israel is the land-bridge needed for a two-pronged thrust—one aimed at the Arabian Peninsula, the other aimed at Africa." "As God sees it," he wrote in 1977, "this Soviet power grasp will be His opportunity

---

59. Cassette tape, "Pat Robertson Teaches: Biblical Prophecy," side 1A.
60. *200 questions*, 118.
61. James A. Barnes, "Looking for Credibility," *National Journal* 19 (25 April 1987): 990.
62. A quotation of a Robertson speech in Dallas, 20 February 1988, and cited in Kenneth F. Bunting and Kaye Northcott, "Robertson Says He's Target of Dirty Tricks," *Fort Worth Star Telegram*, 21 February 1988; see also "Robertson's Grand Design," *U.S. News & World Report*, 22 February 1988, 17.
63. "Robertson's Grand Design," 17.
64. *Perspective*, September 1977, 2.

to rescue Israel and destroy the pretensions of atheistic communism. *As the Soviet mouth opens to seize the Bait, God says He will 'put hooks into their jaws'.*"[65]

Just what is involved in putting those hooks into the Soviet jaws? For quite a while, Robertson seemed to believe that a nuclear war was probably imminent. From 1977 through about late summer 1980, he talked in definite nuclear war terms. In the fall of 1980, however, he began to back off nuclear war talk and started to couch the defeat of the Soviet Union in language referring to natural disasters brought about by God. More than likely, Robertson's growing belief that Armageddon will be fought after the Millennium is responsible for this posture. This puts the big war at least a thousand years into the future.[66]

In 1984, however, Robertson alluded to nuclear war again when he wrote: "We have seen occurrences of some very significant events that convince me that these are the last days. . . . we have the ability, with nuclear weapons, to obliterate all life, or to kill, as Revelation puts it, at least one-third of all people in a single war."[67] Obviously, the inference to be drawn here is that nuclear war would be one sure way to fulfill the prophecy in Revelation regarding the death of one third of the world's population at the end of the age. In his 1982 book, *The Secret Kingdom*, Robertson described the Revelation passage where "fire" is to reign down on Magog by writing that, "This could, of course, be a vision of nuclear bombing. But it may also be the direct, miraculous intervention of God, for the prophecy says the following very pointedly: 'And My holy name I shall make known in the midst of My people Israel.' "[68] In the Fall of 1985, he told *The Wall Street Journal* that "he no longer believes—as he once told his followers—that the Bible predicts a nuclear war and the beginning of the end of the world in the 1980s."[69]

Though Robertson has stopped predicting a nuclear war, he remains convinced that the Bible predicts that the Soviet Union will invade Israel. In 1986, when asked by *Time* magazine about the Middle East and the possibility of a Soviet attack on Israel,

---

65. Ibid.
66. For nuclear war references, see *Perspective*, December 1977, 1; *Perspective*, May-June 1978, 2; *Perspective*, September-October 1978, 2-3; *Perspective*, June 1979, 2; *Perspective*, November-December 1978, 3; *Perspective*, July 1979, 2; *Perspective*, January 1980, 4; *Perspective*, June-July 1980, 3; Cassette tape, "Pat Robertson Teaches: Biblical Prophecy," side 1B.
67. *200 questions*, 31, 153.
68. Ibid., 214.
69. *Wall Street Journal*, 17 October 1985.

he did not take the opportunity to say that he no longer believed that the Bible called for such an attack. Instead, he indicated his belief that "if they [Soviets] begin a venture in the Middle East as I read the Bible, God is going to bring it to pass."[70]

What will the role of the United States be in this apocalyptic (conventional?) war? Does the Bible address it? In 1980, in an issue of his *Perspective* dedicated to "Prophetic Insights," Robertson stated that the United States should be identified with "the young lions of Tarshish (Ezekiel 38:13)," among those who will question and perhaps resist the invasion.[71] Robertson confirmed this biblical identification in an interview conducted during the summer of 1987 and published in *U.S. News and World Report* in early 1988. In response to David Frost's question about whether the United States is mentioned in the Bible, Robertson offered his reply without spelling out the apocalyptic implications contained in his answer: "I think the 'young lions of Tarshish.' Tarshish was a place near Cádiz, Spain, and those were Phoenician traders who . . . had ships that came over to the United States. They were found as far away as Davenport, Iowa. They mined iron in Pennsylvania, and there were evidences of them in Vermont."[72] Robertson's recent apocalyptic identification between the United States and the "young lions of Tarshish" underscores the fact that, though he has personally backed off of predicting timetables regarding apocalyptic events, he does not question the fact that these prophecies will still unfold in the near future.

Nuclear Disarmament and Peace Negotiations

How seriously would a Robertson presidency negotiate for disarmament and work for peace? In discussing SALT II, Robertson wrote that "the Soviets have never kept any agreements under which there is no self-enforcing mechanism. They laugh at treaty obligations. . . . We have unilaterally disarmed while

---

70. *Time*, 17 February 1986.
71. *Perspective*, February-March 1980, 3. For other passages that indicate some kind of American involvement in this apocalyptic event, see *Perspective*, May-June 1978, 1; *Perspective*, March 1979, 1; *Perspective*, June-July 1980, 2. In his tapes on "Biblical Prophecy," side 2A, recorded in 1980, he indicated that American support might not include actual fighting: "the United States probably will not be involved in that war . . . it seems as if God Himself is going to get glory in it and therefore He doesn't want the United States taking glory from Him."
72. "The Gospel According to Robertson," Interview conducted by David Frost, *U.S. News and World Report* (22 February 1988): 21.

they have amassed the most formidable military machines in history." With this point as background, Robertson, in 1979, called for what is now known as "Star wars" or the "Strategic Defense Initiative:" *"On our side, there should be a crash program to develop anti-ballistic missiles, or better still, laser beams capable of destroying aggressive weapons or missiles."*[73] In his view, "unilateral disarmament moves in light of the Soviet buildup are interpreted as weakness and gain nothing."[74] Just prior to the 1985 summit between the Soviet Union and the United States, Robertson told Richard Allen, former national security adviser to President Reagan, that America

will never achieve anything meaningful with the Soviet Union unless it will be to their benefit. And they will not keep any treaty that does not benefit them . . . because lying, according to Lenin, is part of their strategy. And they don't mind lying in written documents. If it's to their benefit to keep the agreements then they'll do it, but basically speaking, their mindset is one of deceit and harassment and oppression. Ours is one of openness and truthfulness and from the Judeo Christian point of view. We come at these things from totally different cultures, totally different mindsets and I personally don't think anything meaningful is going to come out of it.[75]

With regard to the whole question of peace, Robertson reminded his readers of the words of the Apostle Paul: *"When they say peace and safety, then sudden destruction* will come upon them as travail upon a woman with child."[76] Thus Robertson is more than a little skeptical regarding peace initiatives with the Soviet Union. In his 1984 book, Robertson wrote

There is no way that a United Nations, a League of Nations, peace treaties, disarmament treaties, or any other human instrument can bring about peace. Such things mean nothing when one nation desires the land and resources of another. A lasting peace will never be built upon man's efforts, because man is sinful, vicious, and wicked. Until men are changed and Satan's power is removed, there will not be peace on earth.[77]

In March 1986, in response to a question asking what he would do as president to achieve world peace, Robertson replied:

. . . the only way we are going to have world peace is when the Lord himself brings to this world the peace of Jerusalem but in the meantime

---

73. *Perspective*, March 1979, 1-2; see also his massive support for SDI, for example, as expressed on the 700 Club 10/25/85 and in Pat Robertson, *America's Dates with Destiny* (Nashville: Thomas Nelson, 1986), 289.
74. *Perspective*, September-October 1978, 2.
75. 700 Club 15 November 1985.
76. *Perspective*, September-October 1978, 3.
77. *200 Questions*, 28.

we can do everything in our power to put into effect what is called the "law of Reciprocity," where as we do unto others we expect them to do unto us. As long as there are lawless and ungodly nations who are determined and bent on the subjugation of other people we will not have peace, until such time as the Lord brings it about. And then it will only come through divine intervention or through the prayers of people.[78]

This reference to the time when "the Lord brings it about," links Robertson's skepticism about peace negotiations to his apocalyptic world view. He believes that the war in the Middle East will bring mass destruction in its wake. Robertson is not overly concerned about this possibility. In the past, he has indicated that the killing of up to two and one-half billion people will be toward the end that "men will learn and repent."[79] Further, this is a time of great hope and rejoicing for Christians, "a time when God's people begin to shine in a world of darkness and confusion."[80] "To the Christian," Robertson writes, "the coming of such events means that his finest hour is about to begin."[81] The end of the age, with all its killing, "is the most exciting time of all history" for "when these things begin to happen, we are to lift up our eyes, for our redemption is drawing near."[82] One can see quite clearly that apocalyptic theology of this particular variation does not offer much motivation for serious peace negotiation.

Robertson criticizes other Christians who view pacifism as an appropriate Christian posture. "Pacifism," he told *Time* magazine in 1986, is not biblical." All Americans "have to realize . . . that we are dealing with a malevolent power that over the last four decades has resulted in the death of over 250 million human beings." "There has never been a force in the history of the world," he told the *Time* reporter, "that has been as vicious, as malevolent, and at its core, atheistic and desirous of destroying the liberties of people." His view of the Soviet Union as an ideological monster bent on destruction of all free peoples makes impossible the prospect of negotiation with Soviet leadership. "We have no obligation to assist the enemies of the United States or the enemies of the Lord or the enemies of freedom."[83] This philosophy undergirds Robertson's current opposition to the recently signed INF treaty.

---

78. 700 Club, 7 March 1986.
79. Cassette Tape, "Biblical Prophecy," side 2A.
80. *Perspective*, February 1982, 4.
81. *Perspective*, March 1981, 2.
82. *Perspective*, May 1979, 4.
83. *Time*, 17 February 1986. Quoted in Castelli, "Extremist," 11.

EUROPEAN COMMON MARKET

One other major area of Robertson's apocalyptic theology and its potential impact on foreign policy remains to be explored. Robertson predicts that "a catastrophic upheaval" will result from the biblically mandated Soviet invasion of Israel. After the invasion, Robertson asserts, all "oil supplies to Europe and elsewhere [will be] but off."[84] After these events, Robertson reports, "Europe will be in shambles" and "unfortunately ready for another Hitler."[85] This condition will enable "*a powerful charismatic leader with dictatorial powers* to mobilize the resources of these nations."[86] According to Robertson, this figure will be the Antichrist spoken of in Revelation.

The Antichrist is described in Revelation 17:11-12 as "a beast" with "ten horns that . . . are ten kings." In the view of most premillennialists, Robertson included, these kings represent ten nations commonly identified with nations in the area of the old Roman Empire. Throughout Robertson's years of detailing the meaning of these prophecies, he identified these ten nations as those comprising the developing European Economic Community.[87] Of course today, the European Community, commonly referred to as the European Common Market, has twelve members. Yet, Robertson admitted in the fall of 1980 that this group could, by the time of the rise of the Antichrist, have grown to eleven nations that will merge in some way to eventually arrive at the magic number of ten.[88] The Antichrist will make a temporary peace with Israel for three and a half years and then turn on Israel. Christ will return at the end of another three and a half years and defeat the forces of Antichrist, bind Satan, and establish the millennium.

How this particular vision might impact a president's dealings with Europe is anybody's guess. However, one might assume that a serious apocalyptic world view would make a president's support for the European Community, or the Common Market, less than enthusiastic.

---

84. These details are spelled out in *Secret Kingdom*, 215-216.
85. *Perspective*, February 1982, 8.
86. *Perspective*, February-March, 1980, 7.
87. Ibid., 6-7; *Perspective*, June 1979, 1; and Cassette Tape, "Pat Robertson Teaches: Biblical Prophecy," side 2A.
88. Cassette Tape, "Pat Robertson Teaches: Biblical Prophecy," side 2A.

Conclusion

Pat Robertson has recently said that Armageddon is "an act of God Almighty that has nothing to do with human abilities whatsoever" and that he "has no intention of helping God along in this respect."[89] When set side by side with what Pat Robertson has claimed as the purpose of his work at CBN for years, this recently expressed disclaimer might not be very persuasive. Consider, for example, the statement authored by Pat Robertson and written on an expensive and beautifully embossed invitation to become a CBN Founder: "We have been chosen since the foundation of the earth for this day and this time. To help usher in the Second Coming of our Lord Jesus Christ."[90]

Or consider yet another Robertson claim. This claim has its foundation in a prophetic word uttered nearly twenty years ago. In 1968, Harald Bredesen, another charismatic minister, placed his hands on the head of Robertson and uttered prophetic words which Robertson repeated to his CBN followers in an April 1982 letter: "The days of your beginning seem small in your eyes in light of where I have taken you. . . . but these days shall seem small in light of where I am going to take you, for I have chosen you to usher in the coming of My Son." In 1982, in this letter to his supporters, Robertson described these words by saying "I knew God Himself was speaking to us at that very moment."[91]

This particular prophetic utterance has been used in several ways by Robertson to describe the work of his CBN ministry.[92] The context for the original prophecy in 1968 was a meeting at the dedication of the new CBN Portsmouth facility. In recent years, since Robertson decided to pursue the presidency, Bredesen has stated that this prophecy applied to the CBN ministry and not to Robertson himself. Bredesen's statement, however, is not very convincing. The prophecy did use the personal pronoun "you" rather than "it" and was uttered while Bredesen's hands were placed on Robertson's head. For these

---

89. Ed Dobson and Ed Hindon, "Apocalypse Now? What Fundamentalists Believe About the End of the World," *Policy Review* (Fall 1986), 22.
90. All that was needed to become a Founder was a faith pledge of $10,000 dedicated to the building of the CBN International Conference Center. This is not an isolated statement. Take for example, the statement made in a letter mailed to all CBN 700 Club members on 8 November 1982: "CBN Center would be used by God to establish the Kingdom of God on earth."
91. Robertson letter to "Dear CBN Friend," April 1982, see 2-3.
92. In April of 1985, for example, these words were placed on a brochure celebrating three years of CBN ministry in Middle East television.

reasons, it appears to have been directed more toward Robertson than the CBN ministry.

Robertson, however, is probably sincere when he says that he has no intention of helping God bring in the kingdom. Yet, his many apocalyptic statements over the years, including some made in the last one to two years, do seem to indicate that he does believe that his ministry includes the intention of seeing that America is prepared for the end of the age. Such an understanding undoubtedly supports both his apocalyptic posture on foreign policy issues and his fervent desire to return America to a "biblically" based moral agenda.

His dominion theology should be considered in this context as well. As evidenced by his comments on the 700 Club on 16 May 1986, Robertson certainly does see the hand of God in the increasing success of fundamentalist and evangelical people in attaining to political leadership:

The Evangelicals [are] a force that nobody else really has been reckoning with, but they're going to be one to be reckoned with because God is establishing this . . . God is going to be prospering but the intention of the Lord is that His people should reign and rule with Jesus Christ. That's what the Bible says. . . . we are at the edge of something simply marvelous . . . it's waiting for you like the promised land . . . it's yours but you have to move into the promised land . . . you have to do something about it.

Is Robertson's ultimate motive behind his desire to seek the presidency (perhaps again in 1992) somehow tied to his belief that he has been "chosen" to help "usher in the second coming of Jesus" by preparing America for the inevitable apocalypse?[93] In the year prior to his formal announcement for the presidency, Robertson, on the stationary of his PAC "Committee for Freedom," mailed several letters to potential contributers emphasizing his belief that Christians are chosen of God to rule in these "final days." The PAC, he wrote, "can urge the defeat of those who are enemies of righteousness and support those who uphold good government, traditional family values and Biblical morality."[94]

Robertson obviously links his own presidential candidacy to this overall program of the coming apocalyptic rule of the righteous. "I am persuaded," he wrote in February of 1985, "that

---

93. Robertson used this kind of language in describing why he had worked so hard to open his CBN television station in Southern Lebanon in October 1981. In a letter to his supporters addressed to "Dear CBN Friend," he wrote that the station was opened because *"The time had arrived to usher in the second coming of Jesus."*
94. Letter to CBN contributers, 5 November 1985. The original of this letter is in the archives at CBN University.

our Lord has a plan for the next several years which involves lifting His people to a level of responsibility, wisdom, and material prosperity that is unprecedented in history."[95] By 1986, he was more explicit about making the connection between his own candidacy and these ideas:

Would I desire to leave what I now have for the cutting, brutal, often deceitful and usually frustrating world of political service? *The answer is an emphatic no! But my desires aren't what matters. What matters is the will of God* . . . *But what of me personally? Do I know God's will for my life and what decision He wants for me? Of course I do.* He wants once again to see America as "one nation under God." We all want a time when, as the book of Proverbs puts it, "the righteous are in authority and the people rejoice."[96]

Whatever Robertson may be saying publicly, there can be little doubt that privately he sees himself as part of a messianic plan to save America by the rule of the righteous, among whom he counts himself the most qualified to serve as president. The question facing American voters during the next few presidential elections, however, is whether they want to agree with him or not. The campaign of 1988 proved, for the time being at least, that Americans are not quite ready for Robertson to act out his apocalyptic visions from headquarters located on Pennsylvania avenue.

---

95. Letter to CBN contributers, 8 February 1985. The original of this letter is in the archives at CBN University.
96. Letter to CBN contributers, 8 April 1986. Robertson's comments are also indicative of why a premillennialist evangelist would decide to move his otherworldly theology into this world. In September 1982 ("Pat Robertson Teaches: The Kingdom of God, *Touch Point*, 4), he wrote, "I believe in the millennium. But I also believe that the principles of the kingdom of God can change the world. These principles are so revolutionary that they can change government, education, and social life. One day these principles of the kingdom will be totally accepted by all men everywhere. But I believe that they will have to be enforced before *all* men will receive them." Robertson believes that Christ will be the one who does the enforcing at the time of the millennium. Robertson is an example, therefore, of how this-worldly the premillennialist can get: concern for a prosperity theology, author of a program to influence the morality of Americans (and the accompanying concern that America be on the right side of the millennial issues), a great television network using all the latest technology which requires wealthy contributers, and a fine record of parading a great list of wealthy and celebrated personalities on his network to demonstrate how successful people of the world owe a great deal of their success to Christianity.

Paul M. Weyrich

BLUE COLLAR OR BLUE BLOOD?
The New Right Compared with The Old Right

One of the most powerful and vigorous political voices of the New Right, Paul Weyrich is among the few people I have heard whose practical statements are impressive in Washington but can be understood without translation in South Boston or West Virginia. Mr. Weyrich is Director of the Committee for the Survival of a Free Congress in Washington, D.C. How the Washington New Right developed and what it is trying to do on Capitol Hill is explained here with the clarity of a practitioner.

48

The phrase "New Right" was first used in 1975 by Kevin Phillips in a headline discussing the "Coors/Richard Viguerie/New Right Complex." The phrase was used to distinguish the coalition thus indicated from the network of older groups acting in the name of conservatism. From Phillips, the national media picked up the term, and introduced it into common parlance. One virtue of common parlance is that it can speak meaningfully of an entity which in scholarly parlance would be difficult to define. So it is with the phrase "New Right." A political observer could look at, for example, the Conservative Caucus, and say with promptness and accuracy that it is a "new right" group. Similarly, the observer could look at a well-known conservative journal, pronounce it "old right," and be equally correct. The observer might not fully understand why his nomenclature is accurate. It is the purpose of this essay to elucidate some of the points of distinction between the two political groups, which, let it be said at the outset, are not opponents in any important context.

49

The New Right differs from the Old in its political origins, its philosophical/political motivations, its strategic/tactical operations, and its self-conscious goals. The New Right shares with the Old a common adherence to general conservative principles; it differs, however, in articulation of those principles, and in the emphasis given them in the respective politics.

In speaking of origins of a movement, one is speaking of people. It is difficult to separate politics from the influence of social class and education, particularly in America. Prior to the 1970s conservatism tended very much to be a phenomenon of the upper classes, of the genteelly educated. That made for a highly intellectual strain, of which William Buckley's *National Review* is quintessential. Buckley has acknowledged that most of the *NR* circle had been brought up on James Burnham's *Suicide of the West* doctrine —a pessimistic, almost Spenglerian point of view—and that the possibility of arresting the decline of the West was not part of their consciousness at all. Despair, in varying degrees and countenances, was the logical conclusion. In 1978, William Buckley admitted to me that where political action was concerned, *National Review* had been guilty of the theological sin of otherworldliness: the belief that, as long as one's own life was free of sin, one needn't worry about the affairs of this world.

The Old Right was strong on intellectualism. This is worthy in itself, but unfortunately that was as far as it went. In criticizing proposed programs like the Great Society schemes, the Old Right could make its objections soundly and completely, in scholarly publications. The only problem was that it was not speaking in the language of the ordinary man. The language was incomprehensible, and what is incomprehensible is politically irrelevant. We need intellectual discussions, and studies, and experts who know their field through and through, no matter what it is. I believe in truth, and that we should in human affairs get as close to it as human nature will allow. But we also need someone to translate the significant points and the ramifications, if we are to pursue truth in political life.

The intellectualization of conservatism was particularly unfortunate because it completely lost touch with the other branch of the Old Right: working class anti-Communism. Call it knee-jerk, if you will; in truth a debt to Senator Joseph McCarthy must be acknowledged for his role in its political awakening. McCarthy had an enormous following throughout the nation. The tragedy was that that following was never made politically cohesive. When McCarthy died, that was it. Those people never got further into politics. And, to this day, the working class anti-Communist element has not been activated, due to lack of leadership.

I must fault Senator Barry Goldwater for that lack of leadership. Goldwater tried, he fought the good fight. He was vilified as was no other political figure in history. Certainly I do not want to diminish the merits of all that. Despite the vilification, he energized 27 million voters. But then—after the election—he left those 27 million hanging there. He disappeared from public view until he was re-elected to the Senate, as a personal vindication, but not as a leader. What could have been the beginning of a national movement of tremendous significance was nothing without a leader.

The intellectuals behind Goldwater, the Bill Buckleys and Brent Bozells, presented Goldwater as a standard-bearer of truth, a philosopher-politician. That was not the man. Fundamentally, Goldwater is a straight-shooting Westerner who wants to get the government onto a more sensible path. That's what he was in 1964. But those of us who were galvanized by that campaign expected him to be more; the people he drew to his cause then waited for him, or someone else, to continue to lead them. It didn't happen. Because it didn't happen the Right lost a generation of political achievement, of leadership, and of educating the nation.

The seeds of the contemporary New Right were sown by the Goldwater campaign. Most of us can, in our personal histories, mark that campaign as the beginning of the motivation that has never left us. Even if we did nothing but wear a Goldwater button, or attend a rally—and some of the New Right are so young   is all they did—it made a mark, and had an impact. To a limited extent, the organization of Young Americans for Freedom kept in touch with the young people who had been impressed by Goldwater, and kept them politically viable. *Triumph* magazine, which was founded shortly after 1964 by Brent Bozell, Goldwater's chief speechwriter, deserves mention for keeping the Catholic element politically together because it maintained some thread of continuity between the Catholics who had been Goldwater supporters and current politics. The previously existing Young Republicans became a battleground and a training ground for some of the young people who had been galvanized by Goldwater. But the YRs, like the larger party, by and large did not meet the standards of conservatism that Goldwater had set. For sure, the Republican Party had no idea of what it had launched, and reacted to Goldwater's defeat by being tremendously embarrassed, rather than by helping launch a movement.

I said earlier that the Old Right tended to be intellectual and upper class. It is as accurate a generalization that the New Right tends to be middle class, blue-collar and ethnic in its origins. Eighteenth century British economic theory did not pertain very clearly to a German workingman's family in the 1950s. Though the upper classes had more intellectual expertise, they tended to become deficient in something that was strong in the working middle classes: values. In blue-collar areas, especially among the first and second generation ethnics, be they Russian Jews or German Catholics, tradition was as real a part of life as paying taxes, and old world culture as close to home. Well-bred, well-heeled youth allowed right and wrong to become blurred, and tradition to become a romantic decoration. Respect among working people was a consciously instilled value, the cornerstone of everything else—respect for father and mother and grandparents, for priest or rabbi, for the institutions of society: teachers, police, law, government. Respect engenders discipline, and hard work was the means to achieve desired goals.

In the 1960s there was among ethnic Catholics a rush of enthusiasm to share in the Kennedy liberalism. President Kennedy was a Catholic, a Democrat, and was therefore loved as an adopted "favorite son" by most ethnics. By the 1970s, though, we were seeing a large-scale end to this honeymoon, as the bitter fruit of liberalism became known: the fostering and propagating of policies and values that were increasingly destructive to society, policies which are anti-family, anti-religion, and devoid of respect for traditional values. Few of the leaders of today's New Right, despite their often "ethnic" backgrounds, were ever on the liberal bandwagon. This fact, I suspect, had to do with farsightedness, or perhaps with history properly studied. Many of the Catholic New Right activists have a further element in common: Their parents were often faithful listeners to the radio broadcasts through the 1930s and 40s of Father Charles Coughlin, the noted political commentator.

Thus, the blue-collar, middle class origins of the New Right help explain its philosophical motivations. The New Right differs from the Old in its value-orientation, which translates to the "social issues" in the current political jargon. The Old Right gives a primacy to laissez-faire economics. To be sure, we of the New Right believe strongly in free enterprise and individual initiative, and we oppose the expansion of government interference with individual lives. However, the New Right also believes that the individual as an individual does have personal responsibility to society and that each individual has intrinsic moral worth. The Old Right's "live and let live" idea is not reflective of Christian social teachings. A common assumption of New Right activists is that government should support certain moral truths.

Having experienced life in working class America, the New Right leadership realizes that people have come to expect certain things of their government, and that it is possible to give those things to the people without destroying the free enterprise system. Christian social doctrine teaches that, just as individuals have a certain responsibility to individuals, so does government. We reject the total indifference advocated by libertarians, just as we reject the extremes advocated by liberals. I would, for instance, want to see government—through churches and private institutions—ensure care for the helpless. I want to see government by law protect the helpless, be they unborn or senile, against the self-interest of others.

Culturally destructive government policies—racial hiring quotas and busing come to mind as examples—are to the New Right more immediately important in the realm of action, since the damage they can do is enormous and practically irremediable. Given a choice between focusing attention and effort on the defeat of a pork barrel public works bill, and focusing effort on the defeat of an abortion funding bill, the New Right would work to defeat the abortion bill.

Through New Right efforts the Hyde Amendment was successfully preserved through the 95th Congress, something which had not been possible in the 94th Congress when the measure had first been introduced. What caused the difference? This first New Right success was a combination of the distinguishing factors I have described previously between Old and New Right. First, we did not see ourselves as a defensive force in a crumbling society. We expected to win, and we developed a strategy to win.

I came to Washington in 1966, hoping to be a support staffer to a conservative leader. The Senator for whom I worked was a fine conservative of the Old Right school of strategy and tactics. What were the characteristics of that school?

First, there was an actual absence of strategic thinking, by which I mean large-scale manner, long-range planning. On small matters, tactics, there was some activity, but even that was very limited. Conservative Senators on Capitol Hill did not understand or believe in organization. In part, I think this was due to their rugged anti-collectivist philosophy; in part it was also probably due to the lack of a leader around whom they could organize. Their activities were totally reactive. They didn't take the initiative to go out and make an issue, and then let the liberals start talking about *their* issue. Of course, to do that sort of thing pretty much requires some supportive structures. The liberals had their Members of Congress for Peace through Law, their Institute for Policy Studies, their Brookings Institute, their Democratic Study Group. Conservatives had nothing comparable, and prior to the late 1960s did not even have their share of aggressive staff personnel, which the liberals had been acquiring for a decade.

In working with these Senators, I noticed a reluctance to carry matters to their logical conclusion, a personal reluctance to push a point to its last step, an unwillingness, figuratively speaking, to go for the jugular. Part of this was a reluctance to take risks. A lot of this reticence was due to the Old Right's enormous fear of the media. I'll talk more about that later, because I think it's very critical.

For all these reasons, the Old Right was not taken seriously as a political force in Washington. To some degree that was the result of a self-fulfilling prophecy, since these conservatives viewed themselves as the last, futile fingers in the dike of rampaging liberalism. I emphasize the word futile. They had resigned themselves to the inevitable defeat of their principles. They were intending to go down gracefully, preserving the status quo of the nation a little longer, prolonging the death agonies of the American republic, lessening the pain of disintegration of American society.

That was how they viewed themselves. I know that because I had conversations with them, and upon occasion tried to initiate some action, tried to get them to have a more positive approach to things. And I was not successful.

During the height of the anti-Vietnam activism, the Left was bringing up its issues, such as the various end-the-war amendments, time and time and time again. They were always defeated, but by smaller and smaller margins each time. Our people were able to observe the other side practicing this routine, but did not emulate it. Our Senators would bring their issue up for a vote. They would have marshaled their colleagues for a single loss, and that would be the end of it. Six months or a year or two years later if someone suggested, "Why don't we try this?" the decisive answer would be, "Oh no, we tried that a year ago and it didn't work." Period. End of discussion. Here is what I mean by a lack of strategy resulting from a sense of resignation to Fate.

Let me tell you an interesting story, of the one conservative victory our side had during this Old Right era. This was when we managed to stop President Lyndon Johnson from naming Abe Fortas as Chief Justice. It was actually a double victory, because if Fortas had become chief justice, LBJ had a liberal Texas judge lined up to appoint to the Supreme Court. As it turned out, Justice Douglas did not step down, so Fortas was not named Chief Justice. The irony is that this whole effort was engineered by Senator Robert Griffin of Michigan, a moderate. Republican, not a staunch conservative. Griffin had gotten 27 Senators to sign a pledge to oppose Fortas's nomination. When the going got tough, just before Johnson gave in under the pressure, a number of Old Right Senators wanted to cave in and give up fighting. It took Griffin to hold them in line. That's what I mean about not being willing to carry things to their logical conclusion. It reminds me of the old joke that the Republican Party is so good at snatching defeat from the jaws of victory. It was a case of that almost happening. (Of course, the Left got its revenge. When Richard Nixon was President, the embittered Senate refused to consent to the nominations of Carswell and Haynesworth in direct retaliation for the blockage of Fortas.)

I think a lot of the Old Right reluctance to engage in visible activity was motivated by a genuine fear of the media. These were people who had been burned, and burned badly, in the McCarthy era. As a result, they did everything in secret. If they had a regular meeting at the same time each week, and a reporter found out about it, they would cancel the meeting. We of the New Right have a far different attitude toward the media. We invite them to our meetings if they want to come. The Old Right Senators did not understand that you can get fair coverage if you handle the reporters fairly. The media want and need access to the newsmakers. They want to feel they can ask you about something. If a Senator is cold and unfriendly to a reporter, the reporter will know it, and is likely to reciprocate.

Also, I think the Old Right did not know how to do and say things in an interesting way. When I was a news reporter on the City Hall beat in Milwaukee, I didn't want to give coverage all the time to the liberals. But they were the ones who were holding press conferences, who were saying quotable things, who were voicing opinions that were newsworthy. So I had to cover them. The Old Right, whether intentionally or not I can't be sure, did not do things that were newsworthy. Of course, there was not much intrinsic news value to preserving the status quo. Innovation is always more interesting, which was a natural advantage for the Left. The Old Right did not understand anything at all about mass psychology, since they came from a different, pre-television era. It never did much good to try to persuade them to be dramatic, to think big. There was also a barrier to using technology. The New Right recognizes that technology, like the media, is morally neutral and exists to be taken advantage of by anybody. The Old Right seemed to have had the idea that because the Left had exploited the media they could not exploit it themselves without danger of moral corruption. It was a confusion of ideology with an application of technology.

The difference in coverage given the Old Right and the New Right is considerable. In quantity, first of all—media coverage of the Old Right was scarce as hen's teeth. We get a lot of it. For instance, on the day President Jimmy Carter announced he was selling out Taiwan, right away on the AP wire, left-wing Senator Alan Cranston had 500 words' worth of coverage, applauding this decisive move and so forth, as was only to be expected. But also . . . Representative Philip Crane had 500 words on AP! Equal coverage, you could say. That's evidence of progress. *The Washington Post* in its front page story mentioned the Committee for a Free China, the New Right organization long dedicated to preserving Taiwan's freedom. That's evidence of progress, too.

In 1978, the New Right set up a Truth Squad, aimed at exposing fallacies behind the Panama Canal Treaties. We held press conferences wherever we went, and welcomed inquiry from reporters on any subject. One of the questions that reporters will always ask is, "How are you funded?" Now, the Old Right, even assuming that they undertook or participated in such a venture as the Truth Squad, would have been defensive about that question, and responded with some remark amounting to "It's none of your business." This, naturally, would have been the beginning of a big story for some newsman. Not so with the Truth Squad. In the press kit which we routinely handed out was an enumeration of the organizations contributing financial support to this endeavor. Sure enough, at the very first press conference, that question came up. We were able to say, "Uh, fellas, it's in your press kit." So the question never came up again, in all the trips we made. Five years ago, that question would have been the beginning of a juicy story about right-wing finagling and secrecy. But since we engaged in no secrecy, there was no evasion, and hence no adverse publicity.

Another great advantage of the New Right derives, again, from another of the factors which distinguish our general outlook from that of the Old Right. We are not speaking abstractly of the decline of the West, but concretely about preserving values we know are revered by other middle class Americans.

I think the fact that the New Right does speak the language of the common man helps explain the facility with which we can get coverage when we want it. It is like the analogy of differences between the Roman Catholic and Orthodox theologians. Now, everyone can understand the question of whether you recognize the Pope or not. Things get much more subtle and hard to follow when you start getting into the significance of the epiclesis and *filioque*, and so forth. Ordinary folk can't understand these problems so readily. I'm afraid that conservatives have had more than their share of *filioques* in secular politics. It's a distinction the Left has long understood. For a long time, the measures to force oil companies into vertical and horizontal divestiture were being discussed at high levels, but were not generating much publicity. Then some sharp speechwriter coined the phrase "obscene profits," which Senator Henry Jackson began using. Immediately, that phrase gave a handle to the issue, which gave a boost to the clamor for divestiture. The oil companies cannot get over the impact that polemical phrase had on their life history.

New Right campaigns in 1979 used very emphatic language in establishing their issue positions. Senator Gordon Humphrey of

New Hampshire has been criticized for his "strident right-to-life rhetoric." Maybe it was strident, but it made the point. It was down to earth and simple, and that's what matters in getting the message across. After all, getting one's message across is the whole point of politics.

To me—and I think most other New Right leaders would share this perception—politics is activity in relation to power. To the extent that power in the American system resides in legislative bodies, politics focuses on the election of those legislators. Power is also vested in the executive, i.e., the President; hence the electoral fever every four years. Increasingly, however, power resides in the echelons of the Executive Branch which are not affected by a change of administrations. Both the Right and Left realize this. But only recently has the Right—and that which is generally characterized as the New Right—acted in a manner calculated to directly affect the bureaucratic power structure. "Who will draft IRS regulations?" is as portentous a question today as "Who will be President?" was a century ago. "Who controls the drafting?" is a question that may not even be answerable—regardless of the *de jure* reply.

The Constitution vests the Judiciary with power that was intended, at least to some extent, to be an arbiter of matters assigned to it by the Constitution. The New Right recognizes that the courts are far from immune to the currents of contemporary dispute. In fact, since the establishment of publicly funded legal services programs with a definite advocacy bias, the court process has become directly manipulated by power politics. Because of this advocacy element, the judicial process today is simply not what the Constitution envisioned. The appellate jurisdiction has given the courts a veto power that supersedes legislative will and even executive directions. The abortion decision in 1973 is an example of the courts making the law of the land rather than simply resolving disputes over it.

Power is located in other places today, and a realist recognizes that politics can not ignore the innovations of progress. The Constitution could not have anticipated the electronic media, or the power of the press. The Framers did not expect a national public education system, and certainly did not provide for the nationalized public education system sought by the Left. Yet those institutions have tremendous sway over the thoughts of the millions of citizens who ultimately cast the votes in the electoral aspect of the American political system. Late nineteenth century reformers recognized the power vested in the patronage systems of that era and moved to counter it. The New Right observes that potentially corrupting influence on the governing process is no less today because it comes from a government agency rather than from a Big Boss wardheeler. The control may be more respectable coming from a federal representative than from a ward politician, and he is certainly harder to unseat. But that influence is no less a distortion of constitutional and legislative intent.

When I, and others like Howard Phillips, Ed Feulner and Richard Dingman, came to Capitol Hill, we were looking for a Senator or Congressman to whom we could attach ourselves in a support capacity. We were looking, in other words, for leaders. But we quickly found that there were none. Goldwater had provided some leadership in the early 1960s as had Senator Strom Thurmond and a few others in isolated instances. But by the late 1960s there was no such leader. The Left, I believe, has had Congressional leadership consistently over the past two decades. Men like Senators Birch Bayh and Wayne Morse were politically substantive individuals in and of themselves. To be sure, they had good staff, but the staff could hitch themselves to left-wing stars because they were already there, and doing much of the orchestrating themselves.

Conservatives, by the 1970s, were on the way to forming the organizations necessary to launch and keep afloat a political movement. The Left had the Democratic Study Group in the House of Representatives, an ultra-liberal, member-formed backup operation for left-wing issues, dedicated to cranking out research, thinking up strategy, writing speeches, doing footwork, causing things to happen for the Left in general. There was no comparable conservative operation at all until 1973. Until 1970, conservative members of Congress barely met with each other at all to talk politics and strategy. When Representative Floyd Spence came to Congress on January 1, 1971, he initiated formal meetings among conservative members. By 1973, the Republican Study Committee had been formed; by 1974 the Senate Steering Committee, a comparable body on the Senate side, was in operation.

Once there was a coordinated conservative effort on the Hill, we became sharply aware of how little organized effort there was to help elect specifically conservative Senators and Representatives. So the political action groups began to be formed, the Committee for the Survival of a Free Congress in 1974, the National Conservative Political Action Committee in 1975, and others thereafter. Historically, thus, the New Right started on Capitol Hill. No longer is the Hill the core of New Right operations, however. In further emulation of the Left, we had to begin our own think tanks, our own public interest legal operations, our own grassroots organizations, and even our own lobbying efforts. Common cause is made with "like-minded single-interest groups" whenever possible. The right-to-life issue has what one unsympathetic reporter described as a "symbiotic relationship" with the New Right. Whether they want to or not, right-to-lifers find they have to work with New Right activists, simply because nobody else cares about protecting the unborn.

The right-to-work cause is one which frequently comes into the coalition. Most of our fathers belonged to unions. We are anti-big business. The problem is that big unions turned into part of the problem. The New Right does not believe that unions *per se* are evil, as did the economic purist conservatives of the 1930s; we do not want to abolish unions. We merely recognize that today's big union leadership is unrepresentative of union membership, and, worse, uncaring of membership's concerns. We see that the big union bosses abuse members' hard-earned contributions. When people do not want to be forced to join a union, where else can they turn for help but the National Right to Work Committee? Further, the Right to Work Committee also supports pro-free enterprise measures, and opposes further power grabs by regulatory agencies and big labor.

As circumstances dictate, the single-interest groups organized around anti-busing, tax resistance, defense issues, parents' rights, private school survival, energy selfsufficiency, and other major problems find they are able to make common cause with the New Right, because the New Right is a political force which shares their concerns on these issues. There is nothing underhanded, nothing conspiratorial, nothing sinister about this: It is simply the exercise of practical politics, as predicted by Hamilton, Jay, and Madison in *The Federalist Papers*.

One very interesting and promising development is the broadening of the New Right appeal from strictly Republican lines. In their resigned defeatist attitude, the Old Right had totally written off whole chunks of American life: the Democratic Party, labor unions, most churches, and for that matter, most of the working class. The New Right realizes that the participation of all these groups is necessary to forge a coalition for victory. Conservative influence in the Democratic Party is increasing steadily—some of it planned, some not. The Committee for the Survival of A Free Congress, for example, offered a workshop for conservative Democrats at the 1976 Democratic Convention. We had a major role also in the election of conservative Democrat Kent Hance (Texas 19th), and thus in the defeat of liberal, establishment Republican George Bush, Jr. That Edward King could be elected Democratic Governor of Massachusetts in 1978, being the genuine social-issues conservative that he is, is a tribute to the accomplishments of the New Right coalition. Many of his workers, for example, were trained by the right-to-life movement and his election demonstrated the effect of the working class anti-busing movement at the polls. But more than that, Ed King's election is indicative of a new and promising trend in the electorate. The populace is turning away from worn out liberal appeals, looking to the conservative answer.

At the start of the 1980s, it can be said that the New Right has managed to establish the institutions necessary to have impact on the entirety of the political process. We have within our grasp the mechanisms needed to achieve our goal. That goal is not merely to oppose, but to govern. Unlike the Old Right, which saw as its destiny the supervising of the dissolution of the American nation, we see as our goal a new direction for the American republic. We believe we can achieve this goal, provided the Left does not put us out of business before another few years have passed. (That is no idle possibility: Federal financing of House and Senate campaigns would be a major step in that direction. The elimination of single-issue interest groups, a high priority of the Left in the 96th Congress, would be a *coup de grâce* to the New Right coalition.)

If we, or others of our philosophy, had done ten years ago what we are doing now, the situation for the nation as a whole would have been much better. In so many ways, America is limited now, and will be for a long time to come. Militarily, we are weak; we are energy-dependent; our foreign policy is under many constraints. In the last ten years, the years in which conservatism skipped a generation, we have lost so much time that when the New Right does come to power, as I and my co-workers believe it will, things will be much limited by circumstances beyond our control. The Panama Canal has been given away, Taiwan is gone, the Middle East is going.

Despite all this, I am not despondent. It is basic to my philosophy that God's truth ought to be manifest politically. Collectivism, which is what the Left is ultimately advocating in a thousand guises, is an error. The New Right coalition is the only organized substantial effort opposing and speaking truth to its power. I believe with truth on our side we have great cause for hope.

Sociology of Religion 1994, 55:3 243-261

Premillennialists at the Millennium: Some Reflections on the Christian Right in the Twenty-first Century

Clyde Wilcox

Georgetown University

Although the fundamentalist Right of the 1980s floundered on religious particularism, the Christian Coalition has sought to build bridges to Catholics, African Americans, and others. State-level organizations have recruited some politically extreme candidates for local offices, while the national organization has endorsed moderate, even moderately feminist Republicans. The organization now seems to face a major crossroads, and must decide whether to pursue moderate Republican politics, to remain a faction within the Republican party, or to try to build coalitions with morally conservative Americans who lean toward the Democratic party on nonpartisan issues.

Margaret Atwood's mid-1980s novel *The Handmaid's Tale* imagined a future world in which the Christian Right had triumphed and women were reduced to total subservience. Doctors who had performed abortions before the ascendancy of the Christian Right were executed, and women were taught that rape survivors deserved their fate because they had enticed the man.[1] Although many of the book's reviewers suggested that such an ultimate victory by the Christian Right would be extremely unlikely, others were not so sure. Some noted predictions by Marion (Pat) Robertson that conservative Christians would run America by the year 2000. Indeed, in their fundraising letters both Christian Right leaders and leaders of groups that opposed the Christian Right predicted substantial successes in the future for the Christian Right.[2]

Of course, social scientists have also at times predicted success for the Christian Right. Some sociologists predicted in early 1988 that Robertson would

---

[1] Atwood was not the only writer to imagine an America ruled by the Christian Right. Elgin (1984) imagined that Christian conservatives enforced traditional sex roles after contact with aliens. Other writers depict Christian Right control of portions of the United States (Tepper 1988), or a future incarnation of the Christian Right contending for control (Brin 1989). Still other authors (e.g., Hogan 1991) depict alien equivalents of the Christian Right. (For an overview of the role of religion in science fiction, see Reilly 1985; Bishop 1994.)

[2] Recent direct mail solicitations from People For the American Way and Americans United for Separation of Church and State have suggested that the Christian Coalition is a juggernaut that can be stopped now only with some difficulty.

151

win the Republican presidential nomination. In fact, Robertson spent the largest sum in American history in pursuit of the nomination and failed to win a single primary election.[3] His campaign ultimately sent only 35 pledged delegates into the convention — the second worst dollars-to-delegates ratio since the United States began collecting good data on campaign spending in 1976. Predictions of a Robertson victory seem impossible with hindsight, but the improbable frequently occurs in politics. Las Vegas set the odds against George McGovern's bid for the Democratic nomination in 1972 at 1000:1, and Jimmy Carter's staff thought that Ronald Reagan would be the easiest Republican to beat in 1980. Predicting the political future is an enterprise that is fraught with uncertainty.

The uncertainty inherent in predicting the future of the Christian Right is evident from a quick review of the status of the Christian Right a few months after the most recent presidential elections. In early 1981, Jerry Falwell was a frequent face on television, claiming that his Moral Majority had helped deliver the 1980 presidential election to Ronald Reagan. In 1985, Falwell ranked in most surveys as one of the most unpopular men in America, and although he and other Christian Right figures had been highly visible at the Republican convention, most of the Christian Right portion of the 1980 party platform remained unfulfilled. In 1989, Falwell was disbanding a bankrupt Moral Majority, and Robertson was attempting to revitalize his 700 Club after his drubbing in the Republican primaries. After the 1992 election, the conventional wisdom was that the visible presence of the Christian Right at the Republican convention and the strong pro-life plank in the Republican platform cost the Republicans votes (for a conflicting view, see Green 1993). Yet, Falwell is considering reassembling the Moral Majority (Balmer 1992), and Robertson's Christian Coalition is vigorously contesting school board, county commission, and internal Republican elections, and actively supporting candidates for the United States Senate and for governorships in a number of states. At each turn in its fortunes, the Christian Right has defied those who predicted its triumph or its demise.

This essay will ignore the danger inherent in such predictions, and speculate on the future of the Christian Right into the twenty-first century. The first section will provide a brief history of the Christian Right in the twentieth century. The second will focus on explanations for the ultimate failure of the Christian Right in the 1980s, and the third will consider how the Christian Coalition is currently avoiding many of the problems that plagued the Moral Majority, but some of the dilemmas the Christian Coalition faces nonetheless. The final section will provide some thoughts on the future of the Christian Right.

THE CHRISTIAN RIGHT IN THE TWENTIETH CENTURY

Three times in the twentieth century — in the 1920s, the 1950s, and the 1980s — organized groups claiming to represent fundamentalist Christians have

---

[3] Robertson won several party caucuses, where organized efforts to bring supporters to the balloting are crucial. In these low-turnout elections, Robertson's organized pentecostals swamped the less intense but far more numerous supporters of Bush and Dole. Robertson won in states as diverse as Hawaii and Washington, and probably won the initial balloting in Michigan as well.

formed and been active in the interstitial zone between religion and politics. In the 1920s, groups such as the Flying Fundamentalists lobbied state legislatures to ban the teaching of evolution and eventually agitated against communism. In the 1950s, organizations like the Christian Anti-Communism Crusade preached the perils of international and domestic communism, and lobbied against the teaching of sex education in public schools. In the 1980s, the Moral Majority and Christian Voice focused on the dangers of secular humanism in the classroom and advocated a strong military to fend off the threat of international communism.

Although these three waves of fundamentalist Christian Right activity differed in important ways (Wilcox 1992), there are also important similarities.[4] Resource mobilization theorists have emphasized the importance of sympathetic organizations in providing resources for group formation (McCarthy and Zald 1977). All three sets of fundamentalist groups were started with resources provided by fundamentalist churches. Most of the organizations of the 1920s received financial and organizational support from the World's Christian Fundamentals Association, an organization formed out of the battles between fundamentalists and moderates for control of the Protestant denominations. The anticommunist groups of the 1950s were aided by the American Council of Christian Churches, a fundamentalist group formed in the 1940s. The Moral Majority benefited from the resources of Falwell's electronic ministry and from the organizational apparatus of the Baptist Bible Fellowship. The Moral Majority and Christian Voice also benefitted from resources supplied by the secular right in an effort to mobilize evangelicals into Republican politics (Guth 1983).

Second, all three movements of the fundamentalist right stressed a combined message of educational fundamentals and anticommunism. Although the Moral Majority and the Christian Voice both had wide policy agendas, activists in the Moral Majority in Ohio were most concerned with education, and most of the organization's leadership were more committed to their state Christian schools organizations than to the Moral Majority. Anticommunism was a theme in all three waves of fundamentalist groups as well. The Ohio Moral Majority was formed after a national organizer showed a film about Soviet military power.

In the latter half of the 1980s, Pat Robertson began preparing for his presidential campaign. Where the Moral Majority was based in fundamentalist Baptist churches, Robertson's support was centered among pentecostal and charismatic Christians. Robertson raised more money than any presidential nomination candidate in history and had far more contributors than any other candidate (Brown et al. 1994). After the 1988 election, the Moral Majority ceased operation, and Robertson went back to his 700 Club television station. Robertson formed the Christian Coalition, which began to build grassroots organizations across the country.

---

[4] Some have questioned my claim that there is some continuity between the various waves of fundamentalist Christian Right activity in the twentieth century. Falwell himself, however, notes the continuity between the Moral Majority and the organizations of the 1920s, which he cites as sources of inspiration.

That the Christian Right was active in the 1920s, the 1950s, and the 1980s would seem to suggest a cyclical theory of Christian Right mobilization. Ted Jelen (1991) has suggested just such a theory. He argues that religious belief remains privatized during most periods but spills over into politics whenever it becomes obvious that social groups disliked by orthodox Christians (e.g., feminists, homosexuals) become vocal and visible. These groups become more active in national politics and make gains during these quiet periods of religious privatization, which spurs organizational activity by the Christian Right. Religious activism leads to particularism as denominational differences become politicized, which leads the potential Christian Right to splinter and eventually to retreat into privatization — hence a regular cycle of activity.

It is important to note that fundamentalist Christians were not passively waiting for the second coming between the various waves of organized activity. After the anticommunist groups faded in the mid-1960s, for example, fundamentalists and pentecostals continued to build churches, to establish the televangelist ministries that enabled Christian Right leaders to reach potential followers and to establish bookstores that carried political books, newsletters, and magazines.

WHY DID THE CHRISTIAN RIGHT OF THE 1980s FAIL?

Although it raised millions of dollars and received enormous amounts of media attention, the Christian Right of the 1980s cannot be deemed a success (see also Fowler 1993). Its principal agenda remained unfulfilled after twelve years of Republican rule. Although a more conservative Supreme Court has allowed states to impose some procedural regulations on abortion and has been more supportive of public displays of Christian symbols, Reagan was more interested in enacting the agenda of the financial and foreign policy conservatives than those of the Christian Right. The few pro-life policies that he enacted by executive order were reversed by Clinton within days of his inauguration.

In 1994 abortion remains legal, and public schools cannot legally begin their days with public prayer. Homosexual groups continue to make slow, halting progress toward easing societal discrimination. Women's groups claimed victory in the "Year of the Woman" in 1992, with the election of a number of new, feminist Democratic women to Congress (Cook et al. 1994).

Despite this unfulfilled agenda, the organizations of the 1980s have generally disbanded or receded into obscurity. After eight years of Reagan's presidency, the Moral Majority went bankrupt. The Christian Voice was forced to discontinue its Political Action Committee and rely on financing by private organizations with vastly different religious views. Robertson lost badly to moderate Episcopalian George Bush even in Southern, largely evangelical states in which he outspent Bush 3:1, and then retreated from actively seeking elected office.

Why did the Christian Right fail? Why did it appear to rise rapidly in the early 1980s, only to disband in defeat? The answer has more to do with political institutions than with broad social forces. Mass support for the Christian Right did not surge and decline: data from the National Election Studies in 1980, 1984, and 1988 showed a relatively constant 11-15 percent of whites supported the Christian Right throughout this period.[5] There is no evidence that the public dramatically changed its mind on social issues such as abortion during this period (Cook *et al.* 1992). Press attention did surge and decline, but this reflects the importance of novelty in news stories, not changing popular support.

If support remained constant, then why did the national organizations of the Christian Right disband? The Moral Majority folded its tent because it was no longer profitable to raise money through direct mail. The organization was funded almost entirely by small donations raised by mail solicitations. While I was on the Moral Majority mailing list, I was solicited for contributions every two weeks.[6] In 1984, the organization raised $11.1 million through the mail, but by 1988 that figure had declined to $3 million.

The Moral Majority's direct mail revenues declined sharply for three reasons. First, the continued success of Republican presidential candidates made it difficult to convince the organization's contributors that their money was needed to save America. Direct mail relies on the marketing of fear (Godwin 1988). When Reagan ran in 1984 on a campaign that is was "Morning in America," this seemed to negate any urgency in the mail solicitations of the Christian Right.

Second, the market for conservative mail was becoming saturated. One conservative direct mail professional told me that "every group on the Right rented every list and prospected them. Donors were deluged with solicitations." Falwell had to compete with other, specialized groups like Focus on the Family, Concerned Women of America, and various pro-life groups, as well as anticommunist organizations. When solicitations reach a certain critical level, the direct mail professional suggested, then *all* the mail ends up in the garbage.

Finally, 1988 was a very bad year for televangelists. Jim Bakker was defrocked by the Assemblies of God because of homosexual and extramarital heterosexual behavior, Jimmy Swaggert was caught in the company of a prostitute, and Oral Roberts told his supporters that God was holding him hostage, demanding a ransom or he would be called home. Robertson was forced to settle a libel suit out of court regarding his father's influence keeping him out of military action in Korea, and it was revealed that his official biographies had doctored the date of his marriage to conceal the fact that his wife was *very* pregnant when they were finally married. Such revelations made it difficult for televangelists to raise money for their favorite political causes.

If the Moral Majority went bankrupt because its direct mail operation failed, why were they so dependent on mail? The organization initially had attempted

---

[5] The NES data do not have optimal items to measure support for the Christian Right, but they are adequate. I have defined supporters as those who rate the Moral Majority or Pat Robertson at least 10° more warmly than they rate all societal groups on average. This is a fairly liberal definition, which probably overstates actual support.

[6] My unsystematic observation is that the Moral Majority solicitations went in cycles. I made three small contributions to say on the mailing list. After each gift, the first set of letters were on homosexual rights, then education, then abortion, then feminism. Letters on defense spending and on cultural politics followed. Finally the direct mail experts apparently decided that I was a misguided liberal, and sent a letter showing Falwell with starving children in Haiti, suggesting that the Moral Majority was an organization to feed the children of the developing world.

to build grassroots organizations, first by forming state chapters and then by organizing them at the county level (Liebman 1983). A few state organizations did flourish for a time in disparate states such as Indiana, Georgia, and Alaska, but the grassroots efforts of the Moral Majority were ultimately unsuccessful.[7] The same factors that enabled the Moral Majority to establish state chapters quickly ultimately limited their success.

With only a few exceptions, the Moral Majority built its state and county organizations around pastors of the Baptist Bible Fellowship. Fellowship preachers are religious entrepreneurs, who start their own churches in their homes, eventually rent a larger space, and finally build their church. Falwell himself is one of the success stories of this type of effort, for his Thomas Road Baptist Church is one of the largest in the denomination. These entrepreneurs are also active in forming Christian schools, and were willing to form state and county Moral Majority chapters.

Yet this ready network of leaders proved unable to sustain local chapters, for two main reasons. First, their efforts were spread between their pastoral duties, building their churches, building their religious schools, and the Moral Majority. Inevitably, the Moral Majority was the least important priority. Perhaps more important, Baptist Bible Fellowship pastors are an intolerant lot. At one sermon before an organizational meeting of the Ohio Moral Majority, the preacher railed against Catholics, Methodists, pentecostals, evangelicals, and even other Baptist denominations. One Moral Majority candidate survey in a midwestern state asked candidates whether they were certain that they would go to heaven if they died that night. The follow-up question asked whether their salvation was assured by works, by faith, or by other means. Such doctrinal divisions made forging broader political coalitions difficult.

Not surprisingly, my survey of the Moral Majority membership in Ohio did not turn up many Catholic members. Indeed, more than half of the membership were members of the Baptist Bible Fellowship, a small denomination on which to build a grassroots organization. Georgianna (1989) reported that the membership of the somewhat larger Indiana Moral Majority was even more heavily concentrated among the Baptist Bible Fellowship: fully 75 percent were members of this denomination. Georgianna found no Catholic members of the Indiana Moral Majority.

In my study of the Ohio Moral Majority, I interviewed the only three county chairmen who held regular meetings at length, and discussed the membership of their county organizations. Two were members of the Baptist Bible Fellowship, and their county organizations were comprised entirely of members of that denomination. The third county chairman was a Methodist minister; his organization had the only Catholics in the entire state organization and had members in several other Protestant denominations. Yet he was unable to mobilize the membership of the Baptist Bible Fellowship churches in his county, for the Baptists did not want to mingle with Catholics and pentecostals.

---

[7] Christian Voice also formed state and county chapters, some of which survive today.

Ultimately the Moral Majority failed not because of shifting public sentiments or broad historical trends. Their grassroots efforts failed because of the intolerance and distractions of the Baptist Bible Fellowship preachers, and their direct mail fundraising failed because of political conditions and market saturation. Their potential support remained constant, suggesting that in a different political climate a profitable mail operation might resume. Indeed, Falwell's temptation to resume the Moral Majority presumably centers on the profitability of antihomosexual mail in 1993.

The failure of Robertson's presidential bid was unambiguous, yet even as he lost badly in party primaries, his supporters worked behind the scenes to seize control of state party delegations and committees. Although only 35 delegates were pledged to support him on the first ballot, he clearly had more supporters at the convention. That Robertson was forced to leave politics after this defeat is a function of American political institutions. The most obvious contrast is the state of Israel, where several minority religious parties continue to hold seats in the Knesset because of proportional representation. Robertson's vote share would doubtlessly have won him a few seats in a parliamentary system, where he would head a small religious party whose significance would depend entirely on whether its votes were needed to form a government.

Although I have argued that the Christian Right of the 1980s failed to achieve its policy goals, on one level they were part of a larger success story. The secular New Right and the Republican party lent resources to help form Christian Right groups in order to facilitate the political conversion of white, evangelical Christians to Republican politics. In 1988 and again in 1992, George Bush received a substantial majority of white evangelical votes. Although his share of the evangelical vote fell to 60 percent in 1992, this was far higher than his overall 38 percent, and was remarkable for a moderate Episcopalian running against a ticket of two Southern Baptists.

My reading of the data suggests that the Christian Right did help marginally in this minirealignment, although political issues such as abortion, defense spending, feminism, and gay rights probably would have moved many evangelicals toward the Republicans even without the formation of Christian Right organizations. The available evidence suggests that the Moral Majority appealed primarily to long-time Republican activists. The Ohio chapter of the Moral Majority had very few Democrats, and most of the people I interviewed had been Republicans all their lives.

There is some evidence that the Christian Right may also have moved some votes *away* from the Republicans. Pollsters during the 1992 presidential elections noted a growing number of formerly Republican suburban women who now identified as Democrats. Although Green (1993) has concluded that social conservatism and abortion helped Bush in 1992, my own analysis suggests a different conclusion. When those voters who were ambivalent toward both Bush and Clinton are considered, the net effect of abortion and other social issues in the

1992 election was to cost Bush approximately 2 percent of the vote.[8] As Rich Bond, former chairman of the Republican party, notes, "the Christian Right was the straw that broke the camel's back for many Republican suburban voters" (personal communication). Abramowitz (1993) also found that the abortion issue hurt Bush among pro-choice Republicans and independents, while pro-life Democrats were less likely to be aware of the candidate positions on abortion and were therefore less likely to cross party lines and vote for Bush.

My survey of contributors to the Robertson and other presidential candidates, however, suggested that the activists who contributed to the Robertson campaign included a number of more recent Republican converts (Brown et al. 1994). Approximately one in three had voted for Carter in 1976, compared with approximately 10 percent of those who gave to other Republican candidates. These activists were relatively new to political contributions. Robertson's campaign also attracted some support among Southern Democrats (Wilcox 1992). This suggests that Robertson may have brought at least a few Democrats into Republican politics.

THE CHRISTIAN RIGHT IN THE 1990s: GRASSROOTS ACTIVISM AND DILEMMAS

During the 1990s, the Christian Right has to date focused on building grassroots organizations. Several large national organizations have attempted to build state and local organizations, and have generally sought to avoid the organizational mistakes of the Moral Majority. Many, such as Focus on the Family, have strength in some states or regions but not in others. Among the grassroots oriented Christian Right organizations of the 1990s, the one that has attracted the most media attention has been the Christian Coalition, which is associated with Pat Robertson.

As I finished my book (1992) on the Christian Right in the summer of 1990, I argued that the charismatic Right of Pat Robertson had a far greater potential to build a unified Christian Right than had the fundamentalists of the Moral Majority. Where the Moral Majority impaled itself on its own religious particularism, Robertson was openly ecumenical. Harrell (1988:102-3) quotes Robertson:

> In terms of the succession of the church, I'm a Roman Catholic. As far as the majesty of worship, I'm an Episcopalian; as far as the belief in the sovereignty of God, I'm a Presbyterian; in terms of holiness, I'm a Methodist; in terms of the priesthood of believers and baptism, I'm a Baptist; in terms of the baptism of the Holy Spirit, I'm a Pentecostal. So I'm a little bit of all of them.

---

[8] Abramowitz and Green both focused on those voters who listed abortion and other social issues as among the most salient in their votes or who mentioned them as important. Yet a different set of voters may have been torn between, for example, Bush's weak domestic presidency and Clinton's lack of foreign policy experience. For these voters, social issues may have been the tie breaker, yet not mentioned as salient.

In addition, I argued that Robertson had the potential to appeal to blacks. Although my survey of African Americans in the District of Columbia showed surprising support for Robertson, I doubt if many blacks would have crossed party lines to support Robertson against a Democratic candidate.[9] Moreover, support for Robertson was highest among those who knew least about him, suggesting that as the campaign progressed and information about Robertson's conservative positions on a number of issues became more widely available, black support would have declined.

Yet Robertson made an explicit appeal for black support. He launched his campaign in an African-American inner-city community, featured blacks in his advertising, backed a black Republican candidate for the Virginia Senate nomination, and mentioned blacks in his political rhetoric (Hertzke 1992). Indeed, Robertson paid more attention to the needs and concerns of blacks than any other Republican candidate in 1988, with the possible exception of Jack Kemp.

The potential for Robertson to appeal to members of various races and Christian denominations suggests that his Christian Coalition might be able to build a truly grassroots network. The Christian Coalition has avoided the mistake of the Moral Majority of building within an established denomination, instead attracting more secular activists in an attempt to build a truly ecumenical organization. The leadership of the Christian Coalition has already showed substantial political skill, and the group may be a far more formidable organization than earlier incarnations of the Christian Right.

The Christian Coalition claims a membership of 350,000 with 750 local chapters. The organization has lobbyists in several states and in Washington, and a budget of $8-10 million. Its director, Ralph Reed, is perhaps the most politically skilled of all Christian Right strategists (Sullivan 1993). Reed is a frequent guest on television talk shows, where he routinely makes free exercise claims for the Christian Right and compares the mobilization of evangelicals through the Christian Right to the mobilization of blacks through black churches in the 1960s.

The organization's motto is "Think like Jesus . . . Fight like David . . . Lead like Moses . . . Run like Lincoln." Yet the Coalition's candidates have not quite followed Lincoln's lead, for some have run as "stealth" candidates who do not divulge their connections with the Christian Coalition until after the election. *Harpers* magazine (1993) reprinted portions of a 57-page organizational manual for the Christian Coalition distributed in Pennsylvania, which the magazine claimed contained the following advice: "You should never mention the name 'Christian Coalition' in Republican circles."

The Christian Coalition has pursued a three-pronged strategy. First, state and local activists have attempted to wrest control of local and state Republican party organizations by winning precinct and county positions, by packing party caucuses, and by attempting to elect a majority to the state committees. Second, the Christian Coalition has been active in partisan elections. It has recruited

---

[9] Mark Nuttle, campaign manager for Robertson, claimed that Robertson would win 25-30 percent of the black vote in a general election (see Hertzke 1992:146).

and supported candidates especially for county and city councils, but it has also been quite active in supporting candidates for higher office. Finally, the Coalition has attempted to win control of nonpartisan school boards. The three efforts attract different sets of activists, and quite different coalitions. The organization faces a dilemma in choosing among these three strategies, for it seems unlikely that it can successfully pursue all three.

THE CHRISTIAN COALITION IN THE REPUBLICAN PARTY

Within the Republican party, the Christian Coalition built on the precinct, county, and state party organizations that Robertson's followers controlled following the 1988 convention. Christian Coalition activists have controlled at various points Republican organizations in several states, but that control has been fleeting. In Washington, the Christian Coalition together with other local Christian Right groups won control of the party, and put together a platform that focused on witchcraft and New Age religion. The party lost badly in the 1992 general elections. In late 1992, the Christian Coalition and the Oregon Citizen's Alliance narrowly missed electing the state party chairman in Oregon in a highly emotional contest; Christian Right candidates won in other important state party slots (Egan 1992; Sullivan 1993). In Houston, two parallel party committees functioned in early 1993, one dominated by the Christian Right, the other by party moderates.

In these states and others, the Christian Coalition has forged alliances with other Christian Right groups, often locally or state based. It is unclear how much of the effort to seize state and local party organizations comes from the national Christian Coalition, but it appears at this point that most of these efforts have been the inspiration of local and state activists. The model is that of an issue insurgency in a political party, similar to that of the antiwar and feminist movements in the Democratic party in 1972.

Yet in Michigan and Georgia, the party regulars regained control but worked in coalition with the Christian Coalition. That the relationship between the Christian Right and party moderates is cooperative in some states but conflictual in others may be a function of the personalities involved, or it may be part of a more systematic pattern. In states where the relationship has been more conflictual, Christian Coalition activists have appeared to take more extreme positions and to be centered on divisive issues such as homosexual rights.[10]

The long-run prospects of a Christian Right takeover of the Republican party seem dim. The successes to date have occurred while the party regulars have been distracted. Relatively low turnout precinct, county, and other party caucuses and elections are easily dominated by groups that successfully mobilize their supporters, and when the Christian Right has run "stealth candidates," the party moderates have not been mobilized to participate. When the stakes are ob-

---

[10] One Christian Coalition activist who now heads a county Republican organization in Iowa is pushing the state committee to endorse capital punishment for homosexuals, which is not an official Christian Coalition position.

vious, however, as in the contest for head of the Oregon state party organization, the moderates do participate in force.

Moreover, the party mainstream is remarkably hostile to the Christian Right. In my survey of Republican contributors, fully one in six contributors to candidates other than Robertson rated him at 0°, the lowest possible score on a 100 point feeling thermometer. Nearly one in three rated Robertson more coolly than Dukakis, and one in four rated him below Jesse Jackson (Wilcox 1992).[11] Republican moderates have formed political organizations especially designed to fight the Christian Right for control of the party (Apple 1992).

A survey of Republican voters in January, 1993 showed a party electorate that is not supportive of Christian Right figures or goals (Fabrizio 1993). Only 2 percent of those surveyed named Pat Robertson as their choice for the 1996 nomination — a figure far behind other candidates from the 1988 field. Robertson had lower favorable ratings than did Democratic president Bill Clinton, and nearly 40 percent of Republican voters expressed unfavorable views of Robertson, higher than any other Republican in the survey.

This lack of support for Robertson himself was also echoed in the issue stance of Republican voters. Only 12 percent indicated that they were attracted to the party by its moral conservatism, and only 6 percent mentioned social issues as the most salient. Few candidates mentioned abortion or gay rights in any of their responses, and of those who did, three times as many were bothered by the party's pro-life, antihomosexual stance than supported it. Many more Republican voters supported an absolute right to choose on abortion than supported the 1980-1992 platform stance that abortion should be banned with the possible exception of saving the life of the mother.

All of this suggests that the Christian Right has little chance of gaining control of the national Republican party. They can, however, be useful coalition partners in electing Republic candidates. The Christian Coalition has engaged in this second sort of electoral activity — recruiting, endorsing, and working for candidates.

CANDIDATE SUPPORT

The Christian Coalition has recruited and supported candidates across the country for state legislative races, for county commissions, and for city councils. The activists recruited by state and local Christian Coalition groups have frequently taken quite extreme issue positions and have generally run without acknowledging their ties with the Christian Coalition. There has been no effort to catalog the successes of the Christian Coalition at this level by journalists or academics, although Morken (1993) has described the process and justification in some detail.

The Christian Coalition has been much more pragmatic in national politics, especially in Senate elections after November, 1992. Following Clinton's vic-

---

[11] The Robertson contributors, in contrast, were quite warm to other Republican candidates, including Kemp and Bush.

tory, the Coalition was very active in the Georgia Senate runoff election supporting moderate Republican Paul Coverdale against the incumbent liberal Democrat. In Texas in 1993, the Christian Coalition worked actively on behalf of Kay Bailey Hutchison, despite her moderate feminism. Hutchison received money from pro-choice groups, and favored a basic right to choose, although she also supported some state restrictions such as waiting periods and parental notification. In these low-turnout elections, the Christian Coalition endorsed the Republican candidate and attempted to mobilize supporters, but it is difficult to gauge the role of the Christian Right in these elections. Coverdale won narrowly, and probably benefitted from concerted efforts by the Christian Coalition and the right-to-life movement, but Hutchison won easily and would presumably have done so even had the Christian Coalition bypassed the election.

When the Christian Coalition works in conjunction with other Christian Right groups, they can help to forge a broader coalition. In Virginia, the Christian Coalition helped Mike Farris win the Republican nomination for Lieutenant Governor in 1993. Farris's strongest support came from Christian home-school advocates, many of whom were strong fundamentalists who could not support Robertson. Yet an interview with one of Farris's home-school supporters suggested the potential for a flexible coalition involving the Christian Coalition. One Farris delegate indicated that he could never contribute to the Christian Coalition because he disapproved of Robertson's theology, but he could support Christian Coalition political candidates, including charismatic candidates.

The Christian Coalition promised to mobilize in force behind Farris in the November general election, but in fact spent most of their political capital on behalf of the candidacy of George Allen for governor. Allen won easily, although he trailed badly early in the campaign, while Farris lost a surprisingly close election. Christian Right activists in Northern Virginia were generally critical of the role of the Christian Coalition in the campaign, arguing that they claimed credit for Allen's victory without investing many resources to help Farris.

The electoral support that the Christian Right can provide to candidates in party primaries is potentially substantial. Should the Christian Coalition endorse a secular conservative for the 1996 nomination (e.g., Kemp), they could greatly help his or her candidacy in caucus states where turnout is a premium. Yet it is unclear just how far leaders such as Robertson can go in delivering the votes of his supporters to other candidates. Robertson endorsed Bush with public enthusiasm in the 1992 election, yet only 29 percent of Robertson's 1988 contributors gave money to Bush, and fully 22 percent gave to Bush's intraparty opponent Patrick Buchanan.

In electoral politics, then, the Christian Coalition has shown evidence of principled extremism in supporting candidates with little chance of winning but who take issue positions consistent with the organization platform. In other instances, however, the Christian Coalition has shown itself capable of pragmatic accommodation with Republican moderates by supporting candidates whose positions are quite divergent from Christian Coalition policy against more liberal Democrats.

The activity of the Christian Coalition in recruiting and endorsing candidates poses an interesting dilemma for the organization. Its local activists would generally prefer to nominate candidates with relatively extreme views who would hold the line on the core issues of abortion, gay rights, and school textbooks. Its national coalition partners within the Republican party are pushing the organization to moderate its positions on abortion and gay rights, and to attempt to farm traditional Republican fiscal conservatism to its members.

The national organization appears to be adopting the second strategy. During 1993, Reed attempted to focus attention on the Clinton economic package and taxes, and to downplay social issues. Robertson and later Reed have also publicly moderated their positions on abortion. Robertson has announced that he will henceforth attempt to discourage women from having abortions, rather than attempting to mobilize the role of the state to ban them. In a paper presented at a conference in late 1993, Reed wrote that Christian conservatives want a reversal of *Roe v. Wade* and a return of abortion to state governments. Reed was quite critical of *Roe*, but a policy of states rights on abortion would allow some states to codify a basic abortion right, as many have already.

The pull between moderation and broader coalitions on the one hand, and a firm position on the core social issues and narrower coalitions on the other, is one that the Christian Coalition will need to resolve in the near future. The core activists that I have interviewed and surveyed are all strongly conservative on both social and economic issues, but social issues are far more salient. One publication by the Christian Coalition in the summer of 1993 included articles that mostly focused on economic issues and letters from members that focused mostly on gays in the military. Moreover, the broader evangelical constituency that the Christian Coalition may hope to mobilize is far more moderate on economic issues, and the blacks and Catholics that they seek to include in their broader coalition are somewhat liberal on these issues.

The activists may not need persuading to adopt conservative positions on economic issues, therefore, but the larger potential constituency may be turned off by this focus. Moreover, the activists themselves may not be motivated to spend evenings and weekends working for an organization that compromises on social issues but holds the line on a gasoline tax of less than a nickel a gallon. Elsewhere, I have reported that membership in the Moral Majority was motivated by a belief that their activism was helping fight Satan's inroads into American politics (Wilcox et al. 1991). It is easy to pursuade pentecostals, evangelicals, fundamentalists, and even some Catholics and black Protestants that homosexuality and abortion are part of Satan's war on America. The gasoline tax or national health insurance may be a harder sell.

On the other hand, a willingness to moderate on abortion and other issues might enable the Christian Coalition to focus on a broader agenda of values. A Christian Right that focused on a broader definition of family issues, including crime prevention, the prevention of teenaged pregnancies, and so on would potentially be a far broader coalition than the Christian Right has been able to assemble to date.

THE CHRISTIAN COALITION AND
THE POLITICS OF SCHOOL BOARDS

While some in the Christian Coalition try to gain control of Republican party organizations or work in coalition with other conservative Republicans, another part of the organization has concentrated on electing Christian Right candidates to school boards. Many of these elections are nonpartisan. The Christian Coalition has recruited and trained candidates, and worked to help them gain election. In other states, including Virginia, the Christian Coalition has worked to change the law to allow for the election of school board officials. The political coalitions involved in the school board elections are broader and in many ways more interesting than those in other Christian Coalition efforts.

The Christian Coalition has had successes across the country, most notably in San Diego and New York. The Christian Coalition took control of the San Diego school board for a time, where their members proved more moderate than might have been predicted. After two years, the Christian Coalition lost its majority on the board, although it retains considerable strength. The San Diego candidates were "stealth" candidates, although the Christian Coalition connection of some candidates was leaked to the media.

In New York, the Christian Coalition capitalized on widespread dissatisfaction with a curriculum that included books such as *Heather has Two Mommies*, which described the life of a child with two lesbian parents. In these elections, the Christian Coalition was able to forge the inclusive coalitions mentioned above, for the Catholic church distributed Christian Coalition candidate lists (Dillon 1993a; 1993b), as did the Congress on Racial Equality (CORE), a religiously-based African-American civil-rights group. Ultimately the Christian Coalition candidates won about as often as those endorsed by the liberal groups (Randolph 1993). Much closer to its home ground, however, the Christian Coalition got pounded in school board elections in Virginia Beach in April, 1994.

THE MILLENNIUM AND BEYOND:
THE FUTURE OF THE CHRISTIAN RIGHT

Mindful of the inherent capacity of political predictions to embarrass greatly those who make them, I will finally venture some thoughts on the future of the Christian Right. This future does not hinge on the distribution of public opinion on the key social issues on the Christian Right agenda. Such distributions change only gradually, and for the past several decades that change has been inevitably toward greater liberalism. The American public is more tolerant today than in the 1950s, more feminist, and more supportive of gay and abortion rights. Cohort replacement, rising levels of education, and many other factors make such a creeping liberalization likely to continue.[12] Despite this gradual lib-

---

[12] Several studies have shown that the youngest Americans are somewhat more conservative on feminist issues than those who came of age in the 1960s and 1970s (Cook 1993; Cook et al. 1992). Yet they are far more liberal than the oldest generations, suggesting a continued liberalization as the oldest cohorts die.

eralization on these key social issues, a basic conservatism persists on core values, especially those focusing on the family.

The fortunes of organizations of the Christian Right and its opponents are not greatly influenced by mass opinion, however, but rather depend on their ability to mobilize the faithful. Consider the pro-life and pro-choice efforts of the past two decades. Throughout this period aggregate public opinion has remained quite stable — the modal American position is to favor allowing abortion in most but not all circumstances (Cook et al. 1992). Between a third a forty percent of Americans generally show up as consistently pro-choice in national polls, and between five percent and ten percent oppose abortion in all circumstances. Yet the organizational fortunes of National Right-to-Life and NARAL ebbed and flowed as they found issues, Court decisions, and political candidates that would mobilize their supporters to vote the abortion issue and contribute to their organizations.

Wuthnow (1993) notes that there remain important resources for the Christian Right in the 1990s and beyond. A core of support exists for Christian Right groups and policies, although it is unlikely that a Christian Right focused on social issues can expand much beyond that base (Wilcox 1992). There remains sufficient local talent to provide leadership for organizing. Denominations, churches, and television ministries possess important resources that can aid in mobilization.

Some Christian Right groups are currently getting a good return on direct mail opposing the "radical agenda of gays and lesbians." It seems likely, however, that the funding for large, national groups will never consistently reach the levels of the early 1980s, and will ultimately decline. In part, this is because direct-mail contributions for conservative religious groups appears to be a generational, rather than a life-cycle phenomenon. Direct mail experts in Washington tell me that the average age of contributors to political groups that stress religious issues is old and getting older, and it appears that when this generation of contributors moves on to their final reward or punishment the potential for direct-mail fundraising by the Right will be greatly diminished.

The membership of many pentecostal and fundamentalist churches, on the other hand, is quite young. This suggests that instead of national, direct-mail organizations such as the Moral Majority, looser coalitions of local and regional groups are more likely. There may be greater potential for inspiring these younger conservative Christians to vote in a school board election or to run phone banks for a local Christian candidate than for inspiring them to send $25 monthly to a national organization. The real pool of volunteer talent is the women of these orthodox churches, many of whom have real political skills and interests, but who accept the religious ideology that tells them they should stay at home and rear their children. These women need a justification to become involved in projects outside the home, and political issues that at least appear to be a defense of their culture can provide such a rationale.[13]

It seems to me unlikely that the Christian Right can win control of the Republican party at the national level, and I suspect that most state party organizations will again be controlled by mainstream Republicans in the next several years.[14] The majority of party voters and activists are conservative, but they do not share the Christian Right's enthusiasm for using the authority of government to dictate private moral behavior. They are quite negative toward Christian Right candidates, who are generally unelectable in general elections in any event. They are generally pro-choice on abortion, although supportive of some restrictions. The Christian Right will remain a potent force in party politics, perhaps on the level of African Americans in the Democratic party. In the near future, it is likely that the Republican party will abandon its support for a human life amendment and attempt to appear more moderate on social issues.

The future of Christian Right support for political candidates is less certain, because the Christian Coalition has followed both a purist ideological strategy and a pragmatic, accommodating one. Neither strategy seems likely to be ultimately successful. It will be difficult to explain to newly mobilized pentecostals and fundamentalists why they should consistently support Republican moderates who support abortion and who refuse to center their campaigns around Christian Right leaders. Despite Robertson's endorsement, his contributors did not rally to help finance the campaign of George Bush. Conversely, it will be difficult to mobilize support repeatedly for purist candidates who will generally lose party primaries or badly lose general elections when they do win the nomination. After a few sound defeats, premillennialists may decide that the political world cannot be saved.

Moreover, by consistently supporting Republican candidates, the Christian Right risks alienating independent or Democratic evangelicals who may support much of the Christian Right's agenda. Although Guth (1993) is correct that the party system seems to be aligning itself in part around a religious cleavage, there remain large numbers of Democratic evangelicals who must be included if the Christian Right is to expand its support. Moreover, the consistently conservative economic message of many of the Republican candidates supported by Christian Right leaders will not always be popular. In times of economic stagnation, many evangelicals will be tempted to return to their Democratic roots. If national health insurance ultimately proves successful, it will benefit the somewhat less

---

[13] Many of the fundamentalist women active in politics in Ohio whom I interviewed in 1982 seemed indirectly to suggest such a motivation. One young woman noted that she had always wanted to be more active in politics or social groups, but had always felt that she needed to spend all of her time with her young children. When the local pro-life group informed, however, she felt that defending the life of "unborn children" was sufficiently important to justify her hiring a babysitter for several hours a week.

[14] Of course, the Republican party has alternated control by moderates and conservatives for many years, and was controlled by the Right in three nominations in my lifetime. In the cases of Goldwater and Reagan, it was a coalition of defense conservatives, economic conservatives, and religious conservatives that controlled the party.

affluent evangelicals and Catholics that constitute a potential constituency for the Christian Right.

The Christian Right has its greatest potential in mobilizing diverse constituencies in support of local (and occasionally national) moral crusades. These diverse constituencies were not welcome in the Moral Majority, and it is unlikely that they will ever come together in one political organization. Yet they need not do so, for coordinated efforts at the elite level will produce the same results. Catholics in New York did not need to attend Christian Coalition meetings to receive lists of endorsed candidates — the Catholic church distributed them. African Americans did not need to attend meetings filled with white Republicans to know which candidates opposed the curriculum — the lists were distributed by CORE.

Ralph Reed (1993), director of the Christian Coalition, foresees a loose web of interconnected local groups that will cooperate on many but not all issues. A great many local groups exist already, so the real question is whether they can consistently cooperate as in the New York school board elections. I doubt if they can. The New York curriculum was perhaps the most extreme in the country, and opposition was widespread. Short-term cooperation in New York was easy, but longer-term bridges are more difficult to build. The cultural gap between conservative Catholics and fundamentalist Baptists is a wide one, and antipathy still runs deep.

Moreover, local political activists are notoriously difficult to control. The Moral Majority was consistently embarrassed by the activities of local chapters, for those with the most extreme views are generally most willing to volunteer more of their time than more moderate members, and therefore usually end up in leadership roles. The Maryland Moral Majority spent considerable effort trying to get the state assembly to pass laws outlawing anatomically correct cookies, and succeeded only in drawing national attention to one baker on the Eastern Shore who did a short-term boom mail-order business as a result. Already several state and local Christian Coalition leaders have taken astonishingly extreme positions, and seem obsessed by the apparent increase in the prevalence of witches.[15] Such local leaders do not build stable coalitions.

Finally, if the Christian Coalition continues to pursue an electoral strategy within the Republican party, it will become increasingly difficult to work well with Catholics and African Americans. Although the Republicans have made great inroads among Catholics in the past decade, many Catholics have deep Democratic roots. Among African Americans, the Republican party is quite unpopular, and any organization associated with Republican candidates will be suspect.

In the short run, then, I predict that the Christian Right will fight for but ultimately lose control of the Republican party. It will finally become a major interest group within the party. It will continue to endorse both ideological and pragmatic candidates, but find that it cannot deliver the volunteer efforts that it

---

[15] Witchcraft is alleged in current public school curricula. In addition, at least one Christian Right activist in California charges that the United States Air Force has employed official witches.

seeks in support of the candidates, nor even deliver evangelical votes in times of economic recession. It will build bridges with other groups at the national level and form ad hoc coalitions on trigger issues. But these coalitions will not endure because of religious particularism and real political divisions between the Christian Right and other conservative Christians.

As American nears the millennium, Christian Right activity and energy will likely increase. Many will believe that the millennium portends the second coming of Christ; others will devise different prophetic schemes. If the year 2002 arrives with no apocalypse, perhaps Christian Right activity will subside for a time. But Christian Right activity has waxed and waned for most of this century, and it seems likely to come again in the twenty-first century.

REFERENCES

Abramowitz, A. 1993. "It's abortion, stupid." Paper presented at the annual meeting of the American Political Science Association, Washington, DC.

Apple, R. W. 1992. "Republicans form group to regain centrist votes." New York Times (Dec. 16): A24.

Atwood, M. 1987. The Handmaid's Tale. London: Virago.

Balmer, R. 1992. "The Moral Majority's revival." The Arizona Daily Star (Nov. 16): A11.

Bishop, M. 1994. Close Encounters with the Deity. Atlanta: Peachtree.

Brin, D. 1989. Sundiver. New York: Bantam.

Brown, C., Jr., L. Powell, and C. Wilcox. 1994. Serious Money. New York: Cambridge University Press.

Cook, E. 1993. "The generations of feminism," pp. 57-67 in L. Duke (ed.), Women in Politics. Englewood Cliffs, NJ: Prentice-Hall.

Cook, E., T. G. Jelen, and C. Wilcox. 1992. Between Two Absolutes. Boulder, CO: Westview.

Cook, E., S. Thomas, and C. Wilcox. 1994. The Year of the Woman. Boulder, CO: Westview.

Dillon, S. 1993a. "Catholics join bid by conservatives for school boards." New York Times (Apr. 16): 1.

_____. 1993b. "Fundamentalists and Catholics." New York Times (Apr. 17): 23.

Egan, T. 1992. "Oregon GOP faces schism over agenda of Christian right." New York Times (Nov. 14): 6.

Elgin, S. H. 1984. Native Tongue. New York: Daw.

Fabrizio. 1993. Survey of Republican Voters. Alexandria, VA: Fabrizio, McLaughlin & Associates.

Fowler, F. B. 1993. "The failure of the religious right," pp. 57-75 in M. Cromartie (ed.), No Longer Exiles. Washington, CD: Ethics and Public Policy Center.

Georgianna, S. L. 1989. The Moral Majority and Fundamentalism. Lewiston, NY: Mellen.

Godwin, R. K. 1988. One Billion Dollars of Influence. Chatham, NJ: Chatham House.

Green, J. 1993. "Religion, social issues, and the Christian right." Paper presented at Colloquium on the Religious New Right and the 1992 Campaign, Ethics and Public Policy Center, Washington, DC.

Guth, J. 1983. "The politics of the new Christian right," pp. 18-43 in A. Cigler and B. Loomis (eds.), Interest Group Politics. Washington, DC: CQ Press.

_____. 1993. "Religion and the party system." Paper presented at the annual meeting of the American Political Science Association, Washington, DC.

Harrell, D. E. 1988. Pat Robertson. San Francisco: Harper & Row.

Hertzke, A. D. 1992. Echoes of Discontent. Washington, DC: CQ Press.

Hogan, J. P. 1991. *Ectoverse*. New York: Del Ray.

Jelen. T. G. 1991. *The Political Mobilization of Religious Beliefs*. New York: Praeger.

Liebman, R. 1983. "Mobilizing the Moral Majority," pp. 50-75 in R. Liebman and R. Wuthnow (eds.), *The New Christian Right*. New York: Aldine.

McCarthy, J. and M. Zald. 1977. "Resource mobilization and social movements." *American Journal of Sociology* 82:1212-41.

Morken, H. 1993. "The San Diego model." Paper presented at the annual meeting of the American Political Science Association, Washington, DC.

Randolph, E. 1993. "In NY school board 'holy war,' vote is split but civics triumph." *Washington Post* (May 22): A5.

Reed, R. 1993. "What do Christian conservatives really want?" Paper presented at Colloquium on the Religious New Right and the 1992 Campaign, Ethics and Public Policy Center, Washington, DC.

Reilly, R. 1985. *The Transcendent Adventure*. Westport, CT: Greenwood.

Sullivan, R. 1993. "An army of the faithful." *New York Times Magazine* (Apr. 25): 32-44.

Tepper, S. S. 1988. *The Gate to Women's Country*. New York: Bantam.

Wilcox. C. 1992. *God's Warriors*. Baltimore, MD: Johns Hopkins University Press.

_____, T. G. Jelen, and S. Linzey. 1991. "Reluctant warriors." *Journal for the Scientific Study of Religion* 30:245-58.

Wuthnow, R. 1993. "The future of the religious right," pp. 27-47 in M. Cromartie (ed.), *No Longer Exiles*. Washington, DC: Ethics and Public Policy Center.

Sean Wilentz

THE TRIALS OF TELEVANGELISM

Jerry Falwell and the Enemy

In 1987, at the outset of the PTL ("Praise the Lord") scandal, the Reverend Jimmy Swaggart solemnly announced that "the gospel of Jesus Christ has never sunk to such a level as it has today." Never mind the Inquisition: it had taken Jim and Tammy Faye Bakker to drag Christianity to the very depths of depravity. Nobody could have guessed that a year later it would be the Reverend Jimmy's turn to cry, once his sexual carryings-on came to light. We may never know if Swaggart's denunciation of the Bakkers projected his still-secret guilt upon a pair of vulnerable rivals. What is clear is that Swaggart's disgrace (and the Bakkers'), along with Pat Robertson's cranky presidential crusade in 1988, made a mockery of what was supposed to be the great awakening of conservative evangelicalism. Rarely in modern times has a movement of such reputed magnitude self-destructed so suddenly.

Yet, as with everything connected to evangelical politics, appearances were deceiving. Although the evangelical right failed to turn itself into a successful Christian party (or fully convert the GOP), it nonetheless changed the nation's cultural and political life during the 1980s. The key to this change lies in the career of Jerry Falwell. Before he disbanded the Moral Majority and beat a strategic retreat to his church and university in Lynchburg, Virginia, Falwell gave the country a sense of what it would be like to have an American mullah. During most of the Reagan years, Falwell seemed to be everywhere

at once—standing up for Star Wars, denouncing sodomy, fighting secular humanism, and urging patriotic Americans to buy all the Kruggerands they could afford.

Born in 1933 to a pious, dutiful homemaker and a successful Lynchburg bootlegger-businessman ruined by drink, Falwell was less the dour backwoods Bible thumper than a middle-class striver. He studied for two years to become an engineer before receiving God's call and transferring to a fundamentalist Bible college. Although loyal to fundamentalist doctrine, he also encouraged his congregation to compete successfully in the race of life. "Lessons in worldly success," Frances Fitz-Gerald has called his early sermons, "how-to-do-it manuals in the mainstream tradition of Billy Graham and Norman Vincent Peale."

Falwell's Lynchburg congregation consisted not of the amorphous rural classes, so commonly invoked as the mainstay of postwar fundamentalism, but of city people, many of them on the way up, with hardscrabble rural backgrounds. They had come to Lynchburg with the arrival of major national corporations during the 1950s, and they formed the boundary of a rapidly growing middle class. With his methods of "saturation evangelism"— equal parts Christian stewardship and relentless door-to-door salesmanship—Falwell reached out to these people and built his Thomas Road Baptist Church into one of the largest "super churches" in the nation. By the early 1970s it had a splendid new sanctuary, a Christian academy and elementary school, a syndicated television ministry, a rehabilitation center for

An earlier version of this essay appeared as "God and Man at Lynchburg" in *The New Republic*.

alcoholics, and a membership of thousands. If not quite of the mainstream secular world, Falwell and his congregation were certainly in it in a way their parents and grandparents never were.

The trouble was, the world was rapidly changing in ways that deeply wounded fundamentalist sensibilities. Just as they began to climb out from behind the walls of social inferiority and cultural isolation, fundamentalists felt attacked on all sides. For many, the 1962 and 1963 Supreme Court decisions banning prayer in public schools were the first of these troubling changes. For Falwell, the decisive challenge was the civil rights movement.

In 1965, at the time of the Selma marches, Falwell used his pulpit to blast activist clergymen, especially Martin Luther King, Jr., for getting mixed up in politics and ignoring their duties as servants of Jesus Christ. Four months later, when a band of civil rights demonstrators targeted his church for nonviolent protests, they were evicted and arrested. Twenty years later, Falwell called these events a personal turning point: first, because they began a spiritual journey that led him to reject his racism (he now calls the civil rights workers of the 1960s "courageous"); second, because they taught him that religion and politics need not be kept separate. But in the 1960s no such calming perspective was possible. Fundamentalists like Falwell, who believed in a doctrine of pietistic withdrawal, had their backs to the wall. Their continued abstention from politics meant acquiescing to the elimination of structures of white supremacy that were deeply embedded in Southern fundamentalist life. As it happened, the crisis atmosphere abated in Lynchburg over the next few years. Falwell and his congregation found ways to make their peace with civil rights while preserving their church as an overwhelmingly white community.

But by the 1970s the sense of frustration and panic returned. Falwell has cited the 1973 *Roe v. Wade* ruling as his moment of awakening. So too for others who wound up in the Moral Majority. From that moment on, opposition to abortion became a key element in the rise of evangelical political fervor. Abortion did not stand alone, however. Other developments also fed the simmering revolt. There was the duplicity of Watergate, the disgrace of America's defeat in Vietnam, the waning of patriotic anticommunism, the gay rights movement, Jimmy Carter's "betrayal" of his evangelical heritage once in office, and a shaky economy, as seen in the ascendency of OPEC.

Earlier generations of fundamentalists might have been able to distance themselves from such changes, shrug their shoulders, and wait for the Second Coming. But Falwell and untold thousands were already too much in the world for that. Every day they witnessed horrifying spectacles of libertinism, permissiveness, and disorder. Unless something was done, "the Enemy"—Falwell's term for the forces of Satan—would destroy America and prevent it from being the providential nation that would help usher in the millennium.

Television became the critical instrument in this perception of the world, and in Falwell's hands it would also be the critical instrument in rallying the faithful. At the outset, what became known as televangelism was a natural continuation of the older evangelical radio ministries (one of which, Charles Fuller's "Old Fashioned Revival Hour," Falwell credits for his conversion). Emboldened by a 1960 FCC directive allowing paid religious broadcasts to be considered part of the public-service programming required of all affiliates, Falwell and other ministers expanded their outreach, taking advantage of the latest breakthroughs in video technology. By 1971 more than three hundred stations carried Falwell's services from Thomas Road Baptist Church.

There were, of course, problems with this success. A television ministry threatened to undercut the fiercely independent communal autonomy that had long been a pillar of American evangelical Protestantism. An electronic church whose "congregants" tuned in to Falwell was a financial threat to local churches. It might even undermine the traditional subordination of a preacher to his own congregation. A successful television preacher could have a huge audience and at the same time minimal pastoral obligations. If he chose, he could simply turn church government over to the little oligarchy surrounding him.

Better than most, Falwell was able to finesse these problems. He did, after all, have his Thomas Road Church (administered by a close-knit group of local advisers). He approached religion, including televised religion, as a growth industry with room for everyone. On the one occasion when his pastoral leadership and personal integrity came under serious question—a 1973 SEC investigation involving improper bond issues—Falwell was able to plead inexperience and save face. Rarely, however, was it necessary for him to make excuses. He quickly learned to apply his masterful door-to-door hucksterism to the airwaves, raising millions of dollars while cultivating an appealing image.

The image was crucial. Although viewed by liberals as a loudmouth bullyboy, Falwell came as close as someone in the conservative fundamentalist fold could to a generic pan-Protestantism. He was most emphatically not a charismatic or holiness ranter. There was no faith healing or talking in tongues at Thomas Road Baptist. In his tasteful, postmodern colonial church, Falwell rarely raised his voice for long. His delivery, if not particularly stirring, was recognizably avuncular and down-to-earth. The whole operation strove for a touch of class. Aware of the importance of tradition in his native Virginia, Falwell even modeled his church's buildings on Thomas Jefferson's architectural designs. There was something safe and reassuring about his broadcasts. To an uninitiated viewer, it all might have looked like nothing more than, well . . . church. One had to listen awhile to catch Falwell's message.

At the heart of the nation's problems, Falwell declared—the main cause of America's loss of prestige, the decline of patriotism, and the triumph of pervasive liberalism—was a moral rot that derived from the breakdown of sexual rules and of the "traditional family." It was not the first time that American religion and politics had become entangled with profound changes in sexual norms. The evangelical outbursts of the 1820s and 1830s helped legitimate the very model of bourgeois family life and domestic bliss that Falwell and others mythologize as the biblically inspired nuclear unit established for eternity. The fundamentalist uprisings of the 1920s involved a reaction against the New Woman and against the alleged effeminacy of the liberal, modern man whom Billy Sunday called "a wishy-washy sissified sort of galoot that let everybody make a doormat out of him."

Falwell tapped into the deeply sexualized anxieties that followed from the social upheavals of the last twenty years. These anxieties didn't just involve fears of androgyny and male lust; they entailed elemental distinctions between order and chaos, cleanliness and pollution. For Falwell and other fundamentalists, as well as millions of Americans, the qualities of maleness and femaleness are not malleable. They are divinely ordered essences, "intimately woven," as Falwell wrote in 1980, "in the overall fabric of personality."

Fully mature persons are either completely masculine or completely feminine, qualities that Falwell attaches to his long-suffering mother and his tragically doomed father, as well as to his own "Christian marriage." At Thomas Road Baptist, these distinctions are reinforced less in the liturgy (though Falwell always projects a beefy ex-jock presence) than in the visual imagery of Falwell's sermons. On one occasion, Falwell instructed his congregation to reject the prevailing depiction of Jesus Christ as a meek, diaphanous hippie-type with long hair and a billowing robe: "Christ wasn't effeminate. . . . The man who lived on this earth was a man with muscles. . . . Christ was a he-man!"

Yet everywhere they looked in the late 1960s and 1970s, Falwell and his congregation saw a mainstream culture hell-bent on androgyny (and with it the destruction of the American family and the loss of national virility). Worse still, they saw politicians going along with it all. One day the sissified galoots in Washington were proposing constitutional amendments that would force Christian women to be drafted for combat duty. The next day they were touting legislation that would make homosexuals a legally protected minority, thereby thrusting perverts on unwilling Christian employers and school boards.

Male lust, the flip side of androgyny, showed its face everywhere from the porno houses to the divorce courts. More important, the calls for equality by ERA feminists, prochoice groups, and other proponents of women's rights promised to let men evade their responsibilities, prey upon women's bodies, and deny women the legal and moral protections they deserved. A hideous vision unfolded before fundamentalists' eyes: sexual and mental abuse of women and children, babies slain in their mothers' wombs — all in the name of sexual freedoms that did more to oppress women than to liberate them.

By the end of the 1970s, the cumulative effects of fundamentalism's encounters with the postwar world had raised the possibility of launching a conservative Christian crusade around moral and sexual issues unlike any seen for half a century. It took secular right-wing organizers like Paul Weyrich to suggest the contours (and the name) for the Moral Majority and complete Falwell's entry into politics. But Falwell also proved himself an enormously capable organizer.

Very quickly the Moral Majority, along with its sibling organizations the Christian Voice and the Religious Roundtable, attracted attention, raised planeloads of money, and added conservative Protestants to the election rolls. Exact figures are hard to come by, but estimates put the number of voters registered by the Moral Majority and the other religious groups at two million. The new vote was solidly behind the man who endorsed the evangelical revolt, Ronald Reagan. In 1976 two-thirds of the combined evangelical-fundamentalist vote went to the born-again Jimmy Carter. Eight years later, the Reagan-Bush ticket garnered an astounding 81 percent.

The payback for this loyalty was a combination of rhetorical support for the fundamentalist cause and the appointment of friendly federal officials, especially in the courts. It will take future historians to determine just how much of a role Falwell and his friends played in Reagan appointments to the bench, but by the end of the 1980s, they certainly had every reason to be pleased with the results.

Within the churches, meanwhile, Falwell's activities bolstered the fundamentalists' efforts to recapture the leadership of various major fellowships. The most dramatic and wrenching shift came within the Southern Baptist Convention (SBC), the largest Protestant fellowship in the United States. By 1980 fundamentalist conservatives, spearheaded by Bailey Smith, had taken command of the SBC's national offices and done all they could to root out moderate influences. Fundamentalist and charismatic precepts also began to seep into mainline churches and the popular culture. By mid-decade it was common for rock-ribbed Presbyterians to sing evangelical hymns (not in the approved hymnal), to touch and squeeze each other, to attend workshops on *glossolalia*. Even athletics were now affected by religion. It seemed impossible to watch a sporting event without hearing the winner credit his or her victory to a personal relationship with Jesus Christ.

Falwell's rise also contributed to the literal-minded, absolutist temper that permeated public discussion in the 1980s. We must be careful here about grouping him with others who came on the public scene with moral and cultural prescriptions. The Moral Majority emerged from a very different part of the forest than the pop Platonism of Allan Bloom or the curdled feminism of Women Against Pornography. Where they converged was in their willingness to take words or symbols (the Bible, long hair, dirty pictures) as a transparent text with a meaning that would impel people to act, either for good or ill. America, awash in bad symbols, had to exorcize the devil behind them — be he Nietzsche, Larry Flynt, or Satan himself — and bring back good standards and good symbols. By the mid-1980s American discourse was full of in-your-face affirmations about duty, flag, and family — no questions asked.

But as far as consolidating a national political base and changing America's views on other important issues, Falwell's achievement is much cloudier. In 1982, despite some mild boasts by Falwell, the religious right made little difference in the congressional vote nationwide. In some states Moral Majority chapters gained control of seats on local school boards and Republican committees, but generally they failed to capture the political machinery. By 1985 candidates discovered that direct endorsement by political evangelicals could lead to a net loss in votes. On the national level the Reagan White House kept up its rhetorical support of the Moral Majority (and made the necessary appointments), but fairly quickly backed away from the evangelical legislative program.

Explanations abound for why the Moral Majority so soon reached the limits of its power. Most of these center on specific aspects of Falwell's fundamentalist background—which, for all his aspirations to ecumenicism, he could never quite shake. His mounting belligerence, for example, shaped as it was by his Manichean faith, violated what the sociologist James Davison Hunter calls an "ethic of civility" in American politics, a shared unspoken scruple that compels people not only to tolerate others' beliefs but to be tolerable to others. In Falwell's case his television mask turned him into the kind of "hot" personality that leaves the public cold.

The Moral Majority's organizational structure also displayed some of the weaknesses of Falwell's fundamentalist background. Although Falwell claimed that his organization represented a broad spectrum of conservative Protestants, Jews, and Roman Catholics, its foundations were far narrower. In actuality the whole operation resembled a national fundamentalist parachurch with its base in the local congregations. This organization helped the group grow quickly (by 1981 there were an estimated 400,000 Moral Majoritarians), but it also hindered any coordinated effort on political issues outside of presidential elections. It disguised the unevenness of the Moral Majority's development state by state, all but ensuring that Falwell would be continually embarrassed by the outrageousness of an independent spokesman or chapter.

The notion that there really was an absolute moral majority in the country that thought the same way Falwell did and was ready to fight for its vision also turned out to be a myth. Although polls showed that a large number of Americans—perhaps one-third—said they supported all of Falwell's key positions on homosexuality, school prayer, abortion, and the "traditional family," they also showed that the rest held to more liberal positions. Even evangelical Christians hardly formed a moral and political bloc. As Falwell himself admitted, some of the sharpest attacks on him came from such bastions of determined ultrafundamentalist separatism as the Fundamentalist Baptist Fellowship and Bob Jones University.

In the end, though, it was Falwell's politics that evoked the most negative reactions—the widespread suspicion, even among conservative believers, that he and the evangelical right represented a dark, antidemocratic strain in modern American politics. Being called a fascist, a bigot, and a warmonger clearly stung Falwell, and he has devoted a good deal of energy to settling scores with the liberal press for allegedly misrepresenting his views. No doubt he was prejudged in some quarters. But his political pronouncements did often slide off the edge of Christian moralism, "free enterprise" economics, and hard-line anticommunism into tropes reminiscent of the right-wing zealots of the 1930s and the McCarthyites of the 1950s. The irony is that some of his nastiest rhetoric accompanied his early efforts to make his movement more pluralistic.

When Falwell began his crusade, he underestimated the importance of grounding it in one of the great shibboleths of postwar American life—the "Judeo-Christian tradition" that supposedly forms the nation's ethical foundation. As Mark Silk detailed in an illuminating little book, *Spiritual Politics,* Judeo-Christianity emerged after 1945 as the latest in a series of American adhesional faiths—an attempt to provide everyone with a common religious cause and a "quasi-spiritual alliance to the religiously impartial state." Falwell was not blind to such ecumenicism. Early on, he said nice things about Israel, which, to many people's surprise, turned out to be perfectly consistent with his fundamentalist beliefs. (Israel plays a significant and heroic role in fundamentalist eschatology, as derived from the Book of Ezekiel.) But like other fundamentalists, Falwell still believed America had been founded "by godly men upon godly principles to be a Christian nation."

A storm of protest, particularly from Jews, forced Falwell to reshape himself into an unswerving advocate of Judeo-Christian pluralism. But who then was "the Enemy"? Back in the 1950s both liberal and conservative Judeo-Christians thought they knew the answer. "The Enemy" was godless totalitarianism, specifically international communism, including its American adherents and fellow travelers. By the 1980s, however, domestic anticommunism was an inauspicious rallying point for building a broad consensus on moral conservatism. So the religious began talking about a new enemy—secular humanism.

Until 1970, only a few thousand Americans had even heard of the secular humanists, that hearty little band of atheists and world-government types. Conservatives might have missed them altogether if Justice Hugo Black, in a celebrated 1961 decision, hadn't mentioned secular humanism, along with Buddhism, Taoism, and Ethical Culture, as one of several atheistic religions to be guaranteed full First Amendment rights. By 1980 fundamentalists like Falwell's colleague Tim LaHaye had picked up the term and invested it with conspiratorial powers—the many-horned beast of modern liberalism, with its pornography, homosexuality, feminism, and big government. Here a line could be drawn, not between Christian and non-Christian, but between Judeo-Christianity and "the Enemy," secular humanism. And here a new political line could also be drawn between the Judeo-Christians who acknowledged that the United States had been founded on Holy Writ and the heathen who did not.

The invention of secular humanism helped Falwell and the Moral Majority open lines of communication to politically important conservative and neoconservative Jews. But demonizing secular humanism also had disastrous costs. The term was so capacious as to suggest that everyone from Thomas Jefferson to Madonna

shared the same basic beliefs. Most of secular humanism's presumed tenets—the vaunting of personal freedom, the toleration of different personal beliefs—were so deeply enshrined in American culture that it was hard for most Americans to see where they ran afoul of basic American principles. The actions undertaken by pious conservatives to uproot secular humanism in the schools—notably the suit that led to a 1987 decision barring forty-four "secular humanist" texts from Alabama public schools—seemed at odds with Falwell's announced opposition to censorship. Such actions also raised a dilemma: If conservative evangelicals could remove works of secular humanism from public institutions, what was to stop secular humanists from demanding the exclusion of Judeo-Christian materials as prejudicial to *their* religion?

The more Falwell and his allies tried to build a coalition atop their fundamentalist following, the more they confirmed that they were out of touch with the prevailing ideas about democracy. In 1984 the historian Martin Marty concluded that the fundamentalists could succeed on their own terms only in the event of an utter political and economic collapse, leading to "a state religion, compulsory in character, authoritarian in tone, and 'traditional' in outlook." How much of this Falwell understood at the time is unclear. In the mid-1980s, he did, however, begin to soften his public posture.

In 1980, for example, Falwell appeared sympathetic to banning all homosexuals from public-school teaching, but later he insisted he would not abridge their right to teach "as long as they don't use the classroom to promote homosexuality as an alternative lifestyle." Similarly, he kept repeating that abortion is murder but added that abortions are permissible in cases of rape or incest. Falwell even took pride in the fact that his Liberty University trained men and women for professional careers, thus raising the question of what his idea of the "traditional" family and the "traditional" wife now meant.

During Reagan's second term Falwell could still launch into fire-and-brimstone oratory. "Satan had mobilized his own forces," he reflected in his 1987 autobiography, "to destroy America by negating the Judeo-Christian ethic." But the jeremiads now came in passing. So beholden to White House friends had Falwell become that well before the 1988 campaign, he endorsed George Bush, a man who had waffled on the abortion issue and who, for all his protestations about being born again, couldn't seem to get straight the simplest biblical reference. The result is a situation that has enraged fundamentalist purists, who in 1988 cast their lot with Pat Robertson's campaign.

Falwell and his followers are in some ways better off than they were when he began the Moral Majority. Although mired in continuing controversy—above all, the PTL fiasco—Falwell ended the decade with more dignity than virtually all the other high-profile televangelists. He is now free to devote himself to institution building (in particular to his dream of turning Liberty University into a fundamentalist Notre Dame), knowing that the new conservative Supreme Court may yet overturn *Roe v. Wade* and that he has secured for fundamentalist believers a national respectability that was unimaginable twenty years ago.

But he has failed to secure the long-term political initiative. In 1989, politicians who had supported Falwellian and New Right positions on abortion stammered and stumbled, surprised by the public's reaction to the *Webster* decision. Growing portions of the Republican party now predict a political disaster unless the party finally loses its identification with the religious right.

It is one thing to affect the nation's cultural tone, quite another to translate that into enduring political power. Jerry Falwell had to learn this lesson the hard way. While he was learning it, he contributed mightily to the political dreariness of the Reaganite Gilded Age and won his share of victories. We are only beginning to recover. □

LOBBYING FOR THE LORD: THE NEW CHRISTIAN RIGHT HOME-SCHOOLING MOVEMENT AND GRASSROOTS LOBBYING*

Vernon L. Bates

Pacific University

Review of Religious Research, Vol. 33, No. 1 (September, 1991)

This study, based on interviews and participant observation, analyzes the lobbying efforts of participants in the New Christian Right home-schooling movement (HSM) as they pressure a state legislature to write a bill favorable to home-schooling. A resource mobilization approach is employed, but with some attention paid to the importance of grievances and ideology in conservative Christianity as contributors to mobilization. In this essay I consider the growth of home-schooling, the development of home-schooling support groups— originally intended as a network for educational and moral support—-and the transformation of those support groups into grassroots lobbying bodies working for home-schooling legislation.

INTRODUCTION

The analysis of religious organizations' political behavior has recently become the focus of some attention. New Christian Right political action committees (PACS) as they are involved in electoral politics have received much of this attention (Johnson and Tamney, 1982; Himmelstein and Latus, 1983; Wilcox, 1988; Woodrum, 1988). Alan Hertzke's book, *Representing God in Washington*, focuses on the national lobbying efforts of religious interest groups and addresses the effectiveness of grassroots mobilization by conservative Christians (Hertzke, 1988). The particular issue to be considered in this paper is grassroots lobbying at the state level engaged in for the single issue interests of one specific arm of a larger social movement. In 1986, the New Christian Right home-schooling movement (HSM) successfully lobbied the Oregon state legislature for a law in support of their actions and blocked the efforts of the counter-movement to amend this law in the following legislative session.

To understand this lobbying effort a resource mobilization (RM) perspective is useful (Oberschall, 1973; McCarthy and Zald, 1973, 1977, 1979; Tilly, 1978; Zald, 1982). The RM approach has become the dominant perspective for the study of social movements and has replaced traditional social-psychological theories which tended to focus on movement participation as deviant and irrational (Klandermans, 1984). More recently, however, there has been a general criticism of resource mobilization theory for underestimating the significance of "grievances and ideology as determinants of participation in social movements" (Klandermans, 1984). One need not abandon the RM approach to acknowledge the importance of grievances and ideology (Rose, 1982; Klandermans, 1984). On the one hand, Swidler's contention that "Bursts of ideological activism occur in periods when competing ways of organizing action are developing or contending for dominance," (Swidler, 1986:279) and Geertz's discussion of "the struggle for the real," where he says, "the brute empirical fact is that the growth of science has made almost all religious beliefs harder to maintain and a great many virtually impossible to maintain" (Geertz, 1968:103), recognize the importance of ideology in religious social movements. On the other hand, in discussing religion-based social movements, Zald says of the RM perspective, "It does not deny that grievances exist, that actors with grievances can be mobilized into social movements, [but] RM does argue that a focus upon grievances has often led scholars to miss the central social processes that help create and sustain social movements" (Zald, 1982:322).

I will argue that the general anxiety faced by conservative Christian adults when their children encounter a perceived hostile secular world creates a need for a specific type of objective alternative and a plausibility structure that supports the conservative Christian subculture (Ammerman, 1987) and provides for certain social-psychological needs of its participants. The Christian school movement (Peshkin, 1986; Rose, 1988) and more recently the home-schooling movement provide such a plausibility structure that can then be mobilized to lobby for social and political change (Berger and Luckmann, 1963). One cannot argue that grievances and ideology alone make a social movement; after all the conservative Christian reaction to modernism reaches back to the beginning of the 20th century and mobilization has occurred only sporadically. Most recently this has developed as the New Christian Right, which has been considerably aided by advances in technology (Zald, 1982). However, conservative Christian leaders do not attribute their successes to technology alone, but to the commitment of their followers (Hertzke, 1988; 51).

In this research, the successful efforts of the New Christian Right HSM in lobbying for a favorable law will be evaluated as a case where the mobilization of home-schooling participants has a strong ideological base. Lobbying is the result of a specific grievance with the school system, or of what Oberschall has called the "conflict over control of the means of cultural reproduction" (McCarthy 1984:317; Heinz, 1983). It may be that the deep-seated passion of conservative evangelicals, their religious zeal, is something that the opposition does not possess. This can be an important variable in grassroots efforts to have one's cultural morality turned into material reality in the form of law. The potential of ideology as a force for mobilization is well phrased by Latus:

> Their religious motivation provides a value framework for everything they do in life, and this is true of politics no less than of anything else. Related to this religious zeal is the fact that other incentives for participation (such as premiums) are less necessary for individuals driven by the convictions of their faith. Leaders have merely to ask and it shall be given unto them (Latus, 1983:98-99).

The home-schooling law in Oregon came into being not because people were not permitted to home-school their children, but because some people wished to transform their ideology into reality in order to protect their religious convictions and to have some official control over the means of cultural reproduction.

As a nonbeliever and former evangelical I have had a long personal and sociological interest in conservative Christianity dating back to my graduate school years studying the Creation Science Movement in California. My interest in the HSM was generated by contact with a home-schooling neighbor who provided me with my first list of names of participants and leaders and made some supportive phone calls to some of these same persons attesting to my relative neutrality and serious interest in their enterprise. Further lists of names were provided by state legislators, interviewees who gave me names of people who also home-schooled, and participants in groups and conferences. *The Teaching Home*, a magazine for home-schooling families, gave the names, phone numbers, and addresses of home-schooling support group leaders. In my interviews and contacts with these group leaders further lists were provided to me. The majority of initial contacts were made by telephone. Only three of the contacted families refused to be interviewed citing personal reasons for this refusal. I was unable to interview some of the more militant anti-state, home-schooling families because they did not comply with Oregon law and did not wish to be known. Support group leaders acknowledge the existence of these persons but protect their privacy. I interviewed only Christian home-schooling participants. I interviewed 47 home-schooling families in their homes, several other New Christian Right activists, state legislators and their aides, and members of the counter movement (see Appendix for further detail).

During a sabbatical I devoted nine months to data collection, analysis and writing. In the subsequent year of full-time teaching I collected further data, engaged in more analysis, and wrote early drafts of two papers. As an interviewer and participant observer I presented myself as a sociologist and nonbeliever. I do not feel my nonbelief hampered access to the subjects because they believed that I could be saved and that God was guiding me into this enterprise.

Analyzing Social Settings (Lofland and Lofland, 1984) and *Qualitative Sociology* (Schwartz and Jacobs, 1979) were invaluable guides to fieldwork and analysis. I took notes in all settings and in all interviews, refined them immediately upon leaving the setting, and developed mundane files, fieldwork files, and analytic files (Lofland and Lofland, 1984) based on the interviews and observations. These files provided the basis for an ongoing analysis that began on the first day of the research. I tried to approach the data as information about units of social settings, with particular focus on the home-schooling movement as a unit between a group and an organization. I could then begin asking questions of the data about the unit's structure, frequency, causes, processes, consequences, etc. (Lofland and Lofland, 1984). 1 could also begin to ask questions about the motives, intentions, and meanings of the actors in the movement. To a large extent the analysis lies in repeatedly asking these kinds of questions and further sorting and refining the analytical files until some conceptions of the real world of the home-schooling participants begins to emerge in a way that seems to capture their daily life. Upon completing my field work I presented some preliminary results at a professional meeting where I met a fellow panelist who had studied the same group in Oregon using primarily survey research methods (Mayberry, 1988). Our results on socio-economic variables, motivations, practices and beliefs were highly similar, thus giving some credence to my approach. In addition, I gave a public lecture on the movement to an audience that included many home-schooling participants. Their response to my presentation indicated to me that they felt fairly treated by my presentation and analysis.

MOVEMENT DESCRIPTION

Before discussing the political mobilization of the New Christian Right HSM it is appropriate to provide a brief description of the national HSM and a more specific description of that movement in Oregon. In my sample, parents' stated reasons for home-schooling include their religious training and present religious convictions, a belief in "family values," negative peer influence, and the secular climate of public education. They choose home-schooling where they can have a 24 hour influence over their children not provided by "total institution" Christian schools (Peshkin, 1986:259) which have their charges for less than 8 hours per day in an environment where some of their peers are not totally committed Christians (Bates, 1988).

As with many social movements, counting members is difficult, but the most accurate estimate appears to come from Patricia Lines, a policy analyst with the U.S. Department of Education (Lines, 1987). She estimates that the 1987 membership ranges from 120,000 to 260,000 and that the growth will probably continue at a moderate rate. In the State of Oregon, according to figures provided by the State Department of Education, by December 1, 1987, there were 3,098 children registered for home-schooling. This represents approximately 1% of the total school population in Oregon. In my sample there were six families not registered with the state as required by law. The total number of non-registrants is unknown, but many of the interviewees knew a few families that do not comply with the law. The reasons for non-registration are usually ideologically based, part of a right wing, anti-state perspective, but reasons also included lack of motivation and ignorance of the process for registration. No exact figures exist on the percentage of those children who are home-schooled for religious reasons and those home-schooled for other reasons, but available information appears to suggest that conservative Christian home-schoolers make up from 60-80% of those home-schooled in the state of Oregon (Mayberry, 1987).

SOCIAL MOVEMENT ORGANIZATIONS AS PLAUSIBILITY STRUCTURES

One might expect that the very nature of home-schooling would lead to relative isolation for the home-schooling families as they isolate themselves from public institutions. However, just as with many religious organizations in this secular world, the desire for legitimation and an approving and supportive plausibility structure explains in part the rise of a variety of social movement organizations (SMOs) within the broadly defined New Christian Right (Wilson, 1966; Berger and Luckmann, 1966; Zald and Asch, 1966; Peshkin, 1986; Ammerman, 1987; Rose, 1988). In addition, there exists a fairly elaborate set of interconnections with other SMOs which may or may not share their religious goals, but which do share similar social and political goals (Gerlach and Hine, 1970).

I interviewed only New Christian Right home-schooling families whose reasons for home schooling were declared to be primarily religious; thus, for many, a primary supporting organization is their church. However, the extent to which the

180

church supported this home-schooling endeavor varied. Only two of the churches that parents in my sample attended actively promoted home-schooling. One was a charismatic church that actively promotes political action from the pulpit and actively discourages parents from sending their children to public schools. The other was a reconstructionist church (see Clapp, 1987) where home-schooling is viewed as central to their ideological position, a position which holds that home-schooling is the best way to prepare children to be government leaders who will be in charge when Christ returns. Other churches ranged from those that discouraged home-schooling (churches that promote an active Christian witness by children in the public schools) to churches that did not actively promote any specific kind of schooling and were open to public, private and home-schooling as options. This mix of church responses to home-schooling does not provide home-schooling parents with strong institutional religious support for their choice. In addition, virtually all of the parents reported active opposition to their choice from parents, relatives, friends, neighbors, and school personnel. The parents do place a great deal of faith in their churches for spiritual support, but describe a need for other sources of support for home-schooling.

Home-schooling support groups range in size from five to 100 families, are generally organized geographically, and usually meet on a regular basis. The stated purpose of the groups is to provide academic, structural, emotional, and spiritual support for the parents of home-school children. Support groups provide families with new curriculum materials, arrange group activities such as field trips and physical education activities, discuss common problems and common solutions in teaching at home, complain about the poor quality of the public schools, pray for God's guidance and wisdom in their home school, share information about other support groups and schedule home-schooling events such as workshops, discuss politics, and engage in a variety of other activities one might expect from a group of like-minded individuals. As one parent indicated,

The support group is like an extended family that keeps you on the right track and helps you when you get discouraged. I have gotten a lot of neat ideas from other mothers and I have made several friends and found friends for my children. The most important thing of course is that the group helps me keep my eyes on Jesus.

Further support is sought through more formal connections to satellite programs provided by private religious schools. Ray Moore, the head of Hewitt Research Foundation and one of the ideological leaders of the movement, who writes books on home-schooling, appears on James Dobson's program called Focus on the Family to promote home-schooling, and makes public appearances to promote home-schooling, also operates a satellite program. These satellite programs provide testing for children, curricular guidance, athletic facilities, and sites for home-schooling workshops and activities.

Many home-schooling parents also seek support through workshops, public lectures, and radio programming—specifically *Focus on the Family*, which has a decidedly New Christian Right political perspective, encourages political activism, and is a proponent and supporter of home-schooling. Contrary to what one might expect based on recent sociological research, very few families in this sample seek support from religious television broadcasting such as Pat Robertson's *700 Club*, Jerry Falwell, or Jimmy Swaggart (see Stacey and Shupe, 1982). One might speculate that this may be due to the high educational expectations these parents have for their children, expectations often associated with an anti-television bias. Many parents indicate a dislike for television and many do not like television ministers. These sentiments were expressed before the scandals in the late 1980s surrounding the sexual escapades and financial dealings of some television evangelists.

The Teaching Home, an 8-year-old, Portland, Oregon based, internationally distributed magazine, which is an important source of information on everything from curricular materials for home schools to a listing of the support groups in each state, serves to give the HSM a centralized organizing tool that can be used locally, regionally, statewide, and nationally. This magazine, produced in a converted garage on a relatively low-end desk top publishing piece of hardware, may say something about the importance of new technology for the development of social movements, a topic rich in research possibilities. The ease and low cost of this form of communication is a significant development for mobilizing resources.

Further support is provided by friendship networks. Most of the parents who home-school have close friends who also home-school and much of their time is spent socializing with these persons, often to the exclusion of other like-minded religious friends who do not home-school. Berger's notion that religious systems remain plausible only as people articulate them in their conversation and dramatize them in their social interaction is an appropriate framework for understanding this social movement (Berger, 1966; Berger, 1967). The network, here described, provides the knowledge and values necessary to legitimate the choice to home-school and further reinforces existing religious values that are perceived to be threatened in a secular environment.

IDEOLOGY

RM theory stresses the importance of resources and organizational networks, means that can be brought to bear on problems, in explaining the development of social movements and SMOs. Both resource mobilization and ideology are necessary components in the HSM and are central to understanding how they were able to move a bill through the Oregon legislature. Let us first consider ideology.

The importance of ideology in the New Christian Right HSM should not be underestimated. Latus, in her work on ideological PACS, argues for the force of religious conviction in motivating participation:

> . . . *the task of grassroots organizing is usually already partly done, since there is a foundation of existing church congregations on which to build. Furthermore, the religious motivation for behavior can be pervasive and powerful. Related to this religious zeal is the fact that other incentives for participation are less necessary for individuals driven by the convictions of their faith (Latus, 1983:98).*

Commitment to the HSM is ultimately a political choice rising out of the ideology of the New Christian Right. In this sense, this movement may be viewed as a social movement organization in a multiple-issue group (Gamson, 1975; Zald and McCarthy 1966). It is in this discussion of ideology that the RM perspective and the social psychology of collective behavior can be united to help us understand this particular social movement. Certainly, strongly held beliefs alone do not result in social movements; even collectively held strong beliefs do not necessarily result in collective action. The RM perspective makes this clear. On the other hand, the RM perspective may underestimate the significance of ideology as a qualitative difference among social movements. Some movements have more passion and zeal than others. In the HSM one must pay attention to the importance of ideology, commitment and passion.

Home-schooling parents are participants in a multiple issue movement, the New Christian Right. They are also participants in an SMO that shares goals with the New Christian Right and that has an additional set of long-range and short-range goals that are specific to their movement. New Christian Right home-schooling parents participate in several related activities. They are typically active church-goers (many attend church several times a week) they belong to Bible-study groups, prayer groups, children's activity groups such as Awana (a kind of Christian scouting group), and musical and drama groups associated with their churches. In addition to these church-related activities, they listen to Christian radio on a regular basis and they attend Christian concerts and some traveling evangelists' presentations. At another level, they are affiliated with and active in home-schooling networks, and at a third level they are involved in a variety of New Christian Right political organizations such as anti-abortion groups, anti-pornography groups, and educational lobbying groups. However, not all parents who home-school are equally invested in these activities. Attendance and participation are not uniform even for one group of parents over time. At one time or another, nevertheless, most of the parents become involved with many of these cited activities.

The common thread connecting these activities is a shared ideology that has an historical foundation in conservative Christian ideology. It is true that disenchantment with modernism and secularism has a long history among conservative Christians, particularly fundamentalists, and that mobilization of those who adhere to this ideology occurs only sporadically, an obvious support for the RM approach; but it is also true that the conservative Christian utopia depicted in "the end times" has always been an ideological challenge to the existing social structure (for two differing perspectives on this issue see Sandeen, 1970, and Marsden, 1980). Thus, it may be argued that conservative Christian ideology and a strong commitment to that ideology must exist as a component of mobilization in the HSM.

It is appropriate to view mobilization as a variable among conservative Christians, with the various SMOs, such as the anti-abortion movement, anti-pornography movement, creation science movement, and the HSM representing some of the most extreme possibilities of movement mobilization—what John Lofland calls the "white hot" state of maximum mobilization (Lofland, 1979). It may be that "white hot" mobilization occurs when there is a perceived immediate threat to ideology and acceptable material circumstances. One example to illustrate this point comes from the controversies surrounding the theory of evolution. Many feel that the fundamentalists were soundly defeated, in an ideological sense and in a material sense, even though they won the Scopes Monkey Trial of 1925. However, Grabiner and Miller point out that the fundamentalists successfully kept the teaching of evolution out of most public schools until the mid-1960s. Thus, political mobilization of conservative Christians was not necessary until the federal government sponsored a series of textbooks that promoted evolution, the BSCS series, and the creation science movement arose to fend off this threat (Grabiner and Miller,

1974; Bates, 1975). In addition, the banning of prayer in the public schools presented another challenge to their desire for a particular sacred canopy (Berger, 1967). Their definition of America was questioned, and this struck at the heart of their ideology and their desire for a particular way of life. To continue to believe what they believe and to practice what they consider central to their existence in the face of an alternative cultural definition they mobilized in a variety of ways that has recently come to be known as the New Christian Right (Heinz, 1983). Hammond argues that since the 1960s a modernist liberal moral revolution has taken place in America, evoking a morally conservative counter revolution (Hammond, 1985). The central ideology of conservative Christianity contributes to constant mobilization that is variable in intensity and becomes "white hot" as perceived threats become more real.

The mobilization of New Christian Right parents takes many forms. The HSM is a logical outcome of the New Christian Right perspective on public education. Donald Heinz captures the sentiments of many of the parents in the HSM:

> *For the New Christian Right, the public school stands as a primary symbol of their control, or lack of control over decisions that directly affect their lives. The school is a symbol of the neighborhood, of grass-roots, of the family extended. Federal intervention in the school is experienced as the intrusion of the government at a deeply resonant symbolic level. Whatever else, the rapid growth of alternative schools in recent years—and it may mean virulent racism and resurgent know-nothing-ism—it means a war over competing mythologies and a battle for access to symbol production (Heinz, 1983:139; also see Peshkin, 1986; and Rose, 1988).*

Home-schooling promises total control over symbol production and socialization into the world of a very specific ideology. The majority of home-schooling parents are even wary of private Christian school alternatives, because they do not have control over what other students and families may bring to their children (Bates, 1988).

GRASSROOTS POLITICAL ACTION

On the one hand, work on the New Christian Right reveals a mixed message, with some claiming that moral conservatism can have an influence on the outcome of electoral politics: "The politicalization of conservative moral issues contributed to Reagan's victory by attracting voters who traditionally support the Democratic party" (Woodrum, 1988). On the other hand, some claim that religion, religious conservatism in particular, does not play a significant role in American politics: "The evidence presented here indicates rather conclusively that this movement had very little, if any, effect on people's vote for President" (Johnson and Tamney, 1982). In another light, however, in this research we are not dealing with a vote for President; we are dealing with a single issue, the passage of a home-schooling bill, and the mobilization of support for that bill.

In 1986, a variety of Oregon home-schooling groups and PACS came together to lobby for the passage of the home-schooling bill. Those choosing to home-school had already made an ideological and organizational commitment which could easily be mobilized. To choose to take on so intimidating a task suggests a strong commitment to relatively drastic action. Consider this mother's account: "When we started we did not know if we were doing the right thing. My parents were very upset and still are. I was not trained as a teacher like some of my friends who home-school. I knew there were going to be problems with organization, and disciplining myself, and being consistent. I just knew if God was asking me to do this he would help me get through it and he has." Most families indicate that they will continue to home-school their children regardless of the law, and they will go to jail or leave the state if it becomes necessary. To speak, write, lobby and support lobbying organizations involved in passing a home-schooling bill seems to them a small step taken to further their primary goal of protecting their children from the brainwashing of secular humanists in the public schools and thus saving them from eternal damnation.

It is difficult to trace the origins of support for the 1986 home-schooling bill because it is one portion of a larger package of other educational issues and New Christian Right causes. It may be argued cogently that the HSM is, in part, a result of ideas expressed by publicists for the New Christian Right. Home-schooling is presented as a political option to parents without the resources for private Christian schooling, or who feel very strongly about exposing their children to the outside world; thus, the HSM exists, in part, because of the New Christian Right, and in turn, the HSM provides further support for the larger organization. The home-schooling SMO and the New Christian Right are intertwined, if not quite interdependent. The actual organizations that did the lobbying for the home-schooling bill in the state of Oregon were a mixture of older Christian lobbying organizations, older right-wing organizations, and new lobbying organizations. These older organizations are a part of the Old Christian Right in that their existence precedes such organizations as the Moral Majority (Shibley and Johnson, 1987). In addition, New Right and New Christian Right organizations, with broader agendas, see home-schooling as ideologically sound and compatible with their broad agendas and support the effort. And finally, specific home-schooling political action committees and lobbying organizations coordinated the campaign. Most of these groups came together during 1987, in Salem, the State Capital, as the Monday Night Forum, organized by a conservative Representative from a rural area to lobby Republican legislators on a variety of issues, among which education was preeminent.

The one organization that did the majority of the initial work on writing a bill and contacting other SMOs and lobbyist groups was an organization called PEAPAC, Parents Education Association Political Action Committee. It was headed by one very dedicated individual, a Christian Reconstructionist, who became the organizational leader of the lobbying effort. In this case, a charismatic leader seems less important than an organizational leader, as the passion of home-schooling parents appears already assured. Mobilizing already committed individuals is simply a matter of organizing their energies for a directed effort. PEAPAC was able to call upon an umbrella organization for help in the actual lobbying. This group, OCEAN, Oregon Christian (Home) Education Association Network, serves to help home-schooling support groups become established and provides them with non-political home-schooling resources as its primary function. OCEAN distributes a newsletter and has a telephone tree network. In this way, an organization that is set up for essentially non-political purposes can become a central resource in a grassroots lobbying effort. PEAPAC was also able to call upon the editor of *The*

Teaching Home (a magazine also originally devoted to educational issues surrounding home-schooling and not to the political agendas of the New Christian Right) to rally its readers to the cause. Sue Welch, the editor of the magazine, indicated that the leader of PEAPAC spearheaded the changes in the law, and that the editors of the magazine were then asked to support the campaign which they did. After the home-schooling bill became law Sue Welch, with the help of members of the State Department of Education, devoted some energy to drafting the administrative rules. Through OCEAN's newsletter and *The Teaching Home*, home-schooling families were made aware of when key hearings on the bill were to be held and were asked to attend the hearings, write letters, and make telephone calls to key legislators. Welch indicated that a large majority of home-schooling parents responded to this plea for lobbying help.

The chair of the Oregon House Education Committee and his assistant indicated that lobbying for the home-schooling bill was the heaviest lobbying they had ever received. They received more letters and phone calls than they had for any other bill both when it was first drafted and when it was up for possible reconsideration in the next legislative session. They further explained that while hearing rooms typically have 25-30 persons in attendance when bills are being considered, the hearings on the home-schooling bill filled the 140 person capacity room every time, with a large spillover into the hallway. The House Education Committee chair felt that this kind of lobbying did have an effect on the outcome of the bill.

The interconnections among the various home-schooling lobbying groups, New Christian Right lobbying groups, and New and Old Right lobbying groups increased the capabilities of the home-schooling lobbying effort. The head of PEAPAC reported receiving names, telephone numbers, contact persons, and various other forms of assistance from such diverse sources as the Libertarian Party, figures in the Republican Party in the State of Oregon, and a variety of churches and other New Christian Right lobbying groups.

Virtually all of the home-schooling parents who were interviewed indicated that they had participated in the lobbying effort in some fashion. Many felt that they had not done enough in the initial campaign and were planning to do more as the bill came up for reconsideration. All who lobbied felt they were heard, and this increased their motivation to become more politically involved. Many were moved to become involved in the Joe Lutz campaign. Joe Lutz is a Baptist minister who challenged Oregon Senator Robert Packwood for the Republican nomination in the 1986 primaries and surprised many with 41% of the vote. It would be simplistic to suggest that home-schooling parents were a large portion of this 41%, but Joe Lutz, who home-schools his own children, provided an image that led many of them to participate as they had not in the past. Many of these parents have subsequently become more centrally involved in the Oregon Republican Party, as precinct chairs and in general campaign activities. The New Christian Right, beginning with the Joe Lutz campaign in 1986, has discovered its potential at the state level in Oregon and has subsequently come to dominate the Oregon Republican Party through a group called the Oregon Citizens Alliance (The Oregonian, 1988).

Participants in the home-schooling movement who had chosen to live out the passion of their convictions by pulling their children out of what they perceive to be a corrupt public educational system began to see that this passion could be turned into real political power. Of course some were politically involved long before they chose to home-school; a few were involved in the creationist controversy in the

186

1970s, but a much larger number of home-schooling parents were introduced to the political process through lobbying for the home-schooling bill. The depth of their convictions seems to be something that the opposition lacks.

THE WEAKNESS OF THE COUNTER-MOVEMENT

A variable that may have contributed to the effectiveness of the home-schooling lobby was the absence of an effective counter-movement. The Oregon Education Association, cited often by the press and political writers as one of the most powerful lobbies in the State of Oregon, did not participate in the home-schooling debate and mounted no counter-offensive. The two lobbying groups that opposed the bill actively, COSA, the Confederation of Oregon School Administrators, and OSBA, the Oregon School Board Association, filed formal letters of opposition with the House Education Committee and sent single professional lobbyists to the hearings, but mounted no grassroots counter-offensive. It may be that the resources of time, money, and stamina had been spent in the campaign to alter the Oregon tax system so that individual school districts all over the state would not be threatened with shutdowns. It is also possible that the passion of professional lobbyists does not match that of grassroots members of the New Christian Right. As organizations become more professional, bureaucratized, and organized they often lose their original drive.

THE CITIZEN LEGISLATURE

One further variable that may allow for a more effective grassroots lobby in the State of Oregon is the existence of a citizen legislature. Elected representatives in the State of Oregon are not full-time legislators; they meet every other year and most must have other means to make a living. Salaries are small in comparison to many other states, as are per diem expenses. Some argue that a non-professional legislature leads to a more democratic system because the material rewards for staying in office are not great, and thus the pressures of entrenched special interests are lessened. Grass roots lobbying campaigns may then have a greater chance of success, because there is less fear of larger and more powerful interest groups. In addition, in this particular case, that two of the members of the House Education Committee, the committee responsible for drafting the home-schooling bill, were conservative Christians made the lobbying efforts of the home-schooling lobby a bit easier.

SUMMARY

Conservative Christianity can be viewed as a social movement that is in a constant state of mobilization due to an ideology which has consistently been opposed to the 20th Century growth and encroachment of secular culture as an alternative meaning system. The heat of this mobilization waxes and wanes as perceived threats to their value system and way of life are more or less dire and the ability to mobilize resources is greater or lesser. The forms that mobilization take

187

include special interest SMOs. A kind of reinforcing circularity occurs wherein the ideology of conservative Christianity spawns SMOs such as the HSM. In turn, the HSM is, in part, a result of the rise of the New Christian Right. The success of the New Christian Right in the political arena has led to a renewed and widespread discussion of educational issues. This discussion has led some to conclude that the only reasonable alternative is to home-school. Home-schooling reinforces values and, in turn, reinforces further political action. The passion of one's faith leads to further passions, a passion for home-schooling and a particular lifestyle, as well as a desire to protect that lifestyle by making it legally acceptable. The importance of mobilizing resources to carry this out is clear, but so is the role of grievances and ideology.

NOTE

*An earlier version of this paper was presented at the annual meetings of the Society for the Scientific Study of Religion. October 1988, Chicago, Illinois.

REFERENCES

Ammerman, Nancy Tatum.
   1987   Bible Believers. New Brunswick: Rutgers University Press.
Bates, Vernon L.
   1988   "Motivation and resource mobilization in the fundamentalist home-school movement." Paper presented at the annual meeting of the Pacific Sociological Association, April, 1988.
   1975   Christian Fundamentalism and the Theory of Evolution in Public School Education: A Study of the Creation Science Movement. Unpublished Ph.D. dissertation. Davis, CA.
Berger, Peter L.
   1967   The Sacred Canopy. Garden City, N.Y.: Doubleday and Co., Inc.
Berger, Peter L. and Thomas Luckmann.
   1966   The Social Construction of Reality. Garden City, N.Y.: Doubleday and Co., Inc.
Caplan, Lionel (Ed.)
   1987   Studies in Religious Fundamentalism. Albany, N.Y.: State University of New York Press.
Clapp, Rodney.
   1987   "Democracy as heresy." Christianity Today. February 20, 1987.
Gamson, William.
   1975   The Strategy of Social Protest. Homewood, Ill.: The Dorsey Press.
Geertz, Clifford.
   1968   Islam Observed. New Haven: Yale University Press.
Gerlach, Luther P. and Virginia H. Hine.
   1970   People, Power and Change. New York: The Bobbs-Merrill Co., Inc.
Grabiner, Judith K. and Peter D. Miller.
   1974   "Effects of the scopes trial." Science 183:836.
Hammond, Phillip E.
   1983   "Another Great Awakening?" Pp. 208-28 in Robert C. Liebman and Robert Wuthnow (Eds.), The New Christian Right. New York: Aldine Publishing Co.
Hertzke, Allen D.
   1988   Representing God in Washington. Knoxville: The University of Tennessee Press.
Heinz, Donald
   1983   "The struggle to define America." Pp. 133-49 in Robert C. Liebman and Robert Wuthnow (Eds.), The New Christian Right. New York: Aldine Publishing Co.

Himmelstein, Jerome.
1983   "The New Right." Pp. 15-30 in Robert C. Liebman and Robert Wuthnow (Eds.), The New Christian Right. New York: Aldine Publishing Co.

Johnson, Stephen D. and Joseph B. Tamney.
1982   "The Christian Right and the 1980 presidential election." Journal for the Scientific Study of Religion 21:123-30.

Klandermans, Bert.
1984   "Mobilization and participation: Social-psychological expansions of resource mobilization theory." American Sociological Review 49:583-600.

Latus, Margaret Ann.
1983   "Ideological PACS and political action." Pp. 75-103 in Robert C. Liebman and Robert Wuthnow (Eds.), The New Christian Right. New York: Aldine Publishing Co.

Lines, Patricia M.
1987   "An overview of home instruction." Phi Delta Kappan. March:510-517.

Lofland, John.
1979   "White-hot mobilization: Strategies of a millenarian movement." Pp. 157-66 in Mayer N. Zald and John D. McCarthy (Eds.), The Dynamics of Social Movements. Cambridge, MA.: Winthrop Publishers, Inc.

Lofland, John and Lyn H. Lofland.
1984   Analyzing Social Settings. Belmont, CA.: Wadsworth Publishing Company.

McCarthy, John D.
1984   Book review of The New Christian Right: Mobilization and Legitimation, edited by Robert C. Liebman and Robert Wuthnow. Journal for the Scientific Study of Religion 23:137.

Mayberry, Maralee.
1988   "1987 Summary of Oregon home educators." A preliminary report of some of the data for Ph.D. dissertation provided to me by the author. This material was presented at the annual meetings of the Oregon Academy of Sciences, Sociology section, February, 1988. Portland, OR.

Marsden, George M.
1980   Fundamentalism and American Culture. New York/Oxford: Oxford University Press.

McCarthy, John D. and Mayer N. Zald.
1977   "Resource mobilization and social movements: A partial theory." American Journal of Sociology 82:1212-1239.

1973   The Trend of Social Movements in America: Professionalization and Resource Mobilization. Morristown, N.J.: General Learning Corporation.

Oberschall, Anthony.
1973   Social Conflict and Social Movements. Englewood Cliffs, N.J.: Prentice Hall Oregonian.

1988   "GOP hopeful rebuffs conservative group." Oregonian, July 6.

Peshkin, Alan.
1986   God's Choice. Chicago: The University of Chicago Press.

Rose, Susan D.
1988   Keeping Them Out of the Hands of Satan. New York: Routledge, Chapman and Hall, Inc.

Sandeen, Ernest R.
1970   The Roots of Fundamentalism. Chicago: The University of Chicago Press.

Shibley, Mark A. and Benton Johnson.
1987   "The political posture of New Christian Rightists: A study of continuity and change." Paper presented at the annual meetings of the Pacific Sociological Association, Eugene, Oregon, April, 1987.

Stacey, William and Anson Shupe.
1982   "Correlates of support for the electronic church." Journal for the Scientific Study of Religion 21:291-303.

Schwartz, Howard and Jerry Jacobs.
1979   Qualitative Sociology. New York: The Free Press.

189

Swidler, Ann.
    1986   "Culture in action." American Sociological Review 51:273-86.
Wilcox, Clyde.
    1988   "Political action committees of the New Christian Right." Journal for the
            Scientific Study of Religion 27:60-71.
Wilson, Bryan.
    1966   Religion in Secular Society. London: C.A. Watts and Co. Ltd.
Woodrum, Eric.
    1988   "Moral conservatism and the 1984 presidential election." Journal for the Scien-
            tific Study of Religion 2:192-210.
Zald, Mayer N.
    1982   Theological Crucibles: Social Movements in and of Religion." Review of Reli-
            gious Research 23:317-336.
Zald, Mayer N. and Roberta Asch.
    1966   "Social movement organizations: Growth, decay and change" Social Forces,
            44:327-41.
Zald, Mayer N. and John D. McCarthy.
    1979   The Dynamics of Social Movements. Cambridge, MA.: Winthrop Pub

APPENDIX

Data came from the following sources:
1. In-depth interviews with 47 home-schooling families in their homes and home-school classrooms, using a standardized, open-ended interview schedule. The questions in all interviews were open-ended to allow for "recursiveness" (Schwartz and Jacobs, 1979:45). Some of these family members were movement leaders and lobbyists. Interviews usually lasted from one and one-half to two hours. Typical face sheet questions on the social characteristics of interviewees were asked, followed by questions specific to the study. Care was taken to word the interview questions as neutrally as possible. The topics covered ranged from questions about religious background and current beliefs, to motivations for home-schooling, to participation in New Christian Right political activities. The questions asked of other interview subjects were changed as it became appropriate.
2. Interviews with other, non-home-schooling, New Christian Right political activists and other conservative groups. These interviews explored the inter-connections among these groups.
3. Interviews with three ideological leaders of the movement. These were individuals whose written work and workshops provided a rationale and varieties of plans or programs for home-schooling.
4. Interviews with two key Oregon state legislators who serve on the House Education Committee, and interviews with their legislative aids. These legislators played a role in the passage of legislation regulating home-schooling. In addition, I was given full access to, and allowed to make copies of, all correspondence relative to the home-schooling bill. The correspondence numbers several hundred pages. I categorized this correspondence in a variety of ways, such as, did it favor or not favor a home-schooling bill, and was it written by a person identified by religious affiliation?
5. Interviews with the leaders of two separate, counter-movement, education organizations who oppose the home-schooling bill. These interviews were carried out in the professional lobbying offices located in the Oregon state capital, a clear contrast to the facilities available to the home-schooling grassroots effort.
6. Interviews with some of the public school personnel who are charged with carrying out the provisions of the home school bill.
7. Interviews with two private Christian school administrators who supervise satellite programs for home-schooling parents and children.
8. Participant observation during a day-long home-schooling workshop for home-schooling parents and interviews with some of the attendees. As a participant observer I

attended sessions on a variety of issues, conversed with participants, collected pamphlets and purchased books on home-schooling, interviewed some of the attendees and set up future interviews.

9. Participant observation at a New Christian Right lobbyist dinner given for Oregon State legislators at the state Capitol. After some initial resistance from the secretary of a legislator affiliated with New Christian Right causes who played a role in organizing the dinner, I was allowed to attend on the condition of promised anonymity to the participants.

10. Analysis of home school literature and New Christian Right literature, books, magazines, pamphlets, newsletters, home-schooling curricula and curriculum guides, and a variety of advertisements for home-schooling materials.

11. Analysis of programs about home-schooling on Christian radio. I specifically taped and listened most often to James Dobson's program Focus on the Family.

12. Interviews with the officer from the Oregon State Department of Education charged with coordinating state policy for home schools and an evaluation of materials provided by this individual.

CHRISTIAN COALITION PRESENTS

CONTRACT WITH THE AMERICAN FAMILY

A Bold Plan to Strengthen the Family
and Restore Common-Sense Values

Introduction

IN THE 1994 MIDTERM ELECTIONS, the American people elected the first Republican Congress in 40 years in what was the largest transfer of power from a minority party to a majority party in the twentieth century. The message of the election was clear: the American people want lower taxes, less government, strong families, protection of innocent human life, and traditional values.

The 104th Congress devoted its first hundred days to the Contract with America, including a Balanced Budget Amendment, tax relief for families, welfare reform, and term limits. Christian Coalition enthusiastically supported the Contract and launched one of the most extensive grassroots campaigns in its history to support the Contract's passage. The Coalition will continue this effort as the Contract moves through the Senate.

The problems our nation faces are not all fiscal in nature. The American people are increasingly concerned about the coarsening of the culture, the breakup of the family, and a decline in civility. A recent *Los Angeles Times* poll reported that 53 percent of Americans believe the moral problems facing our country are more important than the economic problems.[1] Other survey data indicates that 80 percent of Americans believe there is a problem of declining morality within our nation.[2]

The *Contract with the American Family* is a bold agenda for Congress intended to strengthen families and restore common-sense values. The Contract represents a valuable contribution to a congressional agenda beyond the first hundred days. These provisions are the ten suggestions, not the Ten Commandments. There is no deadline or specified time period during which they are to be enacted. But Congress would be well advised to act with all due and deliberate speed. The provisions in the Contract enjoy support from 60 to 90 percent of the American people.

These items do not represent the pro-family movement's entire agenda. There are many other prominent pro-family organizations that will work on many other issues — women in combat, welfare reform, budget policy — in the months ahead. This contract is designed to be the first word, not the last word, in developing a bold and incremental start to strengthening the family and restoring values.

Restoring Religious Equality

A constitutional amendment to protect the religious liberties of Americans in public places.

ITH EACH PASSING YEAR, people of faith grow increasingly distressed by the hostility of public institutions toward religious expression. Public interest law firms dedicated to preserving religious liberties receive thousands of calls every year on issues pertaining to the rights of students in public schools.

Examples of hostility toward religious values and those who hold them abound. In Nevada, an elementary school student chosen to sing a solo in the school's Christmas pageant was forbidden from singing "The First Noel" because of its religious overtones.[3] At a public elementary school in Rhode Island, the principal announced shortly before the beginning of a Christmas concert that he had censored all of the pageant's songs.[4] A Scarsdale, New York school board banned all religious celebrations from schools, although parties with non-holiday themes were still permitted. According to the Catholic League for Religious and Civil Rights, the ban included "displays or exhibits, such as wreaths, garlands, caroling and menorahs that appear to promote or give approval to religious matters," as well as "candy canes, bells, holiday music, and Hanukkah or Christmas parties and concerts."[5] Teachers in New Jersey

195

were told to avoid references to Easter, including jelly beans and the colors purple and yellow.

Children have been told they cannot read the Bible during silent reading time.[6] In one school, a little girl was told there was a problem with the book she chose to read to her class — it mentioned "God" four times.[7]

This anti-religious bigotry is not confined to the classroom. Nativity scenes are now barred from federal post offices,[8] and from the lawns of public buildings unless accompanied by a non-religious display such as Santa Claus. Some courthouses are prohibited from displaying the Ten Commandments (despite the fact that they are chiseled into the walls of the United States Supreme Court). And landlords have been sued by the state for discrimination because they refused to rent to unmarried couples for religious reasons.[9]

This hostility toward faith is the result of 30 years of confusing and often quixotic jurisprudence in establishment clause cases. The Supreme Court's application of the three-pronged "Lemon test," first developed in *Lemon v. Kurtzman* (1971),[10] has become so tortuous that some court decisions allow states to lend textbooks, but not movie projectors, maps, or laboratory equipment to parochial schools; to supply guidance counseling services outside of parochial schools, such as mobile units, but not within the schools; and to provide bus services to and from parochial schools, but not for school field trips.[11] Justice Scalia, who like many has argued for ending the use of this confusing test, has likened it to "some ghoul in a late-night horror movie that repeatedly sits up in its grave and shuffles abroad, after being repeatedly killed and buried..."[12]

Despite such rollbacks in religious rights, the American public consistently supports freedom of religious expression in the public square. An April 1994 Wirthlin poll indicates that reinstating voluntary school prayer not only continues to receive overwhelming support (78 percent of Americans), but it also enjoys support across a broad spectrum of Americans: 79 percent of African Americans and 80 percent of whites support school prayer; 85 percent of low income and 71 percent of high income Americans support school prayer; and 65 percent of non-Christians and between 80 and 94 percent of

Christians support school prayer.

The Religious Equality Amendment would not restore compulsory, sectarian prayer or Bible-reading dictated by government officials. Instead, we seek a balanced approach that allows voluntary, student and citizen-initiated free speech in non-compulsory settings such as courthouse lawns, high school graduation ceremonies, and sports events.

A survey by the Luntz Research Company found that 78 percent of all Americans support a Religious Equality Amendment. We urge the 104th Congress to pass an amendment that not only protects the rights of students, but the religious liberties of all Americans.

Returning Education Control to the Local Level

Transfer funding of the federal Department of Education to families and local school boards.

T HE NEED FOR EDUCATION REFORM is plainly evident if one considers the trends of recent decades. SAT scores have dropped by more than 75 points since 1960.[13] Ten nations outperform U.S. 13-year-olds in math and science tests.[14] And as education performance drops, the level of school violence in our schools is on the rise. The dramatic increase in shootings and violence-related injuries occurring in our nation's schools is well-known. Because of the prevalence of weapons, many American students are greeted with metal detectors when they arrive for school in the morning. In 1992, 10 percent of tenth-graders admitted they had taken a weapon to school during the past *month*.[15] There are 250,000 crimes committed on school property each year.

Parents are distressed over the failure of schools to teach children basic skills of reading, writing, and arithmetic. Too often, sex education emphasizes contraception and condom use rather than abstinence and self-control. Homosexuality is promoted as an acceptable alternative lifestyle. Outcome-based education (OBE) supplants basic skills. Psychological counseling takes place without parental involvement or notification.[16]

Christian Coalition members believe schools should reinforce rather than undermine the values taught in homes, churches and synagogues.

Parental involvement and local control is the most pressing need in education today. A current report by the U.S. Department of Education, "Strong Families, Strong Schools," corroborates the fact that parental involvement in children's education results in higher student performance.[17] Many local and state reform initiatives focus on increasing parental rights and participation in their children's education.

Despite this trend at the local level, the federal government has done little to advance these initiatives. In 1993 and 1994, Congress tightened the federal choke hold on local schools by passing Goals 2000, the Educate America Act[18] and the Improving America's Schools Act, which re-authorized the Elementary and Secondary Education Act (ESEA).[19]

Christian Coalition seeks to return greater power and control over our children's education to parents and local communities. This reform begins by transferring much of the funding for the U.S. Department of Education to families and local school boards, and applying the remainder to deficit reduction.

The U.S. currently spends approximately $275 billion per year on public education.[20] Yet student performance and educational achievement do not reflect this financial investment. As *Time* magazine recently noted, "The U.S. spends a greater percentage of its gross national product on education (7.5 percent) than any other country except Israel, and yet is out-performed in math and science among 13-year-olds by more than 10 nations, including Hungary, Taiwan and the former Soviet Union."[21] Less than half of federal education dollars reach classrooms for instruction.[22]

Increased spending is not the answer. In fact, the 10 states ranking highest in education performance do not top per-pupil expenditures.[23] Rather, the answer lies in eliminating bureaucracies, administrative costs, and federal restrictions that prevent effective reform at the local level.

Since the time of its creation in 1980, the U.S. Department of Education has grown in magnitude to the point that it now consists of 241 separate programs, a budget of $30 billion,[24] and more than 5,000 employees.[25] Moreover, federal control over education has dramatically increased, ultimately culminating with the 1994 passage of Goals 2000 and H.R. 6, the Improving America's Schools Act.

Goals 2000 established several new federal bureaucracies, including the National Education Standards and Improvement Council (NESIC), which many view as equivalent to a national school board. NESIC has powerful authority to certify national education standards regarding educational content and student performance. Although these standards are not binding on states, they do have national stature, and states have to "voluntarily" develop comparable standards in order to receive a portion of the billions of dollars in federal funding authorized under the Elementary and Secondary Education Act.

When Congress passed Goals 2000, many people predicted it would lead to the establishment of "politically-correct" national education standards, resulting in the introduction of outcome-based education (OBE) on a national scale. Verification of this prediction came quickly.

With 1994's release of national history standards, developed with $2.2 million in federal funding from the National Endowment for the Humanities and the U.S. Department of Education, it became obvious that national education standards would not be objective.[26] Criticism of the biased and distorted views prevalent in both sets of standards — the National Standards for United States History, as well as the National Standards for World History — was widespread. Criticism of the U.S. History standards included the fact that the United States Constitution was never mentioned in any of the 31 standards, and was relegated to the supporting materials;[27] the establishment of the National Organization of Women and Sierra Club were viewed as notable events, but not the first assembling of the United States Congress;[28] and according to one reviewer, the material revealed only one quotation from a congressional leader, and that was Tip O'Neill calling Ronald Reagan "a cheerleader for selfishness."[29] The World History standards drew widespread criticism also, particularly for their anti-Western bias.[30]

The bias in these standards was so grave that the United

States Senate overwhelmingly adopted (99 to 1) a resolution condemning the standards and expressing the sense of the Senate that NESIC not certify them.[31] Nevertheless, 10,000 copies of these standards already have been mailed to school administrators and others throughout the nation.[32] These national standards undermine parental involvement and local control of education.

The time to return federal education control to parents and local communities through elimination of the United States Department of Education is long overdue, and a good first step would include repealing Goals 2000 legislation.

Promoting School Choice

Enactment of legislation that will enhance parents' choice of schools for their children.

SCHOOL CHOICE INITIATIVES are sweeping the nation like wildfire. Sixty-two percent of Americans favor choice among public schools, and 50 percent favor vouchers.[33] School choice legislation was either introduced or pending in 34 states in 1993.[34] These initiatives take a number of forms, including voucher programs, tax credits and charter schools.

Voucher programs provide monetary assistance to parents for use at the school of their choice. Tuition tax credits achieve the same goal of school choice, and are preferred by some communities. Charter schools are a creative new initiative through which states charter and fund alternative schools designed to meet the needs of a diverse student population. Other local initiatives include the privatization of public schools, such as in Baltimore, Maryland and Hartford, Connecticut. As parents and local communities strive to reform our country's educational system, the federal government must do more to assist these efforts.

One possible example of federal school choice legislation is S. 618, the Coats-Lieberman Low-income School Choice Demonstration Act. This legislation would establish up to 20 demonstration projects that would provide financial assistance to low-income parents to help them send their children to the school of their choice, whether public or private. The legislation requires an evaluation of the effectiveness of this demonstration initiative in order to provide objective documentation of the merits of school choice. With almost half of high school students in inner city schools failing to graduate,[35] educational reform for low-income parents in these cities is becoming increasingly urgent.

We urge the swift passage of school choice legislation such as S. 618 during the 104th Congress as a means of promoting school choice for parents. We believe passage of this bill will spur grassroots efforts to reform education and give parents greater choice in selecting the best school for their children.

Protecting Parental Rights

Enactment of a Parental Rights Act and defeat of the U.N. Convention on the Rights of the Child.

T HE UNITED STATES CONSTITUTION does not explicitly set forth protections for parental rights, but a long line of court cases have held that the United States Constitution protects the right of parents to control the upbringing of their children. The rights of parents, however, are under increasing assault in modern day society.

For example, state officials removed an eighth-grade girl from her home because she objected to the ground rules (regarding use of drugs, curfew hours, etc.) her parents had set.[36] One mother's child was removed from her home because the mother refused to continue to take her first-grade child to therapy lessons for hyperactivity.[37] And in 1992, a San Diego grand jury found that 35 to 70 percent of the county's foster children "never should have been removed from their parental homes."[38]

Enactment of a Parental Rights Act will ensure that parental rights are not violated and ensure that parents have the foremost duty and responsibility to direct the upbringing of their children. Representatives Steve Largent (R-OK) and Mike Parker (D-MS) in the House, and Senators Charles Grassley (R-IA) and Howell Heflin (D-AL) in the Senate, are drafting a parental rights act to address this critical problem. While language is still being finalized, the authors intend that the Parental Rights Act of 1995 will clarify that "the right of parents to direct the upbringing of their children," includes overseeing their children's education, health care, discipline, and religious training. Moreover, it requires that any governmental interference in the parent-child relationship be justified by "clear and convincing evidence" that it "is essential to accomplish a compelling governmental interest" and that it is applied in "the least restrictive means" possible.

The threat to the rights of America's parents is very real, as the movement to ratify the U.N. Convention on the Rights of the Child exemplifies. The Convention on the Rights of the Child is a human rights treaty adopted in 1989 by the General Assembly of the United Nations. It has not been ratified in the United States. In the past, the United States has not supported the treaty due to concerns that it may concede jurisdiction over United States citizens to an international body and international court.[39]

Christian Coalition opposes the treaty because it interferes with the parent-child relationship, threatens the sovereignty of U.S. law, and elevates as "rights" such dubious provisions as access to television and mass media. The following are some of the examples of the absolute rights given to children through this treaty:

> • "No child shall be subjected to arbitrary or unlawful interference with his or her privacy, family, home or correspondence ... The child has the right to the protection of the law against such interference or attacks."[40]

> • "The child shall have the right to freedom of expression; this right shall include freedom to seek, receive and impart information and ideas of all kinds, regardless of frontiers, either orally, in writing or in print, in the form of art, or through any other media of the child's choice."[41]

> • With respect to the right of the child to freedom of association or peaceful assembly, "[n]o restrictions may be placed on the exercise of these

rights other than those imposed in conformity with the law and which are necessary in a democratic society in the interests of national security or public safety, public order, the protection of public health or morals or the protection of the rights and freedoms of others."[42]

Under the treaty, parents could well lose their right to prevent their child from associating with disreputable individuals such as delinquents, or receiving literature or gaining access to mass media communication (including films and television) that is not age-appropriate.

Pursuant to the treaty, a Committee on the Rights of the Child has been established to review reports from nations regarding their progress in implementing the treaty. The committee has urged that in the area of sex education, parents be required to give the opinion of the child equal weight. The committee warned that "the possibility for parents in England and Wales to withdraw their children from parts of the sex education programmes in schools" undermines "the right of the child to express his/her opinion."[43]

The committee's concern about soliciting children's views prior to "exclusion from school" should be of particular concern to parents who educate their children at home. It is clear that rejection of this treaty by the United States Senate would be in the best interests of American parents.

Family-Friendly Tax Relief

Reduce the tax burden on the American family, eliminate the marriage penalty, and pass the *Mothers and Homemakers Rights Act* to remedy the unequal treatment that homemakers receive under the Internal Revenue Service Code with respect to saving for retirement.

I T HAS BEEN SAID THAT THE INTACT FAMILY is the most successful Department of Health, Education, and Welfare ever conceived. Yet the federal government, through the tax code, has punished families for working, saving, and staying together. The *Contract with the American Family* addresses not only the cultural pressures on families, but the financial pressures as well.

1. Tax relief for families with children.

In 1950 the average family of four in America paid just 2 percent of its adjusted gross income in federal income taxes. Today that same family sends one out of every four dollars to Washington. When state and local taxes are added, the average family of four pays 38 percent of its entire income in taxes, more than it spends on such essentials as housing, clothing and food.

Christian Coalition's top legislative priority since 1993 has been tax relief for America's hard-working families. We strongly favor the $500 tax credit for children that has been passed by the House and awaits action in the Senate. Our long-term goal is to restore the standard deduction for children to its inflation-adjusted 1946 value: $8,000 to $10,000 per dependent child.

Christian Coalition also supports in concept a flat or flattened tax (with a generous personal exemption for children) as an ultimate goal to simplify the tax code, reward work and savings, and reduce the crushing tax burden on families.

2. Eliminate the marriage penalty.

Under current law, many married couples pay more in taxes than they would if they remained single because their combined income puts them into a higher tax bracket. On April 5, 1995, as part of the American Dream Restoration Act, the House of Representatives voted to restore tax fairness for married couples. H.R. 1215 makes married couples eligible for a tax rebate of up to $145 if their tax liability goes up as a result of being married. In a time when family breakups are so common, the Senate should pass this legislation to encourage marriage and ease the burden on families trying to form and stay together.

3. The Mothers and Homemakers Rights Act.

The *Contract with the American Family* calls for the enactment of legislation such as the Hutchison-Mikulski Individual Retirement Account equity bill (S. 287), which will allow homemakers to contribute up to $2,000 annually toward an IRA, thereby providing equitable treatment to spouses who work at home.

The Internal Revenue Code currently allows a double-income married couple to contribute up to $4,000 per year toward retirement by allowing them to contribute up to $2,000 each toward an IRA. However, in the case of a single-income married couple, the couple can only contribute up to $2,250 per year toward retirement through an IRA, with the homemaker's contribution limited to $250. This inequity in the tax code reflects a disrespect for the valuable role of the homemaker in our society. Christian Coalition urges Congress to remedy this injustice by amending the tax code to allow homemakers to contribute equally up to $2,000 annually toward an IRA. This could provide an increase of up to $150,000 in savings for a couple after 30 years.[44] Furthermore, because the value of families never decreases, the contribution amount should be indexed to inflation.

Restoring Respect for Human Life

Protecting the rights of states that do not fund abortion, protecting innocent human life by placing real limits on late-term abortions, and ending funds to organizations that promote and perform abortions.

IN SPEAKING TO THE NATIONAL PRAYER BREAKFAST in 1994, Mother Teresa delivered an eloquent and stirring defense of the rights of innocent human life. "The greatest destroyer of peace today is abortion," Mother Teresa of Calcutta said at the National Prayer Breakfast in February 1994. "It is a war against the child, a direct killing of the innocent child."[45]

The foundation of all our rights as Americans — to speech, assembly, and religious expression — are all built upon the right to life. The genius of the American idea is that every person is endowed by his Creator with certain inalienable rights, the first of which is the right to life.

Christian Coalition seeks by all lawful and non-violent means to protect innocent human life for the disabled, the elderly, the infirm, and the unborn. We support constitutional and statutory protection for the unborn child. Our ultimate goal is to establish the humanity of the unborn child and to see a day when every child is safe in their mother's womb.

We urge Congress to take the following action as a beginning toward that end.

1. Real limits on late-term abortions by providing legal protection to children in the latter months of pregnancy and ending the practice of "partial-birth abortions."

Most Americans would be shocked to learn about the methods that are used in late-term abortions in America today. These methods have reached the point to where a fully formed child can be completely delivered alive, with the exception of the child's head, and then the abortionist is free to end the child's life. This "partial-birth abortion" procedure is also known as "dilation and extraction," or D&X, in which forceps are used to remove second and third-trimester babies, with only the head remaining inside the uterus. The child's life is then ended, and the dead child is delivered.[46]

Most tragic of all is the fact that the majority of these babies are alive until the end of the proceeding.[47] Indeed, virtually all of the victims are beyond the 24th week of pregnancy, and many can survive outside the womb.

It is difficult to estimate the number of partial-birth abortions performed, because abortion statistics in general are unreliable. The Alan Guttmacher Institute, a research group affiliated with Planned Parenthood, estimates that about 10 percent of abortions occur in the second or third trimester. One abortionist who specializes in D&X procedures testified in 1992 that he had performed 700 of them.[48]

Establishing real limits on late-term abortions is one of the most important steps Congress can take to protect innocent human life. A child has a better than 50-percent chance of survival outside its mother's womb at 26 weeks.[49] But the D&X technique has been used on children up to 40 weeks gestation, which is a full-term pregnancy.[50] One physician experienced in this procedure admitted to having mixed feelings on its morality:

> "I do have moral compunctions. And if I see a case that's later, like after 20 weeks where it frankly is a child to me, I really agonize over it because the

potential is so imminently there. I think, 'Gee, it's too bad that this child couldn't be adopted.'"[51]

We call on the 104th Congress to enact restrictions on late-term abortions and end the practice of D&X abortion. Children at any stage of pregnancy should not be subject to this cruel and inhumane form of death, but such treatment of those who can clearly survive outside the mother's womb is particularly cruel.

2. Protect the rights of states that do not wish to use taxpayer funds to take innocent human life.

In 1993 Congress re-authorized the Hyde Amendment, in effect since 1977, with rape and incest exceptions. Christian Coalition believes taxpayer funds should only be used to pay for an abortion when the mother's life is in danger.

The Clinton administration issued a new interpretation of the Hyde Amendment, and rather than *permitting* states to use Medicaid dollars to fund abortion in rape and incest cases, it *requires* them to do so. This created havoc in the states because 30 states prohibited public funding of abortion, with the life of the mother being the sole exception. Another six states had reporting requirements for abortions due to rape and incest which were invalidated under this new directive. As a result, many states are now involved in litigation over this issue and seven states are facing administrative enforcement proceedings which could ultimately result in the termination of federal Medicaid funding to the state. Moreover, as a result of litigation, two state constitutional provisions have been invalidated and now the states are required to pay for abortion for any reason, with state funds. Enacting legislation to clarify the congressional intent behind the Hyde amendment and to protect states' rights in this area is a matter of urgency for the 104th Congress.

The Coalition urges Congress to adopt the Istook/Exxon Amendment that would protect the rights of the citizens of states that do not use taxpayer funds to take human life.

3. End taxpayer subsidies to organizations that promote and perform abortions.

We call for an end to federal funding for organizations that promote and perform abortions. This includes an end to funding for international family planning organizations that promote and perform abortions.

Christian Coalition, along with numerous American taxpayers, believes that abortion is the taking of innocent human life and that tax dollars should not be used to promote it. Yet, organizations that receive funding under Title X are required to counsel and refer young adolescents on abortion. This implicitly sends the message to these youngsters that abortion is an acceptable method of family planning.

The merits of continued funding of the Title X program have long been questioned. It is estimated that one-third of the clients served through Title X funding are teen-agers.[52] And yet, during the course of the 25 years of Title X's existence, the out-of-wedlock birth rate among girls aged 15-19 has increased 100 percent, the abortion rate for teens has more than doubled, and sexually transmitted diseases among teens also have increased.[53] Today, one out of every four sexually experienced teen-agers becomes infected with a sexually transmitted disease annually.[54]

Family planning expenditures for all ages under Medicaid now approximate $252 million annually,[55] and the annual appropriation to the Title X family planning program is now $193 million,[56] one-third of which is expended on adolescents. The time is long overdue for the United States Congress to eliminate funding for such programs.

Similarly, the American taxpayer should not be forced to fund international family planning organizations that promote abortion overseas. The United States contributed $50 million to the United Nations Population Fund (UNFPA) alone for this year,[57] despite its involvement in China's coercive population-control program that includes forced abortions.[58] Amnesty International USA recently outlined some of the reports coming out of China regarding the method used to enforce its "one-child" policy:

213

[D]etainees were beaten and tortured to accelerate the payment of fines. Some were reportedly hung upside down, others received electric shocks on their tongue with electric batons or live wires...

One man who could not bear to see his wife tortured in a cell for days attempted to sell their children in Beijing... other women pregnant eight or nine months were given — against their will — injections to induce miscarriages.[59]

In fiscal year 1993, the United States contributed at least $580 million toward world family planning programs.[60] Any of this money that is contributed to organizations that encourage or perform abortions should be eliminated. Moreover, the entire budget should be reviewed to determine the success of the program to ensure that, like Title X, we are not subsidizing failed programs.

Encouraging Support of Private Charities

Enactment of legislation to enhance contributions to private charities as a first step toward transforming the bureaucratic welfare state into a system of private and faith-based compassion.

A 1994 REPORT BY THE NATIONAL CENTER for Policy Analysis details the growing evidence that private sector charities do a better job than government "of getting prompt aid to those who need it most, encouraging self-sufficiency and self-reliance, preserving the family unit and using resources [more] efficiently."[61] According to the same report, "94 percent of all shelters for the homeless in the U.S. are operated by private sector organizations."[62] Studies have shown that "as many as 80 percent of low-income people turn to the private sector first when facing a crisis."[63]

In light of this evidence, as well as the growing evidence of the failure of government programs to discourage welfare dependency, the federal government should take steps to encourage donations to private charities which serve the needy.

In their Contract with America, House Republicans have enacted the most dramatic and sweeping welfare reform in decades. By turning welfare spending over to the states in the form of block grants, this reform will encourage innovation at the local level, promoting work and personal responsibility.

The *Contract with the American Family* takes the next step. We propose unleashing the charitable capacity of the American people by providing private, non-governmental solutions to the problems of the underclass. Through the Salvation Army and other private charities, millions of Americans will be able to provide compassionate assistance to those in need without sending more tax dollars to a failed, discredited bureaucratic welfare state.

Many citizens are not as generous in their contributions to private charitable organizations these days because they already are overtaxed. However, if given the choice between having their tax dollars subsidize government welfare programs or subsidize private charitable programs, many would prefer to designate the money to a private charity of their choice. Christian Coalition urges the United States Congress to enact legislation to give taxpayers this opportunity.

One possible means to do so would be to allow individuals to designate on their income tax returns a limited amount of their taxes to qualified private charities. Another would be to create pilot programs through federal welfare block grants that earmark funding to encourage charitable giving and assistance to needy individuals through charities and religious organizations. For every dollar the taxpayer designates toward a private charity, the federal welfare funding to that taxpayer's state would be equally reduced.[64] As a result, "private charities would compete on an equal footing with government welfare programs for the portion of the federal budget that is allocated to poverty programs," thereby increasing competition. This will not only change government, it will change our citizenry's pattern of thinking — people will once again feel more of a civic duty toward their fellow man.

In the words of Acton Institute head Father Robert A. Sirico, "[G]overnment has no monopoly on compassion. Indeed, government is compassion's least able practitioner." Through a private charity check-off or other means, the 104th Congress can replace the welfare state with a culture of caring.

Restricting Pornography

Protecting children from exposure to pornography on the Internet and cable television, and from the sexual exploitation of child pornographers.

P
1. Enactment of legislation to protect children from being exposed to pornography on the Internet.

ORNOGRAPHY, BOTH SOFT CORE and hard core, is freely available on the Internet to virtually anyone with a home computer. Several magazines post pornographic images that can be viewed by anyone, including children, for free. There are also numerous sites on the Internet where hard core pornography depicting a variety of explicit sexual acts, even rape scenes and bestiality, are available free and can be accessed with a few clicks of a computer button.

Christian Coalition urges Congress to enact legislation to protect children from being exposed to pornography on the Internet. Criminal law should be amended to prohibit distribution of, or making available, any pornography, soft core or hard, to children, and to prohibit distribution of obscene hard core pornography to adults.

2. Enactment of legislation to require cable television companies to completely block the video and audio on pornography channels to non-subscribers.

217

Many children throughout the country are exposed to pornography, often hard core, on cable television because of incomplete scrambling of the signal on pornography channels. Cable companies have asserted that it is the parents' responsibility to guard their children. Christian Coalition believes that the responsibility should be on the cable companies to help parents keep pornography out of their homes. Cable companies should not be allowed to transmit pornography to non-subscribers. We urge Congress to require cable television companies to completely block the video and audio on pornography channels to non-subscribers.

3. Amending the federal child pornography law to make illegal the possession of *any* child pornography.

Sexual exploitation of children through child pornography continues to be a major problem in society. Possession of child pornography should be a crime. President Reagan proposed such a law in 1988, hoping that those with collections of child pornography would destroy them for fear of federal prosecution. In an 11th hour compromise on the bill, however, a conference committee of House and Senate members changed the Reagan bill to criminalize only the possession of "three or more" items of child pornography, videos, magazines, etc. Thus, federal law sanctions the possession of some child pornography — less than three pieces. A person with two hour-long videotapes depicting the rape of a child cannot be charged with a federal crime, yet a person with three photos depicting a child in a lascivious pose can. Christian Coalition urges that the federal child pornography law should be amended to make illegal the possession of any child pornography.

Privatizing the Arts

The National Endowment for the Arts, National Endowment for the Humanities, Corporation for Public Broadcasting, and Legal Services Corporation should become voluntary organizations funded through private contributions.

CHRISTIAN COALITION URGES the privatization of the National Endowment for the Arts (NEA) because we do not view such funding as a proper role for the United States Government. The issue is not *whether* the arts should receive funding, but rather *which* entity should do so — the government or the private sector.

Through its grant selection process, the NEA acts as an arbiter of art and places its endorsement or "seal of approval" on certain works. This federal imprimatur is as important to artists as is the funding which accompanies the grant. And yet, as William Bennett pointed out during his testimony calling for elimination of the NEA, this role of arbiter itself should be questioned, as well as the "seal of approval" which gives the "official blessing — the blessing of the people of the United States — to things both worthy and horrible."[65] This federal endorsement is particularly objectionable when it applies to

219

obscenity, pornography, or attacks on religion.

Despite repeated attempts by the United States Congress to place common-sense restrictions on federal funding of the arts, NEA dollars continue to go toward controversial works that denigrate the religious beliefs and moral values of mainstream Americans.[66] William Donohue, president of the Catholic League for Religious and Civil Rights, has joined the call for de-funding the NEA, stating: "We, as Catholics, have rights too, and among them is the right not to be defamed, and this is especially true when defamation is funded with government money."

At a time of fiscal restraint and budget austerity, cultural agencies cannot expect to be exempt from the broader realities of declining federal spending. Americans spend more than $7 billion annually on the arts; only $173 million is derived from federal funding. The privatization of the NEA into a voluntary, charitable organization would unleash the creative capacity of the American people and de-politicize one of the most controversial agencies in recent years. It is an idea whose time has come.

The National Endowment for the Humanities (NEH) also would be improved by privatization. Lynne Cheney, the NEH Chairman from 1986 to 1992, testified in January in support of ending federal funding for the agency. During her testimony she explained, "The humanities — like the arts — have become highly politicized. Many academics and artists now see their purpose not as revealing truth or beauty, but as achieving social and political transformation. Government should not be funding those whose main interest is promoting an agenda."[67] The controversial national history standards, which NEH funding assisted in bringing into existence, are one such example.[68]

William Bennett cites another example of the NEH's use of taxpayer dollars: "[T]he NEH provides funding for the Modern Language Association (MLA) ... Their annual convention attracts over 10,000 professors and students and reveals the type of agenda that NEH grants make possible. Past panels include such topics as 'Lesbian Tongues Untied;' 'Henry James and Queer Performativity;' [and] 'Status of Gender and Feminism in Queer Theory;'..."[69] It is clear that at a time when 24 percent of the average American family's budget goes to the federal government in taxes, we can find a better use for these tax dollars than through continued funding of the NEH.

The Corporation for Public Broadcasting (CPB) is another entity that should rely on private funding. Federal subsidies to the Public Broadcasting Service cost taxpayers $350 million a year, an example of transfer payments from the middle-class to the well-to-do.

Children Television Workshop, producer of "Sesame Street," reaps more than $100 million in licensing fees annually. Its chief executive officer earns $647,000 annually in salary and benefits. A rate card sent out by Washington, D.C. PBS affiliate WETA in 1992 noted that the average net worth of its contributors was $627,000; one in eight was a millionaire; one in seven owned a wine cellar; one in three had been to Europe in the previous three years.

Would privatization cause the death-knell of public broadcasting? Hardly. Private and corporate contributions already make up the vast majority of public broadcasting's revenue. Only 14 percent of the Public Broadcasting Service's (PBS) budget comes from the federal government, and only 3 percent of the National Public Radio's (NPR) budget is composed of federal funds.

Lastly, the Legal Services Corporation (LSC) is a federally chartered corporation established to provide legal assistance to the poor. It received an appropriation of $415 million for FY 1995. What many Americans don't realize is that divorce proceedings are a high priority for many legal services grantees.[70] The LSC alone paid for 210,000 divorces in 1990, at an estimated cost to taxpayers of $50 million. Yet, as study after study has revealed, divorce is not helping our nation's poor break out of poverty. Rather, as historian Barbara Dafoe Whitehead has pointed out: "Children in single-parent families are six times as likely to be poor. Twenty-two percent of children in one-parent families will experience poverty during childhood for seven years or more, as compared with only two percent of children in two-parent families."[71] Therefore, an agency that was established to help ameliorate poverty is instead fostering it through its financing of divorce actions.

Christian Coalition urges Congress to privatize all four entities, the NEA, NEH, CPB, and LSC, and turn them into organizations funded through private contributions.

Crime Victim Restitution

Funds given to states to build prisons should encourage work, study, and drug testing requirements for prisoners in state correctional facilities, as well as requiring restitution to victims subsequent to release.

ODAY'S PRISONS ARE NOT DESIGNED either to punish convicts or provide justice to victims. In Pennsylvania, felons can receive in-cell cable TV.[72] At a facility in Fallsburg, New York, outdoor weight training areas feature televisions prisoners can view as they work out.[73] Hard labor has been replaced in many prisons with recreational activities.

Christian Coalition urges Congress to enact legislation that will encourage states to instill work and study requirements for prisoners. More than one million inmates are imprisoned in our country's correctional facilities - 919,143 in state prisons and 93,708 in federal prisons.[74] Although a majority of institutions have academic programs, many prisoners do not participate in them.[75] In fact, a 1990 census found that "[a]pproximately 570,000 inmates, accounting for two-thirds or more of both sexes in State and Federal facilities, were not participating in any academic activities." Moreover, about a third of the prison population had no work assignment, and 25 percent of the population was idle — meaning prisoners neither worked nor participated in an academic program.[76]

An estimated 70 percent of inmates in U.S. prisons are functionally illiterate. Without the ability to read and write, these individuals are unable to find work outside prison, a contributing factor giving the United States one of the highest prison recidivism rates in the Western world. Literacy programs — many of which can be provided by private charities and prison ministries at low cost — will give prisoners hope and give society a better chance to absorb former inmates upon their release.

Moreover, with one out of four American households victimized by crime each year, as well as more than 700,000 days of hospitalization resulting from crime-related injuries, victim restitution is very necessary.[77] Requiring an offender to make restitution to the victim will not only force the offender to confront the consequences of his actions, but also compensate the victim monetarily.

Christian Coalition urges Congress to remedy this by conditioning the receipt of federal prison construction funding by the states on enactment of work and study requirements. Moreover, we urge that restitution to victims subsequent to release also be required.

Conclusion

THE *CONTRACT WITH THE AMERICAN FAMILY* is the first word, not the last word, on a cultural agenda for the 104th Congress during the post-100-day period. The ideas included in this document are suggestions, not demands, and are designed to be a help, not a hindrance, to Members of Congress as they seek to fulfill their mandate for dramatic change.

Christian Coalition welcomes the support of Republicans and Democrats alike as it seeks passage of the items in this bold legislative agenda. There is no specified deadline on acting on the Contract. The Coalition and its grassroots members will work on behalf of these mainstream proposals in this Congress and in as many subsequent sessions of Congress as necessary to secure passage.

The *Contract with the American Family* emerged from a survey of Christian Coalition members and supporters conducted in March and April, 1995. It has been improved during the drafting process by extensive polling and focus groups and consultations with members of Congress and their staffs. Each item in the Contract enjoys support from between 60 and 90 percent of the American people. More than half of the items in the Contract already have legislative sponsors, and several have already been passed by committee.

The American people now have a Congress that is receptive to their desire for religious liberty, stronger families, lower taxes, local control of education, and tougher laws against crime. With the *Contract with the American Family,* the nation now has an agenda with broad support that addresses time-honored values and cultural issues for the 104th Congress and beyond.

Endnotes

1   Ronald Brownstein, "Dissatisfied Public May Spell Democrat Losses," *Los Angeles Times*, July 28, 1994.

2   Nationwide survey by Luntz Research and Strategic Services, conducted February 11-12, 1995. Sample Size: 1000. Theoretical margin of sampling error: + or - 3.1%.

3   Keith A. Fournier, *Religious Cleansing in the American Republic*, 1993, p. 17. The decision was later reversed after counsel intervened.

4   Catholic League for Religious and Civil Rights, 1994 Catholic League's 1994 Report on Anti-Catholicism, p. 14.

5   Ibid.

6   Keith A. Fournier, *Religious Cleansing in the American Republic*, 1993, p. 16. In both instances, the children were allowed to read their Bibles after legal counsel intervened.

7   Only after the student's parent contacted the school board was the book allowed.

8   Mark Kellner, "Postal Grinch Who Stole Christmas," The *Washington Times*, November 20, 1994; Catholic League for Religious and Civil Rights, 1994 Catholic League's 1994 Report on Anti-Catholicism, p. 17.

9   Catholic League for Religious and Civil Rights, 1994 Catholic League's 1994 Report on Anti-Catholicism, p. 16.

10 403 U.S. 602 (1971).

11 Jesse H. Choper, *The Establishment Clause and Aid to Parochial Schools — An Update*, 75 CAL.L.REV. 5, 6-7. (1987).

12 *Lamb's Chapel v. Center Moriches School Dist.*, 113 S.Ct. 2141, 2149 (1993) (Scalia, J., concurring).

13 William J. Bennett, *The Index of Leading Cultural Indicators* (March 1993), p. 17.

14 "[T]he U.S. spends a greater percentage of its gross national product on education (7.5%) than any other country except Israel, and yet is out performed in math and science among 13-year-olds by more than 10 nations, including Hungary, Taiwan and the former Soviet Union." Claudia Wallis, "A Class of Their Own," *Time*, Oct. 31, 1994, 56.

15 140 *Congressional Record* S9917 (daily ed. July 27, 1994).

16 Maria Koklanaris, "Virginia parents may get option to exclude pupils from counseling," The *Washington Times*, Oct. 28, 1994.

17 U.S. Department of Education, *Strong Families, Strong Schools* (September 1994).

18 Pub. L. 103-227.

19 Pub. L. 103-382.

20 Claudia Wallis, "A Class of Their Own," *Time*, October 31, 1994, p. 56.

21 Claudia Wallis, "A Class of Their Own," *Time*, October 31, 1994, pp. 53, 56, citing a 1992 report by the Educational Testing Service.

22 Claudia Wallis, "A Class of Their Own," *Time*, October 31, 1994, pp. 53, 56.

23 Carol Innerst, "Education Still Lacking Bang for Buck, The *Washington Times*, September 21, 1994.

24 Family Research Council, "Freeing America's Schools[:] The Case Against the U.S. Education Department," Family Policy, p. 5.

25 Letter from Terrel Bell, to The *Washington Post*, February 1, 1995.

26 Carol Inherst, "Some Historians See New Standards as Revisionist Coup," The *Washington Times*, October 27, 1994.

27 Lynne V. Cheney, "The End of History," The *Wall Street Journal*, October 20, 1994.

28 Lynne V. Cheney, "The End of History," The *Wall Street Journal*, October 20, 1994.

29 Ibid.

30 See *Congressional Record*, S1025-1040, January 18, 1995.

31 *Congressional Record*, January 18, 1995, S1025-2040.

32 Statement of Senator Slade Gorton, *Congressional Record*, January 18, 1995, p. S1034.

33 U.S. Department of Education, Center for Choice in Education, Issue Brief, "Public Opinion on Choice in Education" (March 1992), Executive Summary.

34 The Heritage Foundation, "School Choice Continues to Gain Ground," *Business/Education Insider* (June/July 1994).

35 Statement of Senator Coats, *Congressional Record*, March 24, 1995, S4582.

36   In re Sumey, 94 Wash.2d 757, 621 P.2d 108 (1980).

37   Matter of Ray, 408 N.Y.S.2d 737 (1978).

38   K.L. Billingsley, "Sex, Lies and County Government: Abuse Case Shows It All," The *San Diego Union-Tribune*, July 19, 1992.

39   *Human Events*, February 24, 1995.

40   United Nations Convention on the Rights of the Child, Article 16.

41   United Nations Convention on the Rights of the Child, Article 13.

42   United Nations Convention on the Rights of the Child, Article 15.

43   Committee on the Rights of the Child, Eighth Session, Consideration of Reports Submitted by States Parties Under Article 44 of the Convention, p. 3.

44   Statement of Senator Kay Bailey Hutchison, *Congressional Record*, January 26, 1995.

45   Mother Teresa of Calcutta, remarks at the National Prayer Breakfast, February 3, 1994.

46   Illustration Adapted from Drawings Appearing in the February 1993 Issue of "Life Advocate," *National Right to Life News*, July 14, 1993, p. 12.

47   Diane M. Gianelli, "Shock-tactic ads target late-term abortion procedure," *American Medical News*, July 5, 1993 (emphasis added to quotation).

48   Douglas Johnson, "AMA Newspaper Investigative Report Supports NRLC Statements on Brutal 'D&X' Abortion Method," *National Right to Life News*, July 14, 1993, pp. 12, 13.

49   Ibid., p. 13.

50   Douglas Johnson, "AMA Newspaper Investigative Report Supports NRLC Statements on Brutal 'D&X' Abortion Method," *National Right to Life News*, July 14, 1993, p. 12.

51   Diane M. Gianelli, "Shock-tactic ads target late-term abortion procedure," *American Medical News*, July 5, 1993.

52   Family Research Council, "Suffer the Children: Title X's Family Planning Failure," Insight, by Gracie S. Hsu; Family Research Council, "An Estimate of Federal Spending on Contraceptive-'Safe Sex' Services for Adolescents 1970-1993," *Insight*, by Charles A. Donovan, Sr., p. 2.

53   Ibid.

54   Ibid.

55   Family Research Council, "An Estimate of Federal Spending on Contraceptive-'Safe Sex" Services for Adolescents 1970-1993," *Insight*, by Charles A. Donovan, Sr., p. 2.

56   H.R. CONF. REP. NO. 103-733, 103d Cong., 2d Sess. 64 (1994).

57   National Right to Life Committee, Inc. Memorandum, From Douglas Johnson, Legislative Director, to "Interested Parties," April 20, 1995, p. 2.

58 Ibid.

59 Amnesty International USA, "People's Republic of China[:] Catholic Villagers in Hebei Province," March 14, 1995.

60 National Right to Life Committee, Inc., "The Clinton Administration's Promotion of Abortion as a Tool of Population Control in Less-Developed Nations," June 1, 1994, page 2.

61 National Center for Polcy Analysis, "Why Not Abolish the Welfare State?" (October 1994), Executive Summary.

62 Ibid.

63 Ibid.

64 For a general discussion of this concept, see National Center for Policy Analysis, Why Not Abolish the Welfare State? (October 1994), p. 30.

65 Written Testimony of William J. Bennett, Before the House Appropriations Subcommittee on Interior, January 24, 1995, p.3.

66 Rod Dreher, "S&M 'Art' Video Exceeds Shocking Stage Version," The Washington Times, January 26, 1995.

67 Written Testimony of Lynne V. Cheney, Before the Interior Appropriations Subcommittee on January 24, 1995, p.1.

68 Congressional Record, January 18, 1995, S1025-40.

69 Written Testimony of William J. Bennett, Before the House Appropriations Subcommittee on Interior, January 24, 1995.

70 Kathleen B. DeBettencourt, Office of Policy Development, Legal Services Corporation, "Legal Services Corporation vs. The Family," March 1988, p. 15.

71 Barbara Dafoe Whitehead, "Dan Quayle Was Right," The Atlantic Monthly, April 1993, p. 47.

72 Robert James Bidinotto, "Must Our Prisons Be Resorts?" Reader's Digest, November, 1994, pp. 65, 76.

73 Robert James Bidinotto, "Must Our Prisons Be Resorts?" Reader's Digest, November, 1994, p. 65.

74 U.S. Department of Justice, "State and Federal Prison Population Tops One Million," October 27, 1994.

75 U.S. Department of Justice, Bureau of Justice Statistics, "Census of State and Federal Correctional Facilities, 1990," p. 11.

76 U.S. Department of Justice, Bureau of Justice Statistics, "Census of State and Federal Correctional Facilities, 1990," p. 12. A survey of state prison inmates in 1991 also substantiated that approximately one-third of the inmates had no work assignments. See Bureau of Justice Statistics, "Survey of State Prison Inmates, 1991," p. 27.

77 H.R. Rep. No. 104-16, 104th Congress, 1st Sess. at 4 (1995).

Transcript of "No Sex. No Drugs. But Rock 'n' Roll"
By Nicholas Dawidoff
New York Times Magazine February 5, 1995

No Sex. No Drugs. But Rock 'n' Roll: (Kind Of).
Christian music is the fastest-growing form
of popular music, driving its message home
to the tune of $750 million a year."
By Nicholas Dawidoff*

It's a special Friday evening service at the Fletcher Emmanuel Chruch Alive in
Lumberton, a quiet East Texas suburb 20 minutes beyond the oil and gas refineries of
Beaumont. The parishioners—mostly white-bread kids in jeans, high tops and T-shirts
that say "Do It God's Way"—have crammed the pews, lined the walls, packed the
gallery and spilled into the foyer. They are listening to Todd Foster, a traveling
Louisiana evangelist wearing tonic in his hair and a crisp yellow shirt. "God knows your
name and he saw you last Friday night," Foster says, thrusting his head forward and
gazing around the room. "Life doesn't always work out the way you want it to, but you
listen to me, you praise Him anyway. Some of you young men, if you were to die
tonight, you'd go to hell."

    Foster is at pains to punctuate his sermon with some phrases of the moment—
"Hey, homeboy, get a clue," he advises at one point. But what he's really offering up to
these middle-class kids and their chaperones is old-time religion, and the congregation
responds with plenty of fervent nods, murmers and amens.

    Still, it's not until a disk jockey from the Beaumont all-Christian radio station
mounts the pulpit and asks, "How excited are you about Jesus Christ?" that the place
explodes. At once everyone is flowing into the aisles, stomping, clapping and shrieking.
The whole church is suddenly wired, keening with the sort of thrilled excitation that you
find, well, at a rock concert. Which, suddenly, this Friday night service has become.
Four pretty young women with microphones sweep onto the altar. A soundtrack pulsing
with synthesizers, drum machines and a horn section begins blasting loud and hard.

    "Are any of you believers?" cries out one of the singers. And as a roar of
affirmation rolls back to her, Point of Grace, the hottest new act in Christian rock, rips
into their hit single "I'll Be Believing." So far as Fletcher Emmanuel Church is
concerned, the Pointer Sisters have nothing on Shelley Phillips, Denise Jones, Heather
Floyd and Terry Jones.

    Of course, that's the idea. Point of Grace is a cleverly derivative confection
adapted for Christian teen-age consumption from a series of mainstream pop girl-group
templates: the Andrews Sisters, the Supremes and En Vogue. The lush harmonies are
the same; only the lyrics are different. Here at Fletcher, the front row throng of
towheaded girls with braces on their teeth sway to verses like, "When the going gets
tough/When the ride's too rough/When you're just not sure enough/Jesus will still be
there." Instead of singing about boys, bikinis and bourbon, Point of Grace gets 'em with
faith, hope and love.

Between songs, the concert assumes a campfire feeling. "I hope we can laugh and have a good time," Shelley says. "But it's also my prayer that we can lead you in worship tonight." Denise talks gravely about Mercy Ministries of America, an organization that provides care for unwed mothers and their babies and that Point of Grace supports because the band believes that "abortion is not an option." Terry describes Point of Grace's vow to remain "sexually pure" until marriage, and encourages the youth of Lumberton to abstain as well. "We did it, so can you," she says, and the church resonates—almost *writhes*—with approval as the synthesizers kick in for another song. The feeling here is undeniably sensual, which is odd given the fillip for this latest ecstatic outpouring is a call to chastity. Rock-and-roll, the music of youthful rebellion and libidinous abandon—what Jerry Lee Lewis called "the devil's music"— has been blithely co-opted as a piston for churchly proselytizing.

After an hour and a half, the Point of Grace concert ends and much of the crowd streams outside the church to a pair of tables piled with merchandise: $12 Point of Grace T-shirts, $2 black-and-white photos. Behind the second table sits the group itself. If this is a typical session, most fans will ask for autographs, some will seek religious counsel and others will thank the singers for singing songs that helped them through trying times. A few men and women will lean forward and confide, eyes shining, that during the concert they found the Lord. And a couple of men, caught up in the lights and the beat and the mascara, will ask if Shelley or Heather—the two unmarried members of the group—will have dinner with them some time.

All four of the Point of Grace women are in their mid-20's, with glamorously wholesome looks. Indeed, from their airbrushed CD covers and record shop display posters to their carefully scripted concert patter, Point of Grace is not-so-subtly being positioned as the sort of pristine feminine ideal Christian boys are *supposed* to go for. Shelley Phillips is Madonna Ciccone, except that Shelley isn't just like a virgin, she is one. The attractive female performers, devout song lyrics and throbbing rhythms seem calculated to arouse even mildly sentient Christian males, and during this humid night in East Texas, the young Christian men of Lumberton would be missing the point if they didn't take notice.

And, of course, they do. Todd Foster is standing in the church foyer when two boys rush up to him. "Where's Point of Grace?" one of them asks him.

"Out back with 700 guys chasin' 'em," the evangelist replies.

"Seven hundred and two," says the boy, and in a dash he and his friend are off.

Contemporary Christian music (C.C.M., to industry insiders) was created in the late 1950's by a guitar-strumming, longhaired Jesus freak named Larry Norman, who sang hymns about venereal disease to astonished parishioners in California churches. Sometimes Norman was invited back. Mostly he wasn't, and although he had a record contract for a time, eventually his raw lyrics and poor health nudged him into obscurity.

Not so the music, which expanded to embrace everything from the piano-bar pop of Pat and Debby Boone to the glam rock of Stryper, who stirred up their fans in the late 1980's by tossing Bibles from the stage. In the last three years C.C.M., or white gospel, as it is sometimes called to distinguish it from the traditional black gospel of

Mahalia Jackson and Shirley Caesar, has achieved a critical mass, becoming the fastest growing form of popular music in the United States.

Just how fast is somewhat unclear. The Gospel Music Association in Nashville claims that record sales and concert receipts combine to make contemporary Christian music a billion-dollar-a-year industry. A more accurate figure, according to several businessmen I spoke with, is probably closer to $750 million. Regardless, C.C.M. is growing at such a pace that within the next few years it could be what it says it is and more—an entertainment behemoth that accounts for 10 to 13 percent of American popular music sales.

It makes perfect sense that Family Values Pop should be prospering in Newt Gingrich's America, and shrewd corporate executives in the fiercely competitive music business have taken notice. Three years ago, all of the record companies producing contemporary Christian music were independently owned. They have since been snapped up by the likes of the Music Entertainment Group, EMI and the German colossus BMG. In addition, many of Nashville's prominent secular record labels and music-publishing firms from Arista to Sony have been scurrying to create contemporary Christian music divisions.

Of all these transactions, the most signal was the EMI purchase of Sparrow Records, which is, after Word Records, the second-largest Christian label. This was Jimmy Bowen's deal. In 1989, Bowen, then a revered pop producer, took over EMI's country music division. With the help of a pudgy Oklahoman names Garth Brooks, who's been scuffling around Nashville for years, Bowen helped country become, by the early 1990's, the fastest-growing music in America.

Three years ago, Bowen and EMI bought Sparrow. Speaking from his car telephone, Bowen told me that while he happens to be a Christian himself, buying Sparrow had nothing to do with his religious beliefs. "I wanted to be in Christian music because I think it's going to explode very much like country music did five or six years ago," he said. "People never believed such numbers could be done by a minority genre. Now with Christian music, everybody wants to be involved." In December, EMI bought Star Song and placed it beside Sparrow in what Bowen and his partner, Billy Ray Hearn, have somewhat grandly called the EMI Christian Music Group. In effect, Bowen, who made a fortune with lovin'-losin'-and drinkin' songs, has embraced the anti-Country.

Because C.C.M. isn't just rock-and-roll. Christian record companies produce popular music in every category known to your local record dealer: heavy metal, light pop, jazz, folk, grunge, reggae, country, funk and even the wildly popular Christian hip-hop. In each case the sound of the Christian version is virtually identical to its secular counterpart, and so are many of the trappings, from Christian mosh pits to Z Music, a 24-hour cable channel that plays only Christian music videos.

But if much about contemporary Christian music is shamelessly imitative, the lyrics are what set it apart. Besides the obvious distinction that many Christian songs are about biblical subjects, much of the music functions as disapproving foils to mainstream songs, advocating a conservative morality that is anathema to the libertine spirit of mainstream popular music. Where the country band Confederate Railroad sings, "I like my women on the trashy side," the three handsome hipsters who are DC (for Decent

Christian) Talk counter with "I'm lookin' for a girl who's virtuous/'Cause God laid it on my heart to search for this."

High-fidelity salvation sells. "Free at Last," DC Talk's third and most recent album, has sold 910,000 copies, which compares favorably with sales of R.E.M.'s third album, "Fables of the Reconstruction." Other Christian groups are doing as well or better. The seminal Christian heavy metal band Petra has sold five million albums since 1974, and saved tens of thousands of souls at concerts along the way. Sandi Patti's performance at the 1992 Republican National Convention was a hit, as are her records, which routinely sell more than half a million copies. The releases of Michael W. Smith, a blue-eyed-soul singer and keyboard player, sell just below the million mark. "Heaven in the Real World," the latest offering from Steven Curtis Chapman, an earnest blond from Paducah, Ky., is a gold record, and another 500,000-plus seller is "The Standard," a jeremiad on the decline of American moral values by a saturnine man called Carman. In October, 71,000 people attended a Carman concert in Dallas. Outselling them all is Amy Grant, the 34-year-old grande dame of the genre who, in 17 years of writing and singing songs of unstinting sweetness and devotion, has sold 15 million records. (Her recent, more secular albums are responsible for about a third of those sales.)

Point of Grace is experiencing a more modest success. Their first album, released last winter, has since sold 210,000 copies—an impressive debut by Christian music standards, though a quiet one in the mainstream. The four young women were presented a Dove Award—the Christian Grammy—last April for best new artist, and clearly Word Records has high expectations for them. Not long after the Dove Awards I began dropping in on Point of Grace from time to time, to see what it's like to be an ascendant pop star in the Christian music business—and to find out whether evangelical religion, rock-and-roll music and the profit motive are all as compatible as the booming sales figures suggest.

At the end of the summer, Point of Grace arrived in Arkedelphia, Ark., to play what has become an annual concert for the incoming freshmen at Ouachita Baptist University, the group's alma mater. Situated in a dry county speckled with farms and Baptist churches, Ouachita (pronounced WATCH-a-taw) is a sedate, pine-shaded campus where drinking, dancing and dormitory room visits by a member of the opposite sex are all forbidden. "The wildest thing that happens around here is that somebody catches a bigger hybrid bass than was caught before," Ben Elrod, Ouachita's president, told me.

Perhaps that explained the large turnout at the Point of Grace freshman concert. It was the first of many times I would see the group perform its material, and while I wasn't terribly smitten—they seemed like a pale version of Abba to me—mine was definitely the minority opinion. Particularly enthusiastic was a clump of freshman boys from Texas.

"Awesome," said Mark Jansen, who has seen Point of Grace four times.

"The music's something good to listen to," explained Kevin Morgan, who wears a large cross around his neck and a look of intense concentration behind his wire-rimmed glasses. "Something that doesn't influence us negatively. Music has a tremendous power to influence you. I've noticed I can be influenced by secular music,

234

and I don't want to put up with that." I asked what exactly he is wary of. "Girls who look good in a tight dress," he responded. "I've been tempted by that a lot."

James Howard, a classmate, agreed. "To me the music is tempting," he said. "It's nice to have something else. If you listen to secular music, you have to think about what they're saying. Here the message is simple. It's put in simple terms. You can understand it and you don't have to worry about the influences you get in secular music."

It occurred to me that provocation was the whole point of rock-and-roll—the music has always been about confrontation, not comfort. But before I could raise this thought aloud, the students had wandered off, bound for the Family Bowling Center, which the freshman class had rented for the evening.

Three of the four members of Point of Grace grew up in middle-class Republican families in Norman, Okla. Heather, Terry and Denise—who are not related—sang together in church groups at the Trinity Baptist Church in Norman. They all went on to Ouachita. "One night, it was real weird." says Denise, the group's sinewy soprano. "God began to say you can do more with what you have than you're doing." They decided to form a pop group, and invited Denise's roommate, a loquacious blonde from Little Rock named Shelley Phillips, to join them. Three years later, John Mays, the artists-and-repertoire director of Word Records, heard them sing at Praise in the Rockies, a week-long industry convention in Estes Park, Colo., and signed them up.

Point of Grace's current popularity is such that they could be filling midsize auditoriums. But their manager, Mike Atkins, believes the group should make one more pass through the church circuit before moving up. And so through summer and into fall, Point of Grace spent most of each month traveling across what H.L. Mencken called the Coca-Cola Belt, performing virtually the same show day after day from church altars, signing autographs afterward for long lines of middle-class whites, eating hamburgers and sleeping in budget motels. "If we're not careful we'd lose the church," said Heather, looking on the bright side, as she always does. "They might say, 'Well, they're too big to come to our church.' We don't want to do that because our audience is the church and we love the church."

There is also a certain pleasure in being the biggest thing in De Ridder, La., (population 10,400) on a Saturday night. The four women pulled into town to discover that the marquees at the Best Western motel, where they were staying, and at the First Baptist Church, where they would perform, sported Point of Grace welcome messages.

That evening, Point of Grace thoroughly charmed the 700 people who turned out to see them. Among the De Ridder teen-agers they reached was Colleen Nasusako. "A lot of things they talk about, like abortion, it helps me out," she told me. "A lot of my friends drink, smoke, do drugs, have sex. Sometimes it's hard—I want to be in their group, but I don't want to do the things they do. So I'm by myself. Point of Grace understands the struggles we go through and they help me stand up to it."

When I related Colleen's comments to Point of Grace after the show, they were thrilled. The four women are genuinely sweet-natured and seem to live only to encourage Christians in their faith. They are also the model of what a Christian record company wants from its performers. They willingly agree to lengthen their skirt hems and are never so indiscreet as to blaspheme or to take a curious sniff of chardonnay.

235

"We're probably the squeaky clean little Minnie Mouses of the industry," says Terry. "If there's such a thing as an all-American person, that would be neat." Then she reconsidered. "I don't know if I want to be called all-American the way America is today. Maybe all-American from the 50's or earlier."

After the concert the members of Point of Grace returned to their rooms at the De Ridder Best Western. Over a dinner of diet cherry-vanilla Cokes and footlong chili-cheese dogs, the four women talked about their interests and concerns. The conversation unfolded as we traversed East Texas roads, passing Baptist churches and watermelon stands en route to concerts in Tyler, Lumberton and Caldwell.

Christianity consumes Point of Grace. They do not know much about other religions, nor do they care to. Still, they believe that everyone—Buddhists, Muslims, Jews—should worship as Christians and would be happier if they did. "I would love for the whole world to be saved and know Him like I know Him," says Denise.

In devoting their lives to what Terry calls "God's plan," they live lives of quiet uniformity. Shelley and Heather say they are still virgins, although Shelley's current boyfriend is not. "How can we stand before these girls and those guys and say God's greatest grace if forgiveness if I didn't forgive him," she says. "My boyfriend has now made a committment to remain pure until marriage." Like the boys at Ouachita, Point of Grace's religion envelopes them, cushions them against society and obscures them from it. When Point of Grace sings "I have no doubt," they mean it.

"When I grew up, I was a model child," Heather told me, without a trace of irony. "I never did anything bad. My friends were all from church."

As adults, that's still a fair portrait of Point of Grace. They edify believers with their powers of restraint. They don't only resist profanity, short skirts, tobacco and alcohol. They resist nearly everything. They "don't have time" to read books or newspapers and they listen to little much other than Christian music. They have traveled much of the country, but they have investigated very little of it. For them, the next town is pretty much the same as the last: a church and a McDonald's. They are among the nicest, most sincere people I have ever met. They are also quite possibly the blandest.

That is a big part of their appeal. Where soldiers, halfbacks and statesmen falter, Point of Grace and their Christian musical colleagues prevail as exemplars of clean, moral living. Groups like Point of Grace also appear to fill a Christian celebrity void created by the procession of wayward televangelical ministers.

"Preaching in America has really come to a crossroads because of the scandals—the Bakkers, the Swaggarts," Todd Foster told me in Lumberton. "There's a real controversy about preaching because not everybody knows if the guy up there is a genuine man of God. Singers come across more personal, more friendly. That's part of why singers reach people that ministers don't."

But life as a musical paragon isn't easy. "There's a lot of great church singers," John Mays of Word Records says. "There are very few people gifted with the ability to inspire the masses. I'm looking for that." Mays also worries about "morality problems" and "spiritual maturity" in artists. "There have been a lot of people who are really gifted, really talented, sell records, but I can't work with them because of this," he says. "There's tremendous pressure to be perfect when you're in public as a Christian."

Keeping up pristine appearances is, in fact, so important to some Christian record companies that they require artists to sign a "morality clause" in their contracts. One Christian record company even produces album covers that include a message from the president of the label: "You have a right to expect that the singers and songwriters live real Christian lives."

Helping Point of Grace navigate the high road is their manager, Mike Atkins. A conspicuously humble and agreeable man, Atkins is known as one of the best in his business, and when he isn't at their side, Point of Grace consults him constantly by telephone, seeming habitually to defer to the manager. He is always available to them. I encountered him one evening just as he was telling the group that he was going hunting and would be out of touch for a while. He'd be gone, he apologized, until noon the next day.

As Atkins sees it, beyond plotting Point of Grace's career, his responsibility is "to make double sure they maintain their spiritual integrity." "We want to be examples," he says. "I want people to say: 'I want a little bit of what they have. I want the beauty, the selflessness.' To be more Christ-like—that's the bottom line. And they really are that. That's the beauty of it."

One morning, while sitting in his spotless kitchen in suburban Nashville, I asked Atkins how he would respond if a member of Point of Grace committed an unseemly transgression. His leg began shaking under the table. He prayed it wouldn't happen, he said, adding that he hoped he would be forgiving and compassionate. Finally he talked about accountability. "We'd hope we can help them avoid temptations," he said. He'd better. Errant Christian musicians not only lose their credibility—they can also find themselves out of a job.

> *'What they did was protect themselves—*
> *wash their hands of me,'" English says.*
> *'Some people would call that Christian. I call it hypocrisy.'*

Michael English is Mike Atkin's nightmare. When I met English, just after Thanksgiving, he was sitting with his back to me at the House of Judd, the spacious suburban Nashville office of Larry Strickland. Strickland is the husband and manager of Naomi Judd, the country star, and English is his newest client. I knew what English looked like from the covers of the albums he made for Alliance, the Warner Bros. Christian music label. He favored elegant designer clothing and feathered his short hair back, save for a renegade lock that frisked at his temple. A shy half-smile played at his mouth.

Except that now, when the 32-year-old tenor got up from his chair and turned around to greet me, he was transformed. His hair fell lank to his shoulders, he wore an earring and he looked bloated. Outside his black cotton shirt hung a metal cross with "veritas"—Latin for truth—embossed on it. He wasn't smiling. If anything, he seemed a little surly, and in retrospect it's not hard to see why.

English's past half-year has been something of a Christian-rock passion play. Until last April he was contemporary Christian music's poster boy. Then a week after English won six Dove Awards, including best artist and best male vocalist, he returned the statuettes to the Gospel Music Association, explaining that he had been having an affair with Marabeth Jordan, a singer in the group First Call who was also married. Worse, Jordan was pregnant by English. English's confession came just after he and Jordan had both performed in a benefit tour for unwed mothers. Shortly after English's disclosure, Jordon miscarried.

Christian music immediately ostracized English. Christian record stores cleared their shelves of his albums, and Warner Alliance stopped selling them. English says that Neal Joseph, the company's president, told the singer that he planned to exercise the morality clause in his contract and freeze it indefinitely. His life in ruins, English went into seclusion.

In October, English emerged to sign a mainstream recording contract with Curb Records, the label of Lyle Lovett and Merle Haggard. Mike Curb, chairman of the label, believes that "Michael English can be a superstar." That may be, but at the moment English is still smarting from his contemporary Christian music experience.

After selling hundreds of thousands of albums full of songs about love and mercy, English said, C.C.M. showed him neither. When Alliance executives were tipped off about his affair, English said, they forced him to disclose it immediately in a news conference, telling him that if he balked, they'd hold their own news conference and reveal it themselves. "The Christian people are a whole lot more forgiving than the industry," he said. "A lot of people cry, 'Moral, moral,' but they're really thinking, 'What's this gonna do to our pocketbooks?' When things are going great they can label me as a sex symbol, as a GQ man. Whatever you can do to promote that group or that person to make them sell more records they're gonna do. They're pushing me like I'm God. I'm not God. I'm just his messenger. Everything I did I was as humble as I could be. I just made a mistake. I messed up. We all do." After that, said English, "What they did was protect themselves—wash their hands of me. Some people would call that Christian. I call it hypocrisy." (Calls placed to Neal Joseph at Warner Alliance for comment were not returned.)

If Christian music sounds formulaic and homogenized, said English, that's because it *is* formulaic and homogenized. Avoiding strident content is so much the concern that songwriters know that if they want to sell their material to C.C.M. record companies, they had better turn out sunny platitudes. When he wrote a song, English said, it had to go through a committee that included management and the record company. "It's a very closed-in kind of thing," he told me. "You don't want to offend anybody." He said he couldn't use endearments like "baby," and he wasn't permitted to write rhythm-and-blues songs. "They didn't feel like it was me. I said, 'Wait a minute, who is me?' I was a puppet, they held the strings. It's not what you want. It's what they want you to do. Now, I want to do a love song, I can do a love song. If it doesn't sell one record, at least I've got my freedom." He wears the veritas cross because "what I want to be around is truth," he said. "I'm tired of the holy veil."

Leslie Phillips had a similar experience. Once a talented young Christian singer, she fled the fold for the mainstream—where she is now known as Sam Phillips— because of her feeling that Christian record companies would only let her spout dogma. "I started out wanting to write, explore spirituality in music, write about spiritual things," she recently told Vin Scelsa, the host of the New York radio show "Idiot's

Delight." "I thought maybe the church would be a good place to do that. But it wasn't. It turned out to be the very worst place, because they basically wanted propaganda set to music."

Peter Furler remains in Christian music, but he shares some of English's and Phillips's frustrations. Furler is the leader of an Australian Christian new wave band called the Newsboys. Unlike many C.C.M. performers, he listens to mainstream music—he admires the Clash, U2 and the Pet Shop Boys—and says he considers himself a rocker who happens to write songs about Christian subjects. Since he signed on with an American Christian record company, however, Furler said, he has encountered resistance to some of his material. "In Christian music, the majrority, they don't want you to explore the truth further," he told me. "They just want to hear 'God is love.' If you go further than that you could get yourself into trouble. You feel like you have to prove your faith all the time."

Just as the music is homogenized, so, apparently, are the performers. Point of Grace may well be the unstinting models of probity they appear to be, but according to English, there are other Christian music singers who have wandered from the straight and narrow and are hiding their personal troubles for fear of losing their record contracts. "I get tired of people getting up there, saying all the right Christian things and then going home and dealing with problems nobody knows about," English said.

When I called the singer BeBe Winans to discuss some of the things English was telling me about Christian music, he sounded perturbed and indignant. Winans and his sister CeCe have won seven Dove Awards—and seven Grammys as well—for their satiny gospel harmonies. Winans records his Christian albums for Sparrow. He is black, and he thinks he pays for it.

"I still have struggles with my company about how much money is paid to me compared to white artists," he said. "When you ask where the money's going and it's not coming to you, they label you 'a riot,' as a troubled person." He said that he and his sister have sold more than a million Christian albums for Sparrow and have received, at best, $25,000 each annually. "Gospel music is two sides," he said. "There's a ministry side that has nothing to do with a business side. The business side is messed up, totally unfair in what they give to the artists. What frustrates me the most is that we should be showing more of an example of what it should be like, how artists should be treated. Because the message that we're sending through our music is hope, love, unity and virtue. The business side should reflect exactly what we're singing, and it doesn't."

'Are we selling Jesus?' *says Harrell, Amy Grant's brother-in-law.* *'Absolutely. That's our product.'*

"We don't sit here all day thinking God sells our records," Dan Harrell told me one afternoon. Resplendent in a bright red turtleneck, Harrell was sitting in the walnut-toned Nashville office of Blanton-Harrell Entertainment, the most successful talent management firm in Christian music. Tapestries, rare books and fox-hunting prints decorated the walls. A color television was tuned to a cable business channel.

Clearly Harrell and his partner, Michael Blanton, are making a killing. Both men are multimillionaires, and they spend their money as conspicuously as any Hollywood agent with an office in Century City and a table at Spago. They inhabit a world of German luxury coupes, country clubs, personal trainers and ski chalet vacations. Each lives in the exclusive Belle Meade section of Nashville, where they own 20-room mansions with bathrooms that are larger than the average person's living room.

"We don't feel there's some special sanction on us that allows us to be less than professional," Harrell continued. "A lot of people are confused. Mike and I approach this from a business standpoint. Christianity is the undergirding but never the justification. A lot of other industry leaders view it as church work, not as the music business. A lot of them struggle with 'What are we doing? Are we selling Jesus?' Absolutely. That's our product. You can get into more trouble not admitting there is money here to be made than if you don't try to hide it."

Blanton and Harrell are hardly sui generis. It may be easier for a camel to go through the eye of a needle than for a rich man to go to heaven, but you wouldn't know it in the boom-town atmosphere of Christian music. Steven Curtis Chapman sold enough pop music about good Christian values to build this year what he calls his "dream house" on seven choice suburban Nashville acres. Amy Grant already had her dream house, on 200 acres. Point of Grace isn't that prosperous yet—Heather and Shelley share an apartment and a drab brown 1984 Buick LeSabre—but they don't appear to struggle with the prospect of "using God to become rich" the way Michael English did. John Mays of Word Records doesn't think they need to. "The call to Christ is not one of poverty or wealth," he says. "If a plumber gets rich, people wouldn't have the same problems with it."

A plumber, however, is not likely to become rich, and even if he does, he's earning his Mercedes fixing pipes, not souls. When I put all this to Michael Blanton, who was in his office across the hall from Harrell's, he responded in a way that made it very clear why he is such an effective manager. "It's a business absolutely," he told me. "You have to use the same instincts to survive in this thing. Sooner you realize that, you'll do better. This is the entertainment business. We just happen to be guys who are Christian doing it. I think God's in control of the world. I embrace fully my Christianity, but it doesn't mean I can't be a great manager or producer."

Blanton and Harrell formed their company in 1980, because Harrell grew weary of taking telephone calls from his mother-in-law. His wife's teen-age sister, Amy, was an aspiring singer with a record contract from Word, but Amy's mother didn't know the first thing about how to make a career in music. Whenever a question arose, Amy's mom called Harrell at his job at the First American Bank in Nashville to ask his advice. "I looked for a manager for her," says Harrell. "I found that I didn't trust any of these guys. I'm thinking I can do a better job, so I quit my job and became a manager." Harrell knew Blanton, then the artists-and-repertoire director of Word, and he asked him to be his partner. "Mike was real frustrated at Word," he says. "All they wanted to do was put out product. He wanted to develop artists."

There had never been a gold record in Christian music in 1980. The next year, with her brother-in-law Dan Harrell behind her, Amy Grant, still a teen-ager, made the first. "Now we feel we've almost failed if we don't go gold," says Blanton. Besides

Grant, Blanton and Harrell represent her husband—the singer and songwriter Gary Chapman—Michael W. Smith and several other Christian music stars who generate between $70 million and $80 million a year. Reunion, the record company they founded, is flourishing, especially since they sold half of it to BMG.

Now, when record companies send Blanton & Harrell contracts with morality clauses in them, the partners ask the record company executives to sign it, too. Invariably, the clauses quickly disappear from the contracts. When they learned that Gary Chapman had become a substance abuser, they supported him through his recovery.

Just as they engineered Amy Grant's crossover into the pop mainstream, Blanton and Harrell are now contemplating their own crossover. They are trolling Nashville, hoping to sign on some mainstream musical talent. I asked if there were limits to who they could work with. Could they sign up James Taylor? Billy Ray Cyrus? Madonna? Jews? Atheists? "I don't have a problem meeting with anybody," said Blanton. What about representing Michael English? "I'd consider it," said Harrell. "I'd want to know what's going on in his life. If we only worked with people who are perfect, we wouldn't work with anybody."

If Point of Grace is the Sunday morning of Christian music, DC Talk is its Saturday night. DC Talk is Toby McKeehan, Michael Tait and Kevin Max Smith, or "two honks and a Negro serving the Lord," as they like to put it. They met as students at Jerry Falwell's Liberty University in Lynchburg, Va., and today their hip-hop band is the talk of Christian music. They have played for the Pope in Colorado and with Billy Graham in front of 65,000 fans in Atlanta. Their third album, "Free At Last," spent 34 weeks this year as the No. 1 Christian album on the Billboard chart. All three men are in their late 20's and are given to wearing boots, chains, torn baggy jeans, pork-pie hats, sideburns and, in the case of Michael, who is black, earrings and dreadlocks. Their songs range in subject matter from racism, to sexual decadence, to abortion. That Christian kids can't get enough of them was clear at Night of Joy.

Night of Joy is the biggest contemporary Christian music event of the fall, a retreat for thousands of young Christians from all over the United States, held at Walt Disney World in Orlando. Besides all of the usual Disney rides and pleasures, Night of Joy participants can sample any of the six different Christian music groups playing concerts on the Magic Kingdom grounds. It is sanitized music in a sanitized venue. Among the bands invited to perform this year are DC Talk and Point of Grace.

On a stage set up in front of Space Mountain, DC Talk gave its usual high-octane performance. Backed by a four-piece band and three athletic break-dancers, Toby, Michael and Kevin strutted, sneered, preened, rode around the stage on one another's shoulders, hugged, executed flying karate kicks, slam-danced and did the Jagger hip shake thang. They rapped and they sang. Also, they talked. Constantly. "I mean to tell the whole right in front of the mountain, right in front of Mickey Mouse, in front of Donald Duck and Goofy, my Jesus ain't all wrong, my Jesus is all right," said Toby, introducing a hip-hop version of the old Dobbie Brothers song "Jesus Is Just Alright." At one moment Toby was advising, "You ladies need to be ladies after God's own heart." At another, he warned that "all you racists better be careful because there's gonna be all colors up in heaven, baby," to which the audience jubilantly agreed. Later, one dancer, with a terrorist mask pulled over his face, sprinted across the stage, raking the crowd with a high-powered water rifle. The kids pleaded for more.

Offstage, the band seemed not to feel entirely at ease in C.C.M. "People will say, 'You guys are reaching a lot of kids,'" said Michael. "This means stay in the Word, keep writing uplifting, unthreatening songs for our kids. It's like a hidden accountability thing." When Michael grew out his hair and began wearing earrings, "I got some weirdness from the church. They said, 'You've dropped your guard.' I said: 'No I haven't. This ain't gonna keep me out of Heaven.'"

Toby concurred. "We do feel some responsibility, but we feel as long as they realize we cannot possibly live up to their expectations, we're cool. We've freed ourselves from trying to be that perfect role model. We're just three guys trying to pursue a faith in God."

What also troubles DC Talk is that because God is in their songs, they are heard only by Christians. "We actually wish it"—Christian music—"didn't exist," Toby said. "We don't want to play just in front of Christian people. We want to share our music with the people of the world." But their interest in singing for what they call "the MTV generation" going over well with other Christians. "People who share our beliefs want to keep us for themselves," Toby said.

DC Talk was the freshest, most inventive act I saw in Christian rock. To be sure there are some other talented performers in Christian music, but to my ear, most C.C.M. is mediocre stuff, diluted by hesitation and dogmatic formula, inferior to the mainstream popular music it emulates. "It's easy for a Christian artist to go into a church and really impress people," one Christian music producer confessed. "You put that same artist on a level playing field with all the musical talent on the planet, some of it doesn't meet the same standard."

Contemporary Christian music has grown in popularity at a time when Americans are resisting the culture of disbelief and turning to faith. But the music has an ephemeral quality to it: it may appeal to people who haven't listened closely to anything else, but it lacks the artistry and passion of mainstream musicians like Bonnie Raitt and Stevie Wonder. If contemporary Christian music hopes to last beyond its current boom, it needs to loosen up, to cast aside its fearful sensibilities and take advantage of the emotion implicit in the best religious music. Subject matter isn't the issue: when rendered by the likes of Van Morrison and Johnny Cash, Christian music has attracted a large ecumenical audience. There's no reason why contemporary Christian performers, if they allow themselves to explore their talent and emotion more completely, can't successfully combine virtuosity and moral virtue. No doubt when they do, the free market will set in, and their audience will clamor for quality. And people like Bowen, Blanton and Harrell will be there to supply it.

For the moment, however, C.C.M. bands who want to sing about more than faith, hope and love will experience plenty of frustration. On the Monday night culminating Night of Joy weekend, DC Talk were hosts of the first-ever America's Christian Music Awards show. They had a high time of it. They invited Larry Norman to Orlando, and he sang one of his songs with them. They received every award they were nominated for—four in all—and on the rostrum they behaved like scamps. As a gag, they speculated about the pristine Amy Grant's "dysfunctional" marriage. "No, I'm not the ghost of Kurt Cobain," intoned Kevin, who is a ringer for him. The audience didn't laugh. Later, Toby joked that next year's hosts would be Snoop Doggy Dog, Alice Cooper and Roseanne. Again, the response was cold silence.

When Point of Grace was named best new artist, however, the audience erupted with applause. "We just want to thank our Heavenly Father for his grace that he gives us every day," said Denise.

After the awards ceremony, the promoters threw a 1950's-theme bash. Beforehand, Mike Atkins huddled with Point of Grace and urged them "to accept with graciousness what's happening to you." He told them that he was proud of them and gently warned them that from now their lives would be different, that they aren't "the new ones" anymore. He urged them to enjoy themselves, but to rememer that in public, they have responsibilities. At the party, Point of Grace installed themselves at tables and drank soda with their husbands and boyfriends. Industry moguls with fresh Florida golf tans stopped by to congratulate them.

Lounging against a wall off to one side of the room, Kevin Max Smith was brooding behind his sunglasses. He had just learned that many of his wisecracks would be cut out of the delayed telecast of the music awards. He was incredulous. "They edited me!" Then he grew resigned. With his shades, longish blond hair, pretty face and smooth tenor, he is in many ways the picture of the young American rock star. "I realize you can only go so far in a taped program for the Family Channel," he said. "I wish we could have a bit more freedom for ourselves. I've always felt like an alien in this conglomerate, but it's my duty to love these people more than I love myself."

*Nicholas Dawidoff, author of "The Catcher Was a Spy,"
is at work on a book about country music.*

Public Relations Review, 18(3):247–255
ISSN: 0363-8111

The Religious Right's Battle Plan in the 'Civil War of Values'

John S. Detweiler

ABSTRACT: Three family-oriented Christian organizations—
Focus on the Family, Concerned Women for America, and
American Family Associations—are conducting a change-oriented
campaign to restore "traditional values" in America.

The groups are primarily concerned with such issues as
combating abortion, fighting anti-religious trends in schools,
and the morality portrayed in television entertainment.

Dr. Detweiler is chairman of the Department of Public Relations
at the University of Florida, where he has taught for 26 years.

Three conservative Christian organizations with similar
themes and tactics, all supporting "traditional family values," are mobilizing a
potent single-issue group out of adherents who heretofore have been more
comfortable passively sitting in the pew than mounting the picket line.

In the process the "Religious Right," which helped reshape the political
landscape in the 1980 federal elections, is back to full strength. It has survived the
setbacks inflicted upon the movement by wayward TV evangelists during the past
decade. In the 1990s a strong sense of conventional morality seems to be
replacing charisma as the principal credential for Christian leadership.

Using the terminology of warfare or impending crisis, the three leaders of these
groups vividly portray a cataclysmic sense of urgency in their efforts to motivate
the troops.

"Nothing short of a great Civil War of Values rages today throughout North
America," contends Dr. James C. Dobson, president of Focus on the Family.[1]

"The 1990s—Decade of Destiny for America's Children—are moving forward. Many decisions made in this decade will determine the future of our children and grandchildren. Generations to come will be affected by what happens in these ten years, so we must try to make a difference for them and for the future of our nation," says Beverly LaHaye, president of Concerned Women for America.[2]

"This spiritual war was and is the greatest single issue facing Christianity today. Knowing that the entertainment industry, particularly television, was a primary battleground in this war (as is our educational system), I realized that the organized church simply had to be mobilized to join the fight. Only the church has the capacity to fight and win this great spiritual war," challenges Donald E. Wildmon, executive director of the American Family Association.[3]

As a result, their followers have financed lawsuits and lobbying activities; sent postcards by the thousands to networks and TV program sponsors; participated in boycotts of movies, convenience stores, commercial products and abortion clinics; and supported anti-abortion and pro-religion political candidates. The leaders themselves have challenged their rivals in the mainstream media through appearances on talk shows, submission of op ed pieces to newspapers, and their readiness to serve as accessible sources for reporters seeking to balance statements from such organizations as the NOW or People for the American Way.

The movement has won a number of recent skirmishes in this war, erasing what they consider some 30 years of successive defeats. In 1992 they provide a strong base of support for America's quintessential "family man," President George Bush, in the November presidential election.

This study pulls together from materials published by these three organizations a general description of their campaign in support of conventional family values and the tactics which they employ to enlist followers or to influence mass media content or public policy.

The three organizations claim a strong base of support. Focus on the Family's free inspirational, self-help magazine, *Focus on the Family*, is distributed to 1.5 million readers.[4] Its public issues magazine, *Citizen*, has a circulation of 300,000.[5] Concern Women for America, headed by Beverly LaHaye, reports more than 600,000 members.[6] *The American Family Association Journal* reaches 400,000 individuals, pastors or churches.[7]

The groups list an impressive array of enemies in this cultural war: American Civil Liberties Union, National Organization for Women, National Education Association, National Abortion Rights Action League, People for the American Way, Gay Media Task Force, most national staff members of mainline denominations, journalists, television and movie producers, university faculty members, and most of the Washington D.C. establishment—particularly the staff members of the Democratic Party–controlled Congress.

They all contend that the umbrella term denoting the enemy is "secular humanism," a favorite expression of Jerry Falwell's Moral Majority ten years earlier.[8] However, opposing "secular humanism" wins few adherents. It is a confusing and nebulous term, such a campaign itself has a negative slant.

248

Supporting "traditional family values" has proven a much more effective and positive campaign theme. Wildmon changed the name of his organization from National Federation of Decency to American Family Association in 1988. LaHaye changed the name of her publication from *Concerned Women for America* to *Family Voice* in October 1991.

Goals of Focus on Family, American Family Association, and Concerned Women for America are wide ranging, but they seem to focus on a number of key issues: Abortion on demand; sex, violence, and profanity in television entertainment; soft-port and hardcore pornography in print; anti-religious and immoral biases in the mass media and public school books; dial-a-porn services; X-rated rock lyrics; "safe sex" education which dismisses abstinence as impractical; federal funding for immoral art or abortion counseling; governmental programs or media stereotypes which favor working women over homemakers, and similar issues.

The three groups contend they face a stacked deck in the secular mass media. The research most frequently cited to support this contention are studies published by Robert and Linda Lichter with Stanley Rothman—*The Media Elite*[9] and "Hollywood and America: The Odd Couple."[10] These studies show that staffers of America's elite news organizations and Hollywood's creative community, who rarely attend religious services, are likely to consider themselves politically liberal, support legalized abortion, and consider homosexuality a normal sexual orientation.

The organizations maintain that they have struck fertile ground in the discontent among "average parents" over news media coverage and entertainment themes which seem to challenge traditional values. As an example, Dobson cites a poll conducted by *Parents* magazine:

> Two-thirds of those polled said there should be standards to prohibit some material from being shown. Some 74 percent want an end to vulgar, four-letter words on the airwaves; 72 percent feel the same about programs that ridicule and make fun of religion; and 64 percent want TV networks to stop showing programs that ridicule traditional values, such as marriage or motherhood. Not surprisingly, over 70 percent of the respondents thought TV programming overall was mediocre to terrible.[11]

Sensing popular support for their cause, the three organizations seek to supplant the Gay Media Task Force as the organization "recognized by TV insiders as the most powerful lobby in Hollywood."[12]

The entertainment media seem the prime battle ground, but the public schools are just as important. The three Christian groups advocate several alternatives to public schools. They support private Christian schools and home schooling. They also urge their adherents to take an active interest in their children's public school, including running for the school board. However, their weapon of choice for publicly funded schools is the voucher system advocated by President Bush.

Through the voucher system, mothers and fathers become "customers" with the power to follow their choices in educating their children. "For example,"' Dobson comments, "if an offensive sex education program could be expected to cause 300 parents to choose another school alternative, you can be sure moderation would prevail."[13]

The popular theme of diversity, particularly to the degree that it includes homosexuality in the mix, is a growing target of the three groups. *Concerned Women for America* has run several articles based on the reactions of followers who have attended government-sponsored diversity conferences or the national conventions of the National Organization for Women and the National Education Association.

"Joan" was the pseudonym of the woman attending the NOW convention. The *Concerned Women for America* magazine reported: "As a first-time visitor to such conferences, Joan said what surprised her the most was the dominant presence of lesbians. They were everywhere, she said, to such a degree that even the most liberal women would be offended."[14]

"Nancy," the pseudonym of the woman attending the NEA convention, had a similar reaction: "To make its presence felt, the NEA's Gay and Lesbian Caucus embarked on a 'Hot Pink Visibility' campaign during the convention. Each NEAGLC member was told to wear a hot pink ribbon with the homosexual caucus' logo throughout the event." She saw scores of delegates wearing pink ribbons.[15]

Dobson is perhaps the most recognized of the three leaders. He is author of 11 best-selling books on the family. More than 1,300 radio stations carry his daily radio program, and he has served on four national commissions appointed by either the President or Attorney General.[16] He recently moved his headquarters from Pomona California, to Colorado Springs, Colorado.

LaHaye takes advantage of her Washington, D.C., location to personally participate in lobbying activities. She also is in a national media center, providing her an opportunity to serve as a frequent news source on such "woman's issues" as abortion, child rearing, schools, and sexploitation. She has much more ready access to mainstream media than either Dobson in Colorado Springs or Wildmon in Tupelo, Mississippi. LaHaye spends a good deal of her time nurturing her organization. Concerned Women for America has chapters in all 50 states and has a national convention.[17]

Wildmon, executive director of the American Family Association, relishes the "bad guy" role he plays in the fight for traditional values. He has chosen more confrontational tactics than either Dobson or LaHaye, and he has gained a great deal of notoriety in the process—going from a "pipsqueak" preacher in Tupelo, Mississippi, to "Ayatollah of the Airwaves."[18] Wildmon's latest book features this "bad guy" role—*The Man The Networks Love To Hate.* "We're the marines," says son Tim Wildmon, associate director of AFA. The group has 600 chapters nationwide.[19]

The original name of Wildmon's organization, National Federation of Decency, did not carry the family theme. In 1988 he changed the name of the organization to the American Family Association although its basic purposes and tactics remained the same. Wildmon has enlisted volunteer monitors to watch and videotape all network television programs, noting content which seems objectionable and the advertisers of each program. Wildmon then contacts the chief executive officers of companies advertising during offensive programs, inquiring if they wish their ads to be associated with such themes. He utilizes his monthly magazine to publicize these program/advertiser linkages, and he encourages his constituency to write, call or send preprinted postcards to sponsors objecting to the programs which they support.

FINDINGS

In order to gain specific information on the type of issues which these three organizations addressed, this study did a content analysis on 10 issues of the monthly magazines of the three organizations—Focus on the Family *Citizen*, *Concerned Women for America* (now *Family Voice*), and the *American Family Association Journal*. Each group had its own priorities, but six issues accounted for 69% of the articles noted.

American Family Association Journal has a large number of short items. In this survey only articles measuring more than five inches (with headline) were counted. There were 352 articles included in the survey of 10 (January–October) 1991 issues. Focus on the Family *Citizen* had 98 articles included in a survey of 10 (January–October) 1991 articles. *Concerned Women for America* had 123 articles surveyed in 10 issues (June–October 1991). The latter sample was selected because of missing issues in the researcher's file for the first six months of 1991.

The groups differ markedly in the direct actions which they recommend that their followers take. Focus on the Family concentrated primarily on actions which would benefit the pro-life cause or changes in public schools. Concerned Women for America followed a wide agenda, chiefly drawing distinction between liberal

TABLE 1

Percentages of Articles Devoted Six Issues				
Topic	*AFA*	*FOF*	*CWA*	*Average*
Print pornography (soft & hardcore porn, legal actions)	11	9	—	6.7
TV sex, violence, profanity	37	7	2	15.3
Abortion	5	21	43	23.0
NEA controversy (federal funds for objectionable art)	5	2	5	4.0
Public schools (sex education, secularism, anti-Christian bias)	6	16	17	13.0
Homosexuality	7	5	8	6.7
Percent of total content	71	60	75	68.7

TABLE 2

Percentage of Actions Recommended to Followers

Action	AFA	FOF	CWA	Average
Governmental or political contact	9	76	48	44
Collective, nongovernmental action	86	16	42	48
Personal action	5	8	12	8

feminist groups and its own membership. American Family Association concentrated almost entirely on television entertainment. The groups also differed in the type of actions they recommended.

One broad range of action included contacting governmental officials either supporting or opposing various issues. Closely related to this were recommendations for selecting and supporting political candidates with sympathetic viewpoints. A second broad range of action included collective, nongovernmental action such as promoting boycotts, encouraging followers to write or call advertisers to express disapproval or provide positive reinforcement for the programs which they are sponsoring, participating in such activities as Life Chain or Pornography Awareness Week, or joining together in prayer for common objectives. The third type of activity involved individuals taking action to improve their awareness of issues (ordering resources), controlling the television in their homes, or choosing to attend a conference or educational meeting.

The five most recent issues of *Citizen*, *Concerned Women for America* (*Family Voice*) and *American Family Association Journal* were examined to determine specific actions recommended for readers. There were 25 specific actions noted in the *Citizen*, 33 specific actions noted in *CWA—Family Voice*, and 107 specific actions recommended in the *AFA Journal*.

Focus on the Family and Concerned Women for America both gave the heaviest emphasis to the pro-life movement, followed by reforms in the schools. American Family Association placed heaviest emphasis on television content. "Television is the most destructive instrument in our society," Wildmon says. [20]

In addition to changing the content of mass media news, entertainment and advertising or influencing public policy, the groups are also concerned about the terminology used in public discussions.

"Words are bullets" in America's cultural civil war, according to Dobson. He claimed those opposing family, faith, and tradition are able to manipulate words and their meanings over time because they control the communications media. [21]

He uses the term "censorship" as a case in point, calling it a "one-way word."

> It is routinely thrown at citizens who oppose pornography, parents concerned about rock music lyrics, citizen groups who question the appropriateness of some classroom materials, or grass roots organizations who call for boycotts of products or material that attack their values. The reverse is never true. The systematic removal of references to our religious heritage in history books by

publishers is never called censorship. Neither is the harassment or closing by universities of college newspapers which have sprung up in recent years to promote a traditional agenda.

When mainstream bookstores refuse to carry many books with Judeo-Christian themes but carry all sorts of tracts on New Age mysticism, no leading figures take to the airwaves to raise the charge of censorship. Search primetime TV for examples of religion or religious influence in the lives of the characters. It is rare, though religion is a major factor in the lives of Americans.[22]

Some words like "chaste" and "virtue," are disappearing from our vocabulary, Dobson said. Other words, like "evil," are blacklisted. Other words of disapproval have been replaced by non-judgmental substitutes. "Promiscuous" becomes "sexually active;" "pornography" becomes "sexually explicit;" "perversion" or "sexual deviation" becomes "sexual orientation." All three groups abhor the use of "safe sex" to describe anything other than abstinence before marriage and fidelity in marriage.

Semantics is playing an important role in the battle over abortion. The "pro-life" and "pro-choice" advocates complain if their name for the issue is not used by the news media. In addition, the Wichita abortion protests in the summer of 1991 were dealt a semantic blow by U.S. Justice Patrick Kelly, who attempted to block the "Summer of Mercy" demonstrations by a 1871 statute designed to stop the anti-black terrorism of the Ku Klux Klan. Dobson argues:

> Using the Klan Act to Stop Operation Rescue serves an urgent propaganda need of the pro-abortion movement. It undermines the rescuers' self-identification with the civil rights protesters of the 1950s and '60s, and links them instead to groups like the Klan.[23]

The three pro-family groups are beginning to cite a number of achievements as a result of their campaigns. For instance, all three were represented at the Wichita pro-life rally in August 1991 which had a turnout of 30,000 people, about six times larger than the crowd that came to a pro-choice rally the previous day. Operation Rescue, which conducted the summer anti-abortion campaign in Wichita, has been described as an unrepresentative fringe group in the anti-abortion movement, but the visible presence of the three pro-family groups served to "legitimize" it with other Christians.

The editor of CWA's *Family Voice* was able to exclaim:

> After weeks upon weeks of media hype telling Americans that all Wichitans wanted to be rid of Operation Rescue—that they were sick and tired of the abortion issue—the massive turnout at the rally was nothing short of spectacular. It was a resounding rejection of the current line that pro-life is a losing cause.[24]

A prime goal of the three pro-family groups is to propel passive Christians into some sort of action on key issues. The Wichita rally framed such a choice. Six weeks after the Wichita rally, on October 6, a record crowd of 771,000 pro-lifers

251

participated in a less confrontational demonstration. They stood at major inter-sections in 373 cities during National Life Chain Sunday. The demonstrators held signs which said "Abortion Kills Children" or "Jesus Heals and Forgives." Another 65,000 joined the chain in Canada.[26] The number far exceeded previous years' participation. Since the first Life Chain linked up in 1987, an estimated 1,000,000 had participated over a four-year span.[26]

In 1989 Wildmon helped form the Coalition for Better Television (CLeaRTV) with the help of the Rev. Jerry Falwell, who was phasing out his Moral Majority. CLeaRTV now has had 1,600 Christian leaders sign its declaration of principles, representing more than 70 denominations.[27]

The potent group has led to the cancellation of several television programs and have stripped advertising support from others. Wildmon's October membership letter cites a *Wall Street Journal* article (9/30/91) which states that NBC has informed Universal Studios that the studio would be responsible for any losses suffered by advertising pull-out from a "Quantum Leap" episode promoting homosexuality. Earlier Wildmon's group's boycotts led to 7-Eleven removing *Playboy* magazines from its shelves and prevented "The Last Temptation of Christ" from running in first-run movies.

Together the three groups have put enough pressure on Congress that the National Endowment for the Arts has barely survived funding battles for three successive years. Concerned Women for America forced cancellation of funding for a teen sex survey in 1991. The groups also strongly supported the appoint-ment of Justice Clarence Thomas to the U.S. Supreme Court and helped strengthen wavering senators who supported him in his confirmation vote. One of their goals for 1992 will be keeping the election platform of the Republican Party strongly pro-life and then to reelect President Bush in a campaign which reflects that platform.

The work at hand includes court decisions on abortion and church-state issues, legislative action on public schools and morality issues, aggressive enforcement of obscenity laws, and television content which does not affront the conventional family. To some degree the success of these three groups will also be reckoned by their public relations battles in the "court of public opinion" when they square off against opposing groups on such issues as homosexual rights, pro-life vs. pro-choice tests of strength, political campaigns, or issues perceived as censorship of art, TV entertainment or what is taught in the public schools.

NOTES

1. James C. Dobson and Gary L. Bauer, *Children at Risk*, (Dallas: Word Publishing, 1990), p. 19.
2. Beverly LaHaye, *Concerned Women for America*, (July 1991), p. 2.
3. Donald E. Wildmon with Randall Nulton, *The Man The Networks Love To Hate* (Wilmore, KY: Bristol Books, 1989), p. 208.
4. *Focus on the Family*, October 1991, p. 9.

5   Dobson and Bauer, op. cit., p. 269.
6. "Fact Sheet," *Concerned Women for America*, (1991).
7. Wildmon and Nulton, op. cit., p. 176.
8. Ibid., p. 134
9. S. Robert Lichter, and Stanley Rothman, and Linda S. Lichter, *The Media Elite* (Bethesda, MD: Adler & Adler, Publishers, 1986).
10. Linda S. Lichter S. Robert Lichter, and Stanley Rothman, "Hollywood and America: The Odd Couple," *Public Opinion* (January 1983).
11. Dobson and Bauer, op. cit., p. 208.
12. Wildmon and Nulton, op. cit., p. 141, citing Richrd M. Levine, "Family Affair," *Esquire* (March 1984), p. 225–226.
13. Dobson and Bauer, op. cit., p. 226.
14 "Lesbian Clout Felt at NOW Convention," *Concerned Women for America* (September 1991), p. 1.
15. "NEA: Teaching Teachers Radicalism," *Concerned Women for America* (September 1991), p. 7–8.
16. "Focus on the Family Special Introductory Issue," four-page magazine format publication supplied to persons on their initial contact with the organization.
17. "Come Help Save America!," introductory brochure supplied to persons on their original contact with Concerned Women for America.
18. Wildmon and Nulton, op. cit., p. 77.
19. *American Family Association Journal* (September 1991), pp. 19–21.
20. Ibid.
21. Dobson and Bauer, op. cit., pp. 218–219.
22. Ibid., pp. 223–224.
23. "Washington Watch," *Family Research Council* (September 1991), p. 3.
24. "Hope from the Heartland," *Family Voice* (October 1991), p. 10.
25. "Life Chain Draws Record Number," *Charisma*, (December 1991), p. 28.
26. "300 Cities Plan to Link Up for Life," *Concerned Women for America* (September 1991), p. 4.
27. *American Family Association Journal* (September 1991), p. 21.

9

Media and the Arts

One does not need to endure a thousand bleary-eyed evenings with Dan Rather or Tom Brokaw to understand how important a role the media of mass communications plays in our lives. Television, radio, magazines, newspapers, news magazines, the popular press, as well as music, film, theater, visual arts, popular literature, do much more than passively reflect the social and political reality of our times. Like the institutions of public education discussed in the previous chapter, these institutions actively define reality, shape the times, give meaning to the history we witness and experience as ordinary citizens. This outcome is unavoidable in many ways. In the very act of *selecting* the stories to cover, the books to publish and review, the film and music to air, and the art to exhibit, these institutions effectively define which topics are important and which issues are relevant—worthy of public consideration. Moreover, in the *substance* of the stories covered, books published and reviewed, art exhibited, and so on, the mass media act as a filter through which our perceptions of the world around us take shape. Thus, by virtue of the decisions made by those who control the mass media—seemingly innocuous decisions made day to day and year to year—those who work within these institutions cumulatively wield enormous power. In a good many situations, this power is exercised unwittingly, rooted in the best intentions to perform a task well, objectively, fairly. Increasingly, however, the effects of this power have become understood and deliberately manipulated. Is it not inevitable that the media and the arts would become a field of conflict in the contemporary culture war?

There are at least two matters to consider here. First, the contest to define reality, so central to the larger culture war, inevitably becomes a struggle to control the "instrumentality" of reality definition. This means that the battle over this symbolic territory has practically taken shape as a struggle to influence or even dominate the businesses and industries of public information, art, and entertainment—from the major television and radio networks to the National Endowment for the Arts; from the Hollywood film industry to the music recording industry, and so on. But there is more. At a more subtle and symbolic level, the tensions in this field of conflict point to a struggle over the meaning of "speech" or the meaning of "expression" that the First Amendment is supposed to protect. Underlying the conflict over this symbolic territory, in other words, are the questions, "What constitutes art in our communities?" "Whose definition of entertainment and aesthetic appreciation do we accept?" "What version of the news is fair?" And so on.

TAKING ON THE ESTABLISHMENT

We begin by considering a brief vignette of an event that occurred at a pro-life march in Washington, D.C. The day was filled with speeches from politicians, religious leaders, pro-life leaders, and other luminaries. Several hundred thousand people listened attentively, cheered, chanted, prayed, and sang songs. Such are the rituals of modern political rallies. At one point during the rally, however, a number of pro-life advocates spontaneously turned toward a television news crew filming the event from atop a nearby platform and began to chant in unison, "Tell the truth!" "Tell the truth!" Tell the truth!" What began as a rumble within a few moments had caught on within the crowd. Soon, tens of thousands of people were chanting "Tell the truth!" "Tell the truth!" "Tell the truth!" Of all the aspects of the rally covered in the newscast that evening or in the newspapers the following day, this brief and curious event was not among them.

The story highlights the conviction held by virtually everyone on the orthodox and conservative side of the new cultural divide that the media and arts establishment is unfairly prejudiced against the values they hold dear. They do not tell the truth, the voices of orthodoxy maintain, and what is worse, they do not even present opposing sides of the issues evenhandedly. Here is the National Right to Life Committee's direct mail statement: "ABC, CBS, and NBC [have] Declared War . . . on the Movement. . . .We cannot let a handful of network executives and Hollywood writers, actors and directors poison America with their godless attitudes, which are anti-religion, anti-family and anti-life." Tim LaHaye echoed this sentiment in his own mail appeal:

> It's no secret to any of us how the liberal media manages the news and helps to set the national agenda on public debate. They report the news in such a way as to promote the political goals of the left. This censorship of Christian principles and ideas covers many more issues than abortion and the homosexual lifestyle. The media slants what is reported in the areas of national defense, the budget, school prayer, and Soviet expansion in Central America, among others. The truth in all of these areas is being hidden.[1]

Of the film industry, another spokesman said, "The people in Hollywood are so far removed from the people of middle America. They have a hostility toward people who believe anything at all. They live in a hedonistic, materialistic little world."[2]

Exaggerated they may be, but the general perceptions are not totally born out of illusion. Studies of the attitudes of media and entertainment elites, as well as of television news programming and newspaper coverage of various social issues and political events, have shown a fairly strong and consistent bias toward a liberal and progressivist point of view.[3] The field over which these particular battles are waged, then, is uneven—and the contenders recognize it as such. One contender takes a position of defending territory already won; the other strives to reclaim it. There are three major ways in which traditionalists have sought to reclaim this symbolic (and institutional) territory.

One way has been in a direct assault against the media and arts establishment. Acquiring a large-circulation newspaper or a network was something that had been "a dream of conservatives for years," according to Howard Phillips of the Conservative Caucus.[4] Early in 1985, such an assault was made. After years of frustration with what it called "the liberal bias" of CBS, a group called Fairness in Media (FIM) spearheaded a move to buy out the television network. Through its leading spokesman, Senator Jesse Helms, FIM sent a direct mail letter to more than a million conservatives across the country urging them to purchase twenty shares each of common stock in the company, the end of which would be to "become Dan Rather's boss." The plan was not a ruse. Conservative spokesmen called the idea "inspired" and "realistic," and hundreds of people called FIM to find out how to participate. Officials at CBS initially brushed off the proposal but soon were engaged in rearguard action against it, hiring two law firms, an investment banking house, and several public relations firms. Its official response: "CBS intends to take all appropriate steps to maintain the independence and integrity of its news organization." At CBS, a spokeswoman added, "our sole purpose is journalism and our goal is objectivity."[5] Conservatives and others in the orthodox alliance would naturally respond, "whose standards of objectivity?" Ultimately, of course, the bid to take over the network failed but those who supported the idea were not put off. "It may take a while to accomplish [this goal]," one editorialized, "but it's a goal well worth waiting—and striving—for."[6]

The persistent effort of the orthodox alliance to hold the media establishment accountable for the content it presents is another strategy. Numerous national and local organizations are committed to this task, covering a wide range of media. Morality in Media, for example, is an interfaith organization founded in 1962 by three clergymen in order to stop traffic in pornography and to challenge "indecency in media" and to work "for a media based on love, truth and good taste." Accuracy in Media has, since 1969, sought to combat liberal bias by exposing cases where the media have not covered stories "fairly and accurately." The Parents' Music Resource Center, established in 1985, is concerned to raise the awareness of parents about the content of modern rock music, especially heavy metal music. Its specific focus is, according to one of its founders, "not the occasional sexy rock lyric . . . [but] the celebration of the most gruesome violence, coupled with explicit messages that sado-masochism is the essence of sex."[7] One of the most visible of all media watchdog groups is the American Family Association and the affiliated CLeaR-TV, or Christian Leaders for Responsible Television. Founded by the Reverend Donald Wildmon, the American Family Association membership claims ordinary believers and religious leaders from all Christian faiths, Protestant, Catholic, and Orthodox, and together they propose to combat the "excessive, gratuitous sex, violence, profanity, [and] the negative stereotyping of Christians."[8]

These organizations are joined by many others both national and local, including town and city councils around the country that share a similar concern about the content of public information and entertainment. They are effective because they are grass-roots in orientation (or at least they pose as being locally connected to the grass-roots), and they make use of proven techniques of popular political mobilization: letter writing, boycott, countermedia exposure, and the like.

As much a support structure for the various orthodox and conservative subcultures as a weapon in the culture war, communities within the orthodox alliance have created an entire network of alternative electronic media. These alternative media challenge the media and arts establishment a third way, then, through competition, offering programming that defines a fundamentally different and competing reality and vision of America. Conservative Catholics and Orthodox Jews play different roles in some of these media, but it is the Evangelicals who dominate this alternative media industry. Take film as an example. The mainstay dramas produced by Billy Graham's World Wide Pictures have always been deliberately Evangelistic in tone and purpose. More recently, however, Evangelicals have begun to create films that "uphold traditional values." For example, Florida-based Evangelist D. James Kennedy, frustrated and angry about the insensitivities of the Hollywood film establishment toward religiously observant Americans, founded a film company in the late 1980s. "We're tired of sex and blasphemy and immorality, of sadism and influencing people for ill," he said. "We believe there are people who would like to watch something other than drugs and sex. Now, I know there are various kinds of reality in this country, including the reality of the toilet. But how about the *realities of morality and courage and devotion?*"[9] Though Evangelical in nature, Kennedy's initiative has received support from Catholic and Jewish quarters as well.[10]

Even more vigorous challenges have been made by the Evangelical-dominated television and radio industry. Within the Evangelical subculture alone there were over 1,300 religious radio stations, over 200 religious television stations and 3 religious television networks broadcasting in the United States by the early 1990s.[11] The Catholic place in this industry is relatively small by comparison but it does make an important contribution. The programming goes far beyond televised religious services or radio broadcasts of sacred music to include religious talk shows, soap operas, drama, Bible studies, and news commentary. In addition to these enterprises is a billion-dollar book industry (made up, within the Evangelical orbit alone, of over 80 publishing houses and over 6,000 independent religious bookstores) that publish and market books on, for example, how to be a better Christian, how to raise children, how to cope with a mid-life crisis, not to mention a sizable literature on what is wrong about America and what you can do about it. And a multimillion dollar music industry extends far beyond the latest rendition of "Blessed Assurance" by George Beverly Shea to Hasidic and Christian rock and roll, folk, heavy metal (groups called Vengeance, Petra, or Shout singing such releases as "In Your Face"), and even rap music.

THE POLITICS OF FREE SPEECH

What makes these battles over the media and arts especially interesting is that they reveal a conflict that is several layers deeper. The first layer of conflict concerns the nature and meaning of art and music, as well as the nature and meaning of information. Inevitably this conflict leads to the more philosophical and legal disputes over the nature of "speech" and "expression" protected by the First Amendment. There is no end to the number of "headline cases" in which these sorts of issues are worked out. The fact is that each dispute contains within it all the underlying philosophical and legal tensions as well. Collectively, they make the matter a crisis over which actors on both sides of the cultural divide urgently press for resolution.

To demonstrate how this conflict is played out at these different levels, it is necessary to get down to specific cases. The object here is not to comprehensively survey and catalogue the various disputes over media and the arts in recent times. The following sampling of a few widely publicized controversies from different areas of public expression demonstrates a larger pattern of discourse among the contenders, one that ultimately carries us to the deeper issues of expression and censorship in the culture war.

The Avant-Garde and Its Discontents

It begins with the quest for novelty. This impulse is undeniably a driving force in the arts, entertainment, and news media. The quest is based on the premise that the new will somehow be better than the old, a premise that fits well with America's utilitarian demand for improvement. The expectation that the media and arts will continue to innovate keeps an audience coming back for more. Cultural tensions, of course, inhere within the quest and on occasion they erupt into full-blown controversy.

Art

Out of a budget of more than 150 million dollars a year, the National Endowment for the Arts funds literally hundreds upon hundreds of projects in theater, ballet, music, photography, film, painting, and sculpture. In the late 1980s, however, it became widely publicized that the National Endowment for the Arts had indirectly funded two controversial photographic exhibits. One project, by Andres Serrano, included, among others, a photograph of a crucifix in a jar of Serrano's urine, entitled *Piss Christ;* the other project, by Robert Mapplethorpe, included, among many others, a photograph that turned an image of the Virgin Mary into a tie rack as well as a number of homoerotic photos (such as one showing Mapplethorpe with a bullwhip implanted in his anus and another showing a man urinating in another man's mouth). All of this was well publicized. Avant-garde? To say the least! But Serrano and Mapplethorpe are, their defenders maintained, "important American artists." One critic called the photograph *Piss Christ* "a darkly beautiful photographic image."[12] Likewise, the director of the Institute of Contemporary Art in Boston concluded of Mapplethorpe's exhibit, "Mapplethorpe's work is art, and art belongs in an art museum."[13]

For those in the various orthodox communities, the controversial aspects of the Serrano and Mapplethorpe exhibits were not art at all but obscenity. "This so-called piece of art is a deplorable, despicable display of vulgarity," said one critic. "Morally reprehensible trash," said another. Of Serrano himself, a third stated, "He is not an artist, he is a jerk. Let him be a jerk on his own time and with his own resources." The American Family Association responded with full-page advertisements in newspapers asking, "Is this how you want your tax dollars spent?"[14]

These voices had a sympathetic hearing in the halls of government as well. In response to the National Endowment for the Arts funding of these projects and the likelihood that it would fund still other such projects in the future, Senator Jesse Helms introduced legislation that would forbid the endowment from supporting art that is "obscene or indecent." The National Endowment for the Arts agreed to make grants available only to those who pledge not to do anything of this nature. The endowment, a Helms ally argued in support of this proposal, should not showcase "artists whose forte is ridiculing the values . . . of Americans who are paying for it."[15] Conservative columnist Doug Bandow argued similarly, "There's no justification for taxing lower-income Americans to support glitzy art shows and theater productions frequented primarily by the wealthy."[16] Still others cited Thomas Jefferson's dictum that it is "sinful and tyrannical" to compel a person to contribute money for the propagation of opinions with which he or she disagrees.

Music

Rap is just one more innovation in youth-oriented music that began decades before with rock and roll. Serious questions were raised about the form and content of this innovation, however, with the 1989 release of *As Nasty As They Wanna Be* by the Miami-based rap group 2 Live Crew. On just one album, there were over 200 uses of the word "fuck," over 100 uses of explicit terms for male and female genitalia, over 80 descriptions of oral sex, and the word "bitch" was used over 150 times. And what about the work of groups like Mötley Crüe, which invokes images of satanism, and the rap group the Beastie Boys, who mime masturbation on stage, or N.W.A., who sing about war against the police (in "Fuck tha Police"), or Ozzy Osbourne, who sings of the "suicide solution?" Was this really music?

The arts establishment responded with a resounding "yes." Its endorsements were positive and sympathetic. Notwithstanding the violence and irreverence, one essay in the *Washington Post* described rap in particular as "a vibrant manifestation of the black oral tradition. . . . You cannot fully understand this profane style of rapping if you disregard the larger folklore of the streets."[17] A review of 2 Live Crew and rap in general in the *New York Times* claimed that this form of musical expression "reveals the tensions of the communities it speaks to. But with its humor, intelligence and fast-talking grace, it may also represent a way to transcend those tensions."[18] Even at its grossest, one critic wrote in *Time*, this entire genre of music represents "a vital expression of the resentments felt by a lot of people."[19]

Needless to say, the opinions within the orthodox communities were less enthusiastic. One American Family Association member called the work of the rap poets of 2 Live Crew as well as other exemplars of popular music, such as the heavy metal of Mötley Crüe, Twisted Sister, and the like, "mind pollution and body pollution."[20] An attorney involved in the controversy commented, "This stuff is so toxic and so dangerous to anybody, that it shouldn't be allowed to be sold to anybody or by anybody."[21] Because this album was being sold to children, he continued, the group's leader, Luther Campbell, was nothing less than "a psychological child molester."[22] Judges in Florida agreed with the sentiment, finding the lyrics to *As Nasty As They Wanna Be* to violate local obscenity laws. Police arrested Campbell for performing the music in a nightclub after the decree, as well as record store owners who continued to sell the album. In response, Campbell promised two things: a legal appeal and a new album—"this one dirtier than the last."[23]

Film

Of all the films produced by Universal Studios perhaps none has been more controversial than *The Last Temptation of Christ*, based on the 1955 best-selling novel by Nikos Kazantzakis. The intent of the film, according to its director Martin Scorsese, was to present the basic humanity of Christ who discovers—nay, chooses—his divinity. The film portrays a Jesus plagued by human doubt and subject, though not quite vulnerable, to the range of human temptations, including lust, pride, anger, power, and the fear of death. Christ, for example, is shown to fantasize about being married to Mary Magdalene and having sexual intercourse with her; later, after she has died, he imagines marrying Mary (of Mary and Martha) and then still later, committing adultery with Martha. He is also shown confessing in anguish, "I am a liar, I am a hypocrite. I am afraid of everything . . . Lucifer is inside me." In the end, however, he is shown renouncing the final temptation, the offer by Satan to reject his role of Messiah, and accepting his destiny to die for humankind.

A biblical costume epic this certainly was not. Although the film critic establishment was not entirely enamored with the technical aspects of the film, overall they gave the film high marks for its sensitivity and artistry. *USA Today* called it "an extraordinary accomplishment." The *Los Angeles Times* deemed it "an intense, utterly sincere, frequently fascinating piece of art by a director for whom, clearly, the message of Jesus' life had immediacy and meaning." The *Washington Post* called it "a work of great seriousness by one of this country's most gifted filmmakers." In the words of the *New York Daily News* the film was a work of "integrity, reverence and a good deal of cinematic beauty." And finally, the *Los Angeles Herald Examiner* called Scorsese's work "one of the most serious, literate, complex and deeply felt religious films ever made."[24]

It is not surprising that progressivist opinion in the denominations was generally sympathetic to this view. A spokesman for the National Council of Churches called the film "an honest attempt to tell the story of Jesus from a different perspective." The Episcopal bishop of New

York called the film "theologically sound."[25] And a theologian at Notre Dame was quoted as saying, "This film is . . . fairly distinguished art."[26]

To say that the conservative Catholic and Evangelical communities did not share this view of the film is to understate their position monumentally. The universal conclusion was that *The Last Temptation of Christ* was "sacrilegious." Morality in Media judged the film to be "an intentional attack on Christianity."[27] "Utter blasphemy of the worst degree," was the way Reverend Falwell put it. "Neither the label 'fiction' nor the First Amendment," he continued, "gives Universal [Studios] the right to libel, slander and ridicule the most central figure in world history."[28] Official Catholic opinion complained that the Christ portrayed in the film was "not the Christ of Scriptures and of the church."[29] But even this was an understatement in the eyes of the more orthodox Catholics and Evangelicals. Christ, they claimed, was made "an object of low fantasies." Focus on the Family concluded that Jesus was portrayed "as a confused, lustful wimp who denies his divinity and struggles with his sinful nature."[30]

Intense hostility led to sustained protest within the larger community of conservative Catholics and Evangelicals. Mother Angelica, a nun who has run the nation's largest Catholic cable network, called on protesters to drive with their headlights on leading up to opening day to signal their opposition to the film. The American Society for the Defense of Tradition, Family and Property published a full-page "open-letter" to Universal Studios in the *New York Times* with the word "Blasphemy" printed at the top. Concerned Women for America asked all MCA stockholders (MCA owns Universal) to sell the company's stock. The American Family Foundation sent out 2.5 million mailings protesting the film and anti-*Temptation* spots appeared on 700 Christian radio stations and 50 to 75 television stations. These actions spawned a massive letter-writing campaign, street protests, and picketing at film openings in cities across the country, (roughly 25,000 people staged a protest rally at Universal City on one day alone), and, of course, a nationwide boycott called by leaders in the Eastern Orthodox, Catholic, and Evangelical Protestant faiths. Moreover, one Evangelical leader, Bill Bright of Campus Crusade for Christ, offered to raise money to reimburse Universal for all copies of the film, which would then "promptly be destroyed."[31]

Publishing

Of "teen" magazines, there seems to be no end. Yet the publication of one of them, *Sassy*, caused quite a stir. Modeled after the popular

Australian teen magazine *Dolly, Sassy* would offer American teenagers the most candid presentation of teen problems and issues available. Early issues carried articles such as "Sex for Absolute Beginners," "So You Think You're Ready for Sex? Read This First," "Should I Talk During Sex?" "The Truth About Boys' Bodies," "The Dirty, Scummy Truth About Spring Break," "Laural and Leslie and Alex and Brian Are Your Basic Kids. They're dating. They go to movies and concerts. They fight over stupid things. They make up. They're sad sometimes. They're happy. AND THEY'RE GAY," among others. In times like these, editors reasoned, it is important to build up "a spirit of openness in talking to teens about sex," drugs, and other issues that they confront. Thus *Sassy* promised, according to an introductory letter, to "help you with some of the really tough decisions you have to make, such as how to know when it's the right time to say no or yes to that special guy and plenty of other things that your mother forgot to tell you." After all, the letter continued, "There are times when you really need to talk with a friend, not with parents or teachers or other people."[32]

The criticisms that followed the publication of *Sassy* carried much the tone of the other moral criticism we have seen. According to traditionalists, the magazine could only have a negative effect on the minds and morals of teenagers, for it encouraged promiscuity and discouraged respect for parental authority by usurping their role in the task of moral and sexual education. Concerned Women for America, Focus on the Family, the American Family Association, and others were incensed by the arrogance and intrusiveness of such a venture and staged a boycott of the advertisers of the new magazine. Hundreds of letters were written to these advertisers complaining of their indirect support for the undermining of morality among children and in the end, five major advertisers and several smaller ones pulled out. The editor, in an interview, admitted that the effect had been "very damaging" financially and, moreover, that the episode had had an impact on editorial policy.

Television

Every year during the ratings sweep, the major networks display their raciest and most innovative programming. In years past, television shows like "Miami Vice," "Dream Street," "Knots Landing," "thirtysomething," "A Man Called Hawk," "The Cosby Show," among many others have made strong showings within the national television audience. These, in turn, become strong draws for corporations wanting to advertise their products. Critics admit that the amount of sexual intimacy outside of marriage, violence, and profanity portrayed on some of these shows is very high, yet they also have been quick to point out that many of these shows are technically innovative and treat many issues such as homosexuality, child abuse and incest, and the ambiguities of ethical behavior in law enforcement, marriage, student culture, and the like, with great sensitivity.

Sensitivity is the last thing these television shows display, in the view of many with orthodox commitments. To the contrary, "television," claimed a letter from the American Family Association, "is undermining the Judeo-Christian values you hold dear and work hard to teach your children."[33] For this reason, leaders from CLeaR-TV visited with executives from the three major networks in order to express their concerns. According to Reverend Wildmon, "They used the same words that I used, but we certainly didn't mean the same thing by them." From this point on, the leaders decided to approach the advertisers rather than the networks. "Advertisers don't give you a cold shoulder. They want to be your friend."[34] In line with this strategy, the American Family Association and CLeaR-TV began to approach advertisers. Sponsors who did not respond positively to their concerns very often faced the threat of a boycott. PepsiCo, for example, pulled a commercial featuring pop star, nude model, and actress Madonna and their promotion of her world tour; General Mills, Ralston Purina, and Domino's Pizza pulled advertising from "Saturday Night Live"; Mazda and Noxell were also influenced in this way; and of the 400 sponsors of prime-time television in the 1989 ratings sweeps, CLeaR-TV focused on the Mennon Company and the Clorox Corporation, pledging to boycott their products for a year for their sponsorship of programs containing sex, violence, and profanity. Of this latter boycott, Roman Catholic Bishop Stanislaus Brzana of New York (one of more than one hundred bishops nationwide who endorsed CLeaR-TV) argued, "We believe our cause will benefit *not only our group but the whole country*."[35] The work of CLeaR-TV has not been isolated. Kimberly-Clark and Tambrands pulled ads from "Married . . . with Children" after a Michigan homemaker threatened action.[36] The National Decency Forum and the American Family Association have sought to press the Federal Communications Commission, even with legal action, to enforce its "decency code."[37] And finally (though the list could go on), "dial-a-porn" companies who advertise on television have been pressured and a few shut down through legal prosecution and popular pressure by such groups as Citizens for Decency through Law, Concerned Women for America, and Morality in Media.

Decoding Art and the Avant-Garde

The preceding examples are but a few well-publicized illustrations of cultural warfare in various media and forms of public expression. The point of reviewing them was to demonstrate, across media, certain patterns of cultural conflict. Despite the variations of situation and media, one can trace a common and consistent thread of sentiment on each side of the new cultural divide.

On the progressivist side, there is a tendency to value novelty and the avant-garde for their own sake. This in itself is not controversial. What is controversial is *how* avant-garde is defined. Progressives implicitly define the "avant-garde" not so much as the presentation of classic social themes in new artistic forms, but rather as the symbolic presentation of behavior and ideas that test the limits of social acceptability. More often than not this means the embrace of what the prevailing social consensus would have called "perverse" or "irreverent," what Carol Iannone calls "the insistent and progressive artistic exploration of the forbidden frontiers of human experience." Lucy Lippard acknowledges as much in her review of the Serrano corpus in *Art in America:* "His work shows," she contends, "that the conventional notion of good taste with which we are raised and educated is based on an illusion of social order that is no longer possible (nor desirable) to believe in. We now look at art in the context of incoherence and disorder—a far more difficult task than following the prevailing rules."[38] A similar theme can be found in each of the other cases reviewed. In rap music and in television programming, the boundaries of social consensus around human relationships are tested through excessive sex and violence; in the film *The Last Temptation,* they are tested through the demythologization of ancient Christian belief; in publishing the magazine *Sassy,* the boundaries of adolescent innocence (at what age and how kids should learn about sexuality) are tested. In each case, an earlier consensus of what is "perverse" and what is "irreverent" is challenged, and as it is challenged, it inevitably disintegrates.

The issue is sharpened when considering the special case of art. Here too the underlying controversy is over how art is to be defined. In general, progressivists tend to start with the assumption that there is no objective method of determining what is art and what is obscene. Historical experience demonstrates time and again that even if a consensus declares that a work has no enduring artistic value, the consensus may change; the work could, over time, come to be viewed as art.[39] For this reason one must recognize and at all times respect and defend the autonomy of the artist and of artistic effort. Artists should not be bound by legal constraints or inhibited by social conventions, for artistic genius may yet emerge, if it is not already evident. Indeed, modern criticism does regard art "as a 'sacred wood,' a separate universe, a self-contained sovereignty" and the artist, in writer Vladimir Nabokov's words, as responsible to no one but himself.[40] One artist expressed this theme when he said, "It is extremely important that art be unjustifiable."[41]

Out of this general perspective comes the implicit understanding that a work is art if "experts" are willing to call it art and if it symbolically expresses an individual's personal quest to understand and interpret one's experience in the world.[42] Both themes were evident in the expert testimony given at the 1990 obscenity trial of the Contemporary Arts Center in Cincinnati where the question "What is art?" was posed directly in view of the Mapplethorpe retrospective. Jacquelynn Baas, director of the University Art Museum at the University of California at Berkeley, responded to the question of why one should consider Robert Mapplethorpe's work as art by declaring: "In the first place, they're great photographs. Secondly, in this work he dealt with issues that our society, modern society is grappling with . . . what it means to be a sexual being, and also race, that was an important part of the show." Robert Sobieszek, curator of the George Eastman House International Museum of Photography reiterated the same two themes. "I would say they are works of art, knowing they are by Robert Mapplethorpe, knowing his intentions. They reveal in very strong, forceful ways a major concern of a creative artist . . . a troubled portion of his life that he was trying to come to grips with. It's that search for meaning, not unlike van Gogh's."[43] Both experts declare, prima facie, the work to be art; both point out how it symbolically expresses Mapplethorpe's quest to interpret the world and his place in it.

For the orthodox and their conservative allies, expert opinion is not a reliable measure of artistic achievement and the artist's intentions are completely irrelevant to determining whether a work is art. Rather, artistic achievement is measured by the extent to which it reflects the sublime. Critic Hilton Kramer endorses this view in speaking of federal funding for art that reflects "the highest achievements of our civilization."[44] George F. Will similarly favors the view that art, at least art worthy of support, is recognized in its capacity to "elevate the public mind by bringing it into contact with beauty and even ameliorate social pathologies."[45] Art worthy of government funding, therefore, should be justifiable on the grounds that it serves this high public purpose. Congressman Henry Hyde, in reflecting about his role in the public policy process, argues that "art detached from the quest for truth and goodness is simply self-expression and ultimately self-absorption."[46] Again, what all of the voices on this side of the cultural divide hold in common—whether orthodox theists like Hyde or secular platonists like Kramer and Will—is a belief in a metaphysical reality for which art is to be a symbolic expression.

In sum, for the orthodox and their conservative allies artistic creativity is concerned to reflect a higher reality. For their opponents, art is concerned with the creation of reality itself. Art for the progressivist is, then, a statement of being. To express oneself is to declare one's existence. Hilton Kramer may be correct that the professional art world maintains a sentimental attachment to the idea that art is at its best when it is most extreme and disruptive, but he is probably wrong if he believes this to be its chief or only aim. More fundamentally, if only implicitly, the contemporary arts project is a statement about the meaning of life, namely that life is a process of self-creation. As this enterprise takes public form, however, contemporary art and the avant-garde come to represent nothing less than the besmearing of the highest ideals of the orthodox moral vision.

When all is said and done, however, the events taking place in each of the contexts mentioned earlier—the action and reaction of progressivists and cultural conservatives—represent only the first stage in the development of a deeper debate about the limits of public expression in American society.

CENSORSHIP

Progressivist Accusations

The immediate reaction of the progressivists is that those who complain about art do so because they "do not know enough about art," or simply "do not care about art."[47] All of the protest demonstrates, as the *Washington Post* put it, "the danger of a cultural outsider passing judgement on something he doesn't understand."[48] Such comments may sound elitist (and undoubtedly are), but their significance goes beyond implying that those who do not share progressive aesthetic taste are simple philistines. The real significance of such sentiments is that they reaffirm the basic characteristic of the contemporary culture war, namely the nigh complete disjunction of moral understanding between the orthodox and progressivist communities—in this case, on what constitutes art. The progressivist communities and the arts establishment display a certain arrogance in believing that their definitions of "serious artistic merit" should be accepted by all, and this leads them to categorize various cultural conservatives as "Know-Nothings," "yahoos," "neanderthals," "literary death squads," "fascists," and "cultural terrorists."[49]

The response of progressivists to this situation, however, quickly evolves beyond this. In a way, what we hear after this initial response is less of an argument than it is a symbolic call to arms, a "Banzai!" that reveals a spontaneous, unified, and passionate indignation every bit as deep as that expressed by the orthodox in reaction to tarnishing of their ideals. Irrespective of the circumstances or media, the orthodox protest evokes among progressives the cry of "censorship."

Nowhere has this alarm sounded more loudly than in the case of the protest against network television. People for the American Way, Americans for Constitutional Freedom, *Playboy*, and many others have viewed the boycotting of corporate advertisers of television programming as acts of "economic terrorism" that are tantamount to censorship. "What is more intrusive than the attempt by fundamentalist censors to dictate what we can watch in the privacy of our own homes?" asked the founder of Fundamentalists Anonymous. Donald Wildmon, whom *Playboy* called the "Tupelo Ayatollah," is nothing short of "dangerous." Said the executive director of Americans for Constitutional Freedom, "We intend to do everything to prevent him from setting himself up as a censor who can remake America in his own image."[50]

Similar accusations are leveled in every other situation where the orthodox protest the content of public media. The music industry viewed the efforts of the Parents' Music Resource Center to have albums labeled "contains explicit lyrics" as an act of censorship. Frank Zappa called it a conspiracy to extort. Outside observers viewed the orthodox influence on *Sassy*'s editorial policy (through the threat of corporate boycotts) as "horrifying," tantamount to the suppression of ideas. The varied protests against *The Last Temptation of Christ* (particularly the boycott) were viewed by many progressives as acts of censorship, born out of "intolerant narrow-mindedness," "bigotry," and "pharisaism."[51] Universal Studios responded to Bill Bright's offer to purchase all copies of the film with full-page newspaper advertisements in four cities, stating that the right to free expression was not for sale. Economic pressure (in the form of the boycott) against hotel chains that make adult films available to their patrons has been called censorship. Proposals to defund the National Endowment for the Arts were viewed as a move toward censorship. Even the refusal of printing companies to print "controversial" materials has been deemed "printer censorship."[52] And, finally, efforts to prohibit flag burning have been called political censorship.

Implicit within this accusation, of course, is the legal judgment that the constitutionally guaranteed right to freedom of speech is either threatened or actually violated by conservative protest. For this reason, the Bill of Rights is almost always invoked by progressives or by artists themselves. When, for example, Nikki Sixx of Mötley Crüe was told in an interview that there were those who objected to the band stating on stage that their "only regret is that [they] couldn't eat all the pussy [they] saw here tonight, he responded, 'I say fuck 'em. It's freedom of speech; First Amendment!' "[53] Thomas Jefferson himself might not have put it quite that way or even necessarily agreed with the application, but without fail, the legacy of Jefferson directly informs the content of the progressivist reply. Luther Campbell of 2 Live Crew echoed this sentiment when he said, "We give America what they want. Isn't there such a thing as free enterprise here? Isn't there such a thing as freedom of speech?" The record store owner in Florida arrested for selling *As Nasty As They Wanna Be* put the matter in a slightly larger context. "We tell the Lithuanians, you know, fight for freedom . . . And yet, we're trying to censor our own country. . . . We don't need nobody to censor us and they're violating our civil rights and our freedom of speech. And next—what else will it be next?"[54] And finally, a purveyor of "adult art" was perhaps the most articulate on this matter. "The fact that speech is offensive to some people," he said, "the fact that it is controversial, is exactly the sort of speech that the First Amendment was designed to protect. Speech that is acceptable to everyone, that's not controversial, doesn't need protection, because nobody is going to try to suppress it."[55]

The pounding repetition of this accusation is in accord with the general position taken by the People for the American Way, who believe that this brand of censorship is not only on the increase, it "has become more organized and more effective" with haunting implications.[56] The very language employed by cultural conservatives when they insist it is time to "clean up our culture" or to "stop subsidizing decadence" is, as several writers contend, "chillingly reminiscent of Nazi cultural metaphors."[57] Robert Brustein, writing in the *New Republic*, goes so far as to dismiss the distinction between censorship and the effort to influence the distribution of taxpayers' money (as in the effort to defund "offensive art" at the National Endowment for the Arts), insisting that defunding art is a form of censorship. He concludes that "only government—in a time when other funding has grown increasingly restrictive and programmatic—can guarantee free and innovative art. And that means acknowledging that, yes, every artist has a First Amendment right to subsidy."[58]

The progressivist response to this backlash has gone beyond rhetoric into direct political action as well. Full-page newspaper ads criticizing the censorious impulse have appeared. Individual artists, the ACLU, Playboy Enterprises, *Penthouse*, the American Booksellers Association, and many other individuals and organizations have initiated litigation against a number of organizations, such as Concerned Women for America and the American Family Association. Counterboycotts were formed, such as the one called by Fundamentalists Anonymous against Pepsi in order to "protest Pepsi's capitulation to censorship." ("No Madonna, no Pepsi," they claimed. We will make Pepsi "the choice of the fundamentalist generation"—"only losers will drink Pepsi!")[59] A number of new organizations, such as Americans for Constitutional Freedom, the National Campaign for Freedom of Expression, and the Media Coalition, also came to life as part of the progressivist reaction to these assaults.

Orthodox Counteraccusations

To the accusation of censorship, the reply of cultural conservatives is "nonsense!" *Christianity Today* editorialized that the media and arts establishment

> use freedom of speech as a means to flout standards of common public decency. We must not throw in the towel. Christians must unite in mounting a counteroffensive through our families, churches, schools, and other institutions. The legal issues surrounding public standards may be complex, but the moral imperatives are not. We must not abandon the ring of public debate to those who would use freedom of speech as an excuse to be as morally offensive as they "wanna" be.[60]

Implicit here and in much of the orthodox and conservative rhetoric is the view that communities have the right to decide for themselves what standards will be used to discriminate between art and obscenity. If, through the democratic process, standards are agreed upon, why should communities not be entitled to uphold them through official means?

Donald Wildmon also rejects the idea that he and his compatriots are somehow violating the First Amendment protections of free speech, but he takes a slightly different tack. He insists that artists do have the right to express themselves as they please but that he too has a right to speak out against them. This posture is expressed paradigmatically in his rationale for acting against Pepsi for its plans to fund the Madonna tour.

> Here is a pop singer who makes a video that's sacrilegious to the core. Here's a pop star that made a low-budget porn film. Here's a pop star who goes around in her concerts with sex oozing out, wearing a cross. Now Pepsi is saying to all the young people of the new generation, "Here is the person we want you to emulate and imitate." They can do that. They've got every right to give Madonna $10 million dollars, put it on television every night if they want to. All I'm saying is "Don't ask me to buy Pepsi if you do it."[61]

The same rationale undergirds Wildmon's approach to the television networks. "The networks can show what they want to show. The advertiser can sponsor what he wants to sponsor. And the consumer can spend his money where he wants to. [The idea] that I must spend my money with these companies to help support these programs that I find offensive [—] I don't believe that." To those who wonder aloud whether he is infringing on others' rights, he responds, "I'm not infringing on anybody's rights. I have as much right as any other individual in this society to try to shape society. I have as much right to try to influence people. . . . I'm very cognizant of other people's rights. All I'm asking is for them to be cognizant of mine."[62]

Tipper Gore of the Parents' Music Resource Center called the cry of censorship "a smoke screen," a dodge for taking corporate responsibility for their product. In asking for labels on record albums, her group claimed, they were asking for more information, not less. The group's approach, then, "was the direct opposite of censorship." Morality in Media takes the argument one step further in maintaining that "freedom of expression is not the exclusive right of producers, publishers, authors or a handful of media executives. Freedom of expression belongs . . . to the entire community. . . . [it is only a] vocal, unremitting, organized community expression [that] will bring about a media based on love, truth and good taste."[63]

The debate over censorship becomes even more interesting when the accusation of censorship is leveled at progressives by the voices of orthodoxy. At one extreme Jimmy Swaggart insists that "those of the humanistic stripe want to see all Bibles banned in America."[64] But accusations of censorship also come from more tempered voices within the conservative alliance, with much greater credibility.

The complaint that progressivists and a liberal educational establishment censor, through exclusion, material on traditional religion in the public school textbooks was noted in the last chapter. The same kind of de facto censoring occurs, it is maintained, when major magazines and newspapers, through editorial edict, refuse to review books written and published by conservative Catholics or Evangelical Protestants, or deny them the recognition they deserve by not including these works on their best-seller lists. The Evangelical writer Francis Schaeffer, for example, sold over 3 million copies of his books in the United States, and yet his books were never reviewed in the *New York Times Book Review* or *Time* and never counted on any best-seller list. The same was true of Hal Lindsey's *Late Great Planet Earth*, a book that was the top nonfiction seller in America in the 1970s—for the entire decade. The book was not reviewed by the literary establishment nor did it appear on weekly best-seller lists until it was later published by a secular publishing house. For publishing elites to ignore this literature, for whatever reasons— even if they do not believe such works constitute "serious literature or scholarship"—is, they say, to "censor." As columnist Cal Thomas put it, the "practice of treating the Christian market as a kind of 'Negro league' of publishing creates a false impression that we live in a totally secular society where persons with religious principles have nothing to say. If occasionally they do say something in print, their opinions or ideas are not worth reading or considering."[65]

It was in this spirit that the editors of the conservative magazine *Chronicles* wrote (in a subscription appeal):

Once upon a time in America, you could say you loved your country, believed in God, and held your marriage sacred . . . and *not* be snickered at as a simple-minded innocent.

Your could believe in honesty, hard work, and self-reliance;

you could speak of human *responsibilities* in the same breath as human rights . . . and *not* be derided as an insensitive fool.

You could speak out against profane books, depraved movies, and decadent art; you could express your disapproval of drug-sodden entertainers, America-hating educators, and appeasement-obsessed legislators . . . and *not* be branded as an ignorant reactionary.

And yes, once upon a time in America, you could actually believe in *morality*, both public and private, and *not* be proclaimed a hopeless naif—more to be pitied than taken seriously.

But that was before the "censorship of fashion" took control of contemporary American culture.

This insidious form of censorship is not written into our laws or statutes—but it is *woven* into the very *fabric* of our culture. It reigns supreme in literature and the arts, on television and in film, in music and on radio, in our churches, our public schools, and our universities. And above all else, it is dedicated to the propagation of one agenda—the *liberal activist* agenda for America.

The "censorship of fashion" is not only sinister and subtle, it's also ruthlessly *effective*. It employs the powerful weapons of *ridicule* and *condescension* to stifle the voices of millions of Americans, like you, who still cherish our traditional values.[66]

Assaults on the right to free speech, some orthodox leaders contend, are further evident in lawsuits against those organizations that boycott, picket, or systematically protest against the sale and distribution of "sexually explicit material" or against abortion clinics. Such lawsuits have been based on the Racketeer Influenced and Corrupt Organizations (RICO) Act. For example, *Playboy* and *Penthouse* magazines as well as Waldenbooks filed extortion and racketeering charges against the Florida chapter of the American Family Association for using pickets and boycott threats to get 1,400 stores to stop selling the magazine. Said a spokesman for the defendants, "The expansion of the use of RICO against free expression activities is extremely dangerous to the future of free speech, and *is censorship at its worst*."[67]

The view that the media, arts, and literary establishment is intolerant of orthodox perspectives and ideals is not merely a rhetorical device for getting back at progressives but a deeply held conviction. It is the sense of institutionalized bias and even censorship against the orthodox that has inspired the rise of religiously orthodox equivalents to an anti-defamation league. The Catholic League for Civil and Religious Rights is such a group in the conservative Catholic orbit; though groups like the Rutherford Institute serve such a function within the Evangelical camp, calls for an organization deliberately identified and acting in the capacity of a Christian antidefamation league were issued in the early 1990s.[68] Given the nature of the culture war, such a development is, perhaps, inevitable.

Decoding Free Speech

Back and forth the arguments go. After a time, the details of this conflict become tediously predictable. One side claims that a work is "art"; the other claims it is not. One claims that a work has enduring aesthetic or literary appeal; the other claims it only appeals to the eccentric interests of a deviant subculture. At least on the face of it, one is tempted to agree with Justice John Marshall Harlan who concluded that "one man's vulgarity is another's lyric." Such relativism may not be desirable but it seems to be the necessary outcome of the present cultural conflict. In this light, it is entirely predictable that each side would claim that the other side is not committed to free speech but to a systematic imposition of its values and perspectives on everyone else. Alas, one person's act of "censorship" has become another's "commitment to community standards."

Thus, in the contemporary culture war, regard for rights to the freedom of speech has become a matter of "whose ox is being gored" at the moment.[69] The fact is, both sides make a big mistake when they confuse *censuring* (the legitimate mobilization of moral opprobrium) with *censoring* (the use of the state and other legal or official means to restrict speech).[70] Censuring, say through economic boycott or letter-writing campaigns, is itself a form of political speech protected by the First Amendment and employed legally all of the time whether in boycotts against South Africa, Nestle's, or California lettuce growers, or against the purveyors of sexually explicit or theologically controversial art. But the finer points of distinction are lost on many of the activists in this debate. Even when the protest is merely the expression of disapproval, what each side invariably hears are the footsteps of an approaching cadre of censors. In most cases, however, neither side presents a genuine threat to the rights of the other to free expression. The cry of censorship from both sides of the cultural divide, then, becomes an ideological weapon to silence legitimate dissent.

This being said, it must also be stated that real censorship *is* taking place and the voices of both cultural conservatism and progressivism perpetuate it in their own ways. Censorship, again, is the use of the state or other official means to restrict speech. In every case it is justified by the claim that "community standards" have been violated. The use of the police to arrest the members of 2 Live Crew in Florida and the use of law to shut down the Contemporary Arts Center in Cincinnati because they violated community standards of obscenity are, then, textbook cases of such censorship. Censorship is also perpetuated on the other side of the cultural divide. It is seen in the efforts of student groups and universities to prohibit, in the name of community standards, defamatory remarks and expressions against minorities, gays, and women. (Would progressives throw their support or legal weight behind a similar code that prohibited say, unpatriotic, irreligious, or sexually explicit "expressions" on the community campus?) Censorship is also seen, to give another example, in the suspension of Andy Rooney from his job at CBS in 1990 for making remarks against gays. On both sides of the cultural divide, the concept of "community standards" is invoked as an ideological weapon to silence unpopular voices. Understanding how the standards of one moral community can be so diametrically opposed to the standards of the other takes us back to the root of the culture war itself.

ART, EXPRESSION, AND THE SACRED

A critic quoted earlier warned of the danger of a cultural outsider passing judgment on something he does not understand. The reality of the culture war is that the cultural conservative and the progressivist are each outsiders to the other's cultural milieu. Accordingly, each regularly and often viciously passes judgment on the other. That judgment is not at all bad in itself. Such is the back and forth of democratic discourse. The danger is not in passing judgment but in the failure to understand why the other is so insulted by that judgment. *That* is the measure of their mutual outsiderness.

The orthodox, for example, demonstrate such a position when they view certain artistic work in isolation from the larger aesthetic project of an artist and label it obscene, pornographic, and prurient.[71] Who are these people, progressivists ask, to label the life work of Serrano and Mapplethorpe as vulgarity? That they cannot see the "enduring artistic achievement" of an artist's oeuvre is a gauge of their alienation from "high art" discourse. The same kind of obtuseness is found among progressivists. Consider the controversy surrounding *The Last Temptation of Christ*. A *Washington Post* editorial stated with no equivocation that audiences would not find the film blasphemous.[72] Another reviewer, from *Newsweek*, said, "One can think of hundreds of trashy, thrill-happy movies devout Christians could get upset about. Instead, they have taken to the airwaves to denounce *the one movie that could conceivably open a viewer's heart to the teachings of Jesus.*" Still another reviewer, from Newhouse Newspapers, called the film, "The most realistic biblical film ever made."[73] Who are these people, orthodox Christians ask, to proclaim universally that *The Last Temptation of Christ* was not blasphemous? For millions of Americans it certainly was, and it was a measure of progressives' outsiderness that they could not acknowledge it to be.

This kind of mutual misunderstanding reveals once more that the conflict over the media and the arts is not just a dispute among institutions and not just a disagreement over "speech" protected by the First Amendment. Ultimately the battle over this symbolic territory reveals a conflict over world views—over what standards our communities and our nation will live by; over what we consider to be "of enduring value" in our communities; over what we consider a fair representation of our times, and so on. As a bystander at the Contemporary Arts Center in Cincinnati observed during the controversy over the Mapplethorpe exhibit, "This isn't just an obscenity prosecution. This is a trial of a good part of American culture."[74]

But even more, these battles again lay bare the tensions that exist between two fundamentally different conceptions of the sacred. For those of orthodox religious commitments, the sacred is obvious enough. It is an unchanging and everlasting God who ordained through Scripture, the church, or Torah, a manner of life and of social relationship that cannot be broached without incurring the displeasure of God. On the other side of the cultural divide, the sacred is a little more difficult to discern. Perhaps Tom Wolfe had it right when he observed that art itself was the religion of the educated classes.[75] Maybe this is why Broadway producer Joseph Papp said as he observed the police coming into the Cincinnati Contemporary Arts Center to close the Mapplethorpe exhibit, "It's like an invasion. It's like they're coming into a church or coming into a synagogue, or coming into any place of worship. It's a violation."[76] Such an insight makes sense if we see art as a symbol of conscience. To place any restrictions on the arts, therefore, is to place restrictions on the conscience itself; it is to place fetters on the symbol of being. Such an insight also makes sense if we see art as a symbol of immortality—of that which will outlive us all. To place restrictions on art is to place restrictions on the (secular) hope of eternity. Perhaps this is why the procedural guarantee of freedom of expression has also acquired a sacred quality in progressivist circles.

The idea that the battle over the arts is related to the tensions between two different conceptions of the sacred is not far-fetched. How else can one explain the passion and intensity on both sides of the cultural divide were it not that each side, by its very being and expression, profanes what the other holds most sublime? If this is true, we are again reminded of the reasons that the larger culture war will not subside any time soon.

CHAPTER 9: MEDIA AND THE ARTS

1. National Right to Life Committee, Washington, D.C., direct mail appeal, Spring 1990. LaHaye's direct mail appeal was sent out about May 1988.
2. Helle Bering-Jensen, "A Hell-Bent Crusade Against Pornography," *Insight*, 2 July 1990, p. 12.
3. Three studies, Lichter et al., *The Media Elite;* Research and Forecasts, *The Connecticut Mutual Life Report on Values in the 80s*, 1982; and my own "Religion and Power Survey" funded by the Lilly Endowment, documented these tendencies. Reports from the Center for Media and Public Affairs, Washington, D.C., summarize content analysis of television news programs and newspaper reporting for a wide range of issues (such as abortion) or political events (such as campaigns).
4. Quoted in Thomas Edsall and David Vise, "CBS Fight a Litmus Test for Conservatives."
5. Patrick Buchanan, "CBS: 'Conservative Broadcasting System,' " *Human Events*, 16 February 1985, p. 137.
6. "How Conservatives Can Get Control of CBS," *Human Events*, 26 January 1985, p. 76.
7. Morality in Media brochure, New York, no date. Accuracy in Media brochure, Washington, D.C., no date. Tipper Gore, "Curbing the Sexploitation Industry," *New York Times*, 14 March 1988, p. A19.
8. Don Winbush, "Bringing Satan to Heel," *Time*, 19 June 1989, pp. 54–55.
9. Quoted in Mike Yorkey, "A New Wind Blows Through Hollywood," *Citizen* 3, 5 (May 1989): 10 (emphasis added).
10. For example, when he learned of the Kennedy plan, the film critic Michael Medved of Public Broadcasting Service (PBS) immediately wrote Kennedy a letter of congratulation. "I want to let you know how pleased I was to hear of your plans to produce mainstream movies that promote family and religious values. While I am not a Christian myself, I am an observant Jew and active in my local synagogue in California. Along with many of my

fellow congregants, I share precisely the frustrations and the hopes for movies which you expressed in your article. . . . If there is any way that I can be helpful to you in the months ahead, please let me know. In any event, I wanted to inform you immediately that there is at least one national movie critic who is already sympathetic to your efforts." Quoted in ibid., p. 10.

11. Jeffrey K. Hadden and Anson Shupe, *Televangelism: Power and Politics on God's Frontier* (New York: Henry Holt, 1988), p. 292.

12. Lucy Lippard, "Andres Serrano: The Spirit and the Letter," *Art in America* 78 (April 1990): 238–45.

13. Transcript of ABC's "Nightline," 10 April 1990.

14. Carole S. Vance, "The War on Culture," *Art in America* 77 (September 1989): 39–43. American Family Association quote from direct mailing.

15. The observation was made by Representative Dick Armey, quoted in Alex Heard, "Mapplethorpe of My Eye," *New Republic*, 21 August 1989, p. 11.

16. Quoted in Robert Hughes, "Whose Art Is It, Anyway?" *Time*, 4 June 1990, p. 47.

17. David Mills, "The Obscenity Case: Criminalizing Black Culture," *Washington Post*, 17 June 1990, p. G1.

18. Jon Pareles, "Rap: Slick, Nasty and—Maybe Hopeful," *New York Times*, 17 June 1990, section 4, pp. 1, 5.

19. Richard Corliss, "X-Rated," *Time*, 7 May 1990, p. 94.

20. Bering-Jensen, "A Hell-Bent Crusade Against Pornography," p. 15.

21. Transcript of "48 Hours," CBS News, 27 June 1990.

22. Ibid.

23. Ibid.

24. All quoted in Tom Breen, "Film Found Artistic, but Not Blasphemous," *Washington Times*, 15 August 1988.

25. John Leo, "A Holy Furor," *Time*, 15 August 1988, p. 36.

26. The statement is attributed to the Rev. Michael Himes, quoted in a direct mail solicitation from *Fidelity*.

27. Reported in Leo, "A Holy Furor," p. 34. The conservative Catholic *Crisis* reported that even the movie critic Michael Medved agreed that the film was "only the latest and most flagrant example of Hollywood's consistent hostility toward organized religion." *Crisis* (November 1988): 4. Perhaps this is because he is an observant Jew.

28. Leo, "A Holy Furor," p. 34.

29. "U.S. Catholic Bishops Denounce Movie," *Daily Progress*, 20 August 1988, p. B4.

30. From a Focus on the Family mass mailing, dated September 1988, Pomona, Calif.

31. Advertisement, *New York Times*, 12 August 1988, p. A7.

32. From an interview, "Magazine Publisher and CWA Face Off on *Sassy*," pub-

lished in *Newsletter of Concerned Women for America* 11 (August 1989): 22–23.

33. Direct mail appeal signed by Reverend Donald Wildmon of the American Family Association, Tupelo, Miss., Spring 1989.

34. Wildmon quoted in Winbush, "Bringing Satan to Heel," p. 54.

35. "Boycott Targets TV Sponsors," *Christianity Today* 33 (18 August 1989): 49 (emphasis added).

36. Reported in "Complicity Is Not Cost-Free," *Playboy* 36 (November 1989): 45.

37. Reported in *Focus on the Family Citizen* 2, 2 (February 1988): 11.

38. Carol Iannone, "From 'Lolita' to 'Piss Christ,' " *Commentary* 89 (January 1990): 52–54. Lippard, "Andres Serrano: The Spirit and the Letter," p. 245.

39. Richard Posner makes this point in "Art for Law's Sake," *American Scholar* 58 (Autumn 1989): 513–20. It is endorsed by critic Robert Brustein, "The First Amendment and the NEA," *New Republic*, 11 September 1989, p. 27.

40. Iannone, "From 'Lolita' to 'Piss Christ,' " pp. 52–54.

41. Robert Rauschenberg quoted in George Will, "The Helms Bludgeon," *Washington Post*, 3 August 1987, p. A27.

42. On the first theme consider the following: "Kathleen Sullivan of the Harvard Law School [has] testified [that] a work cannot legally be defined as obscene if it has serious artistic merit, and NEA grants are by definition made to works that fellow artists have validated." John F. Barber, "A War That Must Be Won," editorial, *Publishers Weekly*, 1 June 1990, p. 1.

43. Baas and Sobieszek quoted in Jayne Merkel, "Art on Trial," *Art in America* 78 (December 1990): 47. Later in his testimony, Sobieszek reiterated the view that there are no qualities that inhere in an object that make it art but that art exists when experts define it as such. When asked, "What determines what is a work of art?" he responded: "I think it's the culture at large—museums, critics, galleries."

44. Quoted in Brustein, "The First Amendment and the NEA," p. 28.

45. Will, "The Helms Bludgeon."

46. Henry J. Hyde, "The Culture War," *National Review*, 30 April 1990, pp. 25–27.

47. The first comment was made by Susan Wyatt, executive director of Artists' Space, taken from a transcript of "Mapplethorpe: Obscene in Cincinnati?" on ABC's "Nightline," 10 April 1990; the second comment is attributed to photographer Jock Sturgis, taken from a transcript of "48 Hours," CBS News, 27 June 1990.

48. Mills, "The Obscenity Case: Criminalizing Black Culture."

49. Of course, it is the arrogance of the orthodox in their particular views of art that lead them to accuse the arts establishment of being "smut peddlers."

50. Founder of Fundamentalists Anonymous quoted in "Pepsi: Soda-Pop of Puritans," *Playboy* 36 (September 1989): 42. Director of Americans for Constitutional Freedom quoted in an ACF press release, New York, 1 June 1989.

51. See Peter Bien, "Scorsese's Spiritual Jesus," *New York Times*, 11 August 1988, and a *Washington Post* editorial, "Satanism in Hollywood," 12 August 1988.

52. See, for example, Madalynne Reuter, "Small Firms Claim Printer Censorship Is Growing," *Publishers Weekly*, 29 June 1990, p. 10.

53. Cited in Tipper Gore, *Raising PG Kids in an X Rated Society* (New York: Bantam, 1988), p. 61.

54. Transcript, "48 Hours," CBS News, 27 June 1990.

55. This observation is attributed to Phil Harvey, the founder and president of Adam and Eve adult mail-order company, taken from the transcript, ibid.

56. *Attacks on the Freedom to Learn: 1986–87 Report* (Washington, D.C.: People for the American Way, 1987), p. 9.

57. All of these quotes are found in Vance, "The War on Culture," pp. 39–43. Robert Brustein also sees within the backlash to the NEA the specter of totalitarianism in "The First Amendment and the NEA," p. 28. There he says, "Totalitarianism's campaign against 'degenerate modern art,' and its insistence that art be 'the handmaiden of sublimity and beauty, and thus promote whatever is natural and healthy,' is well-known. The memory of it is still fresh."

58. Brustein, "The First Amendment and the NEA," p. 29.

59. Quoted in "Pepsi: Soda-Pop of Puritans," p. 42.

60. Timothy K. Jones, editorial: "Put Up Your Dukes," *Christianity Today* 34 (17 December 1990): 14.

61. Interview by Winbush, "Bringing Satan to Heel," pp. 54–55.

62. Ibid.

63. See Gore, *Raising PG Kids in an X Rated Society*, p. 10. "You Can Help Turn the Tide of Pornography," brochure, Morality in Media, New York, no date.

64. Reported in Mike Zahn, "TV Evangelist Targeted in Ads," *Journal* (Milwaukee, Wis.), 14 April 1987.

65. Cal Thomas, *Book Burning* (Westchester, Ill.: Crossway Books, 1983), p. 105.

66. *Chronicles* subscription appeal. Emphasis in original. In this same spirit, Father Virgil Blum of the Catholic League for Religious and Civil Rights complained that the views of the league had been "suppressed" and "censored" by a press "dominated and controlled by Secularists." Direct mail solicitation by the Catholic League, Milwaukee, Wis., no date.

67. News item in *Christianity Today* 33 (15 December 1989): 50. Emphasis added.

68. See Ken Sidey, "Open Season on Christians?" *Christianity Today* 34 (23 April 1990): 34–36.

69. Historically, of course, some Fundamentalists have shown reckless disregard for the rights of minority perspectives and values, and such disregard continues to the present. But a similar insensitivity can be found among those

who believe themselves to be champions of liberal toleration. For example, when the *New York Times* criticizes rap music for its sexism and homophobia but completely ignores the vulgarity, it shows this disregard. See Pareles, "Rap: Slick, Nasty and—Maybe Hopeful." When the head of Americans for Constitutional Freedom (ACT) claims that boycotts for liberal causes are legitimate but illegitimate for conservative causes, it also displays this disregard. The 1 June 1989 press release of ACT states: "Wildmon's weapon in his fight for censorship is the boycott. Teicher [the executive director of ACT] acknowledged that the boycott can be a legitimate means of protest when it is used, as it was during the civil rights movement, to fight for expanded rights. 'But, let's not be fooled. What Wildmon is doing is not democratic. The boycotts of civil rights movements expanded freedom. Wildmon's boycotts restrict freedom by cutting access to television shows, movies, books and magazines that are protected by the First Amendment. The television boycott will try to kill popular programs by intimidating their sponsors. These are the same tactics Senator Joseph McCarthy made infamous in the 1950s' " (pp. 5–6).

70. Garry Wills made this point eloquently in his essay, "In Praise of Censure," *Time*, 31 July 1989, pp. 71–72.

71. This was precisely the argument of Lippard in "Andres Serrano: The Spirit and the Letter," pp. 238–45.

72. Breen, "Film Found Artistic, but Not Blasphemous." An article published in the *Post* surveyed the world of film criticism and found that "movie critics across the United States concurred that . . . *The Last Temptation of Christ* . . . is far from blasphemous."

73. Emphasis added. Breen, "Film Found Artistic, But Not Blasphemous."

74. From the transcript of ABC "Nightline," 10 April 1990.

75. "Today educated people look upon traditional religious ties—Catholic, Episcopal, Presbyterian, Methodist, Baptist, Jewish—as matters of social pedigree. It is only art that they look upon religiously." Tom Wolfe, "The Worship of Art: Notes on the New God," *Harpers* 269 (October 1984): 61.

76. ABC "Nightline," 10 April 1990.

Mike and RuthAnn Har[...] with their family. Femin[...] didn't bring equality to th[...] marriage, says RuthAnn[...] religion did.

WOMEN of the

HOLLY STRATTON TAPS the blackboard with her chalk. "Your wedding vows," she posits to the class. **"You say for better or for worse. Do most people mean for better or worse?"**

Heads shake. Negative.

"Do they mean till death do us part?" Negative.

"A vow to be faithful?" More head-shaking. Stratton continues. "It would be more honest to say, 'I will be faithful until someone else more attractive comes along, and then I'll forget you.' We are not people of our word."

Pens scribble in notebooks.

"What are your duties to a spouse?" she asks. "To love your wife as Christ loved the church and to do what? To walk all over her and treat her mean and tell her what to do all the time?"

The men shake their heads. Negative[...] On the blackboard, a list of unke[...] promises grows: debt, unethical busine[...] practices, betrayed friendships. Then [...] list picks up again at its starting poi[...] marriage, love, partnership, respect, tru[...] relationships. "A good name," Stratt[...] instructs from the Bible. "A Christi[...] must have a good name."

Stratton is a teacher in the family [...] consumer sciences department (forme[...] home economics) at the fundamenta[...] Bob Jones University. She is leadin[...] class in American Family. Her stude[...] consist of some 50 young women [...] about a dozen men. The women wear l[...] skirts, loose sweaters, tights and loaf[...] The men are all dressed according to [...] campus's morning dress code of jack[...] and ties (in the afternoon they can w[...] collared shirts without ties) and all lis[...] attentively when the conversation turn[...] what God requires of the Christian ma[...]

Bob Jones University is located [...]

enville, South Carolina, "the buckle on Bible Belt." The women on this cam- are part of a growing movement of tically active right-wing Christians. y take the Bible literally on its admoni- to "submit yourselves unto your own bands as unto the Lord," which in day- ay life means accepting the ultimate ority of the male, allowing a husband's sion to stand in all matters of conflict even abiding by unpalatable prohibi- s and demands.

he women interviewed for this story committed themselves to many of the es made famous by Pat Robertson and Right organizations like his 1.5-mil- -member Christian Coalition. Almost them have led or participated in such rities as pro-life marches, letter-writ- campaigns to oppose gay rights, ol-board elections in which the teach- of creationism and Christian family es are at issue and, when public ols fail to adopt Christian philosophy, e schooling. Their script is the Bible, muse Rush Limbaugh.

me regard this worldview as antiquat- nd dogmatic. But for many of these en, Christian activism and its funda-

By Elizabeth Kadetsky

mentalist soul seem to have delivered what feminism never could. Here, some of these women explain how they have reconciled modern life with ancient scripture.

For the majority of these women, the appeal of the Christian Right as a community is probably enhanced by the promise of sensitive, committed men. "One of the greatest freedoms I think I could ever experience as a woman is to be loved by a man 'as Christ loved the church,'" 35-year-old Stratton tells me after class, quoting from an oft-repeated biblical passage. "Christ gave his life for us, he served us," she says. "That's how my husband is supposed to love me. And he does. I don't feel I have to be sexier or better looking or try to maintain his love. It's totally unconditional. That is really peaceful for me. It gives me a great amount of freedom to grow as a person."

"The widespread sense that marriage is no longer for keeps creates a longing for security," adds Judith Stacey, Ph.D., a secular sociologist whose 1990 book, *Brave New Families*, profiled a fundamentalist community in San Jose, California. Stacey

points out that the minister in that community spoke in the same terms as Stratton does on marriage and divorce. "He would say, 'Marriage is a contract and contracts fail. But Christian marriage is more than a contract: It is a covenant.'"

In an era when leaders of everything from the women's movement to the welfare-reform movement wring their hands about why the modern father is an absent one—either physically or emotionally— some right-wing Christian women *have* found men who belie the pervasive image of the irresponsible or workaholic dad.

Laura Majors, a 23-year-old mother in Texas, is confident that her husband, James, will do better than her own father did. "My dad did not know what was going on in the family," Majors recalls of the household in which she grew up. "He was oblivious. My mom would do everything with us because my dad didn't want to. She took us to softball games, horse shows. James gives his family as much time as I do," she adds. "Where a [non-Christian] guy feels like it's his right to go out, James stays home."

Majors cites a passage from Ephesians in the New Testament that is frequently interpreted to *(Continued on page 247)*

hristian Right

d Sheila Tice
heir five children.
made an
essful run for the
chool board
morality platform,"
for "teaching
right and wrong,"
en decided to
chool her children.

WOMEN OF THE CHRISTIAN RIGHT

Continued from page 231

mean that Christian husbands should participate in their families. While part of that passage grants men the power to make major decisions, it also, according to some interpretations, implies that men must *consult* with their wives. "So ought men love their wives as their own bodies," it reads. "He that loveth his wife loveth himself. For no man ever yet hated his own flesh; but nourisheth and cherisheth it...."

When I first visited Laura and James Majors, they and their one-year-old son were living in a small apartment in a complex of identical, low-slung suburban buildings on the outskirts of San Antonio. Laura had been raised Protestant but did not feel that her family was sufficiently orthodox. By being baptized in her new church, she accepted God as her savior and committed herself to a closer observation of biblical law—a process that many Christians refer to as being born-again.

Like most of those interviewed for this story and many fundamentalists, the Majorses attend a "Bible church," claim no affiliation with any denomination and refer to themselves simply as "Christians."

Though some Christians discern the differences among fundamentalism, evangelicalism and born-again Christianity, some combination of these terms applies to the women and men in this story: fundamentalist, meaning they take the Bible literally; evangelical, believing they must spread the word of God; born-again, having vowed explicitly to "take the Lord as our savior."

A computer expert who does high-level electronic troubleshooting for large organizations, James Majors has been trying to follow the teachings of the Bible more closely since his wife embraced Christianity. When I first met him, James spent his time holed up in a small spare bedroom, operating Christian Connection BBS, a computer network he founded that hosted chats on homosexuality, abortion and other topics of interest to Christian "net-surfers."

"We clashed for the first couple of years," James said about his marriage to Laura, in a rare moment away from the control room. He held a television clicker in one hand and cuddled the willowy Laura in his other arm, flipping through the TV channels before settling on a football game.

"My dad was domineering, and I picked up that message from him," James contin-
(Continued)

ued. "Then I realized that what he was doing was not right and so I tried to change. I'm still trying to change. If the Christian man is not in his place, how can he expect his woman to be in her place? I cannot expect her to be submissive to me if I myself am not willing to be submissive and do the things that God has told me to do, which is treat her with honor and respect."

In the months after my visit, James had sold off his computer equipment, in part to finance Laura's dream—a move to a larger house with room for the couple's second child. James had also given up the BBS, and now comes in contact with computers only at work. "Laura felt that computers distracted me," James says now in a telephone conversation. "I would spend five to six hours after work on the computer and that left Laura alone to care for the baby. Now I'm freed up to take care of the baby, to clean, to cook."

RuthAnn Harvey, a 37-year-old gospel and country singer in rural Pennsylvania who writes, performs and records a rightwing, religio-political repertoire, describes a similar transformation in her husband, Mike. "It wasn't women's lib. It wasn't feminism. It was the Lord that changed his attitude," she says. RuthAnn and Mike are sitting around the kitchen table over a dinner they cooked together and reminiscing about the days before God. A domineering Mike was into drugs and alcohol; RuthAnn was suffering a spiritual malaise.

"Before we were Christians, he would help now and then, but it was like, 'It's your job. You're the woman,' " RuthAnn says of her husband, who now discusses all major decisions with his wife. Mike nods genially as she continues. "There wasn't that Christlike compassion you see today."

A silent Mike rises to clear the dishes and check on the four kids playing in the TV room. When he returns, he explains that he often does the dishes. "In a secular world you're concerned if your neighbor sees you doing the dishes and says, 'What kind of man is this? He should make his wife do that job.' I don't really care what the world says I'm supposed to do. The Bible is my standard."

The Bible is interpreted as demanding emotional sensitivity of men. "Many evangelical women want strong, sensitive men, just as a lot of secular feminists do," observes feminist sociologist Susan Rose, Ph.D., who has studied evangelical women. "They want strong, sensitive men who are not emasculated. There's an emphasis on men being able to show and share their emotions. It's a strength to cry. There's a

model of Christ as a friend and a sensitive man. It frees up men in a whole other way."

Women living in primarily Christian communities feel they're treated with respect, not just by their partners but by men in general. In a Christian context, men cannot catcall, whistle, date rape. "There isn't any sexual harassment. That doesn't go on," Mayme Baker, 22, contends about Bob Jones University, where she was a student until 1994. "We're respected, we're not just pieces of meat walking down the sidewalk," she adds emphatically. "I've never experienced someone coming on to me or any kind of sexual harassment."

While such rules may not be universally obeyed—as the transgressions of religious luminaries have made all too obvious—Mayme's description of the pristine, well-clipped Bob Jones campus and its bevy of well-mannered young men seems accurate. The male students do not leer or make obnoxious comments, though it is hard to believe that no one ever flouts the social code. "At least this is the ideal, at least people are trying to live up to this standard," Carla Clark, 21, a senior at Bob Jones, tells me.

Carla discusses the matter as we drive to Sunday evening church services on the outskirts of Greenville. On this uncrowded freeway, a four-door sedan pulls up and the men inside do what men in sedans do everywhere. Two middle-aged men pucker their lips and gesticulate. We are an all-female carload because university regulations stipulate that male and female students living in the dorms may not leave the campus together if unchaperoned. Carla grips the wheel, stares straight through the windshield and assumes a perplexed expression. "What," she wants to know, "are they doing?"

With lush brown hair, deep green eyes and heavy mascara, Carla gets a lot of unappreciated attention from men. Before she came to Bob Jones University, she worked at a drugstore in Denver, where she grew up in a strict Christian family. "There was the constant belittling," she says, recalling an atmosphere poisoned by a combination of sexual harassment and religious intolerance. "I was ridiculed. My coworkers did everything in their power to undermine my standards. They would try to put lewd images in front of me. They'd try to get me to look at *Playgirl.*"

Christianity, strictly observed, can offer a respite from such pressures, as well as from difficult decisions: whether to sleep with someone in this age of AIDS; whether to go to a raucous frat party that could turn dangerous. "For Christian women there is a certain protection, like the old curfew. You

248

don't have to make choices," says Susan Rose. "You can play out the femininity, the attractiveness, the allure on somewhat safe ground. There really isn't confusion about what 'no' means, because premarital sex is not condoned. There's an escape within the evangelical community."

Later, Carla is sitting in her dorm room with a friend; both are eating a dinner of pizza and soda and discussing the sexual temptations that sometimes sway their commitment to celibacy. But they agree that remaining a virgin is both religiously and personally fulfilling. Each continually returns to the term *respect*.

"Christianity does not mean you don't have hormones," says Carla's friend, who is telling me about her vow to remain a virgin until marriage. "My boyfriend and I have been dating for four years. It's based on friendship and respect for one another. We didn't kiss for the first year and a half. Sex is what so many relationships are based on. If a girl doesn't give a boy what he wants, he'll find a girl who will."

Holly Stratton, the family and consumer sciences teacher, counsels many young women with similar dilemmas. In Stratton's view, refraining from sex preserves self-respect, a pet issue of hers after having counseled numerous Christian students struggling with anorexia, poor body image and the litany of other maladies that afflict college-age women of all persuasions. "Girls have a tendency to feel more used than guys do," Stratton explains. " 'I thought he cared about me,' the girl will say. Maybe they kissed, and she read so much into the relationship. Holding back saves you from that; it protects you from being hurt and enables you to get to know the other person."

For many Christian women, a family-centered life does not preclude social activism and a strong personal voice in the non-Christian community. Bob and Sheila Tice, whose home is announced by a handpainted roadside sign that reads "Abortion Stops A Beating Heart," say that they are what used to be known as 'Jesus freaks.' Shortly after each converted to Christianity, the two met in 1973 in a house where church meetings were held at the University of Delaware. They were liberals then—Sheila voted for George McGovern—but turned Republican when abortion became a political issue a decade later.

At 9 A.M. on a typical morning in Sciota, Pennsylvania, Bob, 39, is in the workshop where he earns the family income repairing guitars. Across the yard in the house, Sheila, 40, has one hand in a sinkful of sudsy water; the other cradles a telephone. Sheila, who is president of the local chapter of Pennsylvanians for Human Life,

watches three-year-old Jonny playing on the floor. The bread maker is percolating. Seven-year-old Danny is choosing a sweater from a stack of used clothing recently procured from a neighbor.

Sheila is chatting on the phone with the producer of a local talk radio show. Both the producer and host know Sheila by name and as "our conservative friend." She calls the show several times a week in what the family refers to as Sheila's "ministry with the radio program," "ministry" being the work one does toward a spiritual end.

Sheila traces her political involvement to the day in 1987 when several community members approached her with the information that a teacher at the local public school was defining various "perverted" terms—*pedophilia, bestiality*—in a sex ed class. Sheila succeeded in pressuring the school board to discipline the teacher and also staged an unsuccessful run for the board. Her "morality platform" called for "teaching what's right and wrong." For example, homosexuality, she insisted, should not be presented as "just another lifestyle."

Partially because of Sheila's personal objections to what she calls the local public school's liberal philosophies, she decided to educate her own children at home. "I *know* what I'm teaching them," she says of her Christian-centric home schooling.

Like Sheila, Carla Clark has found a political forum to express her personal values. She edits the campus newspaper at Bob Jones University, *The Collegian*, in which she has stepped up right-wing opining on topics such as the problems of multicultural curricula and the virtues of Senator Strom Thurmond.

For RuthAnn Harvey, both home and art are infused with politics. Her music often expresses the agenda of the Christian Right: "Nervously the mother of the unborn child is waiting/With her hand she takes a pen and signs away its life/As she walks into the room she feels her body shaking/Nurses reassure her everything will be all right," RuthAnn wrote in her antiabortion song, "Leave 'em Alone."

RuthAnn shares with women like Sheila Tice and Carla Clark a desire to make an impact outside her home. Coming from a traditional family, marrying a man with his own conservative ideas about a woman's role, RuthAnn found that it was Christianity that offered her a way out. "I'm an outgoing person," she says of both her musical work and a ministry she and her husband founded to counsel people who were in what they refer to as cults, namely Mormons and Jehovah's Witnesses. The Harveys were briefly Mormons before converting to Christianity in 1979.

(Continued)

"I was used to demonstrating at organizations, being with people, and suddenly I was in this house," RuthAnn recalls. "I had no neighbors. I felt kind of 'Oh Lord, use me somehow, because I can't stand being here.' Then our ministry started taking off, and it got me out of the house and fulfilled me."

Running for a seat on a local school board, editing a college newspaper or informing music with politics might sound like the endeavors of a feminist—and many Christian women acknowledge a debt to the women's movement. "It's considered normal for me to speak my mind," says Tice. "I'm a woman with an opinion, and that's accepted." But every woman interviewed for this story also reacted with visceral distaste at the mention of feminism. Their political activism and other professional work, they argue, is secondary to caring for their families. They all lament that, today, a woman placing family above all else is considered a throwback.

"My career as a mother of five is thought of in a lower light," Tice says of the cultural attitudes that she attributes to feminism. Carla Clark complains, "If you say, 'I want to be a homemaker,' people look at you like you must be demented. That should be a choice a woman has."

"According to my employers, my family is to come second," says Laura Majors, who has a full-time job. "They will never convince *me* of that. I enjoy homemaking, because that's what it is, homemaking. That's my first love."

Eschewing the material world for the spiritual is a very real trade-off. In order to stay at home and educate her children, Sheila Tice hunts for bargains and collects used clothing. One night I dined with the family on venison collected from a roadside car accident. "I've decided I'm going to stay home, and Bob supports me in that." Sheila says. "We just tighten the belt, burn wood and eat venison."

For many, Christianity also offers a salve against spiritual malaise and despair. "I knew there was God," says RuthAnn Harvey. "I just didn't know how to find Him."

"Without God, my life would be a mess," adds teacher Holly Stratton, who was raised in a fundamentalist family and has observed some of her family members turning to a more secular life. "Everything that we do, we do with an eternal motivation. It would be hard to go through the bumps and all the difficult times without a purpose."

If Christian women have secured self-respect, sexual self-determination, spiritual fulfillment, and satisfaction at work as well as in the family, is it they, and not corporate climbers with full-time child care, who "have it all"? Many of the women interviewed for this story argue that they *do*—but outsiders note that contradictions plague Christian women as much as they do secular women. "What they have has not come without cost," argues sociologist Susan Rose. "They were willing to make certain sacrifices in order to be involved with men who are invested in their families, who are hard workers and primary breadwinners."

One morning at Bob Jones University, Holly Stratton brings me to chapel, the daily Bible service required of all students and faculty. As we take our seats with her husband, Dick, a professor of accounting, I pull out a collection of sermons delivered by the campus's founder and namesake, Bob Jones Sr. "The Bible emphasizes 'keepers at home,'" the well-known fundamentalist preacher wrote more than 50 years ago. "I know some women in this country who run around from place to place and think they are Bible teachers." Jones's words could almost be read as an admonition to Holly, the family and consumer sciences instructor, to stay at home and forget about teaching. "Or they are out in politics where they let their houses go topsy turvey," his words continue. "There is a good deal of old-time religion in soap and a rag." Thinking of Holly and her family-centered Christian counterparts, I ask her whether this view of women doesn't contradict her own view of herself as strong willed, independent and committed to her work as well as to her family.

Before she can answer, the visiting preacher starts to speak. Coincidentally, he has chosen the story of Isaac and Rebecca to illuminate the same theme. "She's something else," the preacher speaks. "What a girl she is, Rebecca, running there, running here, that's a servant's heart. Well, there's something beautiful about that.... Pure is the woman who has a servant's heart. Girls, is that the kind of heart you've got? Fellas, is that the kind of girl you're looking for?"

The preacher wraps up with an anecdote in which he begs of his wife a small favor. " 'Sweetheart, precious darling, what do you want?' " he quotes his wife as asking. He answers that he needs her to substitute-teach a Sunday school class. "She reached over and kissed me on the cheek and said, 'Honey, I'd be glad to.' "

I look over and see Holly laughing. "That's not me," she says. Then she leans over and whispers the same thing to her husband, who lets out a laugh of his own. ●

Elizabeth Kadetsky is a writer in Los Angeles.

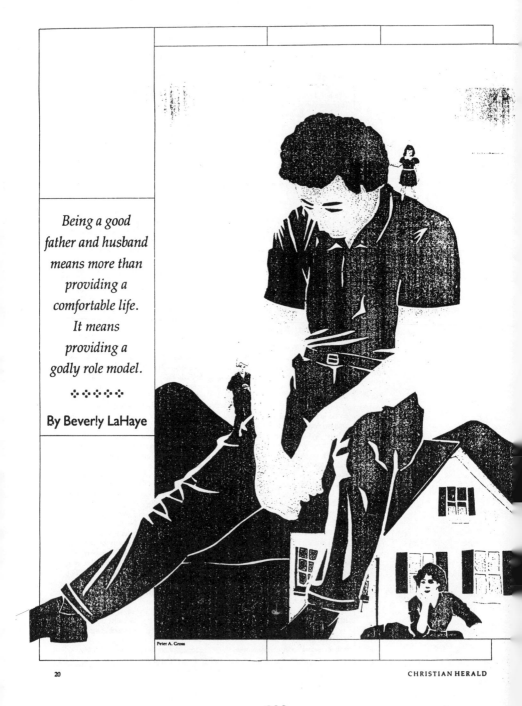

Being a good father and husband means more than providing a comfortable life. It means providing a godly role model.

❖❖❖❖❖

By Beverly LaHaye

Peter A. Gross

CHRISTIAN **HERALD**

As the president of the nation's largest organization for women, I get feedback from all over the country. It's no coincidence that in a time dominated by headlines about failed leadership in government, business, and the church, a recurring concern is the lack of male leadership in the home.

"My husband provides well for our family's material needs, but our spiritual and emotional needs are impoverished," a woman told me in a recent letter, expressing the yearning of many wives.

Another frustrated spouse said her husband spends more time with his hobbies than their children. His work requires him to be around people, so he believes he deserves to be left alone at home, she said. Other women worry about their husband's lack of involvement in church or spiritual activities.

In 1 Timothy 3:5, while talking about the qualifications of a leader, the Apostle Paul writes, "If anyone does not know how to manage his own family, how can he take care of God's church?" Clearly, leadership begins in the home. If we have strong, godly men leading our families, we'll have a stronger church and a stronger society.

I've observed that more women participate in Bible study classes than men, and experience a deeper spiritual growth. Since expectations for husbands are built from the Word, they are disturbed when the husband falls short as

the family's spiritual head.

Women shouldn't expect perfection, of course, but they do need men whose personal lives are in proper relationship with the Lord, who are forgiven for past sins and recognize they can't be the spiritual leader to a wife and family without the Holy Spirit's help.

A godly man will con-

What Women Wish Their Husbands Knew About Leadership

centrate on building up his spouse. He will pray for and with her and encourage her spiritual growth. He will focus his love on her alone. True commitment necessitates fleeing from sexual immorality in his thought life, reading material, glances and actions. There will never be unfaithfulness if the husband turns away from the first lustful thought or glance, if he determines before God he will live a faithful moral life with desires only for his wife.

Being a faithful, loving

partner influences the results of parenting. When children know their parents love each other, they need little explanation about the character of God's love, and it helps prepare them for future adult love.

No Role Models
Not all husbands fall short of this biblical model.

Many take seriously their role as spiritual leader for the family. Unfortunately, a growing number do not. Spiritual training for too many children of Christian couples is bounced between the mother and Sunday school. But Ephesians 6:4 clearly tells fathers to bring up children "in the training and admonition of the Lord."

The Lord can work around a father's lack, of course. Many single-parent moms have to be in charge of their childrens' spiritual training. And

spiritually mature young people have come out of homes where there was no father. My husband, Tim, is an example. His father died when Tim was young, and his mother had a profound spiritual impact on his life. He has spent more than 40 years as a godly husband, minister and author. Still, he recognizes the need for balanced responsibility, and has been a strong model for me and our children.

Moms *can* do a great job when necessary. But the fact remains that fathers are called to lead the family in spiritual instruction.

Recent studies show that dads who spend time alone with their children more than twice a week—giving baths, meals and basic care—rear children who become compassionate adults. A dad's involvement helps the child develop higher self-esteem, better grades, and more sociability.

Women long for their husbands to have more spiritual involvement with the children, who seek a role model. If it isn't Dad or Mom, it probably will be someone not in step with your spiritual values, someone whose values and goals are opposed to yours.

The Right Start
Ideally, dads should start with their children while they are young to capture their respect and admiration. It requires spending time with them—from building with blocks to batting balls around the yard to going fishing and

camping to learning to drive. During these times questions and conversations will develop that let a dad build spiritual character into his children. It's never too late to begin.

One of my favorite stories is about a dad Tim and I knew. He was an active businessman and Christian leader, but he carved his schedule around daily contact with his three sons. He started when they were very young. When we met them, they were 11, 14 and 17, and his daily habit still carried on.

Tim and I were guests when we observed this family in action. Every evening the father made a determined effort to have individual prayer with his sons. If he was home, he would excuse himself and take each son in his own bedroom to pray together. When he was away from home at bedtime, he would telephone and pray with each one by phone. Those few times when it was impossible to make contact with the boys, each knew wherever Dad was, he was praying for them at that time of night.

Once the father was going to travel in Europe for two weeks, and the time difference plus expense would make a phone call difficult. This creative Dad made a cassette tape for each boy to have by his bedside, and every night each could hear Dad praying for him.

The availability and presence of a godly man in the lives of his wife and children has far-reaching

The involvement a father has in his childrens' lives has far-reaching effects, extending to society as a whole.

effects, extending to society as a whole. By loving his wife as Christ loves the church, spending quality time with his children and providing spiritual guidance, a father's influence will continue into successive generations. Psalm 112:1-2 is a promise for all time: "Blessed is the man who fears the Lord, . . . His children will be mighty in the land; each generation of the upright will be blessed."

A man willing to follow the admonition in Deuteronomy 6:5 to "Love the Lord your God with all your heart and with all your soul and with all your strength" *will* be the spiritual leader of his home, will love his wife as his own body, and be a role model to his children. What a pillar of strength this man will be to the family. ▪

Beverly LaHaye, president of Concerned Women for America, also hosts a daily radio talk show, "Concerned Women Live."

2 : Family

Dear to the heart of Christian conservatism lies the family. Surrounding the self, connecting it to and protecting it from society, the family is considered by religious conservatives to be the most important of social institutions. Unlike many of their conservative counterparts, they have embraced the family as a focus of public policy, taking positions on the most intense and intimate of "hearth-and-home" issues, including abortion, homosexuality, and sex education. Considering themselves to be defenders of a besieged Christian culture, they describe the family as a fortress. At the same time, because they think of themselves as soldiers in a struggle to reform secular society, they see it also as a battleground. In either case, they think of the family as fundamental, "the fundamental building block and basic unit of our society," according to Jerry Falwell, "and its continued health is a prerequisite for a healthy and prosperous nation."[1]

In spite of its importance, however, writers within the New Christian Right have had difficulty in defining the family. Criticizing contemporary conceptions, which they see as aberrant and socially self-destructive, they advocate what they call the "traditional" family form.[2] Yet among them there is little agreement as to the meaning of the traditional family itself.[3] In large part, the absence of agreement is inherent in their ideology, for Christian conservative thinkers draw on several different definitions of the family—particularly prominent are Puritan, Victorian, and postwar images of the family as "church," "haven," and "corporation"—combining

296

them into a kind of contemporary collage.[4] Although historically confusing, the result is ideologically consistent, a conception of the family in which men rule, women submit, and children obey. In this conception, says John Kater, "the issue at stake is power."[5]

Religious conservatives have written extensively on the family. In fact, it can be argued that they have treated no other topic so thoroughly. Their books fill the shelves of Christian bookstores, which frequently feature entire sections on family life, marriage, and sexual relationships. The books tend to fall into one of three categories: books about men, usually written by men; books about women, usually written by women, but sometimes also by men; and books about the family, written more often by men than women, and on occasion written by a Christian couple. These books are supplemented by an array of related sources, including sex manuals for married couples, books on dating and sex education for youths, and texts dealing with issues of child rearing and discipline. Autobiographical accounts of family life are also common. Attesting their popularity, many of the books, which tend to be inexpensive paperbacks, boast of frequent printings and massive sales: "National Bestseller," "#1 Best Seller," "Over 1 Million In Print."[6] Albeit perhaps inflated, such sales, when taken together with the proliferation of radio and television shows, cassette tapes, and films, along with conferences, seminars, and rallies that focus on family life, suggest a sizable social movement and an abiding concern on the part of Christian conservatives with family issues.[7]

Although the books do not agree on every point, they do have a clear doctrinal direction. Men are to act as authorities, women are to be submissive, and children are to obey. Sexual roles are clear and distinct, and deviations are disapproved, especially in cases such as feminism and homosexuality. On its face, the theory seems simple and straightforward. Yet when considered more closely, the arguments are more complicated, revealing confusion and self-contradiction. For all its seeming simplicity, Christian conservative social thought can be paradoxical in theory and problematic when put into practice. This chapter considers this theory, including its paradoxes and problems, by focusing on the respective roles of men, women, and children.

Men: Anxious Patriarchs

Christian conservative social theory begins with male authority. Following a patriarchal path established by their early Protestant forefathers, the writers argue that God appointed men to be authorities at the beginning of the world. Tapping later strains of thought as well, especially those established in the Victorian era, they contend that men are predisposed in other ways—biologically, psychologically, even sexually—to exercise power. Few of their beliefs are so fundamental. Yet when it comes to defining how men are to serve as authorities, how they are to exercise power, and even how they are to act as men, the authors exhibit a good deal of uncertainty. Several of the writers admit that their own fathers, for various reasons, provided "no pattern."[8] More often, they confide that in their own lives they have felt unsure about their roles as husbands, fathers, and men, being confused and often humbled, like Pat Boone, at the thought that they were "supposed" to be "the patriarch."[9] Furthermore, they suggest that the situation is getting worse, that today, more than ever, patriarchy is highly problematic. As one writer says, "It has never been so difficult to be a man."[10]

Man's Nature

Men are authorities, appointed by God to rule. For proof of this proposition, these books turn to the Bible. Thus Charles Stanley, the Atlanta pastor, television preacher, and a former president of the Southern Baptist Convention, begins his *A Man's Touch*, a book written for Christian conservative men, by going to the first chapter of Genesis. God made men in his image, says Stanley, a believer in biblical inerrancy. Men are, it follows, the closest thing to God on earth, "the crown of God's creation."[11] Having created Adam, Stanley continues, God commanded him to rule. Specifically, Adam was commanded to rule his wife and family, for in addition to overseeing the earth, God also required Adam to take a wife and, with her, to reproduce, "to bring forth children who likewise would glorify God." From Adam the command has passed down to all men and remains in operation today. "God has not repealed these commands," the fundamentalist Stanley advises. "Today it is still a man's responsibility to rule his world, to produce children in the image of God, and to be faithful to his wife."[12]

In addition to the authority of the Bible, however, many of the books consider biology to be another authorization for patriarchy. In phrases reminiscent of mid-nineteenth-century medical manuals, the authors argue that men differ from women anatomically and physiologically. According to Tim LaHaye, the Southern California pastor, counselor, and writer of marriage manuals and sex studies, there is "a basic, God-created difference between males and females." Because of biology, he argues, men are stronger, having more muscle mass, strength, and stamina. Moreover, biology affects behavior, with men being physiologically influenced by the presence of the hormone testosterone to show attributes of "aggressiveness, dominance, ambition, and sexual initiative." Indeed, LaHaye contends that biology shapes emotions and feelings as well, because dissimilarities in brain construction cause characterological differences between men and women, disposing men to be more courageous, more concerned with productivity, and more capable of leadership than women. According to LaHaye, biochemistry plays a causal role. Thus a boy who has not received the proper amount of testosterone in the womb will be biologically conditioned to exhibit "feminine characteristics," becoming both "effeminate" and "passive." In other words, writes LaHaye, citing "scientific studies," the boy will have a "feminized brain."[13]

The books cite psychological differences as well. Here the treatments seem to be heavily influenced by the popular psychology of the postwar period. One of the best examples is Phyllis Schlafly's *The Power of the Christian Woman*, which relies on "scholarly works," public opinion polls, magazine articles, and interviews with celebrities such as Lauren Bacall, Katharine Hepburn, and Nancy Reagan to conclude that many of the differences between men and women are "emotional and psychological."[14] According to Schlafly, men are psychologically predisposed to be "rational" rather than "emotional."[15] In their thinking, they are "abstract," "discursive," and "logical," while women are "personal" and "mystical."[16] Because they have no "natural maternal need," men tend to be "philosophical," while women, emotionally tied to home and family, are "practical."[17] Indeed, Schlafly goes on to argue that men are innately inclined through a certain "boldness of the imagination" to pursue "higher intellectual activities," while women "tend more toward conformity than men—which is why they often excel in such disciplines as spelling and punctuation."[18] Ironies abounding, the rational, logical, highly intellectual Schlafly concludes that women should above all never seek to act like males. Any attempt to make women into men, she concludes, is "as wrong as efforts to make a left-handed child right-handed."[19]

Even more important, these writers see men as shaped by their sexuality. Men are sexual aggressors. Indeed, at times in these books, men seem like little more than sexual animals. Men are sexually aggressive, writes LaHaye in his *How to Be Happy Though Married*, because of the "constant production of sperm and seminal fluid." In fact, they are almost uncontrollably sexually aggressive. The male sex drive, LaHaye explains, is "almost volcanic in its latent ability to erupt at the slightest provocation."[20] Throughout their marriage manuals and sex studies, the writers presuppose male sexual superiority. Men possess a stronger sex drive than women. They think more about sex, talk more about sex, and, when given the opportunity, engage more in sex, while also enjoying it more than women. In short, men are sexual creatures, for better or worse the product of their reproductive systems—servants, as it were, of their sperm. LaHaye describes the situation: "The hidden force that colors man's thinking, giving him three-dimensional fantasies and stereophonic female perception, is the result of his natural ability to manufacture billions of sperm cells a week."[21]

The Advantages of Sexual Aggressiveness

The authors of these books seem surprisingly at ease with this potentially explosive sexuality, for several reasons. Perhaps most important is that they view sexuality as one of the chief motivations to marriage. In essence, they argue that while women enter marriage out of a desire for security and reproduction, men get married for the sex. In their *The Act of Marriage*, a best-selling sex manual, LaHaye and his coauthor and wife, Beverly, attempt to make marriage more meaningful by stressing its sexual side. Thus this "fully biblical and highly practical" manual comes complete with detailed diagrams of the male and female reproductive systems, discussions of sexual techniques and equipment (including advice on how to clean and reuse condoms), and suggestions on sexual activity ranging from foreplay to sexual positioning to postcoital prayer. Within marriage, the LaHayes seem to say, almost anything is allowed. Writing especially for couples who have been subjected to the sexually repressive standards of their fundamentalist parents and conservative churches, the LaHayes go to some length to deride Victorian strictures against sex, which they label as "nonsense." Quoting Bible verses from the Song of Solomon, they contend that Christianity was never opposed to sexuality, and, for that matter, that many of the Old Testament saints were "good lovers."[22] Indeed, relying on their own social science methods—a public opinion poll which they devised and distributed to some 1,700 couples who had attended their Family Life Seminars—the LaHayes conclude that religious conservatives are able, when properly educated, to have not only more sex, but better sex, experiencing "a higher degree of sexual enjoyment than non-Christians."[23]

At the same time, the authors see male sexuality as serving a larger social purpose. Uncontrolled, it is anarchic and destructive, with men seemingly wandering about in search of sexual conquest. Controlled, however, it allows for stability and social progress. Citing George Gilder's *Sexual Suicide*, Schlafly argues that, when left to its own, male sexuality is mobile, predatory, and violent. The same sexuality, however, when controlled by the boundaries of the family, can serve the cause of stability and security. "Man's role as family provider," states Schlafly, "gives him the incentive to curb his primitive nature."[24] Sexual sublimation has economic implications as well, harnessing energy to drive the engines of progress. According to LaHaye, it "formed the basis of what has come to be known as the Protestant work ethic" and in America "contributed to the great progress and resourcefulness of the United States in technology and industry." Indeed, sexual sublimation is crucial to the continuation of civilization itself, for, writes LaHaye, "social scientists who have studied fallen civilizations note that these cultures declined as strict controls on sexual energy were relaxed."[25]

They admit that sexual sublimation is not easy. According to LaHaye, men's prolific production of sperm creates vast amounts of barely contained sexual aggressiveness. Under these biological circumstances, even the most moral of men, their reproductive systems roaring at full tilt, can wander, or at least their minds can wander. LaHaye, calling for censorship and self-censorship, advises the avoidance of pornographic and sexually suggestive materials of all kinds. Masturbation, a topic treated at length, is equally taboo. Worried, like President Carter, about "lust in the heart," LaHaye recommends self-control: "Get your mind under control by thinking only pure thoughts."[26] Ultimately, however, men cannot be expected to rely only on self-mastery. Women also have a very important role in checking male urges. One way or another, the authors suggest, men will be men, and it is critical that women not lead them on. Thus the LaHayes warn women, including Christian women, to beware of "scanty dress": "If they realized the thought problems which their indecent exposure causes the average man, many of them would dress more modestly."[27]

Issues of Insecurity

Male sexuality becomes troubling only when it is threatened. In particular, the books convey deep concern about male impotence and sexual insecurity. As the authors describe them, modern men are insecure indeed, "less certain of their manhood than formerly."[28] In theory sexual aggressors and sexual athletes, they are in practice fairly flaccid fellows, sometimes impotent, often sexually troubled. Almost always they seem to be worried about their abilities to achieve erection, to hold it, to ejaculate more or less at the right time, and so on. Drawing on his experience as a Christian sex counselor, LaHaye cites examples of even "fantastic physical specimens of manliness" who "on some occasion" proved sexually unsatisfactory and who, as a result, "subsequently became emotionally induced eunuchs."[29] Most striking about these men is their psychosexual fragility, the worries they seem to have of being unable to satisfy their wives, of being compared unfavorably by them to other men, and even of being ridiculed by them. The LaHayes are of course sympathetic: "It can be devastating," they write to wives, "for a wife to joke about her husband's organ."[30]

In charting the causes of male insecurity, the writers look first to wives. Husbands are meant to rule, but, sadly, wives are all too often preempting their prerogatives. Here the writers point to economic considerations, including most prominently the dramatic increase in the number of wage-earning wives. Harkening back to happier times in the 1950s and early 1960s when husbands could support families on their single paychecks, LaHaye argues that women should, if at all possible, stay at home. When the wife works, he says, it "breeds a feeling of independence and self-sufficiency which God did not intend a married woman to have." LaHaye is especially concerned about newlyweds. "I am convinced," he goes on, "that one of the reasons young married couples divorce so readily today is because the wife is not economically dependent upon her husband." If the wife must work, however, LaHaye recommends a joint checking account, with a certain twist, in that the wife is to be allowed to keep from her paycheck "only what she needs for her living and household expenses."[31]

Particularly threatening are aggressive women. Most prominent among these are feminists, who flap through the pages of these books like Valkyries slaying men to take to Valhalla. While reviling feminists as haters of men, the authors seem to accord them grudging respect as fearsome foes in a war in which, according to Schlafly, "man is targeted as the enemy."[32] Of more concern are aggressive wives, including, the authors are sorry to say, many Christian conservative women. While far from considering themselves feminists, these Christian wives have become captives of their culture, taking on more responsibilities and playing more prominent roles; as a result, they have begun to compete, consciously or unconsciously, with their husbands. Hence they pose a threat, depriving their husbands "of a natural need to protect and support," and creating, more generally, "insecurities and fears in them."[33] As a result, men are beginning to lose their manliness and, the writers warn, are becoming "feminized."[34] Furthermore, as the husband comes to rely more on his wife, he risks becoming not only feminized but also infantilized, for he "will subconsciously feel he is married to a second mother."[35] In extreme cases, competition can effectively result in a form of castration, in which the woman can "demasculinize a man by dominating and leading him in everything—including sex."[36]

Men are at least in part at fault. Indeed, presupposing as they do that men are authorized to rule, the authors of these books must almost by definition ascribe to men most of the responsibility for abrogating their authority. The LaHayes, for example, in a chapter in their marriage manual called "For Men Only," cite "inconsiderate" men (i.e., those who ejaculate prematurely) as a cause of female frigidity.[37] Even feminism itself is at points described as following from male failure. In his *Listen, America!*, Jerry Falwell can describe at least some feminists with surprising sympathy, blaming not them for their foibles, but their husbands: "Not all the women involved in the feminist movement are radicals. Some are misinformed, and some are lonely women who like being housewives and helpmeets and mothers, but whose husbands spend little time at home and who take no interest in their wives and children."[38] Constantly the books chide weak-willed husbands. When the husband is weak, says LaHaye, the wife becomes frustrated, nagging, and quarrelsome. Moreover, the situation is self-perpetuating, for as the wife becomes more frustrated, the husband is beaten down until finally, reduced to submission by his wife, he becomes demasculinized and "degenerates into a sub-par human being." The stakes are high, and the authors call on men to be conscious of their male responsibilities. "Remember," LaHaye finds it necessary to remind them, "you should be the initiator because of your stronger sex drive."[39]

Again and again the books denounce the decline of Christian manhood. Symbolizing this decline, and symptomatic of their fears about the fragility of heterosexual masculinity, is homosexuality. The latter, they contend, is unbiblical and unnatural. It is also, like the biblical Sodom, emblematic of a civilization's decline. Most troubling of all is that homosexuality has become "epidemic," prevalent enough to be found even within the church itself.[40] Writes Edwin Louis Cole, an author of books for Christian men: "In recent days I have heard of a Bible college president who had to resign because of homosexuality, a pastor openly admitting it at the time of his resignation, a youth pastor confessing that his desire for ministry was a cover to meet young men, and young men in a church group experimenting with it."[41] Almost as troubling, and more acceptable, is what Cole calls the "androgynous appeal," meaning the blending and confusion of sex roles through which men seem more like women and women more like men. Anxious and unsure of themselves socially, at ease with traditional roles, the authors of these books on manhood insist that there be clear distinctions between the sexes. God intends men to be masculine, says Stanley, "not effeminate": "God made the distinction between men and women very clear. . . . To be masculine means to speak like a man, to move like a man, to think like a man, to act like a man. That is the way God made man." [42]

The problem seems to be pervasive. According to Cole, who has founded a program of rallies and seminars for men called the Christian Men's Network, men have lost their manliness, becoming ambivalent, indecisive, and self-doubting. Intimidated by feminists and gay activists, their sensibilities seduced by humanism and narcissism, they have allowed themselves to become victims of a mass culture that encourages them to be weak and vulnerable. John Wayne has given way to Alan Alda, strength to softness. America once had men, complains Cole in his book *Maximized Manhood*. It now has "pussyfooting pipsqueaks." [43]

As a kind of antidote, the authors turn from decrying the loss of manhood to defining models of masculinity. Here they become a bit self-conscious, for they recognize that not all men need to be told how to be men. After all, writes LaHaye, there are "millions of red-blooded he-man types in all walks of life who can look at their reflections in the mirror and confidently say, 'I am a man.'" [44] Even so, they see the need for a serious revival of virility. Thus they make the case for a new masculinity, calling on men to be not simply men, but "real men," "total men," "men who are men." [45] Counsels Cole, "Don't be a wimp!" [46]

Maximizing Manhood

The men's writers seem to realize that they face a particular problem in reconciling Christianity with virility. In terms reminiscent of turn-of-the-century male religious reformers, they argue that Christianity, dominated too long by women and their male allies in the ministry, has become a religion of women's values, of forgiveness, mercy, and tenderness. Christians, says Cole, have become "Christianettes." [47] Thus they call for a remasculinization of Christianity. Jesus, Cole tells his audiences in phrases reminiscent of a chest-thumping Billy Sunday, was not "sissified." Instead, he was "a fearless leader, defeating Satan, casting out demons, commanding nature, rebuking hypocrites." Indeed, Cole reminds his readers, Jesus could even be ruthless: "To be like Jesus—Christlike—requires a certain ruthlessness." He concludes, "Manhood does also." [48]

Although the authors go first to religion in seeking out models of masculinity, they go more easily and more often to secular culture, especially to sports. In fact, the books by men are filled with allusions to sports of all kinds, from bowling to motorcycling to waterskiing. Most frequent, however, are the references to football. Aggressive and competitive, involving individual initiative but also requiring team play, and featuring lots of barely controlled male aggression, football is particularly popular among these authors. LaHaye, for example, seems to style himself a sort of unofficial chaplain to the San Diego Chargers, and the team's "number one fan."[49] Regardless of the sport, however, the authors emphasize the importance of competing and winning. Says Cole in his *Courage: A Book for Champions*, "Men love winners. They want to be identified with winners."[50]

One other source of masculine modeling is war. The authors of these books are particularly at ease with military metaphors. All of them show the stamp of the postwar period, and many of them seem to be products, in one way or another, of the Vietnam War era. Cole points proudly to the Second World War, seeming less concerned about its moral purpose, which he fails to mention, than its outcome. In that war, he says, "America fought a war until all her enemies were defeated. Whether in Africa, Europe or Asia, they were conquered. Peace resulted." By contrast, Cole considers Vietnam to be a war not of conquest but of compromise. Bypassing any moral or political considerations, he places blame squarely on the politicians who refused to fight. "God didn't call men to be trucemakers," Cole counsels, "but peacemakers. And peace only comes through victory." The same is true, he says, in everyday life: "Men who compromise—who settle for a truce with their sins—live in misery. Only when they fight through to victory do they live in peace."[51]

Ambivalent Authorities

Yet in constructing models of masculinity, the authors are surprisingly ambivalent, arguing that while men should be strong, they should also be sensitive. In fact, their machismo notwithstanding, they pride themselves on their sensitivity. Even the ramrod Cole calls on men to be "tender" as well as "tough."[52] Here they draw comparisons, sometimes explicit but mostly implicit, to earlier generations. Angry fundamentalist fathers at times haunt their pages, but the authors make it clear that they themselves are modern men. As Stanley writes: "I know from experience that many parents grew up in family environments in which men did not hug each other, dads did not hug their sons, and people were generally not very expressive emotionally. . . . [T]he society in which you and I live in is suffering as a result."[53] The writers encourage male readers to be particularly sensitive to their wives. Here their books begin to look suspiciously like manuals on modern manners. LaHaye, for example, expounds on male etiquette: "It is a wise husband who opens doors, including car doors, for his wife and generally treats her as a gentleman should treat a lady."[54] Beverly LaHaye offers a few suggestions of her own to the husband who wishes to "lighten the load" for his wife: "I know of husbands who insist on loading the dishwasher after every evening meal. Others feel the least they can do is vacuum the whole house once a week. Another brave father has arranged to give the three children their bath each night."[55] Tim LaHaye tends to be more conventional, advising husbands, for example, to "be particularly thoughtful during her menstrual period, as she may be unusually emotional then."[56] Still, the advice does suggest at least a nascent sensitivity. Men, concludes Stanley, who takes the argument further, "may even *cry*."[57]

Men should be authorities, not autocrats. There is in fact among these authors a concern that males will abuse their authority. Many confess that they have in their own lives been at times too authoritarian in pursuing their patriarchal role. Stanley is typical: "I thought my family was supposed to serve me, the father, the husband, the pastor. When it dawned on me that it was my responsibility to serve my family, my whole life changed."[58] Most seem to have had personal experience with other men who, while intending to be leaders, have made themselves tyrants. A few go so far as to claim discreetly that they have some knowledge of cases of physical or psychological mistreatment. "Regrettably," write the LaHayes circumspectly, "some husbands are carryovers from the Dark Ages."[59] All of them, however, in one way or another, suggest that strength must be tempered. To be too strong, Stanley states, is to be tyrannical. Indeed, to be too strong is to be weak. "The autocratic father," says Stanley, "lacks deep-down confidence in himself."[60]

The authors show some awareness of the ambivalence that runs through their thinking. Men are to rule, women to submit to them. But men can only rule well when women submit willingly. The position is both principled and practical. As a matter of principle, LaHaye tells husbands that their wives are neither "inferior nor insignificant" and advises men to treat their wives with respect, allowing room for their "opinions, tastes, preferences and good judgment." LaHaye elaborates: "Frankly, I have found that my wife is a more perceptive judge of colors and has better taste in clothes, furnishings, music, and many other areas than I. She is unquestionably a far better authority on our children."[61] Even more important are practical considerations, for the authors advise that it is only when wives are treated well that they submit willingly. Indeed, says LaHaye, the well-treated wife will find it "easy" to submit to her husband "in everything."[62] Others agree, expanding on the role of the responsible husband. "If you want to motivate her to be submissive," writes Stanley, "serve her."[63] It follows, ironically enough, that authority itself requires a kind of submission. Beverly LaHaye takes the argument to its logical outcome. The husband, she writes, must "have a submissive spirit toward his wife. . . . He is God's appointed 'submissive head' of the wife."[64]

Problems of Patriarchy

In the end, however, this ambivalence about authority can lead to problems. At the very least, the books are confusing, calling on men to be strong by being sensitive, to subject others by serving them, to rule by submitting. More than confusing, however, the positions they espouse can be self-contradictory, trapping Christian conservatives in sometimes vicious circles of authority and submission. The problems that result can be overwhelming. Thus in their book *Bless This House*, Bob Green and Anita Bryant, until relatively recently one of Christian conservatism's best-known couples, set the stage for the later dissolution of their marriage in a description of their life together, in which their seemingly happy home life is interrupted by a continuing series of conflicts. At issue is authority, for while Green and Bryant assume that Green should act as patriarchal authority, and that Bryant should submit to him, they both admit that they are unsuited for their respective roles and that each resents the demands of the other. The result, as Bryant freely admits, is anything but a happy home life: "Worse than rough," she writes of their early years together, "it sometimes was hellish."[65]

Trapped in their respective roles, the couple seems aware that their marriage is failing, but they are powerless to save it. Predisposed to accept responsibility rather than to question principles, they seek to solve their problems by reiterating rules. Thus Green can see no alternative but to reassert his patriarchal prerogatives. He explains: "And that brings us back to where we began—with the role of the Christian husband. He *must* assume the leadership of his home because God has told him to."[66]

Thus Christian conservatives persevere in their patriarchal principles, for, in the end, there seems to be no alternative. Cole explains: "It is possible to get spirituality from women, but strength always comes from men. A church, a family, a nation is only as strong as its men."[67] Besides, they seem certain that God is on their side. Says Stanley, "God has promised to be your constant helper as a husband and a father."[68] God, concludes Cole confidently, "has big plans for you. . . . Be a man."[69]

Women: The Paradox of Power through Powerlessness

If Christian conservative social thinkers seem anxious and ambivalent about the character of men, they are even more deeply divided when it comes to defining the nature of women. Tapping into a Protestant tradition that dates from the time of the Reformation, they describe women in two mutually exclusive ways: on the one hand, they are temptresses, self-assertive and sexually threatening; on the other hand, they are helpmeets and mothers, combining self-sacrifice and spiritual virtuousness. At the heart of the theory lies a deep suspicion of women, and in particular of the power they can exert over men. Even women writers, who seem to specialize in books for other women, are suspicious of single women—and are especially resentful of women who are single by choice. At the same time, calling on a conception of Victorian womanhood, and remembering their own mothers and grandmothers, they idealize married women, casting them as strong, competent characters, helping their husbands, bearing and rearing children, sacrificing themselves for others. Their nostalgia notwithstanding, however, the women writers are eager to point out that they themselves are different from their own mothers. All agree that women's roles have changed dramatically even within their own lifetimes. Interestingly, Christian conservative women, like many modern women, admit to being often overwhelmed by these rapidly changing roles. The world, writes Beverly LaHaye, "expects too much of women today."[70]

In describing women, these thinkers begin with the Bible, going to Genesis to depict Eve as the prototypical woman. Their treatment is far from generous, for they describe Eve as the original temptress, the source of original sin. Writing in *A Man's Touch*, Stanley explains that in the beginning Adam and Eve lived happily in the garden in a state of innocence, knowing no sin. According to God's instructions, Adam ruled his domain, and all the world existed in harmony, a kind of heaven on earth. Eve, a part of her husband created from his rib, obeyed him implicitly. Then came the fall, which, Stanley makes clear, came about when Eve rebelled, refusing to abide by her husband's authority and seeking to assert her own power. He writes, "God's command to Adam was that he rule his domain; disaster struck when Eve ignored her husband's instructions."[71] Enticed by Satan, Eve in her willfulness caused the fall. Moreover, her sin was compounded by her seductiveness, for by using her woman's wiles, she tempted her husband to sin as well. Stanley explains: "The conversation between Adam and Eve following Satan's victory shows the influential sway of women over men. Satan had to *persuade* Eve to disobey God, but Eve made only one simple suggestion, 'Have a bite,' to cause Adam's downfall." Following the fall, Eve was properly punished for her rebellion, receiving, according to Stanley, "the devil's due—disillusionment and death." Nevertheless, even today, women continue to sin, and to tempt men into sin, and they continue to be punished for it. Concludes Stanley, "Women can connive to get their way if they are clever enough, evil enough, or un-Christlike enough, but seldom are they happy with the results of their manipulation."[72]

In addition to being temptresses, however, women are also wives and mothers. Here, as in their descriptions of men, the authors apply arguments from biology, expanding on biblical explanations with biological ones. Following the fall, Eve was consigned to motherhood, condemned to suffer the pain of bearing children, her role being, says Beverly LaHaye, "to assist her husband in reproducing life." All of them argue that women are biologically preconditioned to be mothers. Beverly LaHaye belabors the obvious: "Medical science has yet to help a man give birth to a child."[73] Furthermore, they claim that there exists in all women an innate instinct for maternity, so that women can only feel fulfilled when they become mothers. Although they recognize that all women cannot have children, the writers say little about those who are unable to bear their own. Of far more concern to them are the women who seek to avoid motherhood, or even worse, who terminate pregnancy through abortion, which the writers see as woman's ultimate sin, an act of pride and selfishness regardless of the circumstances. Nevertheless, they take consolation in the assumption that most women can and do achieve their final fulfillment in childbearing and child rearing, which comprise the *telos* of their spiritual and biological being. "Motherhood," Beverly LaHaye sums up, "is the highest form of femininity."[74]

Psychologically as well, women are predisposed to be wives and mothers. Here the women's writers seem to draw on social stereotypes, heavily laced with popular psychology, to argue that while men are rational, women are emotional, intuitive, and nurturing. In marriage, comments Shirley Boone, wife of Pat Boone and author of several books on sexuality and family life, men represent "the head," women "the heart."[75] Unlike men, who live their lives logically, women are intuitive, the "intuitive tendency" being, according to the LaHayes, "the primary drive in a woman." Most important, women are psychologically programmed to love. "The one point on which psychologists agree," the LaHayes inform their readers, is that "women have a tremendous capacity for love, both giving and receiving."[76] Particularly important is that while women wish to be loved, they even more seek to love someone else, their "chief emotional need," according to Schlafly, being "active (i.e., to love)."[77] It follows that women are predisposed to be mothers, having a "natural maternal need."[78] It also follows that women are domestic, the "home," says Beverly LaHaye in a line that could have come from *Godey's Lady's Book*, being "an extension of the mother's womb."[79] Thus the "natural longing of every woman's heart," state the LaHayes, is "to be a homemaker."[80] Perhaps most important of all, women are dependent. Beverly LaHaye relates this dependency to spirituality: "I think God has given females a spiritual sensitivity— a special gift of discernment or 'woman's intuition' that leads us to seek spiritual truth. Part of this tendency, I think, is our natural inclination toward dependency, whether focused on our husbands or on the Lord."[81]

As for their sexuality, women are seen as responders. Assuming complementarity, the writers maintain that because men are sexually aggressive, women must be, by definition, sexually passive. Men initiate sex, women await their advances. Moreover, while men are assumed to relish sexual activity, women, while able to enjoy it, more often endure it. Men cannot seem to get enough; women are indifferent most of the time. Schlafly sums up: "The Christian woman recognizes the fact that, when it comes to sex, women are simply not the equal of men. The sexual drive of men is stronger than that of women. . . . The other side of the coin is that it is easier for women to control their sexual appetites."[82]

The Problem of Passivity

Nevertheless, in many of these books, female passivity is presented as a problem, at least when passivity crosses the line to become frigidity. In her popular book *The Total Woman*, Marabel Morgan applies her penchant for catchy phrases and cartoonlike characterizations to the issue, describing the conflict between the mismatched imaginary partners "Nellie Not-Tonight" and her husband, "Herman Hot-to-Trot," who signals his sexual frustrations when "he snorts a few times and paws the ground."[83] Although other women's writers show some embarrassment at Morgan's slightly racy characterizations, most agree with her that the combination of male aggression and female passivity can create problems between the sexes. More often than not, they place responsibility for these problems with women. In fact, according to the LaHayes, who base their writings on their experience as sexual counselors, the most common problem in marriages today is "frigid wives."[84]

The books contend that marriages are in trouble, and the reason is the wives. Christian marriages are on this count no exception. Indeed, in the failure of Christian marriages, wives are seen as particularly at fault, since so many are so sexually passive. To some degree the authors are sympathetic, noting that many Christian women are the product of religiously conservative homes where they have been victimized by Victorian sexual standards. Here they point in particular to the insidious influence of the "little old ladies who were self-appointed evangelists of frigidity," who "having never welcomed the experience of sex" felt "dutybound to keep anyone else from enjoying it."[85] At the same time, they see these same women as having unrealistic expectations about marriage. Marabel Morgan describes the problem in *The Total Woman*, where she uses herself as an example, telling of her own highly idealized preconceptions. She writes, "I believed in the all-American Cinderella story; marriage was ruffly curtains at the kitchen window, strawberries for breakfast, and lovin' all the time." Perhaps most troubling of all is the perception that today's wives, Christian or otherwise, do not know how to be wives. For Morgan, the problem boils down to the fact that they do not know what their husbands expect from them. She again cites her own case, describing the night her husband Charlie, a Miami attorney, drove her to the beach to propose marriage, and while he was talking, Morgan, drowsy after a rich dinner, fell asleep in his arms. She takes up the story from there: "I don't know how long I slept but suddenly Charlie's words jolted me back to consciousness. '. . . and that's what I want in a wife,' he was saying. . . . *What* did he want in a wife? I had missed it!"[86]

Sexual Solutions

As a kind of antidote for the maladies besetting modern marriage, these experts on womanhood embrace female sexuality. Best known on this count is Morgan, the Miami housewife whose *Total Woman*, with its ardent advocacy of female sexuality, became not only a best-selling book in the 1970s but also the basis of a network of Total Woman Seminars, four-week courses on femininity that have proven surprisingly popular among religiously conservative wives. Writing not only for Christian conservative women but for all women who have been taught that sex is somehow morally suspect, Morgan attempts to take the stigma out of female sexuality. Advising women to "hang up their hang-ups," she suggests that after preparing themselves for the return of their husbands from work with a late-afternoon bubble bath (Morgan assumes that her readers are married women who do not work outside the home), wives greet them at the door wearing costumes, including revealing lingerie, lace bikinis, and baby-doll pajamas.[87] (Morgan has become best known for the suggestion, which she has denied making, that women greet their husbands at the door wrapped only in Saran Wrap.) From this point, she counsels the couple to proceed to what she calls "super sex," which is to take place in the hallway, under the coffee table, or in more ingenious locations such as "diving boards, trampolines, bales of hay, sleeping bags."[88] Although such sexual shenanigans can be shocking to her often devoutly religious readers, Morgan's purpose is serious: to take sin out of sex. "Sex," she writes, meaning sex within marriage, "is as clean and pure as eating cottage cheese."[89]

Morgan contends that female sexuality saves marriages. Her books *Total Woman* and the sequel *Total Joy* are in fact filled with testimonials, most of which have a strikingly religious quality. Not surprisingly, many of the testimonies come from husbands, including Christian conservatives. For example, in *Total Woman* Morgan tells of the Southern Baptist layman who found himself being greeted at the door by his devout wife, who was wearing "black mesh stockings, high heels, and an apron. That's all. He took one look and shouted, 'Praise the Lord!'"[90] Even more than husbands, however, Morgan reports the support of wives. "Thank you for teaching me something my mom never cared enough to explain," reads a typical letter. "I've had my first orgasm. Every woman should know what I've just learned—and is my husband ever happy, too!"[91] Some of the letters sound like advertisements, with satisfied customers boasting of their self-improvement and commenting on how cheap, fast, and simple it was. "God bless you!" writes one. "My husband and I are both pooped, but so happy and it was so easy!" But many letters are far more serious, containing intimations of marriages saved from the brink of disaster and of lives, almost lost, being found: "As one woman told me, 'What can I say? At last I know who I am and where I'm going. My children no longer flinch when I hug and kiss them. My husband is thrilled and exhausted with sex. I feel like my life has a new beginning.'"[92]

For Morgan, as for all of these writers, the key to marriage lies in the happiness of the husband. Because they are in authority, husbands cannot be expected to change. Morgan tells of her own realization that she could not reform her husband, that "I couldn't change him and that I was silly to keep trying. I could only change *myself*."[93] Searching for answers, going through marriage books, self-improvement courses, psychology texts, and the Bible, she compiles a set of four simple principles which wives are to apply to their husbands: "accept him, admire him, adapt to him, appreciate him." Resolving to put the principles into practice, Morgan is astonished by the results, for she begins to see changes not only in herself, but also in her husband, the befuddled but undeniably happy Charlie, who starts to gain confidence in himself and show more appreciation for her. She writes, "Right before my very eyes, Charlie began to 'come alive.'"[94] Morgan is candid about the therapeutic role of the wife. Assuming that the home is a haven for the harried husband, she advises the wife to greet her husband at the door, not as a conquering hero, but as a battered knight. She writes, "Put your husband's tattered ego back together again at the end of each day."[95] According to Morgan, husbands are psychologically fragile creatures, needing protection. She advises wives, "Out of your own resources of love and stability, you can choose to protect him from his own emotions . . . you can choose to protect your husband." In effect, the husband becomes a client or patient, the wife his "psychotherapist." Morgan elaborates on the psychotherapeutic role: "Coldly diagnose his problem and then treat him warmly."[96]

The Specter of Feminine Power

Nevertheless, Morgan's course in Christian self-improvement is designed to create not only fewer frustrated husbands, but also more satisfied wives. Indeed, it has been pointed out by critics that graduates from her programs benefit handsomely in several ways. For the upper-middle-class Miami matrons who seem to be drawn to Morgan's seminars, the benefits are most often financial. Thus wives testify to their surprise when their husbands show appreciation for their efforts with refrigerator-freezers, new luggage, and trips to island vacation spots. Morgan herself seems to approve, thinking it only natural that a husband will want to show his appreciation for his adaptable wife and "may even want to spoil her with goodies."[97] Even more important, however, is another benefit, less tangible but more potent. For by following Morgan's precepts, wives gain power, the ability to change their husbands, their marriages, and even themselves. Writes Morgan, "I do believe it is possible, however, for almost any wife to have her husband absolutely adore her in just a few weeks' time. . . . It is really up to her. She has the power."[98]

Admittedly, power can be a problem, especially when it is exercised by women, raising the possibility that males are being somehow manipulated. It is surprising that at least a few of the women among these writers admit to an agenda of control. Birdie Yager, for example, the wife of successful entrepreneur Dexter Yager, writes candidly in her own book for women, *The Secret of Living, Is Giving*, about the power of female sexual submission: "The truth is that submission usually turns the man on and makes him vulnerable."[99] Although more refined, Phyllis Schlafly develops a similar theme, suggesting that women can gain power through the exercise of their femininity. Thus she writes that women have more chances for success in a man's world when men "treat her like a lady." Schlafly continues, "The Christian Woman builds her power by using her womanhood, not by denying or suppressing it."[100] Morgan herself seems

313

to admit that admiration and appreciation are at times strategic. Thus she advises that women make their husbands feel stronger by pretending to be unable to open jar lids in the kitchen. Noting that some husbands may become suspicious of their wives' newfound weakness, she cautions, "Don't overdo it. Give him only the jars you really can't handle." [101] In the wake of considerable criticism, Morgan has become sensitive to charges that her work is meant to be manipulative of men. She defends her philosophy in an article published in *Christianity Today* magazine: "It depends upon your motive. . . . If you're giving to get, that's manipulation, and it won't work." [102] Others, like Beverly LaHaye, are more direct in their condemnation of manipulative wives. To appear weak in order to achieve selfish purposes, she writes, is "counterfeit submission." [103]

In truth, however, the books by women writers are less about wives searching for power than about women protecting themselves from their own weakness. All of the authors who are women show some sense of their relative powerlessness. There is, in fact, a specter that haunts these books: the looming threat of husbands abandoning wives. Predictably, the husbands themselves, while considered irresponsible, are not to be blamed. Men, the authors suggest, are only weak. They "go where they are invited," writes Morgan, "and stay where they're well treated." [104] Fault lies not with men, but with women, including those who work outside the home, such as the "dazzling secretaries" who "surround" husbands at work and "emit clouds of perfume." [105] Playing on women's fears, but also trying to assuage deep anxieties, the writers thus encourage women to be suspicious of other women, warning of the danger that their husbands will be seduced by competing females. "Wherever you live," writes Morgan, " 'out there' is some little sexpot, looking wide-eyed at your husband. . . . She's just waiting to get her clutches on *your* man." [106] Ultimately, men have the upper hand. As Morgan explains it, the wife is queen and exercises great power. But the husband is king and has all the authority. She concludes ominously, with a reference that presumably is to Henry VIII: "A queen shall not nag or buck her king's decision after it is decreed. Remember those speedy trials, gals!" [107]

To the women writers in particular, single women pose problems. Assuming that women are meant to be married and mothers, these writers are confused by those who are neither. Not only do they consider single women to be in sexual competition with married women, thereby threatening their marriages, but they also contend that single women can compete with men in the marketplace, threatening the male sense of masculinity. (Both of these arguments are prominent in Schlafly's case against the Equal Rights Amendment.) Nevertheless, at least some of them treat single women with sympathy, apparently assuming them to be objects of pity for their failure to have attracted a man. It is in this spirit that Beverly LaHaye warns single women to avoid competing with men at all costs, since competition leads to the "masculinization" of women, and, she cautions, "few men are attracted to a macho-feminist."[108] Other concerns go deeper into the realm of sexual insecurity. Thus Beverly LaHaye goes on to warn single women about the attractions of lesbianism: "Beware of an improper physical attachment between you and your roommate. Sad to say, this sometimes happens in today's world, especially if one is lonely, overly affectionate, and lacks a sense of security."[109] In fact, there is a presumption that single women are often lesbians. It is for this reason that Beverly LaHaye prefers that widows not be termed "single." She explains: "This puts her in the same category as the lesbian who has chosen a lifestyle of promiscuity and immorality. Dropping the term *widowed* for the more general term *single* adds dignity and acceptance to the homosexual life-style."[110]

The same arguments apply to feminists. In the case of feminism, however, suspicion seems to have deepened into fear and loathing. In all of the books, the criticism is harsh, sometimes vicious. Most extreme is Schlafly's *Power of the Christian Woman*, which is a relentless attack on what she calls "the disease called women's liberation." To Schlafly, feminism is synonymous with sin, and feminists seem to be the cause of all the world's woes. On this point she waxes uncharacteristically theological:

> The woman in the Garden of Eden freely decided to tamper with God's order and ignore His rules. She sought her own self-fulfillment. She decided to do things her way, independent of God's commandment. She even persuaded the man to join her in "liberation" from God's law. Sin thus entered the world, bringing fear, sickness, pain, anger, hatred, danger, violence, and all varieties of ugliness.

Continuing the medical metaphor, Schlafly describes feminists as psychologically unstable, a "handful of female chauvinists" who "get their psychological kicks" by opposing "an alleged oppression that exists only in their distorted minds."[111] Beverly LaHaye is seemingly more sympathetic, attributing feminism to an unhappy upbringing. In *The Restless Woman* she provides capsule case studies of famous feminists like Gloria Steinem and Mary Calderone, linking their activism to alleged mistreatment as children. Betty Friedan, for example, "was victimized by her parents," according to LaHaye. "She had a weak-willed father who failed to exercise his proper authority in the family and a domineering, scheming mother."[112] Jerry Falwell does not beat around the bush: feminists, he says in a characteristically definitive statement, "are prohomosexual and lesbian. In fact, it is shocking how many feminists are lesbians."[113] Still worse, at least to Schlafly, is that feminists are liberals and even socialists. Thus she argues that the Equal Rights Amendment is a veiled attempt to create higher income taxes, government-controlled day-care centers, and "the federalization of all remaining aspects of our life."[114] Feminism, concludes Beverly LaHaye, is "more than an illness": "It is a philosophy of death. At its core in modern times there is a stridently anti-life motivation. Radical feminists are self-destructive and are trying to bring about the death of an entire civilization as well."[115]

Most threatening about feminism is its alarming attractiveness. Wherever these writers look, they see women asserting themselves. A few tend to see the insidious influence of feminism in conspiratorial terms. Falwell, for example, cites retired Brigadier General Andrew J. Gatsis as an expert on the fact that "the top command structure of our military forces, the Pentagon, is saturated with ERA proponents, and under the complete control of avid supporters of the women's liberation movement."[116] Most, however, point to larger social trends. Beverly LaHaye appears to have the cigarette advertisement "You've Come a Long Way, Baby" in mind when she comments on the fact that there has been "an obvious deterioration in the actions and manners of women in general": "Women first developed a new image as glamorous smokers (a profitable boost to cigarette sales in America), then they were seen in bars. Gradually they competitively shared dirty stories and became aggressive sexually."[117] Others point to changes taking place within the home. Schlafly is concerned that many women are abandoning motherhood for work, choosing to have fewer children, or no children at all. She is particularly concerned about the "refusal of young women to have babies." She writes: "Why should a man marry a woman who refuses to be a mother to his children? He can get everything else he wants from women at a price much cheaper than marriage."[118] Then there is the changing role of women within the church. Here Beverly LaHaye speaks out strongly against Christian feminism, which she sees as "one of the greatest dangers facing the Christian church today": "A philosophy based on selfishness, rebellion, and anger should have absolutely no place in our churches. Feminists should not be allowed to infect Christian women with their alien ideologies, which are based in large measure on Marxist and humanist teachings."[119] While Beverly LaHaye seems to see the problem mostly in mainline denominations, her husband, Tim, referring to surveys taken in his Bible class, finds it in his own fundamentalist church. "The refusal of many Christian wives to accept the principle of subjection," he laments, "is increasingly common today."[120]

All agree on the antidote: submission. Virtually every one of the books on women cites St. Paul on the responsibility of wives to submit. "The Scripture teaches in Ephesians 5:22–23," Stanley preaches, invoking the verse cited most frequently by the writers, "that the husband is to be the head of the wife and the wife is to be in subjection to her husband." [121] Numerous other verses which express similar sentiments are used as well (Morgan's *Total Woman* includes an appendix listing thirty-nine of them). Repeatedly wives are urged to be "totally submissive." [122] Husbands are to be not only admired and accepted, but also obeyed, apparently without any questions asked. If wives disagree, they are told to disagree silently, since, according to Beverly LaHaye, women should have "a consistently quiet spirit." [123] The books are quite explicit, telling women to "watch their tongues" and instructing them that one role of the wife is to "keep her mouth shut." [124] Furthermore, the wife must go well beyond silent subservience, taking positive steps to serve her husband, making "his happiness her primary goal." [125] In fact, to be truly happy, the wife must see herself as an extension of her husband, giving up her own identity to become a part of his: "You can live fully," concludes Beverly LaHaye, "by dying to yourself and submitting to your husband." [126]

In this antifeminist social theory, submission is the rule, and few if any exceptions are allowed. Following the injunctions of Paul, the authors make it clear that Christian wives are to be submissive to husbands who are not themselves believers. Indeed, Beverly LaHaye instructs wives of unsaved husbands to be "extremely careful that you are obedient and respectful." [127] Through their submission, women can become agents of evangelism, placing their recalcitrant husbands on the road to salvation. Tim LaHaye gives an example of the process, describing a "case" from his own "counseling file":

> But when Sara accepted Christ as her Lord and Savior in my office that day, she canceled their divorce proceedings and went home to become a loving, submissive, gracious wife. . . . Within ten weeks Sam also came to a saving knowledge of Christ, and they have enjoyed a compatible relationship for many years.[128]

Somewhat more surprising is that the authors argue that women must obey bad husbands, including even those who abuse them. Charles Stanley seems to have had some experience in this area through his work as a pastoral counselor: "Anytime there is a threat of physical abuse from a husband, I do not hesitate to recommend separation for a time. But I would never recommend that a wife take over the household while her husband is still at home. To do so is to assume a role God never intended for her to fulfill."[129] Considering divorce to be unacceptable, an option to be exercised only in the most extreme of cases, Stanley suggests that women remain committed to even the most troubled of marriages. Recalling the case of a child abused by his stepfather, Stanley points admiringly to the fact that the mother, while herself also being abused, did not divorce the man. Divorce, it seems, would have been even worse. He writes: "Mom, I know it can be tough. But for the sake of your children, submit to your husband. Your obedience in this matter may be their only hope for a healthy childhood."[130] "Even in terrible home situations," adds Anita Bryant, who advises prayer, "there still can be hope."[131]

Nevertheless, it is significant that the antifeminists themselves admit to ambivalence about submission, describing it as both natural and highly unnatural. Women, they argue, are programmed to submit; psychosexually, they are predisposed to surrender. Hence submission comes naturally to them. Tim LaHaye explains: "God would not have commanded a woman to submit unless He had instilled in her a psychic mechanism which would find it comfortable to do so."[132] At the same time, they are realistic enough to admit that submission is often far from easy. Stanley, as is his inclination, traces the problem to Genesis. He writes that "as a result of the Fall there is within every wife a natural resistance to the authority of her husband."[133] Tim LaHaye allows that submission may "take practice."[134] In fact, he concedes that it is "so unnatural" that it "can only be ours through the filling of the Holy Spirit."[135] Nevertheless, submission remains the rule for the wife: "Whether she likes it or not," concludes LaHaye, "subjection is a command of God and her refusal to comply with this command is an act of disobedience."[136]

In the same way that men writers recognize certain contradictions in the male role, the women writers find themselves in the profoundly paradoxical position of asserting themselves by sacrificing themselves. Here their arguments are sophisticated, as they denounce feminism as a form of self-interest, and liberalism, with its emphasis on individual rights, as a philosophy of selfishness. Rights, they contend, have taken the place of responsibilities, leading to a situation of alienated anarchy in which "each of us individually persists in carving out his own personal set of rules, his own so-called rights."[137] Thus they call for a reinfusion of virtue, a turning from rights to responsibilities. The call, however, is gender-specific: while men are assumed to be largely self-interested, presumably a product of their role in the marketplace, women are asked to embrace an ethic of self-sacrifice. Beverly LaHaye considers it a matter of reeducating women to an ethic of sacrifice. She describes her own resentment, beginning shortly after her marriage, at the fact that her husband, Tim, insisted on leaving his socks rolled up in little balls by the side of the bed. On consideration, however, she realized that her resentment was selfish and that by failing to pick up her husband's socks she was refusing to play her proper role as a wife, which was to serve others. With this amended attitude she was able to carry out her responsibilities with a sense of purpose, which was in her case a higher spiritual purpose: "I wasn't just picking up dirty socks for my husband; I was serving the Lord Jesus by doing this, so I had to do it heartily as unto Him." [138] Beverly LaHaye finds comfort in viewing her self-sacrifice in these theological terms. Compared to eternity, she writes, "female equality and personal rights seem trivial and insignificant." [139]

At the same time, the women writers compound the paradox, arguing that submission can serve as a way for women to achieve a sense of self-worth. In essence, they see sacrifice as a means to self-assertion. Morgan, who draws with equal ease on St. Paul and Norman Vincent Peale, is most forthcoming about the individualistic implications of her work. Counseling women to use whatever means they can—including cosmetic surgery—to improve themselves, she advises that in order for their husbands to love them, they must love themselves. "Be true to yourself and be yourself," she writes, sounding suspiciously like an advocate for the "me" generation. "You are a great person to be!" [140]

Through sacrifice, women are able to build their own identities, ironically independent of the approval of men. In finding models of femininity, the women writers seek out some surprisingly assertive women. Beverly LaHaye is predictably most conventional, embracing examples like Margaret Prior, the first missionary of the New York Female Moral Reform Society, Frances Willard, founder of the Women's Christian Temperance Union, and Catherine Beecher, an early advocate of what would come to be called "home economics." [141] Phyllis Schlafly is much more militant, in her own way, citing heroines such as Joan of Arc and Queen Brigitte of Scandinavia, a "Viking warrior who became a Christian heroine." [142] Anita Bryant admits to styling herself after the biblical Deborah, a singer, prophetess, and military leader "who was responsible for bringing the people back to God." [143] Indeed, an even more ironic twist is that many of the women writers find in their femininity a sense of solidarity with other women, or at least with other women like themselves. Thus, writes Beverly LaHaye, it is up to Christian conservative women to "save our society," transmitting "civilization and humanity to the 21st century." She concludes on an almost defiant note: "Make no mistake. It is the women who will do it." [144]

Nevertheless, submission can prove problematic, even for the most committed of these women. Some of them, such as Schlafly, appear to thrive on it. At least in her own life she seems to have found a mutually agreeable relationship with her husband, Fred, a St. Louis attorney. She writes, apparently autobiographically: "A Christian Man is delighted to have his wife pursue her talents and spend her time however she pleases. The more she achieves, the prouder he is—*so long* as he knows that he is Number One in her life, and that she needs him."[145] Others have not been so fortunate. More realistic is Morgan, who admits in her *Total Joy* that her marriage, while happy, is a challenge and a struggle, and that "tomorrow, the bottom may fall out and all our efforts may seemingly go down the drain."[146] Bryant's story is sadder. Her marriage collapsing, Bryant blames not only her husband for his failure to act authoritatively, but also herself for her unwillingness to submit to him. She writes of her remorse in the wake of one particularly painful confrontation: "I felt terrible. I realized it all was of my own doing. I had not had the right spirit with Bob to begin with. I wasn't letting him make decisions. I wasn't upholding him as head of our household. I felt about half an inch high. . . . I asked Bob to forgive me."[147]

Moreover, in addition to blaming herself, Bryant blames others. Her marriage troubled and her family life failing, she strikes out against external enemies in a widely reported campaign to defeat a homosexual rights ordinance in Dade County, Florida. The campaign itself is filled with irony. While Bryant seeks to protect her marriage and family from an external sexual threat—specifically, that of men who do not act like men—she discovers in the course of the campaign that the more real threat is internal, for she becomes increasingly resentful of her husband and the Christian conservative men like him who refuse to take a leading role in the movement—men, ironically, who will not act like men. At one point she breaks down, blurting out her frustrations from the pulpit at a Sunday morning church service: "But where are the men?"[148]

Blaming others, however, like blaming oneself, does not provide solutions. The campaign over, the marriage collapses into continuing mutual recrimination. While Green withdraws, Bryant is driven to depression and the verge of suicide before she can admit to herself that the principle of patriarchy on which her marriage was based has been destructive to both her husband and herself. She writes, "I felt like a caged animal, smothered, stymied, and I see that he was miserable, too."[149] Following a particularly painful divorce, she writes with bitterness about the mistaken assumptions of her marriage and predicts similar problems for others who rely on the same patriarchal presuppositions: "Fundamentalists have their head in the sand. . . . Some pastors are so hard-nosed about submission and insensitive to their wives' needs that they don't recognize the frustration—even hatred—within their own households. Some of them are going to be shocked to wind up in my boat." [150]

Admittedly, Bryant is an exception. Within their own marriages, most Christian conservative wives accept the role of submission and self-sacrifice and many accept it willingly. The books by women writers end on a note of resignation. Maintaining a marriage can be costly, requiring much in the way of commitment and effort. In the end, it is a price that the women more often must pay. "Don't be afraid," concludes Beverly LaHaye, "to give and give and give." [151]

Children: Obedience and the Problem of Self-Perpetuation

Christian conservatives are fearful about the future of the family. In terms that recall the earliest American Protestants, they see the family as a little commonwealth, the foundation on which all of society stands. Moreover, they tend to idealize the family, describing it in the sentimental terms of Victorian middle-class morality as a haven in an otherwise heartless world. Their books, like Anita Bryant's *Bless This House*, are suffused with domestic sentimentality, including snapshots of children with Easter baskets and recipes for Grandma Berry's "chocolate toes." [152] At the same time, however, many of them look back on their own childhoods with some pain, such as Tammy Bakker recalling her mother sponging the blood from her brothers' backs after the beatings administered by their stepfather. [153] Perhaps because of the ambiguity of their own memories, they seem to place even more importance on the family, for better and worse. As Shirley and Pat Boone put it, "As wonderful an institution as the family is, it can also be the place where people are everlastingly warped and doomed." [154]

The Character of Children

Theologically, religious conservatives see the character of children as being dominated by sin. In contrast to most mainline Christians, and even to some other evangelicals, they tend to say little about the idea of original innocence. Instead, they look on their children skeptically, almost fearfully, as inheritors of original sin. Beverly LaHaye sees this sin as being passed through the mother. Thus she writes in her *How to Develop*

Your Child's Temperament, one of the most popular of the books on child-rearing: "My mother who conceived me was sinful, not living in sin, but born with sin; therefore, I was born with a sinful nature also." Almost as soon as they are born, children manifest their sinful natures in willfulness, obstinacy, and uncooperativeness. Writing in terms that echo Augustine's *Confessions,* LaHaye describes the infant as a tiny tyrant. "He is born with very selfish desires and thinks only of his own wants," she writes. "When denied his wants, he reacts with rage and fits of anger." Resigning herself to the reality of sin, LaHaye advises parents to consider their children as fallen souls. She writes, "It is of great benefit to the parent when he realizes that it is natural for his child to have a desire for evil." [155]

At the same time, the books about child-rearing argue that children are capable of goodness. Although the pull of sin is strong, children can overcome it through the exercise of will, avoiding evil and choosing good. The choice, however, is conscious, and children must be taught, or trained, to control their instinctual selves. Moreover, they must be taught early, before biological and hormonal changes make control impossible. Beverly LaHaye explains:

> There is great danger ahead for the child that is allowed to just grow up without any training or discipline, and there will be great sorrow and heartache ahead for the parents of such a child. Every child has the potential of becoming a delinquent and a criminal when he is left to his own ways without instruction and correction.

Implicit in the argument is a conception of biology as dangerous and potentially destructive. Explicit is a clear call for control. Parents, explains LaHaye, must "bring their children into subjection." Furthermore, they must begin to bring them under control early, while children remain controllable. "The training must be done while they are young, tender, and still trainable," LaHaye concludes, "because children won't wait." [156]

As to psychology, these books describe children in developmental terms, as having temperaments that must be shaped by training. Many of the authors are acutely interested in child psychology, and some, like Tim LaHaye, who boasts that "family is my business," consider themselves to be child development professionals. Citing her husband as an academic authority (he taught a course in the Biblical Psychology Department at Christian Heritage College, where he also served as chancellor), Beverly LaHaye develops an updated version of Aristotelian temperament theory in which she categorizes characters into four main personality types (sanguine, choleric, phlegmatic, and melancholic). Assuming that each of these temperaments have certain strengths and weaknesses, she argues that each must be developed, or pointed in positive directions, through a process of training that her husband calls "growing a child." [157] Crucial in this training process are the first eight years, for Beverly LaHaye explains that 80 percent of the child's "intellectual and character capacities" are "already determined by the age of eight." Thus the daunting task of shaping the child's temperament falls to parents, who are described by these writers as bearing almost total responsibility for their child's character. Says Beverly LaHaye: "Too few parents seem to comprehend the tremendous impact their teaching or negligence has during the first eight years of their children's lives." [158]

Character must be developed early, prior to the point at which children discover their sexuality. By intervening at an early age, parents can achieve some control over their children. If they wait too long, however, they lose all hope of influencing them, for once children reach the stage of teenage sexuality, they become creatures of passion. In fact, they become extreme examples of sexual passion, captives, in the words of Tim LaHaye, of "the highs and lows of libido." Young males in particular are described as having all of the aggressiveness of the male role, in extremis. Easily aroused, emotionally inexperienced, they seem unable to exercise sexual self-control. The teenage boy, says LaHaye, is "powerless to control his sex drive after it has been brought to a peak." Young women must be forewarned, and they should know in particular, LaHaye goes on, that they "can inadvertently arouse a boy simply by bumping or rubbing against him." Nor are teenage girls totally innocent. Although different, their sexuality is itself at times uncontrollable. Especially during estrus, LaHaye states, "a young woman's emotions are highly combustible." [159] Moreover, teenage girls are seductive creatures, who consciously or unconsciously assert their sexuality by making use of their feminine charms. Beverly LaHaye is particularly interested in alerting teenage girls to their own seductiveness. She writes reprovingly:

> I have seen lovely girls conduct themselves in such a manner that they turn fellows on and cause them to have problems with lust and evil thoughts. One charming young lady was walking out of church with her hand in her date's arm and was very carelessly allowing her breast to rub against the boy.[160]

When brought together, male aggressiveness and female receptivity combine into a potent mixture. Says LaHaye, "An explosion is inevitable." [161]

Thus parents must control their children by training them, and children must be taught that they have an obligation to obey. In defining the respective roles of parents and children, the authors of these books rely on Scripture. Admitting that the Bible says relatively little about the relationship between the parent and the child, emphasizing instead that between husband and wife, they refer to it repeatedly anyway, using it as a kind of manual for parents and a rule book for children.[162] In addressing adults, they cite most frequently Proverbs 22:6: "Train up a child in the way he should go: and when he is old, he will not depart from it."[163] To the children, they recall Colossians 3:20: "Children, obey your parents in all things, for this is well pleasing to the Lord."[164] Other verses are applied to more specific audiences. For example, addressing teenage girls in her *Spirit-Controlled Woman*, Beverly LaHaye uses 2 Corinthians 6:14 ("Be ye not unequally yoked together with unbelievers") to advise them that the Bible provides practical rules for social relationships: "God," she tells young readers with assurance, "has definite ideas on dating."[165] Still more verses are contributed by other writers, including the aptly named David Jeremiah, a protégé of the LaHayes, who in his *Before It's Too Late* lists no less than 161 separate biblical entries dealing with family that range from Genesis to 1 Peter and cover topics from adultery to widowhood.[166] Finally, for those who are less ambitious in their biblical scholarship, there is always the fifth commandment. "The Bible clearly states," says Beverly LaHaye, "'Honor thy father and mother.'"[167]

Failing Families

According to the authors of these books, the contemporary family has failed in carrying out its critical role of child-rearing. Particularly troubling is the failure of their own Christian conservative families. Continuing a theme that has dominated conservative evangelical thinking in the postwar period, they lament the prevalence of divorce among Christian couples. In fact, says LaHaye in his *Battle for the Family*, "a startling number of veteran Christians are choosing divorce as a solution to marital difficulties."[168] Predictably, Christian children are also paying the price for family failure, most often in sexual experimentation. Few themes trouble religious conservatives so deeply. For while they expect children from secular families to be active sexually, they are taken aback by the sexuality of children from their own homes. Writes LaHaye, "Most parents, ministers, and Christian school officials would be amazed at the sexual activity of youth coming from Christian homes."[169] Indeed, although aware of the irony, a few of them go so far as to suggest that their own children are more active sexually than others in their cohort. "I have learned from girls," reports LaHaye, drawing on his counseling experience, "that many Christian boys can't be trusted as much as some of the other boys."[170] In any case, the writers warn that even the best of Christian conservative families are failing, and the consequences are disastrous. Says Shirley Boone: "So many *ministers* today are seeing their own homes and marriages break up, and the homes and marriages of their church leaders. Their kids are becoming homosexuals and drug addicts, running away from home and living promiscuously with first one person, then another."[171]

Christian families are not alone; the authors present their own domestic difficulties as symptomatic of larger social stresses. Throughout American society, the differences between parents and their children have widened, becoming an unbridgeable generation gap. They discuss the trend in historical terms, pointing to changes appearing first in the postwar period. According to Dr. James Dobson, an Arcadia, California, pediatrician and psychologist whose books on child-rearing have proven to be enormously popular among Christian conservative parents, Americans began to lose control of their children in the 1950s, with the coming of what he calls a theory of "permissive democracy." Apparently blaming thinkers such as Dr. Benjamin Spock, Dobson faults liberal models of child-rearing for their "overindulgence, permissiveness, and smother-love." By applying such theories, he contends, parents lost control over their children, creating a generation that "has grown up to challenge every form of authority that confronts it."[172] The authors trace out the social ramifications of this permissiveness in the 1960s, which they tend to describe as a decade of rock music, sexual experimentation, and opposition to the Vietnam War.[173] In the 1970s and 1980s the trends continued, so that today more than ever, observes the Reverend Charles Stanley, children are being shaped by a corrupt culture: "From rock music stars to political cheats, these people are influencing life-styles and making decisions that affect us all."[174]

Admittedly, these critics are predisposed to be hard on contemporary society. Their lamentations have a timeless quality, complete with calls for a return to some lost paradise in the past. "Where are the days," wonders Beverly LaHaye, "when children were taught respect and answered, 'Yes, sir' or 'No, sir'? Instead, today answers are usually 'Uh-uh' or 'Unhunh,' if you are lucky."[175] There is, however, a sense of urgency in these contemporary jeremiads, with the writers making it clear that the decline is steepening, that families are failing faster all the time, and that if something drastic is not done, children will become foreigners to their parents. Moreover, their own Christian children, far from secure, seem to be most at risk. Observes Stanley, "Unless we retrain our children in some areas and protectively train them in others, they are going to break our hearts."[176]

The authors of these books portray themselves as cultural defenders, protecting the family from any number of insidious enemies. For some, the conflict seems positively conspiratorial, with the family coming under concerted attack from forces dedicated to the cause of secular humanism. In *Battle for the Family*, LaHaye describes the small but committed cadre of secular humanists who make use of their control of "such centers as government, public schools, TV, and pornographic-literature sources" to disseminate a system of thought that is "anti-God, anti-moral, anti-self-restraint, and anti-American," and who are ultimately "determined to destroy the family." [177] While more circumspect in their claims about conspiracy, others see similar enemies. Onalee McGraw, a New Right conservative whose espousal of family causes has won wide support among Christian conservatives, considers the family to be under attack by the "new class," an "unholy alliance" of "liberal politicians" and "government interventionist helping professionals." [178] Jerry Falwell points to efforts by the Internal Revenue Service, the Department of Education, and the Department of Health, Education, and Welfare as proof that the most sustained threat to the family has come from the state itself, from "our own government." Almost always, the specter of communism seems to be present, vying for control of America's children. Falwell continues: "Communists believe in taking children away from the family and raising them separately so they can indoctrinate them with government loyalty. How I fear this will happen to our own children." [179]

In the forefront of the assault on the family are the public schools, which the writers describe as being in a state of moral decline. Describing their own childhoods, they look back longingly to simpler, more moral schools. Falwell, for example, recalling the years he spent at Mountain View Elementary School in Lynchburg, Virginia, emphasizes the prominent place of religion: "Every week we attended chapel. Someone would read the Bible to all of the students and we would have prayer and sing hymns. We were taught to reverence God, the Bible, and prayer." Today's public school system provides a rude contrast. Pointing in particular to Supreme Court decisions limiting prayer in the public schools, Falwell describes the present system as "permeated with humanism." [180] Beverly LaHaye, a staunch advocate of Christian schooling, goes further: "The public school has turned into a zoo today. Drugs, immorality, pornography, violence, and in some places witchcraft, have replaced what once was a great educational system." [181] Phyllis Schlafly, a Christian conservative comrade-in-arms who attended private Catholic schools, seems never to have put much faith in public ones. But she is concerned about the character of colleges and universities, which she considers to be "citadels of atheism" and "training grounds for criminals."[182] Although a few of these thinkers believe that children can endure public school education, most believe the schools to be irredeemable. Thus Beverly LaHaye advises Christian conservative parents to send their children to Christian schools or to educate them at home. She concludes, "Too many children have been lovingly led to Christ at their parent's knee and then thrown to the destruction of the public school system."[183]

Much of the suspicion of the public schools centers on the issue of sex education. For the last twenty years, says LaHaye in his *Sex Education for the Family*, at the urging of "atheists" and "evolutionists" such as those in SIECUS (Sex Information and Educational Council of the United States) and Planned Parenthood, along with the "self-styled sexologists" who create courses in sex education, America's schools have begun to instruct schoolchildren in what he calls "the art of intercourse." The result, he says, has been a "moral holocaust," a "wave of promiscuity, teenage pregnancies, and venereal disease." According to LaHaye, sex education is a family matter, for several reasons. Perhaps most important, LaHaye considers sexuality to be "an intensely private subject." There is, he writes, a "natural reserve between the sexes." Females in particular experience a "certain feminine mystique or modesty" that is "broken down when thirty high schoolers . . . study this subject together." Moreover, even admitting that some sexual information must be taught, preferably in the context of biology and hygiene courses, LaHaye believes that such subjects should be treated in sex-segregated classes lest they serve as an invitation to sexual experimentation. The teaching of sexuality in mixed classes, especially to "hot-blooded teenagers," he writes, is like "pouring gasoline on emotional fires." Above all, LaHaye prefers that any discussion of sex take place within marriage. Pointing to the sex manual he has written with his wife, he contends that most people can be taught "all the basic ingredients in two or three hours just prior to marriage." By contrast, sex education outside of marriage can only lead to sexual experimentation, or even worse, "to an obsession."[184]

Yet the problem goes well beyond the schools. As described in these books, which are graphic and sometimes lurid, America is teeming with sexual deviance. Infiltrating the home, attacking the family with its insidious and pervasive influence, deviant sexuality appears to be all but unstoppable. Most acute is the problem of pornography, which is, according to LaHaye, "the single most inflammatory force for evil in our society."[185] The authors define pornography broadly, including not only magazines and movies but also sexually suggestive material of every kind, including sex education manuals and some biology textbooks, and they see it as having epidemic effects. David Jeremiah considers it to be the chief contributor to child abuse, rape, and (he cites J. Edgar Hoover) crime of all kinds.[186] Falwell finds its influence in adultery, divorce, homosexuality, and the spread of massage parlors.[187] LaHaye claims that "fully two-thirds of the sexual problems in marriage today can be traced to the use of pornography." Especially disturbing are the effects on teenagers, who seem to be almost helpless in its grasp. Thus he tells of the sixteen-year-old Christian girl who, unsuspecting, went with her boyfriend to the home of one of his friends: "The boy distributed his father's *Playboy* magazines, and they all began reading them until they got so worked up that they stripped off their clothes and performed sexual acts in front of each other."[188] Boys in particular are warned to avoid being tempted by pornography. Explains LaHaye, "Nice girls are repulsed by porn users."[189] Even so, no one is immune. Jeremiah offers an example: "Recently, I learned of a gospel minister who attended late-night pornographic films until he was discovered by one of his parishioners who had also fallen into the sin of an unclean mind."[190]

In protecting their children, parents must fight on every front. Movies offer a steady outpouring of sex and violence. Television is even worse; controlled, according to LaHaye, by "humanistic perverts" and "hedonists," it serves up a constantly changing scene of steamy soap operas, sexually titillating talk shows, and foul-mouthed comedians. Rock music surrounds children with a beat that is "capable of destroying the emotions or at least inflaming the fleshly lusts."[191] Even seemingly harmless sexuality takes its toll. Thus Beverly LaHaye opposes "Barbie" and "Ken" dolls, "complete with sex organs," because they "encourage little girls to think of themselves as sex partners instead of mothers."[192] Sometimes the unwitting parents themselves are at fault, as when they allow their children to see them naked. Says LaHaye, "What usually happens is that the child becomes morbidly obsessed with sexual matters and may develop voyeuristic tendencies or begin fantasizing about having sexual relations with his or her parent."[193]

Of all social specters, however, the most terrifying to the Christian conservatives is homosexuality. In and of itself, homosexuality is an abomination to them. The Texas evangelist James Robison, who has won notoriety for his radio attacks on homosexuals, sums up the opinion of these writers: "It is perversion of the highest order. It is against God, against God's Word, against society, against nature. It is almost too repulsive to imagine and describe. It is filth."[194] Many of the writers assert that they have nothing against homosexuals as individuals, being prepared to love them and pray for their salvation. What they oppose vigorously, however, are public statements of homosexuality. Anita Bryant, explaining her opposition to the Dade County gay rights ordinance, describes the difference between homosexuals and "known practicing homosexuals": "Homosexuals do not suffer discrimination when they keep their perversions in the privacy of their homes . . . so long as they do not flaunt their homosexuality and try to establish role models for the impressionable young people—our children." [195]

Among these writers there is unanimous agreement that homosexuals pose a threat to children. Sometimes the threat is subtle, as Tim LaHaye explains, alerting mothers that a "large percentage" of their children's clothes are designed by homosexuals in the clothing industry. [196] More often, the threat is anything but subtle. Warning of "homosexual exploitation," Falwell asks, "Why must they prey upon our young?" [197] Although not said in so many words, there seems to be concern that homosexuals present an appealing, or at least an enticing alternative. As the LaHayes put it, "Every homosexual is potentially an evangelist of homosexuality, capable of perverting many young people to his sinful way of life." [198] Most terrifying of all, however, is that homosexuals are being created all the time, the product of failed families, of weak-willed fathers and overly dominant mothers. Homosexuals, says LaHaye, are not "born that way"; they are led to homosexuality "unintentionally by the influence of one or both parents." [199]

Daring to Discipline

Such passages point to the deepest source of the fears about the family that are so pervasive in the New Christian Right. Society notwithstanding, it is parents who are ultimately responsible for the behavior of their children, and it is parents who are failing to rear responsible children. On this point the defenders of the family draw heavily on the writings of James Dobson, whose books criticizing permissive child-rearing describe in sometimes gruesome detail how parents, in failing to control their children, have made them uncontrollable. In *Dare to Discipline*, his most popular book, he tells the story of a teenage girl, reared permissively, who strikes her mother down in an argument and leaves her in a pool of blood in the bathroom, while she herself proceeds to the backyard to dance with friends. [200] Another of his books, entitled *Hide or Seek*, includes even more sensational accounts based on case studies of famous criminals, all presumably raised permissively, such as Gary

Gilmore, Charles Manson, David ("Son of Sam") Berkowitz, Lee Harvey Oswald, and others. Nevertheless, in both of these books Dobson argues that the most tragic outcome of permissiveness is not rebellion but weakness. For permissiveness is the chief contributor to a larger social problem, the absence of self-esteem, what Dobson calls America's "epidemic of self-doubt."[201]

In shoring up the character of their children, Christian conservatives turn to the tried and true remedy of discipline. Parents are to act as authorities, setting boundaries and rules. Children are to be controlled. Even more important, they are to be taught self-control, showing respect and self-sustaining obedience toward their parents. When children do not obey, they must be punished, and small children in particular should be punished corporally, with spankings. Early punishment is especially important, for attitudes toward authority are strongly shaped from ages two to four, and as a result, parents who do not achieve control over their children at this time may never be able to control them. Dobson explains:

> You have drawn the line in the dirt, and the child has deliberately flopped his big hairy toe across it. Who is going to win? Who has the most courage? Who is in charge here? If you do not answer these questions conclusively for the child, he will precipitate other battles designed to ask them again and again.[202]

Dobson is adamant that authority must be asserted early, or else. Fueling the fears of parents, he tells of tiny tots who were not spanked when they spit in their parents' faces, and who, as an inevitable result, became teenage tyrants: "When a parent loses the early confrontations with the child, the later conflicts become harder to win. The parent who never wins, who is too weak or too tired or too busy to win, is making a costly mistake that will come back to haunt him during the child's adolescence." Thus parents of toddlers must be constantly vigilant, remaining ready to discipline at any appropriate point. In time, their vigilance pays off, with their children learning lifelong lessons of control. Although parents benefit, it is children who gain the most from early punishment. Indeed, says Dobson, children prefer that their parents punish them. "It is the ultimate paradox of childhood," he writes, "that a youngster wants to be controlled, but he insists that his parents earn the right to control him."[203]

It follows that spanking plays a particularly important part in Christian conservative child-rearing. All of the authors of the books on children advocate it. Many seem to recall with some sentimentality the beatings they received as children. Dobson himself describes beatings with belts, shoes, and, on one memorable occasion, his mother's girdle, complete with "a multitude of straps and buckles."[204] Nostalgia notwithstanding, Dobson is cautious in advocating corporal punishment. Children should be spanked only in response to acts of defiance—in effect, only when they question the authority of their parents. Counseling parents to save spankings for particularly antagonistic occasions, Dobson tells them that most of the time "a firm thump on the head or a rap on the fingers will convey the same message just as convincingly."[205] Others disagree; aware of the potential for child abuse, and sensitive to charges made on this count against Christian conservative school administrators, teachers, and parents, LaHaye strictly advises that children never be struck on the face or head, but always on the buttocks, which he calls a "well-cushioned seat of learning."[206] (Fearing lest children be stuck in anger, Beverly LaHaye suggests that parents not spank with the hand, but use instead a paddle—a biblical "rod"—or other instrument. One advantage is that while the child retrieves the paddle, the parent can cool his or her anger. The LaHayes themselves use a large wooden spoon for this purpose.)[207] Spankings should be administered only when the parent is in complete control, never in rage. As soon as the spanking is administered, the parent should embrace the child, making it clear that the punishment is an act of love, what Beverly LaHaye calls "a special kind of love."[208] She explains:

> A wrong spanking would be a cruel, sadistic beating that is given in rage. . . . A right spanking is given with a sound, positive approach. . . . It should be given with a "rod" of correction and much love. One father had a paddle made with these words inscribed: "To my son with love."[209]

Following patriarchal principles, fathers should spank, the mother acting, according to Beverly LaHaye, as "the assistant," and also being able to "fill in when the father is absent."[210] While not sadistic, spankings should be sound, "of sufficient magnitude to cause the child to cry genuinely." Above all, parents should enter into the spanking with some enthusiasm and should never "dread or shrink back from these confrontations with the child." Spankings, concludes Dobson, "should be anticipated as important events."[211]

Indoctrinating, Insulating, Instilling Self-Control

In contrast to the anxious early years, the preteen period, the time approximately from four to twelve, seems considerably calmer. On the whole, the books suggest that during this period issues of control recede, with the child becoming less willful and more pliable. As a result, they depict this stage as most suited to formal learning, a time for children to be "indoctrinated."[212] In discussing ways to educate their children, the authors show a certain amount of ambivalence. Perhaps because many of them look back on this time in their own lives as not particularly happy, largely because of the restrictiveness of their parents, they express some reticence about an excessive reliance on rules. Although certain moral principles do have to be learned, preferably early in this period, the writers argue that learning should be experiential rather than rote. Ironically, the model seems to be a kind of conservative Deweyism, as seen in Beverly LaHaye's advice to parents on how to teach proper sex roles:

> Involve little boys with father's companionship and little girls with mother's. Dad and son can go to the ball game or work on the car. Mother and daughter can work together to develop skills in sewing and cooking. This type of interrelationship must be worked on; it does not just happen.[213]

It is interesting to note that the books allow for at least a few—albeit carefully crafted—lessons in sexuality during the prepubescent period. Admittedly, they are characteristically circumspect in describing these lessons, which LaHaye suggests might center on discussions of how animals reproduce. Nevertheless, they do advocate some discussion, if only as "a matter of self-defense."[214] But most important of all the lessons learned during the preteen period are the biblical and theological ones. Children of this age are seen as malleable creatures spiritually. If they do nothing else, parents will succeed as parents if they bring their children to salvation sometime during these years. Warns LaHaye, "older children should be an increasing object of prayerful concern by their parents, if they have not received Christ before their twelfth birthday."[215]

The teen years are something else again, reintroducing all of the anxieties about authority and control, but now in an atmosphere of highly charged sexuality. On the whole, these experts on the family do not seem to know what to do with teens. Assuming that children who have learned their lessons well in the early years will become responsible youths, and that those who did not learn their lessons will be wastrels, they seem resigned to doing little. At best, parents can try to protect their teens, shielding them from temptation. Thus the authors call on parents to choose carefully the books, movies, and television programs that their children watch. Most also advise that they choose their children's friends, limiting them to children from Christian families, or at least screening friends for Christian values. "One of the biggest mistakes Christian parents make," counsels LaHaye, "is to let teenagers select their own friends."[216] In addition, almost all of the books include long lists of rules, with even the most rule-wary writers drawing up pages of "don'ts" on dating.[217] Although the rules are relatively restrictive, the writers point out that they are far more liberal than those they themselves were forced to follow as youths. While determined to protect their children, they seem resigned to the fact that sometimes compromises must be made. As Pat Boone puts it, the challenge is to rear children so that they will be focused on God "without making them 'sticks-in-the-mud' or fanatics or weirdos."[218]

When it comes to sexual experimentation, however, there is no room for compromise. Teenagers must be made aware of the dangers of sexual arousal. On this point boys receive less attention than girls, the writers taking the attitude that boys are less able to control themselves sexually— that boys, in effect, will be boys. Although LaHaye does remind boys of their responsibilities, his advice is phrased in Victorian terms that stress male prerogatives rather than female rights: "Dating is a sacred trust. You bear responsibility for another man's most treasured possession." Indeed, even in extreme cases, boys get off easy:

> Many "friendship rapes" are caused by boys who get overheated, lose control of their lust, and use their superior force to overpower a girl. The fact that she never intended it to "go all the way" does not lessen the fact that she . . . is partially responsible for the unpleasant situation.[219]

Girls, on the other hand, bear the burdens of sexuality. Applying female sexual stereotypes, the family writers assume that just as women are either temptresses or model mothers, girls are also either bad or good, loose or moral. "Promiscuous girls," LaHaye elaborates, "are only popular for sex, whereas virtuous girls are admired for themselves." In either case, girls must know that the responsibility for any and all sexual activity is borne squarely on their shoulders. As LaHaye explains, "Her body can be a symbol of femininity that ennobles men or a symbol of lust that inflames and causes them to stumble spiritually." Good Christian girls are no exception. In fact, they must be especially careful, because, LaHaye says, "it is usually the nice girls who get pregnant. Naughty girls on dates usually take steps to avoid pregnancy." Furthermore, Christian girls bear a greater stigma if they become pregnant before marriage, and apparently rightly so, for "once a girl violates her virtue, she loses self-respect."[220] In any case, parents must do everything possible to prevent their daughter from practicing premarital sex. At all costs, advises LaHaye, she must be encouraged to "save the flower of her sexuality for marriage."[221]

Assuming that they have taken all the proper steps, parents can rest more easily once the teen years have come to a close. Having controlled their children's development for eighteen or so years, they can begin to withdraw, leaving them to live their own lives. The authors advise parents to remain available, counseling their children on crucial decisions such as the choice of a college—Christian colleges are strongly preferred— or of a vocation. In general, however, while recognizing that the process can be painful, they call on parents to begin to let go, forfeiting control over the day-to-day decisions that govern their children's lives. Says Dobson, "Then we must take our hands off and trust in divine leadership to influence the outcome."[222]

Yet as their children enter adulthood, these parents seem far from confident. Instead, they are surprisingly worried at this point, looking nervously at their children for signs of success. Stanley admits their anxiety: "In some families, the nagging question remains unanswered for years: 'Did we really train our child in the way he should go?'" At least some of their fears can be attributed to the fact that parents can never be certain about the character of their children. Stanley explains: "Fathers are inclined to think, 'My children are not so bad.' Maybe they are not, but what is hidden in their minds and secret memories? Will their actions please you as they grow into more and more freedom? And will they please God?" But even more important, they see in their adult children a reflection of themselves, along with proof of their abilities as parents. Stanley reminds his readers that Proverbs 22:6 ("Train up a child in the way he should go: and when he is old, he will not depart from it") has more than one meaning: it can comfort those parents who are successful, but it can condemn those who are failures. In either case, full responsibility lies with the parents, and no exceptions are allowed. "The problem is not with God's promise," Stanley concludes, "but with our training."[223]

Adding to these uncertainties, the books are unclear about what parents should expect of their adult children. All insist that they be converted and that they live godly lives. But beyond these basic requirements, the conceptions of successful adulthood are at best vague. For some of the writers, like Tim LaHaye, it seems enough that grown children "not encounter trouble with the law."[224] Others, such as Stanley, expect much more, insisting on "initiative, creativity, and self-image."[225] Most fall somewhere in between, and although none of them admit it, their advice is often ambivalent and sometimes contradictory. Emphasizing authority, insisting on obedience, they seem happiest when their adult children emulate their own values, becoming, as it were, reproductions of themselves. At the same time, they allow that adult children must be free to make their own choices. Hence their ambivalence, summed up best by Stanley: "We should strive to produce responsible adults who are able to function independently of parents' authority, yet wholly submitted to God's."[226]

Anxious and ambivalent, parents often respond to this difficult situation by retreating to simple solutions. Advised to act authoritatively, they set rules for their children to obey. "Don't be deterred by their objections," counsels LaHaye. "Set good rules whether they like them or not."[227] Predisposed to punish, they punish, sometimes with a vengeance. Even the seemingly mild-mannered Pat Boone describes how he slapped and spanked his children, on one occasion paddling his seventeen-year-old daughter Debby over his knee until she was "black and blue."[228] Expecting their children to be like themselves, they balefully predict the very worst for those who wander from the prescribed way. In the words of D. James Kennedy, the Fort Lauderdale, Florida, minister and television evangelist, "The Bible says, 'The eye that mocks a father, that scorns obedience to a mother, will be pecked out by the ravens of the valley.' "[229]

Predictably, such authoritarian solutions do not always work. Admitting that many parents prefer to rely on "rules for rules' sake," Stanley sees sometimes disastrous results:

> I am afraid that the objective of many parents is to produce kids that always jump when Mom or Dad gives a command. Parents with that approach, however, often produce adults who cannot function outside an environment of clearly defined parameters; they destroy their children's ability to reason and think for themselves.[230]

Similarly, Boone, frustrated by his failure to reach his four girls, confesses to feelings of failure in a revealing and uncharacteristic passage: "I knew I was doing something wrong, but in my exasperation, I couldn't figure out what it was. I know that a father is to use his authority, and that kids are to obey—but what do you do when the formula doesn't work?"[231] Almost all of the authors admit to at least some failures as parents, usually as a result of erring on the side of strictness. After having reared five children, admits Beverly LaHaye, she has come to realize that "a child needs a certain amount of freedom."[232] Yet in truth such second thoughts are relatively rare. Committed to principles that sometimes do not work in practice, these thinkers seem unable or unwilling to question them, to admit inconsistencies, or to allow exceptions. Instead, they reassert the rightness of their principles and enforce them by doling out discipline, insisting on obedience, calling on God for help, and blaming external enemies for their failures. Thus, her own reservations notwithstanding, LaHaye remains steadfast in advising parents to insist that their children show them nothing less than "absolute obedience."[233]

The children also pay a price, responding to these patterns of child-rearing in a variety of ways, including self-destructive ones. Some of them rebel, like the strong-willed Debby Boone, rejecting the strictures of patriarchal rule by breaking away or placing themselves at odds with their families. She writes of her early teen years: "I loved Jesus and hated my father, and I saw little or no conflict between those two postures."[234] Others attempt to obey the rules set by their parents but find themselves failing through no fault of their own. Observes Stanley, "I have seen many cases in which a child's creativity and individuality has been misunderstood as rebellion."[235] A few, like the Boones' daughter Cherry, a victim of anorexia nervosa, turn inward, seeking to master themselves while at the same time pleasing their parents, and ending in a compulsive and ultimately self-destructive attempt to reconcile self-control with social conformity.[236] But most of the children apparently obey, even at the cost of their own independent identities; when they become parents themselves, they assert the same rules over again, enforcing them on their own children. And the prodigals often return. Having struggled against the authority of her father, says Debby Boone, she realizes her error and resigns herself in the end "to kneel before the head of all authority, my heavenly Father."[237]

Self-Protection and Social Reform

Thus it is that Christian conservatives spell out their social theory. Anxious defenders of a contemporary form of patriarchy, they insist that men act as authorities, that wives submit to their husbands, and that children obey their parents. Men are to be men and women women; differences between the sexes are clearly defined, and deviations are punished severely. They believe that by teaching their children well, they can protect them from secular society, while at the same time perpetuating the principles of their social movement, creating in effect a self-contained subculture. Their purpose, says LaHaye, is to "insulate the Christian home against all evil forces."[238]

But these cultural defenders argue that religious conservatives must pursue social policies that are aggressive as well as defensive. Condemning complacency and arguing that social change cannot be consigned to the last days before the millennium, LaHaye himself sounds a clarion call to social action. In his *Battle for the Family*, he gives advice on how to form a MAC (Moral Activity Committee) and provides addresses of exist-

336

ing ones, exhorting his readers to become active politically: "Write to your local, state and national officials whenever they are considering moral issues. They need to hear from you. Be sure to participate as you are able in such programs as 'Clean Up TV,' 'Pass the Human Life Amendment,' or anything else that will bring back moral standards in our land."[239]

Christian conservatives can be found adhering to both of these positions. To some extent, they are divided among themselves, with fundamentalists frequently advocating sectarian self-protection, while evangelicals and Pentecostals urge a more aggressive and broadly based strategy of social reform. More often, they are divided within themselves, advocating both strategies at once, like LaHaye, and swinging back and forth, as it were, between them. He writes in *The Race for the 21st Century*:

> Cultural change takes place slowly, so a wise Christian must understand that he is really racing on two fronts at the same time. To change the future, he must fight the forces that are misshaping society. But he must also protect himself and his family from those liberal-humanist influences in society that are already trying to destroy it. It will do your family little good if you neglect it to win the race for our culture in the next century.[240]

In attempting to allay this ambivalence, and to bridge the gap between society and the state, religious conservatives find themselves turning to another domain, that of the economy. Standing strategically between the family and the polity, the marketplace provides an arena for these thinkers to find conservative friends and to investigate conservative ideas, allowing them to extend their movement and to expand their thinking. Sure of the connection between Christianity and capitalism, they seem eager to enter the realm of economics. We consider their thoughts on the economy next.

CHAPTER TWO

1. Jerry Falwell, "An Agenda for the Eighties," in *The Fundamentalist Phenomenon: The Resurgence of Conservative Christianity*, ed. Jerry Falwell (with Ed Dobson and Ed Hindson) (Garden City, N.Y.: Doubleday and Company, 1981), 205.

2. See, for example, Crawford, *Thunder on the Right*, 144–64; Pamela Johnston Conover and Virginia Gray, *Feminism and the New Right: Conflict over the American Family* (New York: Praeger Publishers, 1983), 1–11; on the symbolic role of the family, Donald Heinz, "The Struggle to Define America," in Liebman and Wuthnow, *New Christian Right*, 141–43; and Rebecca Klatch, *Women of the New Right* (Philadelphia: Temple University Press, 1987), 22–25. See also Ammerman, *Bible Believers*, 134–46, Balmer, *Mine Eyes*, 109–37, and Watt, *Transforming Faith*, 93–136.

3. See John L. Kater, Jr., *Christians on the Right: The Moral Majority in Perspective* (New York: Seabury Press, 1982), 88–102.

4. On the family as "domestic church," see Onalee McGraw, *The Family, Feminism, and the Therapeutic State* (Washington, D.C.: Heritage Foundation, 1980),

29. For Victorian family imagery, see Falwell, *Listen, America!*, 123. Neo-Gothic images of the home as "castle" and the family as "kingdom" are found in Morgan, *Total Woman*, 55, and Charles Stanley, *A Man's Touch* (Wheaton, Ill: Victor Books, 1977), 60 (the Stanley book was originally titled *Is There a Man in the House?*). Business and corporation metaphors are common. See, for example, Morgan, *Total Woman*, 82, where she states that "allowing your husband to be your family president is just good business." (Morgan does not explain how it happens that her husband Charlie is vice-president of Total Woman, Incorporated, where she serves as president.) Falwell also appropriates bureaucratic imagery: "The family is the best and most efficient 'department of health, education, and welfare.'" Falwell, *Listen, America!*, 135.

5. Kater, *Christians on the Right*, 88.

6. See Edwin Louis Cole (with Doug Brendel), *Maximized Manhood: A Guide to Family Survival* (Springdale, Pa.: Whitaker House, 1982); Morgan, *Total Woman*; Tim and Beverly LaHaye, *The Act of Marriage: The Beauty of Sexual Love* (Grand Rapids, Mich.: Zondervan Publishing House, 1976). Other popular books include James Dobson, *Dare to Discipline* (New York: Bantam Books, 1977) ("Over 1,000,000 Copies sold"); idem, *Hide and Seek*, rev. ed. (Old Tappan, N.J.: Fleming H. Revell Company, 1979) ("Over half a million copies sold"); and Beverly LaHaye, *How to Develop Your Child's Temperament* (Eugene, Ore.: Harvest House Publishers, 1977) ("Over 250,000 Copies Sold").

7. Many of the Christian conservative thinkers combine media in reaching their audiences. Typical is the Reverend Tim LaHaye, a San Diego, California author, television talk show host, and founder of "family life seminars." Through his Family Life Services, LaHaye and his wife, Beverly, have conducted seminars for over 300,000 people, in addition to writing books and producing movies, tapes, and videocassettes, which are distributed through their "Cassette-of-the-Month Club." They also offer psychological counseling by mail, including the "LaHaye Temperament Analysis." The approach is decidedly entrepreneurial: "Your personal 13- to 16-page evaluation letter from Dr. Tim LaHaye will be permanently bound in a handsome vinyl leather portfolio." Tim LaHaye, *How to Be Happy Though Married* (Wheaton, Ill.: Tyndale House, 1968), 162.

8. Charles Stanley, *How to Keep Your Kids on Your Team* (Nashville, Tenn.: Oliver-Nelson Books, 1986), 35. Stanley's father died when he was seven months old. Tim LaHaye, whose father died when he was a small boy, remembers him as a "strong disciplinarian with a violent temper," but also as a "great father." Tim LaHaye, *Understanding the Male Temperament* (Old Tappan, N.J.: Fleming H. Revell Company, 1977), 18.

9. Boone, *New Song*, 20.

10. LaHaye, *Understanding the Male Temperament*, 12.

11. Stanley, *A Man's Touch*, 9. Surprisingly, Stanley seems to flirt with humanism in making the biblical case. He writes, "God could not have complimented man more than to make man like Himself." One evangelical theologian who has criticized conservative writers for their implicit humanism is Fackre, *Religious Right*, esp. 31–35.

12. Stanley, *A Man's Touch*, 10.

13. Tim LaHaye, *Sex Education Is for the Family* (Grand Rapids, Mich.: Zondervan Publishing House, 1985), 84. On Victorian conceptions of male sexuality, see Charles Rosenberg, "Sexuality, Class, and Role in 19th-Century America," *American Quarterly* 25 (1973): 131–53. See also John S. Haller and Robin M.

Haller, *The Physician and Sexuality in Victorian America* (New York: W. W. Norton and Company, 1974), 91–137.

14. Phyllis Schlafly, *The Power of the Christian Woman* (Cincinnatti, Ohio: Standard Publishing Company, 1981), 23. This book, which is published for sale in Christian bookstores, is virtually identical to Schlafly's *The Power of the Positive Woman* (New Rochelle, N.Y.: Arlington House Publishers, 1977), which is published for sale in mass-circulation outlets. The books differ only in that the words "Christian" and "positive" are interchanged throughout the texts. Additionally, in *Christian Woman*, Bible verses are added as chapter subheadings.

15. Schlafly, *Christian Woman*, 26. Apparently Schlafly considers the lack of emotion in males to be a highly admirable trait. She writes, "The public display of fear, sorrow, anger, and irritation reveals a lack of self-discipline that should be avoided by the Christian Woman just as much as by the Christian Man." Ibid., 24.

16. Ibid., 26.

17. Ibid., 24, 26. Here Schlafly's anticommunism comes into play: "Men may philosophize about how life began and where we are heading; women are concerned about feeding the kids today. No woman would ever, as Karl Marx did, spend years reading political philosophy in the British Museum while her child starved to death." Ibid., 25–26.

18. Ibid., 27, 26. Schlafly here cites Amaury de Riencourt's *Sex and Power in History* (New York: David McKay Company, 1974), 56.

19. Schlafly, *Christian Woman*, 27.

20. LaHaye, *Happy Though Married*, 57, 63.

21. LaHaye, *Understanding the Male Temperament*, 30.

22. T. and B. LaHaye, *Act of Marriage*, 27, 18. See also ibid., viii. According to the LaHayes, Victorian sexual repression was not biblical but cultural, being the product of "a day of biblical ignorance." Ibid., 210. At another point they appear to attribute sexual repression to Catholicism. They write that the equation of sin with sexuality "sprang from the 'Dark Ages' when Roman theologians tried to merge ascetic philosophy with Christian thought." Ibid., 98. The real problem with Victorian morality, the LaHayes point out, was that "Victorians did not seem to distinguish between their premarital and marital taboos." See ibid., 27. Yet it should be said that for all its apparent liberality, the manual is quite restrictive, with the LaHayes making clear their opposition to oral sex, their preference for the "man above" as the "most satisfying" position, and their resolute resistance to sexual pleasure outside marriage. (The LaHayes take the precaution of recommending that couples about to be married wait until their wedding night to read their 315-page book.) Ibid., 84. See also ibid., 65.

23. Ibid., vii. Beverly LaHaye elaborates, "Our detailed sex survey taken from 1700 Christian couples revealed that Christians not only scored themselves ten points higher in satisfaction in this area than non-Christians but that Spirit-filled Christians registered seven points higher than the non-Spirit-controlled." Beverly LaHaye, *The Spirit-Controlled Woman* (Eugene, Ore.: Harvest House Publishers, 1976), 123.

24. Schlafly, *Christian Woman*, 103. Donald G. Mathews and Jane DeHart Mathews have pointed out that this conception of male irresponsibility was used effectively by Schlafly and other opponents of the Equal Rights Amendment. See "The Cultural Politics of ERA's Defeat," *OAH Newsletter*, November 1982, 13–15. See also Jane J. Mansbridge, *Why We Lost the ERA* (Chicago: University of Chicago Press), 90–117, and Jane S. DeHart and Donald G. Mathews, *Sex, Gender,*

and the Politics of the ERA: A State and the Nation (New York: Oxford University Press, 1990).

25. LaHaye, *Sex Education*, 197. See also LaHaye, *Understanding the Male Temperament*, 30: "Eunuchs rarely distinguish themselves in any field."

26. LaHaye, *Sex Education*, 185. LaHaye's protégé David Jeremiah recommends a similar strategy, suggesting that Christians recite Bible verses at times of temptation: "When we have committed many passages of God's Word to memory, we will discover that they come to our minds, at just the right moment, to aid us in gaining victory in this battle." David Jeremiah, *Before It's Too Late* (Nashville, Tenn.: Thomas Nelson Publishers, 1982), 72. LaHaye argues that masturbation leads to homosexuality. He writes: "Most of the homosexuals I know indulged in masturbation early and frequently. This seems to be a crucial step in adopting a homosexual lifestyle." LaHaye, *Sex Education*, 89.

27. T. and B. LaHaye, *Act of Marriage*, 33.

28. Ibid., 285.

29. LaHaye, *Understanding the Male Temperament*, 31.

30. T. and B. LaHaye, *Act of Marriage*, 173.

31. LaHaye, *Happy Though Married*, 29.

32. Schlafly, *Christian Woman*, 18.

33. Beverly LaHaye, *The Restless Woman* (Grand Rapids, Mich.: Zondervan Publishing House, 1984), 128.

34. LaHaye, *Sex Education*, 188.

35. LaHaye, *Happy Though Married*, 106.

36. B. LaHaye, *Spirit-Controlled Woman*, 130.

37. See T. and B. LaHaye, *Act of Marriage*, 87.

38. Falwell, *Listen, America!*, 150.

39. LaHaye, *Happy Though Married*, 106, 66.

40. Tim LaHaye, *What Everyone Should Know about Homosexuality* (Wheaton, Ill.: Tyndale House Publishers, 1988). The book was originally published in 1978 under the title *The Unhappy Gays*. Homosexuality, explains David Jeremiah, is "the cultural culmination of rebellion against God." Jeremiah, *Before It's Too Late*, 43.

41. Edwin Louis Cole, *Courage: A Book for Champions* (Tulsa, Okla.: Harrison House, 1985), 60.

42. Stanley, *A Man's Touch*, 27. On "the new androgynous man" and on "gender castration," see Cole, *Courage*, 17.

43. Cole, *Maximized Manhood*, 35. In contrast to today, many of the writers seem to see the early postwar period as a golden age of American manhood. "It used to be," writes Bob Green, conjuring up images of football games and proms, "that if guys wanted to date a sharp girl they had to polish the car and fix themselves up—and compete." Nowadays, he continues, expressing concern over the fact that girls call boys for dates, "it seems guys are more docile. They're almost feminine in manner and dress, and their attitudes toward girls are very lackadaisical and ungallant." Green fears for the future: "Where you have a bunch of weak males, everything is going to cave in." Green quoted in Anita Bryant, *Bless This House* (Old Tappan, N.J.: Fleming H. Revell Company, 1972), 142, 141–42, 142.

44. LaHaye, *Understanding the Male Temperament*, 12.

45. Cole, *Courage*, 48; idem, *Maximized Manhood*, 35; Stanley, *A Man's Touch*, 96; LaHaye, *Understanding the Male Temperament*, 12.

46. Cole, *Courage*, 48.

341

47. Ibid., 123. On the movement of males to recapture a role in turn-of-the-century mainstream Protestantism, see Gail Bederman, " 'The Women Have Had Charge of the Church Work Long Enough': The Men and Religion Forward Movement of 1911–12 and the Masculinization of Middle-Class Protestantism," *American Quarterly* 41 (1989): 432–65. For background on the role of middle-class women in setting American Protestant values, see Ann Douglas, *The Feminization of American Culture* (New York: Alfred A. Knopf, 1977), esp. 17–139.

48. Cole, *Maximized Manhood*, 63.

49. LaHaye, *Understanding the Male Temperament*, 187. Bob Green and his wife, Anita Bryant, allude to their close friendship with the "angels," a group of Miami Dolphins players. Marabel Morgan, who is also a Miamian, tells how she once offered her Total Woman seminar to the wives of an entire Dolphins team, and she points out, without laying undue claim, that the following year their husbands won the Super Bowl. In his early days as a revivalist, James Robison, whose own athletic interests include baseball, basketball, golf, and tennis, once saved an entire high school football team: "They had a fabulous year, too, going all the way to the district championship." See Bryant, *Bless This House*, 85, Morgan, *Total Woman*, 250–51, and Robison, *Thank God, I'm Free*, 87.

50. Cole, *Courage*, 156. The writers are realistic and admit that they themselves do not always win. Thus, at the age of fifty, the red-blooded LaHaye is able to admit for the first time that he is only a mediocre athlete. At the cost of considerable embarrassment, LaHaye lets it all hang out: "I found the church bowling team a pleasant experience, but I had to endure the humiliation of coming home three-fourths of the time knowing that my wife outscored me by ten to twenty-five pins." LaHaye, *Understanding the Male Temperament*, 187.

51. Cole, *Courage*, 49.

52. Cole, *Maximized Manhood*, 61.

53. Stanley, *Kids*, 122.

54. LaHaye, *Happy Though Married*, 36.

55. Beverly LaHaye, *I Am a Woman by God's Design* (Old Tappan, N.J.: Fleming H. Revell Company, 1980), 100. On the other hand, writes Beverly LaHaye, "if she is home all day, but wastes her time, she cannot expect her husband to come home from a day's work and do what she should have been doing earlier." Ibid.

56. LaHaye, *Happy Though Married*, 120. LaHaye can at times be surprisingly sensitive, as when he suggests that husbands try to see themselves "through wives' eyes." LaHaye, *Understanding the Male Temperament*, 181.

57. Stanley, *A Man's Touch*, 36.

58. Ibid., 116.

59. T. and B. LaHaye, *Act of Marriage*, 129.

60. Stanley, *A Man's Touch*, 58.

61. LaHaye, *Understanding the Male Temperament*, 181.

62. Ibid. LaHaye explains: "The father who insists on rendering a long series of unilateral edicts may encounter vigorous resistance at home. His wife and children will find it much easier to comply with 'the general's orders' if granted a hearing." Ibid.

63. Stanley, *A Man's Touch*, 116.

64. B. LaHaye, *Woman by God's Design*, 50–51.

65. Bryant, *Mine Eyes*, 72.

66. Green cited in Bryant, *Bless This House*, 143.

67. Cole, *Maximized Manhood*, 72.

68. Stanley, *A Man's Touch*, 120.

69. Cole, *Maximized Manhood*, 176.

70. B. LaHaye, *Restless Woman*, 142. For background on Christian conservative women, see Theodore S. Arrington and Patricia A. Kyle, "Equal Rights Amendment Activists in North Carolina," *Signs* 3 (1978): 666–80; David W. Brady and Kent L. Tedin, "Ladies in Pink: Religious and Political Ideology in the Anti-ERA Movement," *Social Science Quarterly* 56 (1976): 564–75; and Kent L. Tedin, "Religious Preference and Pro/Anti Activism on the Equal Rights Amendment Issue," *Pacific Sociological Review* 21 (1978): 55–66.

71. Stanley, *A Man's Touch*, 19. Beverly LaHaye elaborates: "A woman is a necessary part of a man, a part which makes him fulfilled and complete. God created woman very specially from one of Adam's ribs." B. LaHaye, *Spirit-Controlled Woman*, 57.

72. Stanley, *A Man's Touch*, 19. As an example, Beverly LaHaye cites the woman who "had bossed her husband around and tried to dominate him until she had driven him to alcohol." B. LaHaye, *Spirit-Controlled Woman*, 37.

73. B. LaHaye, *Woman by God's Design*, 27, 27–28. Tim LaHaye follows out the logic to make the case for early marriage: "If God designed the female anatomy to bear children in the latter teen years, he must have intended that girls become wives and mothers early in life." LaHaye, *Happy Though Married*, 77–78. It should be pointed out that LaHaye does not take the argument to its logical conclusion of opposition to birth control. Although the LaHayes themselves have five children and prefer large families, they do set limits: "No woman should be expected to keep bearing children from marriage through menopause." LaHaye, *Sex Education*, 176.

74. B. LaHaye, *Woman by God's Design*, 29. It is interesting to compare LaHaye's reproductive determinism to that of mid-nineteenth-century medical descriptions of women: "It was," a physician explained in 1870, "as if the Almighty, in creating the female sex, had taken the uterus and built up a woman around it." Cited in Carroll Smith-Rosenberg and Charles Rosenberg, "The Female Animal: Medical and Biological Views of Woman and Her Role in Nineteenth-Century America," *Journal of American History* 60 (1973): 335. The issue of abortion is discussed in Kristin Luker, *Abortion and the Politics of Motherhood* (Berkeley: University of California Press, 1984), 158–91.

75. Shirley Boone cited in Boone, *New Song*, 204.

76. T. and B. LaHaye, *Act of Marriage*, 38, 39. The LaHayes add a word of warning: "Don't be tricked into thinking that today's 'mod' women are any different, just because some of them wear frumpy clothes and sometimes act as if they care little about manners and etiquette. Something deep down in a woman's heart cries out for romantic love." Ibid., 42.

77. Schlafly, *Christian Woman*, 62. By contrast, Schlafly continues, "a man's prime emotional need is passive (i.e., to be appreciated or admired)." Ibid.

78. Ibid., 23. If the maternal need is not met with natural children, says Schlafly, women will meet it in other ways, such as pursuing careers in care-giving professions such as teaching and nursing, helping to care for the children of others, or adopting pets. She writes, "The maternal need in some women has even manifested itself in an extraordinary affection lavished on a dog, a cat, or a parakeet." Ibid., 24. Beverly LaHaye suggests that maternal instincts may be applied to husbands as well: "Sometimes a wife will also feel like crying out for attention or understanding, but she should not expect her husband to hear her unless she has

already been responsive to his silent pleas. God has given her a mother instinct for this, so it will, of course, come more naturally for her than for him." B. LaHaye, *Spirit-Controlled Woman*, 97.

79. B. LaHaye, *Restless Woman*, 73. On the role of "ladies' magazines" in creating Victorian connections between female biology and feminine domesticity, see Barbara Welter, "The Cult of True Womanhood, 1820–1860," *American Quarterly* 18 (1966): 151–74.

80. T. and B. LaHaye, *Act of Marriage*, 38. Women, says Schlafly, borrowing lyrics from a popular song, desire "a Sunday kind of love." Schlafly, *Christian Woman*, 53. Somewhat surprisingly, she draws frequently from popular songs in advising women. For example, she cites approvingly a song by Burt Bacharach: "Hey little girl, comb your hair, fix your makeup, soon he will open the door." Ibid., 64.

81. B. LaHaye, *Restless Woman*, 114.

82. Schlafly, *Christian Woman*, 23. Writes Tim LaHaye in his *How to Be Happy Though Married*, "The role of a woman is to respond. . . . God has given her the capacity to respond to her husband—if she will just let herself. A full understanding of this feminine response will help a woman overcome her selfish tendency to think first of how she feels when her husband approaches her and, instead, cause her to think how she will feel if she will relax and give herself to him." LaHaye, *Happy Though Married*, 69.

83. Morgan, *Total Joy*, 115. She writes, "Your husband's hunger for sex is as gnawing as his hunger for food . . . a man hardly ever tires of sex." Ibid., 113.

84. T. and B. LaHaye, *Act of Marriage*, viii.

85. Ibid., 99. Like the LaHayes, Morgan begins with the problem of Victorian sexual repression. She describes one wife: "One girl told me how her mother counseled her before her wedding day. 'You have to endure sex,' she said. 'It's a part of marriage. But never act as if you like it, because your husband will think you've been promiscuous.'" Morgan, *Total Woman*, 135. It is interesting to note that at least one writer attributes Victorian sexual repression to an early form of frustrated feminism. The problem with the Victorians, she writes, is that they believed that "somehow a woman should not be totally submissive." Birdie Yager (with Gloria Weed), *The Secret of Living, Is Giving* (Springfield, Mo.: Restoration Fellowship, 1980), 31.

86. Morgan, *Total Woman*, 3, 4–5.

87. See ibid., 139ff. The bubble bath is also intended to be enjoyable for the wife: "Bubble your troubles away at five o'clock." Ibid., 149. Nevertheless, the writers do emphasize that the main object of the preparations is to please the husband. Thus Tim LaHaye counsels newlywed wives that "a bride should begin one ritual immediately after her honeymoon; the last thirty minutes before her husband returns from work she should spend on her appearance. His homecoming should be the high point of her day." LaHaye, *Happy Though Married*, 35. Says LaHaye, "'Clean up, paint up, fix up' is a good motto for every loving wife to remember just before the time of hubby's arrival." T. and B. LaHaye, *Act of Marriage*, 105.

88. Morgan, *Total Joy*, 135.

89. Morgan, *Total Woman*, 141. LaHaye take a similar, if somewhat more staid position, making the case for what he calls the "sanctity of sex." LaHaye, *Sex Education*, 153.

90. Morgan, *Total Woman*, 119–20. Another wife reports that she was "'wearing

my new dress with the no-bra look.' Her husband couldn't quite believe it, but said, 'This is one of the happiest moments of my life; I just don't want it to end.'" Ibid., 120.

91. Morgan, *Total Joy*, 110. The LaHayes point proudly to their finding that 89 percent of the women in their Family Life Seminars have "registered orgasmic experiences." They write, "No Christian woman should settle for less." T. and B. LaHaye, *Act of Marriage*, 113, 117.

92. Morgan, *Total Joy*, 217, 222.

93. "Marabel Morgan: 'Preferring One Another,'" *Christianity Today*, 10 September 1976, 15. Morgan's principles assume attitudinal change on the part of wives, what she calls "interior decorating on your attitudes." Idem, *Total Woman*, 37.

94. Morgan, *Total Joy*, 16.

95. Morgan, *Total Woman*, 75. Advising a similar technique, the LaHayes pass on the report of one successful wife: "There is one time each month when I always try to get my husband to make love to me—the night after he has paid the family bills. It seems to be the only thing that gets him back to normal." T. and B. LaHaye, *Act of Marriage*, 26.

96. Morgan, *Total Woman*, 188, 171, 179. As another part of the therapeutic plan, Morgan emphasizes order and household efficiency. She writes, "When you're organized and efficient, his flame of love will begin to flicker and burn." Ibid., 34. Says Yager, "Don't underestimate your powers. Your approval alone can sometimes be the difference between [your husband's] success and failure." Yager, *Secret of Living*, 45.

97. Morgan, *Total Woman*, 83. She quotes one enthusiastic graduate: "The Total Woman is in heaven—a beautiful suite overlooking the Atlantic Ocean in the heart of San Juan—new, gorgeous luggage in my closet, with the sweetest guy in the world as my companion. That course is powerful stuff!" Ibid., 105.

98. Ibid., 20–21.

99. Yager, *Secret of Living*, 31.

100. Schlafly, *Christian Woman*, 48, 75.

101. Morgan, *Total Woman*, 72. Intimations of behavioral conditioning abound in the books. Thus one woman, whose husband had thin arms, made a point of accidentally squeezing his bicep and saying, "Oh, I never knew you were so muscular." Two nights later she found him in the garage lifting a new set of barbells. Explains Morgan, "He wanted to build more muscles for her to admire." Ibid., 71.

102. Morgan cited in "Marabel Morgan: 'Preferring One Another,'" 15.

103. B. LaHaye, *Woman by God's Design*, 49.

104. Morgan, *Total Joy*, 111.

105. Morgan, *Total Woman*, 113.

106. Morgan, *Total Joy*, 111. The reliance on costumes is in part a response to the problem of sexual competition. Writes Morgan, "I have heard women complain, 'My husband isn't satisfied with just me. He wants lots of women. What can I do?' You can be lots of different women to him. Costumes provide variety without him ever leaving home." Idem, *Total Woman*, 117.

107. Morgan, *Total Woman*, 83–84. Schlafly makes a similar point in opposition to the Equal Rights Amendment: "Marriage and motherhood are the most reliable security the world can offer." Schlafly, *Christian Woman*, 4. See also Klatch, *Women of the New Right*, 138–39.

108. B. LaHaye, *Restless Woman*, 128. Similarly, Schlafly warns women to avoid

competing with men at all costs, lest "by trying to think, act, talk, and react like a man," they lose their "emancipation as a woman." Schlafly, *Christian Woman*, 13.

109. B. LaHaye, *Spirit-Controlled Woman*, 52. In the case of a single woman or an absentee husband, writes Beverly LaHaye, "the minister is to be the figure of authority." Idem, *Woman by God's Design*, 70.

110. B. LaHaye, *Woman by God's Design*, 119.

111. Schlafly, *Christian Woman*, 65, 14, 117, 76.

112. B. LaHaye, *Restless Woman*, 80. In an even more wide-ranging study of early feminists, including George Sand, Mary Wollstonecraft, Elizabeth Cady Stanton, and Karl Marx, LaHaye concludes that "the majority of them were either cruelly treated by their mothers or fathers, or they simply couldn't cope with their rigid, humorless religious upbringings." Ibid., 44.

113. Falwell, *Listen, America!*, 185. Tim LaHaye, who sent a personal "representative" to the 1981 National Organization for Women convention, describes how his representative discovered that "dildos, vibrators, and other lesbian paraphernalia that would shock any decent person were openly displayed." LaHaye, *Battle for the Family*, 139. Schlafly believes that "lesbianism is logically the highest form in the ritual of women's liberation." Schlafly, *Christian Woman*, 18. Her *Power of the Christian Woman* contains an appendix of twelve pictures taken at a demonstration supporting the Equal Rights Amendment that prominently feature "the unkempt, the lesbians, the radicals, the socialists, and the goverment employees [i.e., AFSCME union members] who are trying . . . to force us to conform to their demands." Ibid., 187, and see 187ff.

114. Schlafly, *Christian Woman*, 30. Schlafly considers capitalism to be far more liberating than feminism. She writes, "The great heroes of women's liberation are not the straggly-haired women on television talk shows and picket lines, but Thomas Edison, who brought the miracle of electricity to our homes to give light and to run all those laborsaving devices. . . . Or Elias Howe, who gave us the sewing machine. . . . Or Clarence Birdseye, who invented the process for freezing foods. Or Henry Ford." Ibid., 38.

115. B. LaHaye, *Restless Woman*, 54. Beverly LaHaye is bitter: "All they can think of is their downtrodden rights." B. LaHaye, *Spirit-Controlled Woman*, 79.

116. Falwell, *Listen, America!*, 158–59.

117. B. LaHaye, *Restless Woman*, 14.

118. Schlafly, *Christian Woman*, 60.

119. B. LaHaye, *Restless Woman*, 121. Beverly LaHaye believes that the desire of women to be ordained is "a selfish desire for an elevated position." She writes, "In the Church, authority is in the hands of men because they represent Christ and the great mystery. If you disagree, you are rebelling against Christ's authority as head of the Church." B. LaHaye, *Woman by God's Design*, 68, 67.

120. LaHaye, *Happy Though Married*, 107.

121. Stanley, *A Man's Touch*, 50. According to Stanley, submission is not a badge of inferiority: "God did not make man superior or woman inferior at the Creation. Not one single verse in the Bible suggests that." Ibid., 53–54. Falwell bases his opposition to the Equal Rights Amendment on Ephesians 5:23: "A definite violation of holy Scripture, ERA defies the mandate that 'the husband is the head of the wife.'" Falwell, *Listen, America!*, 151. See Morgan, *Total Woman*, 253–54.

122. B. LaHaye, *Spirit-Controlled Woman*, 71. Beverly LaHaye makes clear that submission is not slavery: "Submission does not mean that she is owned and operated by her husband but that he is the 'head' or 'manager.'" Ibid. Tim LaHaye

elaborates: "When decisions have to be made, the president (or husband) will act as final authority, but he will weigh the thoughts and insights of all the vice-presidents before doing so." LaHaye, *Understanding the Male Temperament*, 181.

123. B. LaHaye, *Woman by God's Design*, 76. Falwell agrees, citing 1 Peter 3:4 that women are to be "the ornament of a meek and quiet spirit." Falwell, *Listen, America!*, 183.

124. T. and B. LaHaye, *Act of Marriage*, 184. "Next to nagging, nothing is less pleasing to a husband than a domineering wife. (It turns the children off too.) There is just nothing feminine about a domineering woman." Ibid.

125. B. LaHaye, *Spirit-Controlled Woman*, 74.

126. Ibid., 73. Schlafly suggests that there are limits, warning that "the total submersion of a wife's identity in her husband's can become more offensive to the husband than to the wife." Schlafly, *Christian Woman*, 63.

127. B. LaHaye, *Spirit-Controlled Woman*, 78.

128. T. and B. LaHaye, *Act of Marriage*, 246. Apparently Tim LaHaye considers submission to be the solution to almost all troubled marriages. In his books, he gives numerous examples of cases from his files as a Christian counselor, in virtually all of which he counsels women to save their marriages by submitting to their husbands. See LaHaye, *Happy Though Married*, 143–60.

129. Stanley, *Kids*, 215.

130. Ibid., 214–15. Says Beverly LaHaye, "Surely it would take heavenly grace and divine wisdom to live with some of the men I have heard women tell about. But God is faithful! Nothing is impossible!" B. LaHaye, *Spirit-Controlled Woman*, 76.

131. Bryant, *Bless This House*, 119.

132. LaHaye, *Understanding the Male Temperament*, 178. A few writers point out that the husband bears some responsibility in the matter, and that submission is "not a major issue in the home unless a husband neglects his role." Stanley, *Kids*, 215.

133. Stanley, *Kids*, 210.

134. LaHaye, *Understanding the Male Temperament*, 38.

135. LaHaye, *Happy Though Married*, 131. Bryant agrees, speaking on the basis of hard experience: "How *impossible* it is to be a wife *unless* you have been born again." Bryant, *Bless This House*, 114.

136. LaHaye, *Happy Though Married*, 106. Says Stanley, "The wife who says, 'I don't like the idea of being subject to my husband,' has a streak of rebellion within her." Stanley, *A Man's Touch*, 52.

137. Bryant, *Bless This House*, 44.

138. B. LaHaye, *Spirit-Controlled Woman*, 63. She writes: "It was almost a time of devotion each day as I lovingly picked up those blessed dirty socks." Ibid., 64. Schlafly makes a similar case: "Are dirty dishes all that bad? It's all in whether you wake up in the morning with a chip on your shoulder or whether you have a positive mental attitude." Schlafly, *Christian Woman*, 58.

139. B. LaHaye, *Woman by God's Design*, 55. She writes, "The feminist ideology is based entirely on a selfish orientation, encouraging a woman to look out for her own self-interests and rights." Ibid., 86.

140. Morgan, *Total Woman*, 45.

141. See B. LaHaye, *Restless Woman*, 116–20.

142. Schlafly, *Christian Woman*, 181. Schlafly also admires Margaret Thatcher, "an old-fashioned, proper, traditional lady. And she cooks breakfast every morn-

ing for her husband (in contrast to Mrs. Gerald Ford, who stayed in bed . . .)."
Ibid., 51.

143. Bryant, *Anita Bryant Story*, 57.

144. B. LaHaye, *Restless Woman*, 126. Here she is citing Connaught Mashner
on the "new traditional woman."

145. Schlafly, *Christian Woman*, 63. On Schlafly's marriage, including the story
of how Fred Schlafly first opposed and then supported his wife's decision to attend
law school, see Carol Felsenthal, *The Sweetheart of the Silent Majority: The Biog-
raphy of Phyllis Schlafly* (Garden City, N.Y.: Doubleday and Company, 1981),
115–17. Says daughter Anne of her father, "I sure wouldn't want to compete with
Mother." Cited at ibid., 117.

146. Morgan, *Total Joy*, 222.

147. Bryant, *Bless This House*, 131.

148. Bryant, *Anita Bryant Story*, 58.

149. Cited in "Anita Bryant's About-Face," *Washington Post*, 15 November
1980, F3.

150. Cited in Cliff Jahr, "Anita Bryant's Startling Reversal," *Ladies' Home
Journal*, December 1980, 67.

151. B. LaHaye, *Spirit-Controlled Woman*, 93.

152. Bryant, *Bless This House*, 29.

153. T. Bakker, *I Gotta Be Me*, 19. She writes: "Most of us, I think, that were
raised in my day and age obeyed our parents because we were so frightened by
what they would do to us if we didn't." T. Bakker, *Run to the Roar*, 22.

154. S. and P. Boone, *Honeymoon*, 178.

155. B. LaHaye, *Your Child's Temperament*, 2, 3. She refers to Psalm 51:5.

156. Ibid., 3, 2, 5. Parents, adds her husband, Tim, "cannot begin too early."
LaHaye, *Sex Education*, 32.

157. LaHaye, *Battle for the Family*, 28, 4.

158. B. LaHaye, *Your Child's Temperament*, 5, 4–5.

159. LaHaye, *Sex Education*, 136, 106, 150.

160. B. LaHaye, *Spirit-Controlled Woman*, 49. On another occasion, LaHaye
writes, "a darling girl snuggled next to her date in church; during the sermon she
reached over and placed her hand on his leg." Ibid.

161. LaHaye, *Sex Education*, 17.

162. Says Beverly LaHaye, "The Bible emphasizes the husband-wife role in
contrast to man-made religions which stress the parent-child and father-mother
relationships." B. LaHaye, *Spirit-Controlled Woman*, 96. By contrast, David Jeremiah sees the family as a biblical priority: "God has always put high priority on
the family." Jeremiah, *Before It's Too Late*, 100.

163. D. James Kennedy, *Learning to Live with the People You Love* (Springdale,
Pa.: Whitaker House, 1987), 129.

164. Stanley, *Kids*, 142–43.

165. B. LaHaye, *Spirit-Controlled Woman*, 43. Tim LaHaye seems to apply the
same method to teenage boys when he advises fathers that a good way to begin
discussing sex with their teenage sons is by recommending to them that they read
Matthew 5:27–28. "You may wish to add," he suggests, "'Do you know what Jesus
meant when he talked about lusting being as bad as adultery?'" LaHaye, *Sex
Education*, 96.

166. See Jeremiah, *Before It's Too Late*, 90–102. Jeremiah lists verses treating

topics such as "contentious wives," "rebellious children," and "sexual deviations." See ibid., 95–96.

167. B. LaHaye, *Spirit-Controlled Woman*, 42.

168. LaHaye, *Battle for the Family*, 14. LaHaye tells how he was saddened, while attending a recent Christian bookseller's convention, "to find three Christian celebrities sporting new wives." Ibid., 15.

169. LaHaye, *Sex Education*, 97.

170. LaHaye, *Happy Though Married*, 87–88. To some extent the problem may be endemic. LaHaye explains, quoting a client from his files: "We met at a Christian group in college, and since we were too spiritual to go to shows and dance we could find little else to do on our dates but park and neck!" Ibid., 151.

171. Shirley Boone in S. and P. Boone, *Honeymoon*, 182.

172. Dobson, *Dare to Discipline*, 11.

173. Perhaps because he is primarily concerned with the relationship between fathers and sons, Stanley sees the war as a watershed. Before Vietnam, he says, it was a truism that "like father, like son." But the war acted as a kind of wedge dividing the generations. He elaborates: "During the Vietnam War, as an example, the college-age sons of the national Secretary of Defense, Army Chief of Staff, Secretary of the Army, and Secretary of the Navy all opposed their fathers' war efforts. How embarrassing, and potentially tragic!" Stanley, *A Man's Touch*, 22.

174. Ibid., 71.

175. B. LaHaye, *Your Child's Temperament*, 136.

176. Stanley, *A Man's Touch*, 71.

177. LaHaye, *Battle for the Family*, 31–32.

178. McGraw, *Family, Feminism, and the Therapeutic State*, 47.

179. Falwell, *Listen, America!*, 131, 132.

180. Ibid., 205.

181. B. LaHaye, *Your Child's Temperament*, 105.

182. Schlafly, *Christian Woman*, 155.

183. B. LaHaye, *Your Child's Temperament*, 77.

184. LaHaye, *Sex Education*, 17, 19, 20, 17, 16.

185. Ibid., 119.

186. Jeremiah, *Before It's Too Late*, 67.

187. Falwell, *Listen, America!*, 200.

188. LaHaye, *Battle for the Family*, 179, 181. David Jeremiah tells the story of "Marty," the son of an affluent family, who at thirteen discovered pornography and became "seduced" by it, turning to a life of "drugs and sexual fantasies." Writes Jeremiah, "Apart from a miracle, Marty will never lead a normal life." Jeremiah, *Before It's Too Late*, 63.

189. LaHaye, *Battle for the Family*, 180.

190. Jeremiah, *Before It's Too Late*, 71.

191. LaHaye, *Battle for the Family*, 109, 195. Boone describes how he and his wife, Shirley, exorcised daughter Debby's room, which was filled with posters of rock musicians, by systematically moving around the room "rebuking Satan in Jesus' name and cutting off any spiritual influence he might have on Debby's rebellion." S. and P. Boone, *Honeymoon*, 62.

192. B. LaHaye, *Spirit-Controlled Woman*, 65.

193. LaHaye, *Sex Education*, 192. The LaHayes advise that such nudity is "expressly forbidden in the Scriptures and is unnecessary for child development." T. and B. LaHaye, *Act of Marriage*, 303.

194. Robison, *Thank God, I'm Free*, 124.

195. Bryant, *Anita Bryant Story*, 129, 62. Following her divorce, Bryant revised her opinions on homosexuality, allowing that people should "live and let live." Cited in Jahr, "Anita Bryant's Startling Reversal," 68.

196. LaHaye, *Understanding the Male Temperament*, 34.

197. Falwell, *Listen, America!*, 185.

198. T. and B. LaHaye, *Act of Marriage*, 279.

199. LaHaye, *Sex Education*, 29. Writes Stanley: "These men [homosexuals] are totally responsible for their behavior. One day they will give an account to God for it. But they are not the only ones who will give an account. Their parents are responsible to some degree." Stanley, *Kids*, 220.

200. See Dobson, *Dare to Discipline*, 17.

201. Dobson, *Hide or Seek*, 20. See 173–74. Also recalling the case of Charles Manson, Morgan connects parental permissiveness to heroin use among their children. See Morgan, *Total Woman*, 212–14.

202. Dobson, *Dare to Discipline*, 16. Beverly LaHaye approves of Dobson's strategy: "The time to disarm that teen-age time bomb is before he is five years old." B. LaHaye, *Your Child's Temperament*, 98.

203. Dobson, *Dare to Discipline*, 21, 16. Writes Marabel Morgan: "When a close friend spanked his three-year-old for hitting the baby, he did it in a loving way. Afterward the child hugged him and said, 'Thank you for saying no, Daddy!'" Morgan, *Total Woman*, 218. See also Falwell, *Listen, America!*, 140.

204. Dobson, *Dare to Discipline*, 19. Boone remembers that his mother kept an old sewing machine belt hanging on the bathroom door as an "enforcer." He recalls receiving his last "flailing" at the age of seventeen. Boone, *New Song*, 31.

205. Dobson, *Dare to Discipline*, 46.

206. LaHaye, *Battle for the Family*, 214. LaHaye goes on: "Parents need to be particularly cautious today when disciplining their children, because some humanists in government spend all their time ferreting out and attacking parents who believe in discipline, accusing them of child abuse." Ibid. See also Falwell, *Listen, America!*, 140.

207. See B. LaHaye, *Your Child's Temperament*, 146. Bob Green describes another system. He writes: "I'm a father to my children, not a pal. I assert my authority. I spank them at times, and they respect me for it. Sometimes I take Bobby into the music room, and it's not so I can play him a piece on the piano. We play a piece on the seat of his pants!" Green cited in Bryant, *Bless This House*, 40.

208. B. LaHaye, *Your Child's Temperament*, 130. Adds Cole, "Tough love is the only kind of love that God knows." Cole, *Courage*, 144. Falwell agrees, stating the case in even stronger terms: "Parents who do not correct their children actually hate them; they do not love them." Falwell, *Listen, America!*, 141.

209. B. LaHaye, *Your Child's Temperament*, 145. Beverly LaHaye continues: "How many times parents have told a child just before a sound spanking, 'This hurts me more than it does you,' and the child absolutely does not believe it. But when discipline and love are bound together, it does hurt the parent." Ibid., 140.

210. Ibid., 135.

211. Dobson, *Dare to Discipline*, 23. The writers see themselves as striking a middle ground between excessive permissiveness and excessive punishment. Says Beverly LaHaye: "Love without discipline is spineless. . . . Discipline without love is cold and militaristic." B. LaHaye, *Your Child's Temperament*, 140.

212. LaHaye, *Battle for the Family*, 25.

213. B. LaHaye, *Woman by God's Design*, 113. In child-rearing, the authors seem particularly insistent that sex roles be unambiguous. It is "extremely important," says Tim LaHaye, "for boys to dress like boys and act like boys early in life!" LaHaye, *Understanding the Male Temperament*, 34.

214. LaHaye, *Sex Education*, 14.

215. LaHaye, *Battle for the Family*, 208. In a scene similar to one described by the seventeenth-century Puritan writer Samuel Sewall, Anita Bryant describes how her five-year-old daughter, Gloria, came to them at night "crying, saying she was scared and going to hell." Bryant points proudly to the fact that Gloria was saved soon thereafter, at the age of five. See Bryant, *Amazing Grace*, 38. Similarly, Beverly LaHaye describes how her four-year-old came to be converted. She writes about a traumatic period in the child's life when her dog was run over by an automobile: "She began to question us if her doggy had gone to doggy heaven. We satisfied her by saying that God certainly must have a place for dogs of little girls. Then she asked if she would go to heaven when she died. Very simply we explained to her that she would, but first she would have to invite Jesus into her heart. She responded, 'I want to invite Jesus in right now.' We all prayed and I firmly believe that on that day, at four years of age, she was saved." B. LaHaye, *Your Child's Temperament*, 75. See also Kennedy, *Learning to Live*, 107: "The eternal salvation of their souls lies primarily in your hands."

216. LaHaye, *Battle for the Family*, 232. LaHaye is especially concerned that children not be allowed to associate with homosexuals: "Remember, homosexuals that would misdirect your son or daughter don't wear badges saying 'I am a homosexual.' Quite the opposite—they do everything they can to appear normal." LaHaye, *Sex Education*, 92.

217. See, for example, LaHaye, *Sex Education*, 130–39. The rules apply to other aspects of life as well: "If you don't want your daughter to wear a bikini," says Stanley, "don't simply tell her to buy something conservative. Tell her you do not want her coming home with a bikini." Stanley, *Kids*, 74.

218. Pat Boone in S. and P. Boone, *Honeymoon*, 71.

219. LaHaye, *Sex Education*, 102, 108. Stanley seems to place partial blame on parents, especially fathers. He writes: "Girls from homes where Dad failed to fulfill his role may make up for his [lack of] affection by finding it through relationships with men. Girls from homes like this are easy prey for guys, especially older ones, with the wrong intentions. Their eyes seem to say, 'Take me, I'm available.'" Stanley, *Kids*, 217.

220. LaHaye, *Sex Education*, 109, 106, 150, 111. Kennedy adds another consideration, citing "studies" that "show that promiscuous girls in their teens have a five to one greater incidence of cervical cancer." Kennedy, *Learning to Live*, 139–40.

221. LaHaye, *Sex Education*, 114. Says LaHaye, "You can't keep your daughter from ruining her life through premarital sex but you can try." Ibid., 113.

222. Dobson, *Hide or Seek*, 113.

223. Stanley, *A Man's Touch*, 65, 66, 67.

224. LaHaye, *Battle for the Family*, 248.

225. Stanley, *A Man's Touch*, 79.

226. Stanley, *Kids*, 69. Beverly LaHaye describes the dilemma in eighteenth-century evangelical terminology: "It is the will that must be broken and not the spirit." B. LaHaye, *Your Child's Temperament*, 18. On the early evangelical theme

of "breaking the will," see Greven, *Protestant Temperament*, 32–43. See also Ammerman, *Bible Believers*, 170–74.

227. LaHaye, *Happy Though Married*, 91.

228. S. and P. Boone, *Honeymoon*, 124. See also ibid., 118–25. Writes Debby in her own autobiography, *So Far*, "Spankings, especially from my father, were not just a perfunctory pat on the behind. He meant for us to remember them and used a slipper, belt, or anything else that stung. . . . Often with tears still fresh in our eyes, the four of us would go up to my room and compare war wounds. Bending over, we'd back up to the mirror to see whose backsides had the reddest marks." Debby Boone, *So Far*, 107.

229. Kennedy, *Learning to Live*, 101.

230. Stanley, *Kids*, 69.

231. Pat Boone in S. and P. Boone, *Honeymoon*, 60.

232. B. LaHaye, *Spirit-Controlled Woman*, 115. In *Your Child's Temperament*, Beverly LaHaye goes so far as to argue that "every child has rights that are due him and the parent who loves with involvement will consider and respect them." B. LaHaye, *Your Child's Temperament*, 161.

233. B. LaHaye, *Your Child's Temperament*, 123.

234. D. Boone, *So Far*, 18. Says Stanley, "A high percentage of the rebellious children I have counseled came out of homes where the principle of wisdom was ignored, where almost everything was made into a moral issue." Ibid., 162.

235. Stanley, *Kids*, 55.

236. Boone discusses his daughter's illness in S. and P. Boone, *Honeymoon*, 126–34. See also Rachel Orr, "Anorexia: My Illusion of Weight Control," *The Daily Tar Heel*, 14 January 1988, 4–5.

237. D. Boone, *So Far*, 192. See also D. James Kennedy (with Norman Wise), *The Prodigal Child* (Nashville, Tenn.: Thomas Nelson Publishers, 1988).

238. LaHaye, *Battle for the Family*, 206. For LaHaye's views on the role of technology in creating a Christian conservative "electronic cottage," see ibid., 239–42.

239. Ibid., 231.

240. Tim LaHaye, *The Race for the 21st Century* (Nashville, Tenn.: Thomas Nelson Publishers, 1986), 150. Pointing proudly to the role of the Moral Majority and other groups in mobilizing millions of new voters, LaHaye compliments them on their "good citizenship that helps to insulate the home." LaHaye, *Battle for the Family*, 225.

'Family Values' And The Religious Right: A Narrow Definition

by Barry W. Lynn

I was up near Boston last month to debate religion and politics with Janet Parshall, a broadcaster who used to work for Concerned Women for America, an ultraconservative Religious Right group.

Although this event was co-sponsored by the American Jewish Committee and Gordon College, the local Christian radio station, which broadcasts Janet's show, managed to have a large banner draped on the podium that said "WEZE — Boston's Family Radio Station." The station's logo consists of a series of silhouettes of a terrier dog, a young boy, a man, a woman and a young girl.

Here it is: their view of the perfect nuclear, traditional family. I pointed out that it looked surprisingly close to my own family (except that my dog is cuter). What bothered me, though, was the implication that only this station was the "family" radio station in town and the depiction of the two-child, one-dog, two-parent household as the quintessential family.

Most people today don't live in relationships like that; only about 20 percent of Americans do. We live in a much more diverse nation of families: single-parent families, families with members of three generations, same-gender families and families with foster children who stay for brief periods of time. *These* are all the American family of 1995.

During the debate, Janet claimed that people routinely disparage the traditional family and as evidence pointed out that sometimes people say, "We don't live in a 'Leave it to Beaver' world anymore." I was starting to feel a little guilty — I've

used that phrase myself. But I caught myself. That line isn't meant to be an attack on traditional families. It is a simple recognition that "Leave it to Beaver" has been "colorized" since the 1950s.

This nation *was* always multi-racial, multi-lingual, multi-religious and multi-cultural. The difference now is that we're more apt to depict it as it really is. And when we work to protect "family values," we need to recognize the diversity of its unmet needs. Those diverse American families too often find themselves located in a world where people fear violence and crime and even hard-working people in two-parent families can't keep their heads above water because wages have slipped and costs for things like medical care, child and elder care and other expenses keep escalating.

When groups like Pat Robertson's "Christian Coalition" (and yes, they do seem to be arrogating to themselves the mantle of the only voice of Christendom) send out questionnaires to political candidates, they claim to be searching for answers to what they often characterize as the great "pro-family" questions. But are these even the questions somebody concerned with real family values ought to be asking?

In preparation for a recent sermon I delivered at the First Baptist Church in Silver Spring, Md., I looked over some Christian Coalition voter guides. One, from a 1994 congressional race in Indiana, caught my attention because of the issues it emphasized. One was "Banning Ownership of Legal Firearms." Incumbent Andy Jacobs supported the ban on "assault weapons," so he was listed as supporting the banning of legal firearms. His opponent, the Christian Coalition's clear choice, opposed such a ban. Where exactly did the Christian Coalition learn that assault weapons are pro-family? Reasonable people of goodwill can differ on the question of gun control, but to imply that those who advocate it are "anti-family" is grotesque.

Some of the other Christian Coalition-highlighted issues are also curious barometers of "family values": term limits, a

balanced budget amendment, tuition vouchers for private schools. Why do these issues, of all the great moral questions of the day, take up so much space in their polls? Where are the questions about child nutrition programs, low-income housing assistance and more law enforcement officers on the streets? They are absent, swallowed up by a morass of moral marginalia.

Frankly, I'm not sure one can readily determine biblically-centered opinions one way or the other on any of these issues, but from my theological training helping children eat is easier to support from the Bible than limiting Senators to 12 years in office.

Last month I watched Christian Coalition Executive Director Ralph Reed unveil his "Contract with the American Family." It includes several extremely dangerous proposals, including a "religious equality" amendment to gut the principle of church-state separation, vouchers for religious schools, an end to international family planning funds and broad new powers for religious groups to exercise a veto over school curricula.

So, as this debate over "family values" continues, all of us need to decide whether we should stand with those who spend their time fussing over whether a book in a school library has too "favorable" a comment on condoms, or those who battle to retain funding so that public schools can become safer, more secure and better at the task of teaching our children. Will we allow our Constitution to be altered, or will we keep the schools free of sectarian domination and let families renew their own commitments to prayer in homes and religious institutions? Will we seek a nation that restricts choice in moral decision making or proclaim real liberty of conscience? In real terms those are the choices we face.

Barry W. Lynn is executive director of Americans United for Separation of Church and State.

The Christian Right's antigay campaign

Part stealth, part muscle

DONNA MINKOWITZ

FOR THE LESBIAN AND GAY community, the 1992 election was supposed to be an apocalypse. Either Bush would be reelected, this time on an explicitly homophobic platform and owing a major political debt to the Christian right; or the United States would elect the first president in history openly to profess support for gay and lesbian civil rights.

The presidential election *was* a life or death matter for my community. Even so, daily life has gotten *more* apocalyptic for lesbians and gay men, not less, in the wake of the Clinton victory. Three-and-a-half months into 1993, we are in a situation we have never faced: The White House supports us—at least theoretically; but our enemies are organized to an unprecedented degree on the state and local levels.

In a dozen states—Texas, Lousiana, Virginia, Hawaii, Washington, Kansas, Iowa, Alaska, Arizona, California, Colorado and South Carolina—Pat Robertson's virulently antigay Christian Coalition holds a majority or strong minority of voting seats on the state Republican committee. Elsewhere, the Coalition has quietly won majorities on local school boards, neighborhood councils, hospital boards and other governing bodies, usually running candidates who do not reveal their affiliations or agendas until elected. The Coalition's strategy is to shore up enough power at the grassroots level to make policy in larger and larger jurisdictions.

This tactic...what opponents and supporters of the Christian right call "the San Diego model" of running stealth candidates—was developed in 1990 when 50 out of 88 Christian right candidates were elected to school boards, water boards, and other local governing bodies in San Diego. These candidates avoided public forums and mainstream media, campaigning only through conservative churches. Because the turnout in local elections is low, the Christian Coalition and related organizations were able to win by appealing to Christian right voters alone.

"We're trying to generate as large a turnout as possible among our constituency by communicating with them in a way that does not attract the fire of our opponents," Christian Coalition executive director Ralph Reed explained to the San Diego *Union-Tribune* September 29, 1991. Since then the Christian right-identified members of San Diego school boards have KO'd free breakfast programs as an attempt to replace "the traditional family," and tried to remove novels

DONNA MINKOWITZ covers gay and lesbian politics for The Village Voice.

about witches from school libraries.

Elsewhere in the country, they've gone further. In Texas, Pennsylvania, and Ohio, Christian right school board members have fought programs that encourage children's self-esteem on the grounds that these programs undermine parental authority. Under pressure from the religious right, a high school principal in Meridian; Ohio imposed a gag order preventing teachers from discussing sex, sexually transmitted diseases, or AIDS. In Pennsylvania, California, and New York City, Christian right school board members have fought curricula or curriculum guides that include gay and lesbian history and culture. A recent ruling by the Utah State Board of Education forbids positive portrayals of homosexuality in the public schools.

Antigay organizations

The Christian Coalition, which boasts a membership of 300,000 and over 550 chapters in all 50 states, holds a stations; a substantial proportion of their editorial content is devoted to the threat homosexuals supposedly pose to children and the public health. Within the past year, the corporation has conducted seminars all over the country to teach grassroots activists how to fight gay rights laws, legislation against AIDS discrimination, city permits for gay pride parades, and gay-inclusive classroom lessons.

"Using the Bible does not always convince your representative, city council, or friend of the soundness of your opinion," advises a Focus handbook called *The Homosexual Agenda: What You Can Do.* "They probably don't believe in the Bible. You need other arguments...that they are more likely to hear and accept." The Family Research Council, Focus's political arm, is headed by Gary Bauer, Reagan's domestic policy adviser and one of the main architects of that administration's homophobic policies.

The American Family Association (AFA), founded by the Rev. Donald Wildmon, led the successful fight to repeal Tampa's gay rights law last November. In Tallahassee, the AFA surrounded a public library that was showing a gay and lesbian film festival, in an attempt to prevent would-be viewers from going inside. The AFA also fights TV programs and movies that depict homosexuality positively. It was one of the major forces behind the attack on the National Endowment for the Arts' decision to fund openly gay and lesbian artists such as the late Robert Mapplethorpe.

Citizens for Excellence in Education (CEE) was founded in 1989 specifically to elect Christian right candidates to local school boards and keep approving references to homosexuality and religious pluralism out of public education. To date, CEE has helped elect over 3,500 school board members across the country. The group works closely with the Christian Coalition and other religious right groups.

'Special rights' rhetoric

Colorado's passage last November of Amendment Two, the first state law prohibiting the government from protecting gays from discrimination, has given the antigay movement much-needed experience in wooing voters who do not identify with the Christian right. Emboldened by the Colorado and Tampa votes, organizers have already begun collecting signatures for similar measures in Idaho, Washington, Michigan, California, and elsewhere. Oregon, where voters narrowly defeated a similar amendment last year, faces 37 *local* antigay ballot measures in towns and counties chosen on the basis of their voters' support for the statewide measure.

In these campaigns, antigay organizers have adopted another strategy: Taking a leaf from anti-Semitic organizers past and present, they paint lesbian and gay men as a wealthy elite whose movement threatens the economic interests of ordinary people. Laws protecting gay people's civil rights, they warn, really accord gay people "special rights" at the

mammoth organizing conference every year in Virginia Beach, Virginia, headquarters of Robertson's Christian Broadcasting Network. The conference, dubbed "the Road to Victory," has focused on teaching state-of-the-art political organizing techniques. So great is its influence that last year, both George Bush and Dan Quayle attended.

In the past five years, the Christian right has come to focus more and more on the issue of homosexuality. Operation Rescue (OR), a national group organized for the sole purpose of disrupting abortion clinics, recently took on the fight against gay rights as its second agenda. On January 8, OR held a national day of actions against lifting the ban on gays in the military.

Focus on the Family has also joined the battle. A $77 million Christian right media corporation, Focus produces 10 magazines and radio shows that are heard on 1800 radio expense of struggling heterosexuals. Colorado for Family Values, the group that sponsored Amendment Two, said it this way in their literature:

> What's fair about an affluent group gaining minority privileges simply for what they do in bed?... What's fair about people who enjoy all the right and privileges of American citizenship asking for special status?... Special rights for homosexuals just isn't fair—especially to disadvantaged minorities in Colorado.

Recent antigay pamphlets from Oregon to Maine are studded with references to homosexual wealth, from bogus statistics on "the average homosexual income of $55,000" to the claim that queers are 13 times more likely to be Frequent Fliers.

Though some *machers* in the Republican party are currently trying to distance the GOP from the Christian right zealots, it is important to remember just how deep the GOP-Christian right connection is.

According to Reed, the Chrisitian Coalition was started with $64,000 in "seed money" from the Republican Senatorial Candidates' Committee. Not only does the GOP benefit from access to the Christian right's voter base in right-wing churches nationwide, but the party also gains from "special rights" rhetoric. Homosexuals provide a convenient scapegoat for workers' suffering. And unlike racist appeals to the white working class, antigay appeals can be made in every community, without respect to color or income.

Changing constituencies

Because the media depict the Christian right solely as white, polyester-clad fundamentalists who preach on TV, it may be easy to overlook links between its traditional Protestant memebership and other Christians organizing around many of the same issues. Among Roman Catholics, for example, conservative bishops and grassroots groups who have enjoyed spectacular successes in campaigns against abortion rights and gay rights, especially in areas without a large Protestant evangelical population, frequently escape media scrutiny.

In fact, Robertson's Christian Coalition aims to bring together conservative Catholics, evangelicals, and other right-wing Christians under its banner. Many of the most important figures in the Christian right movement nationally are Catholics, including Pat Buchanan, Phyllis Schlafly of the Eagle Forum, and Richard Viguerie, the godfather of right-wing direct-mail political organizing. Robertson and Reed speak of "evangelicals and pro-family Catholics" when describing their constituency. And in New York City, John Cardinal O'Connor and Bishop Thomas Daily have led the fight against a public school curriculum guide that encourages sensitivity to lesbians and gay men [*Editors' note:* see "Tolerance in the Schoolroom," by Maxine Phillips and Tom Roderick, Feb. 15].

Nor is the broader movement so exclusively white as its popular image suggests. Though some national figures of the Christian right have ties to the white supremacist right, the Christian right has begun recruiting among Latino evangelicals and Catholics and among Black and Asian-American conservative Protestants.

While its greatest strength is currently at the grassroots level, the Christian right's influence in national politics should not be underestimated. Recently, Pentagon officials distributed hundreds of copies of a video called *The Gay Agenda* to members of Congress in order to discourage them from lifting the ban on homosexuals in the military. The video has been produced by Christian Coalition affiliates for use in passing antigay ballot measures in Oregon.

My life still depends on the success or failure of antigay organizers from the Christian right. The difference now is hundreds more battles exist, and the stakes are even higher. ☐

The Preacher Versus The Teacher

By Matthew C. Moen

With few exceptions, professional educators consistently misunderstand the Christian Right. They fail to appreciate the shifting nature of its constituency; the personal rivalries and theological fissures in its ranks; the striking reorientation in its language and tactics since 1985; the uniform rise in the political sophistication of its leaders.

The lack of understanding about the Christian Right reflects the reality that educators have things to do other than chronicle the evolution of a conservative social movement, whose followers prefer that their children attend religious schools anyway. It also reflects the distinct arenas that operate within a supposed "global village."

Just as many conservative Christians cannot distinguish between a traditionalist and a deconstructionist in a modern-day English department, many educators cannot state the theological differences between fundamentalists and evangelicals. The secular teacher and the conservative preacher are "ideal types," to be sure, that are not applicable to all in the ranks, and who do interact even when mutual antipathy exists.

Yet, the idea advanced by Alexis De Tocqueville (1848) that Americans are "careful to break up into small and distinct groups in order to taste the pleasures of private life" seems more accurate than ever. The educator reads a book to relax, tunes into PBS for visual entertainment, and considers the contemplative life the good one, in

Matthew C. Moen *is associate professor of political science at the University of Maine. He received his bachelor's degree from Augustana College and his doctorate from the University of Oklahoma. He is author of numerous journal articles and several books, including* The Transformation of the Christian Right *(1992) and* The Christian Right and Congress *(1989).*

Religious conservatives conjure up the spectre of a monolithic force indoctrinating children in "leftist" causes.

the best tradition of Aristotle; the fundamentalist attends Bible study, watches Bonanza on Pat Robertson's Family Channel, and considers the spiritual life best, as Jesus teaches. Those occupying each camp consort with like-minded individuals and do not search out information on the other side.

The lack of understanding is a constant source of friction. Educators assume that those with a literal understanding of the Bible cannot have a particularly high intelligence quotient. (How can any thinking person blithely ignore fossils?) They lambast religious conservatives for their "backward looking" attitudes; psychologists and sociologists lead the way, solemnly explaining the behavior and objectives of those associated with the Christian Right in terms of "authoritarian personalities" or "status anxiety" (Adorno et. al., 1950; Lipset and Rabb, 1978).

Social scientists thereby reduce the concerns of fellow human beings to the realm of personality disorders and highly symbolic crusades to assert cultural hegemony. Given that restricted prism of understanding, it is hardly surprising that educators cannot fathom the significance of issues such as prayer in schools and that they fall back on Thomas Jefferson's metaphor about a "wall of separation" between church and state, whenever serious questions arise about the intersection of religiosity and public policy. Perhaps it is this political scientist's erroneous observation, based on experiences with students in American Government, but I doubt whether those who cite a "wall of separation" know that the phrase appears nowhere in the Constitution, nor that it is only one possible interpretation of the Establishment Clause.

Religious conservatives exhibit the same lack of understanding. They conjure up the spectre of a monolithic force indoctrinating children in "leftist" causes, beginning with the primary school teacher who encourages children to protect the earth's environment, continuing with the secondary teacher who offers a contrary vision of American history, and ending with the college professor who

The lack of genuine understanding between the teacher and the preacher imperils the quality of American public life.

supports women's studies programs or multiculturalism (Schlafly, 1992).

Educators are portrayed as hell bent on disassembling the body politic, substituting their squishy values for bedrock beliefs. Religious conservatives also oversimplify while registering their objections, combining the seventh-grade art teacher in Alaska with the Marxist history professor at an Ivy League university, under the rubric of the "education establishment." That pejorative label dulls the critical faculties and fomentshostility among a citizenry that loathes bureaucracy, whether real or imagined.

Finally, religious conservatives claim that the Bible contains all of the answers to life's questions, a proposition that intrinsically justifies a lack of inquiry, and that renders its advocates unable to grasp the desire to push the boundaries of human knowledge. St. Thomas Aquinas, the medieval philosopher who worked to reconcile revelation and reason, would abhor the combination of blissful ignorance and ideology.

The lack of genuine understanding between the teacher and the preacher imperils the quality of American public life, because neither party will soon vacate the public square, despite firm predictions of the "fall of the Christian Right" (Bruce, 1988; D'Antonio, 1990). The mutual ignorance of the other side breeds a level of suspicion that, to borrow a phrase, proceeds beyond "our poor power to add or detract."

A step in the right direction, though, is to illuminate the existing state of affairs. This essay clarifies the development of the Christian Right over time, identifying the real (and imagined) challenges that it presents to educators. I purposely sketch the big picture, since a voluminous literature containing the details is available. Although Christian-Right supporters may judge this effort to be giving away "trade secrets" in a competitive environment, and educators may judge it an attack upon "us" rather than "them," the intent is to expose each side to the other area of the global village.

The preacher judged the teacher
ill-equipped to perform the role
requiring that moral statements
accompany clinical explanations.

Who's Right and Who's Wrong?

The Christian Right has a lineage traceable throughout the 20th century (Wilcox, 1992). Its most recent permutation arose in the late-1970s in response to a variety of developments. One long-term factor was the blossoming of the rights movement of the 1960s, which began with civil rights for African Americans and gradually extended to women's rights and gay rights (Morgan, 1984).

Many welcomed those crusades as progress against racism, sexism, and cultural oppression; Christian-Right leaders viewed them as attacks upon traditional values and as positive proof of moral degeneracy.

The Supreme Court's decisions banning school prayer (*Engel v. Vitale*, 1962) and legalizing school busing (*Swann v. Charlotte-Mecklenburg Board of Education*, 1971) and abortion (*Roe v. Wade*, 1973) also played a part, but not in the immediate way suggested by journalists.

The Christian-Right organizations coalesced too many years after those decisions for such direct causation. The decisions merely fostered discontent. The school prayer and abortion decisions signaled moral decay, while the school busing decision made it more difficult for white religious conservatives to avoid school desegregation.

The other long-term factor at work was the growth of the federal government. It pressured the traditional family structure through a higher tax burden, and fostered government assumption of tasks historically performed by the family. Examples abound, with the most obvious being programs for the elderly and the unwed mother.

Another very sensitive issue, which exploded in public schools around the nation, was sex education. The preacher judged the teacher ill-equipped to perform that role, which required that moral statements accompany clinical explanations. This area remains a battleground today, with struggles over the distribution of condoms in schools, and the introduction of "value-free" school curricula. The

President Carter dispatched an
emissary to repair relations with
fundamentalist leaders, but his
overture was too little, too late.

most salient fight has occurred in New York City, where the curriculum included books that taught primary school-children about gay lifestyles through titles such as *Heather Has Two Mommies* and *Daddy's Roommate*. (If you are unaware of the incendiary effect of the "lifestyles" language on religious conservatives, you are due for consciousness-raising).

The specific events that triggered the rise of the Christian Right were the decision of the Federal Communications Commission to consider restrictions on religious broadcasting and the effort of the Internal Revenue Service to revoke the tax-exempt status of private, religious schools practicing racial discrimination. Both of those issues arose during the Carter administration, which was already a disappointment to religious conservatives because of the President Carter's opposition to prayer in public schools, aid to parochial schools, and abortion restrictions.

The FCC and IRS controversies surfaced in 1977-1978, and the major organizations of the early Christian Right (Moral Majority, Christian Voice, and the Religious Roundtable) formed within the space of several months, beginning in December 1978.

Even with a "born-again" Baptist at the helm, the Carter administration failed to anticipate the rise of the Christian Right and the resurrection of previously dormant issues, such as school prayer and tuition tax credits. Once he sensed the depth of the unrest, President Carter dispatched an emissary to repair relations with fundamentalist leaders, but his overture in an election year was too little, too late (Vecsey, 1980).

Journalists were also caught flat-footed. They wrote just two articles about the Christian-Right in the year that it came together, as measured by citations in the *The Reader's Guide to Periodical Literature*, compared to 68 the following year (Moen, 1989). Those responsible for "breaking news" missed one of the major religious and political stories of the past quarter-century, perhaps because of their collective distance from the conservative Christian subculture.

Prominent public officials missed the boat in a different way.

Some scholars missed the genuine outrage that existed, and too easily dismissed the reverberations echoing about the body politic.

Patricia Harris, Secretary of Health and Human Services during the Carter administration, skipped over the messy details of law, personality, culture, and theology to compare Jerry Falwell to Ayatollah Khomeni ("Christian Right Equated with Iran's Mullahs," 1980).

Scholars also misunderstood these events. Hadden and Swann (1981) paved the way for much subsequent scholarship and public discussion, by adding the phrase "televangelism" to the nation's vocabulary. They argued that the Christian Right was built from the "top down" by clever television evangelists. Their reasoning provided a convincing explanation to people far removed from the fundamentalist subculture: whiz-bang technology explained the rise of the bumpkins, in an era where modernization and secularization were gradually eradicating religious belief.

The scholars who followed that cue completely missed the genuine outrage that existed, and too easily dismissed the reverberations echoing about the body politic. They identified Pat Robertson, Jimmy Swaggart, Jerry Falwell, Oral Roberts, and Jim Bakker as master manipulators, not pausing to consider whether their television audiences were not so much an empire as an edifice. It is little wonder that they and so many others were astonished by the "resurgence" of the Christian Right in the 1992 election. It is easy to draw the wrong conclusion when one starts with the wrong premise.

Up, Over, Around, and Through

Since its rise in the late-1970s, the Christian Right has evolved and changed. It has passed through two distinct phases, and is in the midst of a third (Moen, 1992). A brief synopsis of those phases is warranted, so as to inform the discussion of the challenge the Christian Right currently presents. Table 1 provides a reference point for what follows, listing the movement's formal organizations.

The first period of activism lasted from the inception of the Christian-Right organizations in 1978 through 1984. It is properly

TABLE 1

The Organizations of the Christian Right

Year	The Organizations of the Christian Right
1978	National Christian Action Coalition
1979	Religious Roundtable
	Christian Voice
	Moral Majority
	Concerned Women for America
1980	
1981	Freedom Council
1982	
1983	American Coalition for Traditional Values
1984	
1985	
1986	Liberty Federation
1987	American Freedom Coalition
1988	Family Research Council
1989	
1990	Christian Coalition

labeled the *expansionist period*. During that time, the Christian Right grew to seven national organizations, whose membership rose almost monotonically.

The distinguishing characteristics of this period were: a high public profile, evidenced by countless news stories and opinion polls on organizations like Moral Majority; a clique of prominent fundamentalist leaders who arranged and rearranged organizations in kaleidoscopic fashion to foster a perception that an unrivaled political force now existed; a concerted effort to achieve substantive victories on Capitol Hill, cresting in the 98th Congress (1983-1984), with passage of "equal access" legislation that allowed voluntary student groups to use public school facilities for religious activities; a tone that was distinctly moralistic, evidenced in Pat Robertson's oftquoted statement about "getting God back into government," and in an agenda centered on social issues such as prayer in schools, abortion, and gay rights; a proclivity for amateurishness, as the new political players learned the game of politics.

During this initial phase of the movement, President Reagan provided constant rhetorical support, but limited legislative assistance. The net result was a Christian Right that influenced greatly the public and congressional agendas, but fell short of enacting its statutory objectives, which included constitutional amendments to permit school prayer and ban abortion. Both of those "big-ticket"

During this phase of the movement, President Reagan provided constant rhetorical support, but limited legislative assistance.

items were considered on the Senate floor in 1983-1984, for the first time in more than a decade, but each one failed to secure the two-thirds vote needed for passage.

The combination of winning attention and losing legislative struggles knocked items off the agenda and caused the Christian Right to atrophy following President Reagan's reelection in 1984.

The second period of activism lasted during 1985-1986, and may be properly described as the *transition period*. Its major feature was retrenchment.

The National Christian Action Coalition, American Coalition for Traditional Values, and Freedom Council all disbanded; the Religious Roundtable and Christian Voice were allowed to atrophy; Moral Majority was collapsed into the newly formed Liberty Federation, for the express purpose of giving Reverend Falwell a graceful exit from politics. He started shifting funds from his political operations to his religious ministry in 1985, collapsed Moral Majority into the new group in 1986, and announced his retirement from an active political role in 1987.

When Reverend Falwell announced that he was going "back to the pulpit, back to preaching, back to winning souls," many fundamentalists followed (Miller, 1987). The loss of its titular leader reduced the Christian Right's influence on the political agenda for a time, which was reinforced by the closure of its lobbying operations on Capitol Hill. The changes did not mark the end of the Christian Right, however, but the beginning of a new phase of activism more focused on low-profile grassroots work. The Christian Right emerged a more potent political force.

Money, Politics, and Back to the People

The third period of activism started in 1987 and continues to the present. It is properly labeled the *institutionalization period*. Its distinguishing feature is the existence of several organizations that are well-positioned to exert influence for years to come; a secondary

This did not mark the end of the Christian Right, but the beginning of a new activism focused on low-profile grassroots work.

feature is a reorientation that makes it much more likely to combat educators.

Why is the Christian Right better positioned today than ever before, and more likely to challenge public education? One reason is that its current organizations are on firm financial footing. During the Christian Right's early years, its organizations were funded through direct-mail solicitation; their financial backing rose and fell with response rates.

Christian Right elites learned that it was difficult to sustain interest via solicitation, in part because it required increasingly strident rhetoric in order to motivate people to send money. (One can cry "secular humanist conspiracy" only so many times). Leaders remedied that problem in two different ways. One was to quietly tap the deep pockets of controversial figures, such as Reverend Sun Myung Moon, who gave funds to launch the American Freedom Coalition (Judis, 1989). The other was to erect genuine membership organizations, replete with annual dues, local and national meetings, and specific benefits. That tack was taken by Concerned Women for America. Both approaches provide secure financial footing.

Second, the Christian Right consists of fewer fundamentalists and more evangelicals. Early leaders and followers were mostly fundamentalist (Wilcox, 1986), but they gradually yielded to an evangelical contingent attracted to politics by Pat Robertson's 1988 presidential candidacy (Hertzke, 1993).

Scholars have shown that fundamentalists and evangelicals are suspicious of each other (Wilcox, 1986; Jelen, 1991), with a literal interpretation of the Bible a particular point of cleavage. The replacement of fundamentalists by evangelicals over time decreases the intensity of theological fissures; it also means that those currently associated with the Christian Right are more intellectually oriented (Hoffman and Rigney, 1992).

Third, the Christian Right is operating with a more full political agenda. In the early 1980s, the Christian Right had an abundant

> *The Christian Right consists of
> fewer fundamentalists and more
> evangelicals. Early members were
> mostly fundamentalist.*

agenda that included opposition to abortion, pornography, and the Equal Rights Amendment, as well as support for prayer in schools and autonomy for religious schools; it was on the cutting edge of other issues too, such as the effect of the tax code on families.

Over the course of the 1980s, the Christian Right's agenda withered, partly because its issues were disposed of (such as the ERA and the school prayer issue, because of enactment of "equal access" legislation), and partly because its leaders subordinated their issues to Reagan administration objectives. Christian-Right leaders ambled into debates over budget cuts, strategic weapons systems, and aid to the Contras—all issues where they had neither credentials nor expertise.

Their role as mouthpieces for the Reagan administration reached absurd heights when Reverend Falwell took a trip to South Africa and announced that the apartheid structure was misunderstood, and that economic sanctions against the regime were ill-conceived (Cowell, 1985; Pear, 1985). The result of justifying the Reagan administration's policies was that Christian-Right leaders stopped cultivating and springing their own issues, causing a once full agenda to wither.

This decline was symbolized by their focus on Oliver North in 1987, who was made the *cause celebre* because there was little else to advance. In the late-1980s, Christian-Right leaders grasped that problem, and began developing new agenda items. Many of those items focus on education: support for school choice and for forms of religious expression; opposition to university speech codes, "dirty" school textbooks, and federal agencies that dispense money to scholars, such as the National Endowment for the Arts and the National Endowment for the Humanities (these issues are revisited soon).

Fourth, the Christian Right's current leaders frame issues better to attract support for their cause. In the early 1980s, they focused on the rhetoric of morality, spawning organizational titles like *Moral* Majority and the American Coalition for *Traditional Values*. They

"Moral report cards" were issued to Congress—a key to a low "moral approval rating" was a vote for a Department of Education.

issued "moral report cards" that rated members of Congress (one key to a low "moral approval rating" was a vote in favor of creating a Department of Education); they also offered issues with strong moral overtones, such as abortion, school prayer, and pornography. Jorstad (1981) described the moralism of the early Christian Right, arguing that it was the predominant theme. Over time, the rhetoric of moralism was replaced by the language of liberalism, with its emphasis on equality, freedom, and rights.

The most obvious manifestation was organizational titles like the American Freedom Coalition and the Family Research Council, names that were etymologically liberal or else relatively neutral. The more crucial development, however, was the recasting of issues.

Abortion became a civil rights issue that involved "the rights of the unborn" (Operation Rescue even mimicked the tactics of the civil rights movement); school prayer became a matter of children having "the right to pray"; student religious groups in public schools became a matter of "equal access," or a matter of "religious apartheid" if they were to be excluded; school-textbook content became an issue of "parental rights" to monitor their children's learning, as well as a "free speech" issue because of the suppression of religious references in textbooks.

Beyond those clever reformulations, Christian-Right leaders lashed out against "discrimination" and "bigotry" in the press, arguing that Pat Robertson (but not Jesse Jackson) was labeled by his religious beliefs in his run for the presidency. The increasing use of the language of liberalism means that the Christian Right is promoting its issues in the terms most Americans are accustomed to hearing; its use of invective places its opponents on the defensive.

Fifth and lastly, the Christian Right is more oriented toward the grassroots. At the outset, Christian-Right leaders focused on Capitol Hill. It was accessible to interest groups as a result of reforms in the 1970s (Rieselbach, 1986); it provided a perfect opportunity for fledgling groups to institutionalize themselves, through involvement in titanic legislative struggles; it was the only sensible option.

What careless observers saw as the "fall of the Christian Right," was really a calculated decision to build grassroots structures.

The executive branch was in friendly hands with President Reagan, the judiciary was impervious to rapid change, and state and local avenues provided limited victories. After the "high-water" mark of the 98th Congress (1983-1984), however, Christian-Right leaders soon realized their future lay elsewhere. They needed to staff the bureaucracy, bring test cases before an increasingly conservative judiciary, and infiltrate the Republican Party.

What careless observers described as the "fall of the Christian Right," was actually a calculated and prudent decision to build grassroots structures. (Those structures were to be quietly erected, in order to avoid the filter of an antagonistic media). All of the groups active in the late-1980s operated from the premise expressed by Pat Robertson's deputy, Ralph Reed:

> We believe that the Christian community in many ways missed the boat in the 1980s by focusing almost entirely on the White House and Congress when most of the issues that concern conservative Catholics and evangelicals are primarily determined in the city councils, school boards, and state legislatures . . . [we will organize] one precinct at a time, one neighborhood at a time, one state at a time. ("Robertson Groups Vows to Fight for Sectarian Sex Ed," 1990).

The Christian Right's presence in the Republican Party during the 1992 campaign was the natural result of that strategic reorientation.

At the risk of summarizing the matter too starkly, the early Christian Right consisted mostly of fundamentalists, who advanced an agenda on Capitol Hill that was squarely centered on issues of morality; the contemporary Christian Right consists predominantly of evangelicals, who organize in the grassroots and frame issues in the language of liberalism.

Accompanying those changes is a marked rise in the political sophistication of Christian-Right leaders, owing to the experience gained by a decade of political activism, as well as the replacement of

The contemporary Christian Right consists predominantly of evangelicals, who frame issues in the language of liberalism.

less politically astute people by those with proven skills and credentials. A sterling example is Gary Bauer, head of the Family Research Council, who used to be President Reagan's domestic policy advisor. His background is a far cry from the largely apolitical fundamentalist minister.

Those who fail to recognize the transformation of the Christian Right, and therefore do not differentiate between its early and later stages, make a serious mistake. They understate the challenge that the Christian Right is capable of presenting; they exhibit the lack of understanding that surfaced when the sexual escapades of Jimmy Swaggart and Jim Bakker were reported in 1987. Observers predicting devastation to the Christian Right back then missed the simple fact that those ministers were hardly involved with the movement. The happy, spirit-filled pentecostals who visited Jim Bakker's Heritage U.S.A. amusement park were a different clientele than the determined evangelicals who quietly organized to win the "culture war" (Hunter, 1991).

Rhetoric Revisited

The transformed Christian Right presents a much more serious challenge to public education than its earlier counterpart. It is better-funded and more ably led; it is focused on the grassroots, where it is easier to bring effective pressure to bear on public officials (think about the effect of one letter to Capitol Hill, which gets 200 million pieces of mail annually, compared to that person's input into a school-board meeting or party caucus). The Christian Right also has developed new issues to fill the vacuum left by the passing of the Reagan administration and has learned to frame them in ways that maximize their appeal.

School choice probably tops the list of issues that seriously challenge education professionals. (Note the emphasis on "choice," the language of liberalism.) It would usher in sweeping changes in the way that America educates its children. Religious conservatives

Religious conservatives push "choice" as a way of shoving children into private schools, and emasculating the effect of NEA.

push it as a way of shoving children into private schools, and emasculating the effect of the National Education Association.

The concept of choice is inherently attractive to Americans, for whom it has become an entitlement (e.g., students should be allowed to avoid dissection while learning biology; careers should be open to all, even if it means dropping physical standards once deemed crucial). The attractiveness of choice combined with the egalitarian notion that everyone should be able to pick the school their children attend (not just the rich) creates an intriguing package.

Then too, school choice is pushed on a trial basis, making it harder to argue against. (What ogre will deprive little children of a chance to do better?) President Clinton may resist that path, but his record of experimentation in Arkansas and his decision to keep his daughter out of the Washington public schools makes him vulnerable to charges of hypocrisy.

Another issue that looms large is the extent of religious expression in the public schools. Religious conservatives have created organizations such as the National Legal Foundation, Christian Legal Society, and one arm of Concerned Women for America, whose specific purpose is to develop test cases ("Doing the Right Thing: Other Legal Aid Groups," 1990).

These groups challenge the extirpation of religion from public schools—the prohibition against school prayer and the abolition of prayers at commencement and the celebration of religious holidays in wholly secular fashion.

The conservatives believe the future holds promise, however, since the Reagan and Bush administrations remade the federal judiciary and the Supreme Court struck a more accommodationist pose. The case upholding the constitutionality of the Equal Access act showed the Court's new attitude (*Board of Education of the Westside Community Schools v. Mergens*, 1990). Since Christian-Right elites view religious expression in the schools as a barometer of the culture, they will continue to advance test cases.

A final issue that challenges educators is the content of school

Since Christian Right elites view expression in the schools as a barometer of the culture, they will continue to advance test cases.

textbooks. This issue has been around for some time, in the form of religious conservatives seeking to ban books with sexual overtones from the public school system. It has new impetus these days, however, as Christian-Right leaders have pressed their own claims of censorship against those who portray historical events in a largely secular context.

"Which is the greater evil," they ask rhetorically, "to take books off the shelves (that contain sexual imagery), or to put books in the classroom that cast the Pilgrims as happy adventurers, rather than as religious believers escaping persecution?" Which is worse, to ban classics like George Orwell's *1984* because of its sexual component, as religious conservatives seek, or to remove Mark Twain's *Huckleberry Finn* because of its racist stereotypes, as minority groups seek?

An issue that was once confined is now expanded (Cobb and Elder, 1983). These particular controversies attract the attention of parents, because children bring the books in question into the home. Parents ask what the children are reading and who selects the books. The issue has an impact and immediacy that arcane legislative struggles on Capitol Hill do not.

In a different vein, issues that claimed attention in the past are now *passe*. The issue of prayer in schools was gutted by passage of Equal Access legislation, which Christian-Right leaders came to prefer because a serious Bible study after school seemed like a better idea than an eviscerated voluntary prayer at the start of the day. Tuition tax credits are also moot, killed by a federal budget deficit that does not permit a tax break for parents able to afford private schools for their children.

Finally, the issue of creationism is dead. It gained notoriety during the 1980s when Ronald Reagan publicly supported teaching creationism alongside evolution ("Religious Right Talks Politics," 1980); it was manifested in a bill passed in Louisiana that required instruction in "creation-science." The Supreme Court struck down that bill in *Edwards v. Aguillard* (1987), however, and Christian-Right leaders saw that creationism was among their least popular

> *Their political evolution, so to*
> *speak, caused Christian Rights*
> *leaders to end seeking fights with*
> *Darwin outside of church.*

causes. Their political evolution, so to speak, caused them to end seeking fights with Darwin outside of church.

Higher Ed Already Has 'Choice'—K-12 the Real Focus

The challenge the preacher presents to the teacher in the 1990s is not uniform across educational levels. The challenge to higher education is infinitesimal. Students demanding a conservative Christian environment during their matriculation will attend an Oral Roberts University or a Liberty University. The truest of the true believers are thus siphoned off.

Those left attending the public universities confront institutional missions that are understandably secular, faculty who are predominantly liberal, especially in the social sciences and humanities, and institutional norms that promote egalitarianism (Wildavsky, 1991). Students at public universities are probably as attuned to the importance of saying the gender-neutral "chairperson," as they are cognizant of the Golden Rule.

The Christian Right's challenge is also defused, because many issues that incite controversy at lower levels have less relevance with higher education. School choice already exists in higher education, with students able to attend any institution in the nation that they can get admitted into and afford. Likewise, religious expression is tacitly encouraged by a general climate of free expression. Itinerant preachers proselytize on campuses and Gideons dispense copies of the New Testament. Finally, the content of textbooks is a non-issue. Those focused on that issue concern themselves with impressionable schoolchildren, not college students. Campus libraries and bookstores have treatises promoting every conceivable viewpoint.

The Christian Right challenges higher education, but not in any sustained or successful way. Its leaders complain about the phenomenon of "politically correct" speech, for instance, but that issue is driven more by defenders of the First Amendment, such as the

374

The impact on higher ed has been restricted to the spillover effect of bad publicity and the "chilling effect" on proposed projects.

American Civil Liberties Union than by the Christian Right.

Its top leaders also decry the goods produced by scholars from grants bestowed by the National Endowment for the Arts (NEA) and the National Endowment for the Humanities (NEH). Many of the projects coming under fire in recent years, however, such as "Piss Christ" supported by the NEA, were produced by free-lance artists, rather than university employees. The impact on higher education has been largely restricted to the spillover effect of bad publicity and the "chilling effect" on proposed projects (Burd, 1992). Those are real but ephemeral concerns. Moreover, in spite of all the hoopla surrounding the NEA, Congress cut its budget a total of .0003 of 1 percent in 1989, when the controversy surfaced. It reduced a $144.5 million budget by $45,000—the amount equal to the two grants that created the most controversy.

Recent developments portend an end to those struggles. The reauthorization of the NEA in 1990 for three years, and the early resignation of Lynne Cheney as head of NEH, decreases the salience of those agencies. Moreover, the Clinton administration is less likely to kowtow to religious conservatives, as the Bush administration did. (Bush fired John Frohnmayer, head of the NEA, as a sop to conservatives during his intraparty struggle with Pat Buchanan).

Christian-Right leaders may well scour the countryside looking for offensive projects in order to whip up the faithful and raise money, but they will be unable to sustain attention even if they find one. People who see a grave threat to higher education from the Christian Right are crying "wolf" in the presence of a bunny.

That is not the case for those involved in primary and secondary education, however, who face a Christian Right that is well-positioned and determined to prevail. The combination of factors cited—a grassroots emphasis, a more sophisticated way to frame issues, better set of leaders, solid financial base, and full political agenda—means a protracted struggle in school districts all across the country.

In 1992, Christian-Right forces effectively organized support for

375

their invisible "stealth candidates" in school board, city council, and state legislative elections. They won an estimated 40 percent of the 500 races they contested (Mydans, 1992). That figure signals the changes afoot, and provides a perspective on the challenge the Christian Right presents in state and local arenas.

Hard to document, but an important dimension to the struggle is the sense of patience now instilled in Christian Right followers. In the early 1980s, a newly formed political movement burst onto the national scene and demanded immediate and extensive action. Its uneven record of success caused many to drop out. For those who stayed and those who joined the ranks in later years, though, a sense of realism was inculcated about the prospects and pace of change. Those now in the trenches will not retreat from the cultural war.

The struggle between the preacher and the teacher will wax and wane and be unevenly manifested across the country. It will not soon cease, however, because each side is well-equipped and determined to prevail. Bill Billings, of the National Christian Action Coalition, once said that his people were ready to "charge hell with a squirt gun" (Sweeney, 1980). They have since upgraded their weaponry, and are prepared to douse an incendiary "education establishment."

References

Adorno, T., Frenkel-Brunskik, W., Levinson, D., & Sanford, R. (1950). *The authoritarian personality*. New York: Harper.

Bruce, S. (1988). *The rise and fall of the new Christian Right*. New York: Oxford University Press.

Burd, S. (1992, April 22). Chairman of humanities fund has politicized grants process, critics charge. *Chronicle of Higher Education*, 1.

Christian Right equated with Iran's Mullahs. (1980, September 24). *Washington Star*, 4.

Cobb, R W. & Elder, C.E. (1983). 2d ed. *Participation in American politics*. Baltimore: Johns Hopkins University Press.

Cowell, A. (1985, August 20). Botha sees South African churchmen and Falwell. *New York Times*, 6.

D'Antonio, M. (1990, February 4). Fierce in the '80s, fallen in the '90s: The religious right forgets politics. *Los Angeles Times*, M3.

Doing the right thing: Other legal aid groups. (1990, May). *Church & State*, 11.

Hadden, J.K. & Swann, C.E. (1981). *Prime time preachers: The rising power of televangelism*. Reading, Mass.: Addison-Wesley.

Hertzke, A.D. (1993). *Echoes of discontent: Jesse Jackson, Pat Robertson, and the resurgence of populism*. Washington, D.C.: CQ Press.

Hoffman, T.J. & Rigney, D. (1992, September). Is American Catholicism anti-intellectual? Paper presented at the Annual Meeting of the American Political Science Association, Chicago, Illinois.

Hunter, J.D. (1991). *Culture wars*. New York: HarperCollins.

Jelen, T. (1991). *The political mobilization of religious beliefs*. New York: Praeger.

Jorstad, E. (1981). *The politics of moralism*. Minneapolis: Augsburg.

Judis, J.B. (1989, March 27). Rev. Moon's rising political influence. *U.S. News & World Report*, 27.

Lipset, S.M. & Rabb, E. (1970). *The politics of unreason*. New York: Harper & Row.

Miller, M. (1987, November 16). Goodbye to all that. *Newsweek*, 10.

Moen, M.C. (1992). *The transformation of the Christian Right*. Tuscaloosa: University of Alabama Press.

———. (1989). *The Christian Right and congress*. Tuscaloosa: University of Alabama Press.

Morgan, R.E. (1984). *Disabling America: The 'rights industry' in our time*. New York: Basic Books.

Mydans, S. (1992, November 21). Quietly, Christian conservatives win hundreds of local elections. *New York Times*, 1.

Pear, R. (1985, August 22). Falwell denounces Tutu as phony. *New York Times*, 10.

Religious right talks politics. (1980, September 3). *Guardian*, 4.

Rieselbach, L. (1986). *Congressional reform*. Washington, D.C.: CQ Press.

Robertson goup vows to fight for sectarian sex ed. (1990, June). *Church & State*, 14.

Schlafly, P. (1992, November 1). Whistleblowing on social engineers. *Washington Times*, B4.

Sweeney, J. (1980, May 19). Evangelicals seeking to establish political force. *Los Angeles Times*, 1.

Tocqueville, A. D. (1848). *Democracy in America*. Garden City, New York: Doubleday & Co. (Reprint, 1969).

Vecsey, G. (1980, January 21). Militant television preachers try to weld fundamentalist Christian's political power. *New York Times*, 21.

Wilcox, C. (1992). *God's warriors*. Baltimore: Johns Hopkins University Press.

———. (1986). Evangelicals and fundamentalists in the new Christian Right. *Journal for the Scientific Study of Religion*, 25, 355-363.

Wildavsky, A. (1991). *The rise of radical egalitarianism*. Washington: American University Press.

Does welfare bring more babies?

CHARLES MURRAY

LAST OCTOBER, I published a long piece on the op-ed page of the *Wall Street Journal* entitled "The Coming White Underclass." Its thesis was that white illegitimacy—22 percent of all live births as of the latest (1991) figures—is now moving into the same dangerous range that prompted the young Daniel Patrick Moynihan to write about the breakdown of the black family in 1964, and that the ensuing social deterioration in lower-class communities may be as devastating for whites in the 1990s as it was for blacks in the 1960s. The centerpiece of my solution was to abolish all federal support for single women with children.

The response was, for me, unique. It is not just that the piece aroused more intense reaction than anything I have written since *Losing Ground*, but that so many people agreed with me. This is not normal. After I publish something, my mail and phone calls are usually split about 50/50 pro and con. This time, almost everyone agreed that the problem of illegitimacy was just as bad as I described, and a surprising number of people, including some ordinarily prudent people in the public eye, endorsed my radical notion of ending welfare altogether.

All this leads me to believe that illegitimacy is about to replace abortion as the next great national social debate. It should; not because the nation spends too much on welfare but because, as Moynihan said first and best, a community that allows a large number of young men to grow up without fathers "asks for and gets chaos." I believe it is not hyperbole but sober fact that the current levels of illegitimacy already threaten the institutions necessary to sustain a free society.

And so I want to end welfare. But this raises an obvious question: do we have any reason to believe that ending welfare will in fact cause a large-scale reduction in illegitimacy? Does welfare cause illegitimacy?

The answer has seemed self-evident to people ranging from the man in the street to Nobel laureate economists. The answer has not been nearly so clear, however, to social scientists who have studied the problem, nor has the search for an answer been conducted with stately scholarly detachment. It has instead been a hard-fought battle stretching back many years. Almost everyone has brought convictions about what the answer ought to be, for few issues have been so politically charged. But with a few lapses, the combatants have played by the technical rules in making their points, and, after all this time, we have learned at least a few things on which we can agree.

Two detailed reviews summarize the academic evidence. One, by Brown University economist Robert Moffitt, is called "Incentive Effects of the U.S. Welfare System: A Review," and it appeared in the *Journal of Economic Literature* in March 1992. I wrote the other one, called "Welfare and the Family: The U.S. Experience," as part of a special issue of the *Journal of Labor Economics* in January 1993, devoted to a set of articles comparing American and Canadian social policy.

What follows summarizes the major area of agreement that has developed over the last ten years—necessarily simplifying many findings and ignoring nuances. Then I turn to the major remaining area of disagreement. It brings to the attention of a general audience—for the first time, to my knowledge—a major technical error in the understanding of black illegitimacy that has large consequences for the subsequent debate. Bluntly: an important and commonly used argument of those who say that welfare does not cause illegitimacy is 180 degrees wrong.

Where analysts agree

If the agreement could be summed up in a single sentence, it is that moderate differences in welfare benefits produce some differences in childbearing behavior, but only small ones. The main research strategy for reaching this conclusion has been to explore the effects of variations in AFDC (Aid to Families with Dependent Children) benefits across states. The hypothesis has been that since benefits vary widely, there should be differences in childbearing behavior as well, if indeed welfare is a culprit in producing illegitimacy.

Back in 1983, David Ellwood and Mary Jo Bane—both now senior officials in Clinton's Department of Health and Human Services—wrote the early version of a paper (still being circulated in typescript) during the debate over *Losing Ground* that everyone interpreted as proving that welfare doesn't cause increases in illegitimacy. That's not exactly what the analysis found— their approach to the issue was indirect and used a methodology so complex that evaluating the results is difficult even for specialists—but "Ellwood and Bane" is nevertheless still cited in the media as the definitive study that welfare does not affect illegitimacy.

Since then, several studies have explored the issue more directly, and the consensus has shifted to a tentative conclusion that welfare is implicated, but not dramatically. The results from the recent studies have many differences, and it would be unrealistic to try to draw a consensus from them about the magnitude of the effect of welfare. One study found a fairly large effect on childbearing behavior (for example, a predicted increase of 16 percent in the probability of teen births if welfare benefits rose 20 percent), but the effect was statistically insignificant. (This can happen when samples are small or the variation in results is very large.) Another found an effect that was in the same ballpark (a 6 percent increase in childbearing by unmarried women in response to a 10 percent increase in welfare benefits) and was also statistically significant. Other studies have found statistically significant effects without reporting the magnitude.

Until recently, studies of this issue have concluded that the effects of welfare are much easier to find among whites than among blacks. In two of the studies mentioned above, all of the

apparent effect of differing welfare benefits on childbearing behavior was accounted for by the behavior of whites. An additional study that was limited to black teenagers found only a
small, statistically insignificant effect.

But the situation is changing. A recent detailed study by
Mark Fossett and Jill Kiecolt in the *Journal of Marriage and the
Family* using 1980 census data found a substantial and consistent
relationship between the size of public assistance payments and
illegitimacy among black women ages 20–24, even after controlling for a wide variety of economic, social, and demographic
factors. Why did this study find a relationship where others had
not? Partly because the analysis was more tightly focused than
the others, using metropolitan areas rather than states; partly
because the study focused on a particular age group (women
ages 20–24) instead of lumping all women together. Much more
work remains to be done regarding black illegitimacy and welfare, but the best bet at this time is that the results for blacks
and whites will converge. Using what the social scientists call
"cross-sectional data"—comparing different places at the same
historical moment—it seems likely that welfare will be found to
cause some portion of illegitimacy, but not a lot.

The area of agreement, limited though it may sound, has
important policy implications. Even taking the studies showing
the largest statistically significant effect of welfare on childbearing,
there is no reason to suppose that reducing welfare benefits by
10 percent will produce more than about a 6 percent drop in
childbearing among single women. This is not enough to make
much difference in anything. More generally, if you were to ask
scholars of various political viewpoints in the welfare/illegitimacy
debate about the prospective effects of other welfare proposals
that have been in the news recently—stopping the increase in
benefits that kicks in when a second child is born, toughening
workfare requirements, linking welfare to school attendance, and
so forth—almost all of us would be pessimistic. We have different reasons for thinking that such changes would be good or
bad, but the available data do not give much cause to think that
such small changes will produce more than small effects.

There is another intriguing implication of this research, however, that has gone unremarked. The same regression coefficients that show small effects from small changes imply that

getting rid of welfare altogether would have large effects. If a 10 percent increase in welfare benefits elicits a linear 6 percent increase in extramarital childbearing (to take a middle-of-the-road finding), what would a 100 percent decrease produce? A 60 percent reduction in extramarital childbearing? The coefficients might not behave linearly in the real world, of course. The effects of reductions could diminish as the magnitude of the reduction in welfare approaches 100 percent, or they could as plausibly grow. The effects need not be symmetric for increases and decreases in welfare. None of the authors of the various studies has yet explored these tantalizing possibilities, but they obviously call for such exploration.

Where analysts disagree

The favored way of examining the effects of welfare, taking advantage of the natural variation in AFDC payments across states, has a number of defects.

One problem with drawing comparisons across states is that state-by-state differences in welfare benefits are not so great as they seem. When you are first told that Louisiana has an average monthly AFDC payment of $169 and California has a monthly payment of $640 (the 1990 figures), the difference looks huge. But some federal benefits (such as food stamps) are more generous in low AFDC states, and Medicaid is available everywhere. Adding in everything, the proportional differences in the welfare packages available in different states shrink. And when you then put those differences in terms of the local economy, the difference nearly disappears. When the General Accounting Office compared the value of welfare packages in thirteen locations across the country in the late 1970s, when state-by-state AFDC differences were near their peak, the agency found that the San Francisco package turned out to provide an income equivalent to 66 percent of the median household income in San Francisco, while the New Orleans package provided an income equivalent to 65 percent of the median household income in New Orleans. Should we be surprised to find that welfare differences between Louisiana and San Francisco do not produce much difference in out-of-wedlock childbearing?

Another problem is that a powerful factor masks the effects of welfare on blacks when scholars base the analysis on states.

The black-white difference in illegitimacy goes back to the earliest post-Civil War data. No scholar has ever succeeded in explaining away this racial difference with any combination of economic, social, or educational control variables. The residual difference is astonishingly large. Based on the data from a large national database (the National Longitudinal Study of Youth), the probability that a baby will be born to a single woman is more than twice as high for blacks as whites after controlling for age, education, socioeconomic background, and poverty. For reasons that are still not understood, something in black culture tolerates or encourages birth out of wedlock at higher rates than apply to white culture in any given year, and this has been true before and after welfare was introduced. The problem is that "black culture" (a term I am using because no one knows how to describe it more specifically) is not spread evenly across the United States. The states in which blacks have the very lowest illegitimacy ratios are places like Idaho, Montana, North and South Dakota, Alaska, Hawaii, New Hampshire, and Maine, where AFDC payments are often well above the national average, but a very small black population lives in the midst of a dominating white culture (with its much lower illegitimacy ratios). Most of the states with the very lowest AFDC payments are in the Deep South, where blacks not only constitute a major portion of the population, but are densely concentrated in given areas—also, in other words, where whatever-it-is about black culture that produces high illegitimacy is likely to permeate the world in which black youngsters grow up. In statistical terms, this means that a great deal of noise is introduced when one analyzes the effect of varying AFDC payments. The same data that show no relationship between welfare and illegitimacy among blacks across states suddenly show such a relationship when one controls for the size and density of the black population.

The main problem with comparisons across states is that they ignore the overriding historical reality that welfare went up everywhere in the United States in a concentrated period of time, producing an overall national change that dwarfs the importance of between-state differences. Focusing on differences between states ignores the main effect.

Even when one takes a historical perspective, the story is a complex one. Here, pictorially, is the main battleground in the

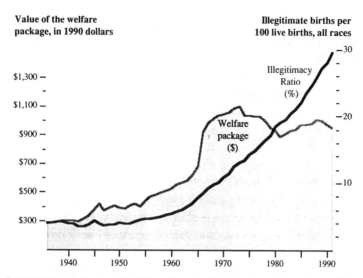

Value of the welfare
package, in 1990 dollars

Illegitimate births per
100 live births, all races

Source: Illegitimacy data since 1960: National Center for Health Statistics, "Advance Report of Final Natality Statistics,"*Monthly Vital Statistics Report*, vol. 42, no. 3 (S) (Sept. 9, 1993), table 16, and comparable tables in earlier volumes. Data prior to 1960: National Center for Health Statistics, *Vital Statistics*. Computation of the welfare package uses budget data from U.S. Bureau of the Census, *Statistical Abstract of the United States,* on AFDC, food stamps, public housing, and Medicaid. The method of computation is described in Charles Murray, "Welfare and the Family: The American Experience," *Journal of Labor Economics*, vol. 11, no. 1, pt. 2 (Jan. 1993).

debate over whether welfare causes illegitimacy.

There are many things to argue about in this figure. Probably the one you have heard most often involves the size of the welfare package. I have shown it as a combination of AFDC, food stamps, Medicaid, and public housing subsidies, using conservative methods for valuing these components. Those who argue for an expansion of welfare benefits would have shown a much different figure, showing just the AFDC benefit, which in real terms has retreated to 1950s levels.

But to focus on just the AFDC cash payment is an example of the bogus part of the welfare/illegitimacy debate that most parties to the debate are now beyond, at least when they talk among themselves. Statements such as "welfare benefits are now back to 1950s levels" often show up in congressional testimony and the network news shows, but no serious student will deny that food stamps, Medicaid, and housing benefits are part of the relevant package available to a young woman with a baby and that those have expanded dramatically, along with a hodge podge of other benefits both federal (the Special Supplemental Food Program for Women, Infants, and Children for example) and state or municipal (heating fuel subsidies, eviction protection, for example). Arguments about the specific value of Medicaid and public housing subsidies could result in minor shifts in the trend line shown in the figure, but the overall shape must remain the same by any method of computation: a very large increase in the last half of the 1960s, a smaller drop in real value in the last half of the 1970s (because of inflation—the nominal value of benefits continued to rise), and only small changes since the early 1980s, when inflation subsided. This basic shape of the trend in welfare benefits sparks the authentic part of the debate, which may be summarized as follows.

Looking at the figure, we see that the real value of the welfare benefit first available in 1936 begins to rise in the mid-1940s. By the end of the 1940s, the illegitimacy ratio begins a modest rise too. The increase in the welfare package steepens somewhat in the mid-1950s, and within a few years the slope of the illegitimacy ratio steepens as well. Then in the mid-1960s the trend lines for both the value of the welfare package and illegitimacy shoot sharply upward. All of this is consistent with an argument that welfare is an important cause of illegitimacy.

But there is another side to this story, as shown in the graph after the early 1970s. After 1973, the value of the welfare package begins to drop, while illegitimacy continues to increase. This is inconsistent with a simple relationship of welfare to illegitimacy. Why didn't illegitimacy decrease a few years after the value of welfare began to decline?

At this point, the published research literature is little help. The "research," if it may be called that, has consisted mostly of pointing to the part of the graph that is consistent with one's position. But the contending parties in the debate must hold certain underlying assumptions about how causation is going to work in such a situation. Let's suppose you want to argue that the trend in illegitimacy should have flattened and reversed when the real value of welfare benefits stopped climbing. It seems to me that this implies two assumptions: (1) fertility behavior is highly sensitive to incremental changes in welfare benefits, independent of existing fertility trends among single women, and (2) young women accurately and quickly discount nominal increases in welfare in keeping with changes in the Consumer Price Index.

I do not find either of those assumptions plausible. In the late 1970s, social scientists knew that the real value of the welfare benefit was declining, but the young woman in the street probably did not. She was, after all, seeing her friends on welfare get checks that were larger every year, and health care and housing benefits that were more important every year as prices went up.

People like me also have to meet a burden, however. The main one, as I see it, is to spell out how a complex causal sequence is working, for, clearly, a simple causal link (fertility behavior among single women goes up and down with the value of the welfare check) doesn't work. One of the key features of my explanation is the assumption that many of the social restraints on illegitimacy erode as out-of-wedlock births become more common. Thus we may argue that the very large increase in benefits in the 1960s was indeed a major culprit in jacking up the illegitimacy ratio, but that the increased prevalence took on a life of its own in the 1970s. I find this plausible but, obviously, many who use the 1970s as evidence that welfare does not cause illegitimacy must not find it plausible. Here, the prescription to improve the quality of the debate is for both sides to spell out the assumptions that go into their causal arguments and test them against the data.

The great black fertility illusion

This brings us to the issue I mentioned earlier, that on one argument crucial to the debate, the accepted wisdom is 180 degrees wrong. It involves black illegitimacy, which has always been at the center of public concern about illegitimacy, and at the center of debate about causes. Many of you who have followed the welfare debate will recognize it, for the argument is made frequently and volubly. It goes like this:

Yes, the proportion of black children born to single women started to shoot up rapidly during the 1960s. But during that same period, the incidence of births among single black women was actually going down. If the increases in welfare during the 1960s had such terrible effects, why were fewer single black wo-

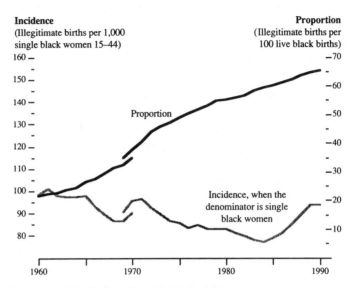

Incidence
(Illegitimate births per 1,000
single black women 15–44)

Proportion
(Illegitimate births per
100 live black births)

Line segments. 1960–70: All nonwhites. 1968–90: Blacks only.
Source: Computed from National Center for Health Statistics, "Advance Report of Final Natality
Statistics,"*Monthly Vital Statistics Report*, vol. 42, no. 3 (S) (Sept. 9, 1993), tables 1 and 17, and
comparable tables in earlier volumes.

men having babies? Here are the trend lines for the proportion
(represented by the line labeled proportion) and incidence (represented by the line labeled incidence).

As one writer put it: "Unmarried black women were having
babies at a considerably lower rate in 1980 than they were in
1960. Further, the birth rate among black single women had
fallen almost without a break since its high in 1961." The author? Me, writing in *Losing Ground*. At that time, like everyone
else involved in the welfare/illegitimacy debate, I took for granted
that the production of black illegitimate babies was falling, even
though the proportion of black children born to single women
was rising, and that this was something that those who would
blame welfare for illegitimacy would have to explain away.

Such explanations are available because fertility rates were
falling for married women as well. One may acknowledge that
broad social forces can have an overriding influence on the propensity of women to have children and still argue that welfare has an independent role in shaping the marital circumstances surrounding the children who are born. But, given the

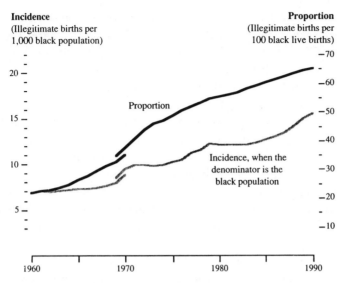

Incidence
(Illegitimate births per
1,000 black population)

Proportion
(Illegitimate births per
100 black live births)

Line segments. 1960–70: All nonwhites. 1968–90: Blacks only.
Source: Computed from National Center for Health Statistics, "Advance Report of Final Natality Statistics,"*Monthly Vital Statistics Report*, vol. 42, no. 3 (S) (Sept. 9, 1993), tables 1 and 16, and comparable tables in earlier volumes.

figure shown here, it becomes implausible to make the more ambitious argument that welfare bribes women to have children, no matter how often social workers tell you that they know of many such cases. That is why, in the example of Harold and Phyllis, which became one of the best-known sections of *Losing Ground*, I was careful to begin the scenario with Phyllis already pregnant. I was persuaded by the evidence summarized in the paragraph above that a case could not be made that welfare caused more births, only that welfare raised the probability that a given birth would be illegitimate.

I was wrong. The figure on the previous page reflects a statistical illusion. Here, in the next figure, is the appropriate way to view the production of black babies out of wedlock from 1960 to 1990.

The line for the proportion remains unchanged, but what a dramatic difference in the measure of incidence. The incidence of black illegitimacy did not peak in 1960; on the contrary, it increased slowly until the late 1960s, when it shot up and then continued increasing with only short breaks through the end of the 1980s.

What statistical game has been played? If you take a careful look at the labels in the figures, you may be able to figure it out for yourself—notice the difference between "illegitimate births per 1,000 single black women 15-44" in the first graph and "illegitimate births per 1,000 black population."

Statistics don't lie, as long as everyone is clear on precisely what question is being asked and precisely what the statistic measures. Here, we are interested in two separate phenomena: proportion and incidence. Proportion can be measured only one way (divide the number of illegitimate babies by the total number of live births). But in the second and third figures, we used two different ways of measuring incidence, and they showed utterly different results. They cannot both be right. Which one is?

The underlying sense of "incidence" is "frequency relative to a consistent base." If the size of a population were constant, then we could simply use the raw number of illegitimate births as our measure of incidence. But populations do not remain constant. Therefore we need to divide the number of births by some denominator that will hold the population factor constant. The usual way to do this is by using the number of single women as the denominator. This makes intuitive sense, since we are talking about illegitimate births. But it is an inferior measure of incidence because the real issue we are interested in is the production of illegitimate babies per unit of population. What few people, including me, thought about for many years is that it is possible for the production of illegitimate babies per unit of population to go up even while the probability that single women have babies goes down.

This seeming paradox can occur if the number of single women suddenly changes far out of proportion to the increase in the overall population, and that's what happened to blacks during the 1960s. In a mere five year period from 1965 to 1970, the proportion of black women ages 15–44 who were married plummeted by 9 percentage points, from 64 to 55 percent—an incredible change in such a basic social behavior during such a short period of time. (During the same period, the comparable figure for whites fell from 69 to 66 percent.) Black marriage continued to fall throughout the 1970s and 1980s, standing at about 36 percent in 1990.

To see what this does to the interpretation of fertility rates, think of the familiar problem of interpreting Scholastic Aptitude Test (SAT) scores. Whenever the scores go down, you read news stories pointing out that maybe education isn't getting worse but that more disadvantaged students (who always would have scored low, but had not been taking the SAT) have entered the SAT pool, therefore causing the scores to fall. It is a similar scenario with the pool of black single women: By 1970, a large number of black women who would have been married in the world of 1960 were not married. The pool was being flooded. Did these new additions to the pool of single women have the same propensity to have babies out of wedlock as the old pool of single women? The contrast between the two figures suggests that the plausible answer, no, is correct.

The crucial point is that the number of illegitimate babies in the black population—not just the proportion, but the number— produced in any given year among a given number of blacks nearly doubled between 1967 and 1990, even though the fertility rate among single black women fell. It increased most radically at the end of the 1960s, tracking with a plausible time lag the most rapid rise in welfare benefits. Or in other words, black behavior toward both marriage and out-of-wedlock childbearing during the period in which welfare benefits rose so swiftly be- haved exactly as one would predict if one expected welfare to discourage women from getting married and induce single women to have babies.

When we then take the same measure and look at it over the fifty year sweep from 1940 to 1990, comparing black incidence of birth within marriage and outside marriage, all against the backdrop of the value of the welfare package, the figure on the following page is how the picture looks.

The figure is not in any way "proof" of a causal relationship. But it is equally important to confront the plain message of these data. At the same time that powerful social and economic forces were pushing down the incidence of black children born to married couples, the incidence of black children born to un- married women increased, eventually surpassing the rate for mar- ried couples. Something was making that particular behavior swim against a very strong tide, and, to say the least, the growth of welfare is a suspect with the means and opportunity.

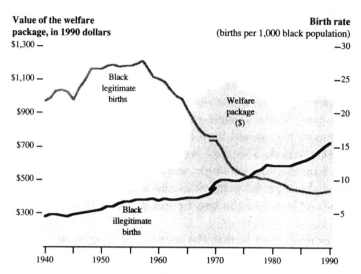

Value of the welfare
package, in 1990 dollars

Birth rate
(births per 1,000 black population)

Line segments. 1960–70: All nonwhites. 1968–90: Blacks only.
Source: Sources used for figure 1.

This new look at black illegitimacy, then, contradicts one of the main arguments that has been used to exculpate welfare's role in promoting illegitimacy. This will not stop the debate. The map linking welfare and illegitimacy still has big gaps. Optimistically, the progress we have been making in the last decade will continue. Pessimistically, it had better. For if illegimacy is as serious a problem as I think, we cannot afford to waste much more time in deciding what needs to be done.

ANTIABORTION, ANTIFEMINISM, AND THE RISE OF THE NEW RIGHT

ROSALIND POLLACK PETCHESKY

INTRODUCTION

Since the 1980 elections, it has become all too clear that American society and the state are plunging day by day more deeply into right-wing reactionism. We confront an emergent power structure and political culture that are openly racist, antifeminist, and also antiliberal. To characterize such a basic political shift in terms of the conspiratorial maneuvering of a tightly organized New Right seems tempting but simplistic, given the pervasiveness of the rightward pull. For what we are surely seeing is not only a well-orchestrated right-wing offensive, but also the demise of the liberal state and, along with it, some of its more progressive ideas—ideas such as individual freedom, "equality," and the responsibility of the state to provide for social welfare needs—in short, the tenets of bourgeois democracy. In practice, these ideas have historically stood in marked contrast to a capitalist, racist, and male-supremacist society. Although they were never either carried to their logical conclusions or made real for large groups of people, they nevertheless, until now, had a widespread ideological legitimacy, and as such were taken up and transformed by progressive movements, sometimes effectively, in the fight for radical social change. The antiliberal reaction obviously poses serious contradictions for socialists, feminists, gay rights activists, and others who have fought to transform the liberal state; at the same time, the attack on liberal reforms pushes those groups to organize on a much broader basis than they have done in the recent past.

Clearly, the New Right is not alone in abandoning liberalism. The dogma that social programs for the poor and working people represent "intrusiveness" and "overregulation" by the state, and that feminism and the sixties' counterculture represent "permissiveness" and "hedonism" (or "narcissism") in the society, emanates not only from the Moral Majority, but also from the domi-

Feminist Studies 7, no. 2 (Summer 1981). ⓒ 1981 by Feminist Studies, Inc.

nant media and intellectual organs, the centers of corporate and
state power, and even from some self-defined leftists. It is important to recognize the generality of these trends and also the fact,
which Zillah Eisenstein demonstrates in this issue, that Reagan's
election cannot be read as a popular "mandate" for conservatism.
And yet it is still the case that the New Right *is* an identifiable
political reality, which had visible success in mobilizing conservative voters and in creating an effective organizational machine in
recent elections.[1] Above all, I shall argue that what has given the
New Right both ideological legitimacy and organizational coherence in this period has been its focus on reproductive and sexual
issues. If there is anything genuinely "new" about the current
right wing in the United States, it is its tendency to locate sexual,
reproductive, and family issues at the center of its political program—not as manipulative rhetoric only, but as the substantive
core of a politics geared, on a level that outdistances any previous
right-wing movements in this country, to mobilizing a nationwide
mass following. The politics of the family, sexuality, and reproduction—and most directly, of abortion—became a primary vehicle
through which right-wing politicians achieved their ascent to state
power in the late 1970s and the 1980 elections. My purpose here
is to analyze the role of antiabortion and antifeminist politics in
that rise to power.

No doubt there is plain old opportunism involved in long-time
arch-conservatives (for example, Phyllis Schlafly, Richard Viguerie,
Paul Weyrich, and others) attempting to co-opt "single-issue"
movements which they themselves did not create and to capitalize
on widespread popular feelings of insecurity and personal loss.[2]
But the motives of politicians should not be confused with the
social and cultural forces that determine the course of the movements they lead or attempt to call forth. The point is that issues
related to sexuality and the family *are* the focal point of New
Right politics, not only on a rhetorical level, but also on the level
of mass organizing, intraparty and legislative struggles, and organizational alliances. At the 1980 Republican convention, for example, it was through sexual/reproductive politics that New Right
forces made their strength felt on the platform committee and
among the delegates generally. Throughout the election, it was
not an aggressive defense-spending and tax-cutting program (which
liberal Democrats supported as well) but opposition to abortion
and the Equal Rights Amendment (ERA) which *identified* the New
Right and its distinctive ideology. Furthermore, those politics
were used to galvanize a substantial segment of voters, funds, and
resources on behalf of right-wing candidates and against candidates

associated with liberalism and feminism. It is true that, with presidential and congressional power apparently in their hands, Ronald Reagan and other conservative politicians are now attempting to dissociate themselves from the prolife elements who focused on sexual-family issues and abortion during the campaign, and to appear to buckle down to the "serious" issues like the economy and foreign policy.[3] Nevertheless, this posturing must be put into a feminist perspective. First, it can't explain away the persistent reliance on sexual and family politics in the Right's concerted effort to win power. Second, the posturing betrays an underlying hostility to feminism and things "female"; as Eisenstein reminds us, the chauvinism implicit in definitions of "serious" politics as economic and military, and unrelated to the familial and personal, is an essential part of that politics. What feminists for generations have been urging—that issues related to the family, sexuality, and reproduction are political at their roots, that they ramify on every level of public and social life—has been squarely brought home to everyone by the staunchest foes of feminism.

Embedded in the New Right's "moral" offensive are two interlocking themes. The first is the *antifeminist backlash*, aimed initially at abortion, but extending from abortion to all aspects of sexual freedom and alternatives to traditional (patriarchal) family life. The second is the *anti-social welfare backlash*, aimed at the principle (given a certain legitimacy during the New Deal and the 1960s) that the state has an obligation to provide for economic and social needs through positive government-sponsored programs. What we need to understand is the relationship between these two aspects of the Right's current politics, how they reinforce one another. For it is now becoming clear that the moralistic fervor applied in the antiabortion campaign is being extended to political goals that appear unrelated to sex, religion, or the family; to more traditional right-wing goals such as racial segregation, welfare cutbacks, and militarism. The analysis that follows will attempt to show not only the centrality of antifeminism and antiabortion politics to the New Right's ideology and political organization, but also some of the connections between antifeminism and the attacks on liberalism and social welfare. In particular, I shall stress the ideology of "privatism" and "private morality" as that element of the antiabortion/antifeminist thrust which has provided the critical link between family-and-sexual politics and traditional economic and social conservatism.

Nowhere is this link clearer, in fact, than in the measures to cut off medicaid funding for abortions. The Hyde Amendment (which curtails funding in practically all cases except when the

woman's life is in danger) and the Supreme Court's decision in
Harris v. *McRae*, which upholds that amendment,[4] contain the
antifeminist and the antisocial welfare components of New Right
politics in a nutshell. These measures are at one and the same time
an attack on the idea of women's right to abortion as so fundamental that no woman, however poor, should be denied it; and
an attack on the idea of decent health care as a basic human need
which the society should meet regardless of people's ability to pay.
In its backward-turning 1980 decision, the Supreme Court held
that a presumed "constitutional right" to "medically necessary"
abortions (which it had granted for *all* stages of pregnancy in its
1973 decision in *Roe* v. *Wade*) does not entitle anyone to the
material means needed to exercise that right in practice:

it simply does not follow that a woman's freedom of choice carries with it
a constitutional entitlement to the financial resources to avail herself of the
full range of protected choices. The reason why was explained in *Maher*
[1977] : although government may not place obstacles in the path of a
woman's exercise of her freedom of choice, it need not remove those not
of its own creation. Indigency falls in the latter category.[5]

The implications of this disclaimer illuminate why the crusade
against abortion was taken up by the New Right as the pivotal
issue in a drive to impose conservative thinking on many areas
of policymaking and social life. The court's decision in *Harris*
v. *McRae* occurs in the larger context of economic crisis, military
buildup, massive cutbacks in social services, and a strong effort,
endorsed not only by the New Right and Reagan but also by most
major corporations, to "deregulate" many areas of American business. It is the general conservative push toward reprivatization of
the state's social welfare functions, the dismantling of the welfare
state, that gives *Harris* v. *McRae* major political significance.
Focused on an area of human activity that appears to be the most
deeply associated with a "private," "personal," realm, and affecting
the most vulnerable, least powerful group in society (poor, mostly
Third World women, many of them teenagers), the Court's decision
offers a politically acceptable wedge for the agenda of "reprivatization" to be applied on a larger scale. In *Harris* v. *McRae*, the
Court is saying that the state is under no constitutional obligation
to provide benefits necessary to make good the social welfare
rights it has itself bestowed (or to redress the social evils it has
not itself created). The tacit assumption is that those benefits
must therefore come from the private sector if they are to come
at all. Clearly, this reasoning could be extended from abortion
to the entire medicaid program—indeed, to any social service whatsoever that conservative legislatures decide to take away.

But the crisis of capitalism surely provides only half the explanation for *Harris* v. *McRae*; the other half comes from the crisis of patriarchy. Abortion is not simply an aspect of social welfare; it is above all a condition of women's liberation, and by the turn of the seventies had become recognized by advocates and foes as deeply symbolic of feminist aspirations for sexual autonomy, as a paradigmatic feminist demand. Although often unarticulated even by feminists, the meanings resonating from abortion politics have more to do with compulsory heterosexuality, family structure, the relationship between men and women and parents and children, and women's employment, than they do with the fetus.[6] Above all, abortion has to do with the possibility for women, especially young women, to be sexual beings, in a context where birth control alternatives are inadequate and heterosexual relations often undependable. Thus, the defeat of abortion, in the courts, the legislatures, and through electoral politics, is—in some ways that are more devastating than the defeat of the ERA—a direct and deliberate attack on the feminist movement. By the early 1970s, that movement had become the most dynamic force for social change in American society, penetrating every institution, public and private—education, government, business, sports, families, and not least, churches. That it has been perceived as a threat to male dominance in all those institutions goes without saying. Thus the attacks on abortion—like the attack on feminism generally—must be understood as necessarily central to the Right's drive for power.

Ironically, while feminists thought the right to abortion meant their "right to privacy," to personal control over their bodies without state (or church) interference, the right wing has used antiabortion politics to reassert its own view of "privacy"—privacy for the patriarchal family, for the church, the schools. "We oppose any move that would give the federal government more power over families," declared the Republican party platform—and by that they meant opposition to federal programs against domestic violence, to federally sponsored family planning programs or birth control for teenagers, to the ERA, which is perceived as encouraging divorce and women's work outside the home; to any federal resources supporting gay or lesbian activity or women's studies; to federal enforcement of school integration and busing. In what follows, I want to address three major questions. First, how did the New Right use the antiabortion and "profamily" crusades to build an organizational mass base and a mass ideology? Second, how is it now extending the politics of antifeminism—that is, of patriarchal family supremacy—to other, seemingly nonsexual or nonfamily domains? And third, what are the social and material conditions that allow this right-wing politics a certain popular resonance at the present time?

THE ORGANIZATIONAL BASE:
CHURCHES AND REPRODUCTIVE POLITICS

"Bible-believing churches of America constitute the largest single minority bloc of America." (Moral Majority flyer)

Prior to the 1980 elections, the media abounded with stories about the religious and evangelical manifestations of the New Right; Jerry Falwell and the Moral Majority captured nearly as much attention as the major candidates. A moralistic, crusading fervor, however, is not new to American right-wing movements; witness Father Coughlin, the fundamentalist Anti-Communist Christian Crusade, the Reverend Billy James Hargis, and others.[7] As Seymour Martin Lipset and Earl Raab suggest, extreme right-wing movements—which they identify as "backlash" movements—are typically an expression of the "preservatist" impulses of social groups who feel their "way of life" threatened:

Desperately preservatist or restorative movements—that is backlash move-ments—require an aggressively moralistic stance and will find it somewhere. There needs to be invoked some system of good and evil which transcends the political or social process and freezes it.[8]

What this "system of good and evil" is, however, is not arbitrary, but a product of the particular historical moment and of a con-junction of material and social forces that bring specific social conflicts to the fore. If the embodiment of absolute evil for an earlier generation of the Right was international communism, the Left, and labor movements in the United States, in the recent per-iod, it is feminism and homosexuality—both representing move-ments for transcendance of a patriarchal form of family and for sexual liberation. This shift is not surprising given the weakness of the Left and labor movements at the present time; whereas the women's liberation movement in the 1970s had become the most dynamic force for social change in the country, the one most directly threatening not only to conservative values and interests, but also to significant groups whose "way of life" is challenged by ideas of sexual liberation. And of all feminist demands, the *right to abortion* is that which somehow appears most threatening to traditional sexual and social values.

The antiabortion movement, which began in the Catholic church

and, despite disclaimers, has remained an essentially *religious* movement, has been the main vehicle through which the New Right has
crystallized and developed both its mass base and its mass ideology.
This particular crusade—which existed before the New Right and,
I would argue, in many ways laid the groundwork for it—has provided the existing right wing with the perfect issue to "freeze" the
political process into an absolute struggle between good and evil;
an intensely palpable symbol of martyrdom, something "positive
to fight for." But, while the religious, moralistic, and often mystical terms in which this crusade is couched resonate for many of
its followers, religion should not be mistaken for the *content* of
right-wing politics. Religion provides an "apocalyptic framework
which validates [moral] absolutism,"[9] but the content of this
framework is political in the most conventional sense: it has to
do with how and by whom power is exercised—in the economy,
the state, the family, and the churches.

From this perspective, it becomes clear that the major role of
organized religion for the Right in the period prior to the 1980
elections was to serve less as an ideological force than as a major
organizational infrastructure, a nationally and locally established
institutional network, one that exists outside the framework of
the Democratic and Republican party structures, but which would
give the Right access to an organized mass constituency.[10] The
two main institutions comprising this infrastructure, and around
which New Right organizing strategy has revolved, are, first, the
conservative wing and hierarchy of the Catholic church; and, second, the fundamentalist Protestant churches, particularly those
affiliated with the Moral Majority. Both of these groups are already organized through the "right-to-life" movement, as well
as through their own internal congregations and networks—a
reality on which the New Right has sought to capitalize. Through
a vigorous use of these conservative religious organizations, the
New Right—and indirectly the Reagan forces—sought to achieve
certain key ingredients of political power: votes and funds; active
recruits and foot soldiers; and legitimacy (through association with
a morally righteous cause.)[11] Already by 1978, its spokesmen
were claiming that this base would give them potential access to
one hundred million voters, and they were confident of commanding sufficient votes in the elections to give them control over the
Senate, the Republican party, and, indeed, the presidency.[12] Regardless of how one analyzes the deeper causes of the right-wing
electoral victories in 1980, it is undeniable that a key element in
the Right's strategy was to use the churches and particularly the
"right-to-life" movement as an organizational model and base.

In contrast to the peace, environmental, and antinuclear movements, which also contain many religious activists and groups, the antiabortion movement, although cross-denominational (it encompasses not only Catholics and fundamentalist Protestants, but also Orthodox Jews, Mormons, and Black Muslims), is narrowly religious and antisecular. As Judge Dooling commented in *McRae* v. *Harris*, "the right-to-life movement . . . does use religious language, invokes religious motivations, and enlists prayer as an aid."[13]   However, its leadership is hostile to those it associates with "social" or "liberal" Christianity (such as the National Council of Churches or the left-wing Catholic clergy in Latin America)—hardly a position of ecumenism. While various denominations participate, the unquestioned direction of the "right-to-life" movement—doctrinal, organizational, financial—has from the outset come from the Catholic church hierarchy.[14]   According to Judge Dooling:

Roman Catholic clergy and laity are not alone in the pro-life movement, but the evidence requires the conclusion that it is they who have vitalized the movement, given it organization and direction, and used ecclesiastical channels of communication in its support. The union of effort with representatives of other denominations is based on shared religious conviction.[15]

The "right-to-life" movement was originally a creation of the Family Life division of the National Conference of Catholic Bishops (NCCB), the directing body of the Catholic church in America. Immediately following the Supreme Court decision in *Roe* v. *Wade*, the NCCB Pro-Life Affairs Committee declared that they would not "accept the Court's judgment," and called for a major legal and educational battle against abortion. Since then, in numerous documents the bishops have summoned Catholics, both lay and clergy, to enter the antiabortion struggle: to defeat liberal abortion laws and proabortion candidates, and to work for a constitutional amendment that would, in accordance with Roman Catholic doctrine, declare the fetus a full human person from the moment of fertilization, and abortion thus a homicide.[16]   In 1975, the NCCB presented a detailed strategy for the church's antiabortion crusade, its "Pastoral Plan for Pro-Life Activity." It calls for the establishment of a network of "prolife committees" based in the parishes, that would (1) effect the passage of a "prolife" amendment; (2) elect "prolife" sympathizers to local party organizations; (3) monitor officials on their abortion stands; and (4) "work for qualified candidates who will vote for a constitutional amendment and other prolife issues."[17]   In other words, from the outset, the "right-to-life" movement was set up to be a political action machine to influence national and local elections, but working primarily through the churches and the financial and organizational leadership of the hierarchy.

The most important strategic base for carrying out the antiabortion crusade is the churches. Pastoral letters have been sent regularly to be read from the pulpits, urging parishioners to get involved in "prolife" political work of all kinds. Church services and mass have become a regular source of financial support for the movement, with hundreds of thousands of dollars collected annually through Sunday service collections and then channeled to local and national "right-to-life" committees.[18] More important than financial assistance, local churches and parishes provide the "right-to-life" movement with the organizational and communicational system that allows it immediate access to material resources and recruits. Churches supply rooms for meetings, telephones, and duplicating equipment, buses—and bodies—for rallies and demonstrations, and highly effective organizers in the person of the priests. Clergy distribute "prolife affirmation cards" at mass and hold special prayer meetings, masses, and diocesan rallies to coincide with particular electoral and lobbying efforts. Indeed, it is important to note the key role that many (though not all) priests and pastors have played in the building of the "right-to-life" movement. Recruited through the hierarchy, they have served as organizers, theoreticians, and militants. Above all, they use their pastoral authority to engage in moral exhortation, in terms clearly evoking religious guilt and linking "prolife" activism with Christian duty and eternal salvation. The pulpits have become the central platforms from which antiabortion statements are delivered regularly and parishioners are directed to attend marches, rallies, clinic sit-ins, and other activist events.[19] For Roman Catholics and fundamentalist Christians who believe literally in the metaphysical reality of the soul and the "innocence" of "fetal life," this appeal receives a powerful stimulus from the concern for one's own salvation.[20]

The most politically crucial function of the churches has been their contribution to the "right-to-life" electoral strategy. "Prolife" Catholic and Protestant clergy have not hesitated to use the power of the pulpit to condemn political candidates who have been targeted by antiabortion "hit lists," attempting to influence votes on the very eve of elections.[21] More generally, the churches serve as recruiting grounds from which voters of both major parties are enlisted into "right-to-life" electoral politics. "Prolife" political action manuals give local organizers detailed instruction about how the electoral process works at every level and how to penetrate it.[22] Because of the steadily declining voter turnout in the United States,

most political candidates are really elected (or defeated) by only a
very small margin. The antiabortion movement in the mid-1970s
thus adopted a complicated electoral strategy whose nucleus was
the "voter identification survey." According to Sharon Thompson's preelection analysis:

The 1980 right-to-life strategy is to pack the state legislatures with anti-
abortion representatives as a means of getting as many of the requisite 38
states as possible to call for a Constitutional Convention . . . [or, failing
that,] to use this leverage to force Congress to report the Human Life
Amendment out of committee. In either case, their electoral goals are
on the state level, where they feel they have a better chance of having
immediate impact. Toward this end, they have conducted voter identification surveys in 36 states. In New York State alone, they have can-
vassed over a quarter of a million primary voters to locate those people
who will vote against pro-abortion candidates in 1980.[23]

The New Right could not help but be drawn to these winning
ingredients: a tightly controlled organization geared to recruiting
and influencing voters across party lines; an alleged eleven million
members and three thousand chapters throughout the United
States; and a sense of moral righteousness on behalf of conservative values and "a cause." It would seem that the "right-to-life"
movement became for the New Right a *model* for building a mass
base. In addition, the New Right has been the direct beneficiary
of mass antiabortion organizing, which has helped to create a constituency and a consciousness that is both responsive to the New
Right's "profamily" ideology (see below) and committed to participating in the electoral process. In a political climate in which
the majority of liberals and radicals are disaffected nonvoters
(see Eisenstein, this issue), such political socialization undoubtedly
contributed to the Right's margin of victory.

But in 1978, the New Right began to take the "prolife" message
outside of the "right-to-life" committees, setting up its own network of "prolife" Political Action Committees (PACs), "leadership
conferences," and "conservative Christian" organizations, all under
the rubric of the "profamily" movement. The strategy adopted in
1977 was to absorb "groups devoted to preservation of the traditional social roles of the family, the churches, and the schools"
(that is, groups that were antiabortion, antibusing, anti-ERA, and
antigay rights) into a single coalition organized around four main
planks: "prolife," "profamily," "promoral," and "pro-American,"
with "family" as the keystone.[24] New Right organizers have
launched direct-mail campaigns aimed at politicizing the country's
fundamentalist preachers and have organized a series of "leadership

conferences" and religious coalitions. In addition to the highly
publicized Moral Majority, conferences and groups with names
like Religious Roundtable, Christian Voice, and American Family
Forum proliferate, with the same speakers and leaders appearing
continually on their rosters: New Right leaders such as Paul Weyrich, Phyllis Schlafly, Richard Viguerie, and Howard Phillips; its
representatives in Congress such as Sens. Gordon Humphrey (R.-
N.H.), Paul Laxalt (R.-Nev.), Orrin Hatch (R.-Utah), Jake Garn
(R.-Cal.), Henry Hyde (R.-Ill.), and Larry McDonald,(R.-Ga.); and
its favorite religious figures, such as Rev. Jerry Falwell and Pat
Robertson. Moreover, New Right strategists have set up a number of "prolife" organizations outside the framework of the National Right to Life Committee (NRLC), such as the Life Amendment Political Action Committee (LAPAC), the American Life
Lobby (ALL), and the National Pro-Family Coalition. Alan Crawford suggests that organizations such as these—used to appeal to
sympathizers on behalf of a "moral" cause—may "function as
fronts for direct-mail campaigns and primarily to make money
for themselves." He cites evidence that New Right-sponsored
"single-issue" organizations become conduits both for campaign
funds for right-wing candidates (including Reagan) as well as for
building a well-financed political organization.[25]

The main constituency "profamily" leaders have sought to
organize is the estimated fifty million "born-again" Christians
in this country, reached through both the evangelical church pulpits and, even more directly, the vast broadcasting network (thirteen thousand radio stations, thirty-six television shows) to which
the evangelical churches have access. As in the "right-to-life"
movement, the key to this strategy is the *preachers*, but particularly the nationally known Bible-preaching broadcasters.[26] For
millions of evangelical Protestants, who are the most frequent
listeners to religious broadcasts, radio and television have taken
the place of the local church, reaching people in their cars and
homes, not only on Sunday, but also on every other day all across
America. Religious broadcasting for right-wing political purposes
has long been a tool of right-wing preachers.[27] But today the use
of high-wave frequencies and satellite technology magnifies the
potential impact of such broadcasting, and its costs, tremendously.[28]
What is of interest here, of course, is not the high-powered technology of the fundamentalist broadcasters, but the large financial
backing which allows the application of that technology on a massive scale; and the political and ideological purposes for which the
"electronic church" has been created. An important example is
Falwell, founder of the "profamily" Moral Majority, which has a

mailing list of seventy thousand pastors. Falwell broadcasts *daily* over 300 television stations and 280 radio stations in thirty-one states. The message he communicates through the electronic church is the essence of "profamily" ideology: antihomosexuality ("the bisexual and homosexual movements in America are anti-family, . . . the number one offender . . . in traditional man-woman relationships"); antifeminism ("we believe in *superior* rights for women"); antiabortion and antidivorce.[29]

An alliance between Protestant fundamentalist preachers and the political right wing is far from new. This writer remembers only too well growing up in Tulsa, Oklahoma, in the 1950s, where Anita Bryant was the football queen of our rival high school one year, where the fundamentalists (Oral Roberts, Billy James Hargis) maintained their headquarters, where "Athletes for Christ" made regular rounds of the high schools and where, above all, the connection of these groups with anticommunism and the John Birch Society were commonly known. That connection is documented in an article published in 1962 by David Danzig, who describes "extreme Protestant fundamentalism," linked to ultra-Right organizations, as "a growing socio-religious force in America."[30] In the early 1960s, this force was still fiercely anti-Catholic, but cut across various Protestant sects, uniting them in a general belief in the Bible's "inerrant truth" as literally interpreted, in "salvation by faith alone and the pre-millenial return of Christ." These beliefs, Danzig points out, lend themselves to both "an anti-historicism which readily supports the conspiracy theory of social change," and an "apocalpytic conception of the world" which sees everything in terms of "the unending struggle between God and the devil."[31] Fundamentalist thinking is thus ripe to be won over by a political ideology that is similarly absolutist and apocalyptic, projecting a vision of society as ridden by demons (communists, homosexuals, "liberated women") from whom the innocent and God-fearing must be saved. Interestingly, Danzig points out that by the late 1950s and early 1960s, the *class base* of Protestant fundamentalism in the South and Southwest (where it was still largely contained) had changed. It was no longer mainly the rural poor, but included the wealthy beneficiaries of what later would be known as the "sun belt revival":

Many fundamentalist churches are modern and imposing, financed by wealthy oilmen from Texas and Oklahoma and prosperous farmers in the wheat and corn belts. Rich and influential lay leaders . . . now make their influence felt in the power structure of the community and state. The fundamentalists also operate a vast network of colleges, training schools, Bible institutions,

Bible prophecy conferences, prayer meetings, and study groups. They have many large publishing houses which blanket small towns with conservative tracts and pamphlets.[32]

The fundamentalists have thus developed a formidable base of financial and corporate support. The main purpose of "profamily" organizing prior to the elections was to mobilize the growing social force of Christian fundamentalism into conservative political activity, and to weld it to the already politicized and Catholic-dominated "right-to-life" movement. An alliance between conservative Catholics and Protestants would be historically unprecedented in the United States; and New Right leaders believe that the politics of "morality"—that is, conservative family and sexual politics—is the key to forging such an alliance, and thus to uniting a potential "100 million Americans" into right-wing political identity and votes.[33] Their method is to tap—as the "right-to-life" movement has done so successfully—both religious guilt and emotional vulnerability to all the symbolic meanings of "family" and "morality." The "profamily" movement promises not only to save fetuses, but to save "the family" itself and the moral foundations of "Christian civilization." Through citation of scripture and an urgent appeal to Christian conscience ("out of the pew, into the precinct"), Christians are urged to get involved in politics for the sake of the family and morality. But the vision implied in Moral Majority rhetoric transcends the family. It is one of a Christian theocracy, a transformed political system in which the (conservative) clergy is at the center of state power, and the state is avowedly "Christian"—and patriarchal.[34]

Yet, the relationship between the group of conservative politicians and political promoters who call themselves the New Right and the right-to-life movement is a complicated one, involving both close ties and potentially deep divisions. From its origins in the early 1970s, the right-to-life movement has been courted by and wedded to a whole series of right-wing political veterans, whose affiliations include the John Birch Society, the Young Americans for Freedom, the World Anti-Communist League, and the Conservative Caucus.[35] These relations have developed into a symbiosis in which New Right organizers lend to prolife groups their expertise in direct mailings, targeting candidates, and managing PACs, in return for securing a mass base of voters and local organizers. Rhonda Copelon, attorney for the plaintiffs in *Harris v. McRae*, speculates that the New Right politicos see the right-to-life movement as genuinely broad-based and thus a vehicle through which conservative forces can make inroads into the (majority)

liberal-democratic electorate.[36] In the 1980 elections, the New
Right succeeded in combining its direct-mail fundraising techniques
with the church-based electoral machinery of the "prolife" movement to elect an impressive number of conservatives to national
office, and to defeat liberals.[37]

At the same time, the New Right's political aims go well beyond
the abortion issue. The goal of their electoral strategy is to get
rid of legislators considered liberal on *any* of the Right's favorite
issues, including environmental regulation, welfare, defense spending, and civil rights. It is this connection of abortion to a much
larger and more traditional set of rightist political ends that has
sown the seeds of difference between hardcore "right-to-lifers"
and their New Right and fundamentalist patrons. Even prior to
the elections, some antiabortion leaders expressed suspicion of
the New Right's motives and were reluctant to let their "single-
issue" focus become absorbed in the larger "profamily"/"pro-
America" agenda.[38] Indeed, much of the rhetoric and organizing
of the NRLC has attempted to appeal to liberal and "humanist"
religious people who identify with the poor and the oppressed, to
connect the "rights of the unborn" to other human rights issues.
(There is even a "Prolife Feminists" caucus which meets at the
NRLC national convention, as well as a small, but growing, "left"
wing of the movement which opposes population control and
nuclear power and favors welfare benefits.)[39]

While the actual ideas and priorities of the antiabortion movement very much contradict the appearance of liberalism and grassroots populism (to say nothing of feminism), the desire to maintain
that appearance, in order to win on the abortion issue, is very real.
A too-close association with the New Right could be damaging to
the "right-to-life" movement's support among liberal Catholics
and others who identify with humanist and pacifist traditions,
who strongly favor many of the services and institutions (daycare,
labor unions, environmental protection laws) that the New Right
loudly condemns. In an editorial in early 1976, the liberal Catholic journal *Commonweal* gave prophetic warning to the Church
hierarchy about the fellows it was bedding down with in the anti-
abortion campaign:

The anti-abortion amendment is a right-wing issue, and the bishops will
quickly become the tools of conservative so-called "pro-life" (and perhaps
anti-busing, anti-'welfare chislers,' pro-arms race, pro-CIA) candidates in
the 1976 elections. The effort will fizzle and the church will have been had.[40]

More recently, there have been efforts to distinguish the very
broad and disparate assortment of Christian evangelists—some of

whose churches have opposed the Ku Klux Klan, joined with the black freedom movement, or staunchly maintained an indifference to politics—from the right-wing fundamentalists and Falwell's reactionary Moral Majority.[41]   The group of self-defined leftist, pacifist, and "feminist" Christians who also define themselves as "prolife" (a disturbing phenomenon for feminists in the reproductive freedom movement) have emphatically dissociated themselves from the New Right and its politics.   Thus the leftist Christian *Sojourners Magazine*, in an issue proclaiming its *conversion* to "prolife" doctrine, writes:

The political strategy of these Christian groups is being formulated by long-time Washington veterans of the extreme right wing who have not been known for their religious devotion. Their motivations have always had more to do with military and economic goals than with abortion. Their pro-military and pro-business agenda is decidedly anti-poor, anti-black, and anti-feminist. . . . The unholy alliance between the anti-abortion movement and the right wing must be directly challenged by those who seriously and consistently espouse a pro-life commitment.[42]

In the aftermath of the elections, it begins to appear that, just as the Reagan forces used the New Right to develop a popular base, so the New Right has used the antiabortion movement. Yet the question remains, *why* were abortion, sexual, and family issues so centrally the focus of 1980 politics for a rising conservatism?   Is the connection between opposition to abortion and other conservative political and social goals really just a matter of opportunism, or is it rather an intrinsic and basic connection, both ideologically and politically?

THE IDEOLOGICAL MESSAGE: FAMILY, SEXUALITY, AND THE REPRIVATIZATION OF POLITICS

The New Right found in the anti-abortion movement not only an efficient organizational network, but also the source of its ideological coherence and legitimacy. As previously suggested, the abortion issue resonates many social and political meanings—about the family, sexuality, the position of women—that go far beyond the status of the fetus; and thus *the organized opposition to abortion has never, in fact, been a "single-issue" movement.* The underlying message of the crusade against abortion—the message which the New Right itself has embraced as its ideological centerpiece— is that conveyed in the defensive response by Dr. J. C. Willke, current president of the NRLC, to accusations about firebombings and harrassment of abortion clinics:

It is they who are doing violence to our beloved nation by their systematic undermining of the basic unit of our society, the family. They do violence by their so-called sex education which is encouraging sexual promiscuity in our children and leading to more and more abortions. They do violence to us by driving wedges, barriers, and suspicion between teenagers and parents. They do violence to marriage by helping to remove the right of a husband to protect the life of the child he has fathered in his wife's womb.[43]

Abortion, Willke suggests, is just the opening wedge in an avalanche of "moral" assaults on the traditional nuclear family, including sex education, teenage sexuality and autonomy, and the sexual and reproductive freedom of women. Preservation of the fetus, note, is not the central issue here, but rather the patriarchal dominion of the husband over "his wife's womb."

In this section, I shall examine how antiabortion ideology becomes the basis, in the hands of the Right, for a much broader counteroffensive to restore conservative ideas and practices regarding the family and sexuality.

"We oppose any move that would give the federal government more power over families." (Republican party platform, 1980)

In his strategy for "Building the Moral Majority," Paul Weyrich explains how the new right-wing religious coalition will go beyond the goal of "saving babies" in its larger program for saving "the family":

What the right-to-life movement has managed to put together on the abortion issue is only a sample of what is to come when the full range of family and educational issues becomes the focus of debate in the 1980s. The threat to the family has caused leaders of various denominations to put aside their sectarian differences and . . . agree on basic principles worth fighting for . . . our very right to worship as we choose, to bring up our families in some kind of moral order, to educate our children free from the interference of the state, to follow the commands of Holy Scripture and the Church, are at stake.

Building on the emotional response that abortion and the invocation of family and religious autonomy generate, the organized Moral Majority will move on to other, less obviously "moral" agenda items: "The alliance on family issues is bound to begin to look at the morality of other issues such as SALT and the unjust power that has been legislated for union bosses."[44]

Sexual and family politics, then, beginning with abortion, be-

came for the New Right intrinsic elements in a larger program that
encompassed more traditional right-wing aims: anticommunism,
antidetente, antiunionism, racial segregation and antifederalism.
Election propaganda appealing to potential constituents typically
listed many targeted issues on which every member of the Christian Right was expected to share a common view, interlacing
"moral" questions with economic and foreign policy questions:
"abortion," "family," "ERA," "homosexuality," "pornography,"
moving on to "public school prayer," "government intervention
in your private Christian school," "the right to bear arms" (gun
control), "high taxes," "balanced budget," and "America's failing
military strength."[45]

Yet if we are to understand the specificity of New Right politics,
we need to analyze the complex relationships between "economic,"
"political," and "moral" issues in their thinking. What I want to
argue is, first, that the politics of the New Right seek legitimation
from a common ideological core, the idea of *privatization*; and
second, that the "privatization" impulse itself cuts in two interrelated directions: against social welfare and the poor, and against
feminism and women. What is particularly important here is the
ideology of the "private sphere" and its relation to both the family
and states' rights. The New Right in its "profamily" program invokes deep fears of loss of control over what is considered most
"private," most "personal." Historically, the concept of "privacy"
for American conservatives has included not only "free enterprise"
and "property rights," but also the right of the white male property owner to control his wife and his wife's body, his children
and their bodies, his slaves and their bodies. It is an ideology that
is patriarchal and racist, as well as capitalist.[46] Part of the content
of the formal appeal to "states' rights" is the idea of the family as
a private, and above all male-dominated, domain. Control over
families (one's wife and children) and control over local and state
power structures are closely related conservative values, insofar as
the latter is the means whereby the former is sought as an end.
Thus what appear to be attacks on federalism are simultaneously
attacks on movements by women, blacks, and young people to
assert their right to resources, services, and a viable existence outside the family and the ghetto.

In the "profamily" movement's first, and apparently successful,
campaign, the battle against the ERA, the connection between
"family rights," "property rights," and "states' rights" has been
made continually. The *Conservative Digest* characterizes the ERA
as a "federal power grab," charging that "it would shift vast
amounts of power from states to the federal government."[47]

Similarly, in a fund-raising letter on behalf of "Stop-ERA" in Florida, Senator Orrin Hatch has written that the ERA would

allow federal bureaucrats to answer and dictate areas of yours and my personal lives where they have never been able to intrude before. . . . Under ERA, our states will have to surrender to the federal bureaucrats their law-making rights covering marriage, divorce, property settlements and even the raising of our children.[48]

Feminist theory, I suggest, can help us clarify and critique the dominant mode of discourse, the dominant ideology of legitimation, that an ascendant conservatism has adopted. For if feminist theory has contributed any insight to an understanding of modern capitalist society, it is in having revealed the illusion of a split between a "private" and a "public" world that bourgeois culture embodies. Feminism penetrates this boundary between "public" and "private," revealing for political scrutiny the realms of life that bourgeois society had consigned to a sacred "privacy"—marriage, the family, childrearing, maternity; sex, of whatever variety; personal, "private" relations, especially between women and men, wherever they occur. Feminism calls forth all these unspoken, "personal" relations and renames them as political questions, questions of power and social determination. Earlier, Marxism had illuminated the social character of "private property," the mystification in the notion that "property"—capital, labor power, ground rent—was a personal attribute. But feminism goes further to the root of the problem because it demystifies the category of privacy itself.

The New Right must be understood as a response to feminist ideas and to their strong impact, in the 1970s, on popular consciousness. Joined by major segments of the corporate capitalist and state power structures, the New Right is trying to designate the private as "private" once again, but in a particular sense. The aim is surely to *reprivatize* every domain of social, public intervention that has been created through the struggles of working people, blacks, the poor, and women for the last twenty years. Not only abortion, sex education, and domestic violence services, but health care, education, the right to equal education, legal services, health and safety at work, access to the broadcasting media are all being pushed back into the unregulated anarchy of the private sector. The legitimation for this massive attempt to destroy the meager reforms that were won from the liberal state in the 1960s and 70s is the myth of "privatism"—the idea that what's wrong with busing or medicaid abortions or the Occupational Safety and Health Administration (OSHA) or the Environmental Protection Agency is that the federal government is "meddling in our 'private' business"; that, indeed, there even exists some private, safe, secure place—our neighborhoods, our churches, above all, the family—that would give us everything we needed if only the government would stay out.

But, although the language of New Right ideology evokes the sentiment of personal freedom from state interference, what distinguishes that ideology from classical conservatism is that it is spoken on behalf of *corporate* bodies rather than individuals. It is, in other words, corporate privatism—in the service of business, church, private school, and patriarchal family—that is intended, not individual privacy. In this regard, the New Right's appeal to privatism is much closer to fascism than to classical libertarian doctrine and is thus perfectly compatible, in theory as well as practice, with a program of massive state control over individuals' private lives. Of course, the fact that this neoconservative ideology is being propagated widely in a period of severe economic crisis and recession is not particularly surprising. My argument here is that it is the context of a popular feminist movement and an antifeminist backlash that has, in this historical period, fueled that ideology and given it a certain popular momentum. In that context, by focusing on those realms which still have the greatest *appearance* as "private," or "personal," in our culture—sexuality, abortion, the relations between parents and children—the New Right has been able to achieve a much greater ideological legitimacy for its politics of racism and fiscal conservatism than it could have by calling things by their right names.

Probably the most important piece of proposed right-wing legislation designed to defend "family privacy" (that is, middle-class white "family privacy," and patriarchal authority) against federal intervention is the "Family Protection Act," or Laxalt Bill, introduced into both the Senate and the House by Senator Paul Laxalt, spokesman in Congress for the Moral Majority and long-time Reagan collaborator. The Laxalt Bill seeks to reestablish "the family"— defined as the heterosexual married couple with children—as the final authority over all "moral" questions.[49] Specific provisions promote a public policy favoring not only marriage and childbirth, but also heterosexuality and the role of the husband as "household head." Thus federal jurisdiction over wife and child abuse would be subordinated to the states (Title V, Secs. 501-502, "Domestic Relations"). Tax benefits would be provided for married couples filing joint returns; a childcare deduction would be provided for nonworking married women engaged in "volunteer," "charity," or "religious" work (Title IV, Secs. 401-403);

and a one thousand dollar tax exemption would be given to *married couples only* for the birth or adoption of a child during the fiscal year.

The major provisions of the bill, however, have to do with education. They would reauthorize "voluntary prayer" in the public schools (by withholding federal funds from states which prohibit it); authorize parents to "review," that is, censor, any textbooks intended for use in public school classrooms; and reauthorize sex segregation of "sports or other school-related activities" (again, by threatening denial of federal funds to locales that prohibit such segregation on affirmative action grounds). Awareness of the importance of culture and the power of ideas in shaping sexual politics is very much in evidence here, as is the fear the New Right has of feminists, radicals, homosexuals, or anyone who questions traditional ideas about sexual divisions in the classroom. This is sharply underlined in blanket provisions which would prohibit federal funding to: (1) "Any program which produces or promotes courses of instruction or curriculum seeking to inculcate values or modes of behavior which contradict the demonstrated beliefs and values of the community"; or (2) any program which supports "educational materials or studies . . . [which] would tend to denigrate, diminish, or deny the role differences between the sexes as it [sic] has been historically understood in the United States" (a clear reference to women's studies programs!) (Title I, Sec. 101).

In addition to sexual and religious issues, the Laxalt Bill reasserts parental control over education in the service of middle-class economic interests, by providing special tax deductions for parents of private and parochial school students (amendment to the Internal Revenue Code, Sec. 101). It promotes racial and religious segregation, by endorsing "parental schools" (or "Christian schools," as the *Moral Majority Report* calls them) and severely limiting federal jurisdiction over such schools, or any private and parochial schools—which, of course, means ending federal control over desegregation in private schools (Secs. 104 and 301). The restrictions in the bill against "homosexuality advocacy," however, are much broader, extending beyond the classroom "to any public or private individual, group, foundation, commission, corporation, association, or other entity which presents homosexuality, male or female, as an acceptable alternative life style or suggests that it can be an acceptable life style" (Sec. 507).

The Laxalt Bill's provisions would underwrite government witch-hunts and further repression of individual sexual freedom in the name of curbing government "intrusion" into the family.[50] Under the Laxalt program, government would inevitably be more than ever inserted into the private lives and values of individuals, through a kind of moral police. The social and political impact of the bill would wipe out many existing feminist and gay rights programs which depend heavily on federal funds, and reconstitute ·the family and private agencies, such as the church, as the main institutions to which women and teenagers must look for support. This goal is evident in the bill's provisions requiring parental notification prior to teenagers' receiving birth control or abortion services, and "a reasonable effort" toward notification prior to venereal disease treatment. It is even clearer in the bill's provision (Sec. 301) establishing the immunity of all religious and other private welfare and education programs—childcare centers, foster homes, training centers, counseling programs, drug abuse treatment centers, and so on—from any federal government supervision. "Privacy" is, in this view, a *corporate* attribute, not one belonging to individuals as persons.

The idea of "protection" runs heavily throughout the "profamily" literature—protection, not only of fetuses and minors, but of adult women, who are meant to remain dependent on husbands. This idea has been used continually to discredit the ERA, which Schlafly claims will "strike at the heart of women's family support rights."[51] "Protection" encounters contradictions, however, in regard to the issue of domestic violence: how to protect women from the real physical dangers that exist *within* the family? One of the major legislative campaigns of the New Right has been directed against the Domestic Violence Prevention and Services Bill, which would expand federally funded programs to assist domestic violence victims.[52] "Profamily" spokesmen have admittedly found this a tricky issue, since they don't wish to appear "indifferent to the plight of battered women and children." While accepting that domestic violence exists, they dispute feminist theories about its causes. Domestic violence is not, they argue, "the result of sexist cultural norms that dominate American society," but, like homosexuality, the product of individual deviance—in other words, pathology, brought on by alcohol and drug abuse. Behind the New Right's opposition to the Domestic Violence Prevention and Services Bill is their desire not to further subsidize a national network of battered women's centers, often run by feminists, which encourage battered women to leave home. The "profamily" alternative is to return women to the authority of their spouses, offer them counseling, and remove domestic violence services entirely from the public back to the private (preferably church-sponsored) domain.

Having legitimated the principle of a return to patriarchal family values through the campaigns against the ERA, abortion, and homosexuality, the right wing's post-election domestic strategy would seem to be aimed at extending that ideology to other federal domains: to defeat OSHA, environmental regulations, legal services for the poor, federal enforcement of school integration through busing, and even the basic values of public education. Indeed, as the Laxalt Bill demonstrates, a great amount of "profamily" energy has been focused on *schools*,[53] in an effort to reassert local, parental, and church control over them (and thus over the minds of kids). The complexity of this aim becomes evident when we look more systematically at the specific demands that "profamily" organizers have been making in relation to schools: (1) restoration of "voluntary prayer" in the public schools; (2) opposition to any federal jurisdiction over private and parochial schools, especially over racial segregation, as well as busing in the public schools; (3) attainment of tuition tax credits for parents of private and parochial schoolchildren; (4) opposition to unionization of public school teachers; and (5) elimination of all programs or textbooks relating to sex education, homosexuality, or a critical view of traditional sex roles; and firing homosexuals from public school employment.

These are distinct though interrelated ends. Parents among fundamentalist and Catholic conservative constituencies to whom the New Right appeals want control over the local schools for reasons that are in part religious, in part class-based, in part racist, in part sexist and homophobic, and in part expressive of their fears, as parents, of loss of control over their children. Overall, it may be that, in a time of economic and political insecurity, the desire to control one's children (since other aspects of life seem out of control) becomes a kind of conduit for other fears—of racial "mix," of economic loss, of sexuality itself. In this context, invocations of "the family" communicate a complex set of meanings and moral sanctions. "The family" provides a new moral thrust, a new legitimation, for older right-wing values such as racism or prayer in the public schools, which, since the 1960s and the civil rights movement, are no longer so easily justified in their own terms. Thus, to argue that "moralism" is used by the New Right merely as a gloss to obscure its "real" political aims is misleading,[54] for economic pressures, class divisions, and racism are integrally tied to people's concerns about "family autonomy" and to sexual politics.

The pending (at this writing) antibusing legislation illustrates both the interrelation between antifeminist/patriarchal values and

racism, and the use of the antiabortion campaign as a model for
right-wing ideology and organizing. On a strategic level alone,
there are striking parallels between the campaign in the Senate
to curb federal jurisdiction over busing and the campaign against
abortion funding.[55] In both cases, legislation was attached as a
rider to a major appropriations bill, thereby holding hostage the
salaries of those very federal administrators who have been committed to implementing legally sanctioned reproductive and civil
rights. In both cases, the claim is made that the legal "right" (to
abortion, to decent education) still stands, but the political and
material means to implement that right are being vitiated. On the
symbolic level, conservative members of congress have applied the
moralistic scare tactics developed in the antiabortion campaign to
the campaign against busing, driving one liberal senator to complain
"that 'busing' had become a 'buzzword' that 'strikes fear into the
hearts of my colleagues.' "[56] What is most significant, however, is
that "busing" is made to evoke a whole array of associated fears
and feelings of vulnerability that are particularly related to the
autonomy of *families* and parental control over children. In the
name of "family rights" and the defense of "the family" against
"government meddling," right-wing politicians and judges in fact
justify racism, racial segregation, and, I would argue, sexual fear
and repression as well.[57] The sexual component of this ideological
thrust cannot be overstressed. For the "freedom" that white parents want is clearly the "freedom" to keep their children away
from black children; and their fears of "racial mix" are in no small
part bound up with sexual-racial stereotypes and the fear of their
own children's sexuality.

*"God did not ordain sex for fun and games." (Anonymous woman
participant, 1979 National Right-to-Life Convention)*[58]

Antiabortion ideology has been taken up by the right wing not
only for its "profamily" and prochurch message, but also for its
support of conservative sexual values. The "right-to-life" doctrine
of the fetus's "personhood" and the aborting woman's "selfishness"
is directly akin to the antihumanist philosophy of the "profamily"
movement. Antihumanism, as professed by the "right-to-life" and
"profamily" movements, pits itself squarely against every intellectual and philosophical tradition that grew out of the Enlightenment
and secularism. Marxism and feminism both are clearly denounced
by the "right-to-life"/"profamily" movement, but so are all philosophies, including radical Christian movements, whose central focus
is social change on this earth or even human as opposed to divine,

or scriptural, ends. When Weyrich describes the Moral Majority as "a Christian democratic movement rooted in the authentic Gospel, not the social gospel," he is attacking, and distinguishing his politics from, those Christian and Catholic movements in the United States and Latin America who ally with the poor to change oppressive social conditions.[59] All social movements—including labor movements, peasant uprisings, anticolonial struggles, civil rights, antinuclear protests—would thus be categorized by the New Right under "materialistic, atheistic humanism," charged with the sin of making human life and human pleasure on earth the measure of all value.

But a very particular condemnation is reserved for feminism and the movement for sexual liberation. It is this branch of humanism that the New Right associates most closely with hedonism, equated with "doing whatever feels good," with "moral perversity and total corruption." If a woman can control her pregnancies, there is no built-in sanction against her having sex when, how, and with whom she pleases—and this, for the "profamily"/"prolife" movement, is the heart of the matter. As Ellen Willis puts it, "the nitty-gritty issue in the abortion debate is not life but sex."[60] The fetus itself, its "innocence," symbolizes asexuality. Sharon Thompson, who attended a workshop discussion of sex education at a local "right-to life" convention, comments on the antisexual biases of "right-to life" activists:

In a sense, theirs is a movement championing the asexual in a post-Freudian era. The fetus is their purest symbol for that reason. Even babies are sexual, they now admit, but surely not the fetus. (If we could get a photo of a fetus masturbating, we might be able to short-circuit their whole movement.) They hate Planned Parenthood in large part because they perceive it as pro-sex. "Planned Parenthood even thinks old people should have sex!" one speaker called out at lunch, and the whole room exploded with laughter.[61]

Opponents have questioned whether the "prolife" movement is really "prolife" at all. The movement's claim to believe "that *all* human life is precious, and equally deserving of protection under the law," seems hypocritical in light of repeated support by "prolife" politicians for capital punishment, nuclear energy, and increased armaments and their opposition to nuclear regulation, welfare spending, childcare programs, and federal protection of environmental and workplace safety and health.[62] Sociologist Donald Granberg's study of a national sample of "prolife" activists found no correlation between opposition to abortion and "a more generalized prolife stance." Antiabortionists in his sample did not oppose capital punishment, "tended to express somewhat greater confidence in the military and to favor increased spending on the military and armaments." Moreover, "opposition to abortion was inversely . . . related to opposition to the Vietnam War." On the other hand, Granberg found the greatest correlation to exist between opposition to abortion and "a conservative approach to matters of traditional morality," that is, *disapproval* of premarital sex, birth control for teenagers, sex education, and divorce.[63]

Over and over again in antiabortion and "profamily" literature, one is struck with a defiantly traditional middle-class morality regarding sexual behavior and an undisguised antipathy toward *all* forms of sexuality outside the marital, procreative sphere. Male homosexuality, lesbianism, extramarital sex, divorce—all are targets of the New Right's modern "purity crusade." But more than anything else, the subject that excites "prolifers" is premarital sex among teenagers. Increasingly it appears that antagonism to abortion stems less from concern for protecting the fetus than from a desire to prevent teenage sexuality. "Right-to-life" advocates assume as a matter of course that there is a causal relationship between legalized abortion and a rise in sexual promiscuity and illegitimacy, particularly among teenagers.[64] Not only abortion but also birth control and sex education programs sponsored by clinics and schools are seen as giving official government sanction to "illicit" sex—and, therefore, as interfering with parents' control over the moral behavior and values of their children. Conversely, the way to eliminate premarital sexuality, it is thought, is to eliminate abortion, teenage contraceptive programs, and sex education. Indeed, this has been the unenlightened opinion of Ronald Reagan for years, judging from remarks he made in 1973 while vetoing (for the third time) proposed legislation in California to allow teenagers to obtain contraceptives without parental consent:

Simply because sexual permissiveness may exist among certain young people does not mean the state should make it easier for them. . . . The state has no right to even tacitly seem to condone such behavior, particularly among children who, in too many instances, are not yet mature enough to understand the full implications of their actions.[65]

It should be no surprise, then, that the Family Protection Act and Reagan's appointees in the Department of Health and Human Services are aiming to halt all public programs providing contraception, sex education, or sex-related health services to teenagers. Such a policy, in combination with the drive to recriminalize abortion, makes it quite clear that the main goal of antiabortion politics is to "protect" young women from sex;[66] the fetus has little to do with it.

The theme of protecting children has also been applied in the movement's virulent, active campaign against homosexuals and lesbians. On the false pretext that male homosexuals and lesbians are child molesters, New Right legislative and political offensives have sought, with some success, to defeat local gay rights ordinances in cities around the country; to deny federally funded legal services to homosexuals; to bar homosexuals from teaching in the public schools (as in the defeated Briggs Amendment campaign in California);[67] and to revive the ideology (abandoned even by the American Psychiatric Association) that homosexuality is "pathological" and "perverse." A longer-range goal is to prohibit the employment of homosexuals not only in education, but in *any* "public sector" or "high visibility public jobs";[68] as well as to prohibit federal funding of any organization that even "suggests" that homosexuality "can be an acceptable lifestyle." (See previous discussion of the Laxalt Bill.) This campaign is unrelenting and heavily financed.[69] In terms of its civil rights implications, it obviously would open the door to vicious harassment, witch-hunts, and persecution at least as widespread as that which was aimed at communists during the McCarthy period (of which some New Right leaders are veterans).

The ideas behind the New Right's antihomosexual campaign are revealing of the political values that motivate the "profamily" movement, including the movement against abortion. They suggest that, while it may be true that "prolifers" are hostile to sexuality as such, it is really the social aspects of traditional gender identities—and particularly the position of male paternal and heterosexual authority—that they are determined to protect. Homosexuality is characterized by "profamily" representatives as "unnatural," "evil," and psychologically "perverse"; but male homosexuality is even more dangerous than female, in the "profamily" view, because it signals a breakdown of "masculinity" itself—or what one right-wing ideologue calls the "male spirit," or "the male principle."[70] Thus, what is at stake in the New Right campaign against homosexuality is the very idea of what it means to be a "man" or a "woman," and the structure and meaning of the traditional family. These two concepts are clearly related, for the meaning of "masculinity" (as of "femininity")—that is, of gender itself—has been defined historically through the structure of the family and dominant position of the father within it. Paul Weyrich, a leader of the "profamily" movement, expresses an awareness of this reality when he says that there are people who want a different political order, who are not necessarily Marxists. Symbolized by the women's liberation movement, they believe that the future for their political power lies in the restructuring of the traditional family, and particularly in the *downgrading of the male or father role in the traditional family.* [71]

The aim of the "profamily" movement is to restore heterosexual patriarchy, the control of men over their wives and children. Teenage sexuality; homosexuality; the freely determined sexuality of women as wives and daughters; abortion and contraception, insofar as they promote sexual freedom; even "test-tube babies," which hold out the prospect of totally removing procreation from heterosexual monogamy—all are a direct threat to male authority and the identification of men as heads of families. Given this, it is not surprising that all these activities have become the central target of a movement that is led by middle-class conservative men. The men of the "profamily" movement, mainly upper-middle-class professionals,[72] are not immune to the sense of personal loss and threat provoked by feminism and by recent changes in the family and women's work. Weyrich again captures the essence of this middle-class patriarchal *ressentiment* when he proclaims: "The father's word has to prevail."[73] With this unambiguous call to arms, Weyrich speaks not only as a New Right general, but also as a husband and a father. And he speaks, too, as a leading patriarch in his church, aware of the Sonia Johnsons and the Sister Theresa Kanes and the other believing women who would perhaps turn traditional church governance upside down.

In the case of the Catholic Church, one could argue that it is feminism itself, within the church as outside it, that explains the singlemindedness and fury with which the church hierarchy has engaged in the current crusade against birth control and abortion. The hierarchy and the pope have evidenced strong concern about feminist and Marxist stirrings within the church's own ranks and the need to impose "discipline" and patriarchal authority in its own house. This was made clear in the pope's visit to the United States in 1979 and his outspoken endorsement there, and during the recent Synod of Bishops, of the most conservative views on women, birth control, sexuality and marriage—even in the face of widespread lay nonconformism and public appeals by nuns for a more modern approach.[74] Feminism represents to the church a threat of insubordination, but also a threat of depopulation: not only have Catholic birth rates gone down as much as other groups', but Catholics today both approve of and *practice* abortion in nearly as large numbers as do other groups in the United States.[75]

Declining enrollments in parochial schools may play no small part in motivating church attacks on birth control, abortion, and women's control over pregnancy.

Taking feminist ideas more seriously than do many liberals, the doctrinal leaders of the New Right relate women's sexuality to their place in society—only reversing the feminist vision. Connie Marshner, another prime mover behind the "profamily" movement and director of its "Library Court" legislative group, assures women that all they need is "to know 'that somebody will have the authority and make the decision, and that your job is to be happy with it.' "[76] This is exactly what Schlafly and her anti-ERA forces have been vociferously promoting since 1973—the idea that it is women's "right" to be dependent, cared for, subordinate to men, and defined by marriage and motherhood. At the center of anti-ERA ideology is the assumption that it is destructive of the family for married women to work outside the home. From this follows their opposition to federally funded childcare programs and their support for "protective" legislation that would exclude women from certain jobs, due to their "physical differences and family obligations," or would "give job preference . . . to a wage-earner supporting dependents" (meaning men). Most fundamentally of all, however, "prolife" and "profamily" ideology represent the urge to restore the values of motherhood as they have been propagated since the late eighteenth century: as woman's true destiny, her "calling," that which defines her above all else and so must take priority above all other tasks or commitments. Clearly, this is the underlying message of the antiabortion movement, that women who seek abortions are "selfish" because they attempt to deny the "life" of "their own child" and therefore their own "destiny" (both "natural" and God-given) to procreate, nurture, and suffer. One could speculate at length on the deeper cultural and psychological roots of the "promotherhood" backlash, yet it obviously touches something very profound—in men, a long-ingrained expectation of being taken care of, which feminism seems to threaten; in women, a long-ingrained vulnerability to guilt, which antifeminism evokes.

"Profamily"/"prolife" organizers understand all too well that the main threats to maintaining a traditional family structure in which men dominate women and children, and women seek their identity in motherhood, are women's economic independence from husbands and the existence of a strong feminist movement. The massive rise in women's labor force participation, particularly among married women; and, on a much smaller but still important scale, the existence of feminist alternatives outside the home (battered women's shelters, lesbian communities, "returning women's" programs in colleges, feminist health networks), create the possibility for women to imagine existing outside of traditional married life. For married women too, these possibilities have changed how they think about marital relations and motherhood, whether or not they remain married (which most of them do). Far more than an opportunistic appeal to the "irrational," the New Right represents a highly conscious conservative response to these broad and changing social conditions. It is a response that advocates a return to the values of privatism; that would throw the welfare and education of individuals back onto the resources of the family and the church; that would confine sexuality within the strict bounds of heterosexual marriage, and women within a patriarchal version of self-denying motherhood.

CONCLUSION

Describing the ideology and political program of a social movement is not at all the same as understanding the consciousness of the masses of people who make up that movement, much less the material and social conditions that bring a particular consciousness to light.[77] We have to consider why that ideology is able to have a broad impact on people's consciousness; why, in this case, the resurgence of patriarchal authority, in its "prolife" and "profamily" incarnations, has come to play such a central role in American politics and its current bend to the right.

First, the simplest and most obvious explanation for the "prolife" movement's existence and its success in developing a mass-based organization is that the political values and social changes its members are fighting against are real and pervasive. Both the women's and gay liberation movements, on the one hand, and the structural changes in the family that have been both cause and effect of those movements, represent a genuine threat to the type of family system and the sexual morality that the New Right is seeking to preserve. While New Right language and symbolism often take a mystical and irrational form, their ends are nevertheless coherent and clear; the conflict between the values of the New Right and those they oppose, as they perceive better than many liberals, broaches no compromise. In this sense, the antiabortion/antigay/anti-ERA/"profamily" current is indeed a backlash movement, a movement to turn back the tide of the major social movements of the 1960s and 1970s. This backlash is aimed primarily at those organizations and ideas that have most directly confronted patriarchal traditions regarding the place of women in society and the dominant norms of heterosexual love and marriage. But it is also a reaction to the New Left and the counterculture generally, which many white middle-class parents experienced as having robbed them of their children, either literally or spiritually. The strength and determination of this backlash—particularly in regard to abortion, homosexuality, and the ERA—is in part a measure of the *effectiveness* of the women's and gay movements, the extent to which their ideas (and various commercial distortions of their ideas) have penetrated popular culture and consciousness, if not public policy. This ideological impact has, of course, been double-edged because it has brought with it a great deal of uncertainty about what will replace the old forms that are being challenged, and even about people's own identities. But it is also true, as Zillah Eisenstein has argued elsewhere, that there is no corner of the society where the basic liberal feminist idea of women's "equality" with men has not touched people in their daily relationships.[78]

Second, the "profamily" movement is reacting to very real, dramatic changes in family life that have occurred most sharply during the past fifteen years. The kind of family model the New Right would like to restore—in fact, to make morally and legally mandatory—has become practically extinct in America. Consider the following well-known but critical facts:

1. By 1975, husband-wife families with two or more children in which only the husband worked outside the home constituted only 13.5 percent of all husband-wife families.[79]

2. Although the labor force participation rate of all women has risen steadily since World War II, it has risen fastest among married women, and particularly those with young children. By 1977, three-fourths of all married women were working outside the home, and well over one-half of all those with school-age children.[80]

3. Although marriage and remarriage rates are higher than ever before, divorce rates have doubled since the 1960s, and one out of three marriages ends in divorce (in other words, marriage is a phase of the life cycle rather than a lifetime proposition).[81]

4. The number of female-headed households more than doubled since 1960, so that by 1977, one out of seven of all households in the United States was headed by a single woman. Meanwhile, one out of five of all Americans lives as a single individual—that is, alone, not in a family; and over 1 million households consist of unmarried couples, with an eightfold rise in such households since 1970 among persons under the age of twenty-five.[82]

5. The total fertility rate has reached its lowest point in this country's history, reflecting more than anything else a reduction

in average family size. In fact, most women in our society become
mothers, but mothering is increasingly concentrated within a
shorter span of a woman's total life cycle; women on the average
interrupt their work lives for pregnancy and childbirth only for a
few months, and they generally are done with childrearing by their
forties.[83]

6. Finally, while the overall birthrate has declined, the rate of
births to unmarried women under twenty-five has risen, particularly
among teenagers, who account for one-half of all "illegitimate"
births.[84]

These figures, pertaining to changes in family structure, women's
work force participation, and birthrates, only hint at changes in
sexual norms and behavior. That they have been accompanied by
much greater openness, however, about homosexuality, nonmarital
heterosexuality, living arrangements, and childrearing arrangements
that fall outside the traditional heterosexual-married-household
pattern, seems unquestionable. Further, the whole pattern and
social context of motherhood has changed as a result of these
shifts. While most women will raise one or two children in their
lives, they will do so in a context of nearly continuous work outside the home; and, for many, of decreasing economic dependence
on husbands or other men.

These are changes whose major upswing has occurred only during the last twenty years, less than one generation, and whose impact on people's lives and expectations for themselves and their
children has undoubtedly been intense and unsettling. Absorbing
that impact has been difficult for all people, including committed
feminists, who believe strongly in the need for divorce, birth control, and sexual freedom. For those persons whose belief has remained unshaken in their prerogative, as a man, to "have the
authority and make the decision," or their privilege, as a woman,
"to be happy with it"—and that their children after them would
follow suit—it must seem a very alien and treacherous world. To
argue that the New Right's focus on sexual and family issues is
merely a diversionary tactic, to lure people's attention away from
unemployment and other economic distress, is to deny the social
reality of the trends listed above and their effect on people's sense
of who they are, particularly in a climate of economic insecurity.
At the same time, women's employment outside the home, as well
as the women's liberation movement, is once again being blamed
for the economic crisis, for taking jobs away from men, and this
adds fuel to the New Right's antifeminist attack and people's sus-
ceptibility to it.

The New Right's "prolife," "profamily" campaign thus cannot

easily be written off as either religious fanaticism or mere opportunism. It has achieved a mass following and a measure of national
political power because it is in fact a response to real material conditions and deeplying fears, a response that is utterly *reactionary*,
but nevertheless attune. It is not only those conditions and fears,
however, that have given the New Right its leverage, but also the
failure of the Left and feminist movements to develop an alternative vision, based on socialist and feminist values, that gives people
a sense of orientation in dealing with the kinds of personal insecurity and disruption brought by recent changes in the family and
sexual norms. The disjunctions in relations between parents and
teenagers illustrate this lack of vision painfully. For the concerns
of parents about their children getting pregnant, having abortions,
being encouraged toward "sexual freedom," without any social
context of sexual and reproductive responsibility, are rational and
real and neither the Left nor the women's movement has offered
a model for a better, more socially responsible way for teenagers
to live. The "prolife" movement's critique of a certain kind of
"hedonism," the cult of subjective experience and "doing whatever feels good," with no sense of values outside the self, is in
part a response to the moral failure of contemporary capitalist
culture.

In addressing these cultural dislocations, the New Right answers
with the reassurance of moral absolutism: to deal with the problems of abortion, teenage sexuality, conflicts in female-male relations, simply abolish them. There are no decisions to make, no
hard choices, no ambiguities. You have only to listen to "the
word"—of the priest, of the husband, of the father. But this is
a nonmorality, because it absolves human beings (especially those
lacking patriarchal authority) of moral agency, and thus plays on
people's weakness and insecurity. Moreover, it puts its own followers—for example, the activist women of the "right-to-life"
movement—in a terrible dilemma, because the meaning of political activism, to which they are being called, is to think, to act,
to be responsible. Indeed, the most stinging contradiction embodied in the "prolife" movement may be that confronting its
apparently large numbers of female rank and file, most of them
white, middle class and middle aged. On the one hand, we may
speculate that these are the very women for whom the loss of a
protective conjugal family structure and the idea of motherhood
as the core of woman's fulfillment is a truly menacing specter.
On the other hand, what can it mean to be active as a woman
in a political movement, or a church, that stands for women's
passivity and subordination? How will the women of the New
Right begin to confront this dilemma?

Anita Bryant, for three years national symbol and leader of the anti-gay rights movement and a devout fundamentalist, may be a harbinger of a gathering storm. Finding herself divorced, jobless, and denounced by the male-dominated church that has made millions of dollars off her name, Bryant now claims to "better understand the gays' and the feminists' anger and frustration." She sees "a male chauvinist attitude" in "the kind of sermon [she] always heard" growing up in the Bible belt—"*wife submit to your husband even if he's wrong*"; and thinks "that her church has not addressed itself to women's problems":

Fundamentalists have their head in the sand. The church is sick right now and I have to say I'm even part of that sickness. I often have had to stay in pastors' homes and their wives talk to me. Some pastors are so hard-nosed about submission and insensitive to their wives' needs that they don't recognize the frustration—even hatred—within their own households.[85]

But there are also material contradictions that, I believe, will undo the "prolife" movement in the long run. The New Right's rejection of the now dominant ideology of the "working mother," their determination to bring women back into the home, represents a basic misunderstanding of current economic realities, including the long-range interests of the capitalist class as a whole, which continues to rely heavily on a (sex-segregated) female labor force. Emma Rothschild has cogently pointed out that the only real "growth" industries in the American economy in the current period—"eating and drinking places," "health services," and "business services"—are those whose labor force is predominantly women.[86] Corporations are unlikely to fill these low paid, part-time, unprotected, high-turnover jobs with male workers; they are, in the existing division of labor, "women's work."

Finally, neither the practice of abortion and birth control nor the expression of sexual desire has ever been successfully stamped out by repressive religious or legal codes. As Jill Stephenson comments with regard to the failure of Nazi "promotherhood" ideology to raise the German birthrate:

The long history of birth control in Germany, with widespread resort to abortion if contraception had been unavailable, or had failed, could not be eliminated from popular consciousness by a few laws and even a mass of propaganda.... Repression could only drive these practices underground, where popular demand ensured that, somehow, they survived.[87]

In the United States in the 1980s, social needs and popular consciousness will also assure the survival of these practices. But whether survival will transform into political struggle will depend on the existence and strength of an organized popular movement.

NOTES

This paper would not have come to exist without the resource materials, insights, and advice generously shared with me by a large number of people who are also working on, or deeply concerned with, these issues. In particular I would like to thank Sharon Thompson, Rhonda Copelon, Meredith Tax, Bonnie Bellow, Nick Egleston, Sarah Shulman, and Sophie Mirviss for the use of their files and for providing most of the primary materials on which the paper is based; and Suzanne Gaston, for research assistance. While I alone remain responsible for the paper's ideas, those ideas grew out of many discussions: with Rhonda and Sharon, with Bonnie and Nick, with Sarah and Sophie, with Alan Hunter, with Zillah Eisenstein and Beau Grosscup, with Fannie Eisenstein and Hal Benenson, with Judy Newton, and with my sisters in the Committee for Abortion Rights and Against Sterilization Abuse. Finally, thanks to Rayna Rapp for heroic editorial help.

[1] Early attempts to assess the New Right as a growing political force follow: Linda Gordon and Allen Hunter, "Sex, Family and the New Right: Anti-Feminism as a Political Force," *Radical America* 11, no. 6; 12, no. 1 (November 1977-February 1978): 9-25; Sasha Gregory-Lewis, "Danger on the Right," *The Advocate* (originally published as a series, November, June, and August 1977; available in xeroxed form, from Liberation Publications, San Francisco, Calif.); and Peggy A. L. Shriver, "A Briefing on the Right Wing," Report prepared for the Office of Research, Evaluation and Planning, National Council of Churches, Spring 1978. See also the excellent analyses by Dana Naparsteck, "The Politics of the Right-to-Life Movement," *Interchange* (Interchange Resource Center, Washington, D.C., 1979); and Steve Manning, " 'New Right' Forces Expect to Win," *Guardian*, 3 October 1979, p. 3.

More recently, a number of book-length treatments have been published, including Alan Crawford, *Thunder on the Right: The "New Right" and the Politics of Resentment* (New York: Pantheon, 1980); Michael Miles, *The Odyssey of the American Right* (New York: Oxford University Press, 1980); and Bertram Gross, *Friendly Fascism* (New York: W. Evans Co., 1980).

[2] Crawford, who is highly critical of the New Right for betraying what he believes are the true values of "responsible conservatism," implies that a politics that focuses on such issues as abortion, ERA, gay rights, and busing, is *intrinsically* opportunistic insofar as these issues are, in his view, "symbolic" and "nonpolitical, fringe issues at best" (see *Thunder on the Right*, pp. 8-10 and 149). The refusal by some liberals and "moderate" conservatives to take the New Right's sexual politics seriously is, of course, another form of male chauvinism.

[3] According to one southern conservative congressman: "It's economics, strictly economics. . . . We're not talking about abortion or busing, we're talking about budget controls, spending cuts, and tax rate cuts." See Steven V. Roberts, "New Conservative Coalition," *New York Times*, 7 January 1981, p. A15.

[4] *Law-Week* 48 (24 June 1980): 4941.

[5] Ibid., p. 4946.

[6] See Ellen Willis, *Village Voice*, 3 March 1980, p. 8, for an eloquent statement about the sexual and social meanings of abortion, from a feminist perspective. See also the discussion in Committee for Abortion Rights and Against Sterilization Abuse, *Women Under Attack* (New York, 1979), pp. 9-11, of the meaning of "reproductive freedom."

[7] Placing the New Right within a fuller historical perspective is important for understanding its political significance today. While that task awaits more careful historical research, my cursory reading suggests tentatively that the right-wing predecessors to the New Right differ from the latter in important ways. The John Birch Society, for example, has been entirely secular in its approach, as well as focusing on economic issues and anticommunism as the target of its crusade. Moreover, the John Birch Society

"never seriously attempted to build a mass appeal of any kind," but rather saw itself not so much as seeking political power, but as a "striking force" trying to influence other conservatives, and especially the Republican Party. See Seymour Martin Lipset and Earl Raab, *The Politics of Unreason: Right-Wing Extremism in America, 1790-1970* (New York: Harper and Row, 1970), p. 269. On the other hand, right-wing anticommunist movements rooted in the churches—for example, the fundamentalist Anti-Communist Christian Crusade, Rev. Billy James Hargis, and even Father Coughlin in the 1930s—have developed a certain mass following; they have crusaded around "moral" and "family" issues (especially sex education and prayer in the schools), as well as more traditionally economic and political ones. But these movements were never organized as a political machine to move actively into national arenas of state power. See ibid., pp. 269, 273; and David Danzig, "The Radical Right and the Rise of the Fundamentalist Minority," *Commentary* 33 (April 1962): 291-98.

[8] Lipset and Raab, *Politics of Unreason*, p. 117.

[9] Ibid., p. 111.

[10] Rhonda Copelon, talk on "The Catholic Church and the Right-to-Life Movement," meeting of the Committee for Abortion Rights and Against Sterilization Abuse (CARASA), 8 November 1979, New York University School of Law; and David Moberg, "Letting the Left Hand Know," *In These Times*, May-June 1978, p. 3.

[11] Meredith Tax, talk on "The New Right and the Right-to-Life Movement," CARASA meeting, 8 November 1979. See "The Interlocking Directorate," developed by Meredith Tax and Bettie Wallace, a chart which documents the connections between prolife leaders and the leadership of other conservative political organizations. It is available from Bettie Wallace, Center for Constitutional Rights, 853 Broadway, New York, N.Y. 10003.

[12] See Manning, " 'New Right' Forces Expect to Win"; and "Mobilizing the Moral Majority," *Conservative Digest* 5 (August 1979): 15.

[13] McRae *v.* Harris, 491 F. Supp. 630 (1980), 711.

[14] Ibid., pp. 703-707; McRae v. Califano, 76 Civ. 1804, U.S. Dist. Court, Eastern Dist. of N.Y., Plaintiffs' First Amendment Brief, pp. 70-106, hereafter cited as "McRae Brief"; Thomas B. Littlewood, *The Politics of Population Control* (Notre Dame: University of Notre Dame Press, 1977), pp. 148-49; and Naparsteck, "Politics of Right-to-Life Movement," pp. 2-4 and 42.

[15] McRae v. Harris, 491 F. Supp., 712.

[16] The 1974 Declaration, however, allows certain "permissible exceptions," even though it says that "no reason, even the death of the mother, is sufficient to 'confer the right to dispose of another's life.' " This general prohibition may be evaded in cases categorized as "unintended abortion," consequent to treatment or surgery administered to the mother because of grave or life-threatening conditions such as a cancerous uterus or an ectopic pregnancy. But if the fetus is alive in such cases and dies in utero, it must be baptized. More significantly, in cases of rape or pregnancy following "involuntary intercourse," medical treatment soon afterward—when there is still doubt that the egg has implanted—is allowed within the Catholic doctrine. Note that these are precisely the exceptions that are presently written into law in the Hyde Amendment.

[17] McRae v. Harris, 491 F. Supp., 703-705; and "McRae Brief," pp. 78-79.

[18] Evidence presented in the *McRae* case before the federal district court revealed an agreement between the New York State Right-to-Life Committee and Cardinal Cook that funds collected in archdiocesan churches on "Respect Life Sunday" would be split three ways between "the local group," the State Committee, and the National Right-to-Life Committee, "McRae Brief," pp. 101-103. According to the *National Catholic Reporter* (cited in the brief), the National Committee for a Human Life Amendment (a National Conference of Catholic Bishops lobby) received its largest contribution in 1979 from the New York Archdiocese. This sort of lobbying and fund-raising activity by the church apparently enjoys a good deal of legal latitude. As one commentator points out, Internal

Revenue Service regulations permit churches to engage in "insubstantial" amounts of such activity, but "an insubstantial fraction of a budget the size of the Catholic Church's could be large indeed." See Roger M. Williams, "The Power of Fetal Politics," *Saturday Review* 9 June 1979, p. 11.

[19]Examples abound of the use of religious exhortation from the pulpits in antiabortion organizing. In St. Louis, Mo., the "Cathedral Bulletin" urged parishioners to attend the picketing of a local abortion clinic, with the message: "NO CHRISTIAN WILL EXCUSE HIMSELF LIGHTLY ON THIS DUTY." (Cited in "McRae Brief," p. 93). See also "Cardinal Condemns Abortion," *The Catholic Register*, 12 August 1977, regarding the agitational activities of Cardinal Humberto Medeiros of Boston; and my report on an antiabortion rally held by the right-wing Catholic group, "Tradition-Family-Property," in which priests had obviously played a key role in mobilizing parishioners, "Face-to-Face with the Far Right: Tradition, Family, Property," *Heresies*, no. 6 (Summer 1978), p. 59.

[20]In an address before a Maryland right-to-life convention, it was a U.S. congressman, and not a clergyman, Rep. Henry Hyde (sponsor of the antiabortion Hyde Amendment), who conveyed the awesome otherworldliness of this belief:

When the time comes, as it surely will, when we face that very terrible moment, the final judgment, I've often thought . . . that it is a terrible moment of loneliness, you have no advocates there, you are there alone standing before God and a terror will rip your soul like nothing you can imagine. I really think that those in the prolife movement will not be alone. I think there'll be a chorus of voices that have never been heard in this world but are heard very beautifully and very loudly in the next world and I think they will plead for everyone who has been in this movement and they will say to God, "Spare him, because he loved us." And God will look at us and say not "Did you succeed?" but "Did you try?" (Quoted in "McRae Brief," p. 117.)

[21]Michael Knight, "Cardinal Cautions Voters on Abortion," *New York Times*, 16 September 1980, p. A20; and John Herbert, "Anti-Abortionists' Impact Is Felt in Elections Across the Nation," *New York Times* 19 June 1978, pp. A1 and B10.

[22]One such manual stresses that the American political system is full of soft spots just waiting to be filled by conscientious right-to-lifers, for example, at the precinct level:

If the Right to Life movement, in addition to other efforts, were to direct its attention toward the invisible party structure presently supporting public officials, by either persuading, or if necessary replacing such persons, Congress would gladly fall in line and vote for a constitutional amendment protecting the unborn.

See Robert G. Marshall, *Bayonets and Roses: Comprehensive Pro-Life Political Action Guide* (Robert G. Marshall, 1978), p. 3.

[23]See Sharon Thompson's paper, "The Anti-Abortion Movement in New York State: Fall 1979." Thompson's writing on this subject is based on her personal observations and interviews, conducted over a period of many months with great courage and commitment. I am fortunate to be able to draw from her work here and aware of how much my own thinking has depended on hers.

[24]Crawford, *Thunder on the Right*, p. 36; and *Conservative Digest* 5 November 1979: 11.

[25]Crawford, *Thunder on the Right*, pp. 57-70.

[26]The promotional flyer for the Moral Majority states:

Bible-believing churches of America constitute the largest single minority bloc of America. However, this bloc is, for the most part, uninformed and totally disorganized. . . . The only persons who can lead this mammoth bloc are the pastors. . . . Therefore, the burden for stemming the tide of secular humanism rests solely on the leadership of Bible-believing pastors of America.

[27]Billy James Hargis was broadcasting his anticommunist messages over one hundred radio stations by the mid-1960s, having learned the technique for organizing a "radio-based movement" from Gerald Winrod, a virulent anti-Semitic and pro-Nazi of the 1930s and 40s. See Lipset and Raab, *Politics of Unreason*, pp. 167-69 and 273-75.

[28]The Director of Communications of the (liberal) United Church of Christ has emphasized the economic issue in religious broadcasting and that evangelical groups have the finances to pay millions of dollars to broadcasters to buy station time, undercutting smaller (and often more politically moderate) churches that lack such funding and rely on free time. See Ernest Holsendolph, "Religious Broadcasts Bring Rising Revenues and Create Rivalries," *New York Times*, 2 December 1979, pp. 1 and 36. According to Holsendolph's account, the Christian Broadcasting Network alone, headed by Pat Robertson, maintains a new $20 million television programming center in Virginia, including twin satellite earth dishes and transmitting antennas that beam to two different satellites. "The network can reach cable systems across the nation and 150 radio stations and 150 television stations on a 24-hour basis."

[29]*Moral Majority Report* 1: 3 (14 March 1980) and 1: 5 (26 May 1980).

[30]Danzig, "The Radical Right," p. 293.

[31]Ibid., p. 292.

[32]Ibid., p. 293.

[33]Weyrich, a key New Right leader, offers a revealing synopsis of the profamily organizing strategy in the August 1979 *Conservative Digest*. He hails "the new breed of religious leader," "the electronic preachers" like Falwell and Robertson, who "understand the linkage between the religious and moral issues and the politics of our time." "All in all," he ventures, "there may be nearly 100 million Americans—50 million born-again Protestants, 30 million morally conservative Catholics, 3 million Mormons, and 2 million Orthodox Jews—from which to draw members of a pro-family, Bible-believing coalition." See Weyrich, "Building the Moral Majority," p. 15.

[34]See Rev. Robert J. Billings, executive director of the Moral Majority, writing in the *Moral Majority Report*, no. 3 (14 March 1980): 15-16; and Marshall, *Bayonets and Roses*, pp. 226-27. This annunciation of a "Christian" state is bound to stir fears of anti-Semitism among Jews, and not without reason, as Ku Klux Klan and American Nazi Party activity increase.

[35]Since 1977, the personnel links between "prolife" and right-wing groups have proliferated to the point where they presently constitute a rather vast and complicated network (see chart by Tax and Wallace). A number of key leaders and strategists seem to straddle the two sets of organizations and share a common affiliation with such mainstream conservative organizations as the Birch Society, the Young Americans for Freedom (YAF) and the World Anti-Communist League. Most prominent among these are Richard Viguerie, the direct-mail fund-raiser and editor of the *Conservative Digest*; Paul Weyrich, director of the Committee for the Survival of a Free Congress and spokesman for the Moral Majority; Phyllis Schlafly, self-appointed head of "STOP ERA" and the anti-ERA "Eagle Forum"; Howard Phillips, chairman of the Conservative Caucus and also active in all the national "prolife" PACs; and Paul Brown, director of the Life Amendment Political Action Committee (LAPAC), probably the most aggressive of all the national "prolife" groups engaged in lobbying and electoral activity. See Manning, " 'New Right Forces Expect to Win,' "; Naparsteck, "Politics of Right-to-Life Movement, p. 3; Gregory-Lewis, "Danger on the Right" (2 November 1977); Sidney Blumenthal, "Mail-Order Politics," *In These Times*, July 18-24, 1979, pp. 12-13; and *Conservative Digest*, 6, nos. 5-6 (May-June 1980), which provides detailed profiles of the "pro-family" movement's principal leaders, organizational networks and goals.

[36]Personal conversation.

[37]The 1980 elections brought not only Ronald Reagan, a conservative Republican and opponent of legal abortion, to the presidency, but also a shift in the balance of

power in the Senate to a Republican majority for the first time in twenty-six years, and a coalition of conservative Republicans and Democrats—a number of whom chair key committees. In addition, there were considerable conservative gains in elections to the House of Representatives. For further breakdown of these developments, see Roberts, "New Conservative Coalition"; and Martin Tolchin, "Republicans Prepare for Senate Leadership," p. A28, Marjorie Hunter, "Democrats Keep Control of the House," p. A29, both in *New York Times*, 6 November 1980; and "The 1980 Elections: An Analysis," *Planned Parenthood-World Population Washington Memo* (Washington, D.C.: 14 November, 1980), p. 1.

[38] For example, the director of the NRLC in Washington left the organization to form her own American Life Lobby (ALL), reportedly because of NRLC President Carolyn Gerster's opposition to close ties between the organization and Viguerie. The former director is Judie Brown, wife of Paul Brown, who directs LAPAC; her ALL has become Viguerie's first direct "prolife" client. See David Crossens, "The Right-to-Life Movement: Major Force or Guerilla Movement?" Report prepared for Planned Parenthood Federation of America, 16 October 1979, hereafter cited as "Planned Parenthood Report." Another example is that of Ellen McCormack, leader of the "Right-to-Life party" in New York State. When McCormack—who apparently favors federally funded childcare, gun control, and detente with the Soviet Union—insisted on running for president in the 1980 election on a strict antiabortion platform, she met hostile resistance from Reagan supporters both within and outside the "right-to-life" movement. See Frank Lynn, "Anti-Abortion Groups Split on Reagan's Candidacy," *New York Times*, 22 June 1980, p. 28; "Will McCormack Cost Reagan the Election?" *Human Events* (National Conservative Weekly) 40, no. 29 (19 July 1980): 1 and 8; and Crawford, *Thunder on the Right*, p. 36.

[39] The most coherent statement of the "human rights" argument against abortion is John Lippis, "The Challenge to Be 'Pro Life' " (Santa Barbara, Calif.: Pro Life Education, Inc., 1978), pp. 1-3. Workshops at the 1979 NRLC convention in Cincinnati, Ohio, included one called "Pro-Life—Truly a Liberal Cause" and another called "Poverty, Abortion and Genocide." A resolution passed at the same convention links the "right to life" of the unborn to that of "the retarded, mentally ill, physically handicapped, abused children, educationally deprived, the poor, the aged, unmarried parents, the incurably ill, drug-dependent persons including alcoholics, victims of discrimination or [crime], the hungry all over the world." There has always been an attempt to appeal to blacks and other minorities by identifying abortion with racial "genocide" and publicizing the antiabortion views of well-known black and Hispanic leaders such as Jesse Jackson and Cesar Chavez.

[40] Editorial, *Commonweal* (2 January 1976), quoted in McRae v. Califano, 491 F. Supp., 709.

[41] See Timothy L. Smith, "Protestants Falwell Does Not Represent," *New York Times*, Oct. 22, 1980, Op-Ed page; and Robert Booth Fowler, "Evangelical Christians and Women's Liberation," paper presented at the meeting of the American Political Science Association, Washington, D.C., 31 August 1980.

[42] Jim Wallis, "Coming Together on the Sanctity of Life," *Sojourners Magazine* 9, no. 11 (November 1980), p. 4.

[43] Memorandum, National Right to Life Committee, 21 February 1978, signed, J.C. Willke. Willke was at the time national vice-president of the committee, and has subsequently been elected its national president, the first male to hold this office. By "they" he is referring both to Planned Parenthood and to all abortion advocates, liberal family planners, and feminists.

[44] *Conservative Digest* 5 (August 1979), pp. 18-19.

[45] See *Moral Majority Report*, full-page ad in every issue called "Join the Moral Majority"; and William Billings, *The Christian's Political Action Manual* (Washington, D.C.: National Christian Action Coalition, 1980), "Sample Candidate Questionnaire,"

pp. 33-34. This questionnaire was used by the New Right as a rating device for candidates in the 1980 congressional elections. Billings is son of Rev. Robert Billings, the Moral Majority's director.

[46] For an analysis of capitalism and patriarchy as distinct but interrelated *ideological* traditions, see Zillah Eisenstein, Introduction to *Capitalist Patriarchy and the Case for Socialist Feminism* (New York: Monthly Review Press, 1978).

[47] *Conservative Digest* 4, no. 7 (July 1978), p. 16.

[48] Quoted by Gregory-Lewis, "Danger on the Right."

[49] S. 1808, 96th Congress, 1st Sess. Sec. 302 of the bill would amend the *United States Code* by adding the following provision: "Rights of Families—In any action brought under the provisions of this title involving the parent's role in supervising and determining the religious or moral formation of his [*sic*] child, there is a legal presumption in favor of an expansive interpretation of that role."

[50] Robert J. Billings, "Family Protection Act: Now Is the Time for Passage," *Moral Majority Report* 1, no. 4 (11 April 1980): 16, describes the bill's purpose as being "to strengthen the family, the home, the church, and the private school" against "big government's . . . constant intrusion into family matters."

[51] Phyllis Schlafly, "ERA Means Unisex Society," *Conservative Digest* 4, no. 7 (July 1978): 14-16; and her brochure, "Eagle Forum—The Alternative to Women's Lib," (Box 618, Alton, Ill., n.d.).

[52] Onalee McGraw, "Federally Funded Domestic Violence Centers," *Moral Majority Report* 1, no. 4 (11 April 1980): 14-16; and "Senate Jeopardizes Family Values," *Moral Majority Report* 5, no. 3 (14 March 1980): p. 8.

[53] The "Sample Candidate Questionnaire" previously cited contains five out of thirteen questions that relate in some way to schools or education, regarding candidates' stands on busing, school prayer, tuition tax credits, "racial quotas" in private schools, and government-funded childcare. A sixth question, "Should homosexuals be discriminated against in employment?" is indirectly related because a major concern of the Right is to remove homosexuals from employment in public schools.

[54] See " 'New Right' Provides Anti-Union Thrust to Growing Religion-in-Politics Movement," Memorandum from COPE/Committee on Political Education, AFL-CIO, no. 17-69 (3 September 1979); and Crawford, *Thunder on the Right*, pp. 149-59, for versions of this argument.

[55] See Martin Tolchin, "Antibusing Measure Approved by Senate," *New York Times*, 14 November 1980, p. A18; and Steven V. Roberts, "Senate Votes to Bar Justice Department Suits Asking for Busing," *New York Times*, 18 November 1980, pp. A1 and B10.

[56] Roberts, "Senate Votes," p. A1. Indeed, a number of liberal senators, for example, Bob Packwood and Alan Cranston, were apparently intimidated into voting for the amendment.

[57] Thus New Right Senator Jesse Helms defended the legislation, of which he is a sponsor, by arguing that: "The vast majority of people of all races are sick and tired of Government meddling in their schools." Senator Strom Thurmond, the bill's cosponsor, maintained: "We're not favoring discrimination. We're simply saying, 'Let the children go to the nearest school, whether it's all white or all black or whatever.' " See Tolchin, "Antibusing Measure." In his judgment defying a federal district court order to enforce desegregation in a Louisiana school, Judge Richard E. Lee (now a right-wing and segregationist hero) held "that the case *no longer involves desegregation but is solely a matter of 'family law'* over which he, not the Federal Government, has jurisdiction." See John M. Crewdson, "Judge's Stand on Busing Divides Louisiana Town on Racial Lines," *New York Times*, 9 January 1981, p. A10.

[58] Participant interviewed by Bonnie Bellow and Nick Egleston, in a slide show on the abortion struggle and the "right-to-life" movement. I am grateful to Bonnie and Nick for sharing this important set of interviews with me.

[59] "Building the Moral Majority," p. 18. Cf. address by Henry Hyde before the Institute on Religious Life's Conference on "Whatever Happened to Religious Life?" St. Louis, Mo., 22 April 1978 (Mimeographed), where Hyde expressed great concern over the rise of left-wing and feminist dissidents within the church who are critical of the church's social policies, posing "serious problems for the church."

For examples of the fundamentalist attack on "secular humanism" as it relates to the attack on abortion, see Richard L. Ganz, "Psychology and Abortion: The Deception Exposed," in *Thou Shalt Not Kill: The Christian Case Against Abortion*, ed. Richard L. Ganz (New Rochelle, N.Y.: Arlington House, 1978), pp. 26-42; and Francis A. Schaeffer and C. Everett Koop, *Whatever Happened to the Human Race?* (Old Tappan, N.J.: Fleming H. Revell, 1978).

[60] Ellen Willis, *Village Voice*, 5 March 1979, p. 6.

[61] Thompson, "Anti-Abortion Movement," p. 11. I have also learned a lot concerning the sexual connotations of antiabortion politics from the insights of Janet Gallagher. See her article, "Abortion Rights: Critical Issue for Women's Freedom," *WIN* 15, no. 8 (8 March 1979, "International Women's Day" issue): 9-11, 24-26.

[62] "Are 'Pro-Lifers' Anti-Social?—Anti-Abortion Legislators Vote on Social Issues," NARAL/National Abortion Rights Action League Newsletter 2, no. 2 (March 1979): 5-7. Sens. Orrin Hatch and Richard Schweiker (who has been appointed by Reagan as Secretary of Health and Human Services) are cosponsors of a bill to divest the Occupational Health and Safety Administration of much of its enforcement power, as well as being National Advisory Board members of the NRLC.

[63] Donald Granberg, "Pro-Life or Reflection of Conservative Ideology? An Analysis of Opposition to Legalized Abortion," *Sociology and Social Research* 62, no. 3 (April 1978): 421-23. Granberg's findings on antiabortion attitudes were confirmed by a study of Catholic right-to-life advocates done at the Quixote Center for Justice in Washington, D.C. See Maureen Fiedler and Dolly Pomerleau, *Are Catholics Ready?* reviewed in *National Catholic Reporter*, 14 November 1978. Moreover, an unpublished longitudinal study of an interdenominational national sample, by Judith Blake and Jorge Del Pinal from the University of California at Los Angeles, reports that the "attitudinal variables" that most closely correlate with antiabortion attitudes "are not simply a function of generalized prudery toward sex . . . but . . . relate specifically to *disapproval of premarital sexual relations.*" See "Determinants of Attitudes Toward Abortion in the United States," p. 9.

[64] See Planned Parenthood Report, p. 1-48; Lippis, "Challenge to be 'Pro Life,' " p. 16; and C. Everett Koop, "A Physician Looks at Abortion," in Ganz, *Thou Shalt Not Kill*, p. 13.

[65] Quoted in Littlewood, *Politics of Population Control*, p. 138.

[66] "Prolife" lobbyist, Marjory Mecklenburg, who at this writing is the administration's preferred choice for head of the federal Office of Adolescent Pregnancy Programs, has publicly stated that in her view the "front line of defense" against unwanted teenage pregnancies should be, not to provide teenagers with contraception, but to educate them to "postpone sexual involvement" (David E. Rosenbaum, "Abortion Foe is Chief Candidate to Lead Birth Control Programs," *New York Times*, 18 February 1981, p. 16.) Her view is shared by Secretary of Health and Human Services, Schweiker.

[67] See "Sexuality and the State: The Defeat of the Briggs Initiative and Beyond," interview with Amber Hollibaugh, *Socialist Review* 9, no. 3 (May-June 1979): 55-72.

[68] *Conservative Digest* 5, no. 3 (March 1979): 10.

[69] See Gregory-Lewis, "Danger on the Right," on funding of both the antigay rights and the anti-ERA campaigns.

[70] Michael Novak, "Homosexuality: A Social Rot," *Conservative Digest* 5, no. 1 (January 1979), pp. 44-45.

[71] Interview with Paul Weyrich in *Conservative Digest* 6, no. 6 (June 1980): 12.

[72] This is an inference based in part on P. Leahy, *The Anti-Abortion Movement: Testing a Theory of the Rise and Fall of Social Movements* (Ann Arbor: University Microfilms, 1975), pp. 50-52; and in part on descriptions of the "profamily" and right-to-life leadership contained in their own literature and provided through personal observations by individuals of their national meetings.

[73] Quoted in Leslie Bennetts, "Conservatives Join on Social Concerns," *New York Times*, 30 July 1980, pp. 1 and B6.

[74] See Francis X. Clines, "Pope Ends U.S. Visit with Capital Mass Affirming Doctrine," *New York Times*, 8 Oct. 1979, p. 1; and Kenneth A. Briggs, "Archbishop Stresses Stand Against Birth Control," *New York Times* 2 October 1980, p. A14.

[75] See Frederick S. Jaffe, Barbara L. Lindheim, and Philip R. Lee, *Abortion Politics: Private Morality and Public Policy* (New York: McGraw-Hill, 1981), p. 106, summarizing national survey data through 1977.

[76] Quoted in Bennetts, "Conservatives Join on Social Concerns," p. B6.

[77] Some of the most important thinking about the relationship of consciousness to social movements is in the work of Sarah Eisenstein, whose tragic death in 1978 prevented her from completing that work.

[78] Zillah Eisenstein, *The Radical Future of Liberal Feminism* (New York and London: Longman, 1980), chaps. 1 and 10.

[79] Beverly L. Johnson and Howard Hayghe, "Labor Force Participation of Married Women, March 1976," Special Labor Force Report 206, U.S. Department of Labor, Bureau of Labor Statistics (June 1977), pp. 32-34.

[80] U.S. Department of Labor, Bureau of Labor Statistics, *U.S. Working Women: A Databook* (1977), tables 1-4, 18-19, and charts 3-4; and U.S. Department of Commerce, Bureau of the Census: *A Statistical Portrait of Women in the United States*, Current Population Reports Series P-23, no. 100 (February 1980), tables 6-1, 6-2, and 6-6.

[81] U.S. Department of Commerce, Bureau of the Census, "Divorce, Child Custody, and Child Support," Current Population Reports Series P-23, no. 84 (June 1979), pp. 1-2 and fig.1; U.S. Department of Commerce, Bureau of the Census, "Marital Status and Living Arrangements: March 1978," Current Population Reports Series P-20, no. 338 (May 1979), pp. 2-3 and table C; and "U.S. Divorce Rate Rises Again After Levelling Off," *New York Times*, 17 August 1980, p. 53.

[82] "Marital Status and Living Arrangements," pp. 3-6 and tables D-G; Heather L. Ross and Isabel V. Sawhill, *Time of Transition: The Growth of Families Headed by Women* (Washington, D.C.: The Urban Institute, 1975); Frances E. Kobrin, "The Fall in Household Size and the Rise of the Primary Individual in the United States," *Demography* 13, no. 1 (February 1976): 127-38; and "One-Parent Families Rose 79% in Decade, U.S. Report Indicates," *New York Times* 17 August 1980, p. 29.

[83] U.S. Department of Commerce, Bureau of the Census, "Perspectives on American Fertility," Current Population Reports Series P-23, no. 70 (July 1978), pp. 1-4, 21-23, fig. 1-4, and tables 3-1/3-2; and Sandra L. Hofferth and Kristin A. Moore, "Women's Employment and Marriage," in *The Subtle Revolution: Women at Work*, ed. Ralph E. Smith (Washington, D.C.: The Urban Institute, 1979), pp. 102-103.

[84] U.S. Department of Health and Human Services, "Trends and Differentials in Births to Unmarried Women, United States 1970-76," Vital and Health Statistics Series 21, no. 36 (May 1980), p. 3.

[85] Cliff Jahn, "Anita Bryant's Startling Reversal," *Ladies' Home Journal* 97, no. 12 (December 1980): 62-68. Thanks to Judy Stacey for sending me this article.

[86] Emma Rothschild, "Reagan and the Real America," *New York Review of Books* 28, no. 2 (5 February 1981), pp. 12-13.

[87] Jill Stephenson, *Women in Nazi Society* (New York: Barnes and Noble, 1975), p. 71.

■ DAN, MURPH AND ME

Why I Hate 'Family Values' (Let Me Count the Ways)

KATHA POLLITT

Unlike many of the commentators who have made Murphy Brown the most famous unmarried mother since Ingrid Bergman ran off with Roberto Rossellini, I actually watched the notorious childbirth episode. After reading my sleep-resistant 4-year-old her entire collection of Berenstain Bears books, television was all I was fit for. And that is how I know that I belong to the cultural elite: Not only can I spell "potato" correctly, and many other vegetables as well, I thought the show was a veritable riot of family values. First of all, Murph is smart, warm, playful, decent and rich: She'll be a great mom. Second, the dad is her ex-husband: The kid is as close to legitimate as the scriptwriters could manage, given that Murph is divorced. Third, her ex spurned *her*, not, as Dan Quayle implies, the other way around. Fourth, she rejected abortion. On TV, women have abortions only in docudramas, usually after being raped, drugged with birth-defect-inducing chemicals or put into a coma. Finally, what does Murph sing to the newborn? "You make me feel like a natural woman"! Even on the most feminist sitcom in TV history (if you take points off *Kate and Allie* for never so much as mentioning the word "gay"), anatomy is destiny.

That a show as fluffy and genial as *Murphy Brown* has touched off a national debate about "family values" speaks volumes—and not just about the apparent inability of Dan Quayle to distinguish real life from a sitcom. (And since when are TV writers part of the cultural elite, anyway? I thought they were the crowd-pleasing lowbrows, and *intellectuals* were the cultural elite.) The *Murphy Brown* debate, it turns out, isn't really about Murphy Brown; it's about inner-city women, who will be encouraged to produce fatherless babies by Murph's example—the trickle-down theory of values. (Do welfare moms watch *Murphy Brown*? I thought it was supposed to be soap operas, as in "they just sit around all day watching the soaps." Marriage is a major obsession on the soaps—but never mind.) Everybody, it seems, understood this substitution immediately. After all, why get upset about Baby Boy Brown? Is there any doubt that he will be safe, loved, well schooled, taken for checkups, taught to respect the rights and feelings of others and treated to *The Berenstain Bears Visit the Dentist* as often as his little heart desires? Unlike millions of kids who live with both parents, he will never be physically or sexually abused, watch his father beat his mother (domestic assault is the leading cause of injury to women) or cower beneath the blankets while his parents scream at each other. And chances are excellent that he won't sexually assault a retarded girl with a miniature baseball bat, like those high school athletes in posh Glen Ridge, New Jersey; or shoot his lover's spouse, like Amy Fisher; or find himself on trial for rape, like William Kennedy Smith—children of intact and prosperous families every one of them. He'll probably go to Harvard and major in semiotics. Maybe that's the problem. Just think, if Murph were married, like Dan Quayle's mom, he could go to DePauw University and major in golf.

That there is something called "the family"—Papa Bear, Mama Bear, Brother Bear and Sister Bear—that is the best setting for raising children, and that it is in trouble because of a decline in "values," are bromides accepted by commentators of all political stripes. The right blames a left-wing cultural conspiracy: obscene rock lyrics, sex ed, abortion, prayerless schools, working mothers, promiscuity, homosexuality, decline of respect for authority and hard work, welfare and, of course, feminism. (On the *Chicago Tribune* Op-Ed page, Allan Carlson, president of the ultraconservative

Rockford Institute, found a previously overlooked villain: federal housing subsidies. With all that square footage lying around, singles and unhappy spouses could afford to live on their own.) The left blames the ideology of postindustrial capitalism: consumerism, individualism, selfishness, alienation, lack of social supports for parents and children, atrophied communities, welfare and feminism. The center agonizes over teen sex, welfare moms, crime and divorce, unsure what the causes are beyond some sort of moral failure—probably related to feminism. Interesting how that word keeps coming up.

I used to wonder what family values are. As a matter of fact, I still do. If abortion, according to the right, undermines family values, then single motherhood (as the producers of *Murphy Brown* were quick to point out) must be in accord with them, no? No. Over on the left, if gender equality, love and sexual expressivity are desirable features of contemporary marriage, then isn't marriage bound to be unstable, given how hard those things are to achieve and maintain? Not really.

Just say no, says the right. Try counseling, says the left. Don't be so lazy, says the center. Indeed, in its guilt-mongering cover story "Legacy of Divorce: How the Fear of Failure Haunts the Children of Broken Marriages," *Newsweek* was unable to come up with any explanation for the high American divorce rate except that people just didn't try hard enough to stay married.

When left, right and center agree, watch out. They probably don't know what they're talking about. And so it is with "the family" and "family values." In the first place, these terms lump together distinct social phenomena that in reality have virtually nothing to do with one another. The handful of fortysomething professionals like Murphy Brown who elect to have a child without a male partner have little in common with the millions of middle- and working-class divorced mothers who find themselves in desperate financial straits because their husbands fail to pay court-awarded child support. And neither category has much in common with inner-city girls like those a teacher friend of mine told me about the other day: a 13-year-old and a 12-year-old, impregnated by boyfriends twice their age and determined to bear and keep the babies—to spite abusive parents, to confirm their parents' low opinion of them, to have someone to love who loves them in return.

Beyond that, appeals to "the family" and its "values" frame the discussion as one about morals instead of consequences. In real life, for example, teen sex—the subject of endless sermons—has little relation with teen childbearing. That sounds counterfactual, but it's true. Western European teens have sex about as early and as often as American ones, but are much less likely to have babies. Partly it's because there are far fewer European girls whose lives are as marked by hopelessness and brutality as those of my friend's students. And partly it's because European youth have much better access to sexual information, birth control and abortion. Or consider divorce. In real life, parents divorce for all kinds of reasons, not because they lack moral fiber and are heedless of their children's needs. Indeed, many divorce because they *do* consider their kids; and the poisonous effects of growing up in a household marked by violence, craziness, open verbal warfare or simple lovelessness.

Perhaps this is the place to say that I come to the family-values debate with a personal bias. I am recently separated myself. I think my husband and I would fall under *News-*

week's "didn't try harder" rubric, although we thought about splitting up for years, discussed it for almost a whole additional year and consulted no fewer than four therapists, including a marital counselor who advised us that marriage was one of modern mankind's only means of self-transcendence (religion and psychoanalysis were the others, which should have warned me) and admonished us that we risked a future of shallow relationships if we shirked our spiritual mission, not to mention the damage we would "certainly" inflict on our daughter. I thought he was a jackass—shallow relationships? *moi*? But he got to me. Because our marriage wasn't some flaming disaster—with broken dishes and hitting and strange hotel charges showing up on the MasterCard bill. It was just unhappy, in ways that weren't going to change. Still, I think both of us would have been willing to trudge on to spare our child suffering. That's what couples do in women's magazines; that's what the Clintons say they did. But we saw it wouldn't work: As our daughter got older, she would see right through us, the way kids do. And, worse, no matter how hard I tried to put on a happy face, I would wordlessly communicate to her—whose favorite fairy tale is "Cinderella," and whose favorite game is Wedding, complete with bath-towel bridal veil—my resentment and depression and cynicism about relations between the sexes.

The family-values types would doubtless say that my husband and I made a selfish choice, which society should have impeded or even prevented. There's a growing sentiment in policy land to make divorce more difficult. In *When the Bough Breaks*, Sylvia Ann Hewlett argues that couples should be forced into therapy (funny how ready people are to believe that counseling, which even when voluntary takes years to modify garden-ariety neuroses, can work wonders in months with resistant patients who hate each other). Christopher Lasch briefly supported a constitutional amendment forbidding divorce to couples with minor children, as if lack of a separation agreement would keep people living together (he's backed off that position, he told me recently). The Communitarians, who flood *The Nation*'s mailboxes with self-promoting worryfests, furrow their brows wondering "How can the family be saved without forcing women to stay at home or otherwise violating their rights?" (Good luck.) But I am still waiting for someone to explain why it would be better for my daughter to grow up in a joyless

household than for her to live as she does now, with two reasonably cheerful parents living around the corner from each other, both committed to her support and co-operating, as they say on *Sesame Street*, in her care. We may not love each other, but we both love her. Maybe that's as much as parents can do for their children, and all that should be asked of them.

But, of course, civilized cooperation is exactly what many divorced parents find they cannot manage. The statistics on deadbeat and vanishing dads are shocking—less than half pay child support promptly and in full, and around half seldom or never see their kids within a few years of marital breakup. Surely, some of this male abdication can be explained by the very thinness of the traditional paternal role worshiped by the preachers of "values"; it's little more than breadwinning, discipline and fishing trips. How many diapers, after all, has Dan Quayle changed? A large percentage of American fathers have never changed a single one. Maybe the reason so many fathers fade away after divorce is that they were never really there to begin with.

It is true that people's ideas about marriage are not what they were in the 1950s—although those who look back at the fifties nostalgically forget both that many of those marriages were miserable and that the fifties were an atypical decade in more than a century of social change. Married women have been moving steadily into the work force since 1890; beginning even earlier, families have been getting smaller; divorce has been rising; sexual activity has been initiated even earlier and marriage delayed; companionate marriage has been increasingly accepted as desirable by all social classes and both sexes. It may be that these trends have reached a tipping point, at which they come to define a new norm. Few men expect to marry virgins, and children are hardly "stigmatized" by divorce, as they might have been a mere fifteen or twenty years ago. But if people want different things from family life—if women, as Arlie Hochschild pointed out in *The Second Shift*, cite as a major reason for separation the failure of their husbands to share domestic labor; if both sexes are less willing to resign themselves to a marriage devoid of sexual pleasure, intimacy or shared goals; if single women decide they want to be mothers; if teenagers want to sleep together—why shouldn't society adapt? Society is, after all, just us. Nor are these developments unique to the United States. All over the industrialized world, divorce rates are high,

single women are having babies by choice, homosexuals are coming out of the closet and infidelity, always much more common than anyone wanted to recognize, is on the rise. Indeed, in some ways America is behind the rest of the West: We still go to church, unlike the British, the French and, now that Franco is out of the way, the Spanish. More religious than Spain! Imagine.

I'm not saying that these changes are without cost—in poverty, loneliness, insecurity and stress. The reasons for this suffering, however, lie not in moral collapse but in our failure to acknowledge and adjust to changing social relations.

We still act as if mothers stayed home with children, wives didn't need to work and men earned a "family wage." We'd rather preach about teenage "promiscuity" than teach young people—especially young women—how to negotiate sexual issues responsibly. If my friend's students had been prepared for puberty by schools and discussion groups and health centers, the way Dutch young people are, they might not have ended up pregnant, victims of what is, after all, statutory rape. And if women earned a dollar for every dollar earned by men, divorce and single parenthood would not mean poverty. Nobody worries about single fathers raising children, after all; indeed, paternal custody is the latest legal fad.

What is the point of trying to put the new wine of modern personal relations in the old bottles of the sexual double standard and indissoluble marriage? For that is what most of the current discourse on "family issues" amounts to. No matter how fallacious, the culture greets moralistic approaches to these subjects with instant agreement. Judith Wallerstein's travesty of social science, *Second Chances*, asserts that children are emotionally traumatized by divorce, and the fact that she had no control group is simply ignored by an ecstatic press. As it happens, a recent study in *Science* did use a control group. By following 17,000 children for four years, and comparing those whose parents split with those whose parents stayed in troubled marriages, the researchers found that the "divorce effect" disappeared entirely for boys and was very small for girls. Not surprisingly, this study attracted absolutely no attention.

Similarly, we are quick to blame poor unmarried mothers for all manner of social problems—crime, unemployment, drops in reading scores, teen suicide. The solution? Cut off all welfare for additional children. Force teen mothers to live with their parents. Push women to marry in order to attach them to a male income. (So much for love—talk about marriage as legalized prostitution!)

New Jersey's new welfare reform law gives economic coercion a particularly bizarre twist. Welfare moms who marry can keep part of their dole, but only if the man is *not* the father of their children. The logic is that, married or not, Dad has a financial obligation to his kids, but Mr. Just Got Into Town does not. If the law's inventors are right that welfare policy can micromanage marital and reproductive choice, they have just guaranteed that no poor woman will marry her children's father. This is strengthening the family?

Charles Murray, of the American Enterprise Institute, thinks New Jersey does not go far enough. Get rid of welfare entirely, he argued in *The New York Times*: Mothers should marry or starve, and if they are foolish enough to prefer the latter, their kids should be put up for adoption or into orphanages. Mickey Kaus, who favors compulsory low-wage employment for the poor, likes orphanages too.

None of those punitive approaches will work. There is no evidence that increased poverty decreases family size, and welfare moms aren't likely to meet many men with family-size incomes, or they'd probably be married already, though maybe not for long. The men who impregnated those seventh graders, for example, are much more likely to turn them out as prostitutes than to lead them to the altar. For one thing, those men may well be married themselves.

The fact is, the harm connected with the dissolution of "the family" is not a problem of values—at least not individual values—it's a problem of money. When the poor are abandoned to their fates, when there are no jobs, people don't get to display "work ethic," don't feel good about themselves and don't marry or stay married. The girls don't have anything to postpone motherhood for; the boys have no economic prospects that would make them reasonable marriage partners. This was as true in the slums of eighteenth-century London as it is today in the urban slums of Latin America and Africa, as well as the United States. Or take divorce: The real harm of divorce is that it makes lots of women, and their children, poor. One reason, which has got a fair amount of attention recently, is the scandalously low level of child support, plus the tendency of courts to award a disproportionate share of the marital assets to the man. The other reason is that women earn much less than men, thanks to gender discrimination and the failure of the workplace to adapt to the needs of working mothers. Instead of moaning about "family values" we should be thinking about how to provide the poor with decent jobs and social services, and about how to insure economic justice for working women. And let marriage take care of itself.

Family values and the cult of the nuclear family is, at bottom, just another way to bash women, especially poor women. If only they would get married and stay married, society's ills would vanish. Inner-city crime would disappear because fathers would communicate manly values to their sons, which would cause jobs to spring up like mushrooms after rain. Welfare would fade away. Children would do well in school. (Irene Impellizeri, anti-condom vice president of the New York City Board of Education, recently gave a speech attributing inner-city children's poor grades and high dropout rates to the failure of their families to provide "moral models," the way immigrant parents did in the good old days—a dangerous argument for her, in particular, to make; doesn't she know that Italian-American kids have dropout and failure rates only slightly lower than black and Latino teens?)

When pundits preach morality, I often find myself thinking of Samuel Johnson, literature's greatest enemy of cant and fatuity. What would the eighteenth-century moralist make of our current obsession with marriage? "Sir," he replied to Boswell, who held that marriage was a natural state, "it is so far from being natural for a man and woman to live in the state of marriage that we find all the motives which they have for remaining in that connection, and the restraints which civilized society imposes to prevent separation, are hardly sufficient to keep them together." Dr. Johnson knew what he was talking about: He and his wife lived apart. And what would he think of our confusion of moral preachments with practical solutions to social problems? Remember his response to Mrs. Thrale's long and flowery speech on the cost of children's clothes. "Nay, madam," he said, "when you are declaiming, declaim; and when you are calculating, calculate."

Which is it going to be? Declamation, which feeds no children, employs no jobless and reduces gender relations to an economic bargain? Or calculation, which accepts the fact that the Berenstain Bears, like Murphy Brown, are fiction. The people seem to be voting with their feet on "the family." It's time for our "values" to catch up.   □

ARTICLES.

■ DAN QUAYLE'S REVENGE

The New Family Values Crusaders

JUDITH STACEY

On election eve in 1992, I optimistically anticipated a respite from the family wars. After all, Murphy Brown had triumphed over Dan Quayle, and the ultramoralistic Republican convention had self-destructed on national television. The family values brigades seemed routed. Who could have predicted that even the liberal media would scramble to rehabilitate the former Vice President's image and warmly embrace family values before Clinton had survived his blistering first 100 days?

"Dan Quayle Was Right," decreed the April 1993 *Atlantic Monthly*, a magazine popular with the very cultural elite Quayle had blamed for the decline of Western civilized family life. Just as Clinton's job stimulus package suffered a silent demise, Jeremiahs from *The New York Times* to the *Chronicle of Higher Education*, from *This Week With David Brinkley* to *The MacNeil/Lehrer NewsHour*, chanted kaddish for those fifties families, whose romanticized virtues grow ever more mythic with their passing. Because the rhetoric is numbingly familiar, few seem aware that the media's current family fervor signals the considerable success of a well-orchestrated new campaign. Old-style family values warriors like Quayle, Pat Buchanan and Jerry Falwell are reactionary Republicans and fundamentalist Christians—overtly antifeminist, antigay and, at least at the moment, on the defensive. In contrast, the revisionist family values campaign is explicitly centrist and coming on strong.

A creation of academicians rather than clerics, the campaign grounds its claims not in religious authority but in social science. During the late 1980s, a network of research and policy institutes, think tanks and commissions began mobilizing to forge a national consensus on family values and to shape the family politics of the "new" Democratic Party. Central players are the Institute for American Values, led by David Blankenhorn and Barbara Dafoe Whitehead (author of the *Atlantic* article), and its offshoot, the Council on Families in America, co-chaired by social scientists David Popenoe and Jean Bethke Elshtain. President Clinton's domestic policy adviser, William Galston, is one of the council's seventeen academic members, and Louis Sullivan, George Bush's Secretary of Health and Human Services, gave the keynote address at its inaugural meeting.

"This is an attempt to bring people together who could con-

vince the liberal intelligentsia that the family was in trouble and that this was a big problem," Popenoe told me when I interviewed him recently. "Most of us are neoliberal—you know, New Democrats, affiliated with the Progressive Policy Institute. We try to keep to the middle of the road." The political networks of these center-laners entwine tightly with those of the communitarians—a movement characterized by its founder, sociologist Amitai Etzioni, as "struggling for the soul of the Clinton Administration." Galston, Blankenhorn, Popenoe and Elshtain are all communitarians. So is Clinton's housing secretary, Henry Cisneros; and Al Gore spoke at a 1991 communitarian teach-in [see Jamie Stiehm, "Community and Communitarians," July 18]. The groups led by Blankenhorn, Popenoe and Etzioni draw on the same funding sources, according to Popenoe, who concedes that more of their benefactors are conservative than liberal. These include the Randall, Smith Richardson, Mott and Scaife foundations; the Brookings Institution; and the American Enterprise Institute.

***T**hey identify fatherless families as the root of everything—poverty, violence, drug addiction, crime . . .*

Declaring that "the principal source of family decline over the past three decades has been cultural," Whitehead and her colleagues have mounted a crusade to restore the privileged status of lifelong, heterosexual marriage. The effects on intimate behaviors remain to be seen, but these new family values warriors have already achieved astonishing influence over the Clinton Administration. It took scarcely a year to convert Clinton from a proud icon of a single mom's glory into a repentant Quayle acolyte. *Newsweek* published the President's revised family credo last December: "Remember the Dan Quayle speech? There were a lot of very good things in that speech. . . . Would we be a better-off society if babies were born to married couples? You bet we would."

The belief that married-couple families are superior is probably the most pervasive prejudice about family life in the Western world, and the centrists are busy transmuting it into a social scientific "truth." They claim that research demonstrates that having two married, biological parents is the passport to a child's welfare, and thereby to society's welfare. Joining Daniel Patrick Moynihan on the "family breakdown" trail he has trekked since the sixties, they identify fatherless families as the root of everything from poverty, violence, drug addiction, crime and declining standards in education and civility to teen pregnancy, sexually transmitted disease, narcissism and the Los Angeles uprising. Claiming that research proves that divorce and unwed motherhood inflict devastating harm on children, centrists seek to revive the social stigma that once marked these "selfish" practices. They want to restore fault criteria to divorce proceedings and impose new re-

---

Judith Stacey, who teaches sociology and women's studies at the University of California, Davis, is the author of Brave New Families: Stories of Domestic Upheaval in Twentieth Century America *(Basic).*

strictions, like mandatory waiting periods and counseling. They also favor welfare caps on unwed mothers.

By endlessly repeating and cross-citing one another's views, the centrists seem to have convinced most of the media, the public and Clinton that the superiority of the family values they espouse is, as Popenoe puts it, "a confirmed empirical generalization." Their efforts paved the yellow brick road to the shockingly respectful response that Charles Murray, an American Enterprise fellow, has received to his punitive quest to restigmatize "illegitimacy" and to terminate "all economic support for single mothers." The revisionist cultural onslaught has been so potent that even Donna Shalala, Clinton's Secretary of Health and Human Services and the Administration's token progressive feminist, seems to feel compelled to recite its mantra. "I don't like to put this in moral terms, but I do believe that having children out of wedlock is just wrong," Shalala told *Newsweek*, while a "dyed in the wool, but curious White House liberal" confided, off the record, that he'd "like to see the Murray solution tried somewhere—just to see, y'know, what might happen."

Although the revisionists sound like card-carrying conservatives who traded in leisure suits for academic tweed, they take wiser note of present demographic and cultural terrain than do their right-wing counterparts. They eschew antifeminism for a postfeminist family ethic and attempt to address some of the dilemmas currently plaguing working parents. They promote greater public commitment to lifting families out of poverty than conservatives can stomach, as well as more reforms like flextime, family allowances, flexible career paths and paid family leave. Disdainful of the Republicans' crude antifeminism, centrists gesture toward gender equality. Blankenhorn, for example, insists that "strengthening family life in the 1990s cannot and should not mean the repeal of the past

thirty years of new opportunities for women in the workplace and in public life." Centrists also call for greater familial responsibility from men. Blankenhorn has joined forces with Don Eberly, a former aide to Jack Kemp, to form a national organization of fathers to "restore to fatherhood a sense of pride, duty and reward."

No other "advanced" industrial nation subjects working mothers to as anguishing a work/family conflict as does the United States. Burned-out supermoms, devalued housewives and women suffering the effects of divorce, deadbeat dads, feckless sexual partners or asymmetrical job and courtship markets may be excused if they indulge, like unapologetic male chauvinists, in some backlash nostalgia for simpler family times. While centrists effectively exploit this yearning, progressive social scientists have been backed into ideological corners and marginalized. So before the feeble ranks of remnant, "dyed in the wool" liberals succumb to "curiosity" over what the Murray solution might accomplish, I want to expose the most egregious flaws in the centrists' social science and to confront the kernels of truth embedded in their family sermons.

Contrary to centrist claims, most social scientists do not agree that a family's structure is more important than the quality of the relationships. Revisionists employ academic sleights of hand to evade this consensus. For example, they rest claims on misleading comparison groups and on studies, like Judith Wallerstein's widely cited research on divorcing parents, that do not use any comparison groups at all. It is true that, on average, children of divorce fare somewhat worse than those in intact families, but this tells us nothing about how divorce affects children. To address that question, we must compare children of divorce not with all children of married parents but with those whose unhappily married parents do not divorce. Research indicates that high-conflict marriages harm children more than do low-conflict divorces.

Centrists use another statistical trick to exaggerate advantages that some children from two-parent families enjoy over their single-parented peers—treating small and relative differences as though they were gross and absolute. In fact, most children from both kinds of families turn out reasonably well, and when other parental resources—like income, education, self-esteem and a supportive social environment—are roughly similar, signs of two-parent privilege largely disappear. Most research, like that summarized in Frank Furstenberg and Andrew Cherlin's *Divided Families*, indicates that a stable, intimate relationship with one responsible, nurturant adult is a child's surest path to becoming one too. In short, the research scale tips toward those who stress the quality of family relationships over their form. Moreover, it is untenable to appeal to a child-centered doctrine to impugn the "selfishness" of single women who choose to become mothers. Because no child asks to be born, almost all intentional parenting is selfish.

The centrists have it backward when they argue that the collapse of traditional family values is at the heart of our social decay. The losses in real earnings and in breadwinner jobs, the persistence of low-wage work for women and the corporate greed that has accompanied global economic restructuring have wreaked far more havoc on Ozzie and Harriet Land

ILLUSTRATIONS BY ROBERT GROSSMAN

than have the combined effects of feminism, sexual revolution, gay liberation, the counterculture, narcissism and every other value flip of the past half-century.

In all cultures and eras, stable marriage systems have rested upon coercion—overt or veiled—and on inequality. Proposals to restrict access to divorce and parenting implicitly recognize this. Without coercion, divorce and single motherhood will remain commonplace. Marriage became increasingly fragile as it became less obligatory, particularly for women. It seems a poignant commentary on the benefits to women of modern marriage that even when women retain chief responsibility for children, when they earn much less than men with similar "cultural capital" and when they and their children suffer major economic loss after divorce, so many regard divorce as the lesser evil.

Yet most centrists avert their eyes from this injustice. Whitehead, for example, celebrates signs of a "New Familism" in which "both parents give up something in their work lives in order to foster their family lives. The woman makes the larger concession, but it is one she actively elects." Postfeminist family ideology appropriates feminist critiques of traditional masculine priorities while appealing to those maternal values that feminists like Carol Gilligan have made popular. They also build upon a body of thought I once termed "new conservative feminism," whose defining feature is distaste for sexual politics. Revisionists offer tepid support, at best, for abortion rights, often supporting restrictions like spousal and parental notification, partly in the service of making men more accountable. Moreover, as Etzioni puts it, "there are some issues, such as abortion and gay rights, that we know communitarians cannot agree on, so we have completely avoided them."

Homophobia also plays a closeted role in the centrists' campaign, one that could prove more insidious than Buchanan-style gay bashing. Moynihan's conviction that children need to grow up in families that provide a "stable relationship to male authority" is echoed by Whitehead's undocumented claim that research demonstrates "the importance of both a mother and a father in fostering the emotional well-being of children." Elshtain unapologetically concedes that "we are privileging relations of a particular kind in which certain social goods are at stake" by affirming a heterosexual family model. Ignoring consistent research findings that lesbian and gay parents are at least as successful as heterosexual ones, the council she co-chairs refuses to advocate equal marriage, adoption or childbearing rights for gays.

Nor do the centrists seem much concerned with the class and race prejudices their crusade exhibits. Having studied families struggling to sustain body, soul and kin ties in Silicon Valley during the mid-1980s recession, I wonder what sort of bourgeois, bubble world folks like Whitehead, Popenoe and the other communitarians inhabit. I do not know whether their moralistic images of hedonistic adults who place selfish emotional, erotic and "career" ambitions above the needs of neglected children derive from close observation of occupants of some professional/corporate cocoon. I do know that such caricatures bear scant resemblance to the family realities of the working people—married or single, lesbian or straight, employed, laid off or retired—that I studied, nor,

I would venture, to those of most of the rest of us. Few can enjoy the luxury of a "new familism" that places children's needs above the demands of a job. Wherever class bias flourishes, race is seldom far behind. Dan Quayle's attack on Murphy Brown was an attempt to play the Willie Horton card in whiteface. Without resorting to overt racism, he conjured up frightening hordes of black welfare "queens" rearing infant fodder for sex, drugs and videotaped rebellions, such as had just erupted in L.A. The greatest contrast in family patterns and resources in the country today is between steady-earner and single-mother households, and these divide visibly along racial lines. Voting patterns in the 1992 election registered a wider "family gap" than gender gap. Unmarried voters' heavy preference for Clinton shored up his precarious margin of victory. Clearly, a campaign that sets two- and single-parent families at odds has political consequences. Centrist Democrats hope their family values campaign will erode the advantage Republicans now enjoy among the largely white, middle-class, heterosexual, two-parent family set. Such a strategy is unlikely to succeed. As Quayle and Christian right leaders recognize, family values ardor more readily promotes their reactionary agenda.

But to halt the stampede to a conservative cultural consensus, progressives must do more than expose the errors of the centrists. We must also dodge the ideological corners into which they deftly paint us, resisting knee-jerk responses to their reductionist logic, like one feminist bumper sticker—"Unspoken Traditional Family Values: Abuse, Alcoholism, Incest"—that Whitehead cites to mock feminists. Nor should we tolerate an image as an overzealous cheering squad for unwed single motherhood. Certainly, aiding women's struggles to resist unequal, hostile, dangerous marriages remains a crucial project, but one we cannot advance by denying that many women, many of them feminists, want committed, intimate relationships with men. The best interests of women, men and children do *not* always coincide. Some divorces *are* better for the adults, who choose them, than for the children, who do not. Just as there are his and hers marriages, divorce is often better for one spouse than the other.

We should also recognize that in most industrial societies teenage motherhood (married or not) often does not augur well for the offspring. Without rejecting the view that most teens now lack the maturity and resources to parent effectively, we might note that this is as true of those whom Charles Murray would shame and starve into shotgun marriages as of those whose dads lack shotguns. The rising age of marriage since the 1950s is a positive trend, but one of its consequences is more nonmarital sexuality and pregnancy. The drive to restigmatize "illegitimacy" demands a renewed struggle to destigmatize abortion and make it accessible, along with contraception and sex education. It seems time to revive Margaret Sanger's slogan, "every child a wanted child."

To show solidarity with single mothers, we need not deny that two responsible, loving parents generally *can* offer children more than one parent can. Of course, three or four might prove even better. Programs encouraging child-free adults to form supportive ties with the children of overburdened parents (a category from which few parents are exempt) might give many kinds of families common cause. Once we grasp the distinctions between right-wing and centrist family values, we can support the latter's "family friendly" reforms while struggling for a more democratic definition of the term. We can employ family values logic to extend full family rights to gays, but to succeed we should help heal the rift between them and blacks that right-wing family values folks are effectively exploiting.

Unless a full-spectrum rainbow coalition comes to recognize shared stakes in democratizing family rights and resources, the future of no kind of family is secure. Communitarian doctrine urges greater collective responsibility for the common good, but its enthusiasm for privatistic, narrowly defined family values is self-canceling. What we need above all is an inclusive movement for *social* values. We won't find this in the middle of the road.   □

The social-science evidence is in: though it may benefit the adults involved,
the dissolution of intact two-parent families is harmful to large numbers of children. Moreover,
the author argues, family diversity in the form of increasing numbers of single-parent
and stepparent families does not strengthen the social fabric but,
rather, dramatically weakens and undermines society

DAN QUAYLE WAS RIGHT

BY BARBARA DAFOE WHITEHEAD

IVORCE AND OUT-OF-WEDLOCK CHILDBIRTH ARE TRANSFORMING THE LIVES of American children. In the postwar generation more than 80 percent of children grew up in a family with two biological parents who were married to each other. By 1980 only 50 percent could expect to spend their entire childhood in an intact family. If current trends continue, less than half of all children born today will live continuously with their own mother and father throughout childhood. Most American children will spend several years in a single-mother family. Some will eventually live in stepparent families, but because step-

families are more likely to break up than intact (by which I mean two-biological-parent) families, an increasing number of children will experience family breakup two or even three times during childhood

According to a growing body of social-scientific evidence, children in families disrupted by divorce and out-of-wedlock birth do worse than children in intact families on several measures of well-being. Children in single-parent families are six times as likely to be poor. They are also likely to stay poor longer. Twenty-two percent of children in one-parent families will experience poverty during childhood for seven years or more, as compared with only two percent of children in two-parent families. A 1988 survey by the National Center for Health Statistics found that children in single-parent families are two to three times as likely as children in two-parent families to have emotional and behavioral problems. They are also more likely to drop out of high school, to get pregnant as teenagers, to abuse drugs, and to be in trouble with the law. Compared with children in intact families, children from disrupted families are at a much higher risk for physical or sexual abuse.

Contrary to popular belief, many children do not "bounce back" after divorce or remarriage. Difficulties that are associated with family breakup often persist into adulthood. Children who grow up in single-parent or stepparent families are less successful as adults, particularly in the two domains of life—love and work—that are most essential to happiness. Needless to say, not all

children experience such negative effects. However, research shows that many children from disrupted families have a harder time achieving intimacy in a relationship, forming a stable marriage, or even holding a steady job.

Despite this growing body of evidence, it is nearly impossible to discuss changes in family structure without provoking angry protest. Many people see the discussion as no more than an attack on struggling single mothers and their children: Why blame single mothers when they are doing the very best they can? After all, the decision to end a marriage or a relationship is wrenching, and few parents are indifferent to the painful burden this decision imposes on their children. Many take the perilous step toward single parenthood as a last resort, after their best efforts to hold a marriage together have failed. Consequently, it can seem particularly cruel and unfeeling to remind parents of the hardships their children might suffer as a result of family breakup. Other people believe that the dramatic changes in family structure, though regrettable, are impossible to reverse. Family breakup is an inevitable feature of American life, and anyone who thinks otherwise is indulging in nostalgia or trying to turn back the clock. Since these new family forms are here to stay, the reasoning goes, we must accord respect to single parents, not criticize them. Typical is the view expressed by a Brooklyn woman in a recent letter to *The New York Times*: "Let's stop moralizing or blaming single parents and unwed mothers, and give them the respect they have earned and the support they deserve."

Such views are not to be dismissed. Indeed, they help to explain why family structure is such an explosive issue for Americans. The debate about it is not simply about the social-scientific evidence, although that is surely an important part of the discussion. It is also a debate over deeply held and often conflicting values. How do we begin to reconcile our long-standing belief in equality and diversity with an impressive body of evidence that suggests that not all family structures produce equal outcomes for children? How can we square traditional notions of public support for dependent women and children with a belief in women's right to pursue autonomy and independence in childbearing and child-rearing? How do we uphold the freedom of adults to pursue individual happiness in their private relationships and at the same time respond to the needs of children for stability, security, and permanence in their family lives? What do we do when the interests of adults and children conflict? These are the difficult issues at stake in the debate over family structure.

In the past these issues have turned out to be too difficult and too politically risky for debate. In the mid-1960s Daniel Patrick Moynihan, then an assistant secretary of labor, was denounced as a racist for calling attention to the relationship between the prevalence of black single-mother families and the lower socioeconomic standing of black children. For nearly twenty years the policy and research communities backed away from the entire issue. In 1980 the Carter Administration convened a historic White House Conference on Families, designed to address the growing problems of children and families in America. The result was a prolonged, publicly subsidized quarrel over the definition of "family." No President since has tried to hold a national family conference. Last year, at a time when the rate of out-of-wedlock births had reached a historic high, Vice President Dan Quayle was ridiculed for criticizing Murphy Brown. In short, every time the issue of family structure has been raised, the response has been first controversy, then retreat, and finally silence.

Yet it is also risky to ignore the issue of changing family structure. In recent years the problems associated with family disruption have grown. Overall child well-being has declined, despite a decrease in the number of children per family, an increase in the educational level of parents, and historically high levels of public spending. After dropping in the 1960s and 1970s, the proportion of children in poverty has increased dramatically, from 15 percent in 1970 to 20 percent in 1990, while the percentage of adult Americans in poverty has remained roughly constant. The teen suicide rate has more than tripled. Juvenile crime has increased and become more violent. School performance has continued to decline. There are no signs that these trends are about to reverse themselves.

If we fail to come to terms with the relationship between family structure and declining child well-being, then it will be increasingly difficult to improve children's life prospects, no matter how many new programs the federal government funds. Nor will we be able to make progress in bettering school performance or reducing crime or improving the quality of the nation's future work force—all domestic problems closely connected to family breakup. Worse, we may contribute to the problem by pursuing policies that actually increase family instability and breakup.

From Death to Divorce

ACROSS TIME AND ACROSS CULTURES, FAMILY DISruption has been regarded as an event that threatens a child's well-being and even survival. This view is rooted in a fundamental biological fact: unlike the young of almost any other species, the human child is born in an abjectly helpless and immature state. Years of nurture and protection are needed before the child can achieve physical independence. Similarly, it takes years of interaction with at least one but ideally two or more adults for a child to develop into a socially competent adult. Children raised in virtual isolation from human beings, though physically intact, display few recognizably human behaviors. The social arrangement that has proved most successful in ensuring the physical survival and promoting the social development of the child is the family unit of the biological mother and father. Consequently,

any event that permanently denies a child the presence and protection of a parent jeopardizes the life of the child.

The classic form of family disruption is the death of a parent. Throughout history this has been one of the risks of childhood. Mothers frequently died in childbirth, and it was not unusual for both parents to die before the child was grown. As recently as the early decades of this century children commonly suffered the death of at least one parent. Almost a quarter of the children born in this country in 1900 lost one parent by the time they were fifteen years old. Many of these children lived with their widowed parent, often in a household with other close relatives. Others grew up in orphanages and foster homes.

The meaning of parental death, as it has been transmitted over time and faithfully recorded in world literature and lore, is unambiguous and essentially unchanging. It is universally regarded as an untimely and tragic event. Death permanently severs the parent-child bond, disrupting forever one of the child's earliest and deepest human attachments. It also deprives a child of the presence and protection of an adult who has a biological stake in, as well as an emotional commitment to, the child's survival and well-being. In short, the death of a parent is the most extreme and severe loss a child can suffer.

Because a child is so vulnerable in a parent's absence, there has been a common cultural response to the death of a parent: an outpouring of support from family, friends, and strangers alike. The surviving parent and child are united in their grief as well as their loss. Relatives and friends share in the loss and provide valuable emotional

and financial assistance to the bereaved family. Other members of the community show sympathy for the child, and public assistance is available for those who need it. This cultural understanding of parental death has formed the basis for a tradition of public support to widows and their children. Indeed, as recently as the beginning of this century widows were the only mothers eligible for pensions in many states, and today widows with children receive more-generous welfare benefits from Survivors Insurance than do other single mothers with children who depend on Aid to Families With Dependent Children.

It has taken thousands upon thousands of years to reduce the threat of parental death. Not until the middle of the twentieth century did parental death cease to be a commonplace event for children in the United States. By then advances in medicine had dramatically reduced mortality rates for men and women.

At the same time, other forms of family disruption—separation, divorce, out-of-wedlock birth—were held in check by powerful religious, social, and legal sanctions. Divorce was widely regarded both as a deviant behavior, especially threatening to mothers and children, and as a personal lapse: "Divorce is the public acknowledgment of failure," a 1940s sociology textbook noted. Out-of-wedlock birth was stigmatized, and stigmatization is a powerful means of regulating behavior, as any smoker or overeater will testify. Sanctions against nonmarital childbirth discouraged behavior that hurt children and exacted compensatory behavior that helped them. Shotgun marriages and adoption, two common responses to nonmarital birth, carried a strong message about the risks of premarital sex and created an intact family for the child.

Consequently, children did not have to worry much about losing a parent through divorce or never having had one because of nonmarital birth. After a surge in divorces following the Second World War, the rate leveled off. Only 11 percent of children born in the 1950s would by the time they turned eighteen see their parents separate or divorce. Out-of-wedlock childbirth barely figured as a cause of family disruption. In the 1950s and early 1960s, five percent of the nation's births were out of wedlock. Blacks were more likely than whites to bear children outside marriage, but the majority of black children born in the twenty years after the Second World War were born to married couples. The rate of family disruption reached a historic low point during those years.

A new standard of family security and stability was established in postwar America. For the first time in history the vast majority of the nation's children could expect to live with married biological parents throughout childhood. Children might still suffer other forms of adversity —poverty, racial discrimination, lack of educational opportunity—but only a few would be deprived of the nurture and protection of a mother and a father. No longer did children have to be haunted by the classic fears vividly dramatized in folklore and fable—that their parents would die, that they would have to live with a stepparent and stepsiblings, or that they would be abandoned. These were the years when the nation confidently boarded up orphanages and closed foundling hospitals, certain that such institutions would never again be needed. In movie theaters across the country parents and children could watch the drama of parental separation and death in the great Disney classics, secure in the knowledge that such nightmare visions as the death of Bambi's mother and the wrenching separation of Dumbo from his mother were only make-believe.

In the 1960s the rate of family disruption suddenly began to rise. After inching up over the course of a century, the divorce rate soared. Throughout the 1950s and early 1960s the divorce rate held steady at fewer than ten divorces a year per 1,000 married couples. Then, beginning in about 1965, the rate increased sharply, peaking at twenty-three divorces per 1,000 marriages by 1979. (In 1974 divorce passed death as the leading cause of family breakup.) The rate has leveled off at about twenty-one divorces per 1,000 marriages—the figure for 1991. The out-of-wedlock birth rate also jumped. It went from five percent in 1960 to 27 percent in 1990. In 1990 close to 57 percent of births among black mothers were nonmarital, and about 17 percent among white mothers. Altogether, about one out of every four women who had a child in 1990 was not married. With rates of divorce and nonmarital birth so high, family disruption is at its peak. Never before have so many children experienced family breakup caused by events other than death. Each year a million children go through divorce or separation and almost as many more are born out of wedlock.

Half of all marriages now end in divorce. Following divorce, many people enter new relationships. Some begin living together. Nearly half of all cohabiting couples have children in the household. Fifteen percent have new children together. Many cohabiting couples eventually get married. However, both cohabiting and remarried couples are more likely to break up than couples in first marriages. Even social scientists find it hard to keep pace with the complexity and velocity of such patterns. In the revised edition (1992) of his book *Marriage, Divorce, Remarriage*, the sociologist Andrew Cherlin ruefully comments: "If there were a truth-in-labeling law for books, the title of this edition should be something long and unwieldy like *Cohabitation, Marriage, Divorce, More Cohabitation, and Probably Remarriage*."

Under such conditions growing up can be a turbulent experience. In many single-parent families children must come to terms with the parent's love life and romantic partners. Some children live with cohabiting couples, either their own unmarried parents or a biological parent and a live-in partner. Some children born to cohabiting parents see their parents break up. Others see their parents marry, but 56 percent of them (as compared with 31 percent of the children born to married parents) later see their parents' marriages fall apart. All told, about three quarters of children born to cohabiting couples will live in a single-parent home at least briefly. One of every four children growing up in the 1990s will eventually enter a stepfamily. According to one survey, nearly half of all children in stepparent families will see their parents divorce again by the time they reach their late teens. Since 80 percent of divorced fathers remarry, things get even more complicated when the romantic or marital history of the noncustodial parent, usually the father, is taken into account. Consequently, as it affects a significant number of children, family disruption is best understood not as a single event but as a string of disruptive events: separation, divorce, life in a single-parent family, life with a parent and live-in lover, the remarriage of one or both parents, life in one stepparent family combined with visits to another stepparent family; the breakup of one or both stepparent families. And so on. This is one reason why public schools have a hard time knowing whom to call in an emergency.

Given its dramatic impact on children's lives, one might reasonably expect that this historic level of family disruption would be viewed with alarm, even regarded as a national crisis. Yet this has not been the case. In recent years some people have argued that these trends pose a serious threat to children and to the nation as a whole, but they are dismissed as declinists, pessimists, or nostalgists, unwilling or unable to accept the new facts of life. The dominant view is that the changes in family structure are, on balance, positive.

The Family-Values Debate

James Q. Wilson

THERE are two views about the contemporary American family, one held by the public and the other by policy elites. In his presidential campaign, Bill Clinton appeared to endorse the public's view. It remains to be seen which view President Clinton will support.

The public's view is this: the family is the place in which the most basic values are instilled in children. In recent years, however, these values have become less secure, in part because the family has become weaker and in part because rivals for its influence—notably television and movies—have gotten stronger. One way the family has become weaker is that more and more children are being raised in one-parent families, and often that one parent is a teenage girl. Another way is that parents, whether in one- or two-parent families, are spending less time with their children and are providing poorer discipline. Because family values are so important, political candidates should talk about them, though it is not clear that the government can do much about them. Overwhelmingly, Americans think that it is better for children if one parent stays home and does not work, even if that means having less money.[1]

No such consensus is found among scholars or policy-makers. That in itself is revealing. Beliefs about families that most people regard as virtually self-evident are hotly disputed among people whose job it is to study or support families.

A good example of the elite argument began last fall on the front page of the *Washington Post*, where a reporter quoted certain social scientists as saying that the conventional two-parent family was not as important for the healthy development of children as was once supposed. This prompted David Popenoe, a professor at Rutgers who has written extensively on family issues, to publish in the *New York Times* an op-ed piece challenging the scholars cited in the *Post*. Popenoe asserted that "dozens" of studies had come to the opposite conclusion, and that the weight of the evidence "decisively" supported the view that two-parent families are better than single-parent families.

Decisively to him, perhaps, but not to others. Judith Stacey, another professor of sociology, responded in a letter to the *Times* that the value of a two-parent family was merely a "widely shared prejudice" not confirmed by empirical studies; Popenoe, she said, was trying to convert "misguided nostalgia for 'Ozzie-and-Harriet'-land into social-scientific truth." Arlene and Jerome Skolnick, two more professors, acknowledged that although Popenoe might be correct, saying so publicly would "needlessly stigmatize children raised in families that don't meet the 'Ozzie-and-Harriet' model." After all, the Skolnicks observed, a man raised outside that model had just been elected President of the United States.

THE views of Stacey and the Skolnicks are by no means unrepresentative of academic thinking on this subject. Barbara Dafoe Whitehead recently surveyed the most prominent textbooks on marriage and the family. Here is my paraphrase of her summary of what she found:

The life course is full of exciting options. These include living in a commune, having a group marriage, being a single parent, or living together. Marriage is one life-style choice, but before choosing it people weigh its costs and benefits against other options. Divorce is a part of the normal family cycle and is neither deviant nor tragic. Rather, it can serve as a foundation for individual renewal and new beginnings. Marriage itself should not be regarded as a special, privileged institution; on the contrary, it must catch up with the diverse, pluralistic society in which we live. For example, same-sex marriages often involve more sharing and equality than do heterosexual relationships. But even in the conventional family, the relationships between husband and wife need to be defined after carefully negotiating agreements that protect each person's separate interests and rights.[2]

JAMES Q. WILSON is the Collins Professor of Management and Public Policy at UCLA. His many books include *American Government: Institutions and Policies*, *Thinking About Crime*, *Bureaucracy*, and, most recently, a collection of essays, *On Character*. A new book, *The Moral Sense*, will be published by the Free Press in July.

[1] Evidence for these beliefs can be found in the poll data gathered in the *American Enterprise*, September/October 1992, pp. 85-86.

[2] Paraphrased from Barbara Dafoe Whitehead, *The Expert's Story of Marriage*. Institute for American Values, Publication No. WP14 (August 1992), pp. 11-12. Whitehead supplies references to the texts she summarizes. She does not endorse—just the opposite!—the views she has compiled.

Many politicians and reporters echo these sentiments and carry the argument one step further. Not only do poor Ozzie and Harriet (surely the most maligned figures in the history of television) stand for nostalgic prejudice and stigmatizing error, they represent a kind of family that in fact scarcely exists. Congresswoman Pat Schroeder has been quoted as saying that only about 7 percent of all American families fit the Ozzie-and-Harriet model. Our daily newspapers frequently assert that most children will not grow up in a two-parent family. The message is clear: not only is the two-parent family not especially good for children, but fortunately it is also fast disappearing.

Yet whether or not the two-parent family is good for children, it is plainly false that this kind of family has become a historical relic. For while there has been a dramatic increase in the proportion of children, especially black children, who will spend some or even most of their youth in single-parent families, the vast majority of children—nationally, about 73 percent—live in a home with married parents. Today, the mothers in those families are more likely to work than once was the case, though most do not work full time. (I am old enough to remember that even Harriet worked, at least in real life. She was a singer.)

The proponents of the relic theory fail to use statistics accurately. The way they arrive at the discovery that only 7 percent of all families fit the Ozzie-and-Harriet model is by calculating what proportion of all families consists *exactly* of a father, mother, and two (not three or four) children and in which the mother never works, not even for two weeks during the year helping out with the Christmas rush at the post office.

THE language in which the debate over two-parent families is carried on suggests that something more than scholarly uncertainty is at stake. If all we cared about were the effects of one- versus two-parent families on the lives of children, there would still be a debate, but it would not be conducted on op-ed pages in tones of barely controlled anger. Nor would it be couched in slogans about television characters or supported by misleading statistics.

What is at stake, of course, is the role of women. To defend the two-parent family is to defend, the critics worry, an institution in which the woman is subordinated to her husband, confined to domestic chores with no opportunity to pursue a career, and taught to indoctrinate her children with a belief in the rightness of this arrangement. To some critics, the woman here is not simply constrained, she is abused. The traditional family, in this view, is an arena in which men are free to hit, rape, and exploit women. To defend the traditional family is to defend sexism. And since single-parent families are

disproportionately headed by black women, criticizing such families is not only sexist but racist.

Perhaps the most influential book on this subject to appear during the 1970's was *The Future of Marriage* by Jessie Bernard, a distinguished scholar. Widely reviewed, its central message was that the first order of business for marriage must be "mitigating its hazards for women."

Unlike more radical writers, Bernard thought that the future of marriage was assured, but this would be the case only because marriage would now take many forms. Traditional marriages would persist but other forms would gain (indeed, had already gained) favor—communes, group marriages, the *ménage à trois*, marital "swinging," unmarried cohabitation, and limited-commitment marriages. (She did not discuss mother-only families as one of these "options." Nor did she discuss race.) In principle, no one form was better than another because "there is nothing in human nature that favors one kind of marriage over another." In practice, the forms that were best were those that were best for the woman. What might be best for children was not discussed. Children, it would seem, were incidental to marriage, except insofar as their care imposed strains on their parents, especially their mothers.

The main theme of much of the writing about marriage and families during the 1970's and 1980's was that of individual rights. Just as polities were only legitimate when they respected individual rights, so also marriages were worthy of respect only when they were based on a recognition of rights.

This view impressed itself on many who were not scholars, as is evident from an essay published in 1973 in the *Harvard Educational Review*. It urged that the "legal status of infancy . . . be abolished" so that a child would be endowed with all the rights of an adult. Even more, any law that classified people as children and treated them differently from adults "should be considered suspect." As a result, the state "would no longer be able to assume the rationality of regulations based on age." The author of this essay was Hillary Rodham.

A RIGHTS-BASED, individualistic view of marriage is questionable in its own terms, but these theoretical questions would become insuperable objections if it could be shown that children are harmed by growing up in mother-only, or communal, or swinging, or divorced households. The academic study of families during the 1970's, however, did not produce an unchallenged body of evidence demonstrating that this was the case. There were several studies that attempted to measure the impact of mother-only families on their children's school attainment, job success, and personal conduct, but many discovered either no effects or ones that were ambiguous or equivocal.

I first became aware of this in the early 1980's when Richard J. Herrnstein and I were writing *Crime and Human Nature*. One of my tasks was to prepare the first draft of the chapter on the effects on crime rates of what were then called broken homes. I fully expected to find a raft of studies showing that growing up in a mother-only home put the child, especially the boy, at risk for criminality.

I did not find what I had expected to find. To be sure, I ran across the familiar fact that men in prison tended disproportionately to come from broken homes, but men in prison also tended to have parents who were themselves criminal and to come from poor, minority backgrounds. Since these factors—class, race, parental criminality, and family status—tended to co-vary, it was not clear that family background had any effect independent of temperament or circumstance. Similarly, Elizabeth Herzog and Cecelia Sudia reviewed eighteen studies of female-headed families carried out between 1950 and 1970. They found that in seven there was more delinquency in father-absent homes, in four there was less, and in seven the results were mixed. Some studies showed boys in father-absent homes failing to develop an appropriate masculine identity and others uncovered no such effect. (There was—and is—ample evidence that children from cold, discordant homes are likely to have plenty of problems, but there are lots of cold, discordant *two*-parent families.)

Since I wrote that chapter, though, the evidence that single-parent families are bad for children has mounted. There will never be anything like conclusive proof of this proposition unless we randomly assign babies at birth to single- and two-parent families of various economic and ethnic circumstances and then watch them grow up. Happily the laws and customs of this country make such an experiment unlikely. Short of that, the best evidence comes from longitudinal studies that follow children as they grow up in whatever kind of family nature has provided.

One example: when the 5,000 children born in the United Kingdom during the first week of March 1946 were followed for three decades, those raised in families broken by divorce or desertion were more likely than those living in two-parent families to become delinquent.[3]

A second example: for many years, Sheppard Kellam and his colleagues at Johns Hopkins University followed several hundred poor, black, first-grade children in a depressed neighborhood in Chicago. Each child lived in one of several different family types, depending on how many and what kinds of adults were present. In about one-third of families the mother was the only adult present; in another third there was both a mother and a father. (Only a tiny fraction was headed by a father with no mother present.) The remainder was made up of various combinations of mothers, grandparents, uncles, aunts, adult brothers and sisters, and various unrelated adults. By the time the children entered the third grade, those who lived with their mothers alone were the worst off in terms of their socialization. After ten years, the boys who had grown up in mother-only families (which by then made up about half the total) reported more delinquencies, regardless of family income, than those who had grown up in families with multiple adults, especially a father.[4]

By 1986, when Rolf and Magda Loeber of the University of Pittsburgh reviewed 23 studies assessing the relationship of parental absence (usually, father absence) to juvenile delinquency, they found an effect, though smaller than the one caused by discord within a two-parent family.[5] One problem with their overall conclusion was that they lumped together families where the biological father had never been present with those in which he left, as a result of separation, divorce, or death, while the child was growing up. Inspecting their data suggests that if the latter cases are omitted, the connection between family status and criminality is strengthened a bit: fathers never present create greater hazards than fathers who depart (owing to death or divorce) later in the child's life. The greatest hazard of all is found in families where the parents have the greatest number of problems—they are absent, discordant, rejecting, incompetent, and criminal.

THE most recent important study of family structure was done in 1988 by the Department of Health and Human Services. It surveyed the family arrangements of more than 60,000 children living in households all over the country. Interviews were conducted in order to identify any childhood problems in health, schoolwork, and personal conduct. These results were tabulated according to the age, sex, and ethnicity of the child and the income and marital status of the parents.

The results were striking. At every income level save the very highest (over $50,000 per year), for both sexes and for whites, blacks, and Hispanics

---

[3] M.E.J. Wadsworth, *Roots of Delinquency*, Barnes & Noble (1979).

[4] Sheppard Kellam et al., "The Long-Term Evolution of the Family Structure of Teenage and Older Mothers," *Journal of Marriage and the Family*, vol. 44 (1982), pp. 539-554; Kellam et al., "Family Structure and the Mental Health of Children," *Archives of General Psychiatry*, vol. 34 (1977), pp. 1012-1022; Margaret Ensminger et al., "School and Family Origins of Delinquency: Comparisons By Sex," in Katherine T. Van Dusen and Sarnoff A. Mednick, eds., *Prospective Studies of Crime and Delinquency*, Kluwer-Nijhoff (1983).

[5] "Family Factors as Correlates and Predictors of Juvenile Conduct Problems and Delinquency," in Michael Tonry and Norval Morris, eds., *Crime and Justice: An Annual Review of Research*, University of Chicago Press (1986), pp. 29-149.

alike, children living with a never-married or a divorced mother were substantially worse off than those living in two-parent families. Compared to children living with both biological parents, children in single-parent families were twice as likely to have been expelled or suspended from school, to display emotional or behavioral problems, and to have problems with their peers; they were also much more likely to engage in antisocial behavior. These differences were about as wide in households earning over $35,000 a year as they were in those making less than $10,000.[6]

Charles Murray of the American Enterprise Institute has been looking at the people whose lives have been followed by the National Longitudinal Study of Youth (NLSY) since they were in high school (they are now in their late twenties or early thirties). The NLSY not only keeps careful records of the schooling, jobs, and income of these young adults, it also looks at the home environment in which they are raising any children they may have. These home observations rate emotional quality, parental involvement in child care, style of discipline, and the like. The homes, thus observed, can be ranked from best to worst.

Murray has compared the home environments with the economic status of the parents and the legal status of the child. The odds of the children living in the worst home environments were powerfully affected by two things: whether the parents were married when they had the baby and whether they were regular welfare recipients. The child of an unmarried woman who was a chronic welfare recipient had one chance in six of growing up in the worst—that is, emotionally the worst—environment. The child of a married woman who never went on welfare had only one chance in 42.[7]

Being poor hurts children. Living in a rotten neighborhood hurts them. Having cold or neglectful parents certainly hurts them. But so also does being illegitimate and living on welfare. This is generally true for whites as well as blacks.

And so also does being a teenage mother. For many years, Frank Furstenberg of the University of Pennsylvania and his colleagues have been following 300 teenage mothers living in Baltimore. What they have found supports the public's view. Teenage girls who have babies fare much worse than ones who postpone child-bearing, and this is true even among girls of the same socioeconomic background and academic aptitude. They are more likely to go on welfare, and less likely to enter into a stable marriage. The children of teenage mothers, compared with those of older ones, tend to have more trouble in school, to be more aggressive, and to have less self-control. This is especially true of boys.[8]

We have always had teenage mothers, and in some less-developed societies that is the norm. What is new and troubling about the present situation is the vast increase in the number of teenage mothers and their concentration in the same neighborhoods. A girl with a baby presents one kind of problem when she is either a rarity or is embedded in an extended family that provides guidance and assistance from older women living with her. She presents a very different and much more serious problem when she is one of thousands of similarly situated youngsters living in the same neighborhood or public-housing project, trying to maintain an independent household on welfare.

A lot more light will be shed on these issues when Sara McLanahan at Princeton and Gary Sandefur at the University of Wisconsin publish their careful analysis of the best available longitudinal data bases.[9] There are at least four of these files—the already-mentioned National Longitudinal Study of Youth; the Panel Study of Income Dynamics; the High School and Beyond Study; and the National Survey of Families and Households. McLanahan and Sandefur are looking at the effect of family structure, after controlling for income, race, and education, on such things as a child's chances of graduating from high school, a girl's chances of becoming a teenage mother, and a boy's chances of being idle (that is, neither working nor in school). Their results so far suggest that children who grow up in single-parent families do less well than those who grow up in intact families, and that this is true whether they are white or black, rich or poor, boys or girls. These other factors make a difference—it is better to be white than black, rich than poor—but so does family status.

I THINK that the American people are right in their view of families. When they look at the dramatic increase in divorce, single-parent families, and illegitimate children that has taken place over the last 30 years, they see families in decline. They do not need studies to tell them that these outcomes are generally bad, because they have had these outcomes happen to them or to people they know. Divorce may sometimes be the right and necessary remedy for fundamentally flawed marriages and for the conditions created by an abusive or neglectful spouse, but in general divorce makes people worse off: the woman becomes poorer and the children more distressed. Properly raising a child

---

[6] Deborah A. Dawson, "Family Structure and Children's Health: United States, 1988," *Vital and Health Statistics*, Series 10, No. 178 (June 1991).

[7] "Reducing Poverty and Reducing the Underclass: Different Problems, Different Solutions," paper presented to the Conference on Reducing Poverty in America, January 15, 1993, at the Anderson Graduate School of Management, UCLA.

[8] Frank F. Furstenberg, Jr., Jeanne Brooks-Gunn, and Lindsay Chase-Lansdale, "Teenage Pregnancy and Childbearing," *American Psychologist*, vol. 44 (1989), pp. 313-320.

[9] *Uncertain Childhood, Uncertain Future* (Harvard University Press, forthcoming).

is an enormous responsibility that often taxes the efforts and energies of two parents; one parent is likely to be overwhelmed. Children born out of wedlock are in the great majority of cases children born into poverty. Millions of people are living testimony to these bleak facts. If scholars say that the evidence is not conclusive, so much the worse for scholars. But now, I believe, scholars are starting to find hard facts to support popular impressions.

The debate over the effects of family structure continues, albeit with some prospect of a consensus emerging some time in the near future. But there is not even a glimmer of such an accord with respect to the other hot topic in family studies—day care. The dominant view among child psychologists is that day care is not harmful. For a long time Professor Jay Belsky of Pennsylvania State University shared that view. When he changed his mind, he was excoriated. He is now of the opinion that day care, especially in the first year of life, is harmful in some respects to some children.

In a widely-reported 1988 article, Belsky reviewed all the studies measuring the effect of nonmaternal care on attachment and social development and concluded that, subject to many caveats,

> entry into [day] care in the first year of life for twenty hours or more per week is a "risk factor" for the development of insecure attachment in infancy and heightened aggressiveness, noncompliance, and withdrawal in the preschool and early school years.[10]

By "risk factor" Belsky meant that the child in day care was somewhat more likely to experience these adverse outcomes than would a similar child under parental care, especially if the day care was not of high quality.

Some critics argued with Belsky on scientific grounds, saying that the evidence was less clearcut than he suggested, that the measure of emotional well-being he used (observing how a child reacts after it is separated from its mother) was flawed, that children turn out well in cultures where nonparental care is commonplace, and that whatever ill effects exist (if any) do not last.

But many attacked him politically, and even the scholarly critiques had a sharp edge to them. As with family structure, what is at stake in this controversy are not just facts and interpretations but philosophy and policy: if day care has bad effects, then women ought to care for their children in their own homes. And that is a politically-incorrect conclusion. Many scholars feel, I believe, that to support the claim of family decline is to give aid and comfort to conservative politicians and religious leaders who bemoan that decline and call for the reassertion of "traditional values." In short, what is at stake is Murphy Brown.

The Changing Culture

BOTH teenage pregnancies and single-parent families have increased dramatically since the 1950's. Changes in the economy and in the provision of welfare benefits explain some of this growth but not all or even most of it. There are no doubt some features peculiar to American society that explain some of it, but since the decline of the family—that is, in lasting marriages and legitimate births—has happened in many nations, it cannot be entirely the result of American policies or peculiarities.

We are witnessing a profound, worldwide, long-term change in the family that is likely to continue for a long time. The causes of that change are not entirely understood, but probably involve two main forces: a shift in the family's economic function and a shift in the culture in which it is embedded. The family no longer is the unit that manages economic production, as it was when agriculture was the dominant form of production, nor is it any longer the principal provider of support for the elderly or education for the young.

At the same time, the family no longer exercises as much control over its members as it once did, and broader kinship groupings (clans, tribes, and extended families) no longer exercise as much control over nuclear families. Since the Enlightenment, the dominant tendency in legal and philosophical thought has been to emancipate the individual from all forms of tutelage—the state, revealed religion, ancient custom—including the tutelage of kin. This emancipation has proceeded episodically and unevenly, but relentlessly. Liberal political theory has celebrated the individual and constrained the state, but it has been silent about the family.

What is remarkable is how well the family has survived this process. Were the family the mere social convention that some scholars imagine, it would long since have gone the way of cottage industries and the owner-occupied farm, the inevitable victim of the individualizing and rationalizing tendencies of modern life. But, of course, the family is not a human contrivance invented to accomplish some goal and capable of being reinvented or reformulated to achieve different goals.

Family—and kinship generally—are the fundamental organizing facts of all human societies, primitive or advanced, and have been such for tens of thousands of years. The family is the product of evolutionary processes that have selected against people who are inclined to abandon their offspring and for people who are prepared to care for them, and to provide this caring within

---

[10] "The 'Effects' of Infant Day Care Reconsidered," *Early Childhood Research Quarterly*, vol. 3 (1988), pp. 235-272. For a response, see Tiffany Field, *Infancy*, Harvard University Press (1990), pp. 90-93.

kinship systems defined primarily along genetic lines. If kinship were a cultural artifact, we could as easily define it on the basis of height, athletic skill, or political status, and children would be raised in all manner of collectives, ranging from state-run orphanages to market-supplied foster homes. Orphanages and foster homes do of course exist, but only as matters of last resort designed (with great public anxiety) to provide care when the biological family does not exist or cannot function.

If the family were merely a convenience and if it responded entirely to economic circumstances, the current debate over family policy would be far less rancorous than it is. Liberals would urge that we professionalize child-rearing through day care; conservatives would urge that we subsidize it through earned-income tax credits. Liberals would define the welfare problem as entirely a matter of poverty and recommend more generous benefits as the solution; conservatives would define it as entirely a matter of dependency and recommend slashing benefits as the solution. Liberals would assume that the problem is that families have too little money, conservatives that families get such money as they have from the state. There would still be a battle, but in the end it would come down to some negotiated compromise involving trade-offs among benefit levels, eligibility rules, and the public-private mix of child-care providers.

But once one conceives of the family problem as involving to a significant degree the conflict between a universal feature of human society and a profound cultural challenge to the power of that institution, the issue takes on a different character. To the extent that one believes in the cultural challenge—that is, in individual emancipation and individual choice—one tends to question the legitimacy and influence of the family. To the extent that one believes in the family, one is led to question some or all parts of the cultural challenge.

That is why the debate over "family values" has been so strident. On both sides people feel that it is the central battle in the culture war that now grips Americans (or at least American elites). They are absolutely right. To many liberals, family values means a reassertion of male authority, a reduction in the hard-earned rights of women, and a license for abusive or neglectful parents to mistreat their children free of prompt and decisive social intervention. For some liberals, family values means something even more troubling: that human nature is less malleable than is implied by the doctrine of environmental determinism and cultural relativism—that it is to some significant degree fixed, immutable. To many conservatives, family values is the main line of resistance against homosexual marriages, bureaucratized child care, and compulsory sex education in the schools. For some conservatives, the family means a defense against the very idea of a planned society.

Now, reasonable people—say, the typical mother or father—will take a less stark view of the alternatives. They will agree with conservatives that the family is the central institution of society, incapable of being replaced or even much modified without disastrous consequences. They will be troubled by same-sex marriages, upset by teenage girls becoming mothers, angered by public subsidies for illegitimate births, and outraged by the distribution of condoms and explicit sex-education manuals to elementary-school children. But they will agree with many liberals that we ought not to confine women to domestic roles or make them subservient to male power and that we ought to recognize and cope with the financial hardships that young couples have today when they try to live on one income in a big city.

On one issue most parents will squarely identify with the conservative side, and it is, in my view, the central issue. They will want our leaders, the media, television programs, and motion pictures to take their side in the war over what the family is. It is not one of several alternative lifestyles; it is not an arena in which rights are negotiated; it is not an old-fashioned and reactionary barrier to a promiscuous sex life; it is not a set of cost-benefit calculations. *It is a commitment.*

It is a commitment required for child-rearing and thus for any realistic prospect of human happiness. It is a commitment that may be entered into after romantic experimentation and with some misgivings about lost freedoms, but once entered into it is a commitment that persists for richer or for poorer, in sickness and in health, for better or for worse. It is a commitment for which there is no feasible substitute, and hence no child ought lightly to be brought into a world where that commitment—from both parents—is absent. It is a commitment that often is joyfully enlivened by mutual love and deepening friendship, but it is a commitment even when these things are absent.

There is no way to prepare for the commitment other than to make it. The idea that a man and a woman can live together without a commitment in order to see if they would like each other after they make the commitment is preposterous. Living together may inform you as to whether your partner snores or is an alcoholic or sleeps late; it may be fun and exciting; it may even be the best you can manage in an imperfect world. But it is not a way of finding out how married life will be, because married life is shaped by the fact that the couple has made a solemn vow before their family and friends that this is for keeps and that any children will be their joint and permanent responsibility. It changes everything.

Despite high divorce rates and a good deal of sleeping around, most people understand this. Certainly women understand it, since one of their most common complaints about the men they know is that they will not make a commitment. You bet they won't, not if they can get sex, cooking, and companionship on a trial basis, all the while keeping their eyes peeled for a better opportunity elsewhere. Marriage is in large measure a device for reining in the predatory sexuality of males. It works quite imperfectly, as is evident from the fact that men are more likely than women to have extramarital affairs and to abandon their spouses because a younger or more exciting possibility has presented herself. But it works better than anything else mankind has been able to invent.

Because most people understand this, the pressures, economic and cultural, on the modern family have not destroyed it. And this is remarkable, considering the spread of no-fault divorce laws. The legal system has, in effect, said, "Marriage is not a commitment; it is a convenience. If you feel yours is inconvenient, we will make it easy for you to get out of it." This radical transformation of family law occurred, as Mary Ann Glendon of the Harvard Law School has shown, in many industrialized countries at about the same time. It may or may not have caused the rise in the divorce rate, but it certainly did nothing to slow it down.

The legal system has also altered child-custody rules so that, instead of being automatically assigned to the father (as was the case in the 19th century, when the father was thought to "own" all the family's property including the child), the child is now assigned by the judge on the basis of its "best interests." In the vast majority of cases, that means with the mother. I sometimes wonder what would happen to family stability if every father knew for certain that, should the marriage end, he would have to take custody of the children. My guess is: more committed fathers.

These cultural and legal changes, all aimed at individualizing and empowering family members, have had an effect. In 1951, 51 percent of all Americans agreed with the statement that "parents who don't get along should not stay together because there are children in the family." By 1985, 86 percent agreed.[11] Still, these changes have not devastated modern families. The shopping malls, baseball stadiums, and movie theaters are filled with them doing what families have always done. That fact is a measure of the innate power of the family bond.

Yet the capacity for resisting these changes is unequally distributed in society. Christopher Jencks of Northwestern University puts it this way:

Now that the mass media, the schools, and even the churches have begun to treat single parenthood as a regrettable but inescapable part of modern life, we can hardly expect the respectable poor to carry on the struggle against illegitimacy and desertion with their old fervor. They still deplore such behavior, but they cannot make it morally taboo. Once the two-parent norm loses its moral sanctity, the selfish considerations that always pulled poor parents apart often become overwhelming.[12]

Culture and Politics

THE central issue in family policy is whether or not it will be animated entirely by an economic view of family functions and consist entirely of economic solutions to family needs. The principal source of domestic social-policy advice to Bill Clinton during his presidential campaign was the Progressive Policy Institute (PPI), and in particular Elaine Kamarck and William Galston. "The best antipoverty program for children is a stable, intact family," they wrote in their report, *Mandate for Change.* Though not neglecting economic measures, such as a tax credit for each child and an earned-income tax credit to supplement the wages of the working poor, the PPI urged that the divorce laws be changed to protect children better, that efforts be intensified to promote parental responsibility for child care, that pregnant women who use drugs be required to undergo periodic drug testing, and that the earnings of absent parents be taxed to pay for their children. And the report called for the President to use his bully pulpit to reinforce the importance of intact and caring families.

As of this writing, only Galston of all those connected with the PPI has been appointed to even a moderately significant position in the Clinton administration (he joined the White House domestic-policy staff). Clinton's Secretary of Health and Human Services, Donna Shalala, had virtually nothing to say about these matters in her confirmation hearing before the Senate Finance Committee. There will in time be a debate on welfare policy; Clinton has promised to appoint a task force to make recommendations. Perhaps something will happen, though the history of past efforts at welfare reform suggests that few in Congress have the stomach for it and few scholars expect that such reforms as pass will make much of a difference.

The truth of the matter is that the most important features of family life are beyond the reach of policy. The recently passed family-leave bill in large measure merely ratifies opportunities that large firms have been granting to their em-

[11] David Popenoe, "The Family Condition of America," paper prepared for a Brookings Institution seminar on values and public policy (March 1992), citing a study by Norval Glenn.
[12] "Deadly Neighborhoods," the *New Republic*, June 13, 1988, pp. 23-32.

ployees for some time; it will make things a bit easier for middle-class mothers but will do little for poor, teenage ones. The far more contentious issue of welfare reform will not be so easily resolved, but it is hard to imagine any feasible change in the existing rules that will make much of a difference in the chances of a child being born out of wedlock. Expanding the earned-income tax credit may help poor working parents, but do we really want single mothers of two-year-old children to work? Tightening the divorce laws may be a good idea, but it will not make much difference to parents who never got married in the first place. Improving the system for collecting child-support payments is a good idea, but many fathers who desert their children have little money to be collected and, in any event, this is not likely to convert uncommitted impregnators into committed fathers.

I suspect that the culture of the family will have to be rebuilt from the bottom up. Certainly Robert Woodson, head of the National Center for Neighborhood Enterprise, thinks so. He and his associates have been energetically pursuing this goal by supporting local church-related groups that try to encourage men to take responsibility for their children. There are many other local efforts to get men to marry their pregnant lovers and to sign the birth certificates of their children.

But these efforts proceed against the cultural grain, or at least against the grain of the high culture. When the people who deliver mocking attacks on "traditional family values" are the same ones who endorse condom distribution among elementary-school children, the average parent is led to wonder whether he or she is being a sucker for trying to stay together and raise the kids. Most Americans, I would guess, understand very clearly the difference between a traditional family and an oppressive one; they want the former but not the latter. Most women, I would guess, can distinguish very easily between the rights they have won and the obligations they retain; they cherish both and see no fundamental conflict between them, except the inescapable problem that there is not enough time for everything and so everyone must make choices.

It is extraordinary how well most husbands and wives have held up in the face of constant taunts comparing them to Ozzie and Harriet. The family life that most Americans want is regarded by the eminences of the media and the academy as a cartoon life, fit only for ridicule and rejection. When the history of our times is written, this raging cultural war will deserve careful attention, for it is far more consequential than any of the other cleavages that divide us.

Many Americans hope that President Clinton will stand up for "traditional family values," by which they mean, not male supremacy, spouse abuse, or docile wives, but the overriding importance of two-parent families that make child care their central responsibility. Clinton wants to stay in touch with the people at town meetings; fine, but let him say at those meetings that nobody should conceive a child that he and she are not emotionally ready to care for. The best, albeit an imperfect, sign of that readiness is the marriage vow. Let him say that it is wrong—not just imprudent, but wrong—to bear children out of wedlock. Let him meet with local ministers and neighborhood groups that are trying to encourage marriage and discourage predatory male sexuality. Such statements may earn Clinton dismayed groans from sitcom producers and ideological accusations from sociology professors, but at least the people would know that he is on their side.

457

THE CHRISTIAN RIGHT AND THE PRO-LIFE MOVEMENT: AN ANALYSIS OF THE SOURCES OF POLITICAL SUPPORT[1]

Clyde Wilcox

Leopoldo Gomez

Georgetown University

Review of Religious Research, Vol. 31, No. 4 (June, 1990)

Although Christian Right elites predicted a united front between the fundamentalist Right and pro-life groups, the alliance has been an uneasy one at best. Only a minority of pro-life supporters have thrown their support to the Christian Right, and Christian Right supporters do not universally support the pro-life groups. We explore the differences between the supporters of the Christian Right and the pro-life movement using data from a national survey in 1984. We find that religious differences are quite important in distinguishing between the supporters of the two sets of groups, with evangelicals supporting the Christian Right and Catholics supporting the pro-life movement. Among evangelicals, those who attend church frequently are more likely to support both groups, while those who belong to evangelical denominations but do not attend regularly are more likely to support only the Moral Majority. In addition to religious differences, the supporters of the two sets of groups displayed important political differences as well, with the pro-life supporters markedly more moderate on foreign policy and minority politics. Supporters of both groups were decidedly more conservative than those who supported only one set of organizations.

Most studies of public support for the New Christian Right during the 1980's reported that support was limited to between 10% and 15% of whites (Buell and Sigelman, 1985; Wilcox, 1987a; Sigelman, Wilcox and Buell, 1987; Wilcox, 1989). These organizations have been unable to expand beyond their initial base of support, a fate which also fell on the Presidential campaign of Pat Robertson, who drew primarily from charismatic churches. The failure of the Christian Right to expand beyond a small minority of dedicated supporters was not predicted by many early observers, who foresaw the possibility of a united front of the Moral Majority, various pro-life groups, and other sympathetic organizations.

There were good reasons to suspect that the Christian Right would draw support from pro-life citizens. Groups like the Moral Majority made abortion one of their central issues, and Rev. Jerry Falwell, head of the Moral Majority during most of the 1980's, spoke often of the common ground which the two sets of organizations shared. Falwell predicted that his organization would draw support from a number of pro-life Catholics, as well as morally conservative Jews. In fact, however, most of the activists of the Moral Majority were concentrated in independent Baptist churches (Liebman, 1983; Wilcox, 1987b). Practically no activists were Catholics, and support among Catholics was quite low. Although pro-life and Christian Right forces have joined together at the elite level to lobby Congress on abortion, the predicted common front has failed to materialize.

In some ways, elite level cooperation is important, regardless of any mass level coalitions. For many members of the Moral Majority or national right-to-life organizations, membership consists almost entirely of contributing money through direct mail. Hayes (1986) has argued that the nature of interest groups has changed radically over the past twenty years, and that in many of the newer groups membership consists merely of contributing money, with little potential for face-to-face contact for the membership. For these sorts of organizations, elite cooperation on lobbying and the sharing of direct-mail solicitations lists which are the lifeblood of mass organizations (Godwin, 1988) may be important.

Yet neither the Moral Majority nor the right-to-life movement are purely direct-mail organizations. The Moral Majority made a concerted effort to mobilize the grass roots, and succeeded in building state level organizations which varied in strength (Liebman, 1983; Wilcox, 1987b; Pierand and Wright, 1984). There has been even more activism at the local level in the pro-life movement, with many supporters logging long hours of volunteer work (Luker, 1984). The failure of a larger movement to emerge at the grass roots, then, has important political consequences.

In this paper we explore some of the reasons for the failure of the Christian Right to draw greater support among pro-life forces. We present bivariate analysis of national survey data which allows us to compare supporters of the Moral Majority, supporters of the Right-to-Life movement, and those who supported both organizations. We next use multivariate discriminant analysis to help us sort out the sets of variables which best predict which citizens were more likely to support each organization, and which were likely to support both.

We explore two possible explanations for the failure of the Christian Right coalition to emerge. First, it is possible that the intolerance of the fundamentalists of the Christian Right has prevented them from gaining support from Catholics in the pro-life movement. Wilcox (1986) reported that activists in the Ohio Moral Majority publicly expressed anti-Catholic sentiments, and Kellstedt (1988) found that anti-Catholicism was a significant predictor of support for the Moral Majority platform among evangelicals, even after multivariate controls.

A second possible explanation rests in the nature of the pro-life movement. Because pro-life groups have steadfastly resisted attempts by some activists to expand their agenda to incorporate a broader conservative orientation, they may be able to attract support from moderates and occasionally liberals whose religious or moral beliefs lead them to oppose abortion without endorsing other conservative positions. These moderate or liberal pro-life supporters would be unlikely candidates for membership in the Moral Majority. This political strategy makes good sense for right-to-life groups, since Catholics are more likely than Protestants to identify themselves as Democrats, to identify themselves as liberals, and to support spending for social programs. These moderate Catholics, however, may be unlikely converts to a Moral Majority.

The Data

The data for this study comes from the 1984 American National Election Study (ANES) conducted by the Center for Political Studies at the University of Michigan in 1984. This survey was a short-term panel study of a national sample Americans conducted in September and November of 1984. We limit our analysis to whites, because religion among blacks has quite different political consequences from religion among whites. The survey contained two items which were used to identify supporters of the Christian Right and pro-life forces. Respondents were asked to place a number of political groups and figures on an imaginary feeling thermometer ranging from 0°(very cold) to 100°(very warm).

Because there is a good deal of variation in individual responses to feeling thermometer items (Wilcox, Sigelman and Cook, 1989), we have adjusted these items to account for individual differences. Supporters of the Christian Right are those respondents who rated "evangelical groups active in politics like the Moral Majority" at least 10° warmer than their individual mean across all groups in the survey, and supporters of pro-life forces are those respondents who rated "anti-abortionists" in the same manner. This operational approach has been used in other studies of support for the Christian Right (Wilcox, 1987a; Sigelman, Wilcox and Buell, 1987). From these two items, we have identified those which support neither set of organizations, those who support only the Christian Right or the pro-life organizations, and those who support both.

The ANES also contained a number of demographic, religious, and political items which were used to help discriminate among supporters. From these items we have constructed several scales. We have constructed a scale of evangelical doctrine by identifying those who report a born-again experience and who accept the inerrancy of Scripture. We have constructed several political issue scales, including one which measured attitudes on women's issues, foreign policy issues, issues of minority politics, spending on social programs, spending on defense and fighting crime, affect towards minority groups, affect towards liberal groups, affect towards groups of the left, affect towards mainstream liberal groups, general equality values, and sexual equality values[2]

The Christian Right and Pro-Life Forces

Our analysis suggests that in 1984, approximately 6% of the white public supported the Christian Right only, nearly 15% supported only the pro-life movement, and around 6% supported both. Over 25% of the white population supported at least one of these groups. If the united front which Falwell sought had developed, then, they would have constituted a sizable electoral force. Instead, only about a quarter of pro-life supporters also supported the Moral Majority, while approximately half the supporters of the Christian Right gave their support to anti-abortion activists. This imbalance in support suggests that the anti-abortion forces are more negatively predisposed towards the Christian Right than are Moral Majority supporters towards the pro-life movement.

A few important demographic differences emerged from our bivariate analysis. The details are presented in Table 1. Supporters of the Moral Majority were more likely to reside in the South, to be male, and to be drawn from the lower socio-economic stratum than were pro-life forces. Predictably, supporters of the Moral Majority were more likely to belong to evangelical churches and to hold evangelical beliefs than were pro-life supporters, who were more likely to be Catholics. There was a marked inequality of cross-support among those two religious groups, however. Those who supported both groups were very likely to hold evangelical beliefs, and less likely than the population to be Catholic.

460

Table 1

BIVARIATE RESULTS: DEMOGRAPHIC AND ATTITUDINAL DIFFERENCES

Demographics	Neither	MM	Abort	Both
Education:				
Less than High School	14%	24%	20%	21%
College Degree +	22%	13%	17%	15%
Occupation:				
Worker	38%	49%	42%	47%
Professional/Manager	24%	13%	21%	12%
Region: South	27%	35%	30%	37%
Rural Born	30%	35%	37%	46%
Doctrinal Evangelical	18%	50%	31%	72%
Denominational Evang.	13%	25%	21%	29%
Catholic	30%	18%	37%	18%
Male	46%	56%	41%	44%

Political Attitudes				
Affect — Left	41	33	34	22
Affect — Liberals	55	51	54	44
Affect — Minorities	59	50	59	57
Foreign Policy	3.7	4.3	4.1	4.6
Women's Issues	3.2	3.9	3.6	4.6
Minority Issues	3.5	3.3	3.5	3.4
School Prayer	4.6	6.1	6.0	6.7
Spending - Social Progs.	1.8	1.8	1.8	2.1
Spending — Cons. Progs.	2.2	2.3	2.2	3.4
General Equality Values	3.6	3.2	3.5	3.2
Gender Equality Values	3.8	3.2	3.5	2.8
Partisanship	2.9	3.4	3.2	4.0
N	1084	91	215	87

Percentage of cases falling into each category, or mean value on each scale. Affect scales reflect degree of warmth respondent reported for groups in scale. Issue scales and partisanship are reflected so that the higher scores indicate more conservative positions.

Important attitudinal differences emerged as well. The data in Table 1 represent mean scores for each group on three scales which measure affect[2], and a number of issue scales. All issue scales are coded so that high scores indicate more conservative positions. Those who supported both groups were consistently more conservative than those who supported only one group. In many cases, however, the pro-life forces were significantly more liberal than those who supported the Christian Right. This was particularly true for equality values, including gender equality. Moreover, close inspection revealed that there was a sizable bloc of pro-life support which adopted fairly liberal positions on other issues. These bivariate data suggest that one reason for the failure of a larger Christian Right coalition to emerge may be the political moderation of right-to-life activists.

Multivariate Analysis

We next tested the impact of these demographic, religious, and attitudinal varia-

461

bles on support using multivariate discriminant analysis. The three discriminant functions enabled us to correctly predict over half of the cases. We do particularly well predicting those who support both groups—successfully predicting approximately two-thirds of those in this category. Table 1 presents the summary information of the analysis.

The first function explains 70% of the variance, and serves to discriminate degrees of support for the American Moral Right. The group means on this function are fairly linear by number of groups supported—that is, between supporting none of the groups, supporting either one, or supporting both. The function did not help distinguish between those who supported only the Moral Majority and those who supported only the pro-life movement. The most important variables in this function are negative affect for organizations of the left and for mainstream liberal groups, evangelical doctrine, frequent church attendance, conservative foreign policy views, conservative views on women's issues, conservative views on social program spending, Republican partisanship, support for school prayer, and low support for sexual equality values. Table 2 presents the correlations between the variables and the canonical discriminant functions.

The second function explained approximately 23% of the variance. It discriminated between those who supported only one or the other of the two sets of organizations. Variables which correlated highly with this function included general and gender equality values, Catholicism, low levels of evangelical doctrine, affect towards minorities, attitudes on minority issues, gender, and region. Those who supported only the pro-life movement were generally more moderate on political issues such as foreign policy, aid to minorities, and school prayer, and were more supportive of societal equality and warmer towards minorities. It seems likely that these moderate activists might be repelled by the consistent strong conservatism of the Christian Right, and might withhold support on policy grounds.

The final function explained only about 10% of the variance. It discriminates primarily between those who support only the Moral Majority and those who support both organizations. It can therefore be interpreted as distinguishing between two types of Moral Majority supporters—those who do and those who do not also support the Right-to-Life movement. Those who do not support pro-life groups are more likely to come from evangelical denominations, to favor school prayer, to be less supportive of gender equality, to be older, to report Republican partisanship, and to have higher incomes and occupational status, combined with lower levels of education. They are also the least likely of the three groups of supporters to attend church frequently. Closer inspection suggests that those who do not also support the pro-life movement are actually more likely to be infrequent attenders of churches in the fundamentalist wing of evangelical Protestantism. Because these individuals are no less conservative on the abortion issue than those who also support the pro-life movement, the explanation seems to lie primarily with the cultural implications of these demographic and attitudinal variables. Rural-born fundamentalists are generally more anti-Catholic than other evangelicals.

The finding that those who fail to support the pro-life movement are infrequently attending fundamentalists echoes findings of Allport (1966) and Allen and Spilka (1967), who reported a curvilinear relationship between church attendance and prejudice. These authors argued that infrequent attenders were more prejudiced

462

Table 2
MULTIVARIATE RESULTS: PREDICTING SUPPORT

	Function 1	Function 2	Function 3
Evangelical Doctrine	.60	−.41	−.14
Affect — Left	−.54	−.00	−.13
Frequency Church Att.	.48	.35	−.19
Women's Issues	.32	−.15	.27
Spending — Soc. Progs.	−.29	−.17	.03
Affect — Liberals	−.26	.07	.14
Spending — Cons. Progs.	.19	−.14	−.00
Occupation	.09	−.07	−.03
Equality Values	−.08	.40	−.21
Foreign Policy	.38	−.39	.05
Catholic	−.04	.35	.13
Affect — Minorities	−.10	.30	−.16
Male	.12	−.26	.19
Minority Issues	−.09	.20	−.08
Rural Birth	.14	−.15	.00
South	.07	−.11	.01
School Prayer	.31	.11	.39
Evangelical Denomin.	.12	−.06	.36
Republican	.30	−.02	.35
Gender Equality Values	−.27	.24	−.30
Income	.05	.08	.20
Age	−.00	−.00	.18
Education	−.08	.10	−.18

Canonical Discriminant Functions Evaluated at Group Means

	Function 1	Function 2	Function 3
Support Neither	−.34	−.04	−.07
Support Moral Majority	.40	−.86	.39
Support Pro-Life	.36	.50	.19
Support Both	1.75	−.16	−.34

Percentage Predicted Correctly

Support Neither	53%
Support Moral Majority	47%
Support Pro-Life	48%
Support Both	70%
Total	53%

because their religion was extrinsic—i.e. instrumental. Our results differ from theirs, however, in finding that frequent attenders of evangelical denominations were the most likely to also support the pro-life movement. This finding is consistent with the work of Himmelstein (1986), who argued that frequent church attendance exposed church members to appeals by right-to-life activists.

The Failure of a Marriage Made in Heaven

Why has the predicted New Christian Right coalition failed to materialize? We offered above two possible explanations—the first centering on the intolerance of

463

the fundamentalist supporters of the Moral Majority for Catholics, and the second focusing on the narrow agenda of the pro-life movement, which allows moderates and even liberals to support its cause. Our data suggest that there is some truth to both explanations. The results from the discriminant analysis suggest that those who support only the anti-abortionists and do not support the Moral Majority are markedly more moderate than Moral Majority supporters on nearly all measures: foreign policy, spending on social welfare, other women's issues and gender equality, minority issues and minority affect, and affect towards the Left. It seems likely that the consistent conservatism of the Moral Majority is not attractive to these moderates, whose only common ground is opposition to abortion.

Table 3
MULTIVARIATE RESULTS: ANTI-CATHOLICISM AND SUPPORT AMONG PROTESTANTS

	Function 1	Function 2	Function 3
Evangelical Doctrine	.57	-.22	-.09
Affect — Left	-.56	.17	.08
Frequency Church Att.	.45	.28	-.19
Women's Issues	.34	-.08	.09
Spending — Soc. Progs.	-.30	-.22	-.00
Affect — Liberals	-.28	-.26	.27
Spending — Cons. Progs.	.18	-.00	.04
Occupation	.15	-.00	-.10
Equality Values	-.18	.24	-.01
Foreign Policy	.42	-.25	.21
Affect, Catholics	-.13	.27	-.01
Affect — Minorities	-.19	.36	-.03
Male	.17	-.25	-.17
Minority Issues	-.10	.34	-.15
Rural Birth	.09	-.07	.35
South	.01	-.02	.01
School Prayer	.31	.03	.36
Evangelical Denomin.	.09	-.10	.43
Republican	.30	-.02	.35
Gender Equality Values	-.30	.25	-.27
Income	.09	-.00	-.17
Age	-.02	-.13	.16
Education	-.08	.10	-.18

Canonical Discriminant Functions Evaluated at Group Means

	Function 1	Function 2	Function 3
Support Neither	-.43	-.04	-.08
Support Moral Majority	.56	-.86	-.08
Support Pro-Life	.43	.25	-.47
Support Both	1.77	-.28	-.38

Percentage Predicted Correctly

Support Neither	63%
Support Moral Majority	47%
Support Pro-Life	40%
Support Both	69%
Total	58%

The Moral Majority supporters may fail to support the anti-abortion movement in part because of their anti-Catholicism. To further test this explanation, we repeated our discriminant analysis, selecting only Protestant respondents and including a measure of affect toward Catholics as an independent variable. The results were substantively similar to our earlier results, with some interesting differences. The data are presented in Table 3. In this analysis, the second function discriminated between those who supported only the Moral Majority and those who supported the anti-abortion movement, and affect toward Catholic loaded heavily on this function. This would suggest that anti-Catholicism is an important barrier in the expansion of the Christian Right coalition to include pro-life Catholics.

An additional discriminant analysis (not shown) suggests that Catholics may respond to this anti-Catholicism: among Catholics, those who attend church most frequently and those who feel the greatest positive affect toward other Catholics are the least likely support the Moral Majority.

Conclusions

The data suggest that in part we can view support for these two organizations as additive: the function associated with the lion's share of the common variance is best interpreted as tapping support for the Right, with Moral Majority and pro-life supporters equally associated with the function. Important differences between those who support only one or the other of these two organizations emerge, however. Those who support only the pro-life movement are more moderate politically, more likely to be Catholic, to oppose school prayer, and more egalitarian in their values. Among the most important distinguishing variables are religious variables, with evangelicals and Catholics supporting different organizations. Those who support both sets of groups seem to be those who hold evangelical beliefs and attend church frequently, though not necessarily in an evangelical denomination.

Two sets of barriers have kept the predicted Christian Right coalition from emerging. First, those who support the pro-life movement, (and in particular Catholic supporters) are political moderates who support greater equality for blacks and women, as well as spending for social programs. These moderates are doubtlessly not attracted to the consistent conservatism of the Moral Majority leadership and supporters. Second, many of the supporters of the Moral Majority have not attempted to form political bridges, in part because of anti-Catholic sentiments.

NOTES

1. *We would like to thank Elizabeth Cook and anonymous reviewers for helpful comments. The data was collected by the Center for Political Studies at the University of Michigan, and made available by the Inter-University Consortium for Political and Social Research. The authors alone bear the responsibilities for all analysis and interpretations.*

2. For details of scale construction, contact the authors.

REFERENCES

Allen, Russell, and Bernard Spilka
    1967   "Committed and Consensual Religion: A Specification of Religion-Prejudice Relationships." Journal for the Scientific Study of Religion 6: 191-206.

Allport, Gordon
    1966   "The Religious Context of Prejudice." Journal for the Scientific Study of Religion 5: 447-457.

Buell, Emmett and Lee Sigelman
    1985   "An Army that Meets Every Sunday? Popular Support for the Moral Majority in 1980." Social Science Quarterly: 426-434.

Ebaugh, Helen and Allen Haney
    1978   "Church Attendance and Attitudes Towards Abortion: Differentials in Liberal and Conservative Churches." Journal for the Scientific Study of Religion 17: 407-413.

Godwin, R. Kenneth
    1988   "The Structure, Content, and Use of Political Direct Mail." Polity 20: 527-538.

Guth, James and John Green
    1987   "The Moralizing Minority: Christian Right Support among Political Activists." Social Science Quarterly 68: 598-610.

Harris, Richard and Edgar Mills
    1985   "Religion, Values and Attitudes Towards Abortion." Journal for the Scientific Study of Religion 24: 137-154.

Hayes, Michael
    1986   "The New Group Universe." In A. Cigler and B. Loomis (eds.) Interest Group Politics. Washington, DC: CQ Press.

Himmelstein, Jerome
    1986   "The Social Basis of Anti-Feminism." Journal for the Scientific Study of Religion 25: 1-15.

Johnson, Stephen and Joseph Tamney
    1984   "Support for the Moral Majority: A Test of a Model." Journal for the Scientific Study of Religion 23: 183-196.

Kellstedt, Lyman
    1988   "The Falwell Issue Agenda: Sources of Support among White Evangelical Protestants." In M. Lynn and D. Moberg (Eds.) An Annual in the Sociology of Religion. New York: JAI Press.

Liebman, Robert
    1983   "Mobilizing the Moral Majority." In R. Liebman and R. Wuthnow (Eds.) The New Christian Right. New York: Aldine.

Luker, Kristin
    1984   Abortion and the Politics of Motherhood. Berkeley: University of California Press.

Pierand, Richard and James Wright
    1984   "The Moral Majority in Indiana." In D. Bromley and A. Shupe, (Eds.) New Christian Politics. Macon, GA: Mercer University Press.

Shupe, Anson and William Stacey
    1983   "The Moral Majority Constituency." In R. Liebman and R. Wuthnow (Eds.) The New Christian Right. New York: Aldine.

Sigelman, Lee, Clyde Wilcox and Emmett Buell
    1987   "An Unchanged Minority: Popular Support for the Moral Majority in 1980 and 1984." Social Science Quarterly 68: 876-884.

Simpson, John
    1983   "Moral Issues and Status Politics." In R. Liebman and R. Wuthnow (Eds.) The New Christian Right. New York: Aldine.

Tamney, Joseph and Stephen Johnson
    1983   "The Moral Majority in Middletown." Journal for the Scientific Study of Religion 22: 145-157.

Wilcox, Clyde
    1986   "Evangelicals and Fundamentalists in the New Christian Right: Religious Dif-
                ferences in the Ohio Moral Majority." Journal for the Scientific Study of
                Religion 25: 355-363.
Wilcox, Clyde
    1987a   "Popular Support for the Moral Majority in 1980: A Second Look." Social
                Science Quarterly 68: 157-167.
    1987b   "Religious Orientations and Political Attitudes: Variations within the New
                Christian Right." American Politics Quarterly. 15: 274-296.
    1989   "Support for the Moral Majority in 1984: A Test of Alternative Hypotheses."
                Social Science Journal 26: 55-56.
Wilcox, Clyde, Lee Sigelman and Elizabeth Cook
    1989   "Some Like it Hot: Individual Differences in Responses to Group Feeling
                Thermometer Items." Public Opinion Quarterly 53: 246-257.
Yinger, Milton and Stephen Cutler
    1982   "The Moral Majority Viewed Sociologically." Sociological Focus 15: 289-306.

Acknowledgments

Atwood, Thomas C. "Through a Glass Darkly: Is the Christian Right Overconfident It Knows God's Will?" *Policy Review* 54 (fall 1990): 44–52. Reprinted with the permission of the Heritage Foundation.

Berlet, Chip. "The Right Rides High" *The Progressive* 58, no. 10 (1994): 22–24, 26–29. Reprinted with the permission of Progressive Inc.

Boston, Rob. "Operation Precinct" *Church and State* 47 (July/August 1994): 8–13.

Buchanan, Pat. "The Election Is About Who We Are: Taking Back Our Country" *Vital Speeches of the Day* 58 (Sept. 15, 1992): 712–15. Reprinted with the permission of the City News Publishing Company Inc.

Conn, Joseph L. "Playing Broadway" *Church and State* 46 (June 1993): 4–6.

Conn, Joseph L. "Trouble in Texas" *Church and State* 46 (February 1993): 11–12.

Diamond, Sara. "How 'Radical' Is the Christian Right?" *Humanist* 54, no. 2 (1994): 32–34. Reprinted with the permission of the American Humanist Association.

Eastland, Terry. "In Defense of Religious America" *Commentary* 71 (June 1981): 39–45. Reprinted from *Commentary* (1981, June) by permission. All rights reserved.

Gerner, George W. "Catholics and the 'Religious Right': We Are Being Wooed" *Commonweal* 122, no. 9 (1995): 15–20. Reprinted with the permission of the Commonweal Foundation.

Kaufman, Leslie. Transcription of "Life Beyond God" *The New York Times Magazine* (Oct. 16, 1994): 46 ff. Copyright (1994) by The New York Times Company. Reprinted by permission.

Kristol, William. "The Future of Conservatism in the U.S." *American Enterprise* 5, no. 4 (1994): 32, 34–37. Reprinted with the permission of the American Enterprise Institute for Public Policy Research.

Lind, Michael. "Why Intellectual Conservatism Died" *Dissent* 42 (winter 1995): 42–47. Reprinted with the permission of the Foundation for the Study of Independent Social Ideas, Inc.

Moen, Matthew C. "From Revolution to Evolution: The Changing Nature of the Christian Right" *Sociology of Religion* 55, no. 3 (1994): 345–57. Reprinted with the permission of the Association for the Society of Religion.

Persinos, John F. "Has the Christian Right Taken Over the Republican Party?" *Campaigns and Elections* 15, no. 9 (1994): 21–24.

Reed, Ralph, Jr. "Casting a Wider Net: Religious Conservatives Move Beyond Abortion and Homosexuality" *Policy Review* 65 (summer 1993): 31–35. Reprinted with the permission of the Heritage Foundation.

Saberi, Erin. "From Moral Majority to Organized Minority: Tactics of the Religious Right" *Christian Century* 110, no. 23 (1993): 781–84. Copyright (1993) Christian Century Foundation. Reprinted by permission of the *Christian Century*.

Taylor, John. "Pat Robertson's God, Inc." *Esquire* 122 (Nov. 1994): 77–83. Reprinted with the permission of the Hearst Corporation.

Toulouse, Mark G. "Pat Robertson: Apocalyptic Theology and American Foreign Policy" *Journal of Church and State* 31 (winter 1989): 73–99. Reprinted from the *Journal of Church and State*, used by permission.

Weyrich, Paul M. "Blue Collar or Blue Blood?: The New Right Compared with The Old Right" in Robert W. Whitaker, ed., *The New Right Papers* (New York: St. Martin's Press, 1982): 48–62. Reprinted with the permission of St. Martin's Press.

Wilcox, Clyde. "Premillennialists at the Millennium: Some Reflections on the Christian Right in the Twenty-First Century" *Sociology of Religion* 55 (1994): 243–61. Reprinted with the permission of the Association for the Society of Religion.

Wilentz, Sean. "The Trials of Televangelism: Jerry Falwell and the Enemy" *Dissent* 37 (winter 1990): 42–48. Reprinted with the permission of the Foundation for the Study of Independent Social Ideas, Inc.

Bates, Vernon L. "Lobbying for the Lord: The New Christian Right Home-Schooling Movement and Grassroots Lobbying" *Review of Religious Research* 33, no. 1 (1991): 3–17. Reprinted with the permission of the Religious Research Association.

Christian Coalition. *Contract with the American Family* (1995): 1–39. Reprinted with the permission of the Christian Coalition.

Dawidoff, Nicholas. Transciption of "No Sex. No Drugs. But Rock 'n' Roll: (Kind of)" *The New York Times Magazine* (Feb. 5, 1995): 40 ff. Copyright (1995) by The New York Times Company. Reprinted by permission.

Detweiler, John S. "The Religious Right's Battle Plan in the 'Civil War of Values'" *Public Relations Review* 18:3 (1992): 247–55. Reprinted with the permission of JAI Press Inc.

Hunter, James Davison. "Media and the Arts" in *Culture Wars: The Struggle to Define America* (New York: BasicBooks, 1991): 225–49. Reprinted with the permission of BasicBooks, Division of HarperCollins.

Kadetsky, Elizabeth. "Women of the Christian Right" *Glamour* (Feb. 1995): 230–31, 247–50. Reprinted with the permission of Conde Nast Publishing Inc.

LaHaye, Beverly. "What Women Wish Their Husbands Knew About Leadership" *Christian Herald* 113 (November 1990): 20–22. Reprinted with the permission of the Herald House, Ltd.

Lienesch, Michael. "Family" in *Redeeming America: Piety and Politics in the New Christian Right* (Chapel Hill: University of North Carolina Press, 1993): 52–93, 271–85. Reprinted with the permission of the University of North Carolina Press.

Lynn, Barry W. "'Family Values' and the Religious Right: A Narrow Definition" *Church and State* 48 (June 1995): 23.

Minkowitz, Donna. "The Christian Right's Antigay Campaign: Part Stealth, Part Muscle" *Christianity and Crisis* 53, no. 4 (1993): 99–100, 102, 104.

Moen, Matthew C. "The Preacher Versus the Teacher" *Thought and Action: The NEA Higher Education Journal* 9, no. 1 (1993): 125–43. Reprinted with the permission of the National Education Association of the United States.

Murray, Charles. "Does Welfare Bring More Babies?" *The Public Interest* 115 (spring 1994): 17–30. Reprinted with the permission of *The Public Interest*. Copyright (1994) by National Affairs, Inc.

Petchesky, Rosalind Pollack. "Antiabortion, Antifeminism, and the Rise of the New Right" *Feminist Studies* 7 (1981): 206–46. Reprinted with the permission of the publisher, FEMINIST STUDIES, Inc., c/o Women's Studies Program, University of Maryland, College Park, MD 20742.

Pollitt, Katha. "Dan, Murph and Me: Why I Hate 'Family Values' (Let Me Count the Ways)" *The Nation* 255, no. 3 (1992): 88, 90–92, 94. Reprinted from *The Nation* magazine. Copyright the Nation Company, L.P.

Stacey, Judith. "Dan Quayle's Revenge: The New Family Values Crusaders" *The Nation* 259, no. 4 (1994): 119–22. Reprinted from *The Nation* magazine. Copyright the Nation Company, L.P.

Whitehead, Barbara Dafoe. "Dan Quayle Was Right" *Atlantic Monthly* 271, no. 4 (1993): 47–50. Reprinted with the permission of the Atlantic Monthly Company.

Wilson, James Q. "The Family-Values Debate" *Commentary* 95 (April 1993): 24–31. Reprinted from *Commentary* (1993, April) by permission. All rights reserved.

Wilcox, Clyde and Leopoldo Gomez. "The Christian Right and the Pro-Life Movement: An Analysis of the Sources of Political Support" *Review of Religious Research* 31 (June 1990): 380–89. Reprinted with the permission of the Religious Research Association.